A WILD JUSTICE

JUSTICE

THE DEATH AND RESURRECTION
OF CAPITAL PUNISHMENT
IN AMERICA

Evan J. Mandery

W. W. NORTON & COMPANY

NEW YORK   LONDON

"Revenge is a kind of wild justice; which the more man's nature runs to, the more ought law to weed it out." —Sir Francis Bacon

For information about permission to reproduce selections from this book, write to Permissions, W. W. Norton & Company, Inc., 500 Fifth Avenue, New York, NY 10110

For information about special discounts for bulk purchases, please contact W. W. Norton Special Sales at specialsales@wwnorton.com or 800-233-4830

Manufacturing by Courier Westford
Book design by Brian Mulligan
Production manager: Louise Mattarelliano

Library of Congress Cataloging-in-Publication Data

Mandery, Evan J.
A wild justice : the death and resurrection of
capital punishment in America / Evan J. Mandery.
    pages cm
Includes bibliographical references and index.
ISBN 978-0-393-23958-4 (hardcover)
1. Capital punishment—United States.—
History—20th century. I. Title.
KF9227.C2M39 2013
345.73'0773—dc23

                            2013010126

ISBN 978-0-393-34896-5 pbk.

W. W. Norton & Company, Inc.
500 Fifth Avenue, New York, N.Y. 10110
www.wwnorton.com

W. W. Norton & Company Ltd.
Castle House, 75/76 Wells Street, London W1T 3QT

1 2 3 4 5 6 7 8 9 0

Praise for *A Wild Justice*

"Explaining Furman and its implications can be tricky, but Evan Mandery . . . has done both with remarkable ease. . . . Mandery knows how to tell a story, and he's done some terrific research."
—David Oshinsky, *New York Times Book Review*

"Gripping."
—Emily Bazelon, *Slate*

"One of the very best books I have ever read not only on the Supreme Court as an institution, but also on the death penalty itself. . . . One keeps turning the pages in order to find out what happens next. Mandery is scrupulously fair."—Sanford Levinson, *History Book Club*

"Mandery writes about these events like they felt to the people who lived through them—as a thriller. . . . [H]e probes deep into the bumpy lives and brilliant minds of the lawyers and justices. . . . [A] virtuoso performance."
—David Dagan, *Washington Monthly*

"A rare achievement. . . . A piece of legal history that grapples brilliantly with capital punishment, one of the fundamental issues of American justice."
—Sean Wilentz, author of *The Rise of American Democracy*

"The fascinating story of the abolition of the death penalty—and its restoration—has found its ideal narrator in Evan Mandery. At once a page-turner and a work of serious scholarship, *A Wild Justice* puts you inside the justices' deliberations and the advocates' strategizing. Required reading for anyone who cares about the Supreme Court and how it shapes our lives."
—Noah Feldman, author of *Scorpions*

"Much like Jeffrey Toobin . . . Mandery has managed to turn textbook-style legal history into cinematic scenes with memorable characters."
—Maurice Chammah, *Austin American-Statesman*

"Outstanding in every respect."
—*Kirkus Reviews*, starred review

"It takes a gifted writer to craft a thriller out of the efforts to have capital punishment declared unconstitutional, but Mandery pulls it off in this intellectual page-turner."
—*Publishers Weekly*, starred review

"A tour de force. . . . [I]lluminating."
—Harry Charles, *Library Journal*, starred review

CONTENTS

PROLOGUE   ix

PART ONE

AN AUDACIOUS IDEA, 1963–1971

Chapter 1:   AN AUDACIOUS IDEA   3

Chapter 2:   THE MOST IMPORTANT LAW FIRM IN AMERICA   31

Chapter 3:   SURCEASE OF SORROW   48

Chapter 4:   A NEAR KNOCKOUT   71

Chapter 5:   TO LICENSE A LAUNDRY, TO LICENSE A LIFE   98

PART TWO

DEATH, 1971–1972

Chapter 6:   YOUNG LAWYERS   123

Chapter 7:   BOILING IN OIL   143

Chapter 8:   NINE LAW FIRMS   166

Chapter 9:   WHIZZER   202

Chapter 10: Lightning Bolts 218

Chapter 11: A Red-Letter Day 234

PART THREE

RESURRECTION, 1972–1976

Chapter 12: Sobering Up 247

Chapter 13: Behind the Backlash 264

Chapter 14: Proving Deterrence and Rationality 281

Chapter 15: The Lion in Winter 318

Chapter 16: The Sausage Factory 336

Chapter 17: Taking Stock 354

Chapter 18: The Main Event 372

Chapter 19: The Center in Control 400

Postscript: What Might Have Been 432

Acknowledgments 441

Glossary of Key Cases 443

Notes 447

Sources 493

Index 503

A WILD JUSTICE

PROLOGUE

IN 1972 THE SUPREME COURT RULED GEORGIA'S DEATH penalty law unconstitutional. Since Georgia's law was more or less the same as the laws in the thirty-nine other states that had capital punishment, most legal experts believed *Furman v. Georgia* meant the end of executions in the United States. The Court's decision earned a six-column headline in the *New York Times*—as large and as bold as when, equally improbably, men had landed on the moon in 1969. On its editorial page the *Times* praised the Court for curing the "cancer of capital punishment."

The decision was supremely improbable. Just ten years earlier the constitutionality of the death penalty had been axiomatic. Then, in 1963, to the astonishment of his colleagues and the entire legal community, Justice Arthur Goldberg suggested that the Eighth Amendment prohibited capital punishment. His proposal was every bit as brash, and its success every bit as unlikely, as President John Kennedy's exhortation two years earlier for an American lunar landing by the end of the decade. Kennedy's vision took eight years to reach fruition. The crusade to end the death penalty, led by an underfunded band of civil rights attorneys, took nine. It was nothing less than a miracle.

Four years later the Supreme Court reversed itself.

PART ONE

AN
AUDACIOUS
IDEA

1963–1971

CHAPTER 1

AN AUDACIOUS
IDEA

ALAN DERSHOWITZ WAS SWEATING. IT WAS HIS first day on his new job, August 1, 1963, in the heat of a characteristically brutal summer in Washington, D.C. To get to work from his home in Hyattsville, Maryland, he had to endure two sweltering bus rides while dressed in his suit and tie. After the bus deposited him at the station, he had to walk up forty-four marble steps and pass through a portico and under a pediment bearing the words "Equal Justice Under Law."

This was no ordinary office: he was a law clerk to Justice Arthur Goldberg of the United States Supreme Court.

In the receiving area he completed some paperwork and rubbed the sleep out of his eyes. Dershowitz and his wife had a one-year-old at home, and that morning he had woken up extra early to make sure he was on time. But when Arthur Goldberg said he wanted to have a word, Dershowitz snapped awake. He knew what it meant when a judge called a clerk into his office: He had spent the last year clerking for D.C. Circuit Court of Appeals judge David Bazelon, a superstar in the legal universe, who was also known for yelling at his clerks.

Dershowitz hoped it would be different this time around. He had made a huge gamble on Goldberg. Law students count themselves lucky to receive a single offer to clerk for a justice, but Dershowitz, a student of legendary prowess, had received two on the same day—one from Goldberg, the other from Hugo Black. Most young lawyers couldn't have resisted the opportunity to work for the iconic Black, a twenty-five-year Court veteran and one of its two intellectual leaders. Dershowitz saw it differently. "Black had formulated his ideas," he said later. "I would be helping him do the same thing he had done. Goldberg, on the other hand, was a new justice." With that potential, though, came a huge risk. No one knew what his temperament would be like and whether Goldberg would be a transformative justice, like Black, or dull and cautious, like, say, Tom Clark.

With trepidation, Dershowitz entered the justice's chambers. He hadn't been there since his interview more than a year ago. He looked around. Most of the furnishings were standard government issue—a wooden desk with an ink blotter and an ashtray, though Goldberg didn't smoke. The notable exception was the artwork on the walls by Goldberg's wife, Dorothy Kurgans, a respected abstract painter. Dershowitz liked her compositions very much. He paid particular attention to a giant portrait of Oliver Wendell Holmes, brooding behind Goldberg's desk. Beneath the picture Goldberg had reprinted several of Holmes's most famous quotes. Dershowitz noted one in particular:

The life of the law has not been logic; it has been experience.

Goldberg offered him a seat. From across his desk, he tossed him a thick legal brief with a red cover.

"Do you know what this is?

"It's a cert petition," Dershowitz replied, picking it up. "Cert" is short for *certiorari*, which translates from Latin as "to be more fully informed." A writ of certiorari requires a lower court to send the record—transcripts, evidence, and so on—to a higher court for review. When a litigant wants the Supreme Court to hear a case, he or she files a petition for cert. Cert petitions in capital cases have red covers.

"No," Goldberg said. "You're holding in your hands a vehicle that can end the death penalty in the United States. The Eighth Amendment prohibits cruel and unusual punishment. What could be more cruel than the deliberate decision by the state to take a human life?"

Dershowitz smiled. He had chosen the right man.

VIEWED FROM THE STANDPOINT of the twenty-first century, the idea of using the Constitution to strike down the death penalty doesn't seem surprising. In the early 1960s, however, the notion that executions were cruel and unusual punishment seemed fanciful. When the Founding Fathers drafted the Constitution, the death penalty was mandatory for most felonies and used in every state. The Fifth Amendment referenced capital crimes explicitly and implicitly when it said no person should be deprived of "life, liberty, or property" without due process of law. The Fourteenth Amendment, adopted in the aftermath of the Civil War, used the same language. No Supreme Court justice had ever suggested that capital punishment might be unconstitutional. Only one law-review article had even hinted at the notion. Nothing should have suggested to Justice Arthur Goldberg that this idea could succeed.

Then again, nothing in his childhood should have suggested to Arthur Goldberg the possibility of his becoming a justice of the U.S. Supreme Court, but he aspired to become one, and did all the same. And Goldberg's time on the Court, though often overlooked because of its brevity, was among the most consequential in its history. During his three years on the bench, Goldberg fomented an intellectual revolution: a radical transformation of the view of the Court's proper role that had profound consequences for capital punishment specifically and American civil liberties in general.

Even as a child Arthur Goldberg had chutzpah. His parents fled a Ukrainian village northwest of Kiev for the West Side of Chicago. There he thrived even as Polish and Irish Americans shouted anti-Semitic epithets at him and pelted him with stones. The experience fundamentally shaped young Goldberg, who developed a lifelong allegiance to underdogs.

Though well educated, Goldberg's father found work only as a peddler, and died when Arthur was eight. To support the family each of Arthur's seven siblings took jobs; none graduated from high school. The youngest child, Arthur was allowed to finish school, but he did his share of work. By age twelve he was wrapping fish, selling shoes, and vending coffee at Cubs games from an urn strapped to his back.

As a teenager Arthur Goldberg aspired to become a lawyer. "I don't know why," he said. "None of my relatives were lawyers and I guess it may have been a response to that." Shortly after his sixteenth birthday he attended the sensational Leopold and Loeb murder trial, where the defense attorney, Clarence Darrow, successfully saved his clients' lives with an impassioned critique of capital punishment. Later Goldberg reflected that Darrow's performance made a lasting impression on him.

While working nearly full-time, Goldberg graduated from Benjamin Harrison High School at sixteen, took classes at Crane Junior College, and finally enrolled at Northwestern University, from which he graduated in just one year. He advanced to the liberal Northwestern Law School, where he learned, in his own words, "the role of law in limiting the arbitrary exercise of state power." Goldberg supported himself by working construction jobs but still managed to become editor of the *Illinois Law Review* and to graduate with high honors at the age of twenty-one. The Illinois Bar Association refused to admit him because he was too young. Goldberg sued and won.

The top Chicago firms were closed to Jews, even the editors in chief of prestigious law reviews. The best position Goldberg could land was at Pritzger & Pritzger, a firm founded by a family of German Jews. It was a fine law office, but substantially down the pecking order. As things turned out, though, landing at Pritzger was a blessing in disguise. Goldberg developed an expertise in labor law, which sustained his career. In 1938 he represented Chicago's striking newspaper workers and began to develop a national reputation.

During World War II, Goldberg served in the army for the Office of

Strategic Services, a precursor to the CIA. The government's conduct during the war solidified Goldberg's mistrust of authority. Following Pearl Harbor the State Department detained Goldberg's legal secretary, Elizabeth Ho, without any evidence against her. Goldberg successfully used his military influence on Ho's behalf, but he recognized that others weren't as lucky.

Goldberg saw unions as an important force to protect the powerless, and so, after the war, he opened his own office focused exclusively on employment law. Soon Goldberg emerged as the most prominent labor lawyer in the United States. He became general counsel for the Congress of Industrial Organizations, and during the 1950s oversaw its merger with the American Federation of Labor.

In 1960 Goldberg became involved in politics when he pledged early support for John Kennedy's candidacy. He played an instrumental role in maintaining JFK's good standing with the labor movement, which resented Kennedy for supporting John McClellan's committee investigation of union corruption. Rewarding Goldberg for his loyalty, President Kennedy named him secretary of labor in early 1961. Twenty months later, when Justice Felix Frankfurter resigned because of failing health, Kennedy fulfilled Goldberg's childhood dream and nominated him to what had come to be known as the "Jewish seat" on the Supreme Court.

Goldberg spent a restless first year on the bench. Because of his long-standing connections to the labor movement, he had to recuse himself from several cases. He enthusiastically joined as the Court rejected prayer in public schools and required states to provide counsel to indigent clients. But he played no more than a peripheral role in these battles, and he authored no major opinions. Privately Goldberg stewed. He hadn't joined the Court to become a silent partner: He wanted to leave his mark.

During the late spring of 1963, Goldberg couldn't have avoided thinking about crime and justice. On June 12 the civil rights leader Medgar Evers was assassinated in Mississippi. Then, shortly before the first anniversary of Adolf Eichmann's execution, Hannah Arendt published her seminal and controversial account of the Nazi's trial, *Eichmann in Jerusalem: A Study in the Banality of Evil.* Goldberg knew Arendt, who supported capital punishment. Ten years earlier they had both participated in the Jewish Theological Seminary's Fiftieth Anniversary Conference on Moral Standards in New York City.

Throughout the following summer Goldberg thought time and again about overturning the death penalty, which he had abhorred since his childhood. Goldberg drew a direct link between the Holocaust and capital punishment. In the aftermath of the war the revelations of Nazi atrocities revolted Goldberg. He read the theologian Reinhold Niebuhr, who argued that faith in humanity's beneficence died with the Holocaust. Like Niebuhr, Goldberg had no confidence in the ability of politics to produce justice.

Furthermore Goldberg thought capital punishment was bad public policy. He didn't believe that the death penalty deterred violent crime. He thought states applied it discriminatorily: In practice the death penalty was used exclusively against the poor and the politically powerless. Goldberg also worried about the problem of executing innocents. In his mind this included people who didn't commit the crime for which they had been convicted and people who were sentenced under outdated principles.

For all these reasons Goldberg resolved to use his position to end capital punishment. The 1963 Court term seemed like the time to do it. During his first term he felt hamstrung by his law clerks, who had been selected by Frankfurter. For his second year on the bench, he made his own choices. Dershowitz struck Goldberg as perfect for the job. His experience working for Bazelon, a committed opponent of capital punishment, would be useful, and Dershowitz seemed to have a passion for civil liberties. Indeed, Goldberg's proposal elated his law clerk. But Dershowitz also had a scholar's mind. He followed the Court closely and understood its major personalities. While he personally abhorred capital punishment, Dershowitz knew that many people would regard Goldberg's plan as a folly.

✦　✦　✦　✦

THOUGH THE SUPREME COURT of the 1960s would be known as the Warren Court—so named for its chief justice Earl Warren, appointed to the Court by President Eisenhower in 1953—it was in reality dominated by two titans of American law, Hugo Black and Felix Frankfurter, the man Goldberg succeeded. Each was appointed by FDR, though they could hardly have been more different. Black, a former U.S. senator, grew up in poverty in Alabama and was educated modestly. Frankfurter was a legal star, who graduated first in his class at Harvard Law School and helped found the American Civil Liberties Union (ACLU). Black made his greatest mark investigating air mail corruption. Frankfurter became a national star when he wrote an *Atlantic* magazine article defending Ferdinando Nicola Sacco and Bartolomeo Vanzetti, two Italian American laborers and anarchists who were executed for murder in 1927 on the basis of sketchy evidence.

At the beginning of the 1963 term, Black remained on the bench, still vibrant at seventy-seven. Frankfurter had resigned two years earlier because of a stroke, but he continued to wield vast influence from afar. Broadly speaking, though these terms are inadequate, Black took an activist view of the Court's role, while Frankfurter advocated for judicial restraint. On a personal level Black was a political master while Frankfurter was an overbearing pedant. To some extent each of the nine Justices in 1963 defined himself by his ideological or personal relationship to these two men.

In the Black camp were Chief Justice Earl Warren, William Brennan, and William Douglas, each there as much for his antipathy for Frankfurter as his substantial admiration for Black. Warren, the former governor of California, believed Frankfurter attempted to subvert his authority, and therefore instructed his clerks not to speak with Frankfurter's. Douglas, an iconoclastic liberal appointed by FDR in 1939, loathed Frankfurter's lectures and hadn't spoken to him in decades. Brennan, another Eisenhower appointee and a master politician himself, also preferred Black.

In Frankfurter's corner stood, most substantially, John Harlan, a renowned jurist whose grandfather also served on the Court. Harlan shared Frankfurter's belief in judicial restraint and, following his appointment to the Court in 1955, voted with Frankfurter in nearly every major civil liberties decision. Unlike Frankfurter, however, Harlan had an easygoing manner. "Frankfurter without mustard," they called him. His intelligence and style attracted Potter Stewart, a third Eisenhower appointee. Frankfurter also maintained a friendship with Tom Clark, Truman's nominee, who had once been U.S. attorney general.

These three were often joined by Byron White, whom Kennedy appointed to the Court five months prior to Goldberg. White had once clerked on the Court—the first justice ever to have done so—and had been frustrated by Black's activism. When he joined the Court, he said nothing had changed in fifteen years. "The same issues that were here in 1947 are still here, and Hugo still runs the Court." White's first principle was that legislative bodies, not judges, should make social policy. He told a friend, "Judges have an exaggerated view of their role in our polity." To a college classmate White said, "The trouble with these liberals up here is that they think they have all the answers to social problems, like crime and race, and what's worse, they're putting them into the Constitution."

With four men on each side, Goldberg's appointment had the potential to shift the balance of power. Goldberg conceptualized the battle in terms of an ongoing intellectual feud between the faculties of Harvard and Yale Law Schools. The Harvard faculty favored their alumnus, Frankfurter. Professor Paul Freund argued that judicial activism put the Court's prestige at risk. The Yale faculty generally supported Hugo Black. Yale's strongest voice was Charles Black (no relation), who said the fear of risking prestige led the Court to refrain too often from addressing important social concerns.

Goldberg was inclined to Charles Black's view. Shortly before assuming his seat, Goldberg read books by both Black and Freund. Goldberg's wife, Dorothy, wrote in her diary, "Art's got one book that was the Harvard point of view, Paul Freund's book on the Supreme Court, and a Mr. Charles Black's book on 'The People and the Court.' He's on the Yale side." Indeed, during his first term, Goldberg voted with Hugo Black more than 85 percent of the time. But even Hugo Black's philosophy couldn't get Goldberg where he now wanted to go. While Frankfurter and Black disagreed about almost everything, on the death penalty they were in rare accord. Neither of them thought it offended the Constitution.

TO UNDERSTAND FRANKFURTER'S WORLDVIEW we need to step back to a seminal constitutional case from 1905 called *Lochner v. New York*. Joseph Lochner, the owner of a Utica bakery, was arrested for employing someone for more than New York's legal limit of sixty hours per week. With the assistance of his trade group, Lochner appealed. His case went all the way to the Supreme Court, which ruled five to four in his favor. The majority said that New York's law violated a fundamental "liberty of contract." The baker, Aman Schmitter, wanted to work, Lochner wanted to hire him, and that, the Court said, should have been the end of that.

The decision—and the opposition to it—defined an era in constitutional law. The phrase "liberty of contract" doesn't appear in the Constitution. In his dissent Oliver Wendell Holmes argued that the principle was a ruse for the majority to impose its economic theory— laissez-faire capitalism—on Americans. Nevertheless *Lochner* endured for more than thirty years, and almost rewrote American history. In 1935 and 1936, based on *Lochner*'s reasoning, the Supreme Court struck down key parts of the New Deal and New York's minimum-wage law. FDR responded with a plan to pack the Court. A constitutional crisis was narrowly averted by Justice Owen Robert's famous switch in time, in a 1937 case called *West Coast Hotel Co. v. Parrish*, upholding Washington's minimum-wage law. *Parrish* effectively overturned *Lochner*.

The intellectual foundation for repudiating *Lochner* had been laid over the preceding decades by three men operating in complementary fora: Justice Holmes, a public-minded attorney named Louis Brandeis who later joined the Court, and Frankfurter, then a professor at Harvard. Operating in their respective arenas, these three friends defined a constitutional theory that could support a progressive agenda. Judges, they said, should exercise great deference to legislative decisions. Frankfurter outlined the theory in a series of articles in the *Harvard Law Review*. These ideas became the judicial philosophy associated with American liberalism.

Judicial philosophies, however, are inherently neither liberal nor conservative. The controversial principle now most commonly associated with Antonin Scalia—that the Constitution should be interpreted in accord with the intent of the framers—is not on its face politically conservative. It's only so if the framers' intent was politically conservative. Theories are liberal or conservative only in context. Soon after Frankfurter advanced his doctrine of judicial restraint, the context changed. During World War II the Supreme Court emerged as the progressive agent, protecting citizens against wartime hysteria in Congress, fear of Communism, and aggressive crime-control tactics. In these contexts judicial restraint was regressive.

Frankfurter remained consistent, though. The Supreme Court, he said, should be reluctant to change its core principles, lest it squander the public's trust. Frankfurter held himself to the same standard. While the Warren Court transformed America, Frankfurter retained his commitment to democratic processes, often repeating a remark Holmes made in his nineties, "About seventy-five years ago, I learned that I was not God." Frankfurter added, "When the people want to do something I can't find anything in the Constitution expressly forbidding them to do, I say, 'Whether I like it or not, Goddammit, let 'em do it.'"

HUGO BLACK DIDN'T BELIEVE that the Constitution required such deference to democracy. His views were an extension of his roots. Unlike Frankfurter, Black was almost entirely self-taught. The son of a poor storekeeper, Black attended Ashland College, a high school in the foothills of Appalachia, but was expelled at the age of fifteen for defending one of his sisters against a teacher. His parents shipped him to Birmingham for medical school, but he dropped out after one year. Black finally found his way to the University of Alabama Law School in Tuscaloosa. It couldn't have been further from Harvard. The law school had only two faculty members and didn't require a college degree. Nevertheless, following graduation, Black excelled as a trial lawyer. He was a devout Protestant, with a common touch, which also served him well later in his political campaigns. But even when he entered the U.S. Senate at the age of forty, Black felt insecure about his background, and he began an intensive self-education campaign, reading widely in history.

When FDR nominated Black to the Supreme Court in 1937, Black had neither served as a judge nor had he written even a single law-review article. His principal qualification for the job was that he had supported all of Roosevelt's major New Deal initiatives. Normally the Senate approved judicial nominees quickly, but Black's confirmation hearings lasted three days. Unknown to Roosevelt, Black had been a member of Robert E. Lee Klan No. 1, based in Birmingham. The Senate interrogated Black regarding his KKK membership and his lack of judicial experience.

When Frankfurter joined the Court, two years after Black, he was already firmly enmeshed in its culture. He had a deep, long-lasting friendship with Justice Brandeis, routinely placed law clerks, and wrote influential reviews of key cases. Frankfurter's opposition to *Lochner* largely defined his academic career. Black, by contrast, played no role in either constructing or dismantling *Lochner*. In fact, prior to joining the Court he had never thought about most basic questions of constitutional interpretation.

While Black's lack of experience may have been a liability in his candidacy, it was indispensable to his ultimate contribution to American law. After joining the Court, Black extended his self-education project and began reading extensively in constitutional history. While Frankfurter constructed his jurisprudence to advance the New Deal, Black started from scratch. Without allegiances or agendas he wanted to put into play, Black developed a unique jurisprudential philosophy. In his view the language of the Constitution should always be the Court's touchstone. Meaning, Black said, should be determined by examining the Constitution as it would have been understood at the time it was written. This, more or less, is the view maintained by Antonin Scalia on the current Court.

Black's emergent philosophy, "originalism," had deep roots in his religion. Protestants believe that the Bible can be understood independent of the interpretation of the church. Martin Luther and John Calvin argued that the controlling interpretation of the Bible should derive from the original meaning of the Gospels' words. Originalism in biblical interpretation was empowering and democratic: Anyone could do it. Applying this to constitutional interpretation jibed with Black's populist politics—he deplored the idea that interpreting the Constitution should be the province of elites. By contrast, Frankfurter believed that the role of a Supreme Court justice was to seek answers through a combination of constitutional history, legal precedent, and a judge's own individual sense of fairness. Only a select few could do this. Black's and Frankfurter's contrasting writing styles mirrored their contrasting philosophies. Black wrote in clear language aimed at laymen. Frankfurter wrote like a law professor.

Though their conflict was profound, it defies simple labels. It's inadequately framed as a battle of liberal versus conservative or left versus right. Even judicial activist versus restraintist doesn't satisfactorily describe the conflict. Black actually considered himself a *proponent* of judicial restraint. It was only in instances in which the Constitution said something directly that the Court needed to act boldly. Black's expansive protection of the literal meaning of the Bill of Rights sometimes led to judicial activism. For example, Black joined the unanimous Court in *Brown*, for which he was burned in effigy by segregationists in Alabama, and he took an absolutist position on the First Amendment. "No law means no law," he famously said. But where the Constitution didn't say something explicitly, Black often fell on the conservative side of the fence. For example, he dissented from *Griswold v. Connecticut,* in which the Court overturned a ban on contraceptives under a right to privacy. Black rejected privacy since it wasn't mentioned in the Constitution. Frankfurter was more protective of it.

On the death penalty, though, Frankfurter and Black found common ground. For Black the analysis was simple. The framers hadn't intended to ban capital punishment, so that was that. Frankfurter regarded the death penalty as a complex moral question best left to the states. He expressed this in a concurring opinion in a 1947 case, *Francis v. Resweber.* Willie Francis, sentenced to die for robbery and murder, didn't expire after two attempts to electrocute him. His lawyers said a third attempt would be cruel and unusual. Though Frankfurter claimed to be against capital punishment personally, he urged, as always, for deference. Frankfurter wrote, "The Court must abstain from interference with State action no matter how strong one's personal feeling of revulsion at a state's insistence on its pound of flesh."

This rare agreement between Frankfurter and Black increased the substantial inertia securing the constitutionality of capital punishment. In its history the Supreme Court had reversed some death penalty convictions, but never on the theory that the death penalty was itself problematic. For example, in 1931, when the Court reversed the death sentences of the Scottsboro Boys, nine black men convicted of raping two white women, it did so on the grounds that they had been inadequately represented by their attorneys. The Court didn't address whether a state could properly take life. During the first 175 years of its existence, the Court discussed the cruel and unusual punishment clause only ten times, the death penalty merely six. In each of these instances the Court acknowledged the penalty's legitimacy. In the late nineteenth century the Court upheld the firing squad and electric chair as methods of execution.

When Goldberg sat down with Dershowitz in the summer of 1963, not even the ACLU believed that capital punishment posed a potential violation of constitutional rights. Dershowitz knew all this, and he repeated the conventional wisdom to Goldberg. "At the time the Eighth Amendment was enacted, the colonists were executing people all over the place," Dershowitz said. "Certainly the framers of the Constitution did not regard the death penalty as unconstitutional."

"Therein lies the beauty of our Bill of Rights," Goldberg replied. "It's an evolving document. It means something different today than it meant in 1792."

Dershowitz agreed with Goldberg's sentiment, but he also recognized its temerity. Neither Frankfurter nor Black would agree with this claim. Goldberg's premise, expressed so succinctly—"the Bill of Rights is an evolving document"—represented a heretical interpretation of the Court's role, with implications for every important civil liberties question. Dershowitz understood that if Goldberg's view was to prevail, it would require nothing less than a paradigm shift in American law.

DESPITE THE OBSTACLES Alan Dershowitz was optimistic. In Dershowitz, Arthur Goldberg found a kindred spirit and a life story that was in many ways the New York parallel of his own Chicago childhood. Dershowitz's father, like Goldberg's, worked as a salesman. His mother, like Goldberg's, was a smart woman who had to cut her education short to support her family during the Depression. The Dershowitzes' situation wasn't so dire as the Goldbergs', but Dershowitz, again like Goldberg, went to work as a young teenager and supported himself through school. He got his first job in a deli on Manhattan's Lower East Side, where he tied the strings that separated hot dogs. As an adult Dershowitz prided himself on being a superior turkey slicer.

Also like Goldberg, Dershowitz had an aversion to capital punishment that traced back to his childhood. Dershowitz argued against capital punishment as a member of his high school debating team. He wrote a letter to the then–prime minister of Israel, Golda Meir, arguing that the death penalty was inappropriate even for Adolf Eichmann. At Yale Law School, with Charles Black as his mentor, he honed an interest in criminal law. During his clerkship year with Bazelon, Dershowitz worked extensively on the appeal of a young black man who had been sentenced to die for accidentally killing a policeman. Even though the defendant hadn't intended to kill the officer, under the controversial felony-murder rule, the young man's intention to rob a liquor store became the mens rea, or guilty mind, required for murder. Dershowitz and Bazelon drafted an opinion that spared his life.

Dershowitz and Goldberg also shared religious faith. The possibility of molding a new justice may have influenced Dershowitz to choose Goldberg over Black, but their shared Judaism also played a role. Of Goldberg, Dershowitz said, "He was someone with whom I could identify, a Jew from Chicago." Indeed, Goldberg and Dershowitz's shared commitment to Jewish causes would be the starting point for a long and deep friendship. Goldberg and Dershowitz attended synagogue together during Dershowitz's time in Washington. On Fridays, Goldberg's mother-in-law sent Arthur to Court with homemade gefilte fish and mandelbrot—almond bread—which he dutifully circulated among the law clerks and the justices. On holidays she sent rugelach pastries. After Goldberg left the Court to become ambassador to the United Nations—a decision he regretted—he and Dershowitz often shared the High Holidays in New York. This connection extended to a mutual intellectual commitment to civil liberties and tolerance. Through scholarship and advocacy, the two men worked together against the death penalty for the remainder of Goldberg's life.

In 1963, though, Alan Dershowitz's optimism stemmed from neither religion nor morality. An avid reader, Dershowitz had his finger on the pulse of the American intelligentsia, and he sensed something powerful going on. America's thinking regarding race, power, and poverty was changing in ways that Dershowitz thought boded well for Goldberg's legal revolution. From the standpoint of a liberal intellectual, the twelve-month period preceding Dershowitz's summer meeting with Goldberg was among the most fecund in American history.

Michael Harrington's *The Other America* placed poverty front and center. Harrington, a sociologist at the City University of New York, argued that poverty in America was widespread and largely invisible, as it affected politically powerless groups. His book had a wide influence: Lyndon Johnson later called it the driving force behind the War on Poverty; and drawing on Harrington's work, the Students for a Democratic Society issued the Port Huron Statement, which decried poverty and the plight of minorities. Forgotten segments of American society moved up the national agenda. *The Fire Next Time*—two essays about African American discontent—landed its author, James Baldwin, on the cover of *Time* magazine. Betty Friedan's *The Feminine Mystique* articulated the discontent of women. Rachel Carson's best seller, *Silent Spring*, sparked the American environmental movement. Carson's volume carried on its cover an endorsement by Justice William Douglas, also a noted environmentalist.

Dershowitz drew a direct connection between the death penalty and this growing concern with inequality. He felt that if the discrimination inherent in the practice of capital punishment could be properly substantiated and dramatized, the public, and by extension the Court, would find it impossible to support. Following his meeting with Goldberg, Dershowitz exhaustively cataloged the cases in which a rapist had been sentenced to die. He found that each one involved a white victim and a black defendant.

Through the dog days of August, Dershowitz worked tirelessly. The Supreme Court normally begins its term on the first Monday in October, but Dershowitz had an earlier deadline. He wanted to discuss the death penalty with William Brennan as soon as Brennan returned from his summer vacation in Nantucket. Brennan was the Court's clearest liberal voice, and Goldberg intended to abandon the plan if he failed to get Brennan's endorsement. "Goldberg, the rookie, did not want to be out there alone," Dershowitz recalled. At their initial meeting Goldberg urged Dershowitz to reach out to Brennan as soon as possible to take his temperature.

Generally speaking, Supreme Court justices aren't in the business of discussing cases with their colleagues' law clerks. "This was unheard of," Dershowitz later said. But Dershowitz had been the classmate and moot-court partner of Brennan's son at Yale, and Brennan had also met Dershowitz several times at lunch with Bazelon. Though they had never discussed anything weighty, Brennan trusted Dershowitz. So when Dershowitz contacted him, Brennan agreed to a meeting.

At their late-summer appointment, Brennan asked Dershowitz to summarize his research. Dershowitz told Brennan he had found "a widespread pattern of unequal application of the death penalty on racial grounds." Brennan listened carefully. At the end of the presentation, he made no promises about joining Goldberg's mutinous enterprise, but he encouraged Dershowitz to continue his research.

Dershowitz emerged from the meeting even more buoyant than before. Under Supreme Court rules, the votes of four justices are sufficient to grant cert. Goldberg's vote was a given. Dershowitz now regarded Brennan's support as certain. All they needed were two more votes, and Dershowitz believed he had constructed an irresistible legal argument.

DERSHOWITZ'S POSITION FOCUSED ON a 1958 case, *Trop v. Dulles*. There the Supreme Court ruled favorably on the appeal of Albert Trop, who was dishonorably discharged from the army after escaping for one day from a stockade in Morocco. Trop was later denied a passport under the Nationality Act of 1940, which stripped military deserters of their citizenship. Trop claimed that denationalization was cruel and unusual punishment under the Eighth Amendment. The Court agreed in an opinion authored by Earl Warren. "Citizenship is not a license that expires upon misbehavior," Warren wrote, rejecting "the sheer enormity of the punishment." The departure from judicial restraint was a stinging defeat for Frankfurter, who dissented. "It is not easy to stand aloof and allow want of wisdom to prevail, to disregard one's own strongly held view of what is wise in the conduct of affairs," Frankfurter wrote. "But it is not the business of this Court to pronounce policy."

While *Trop* was a defeat for Frankfurter, it wasn't a clear victory for Black. Black supported the result because, on his reading, nothing in constitutional history supported the military's right to deny citizenship. Warren's opinion, though, went a substantial step further than Black would have gone. The Chief said that the Court needed to do more than enforce the Constitution's original meaning. Warren wrote, "The basic concept underlying the Eighth Amendment is nothing less than the dignity of man. While the State has the power to punish, the Amendment stands to assure that this power be exercised within the limits of civilized standards." On the scope of the right, he said, "The cruel and unusual punishments clause must draw its meaning from the evolving standards of decency that mark the progress of a maturing society." Black vehemently disagreed with the word "evolving." In his view the Constitution didn't change.

Trop gave Dershowitz great hope but also presented his greatest obstacle. On its face, *Trop* appeared helpful, and it was easy enough to imagine Warren opposing capital punishment. During his tenure Warren had done more for civil liberties than any of his predecessors. Also, as governor of California, he had shown signs of opposing the death penalty. But, to secure Hugo Black's vote, Warren prefaced his Eighth Amendment analysis in *Trop* with a substantial disclaimer. "At the outset, let us put to one side the death penalty," he wrote. "The death penalty has been employed throughout our history, and, in a day when it is still widely accepted, it cannot be said to violate the constitutional concept of cruelty." Dershowitz had reminded Goldberg of this history during their summer meeting, and Goldberg agreed it presented a formidable challenge. "That is our biggest problem," Goldberg said. "Earl Warren does not change his mind, so we might have to be satisfied for him to agree part of the way with us."

The absence of scholarly opposition to the constitutionality of the death penalty further complicated Dershowitz's task. Ordinarily a law clerk drafting a brief can find support for almost any proposition, but the idea of ruling the death penalty unconstitutional wasn't percolating in the way that nascent legal reforms ordinarily do. Generally speaking the law isn't prone to revolutionary change. Legal paradigms almost always shift the same way. First, law professors write articles advocating a reform. Then, where appropriate, academics support the proposal with research. Finally, courts begin to act. This is how desegregation proceeded. Prior to *Brown*, surely the most revolutionary decision in Supreme Court history, notes in both the *Columbia Law Review* and *Yale Law Journal* questioned whether racial segregation could be reconciled with the Constitution's guarantee of equal protection. Furthermore the Court signaled *Brown* in decisions finding separate graduate and law schools unequal.

By contrast there existed no case law and almost no scholarly sentiment that the death penalty could or should be ruled unconstitutional. The sole exception was an article in the *Southern California Law Review* by Gerald Gottlieb, who wasn't really part of the academic establishment. A Beverly Hills antitrust lawyer and member of the ACLU's California chapter, Gottlieb said, "It may tenably be urged that the death penalty in the present social setting is unconstitutional." He argued that *Trop* and a 1910 case called *Weems*, where the Court struck down a fifteen-year sentence for falsifying public documents, required the Court to examine evolving standards of decency. Under this standard, he said, the death penalty would be rejected. Gottlieb also said the Court had embraced a requirement of necessity for extreme punishments. The touchstones of cruelty, he said, were whether a punishment inflicted pain without necessity or violated human dignity. Both were true of the death penalty. Gottlieb's piece was eerily ahead of its time; many of his arguments would be cited almost verbatim in *Furman*. In the early 1960s, though, Gottlieb was the only one saying such things.

That is, until Dershowitz.

IN EARLY OCTOBER, DERSHOWITZ presented Goldberg the final product of his work. Like Gottlieb, Dershowitz argued that *Trop* and *Weems* had transformed the Eighth Amendment. From these cases Dershowitz deduced a three-part test for assessing the constitutionality of capital punishment. The death penalty was unconstitutional, he said, if it was condemned by evolving standards of decency, or if the goals of punishment could be accomplished by a less severe punishment, or if it was used for an act that didn't endanger life. With respect to the second prong, Dershowitz presented evidence that the death penalty didn't deter, and his study showing its discriminatory application.

The brief impressed Goldberg, who agreed with everything Dershowitz had written. Goldberg wondered, though, whether it made strategic sense to present the evidence of racism. Some justices might be comfortable striking down an excessive punishment on ethical grounds but reluctant to critique the American criminal justice system as racist. Dershowitz said he thought it was an essential part of the argument. Goldberg said he would think about it.

One week later Goldberg decided to abbreviate the race argument and move it to a footnote. This note cited some national prison statistics and said that ending the death penalty for rape "would eliminate the well-recognized disparity in the imposition of the death penalty for sexual crimes committed by whites and nonwhites." Other than weakening the race argument, though, Goldberg made only modest revisions to Dershowitz's draft, most of which aimed to soften some language that Goldberg thought might be perceived as too strident.

The final draft began with a modest, tempered tone. "I circulate this memorandum, which simply raises some of the relevant considerations and does not purport to be definitive—to afford an opportunity for consideration of the matter prior to our discussion." It focused on the disproportionality of capital punishment for certain crimes, another strategic choice. Goldberg thus left open the option of striking down the death penalty only for certain crimes, such as rape and robbery, in case the justices disliked capital punishment but wanted to proceed by baby steps. He asked, "May human life constitutionally be taken by the State to protect a value other than human life?"

Despite his pledge not to be definitive, Goldberg took a strong position in the Frankfurter-Black debate. The Court shouldn't avoid the death penalty because of judicial restraint, he said. If the Eighth Amendment only prohibited punishments already condemned by public opinion, then it would be a "dead letter," since these punishments would already have been abolished by the legislature. "The Eighth Amendment was intended as a counter-majoritarian limitation on government action," Goldberg wrote. "It should be applied to nurture rather than to retard our evolving standards of decency." Goldberg also noted the worldwide trend in favor of abolition. "Most of the civilized nations of the western world have abolished the death penalty, and few that have abolished it have ever restored it."

Goldberg continued with a litany of policy arguments against the death penalty. If an innocent person was executed, the mistake could never be corrected. Furthermore a less severe punishment would be equally or more effective than the death penalty. The death penalty didn't attempt to rehabilitate offenders. Vengeance was widely regarded as an unacceptable goal of punishment. The only argument that could be offered in favor of the death penalty was that it deterred other potential criminals. Dershowitz had reviewed every major study on the effect of capital punishment on murder. His conclusion, and Goldberg's, was that one could neither say that the death penalty deterred nor that it didn't deter: The research was too rudimentary. In the words of University of Michigan law professor Francis Allen, inquiries into the deterrent effect of capital punishment "rarely approached any minimum standards of decent scientific rigor." Goldberg argued that the "onus of proof" regarding to the necessity of taking human life was on the states. Since no state could produce adequate evidence, the death penalty must be rejected.

Goldberg concluded by articulating his vision of the Constitution as an evolving document, harkening back to Earl Warren's opinion in *Trop*. "Whatever may be said of times past," Goldberg wrote, "the evolving standards of decency that mark the progress of society now condemn the deliberate institutionalized taking of human life by the state as barbaric and inhuman." Here was the root of his sedition: Goldberg proposed to measure the constitutionality of capital punishment not by the language or intent of the Founding Fathers but rather by the conditions and needs of modern society.

Just as Black's interpretive model was informed by his religion, so too was Goldberg's. In February 1963 Goldberg spoke at the Waldorf-Astoria at the dedication dinner of the Jewish Publication Society of America. The speech was about the relevance of the Bible, but it might as well have been about Goldberg's view of the Constitution. "We read it, of course, because it is great literature, because surprisingly enough to some, it has much historical validity, and because it contains great dramas like the Book of Job and offers the beautiful poetry of the Psalms. But these are not the only or the most basic reasons for studying the Bible," he said. "We study it and we must study it to learn and profit from the great truths which are to be found in its teaching about God, about the Universe, and about the purpose of life itself."

AT THE END OF OCTOBER, Goldberg circulated the document to his colleagues. It was, in Dershowitz's words, a "bombshell," not only for what Goldberg said but that he had dared to say it. The Supreme Court is an institution of deep, long-standing traditions, and it's rare for a justice to write at length about a case that hasn't been set for argument. Writing about a general issue, as Goldberg had, was nearly unprecedented. Reflecting on this history in 1986, Brennan said, "It was, and still is, most unusual for an individual justice to take it upon himself or herself to write at length, prior to Conference, about cases which had neither been argued nor even set for argument, and then to circulate that memorandum to all of his or her colleagues." Worse still, Goldberg made clear that he also envisioned ultimately publishing his memorandum as a law-review article.

Goldberg breached protocol still further by proposing that the Court take up the constitutionality of the death penalty in six pending capital cases, even though the issue hadn't been raised by any of the defendants. "In none of the six capital cases on the current Conference list has the cruel and unusual punishment issue been explicitly presented to this Court," Goldberg conceded. He made no argument that the Court was obligated to consider the death penalty, and offered only a strained argument that the Court could consider it. "But in knowingly sustaining the death penalty in each of these cases, the courts necessarily passed on the legality of its imposition; and, considering the nature of the issue, petitioners' failure to urge it should not preclude this Court from considering this matter." The idea of the Supreme Court deciding an issue not raised by an appellant was nearly unheard of.

Goldberg had thrown tradition completely aside.

"The first reaction was a shutting of minds," Dershowitz said later. Warren and Black had the strongest negative reactions to Goldberg's breaches of protocol. They each found the memorandum presumptuous. Black was furious. In his twenty-five years on the Court, he had never seen an act as reckless as Goldberg's. As the father of originalism, Black also found the legal argument lacking. At a law-clerk lunch Black teased Dershowitz that he had been wise to accept Goldberg's clerkship offer. "Black said I had made the right decision because he would never have given me this type of assignment." Warren's constitutional analysis was the same as Black's. "Of course the death penalty is constitutional," Warren said. "The framers intended it."

Black and Warren's opposition, though, went deeper than a disagreement over interpretation. Their political instincts told them that Americans wouldn't tolerate the Court overturning the death penalty. The Court had paid a steep price for its decision in *Brown*. No one understood this better than the Chief. He had seen for himself the "Impeach Earl Warren" billboards and bumper stickers defacing the South in the wake of *Brown*. He had endured being called a Communist by Senator James Eastland of Mississippi, and been insulted by Alabama's segregationist governor George Wallace as lacking the "brains to try a chicken thief." He watched as Arkansas governor Orval Faubus openly defied *Brown* in 1957. President Eisenhower ultimately sent federal troops to protect the nine black students who enrolled at Central High School in

Little Rock that fall, but did so only with great reluctance. Frankfurter might be wrong to take judicial restraint to an extreme, but the kernel of his position had merit. Warren understood how close the Court had come to being delegitimized during the late fifties.

The Court had pushed the boundary when it forcibly integrated public schools. Ruling the death penalty unconstitutional would mean stepping in on behalf of black rapists and murderers. This would be more than the public could take. Furthermore, as Dershowitz's research revealed, the Court wouldn't just be championing black criminals, but blacks who had raped whites. Even though the evidence had been buried in a footnote, it remained obvious that Goldberg's concern with racism drove his memorandum. The problem of black-on-white crime was a particular sticking point. Dershowitz later said, "I think Warren was quite concerned about bringing to public attention the perception of interracial rape. I think he wanted to stay away from that issue."

These political considerations carried great weight with the other justices. John Harlan said he thought it "a very poor time to bring the matter up." From afar Frankfurter recoiled in horror at the Goldberg memorandum. Former justice Sherman Minton wrote Frankfurter, "How they must miss you! Mr. Justice Goldberg is a walking Constitutional Convention. Wow, what an activist he is!" Frankfurter referred to his successor derisively as "Goldberg, the scholar."

Even the law clerks were up in arms. One of Potter Stewart's law clerks, Jan Deutsch, railed to Dershowitz about the direction of the Court. Deutsch already viewed *Escobedo v. Illinois*, in which the Court expanded the right to counsel to police interrogations, as the death knell of the Frankfurter era, and with it all moderation. Regarding the memorandum, he told Dershowitz, "This is going to destroy the paradigm."

GOLDBERG EXPECTED THE OPPOSITION. He didn't anticipate, however, the lack of support. Even the justices sympathetic to Goldberg's position appreciated the basis of Warren's political concerns.

Brennan had been noncommittal in his meeting with Dershowitz, and now seemed disinclined to go as far as Goldberg wanted to go. Surprisingly Stewart offered support for the memorandum, but it was tepid and vague and Goldberg doubted it would translate into a vote.

Douglas also discouraged Goldberg from pressing the issue. This disheartened Goldberg. If anyone should have been willing to go against tradition, it should have been Douglas, a maverick who had serious reservations about capital punishment. During one discussion Douglas asked Goldberg, "Would a state law imposing the death sentence for larceny of twenty-five dollars or more be constitutional?" Reporting the conversation later, Douglas said, "He did not think so, nor did I." Nevertheless, when Goldberg approached Douglas for advice, Douglas urged restraint. Douglas said, "It would be best to let the matter sleep for a while."

Goldberg thought long and hard about the issue. He respected Earl Warren, and understood the political sensitivities involved. He also believed that the death penalty would never end unless the Supreme Court led the way. Judicial restraint was particularly inappropriate in this context. America needed a push in the right direction. After a few days Goldberg sought out Brennan. His friend's analysis mirrored his own. Brennan, too, had enormous regard for Warren. He, too, regarded the death penalty as immoral and urgent. Brennan recommended framing the memorandum around a series of questions rather than presenting it as an argument. Goldberg liked this idea, and his resolve solidified.

At the end of October, however, Warren personally appealed to Goldberg not to publish the memo. Face-to-face with the Chief, Goldberg couldn't say no. Goldberg and Warren had a long-standing friendship, and in his professional life Goldberg saw Warren as a force for good. Goldberg didn't want to undermine him. In any event Goldberg didn't have the votes. If push came to shove, he couldn't be sure that Douglas or Stewart would support him. Even Brennan might support the Chief out of loyalty.

So Goldberg compromised with Warren. He wouldn't make the

memo public. Instead he would dissent from the denial of review
in one of the six cases. This itself would be unusual—justices rarely
publish opinions discussing cert—but it wouldn't cause nearly the
stir as a sitting justice publishing an internal memorandum in a law
review. Furthermore Goldberg agreed to soften his argument. His
dissent would focus only on the appropriateness of the death penalty
for less than capital crimes, rather than its overall constitutionality,
and he would further cut the race argument. Warren insisted upon
this, invoking the specter of *Brown*. He said the public wouldn't tolerate the Court casting a soft vote on rape. More than anything else
whites feared sexual violence by blacks. It was for this reason Warren had delayed confronting the constitutionality of laws prohibiting
interracial marriage.

After striking the deal, Goldberg made the rounds. Brennan
endorsed the compromise. Douglas did too. All that remained was
to tell Dershowitz. That afternoon Goldberg called his law clerk into
his office and related the agreement. They wouldn't publish the memorandum. They would publish a dissent, but it would be substantially
pared down. "Alan, you are going to be very disappointed," Goldberg
said. "Bill Brennan and I have decided that we have to do a much more
shortened version of this. It will have to be a more cryptic opinion."

Dershowitz was crushed. The decision to soften the dissent bothered him more than the decision not to publish the memorandum.
Dershowitz wanted to see the supporters of the death penalty exposed
and forced to account for their positions. Years later he said, "I wanted
to see a direct challenge to the death penalty as a matter of principle."

None would follow for almost a decade.

GOLDBERG AND DERSHOWITZ'S ATTENTION turned to decid-
ing which of the six cases to use for the dissent. They chose the appeal
of Frank Lee Rudolph, a black man who had been sentenced to die for
raping a white woman in Alabama. Once they picked the case, they
negotiated with Warren's chambers on what language could remain

regarding race. Warren held firm, and Goldberg's published dissent contained no explicit reference to race. The Chief agreed only to allow a reference in a footnote to the *United Nations Report on Capital Punishment*, prepared by Marc Ancel, a justice of the French Supreme Court. The footnote cited Ancel's report only for some statistics on state and national practices, though the report itself contained data exposing racism. Dershowitz and Goldberg hoped that this oblique reference would be enough to suggest the race argument.

Finally Goldberg focused on getting as much support as possible for his dissent. For a moment a ninth-inning grand slam seemed possible. Stewart again commented favorably on the memorandum and seemed genuinely troubled by the death penalty. Dershowitz believed that Stewart was experiencing a cognitive dissonance between his morality and his view of the proper role of courts. It was as if Black and Frankfurter were battling for his soul. "Emotionally he was on our side," Dershowitz said, but in the end Stewart abided by judicial restraint. Ultimately only Brennan and Douglas joined Goldberg's dissent.

Dershowitz had mixed feelings about Goldberg's opinion as published on October 21, 1963. It consisted of but four short paragraphs, a modest document by any standards, and puny in comparison to the comprehensive treatise he had prepared over the summer. It also felt intellectually insubstantial. Dershowitz's memorandum had laid out the death penalty's history and a careful conceptual framework for showing how its imposition violated the Constitution. All that work was gone. The dissent focused only on the excessiveness of death as punishment for rape. It seemed bizarre to Dershowitz to make no mention of racism in the appeal of a black man who was the victim of systemic racism. Dershowitz feared the dissent would be lost. "It was so delphic and cryptic," he said.

Goldberg had a more pragmatic view of the enterprise. Throughout the summer and early fall he had cautioned Dershowitz that they might not prevail that term. Goldberg saw the dissent as the beginning, not the end of the project. Now they needed to spur the bar into action. Goldberg encouraged Dershowitz to use his connections from law school and his clerkship and get the word out about his summer research. "The memo is confidential," Goldberg told Dershowitz, "but the work is yours. Put out the research as your own research." Dershowitz did precisely this. He made some telephone calls to make sure people were aware of the dissent. Then he mailed copies of his memorandum to the ACLU, several academics, and, most importantly, the NAACP Legal Defense Fund.

CHAPTER 2

THE MOST IMPORTANT LAW FIRM IN AMERICA

IN EARLY NOVEMBER NEWS OF GOLDBERG'S DISSENT circulated through a suite of offices on the twentieth floor of 10 Columbus Circle in midtown Manhattan. Though one would never know it from appearances, this was home to the most important law firm in America. The twenty-six-story tower overlooking Columbus Circle was a grim appendage to the New York Coliseum, designed by Lionel Levy in the International Style, a branch of postmodern architecture the Nazis rejected as too austere. When the building opened in 1956, it had bad plumbing, inadequate heating, and was widely regarded as an eyesore. An architect with offices in the tower said the best thing about working in the building was that he didn't have to look at it.

To add insult to injury, the firm's founder, Thurgood Marshall, had been lucky to get this space. When Marshall tried to move the group from its initial, even more dilapidated home on West Forty-Third Street, real estate developers wouldn't deal with him. Marshall had to turn for help to Hulan Jack, a Harlem politician who had worked himself up from janitor at a paper box company to Manhattan borough president. Jack imposed on Robert Moses, the legendary power broker who controlled the skyscraper under the auspices of the Triborough Bridge and Tunnel Authority, to lease the mediocre space to Marshall.

But to take a left turn out of the elevators and walk across the frayed blue carpet and into suite 2030 was to enter a lawyer's Cooperstown. Here in the first office on the left was Constance Baker Motley, the Columbia Law School graduate who drafted the complaint in *Brown*. She would succeed Jack as borough president and later become the first African American woman to serve as a federal judge. Here three doors down was Derrick Bell, who, with Motley, had led the desegregation fight in Mississippi. Bell would become a professor at Harvard Law School, leave in protest over the school's hiring practices, become dean of Oregon Law School, and help found the field of critical race theory. Here too was Jack Greenberg, Marshall's handpicked successor, who had argued forty cases before the Supreme Court.

The National Association for the Advancement of Colored People Legal Defense Fund, sometimes known as the Inc. Fund or, more simply, LDF, had won countless legal victories since its founding twenty-three years earlier. LDF lawyers won *Smith v. Allwright*, a 1944 decision requiring Texas to allow African Americans to vote in primary elections. They prevailed in *Morgan v. Virginia*, the 1946 case desegregating interstate buses. They won cases protecting the rights of African Americans to serve on juries, striking down real estate contracts that precluded property sales to African Americans, and ensuring equal pay for black schoolteachers. And, of course, they won *Brown*.

In 1957, facing pressure from the IRS about LDF's independence, Marshall broke LDF off from the NAACP. Thereafter the organization extended its already legendary reputation. In 1958 it protected the desegregation of Arkansas schools. In 1961 it won *Holmes v. Danner*, integrating the University of Georgia. In 1962 Bell and Motley won *Meredith v. Fair*, opening up the University of Mississippi. When Goldberg's memorandum arrived in 1963, LDF's lawyers were busy defending Martin Luther King, Jr., against contempt charges stemming from his protest of Birmingham segregation. Soon, thanks to LDF, the Supreme Court would dismiss all prosecutions stemming from the civil rights sit-ins.

Many people perceived the organization's power as limitless. When the man who ran LDF's primitive copying machine got into minor legal trouble, Greenberg offered to help. He replied, "Mr. Greenberg, I just want to get out of the fine, I don't want to go to the Supreme Court."

IN EARLY SPRING THREE LDF attorneys bought sandwiches at a delicatessen on Seventh Avenue, and carried them to the lawn in Central Park, where they sat and discussed the implication of Goldberg's dissent. These three lunch partners could hardly have been more different.

Leroy Clark and Frank Heffron were each graduates of Columbia Law School, but the similarities ended there. Clark was black and a fiery critic of American racism. Heffron was white, and expressed himself more dispassionately; Clark called him "straight arrow." Michael Meltsner was also white but, unlike Heffron, a free spirit. A native New Yorker, Meltsner graduated from Stuyvesant High School, Oberlin College, and Yale Law School, and seemed headed down a conventional path. After graduating from law school, though, Meltsner went to work at a kibbutz, not a law firm. During his lifetime he would write a novel, a play, take acting lessons, and become licensed as a family therapist. He would also run Northeastern Law School and help found a transformative movement in legal education. But he would never, not for even a day, represent clients for money.

Despite their different backgrounds, all three men perceived the same opportunity: Goldberg's dissent had stirred the pot. The *New York Times* praised his opinion, saying it raised a "potentially far-reaching idea." The *Washington Post* called it "an appeal to the brooding spirit of the law, to the intelligence of a future day." Moreover, public support for the death penalty had been waning. In 1953, 68 percent of Americans supported capital punishment. In the recent Gallup poll this figure had fallen to 53 percent. The death penalty had lost momentum.

At the same time the three men understood that abolition wouldn't come easily. Goldberg's dissent also had generated substantial oppo-

sition. William Loeb, the publisher of New Hampshire's conservative *Manchester Union Leader*, said the decision "can serve only to
encourage would-be rapists." The Stanford Law School professor Herbert Packer called out Goldberg's true motives. "If one may venture a
guess," Packer wrote, "what Justice Goldberg may really be troubled
about is not the death penalty for rape but the death penalty." If capital
punishment was to be abolished, he said, this change would need to
come from the people, not the Supreme Court. Packer wrote: "Other
social forces will have to work us closer than we now are to the point
at which a judicial *coup de grace* becomes more than mere fiat." The
editors of the *Harvard Law Review* agreed, saying, "To hold that capital punishment is a method of punishment wholly prohibited by the
eighth amendment would be to confuse possible legislative desirability
with constitutional requirements."

Furthermore Goldberg's failure to mention race posed a daunting
problem. LDF was dedicated to ending racism, first and foremost.
If racism was not the problem, what basis did LDF have to become
involved against the death penalty? Goldberg's omission angered
Clark. Surely racism in capital sentencing merited mention. Heffron
wondered whether the act of publishing the memorandum implied
that racism concerned the Court. After all, Rudolph was a black man
accused of raping a white woman. The reality was that no one could
be sure what the Court or even Goldberg meant. Meltsner worried too
about the difficulties of proving discrimination. The American criminal justice system was a complex scheme, with many variables at play,
and courts generally didn't allow statistical proof of discrimination.

Despite the challenges, Meltsner and Clark felt that LDF should
take on the issue. Even Heffron, generally the voice of restraint, felt
they had nothing to lose. LDF received many requests from black
defendants facing the death penalty. They generally accepted the cases
even though capital cases are expensive to litigate, and LDF had limited resources. The lawyers simply found it impossible to say no. Heffron told his colleagues, "If we aren't able to turn these cases away, we
might as well focus on the real issue—capital punishment."

Later the trio made their pitch to Jack Greenberg. Greenberg saw the complications of the issue, but nevertheless responded by appointing Heffron to study racial discrimination in rape sentencing. Whether this represented a change in LDF policy would later be the subject of some dispute. In his memoir Meltsner would write that at the time of this pivotal lunch, "capital punishment was not on the Fund's agenda." Greenberg would in turn disagree, saying that he had been considering a challenge to the death penalty for some time. Whether Greenberg or Meltsner is correct doesn't matter much. From 1963 on, LDF influenced every major death penalty case in the United States and was the leading voice in the abolition movement, dominating all others.

CAPITAL PUNISHMENT SHOULD HAVE been a natural issue for the American Civil Liberties Union. Formed in the 1920s, by a group that included Clarence Darrow and Felix Frankfurter, the ACLU had its hand in countless civil rights triumphs. In 1931 it successfully defended Yetta Stromberg, who displayed a Communist flag in defiance of California law. In 1943 its lawyers overturned the expulsion of two thousand Jehovah's Witnesses who had refused to recite the Pledge of Allegiance. It was the ACLU that encouraged John Scopes to defy the Tennessee law prohibiting the teaching of evolution. The ACLU had also played a critical role in race cases, joining with the NAACP in successfully arguing against all-white primaries, and filing a friend-of-the-Court brief in *Brown*. With fifty thousand members, the ACLU was the most influential defender of civil liberties in the United States. Nevertheless, in 1963, the ACLU had no position on the death penalty. Officially the organization didn't regard capital punishment as a civil rights matter.

The ACLU's reluctance to become involved on capital punishment stemmed in part from an institutional aversion to being attached to political causes. Many felt that the organization had suffered for becoming excessively associated with the labor movement during the 1930s. In the summer of 1964 the leadership of the ACLU was deeply divided over whether to become involved with the "Freedom Summer," the Student Nonviolent Coordinating Committee's effort to use white college students to register black voters in Mississippi. George Papcun, an Arizona civil rights leader, called on the ACLU to "support the Negro revolution totally." Osmond Fraenkel, an eighty-one-year-old legend in the civil rights movement, successfully urged restraint. Fraenkel said the organization had to limit itself to advocating for civil liberties and not become involved in political issues. The reaffirmation of this principle made it more difficult for the ACLU to support abolition because the organization's leadership didn't see capital punishment as a civil rights issue. Emanuel Redfield, counsel to the New York Civil Liberties Union, argued that procedural abuses had been confused with civil liberties issues. Redfield also saw race as a double-edged sword. Racism by itself couldn't suggest that capital punishment should be abolished, Redfield said, "for logically, this argument would call for the abolition of any other penalty when it can be shown that a higher percentage of a certain race is punished." In his view the racism argument weakened the case against capital punishment.

The ACLU's position would soon change. In the mid-1960s the ACLU asked Norman Dorsen, a law professor at NYU, to draft a memo outlining both sides of the capital punishment issue. Dorsen presented Redfield's view but argued that regardless of the technical merits of the racism argument, the death penalty was "inconsistent with the spirit of civil liberties" and "dehumanizes a society which employs it." At Dorsen's urging the ACLU adopted an abolitionist policy in 1965, denouncing the death penalty as "inconsistent with the underlying values of a democratic system." Even after issuing this statement, though, the ACLU aimed its efforts primarily at state legislatures rather than courts. The ACLU was heavily involved in defending conscientious objectors to the Vietnam War, and its leadership believed the organization didn't have the resources to lead another major litigation effort. During the 1970s they would agitate more actively against the death penalty. By this time, though, LDF was firmly established as the leader of the litigation effort, and neither anyone nor any organization, including the ACLU, would ever challenge its authority in the matter.

LDF's ASCENSION TO ITS position of unquestioned prominence had two profound consequences. The first was that LDF construed the death penalty as a problem of race. Its conception of the issue would evolve, but for the first several years of its involvement LDF would challenge capital punishment primarily on the basis of its discriminatory impact. Greenberg's first initiative following the Central Park lunch was appointing Heffron to conduct a preliminary study of racism in rape sentences in southern states. Greenberg also tried, with limited success, to raise money from private foundations to support race research. The downside of this worldview is that racism is extremely difficult to prove. LDF's first major death penalty case offers a vivid illustration of these difficulties. The chronology of the case also offers a sober reminder of how long it takes a capital case to wend its way through the labyrinth of the criminal justice system.

William Maxwell was a black man sentenced to die for the rape of a white woman. He was twenty-one years old when he committed his crime in 1961. Following his trial in 1962, Maxwell unsuccessfully appealed to the Arkansas Supreme Court. He then began a separate proceeding, known as a petition for a writ of habeas corpus, in which he challenged the constitutionality of his state court conviction.* Maxwell's attorney argued that the jury selection procedure had been racially biased and that the Arkansas rape statute was discriminatorily applied. A federal district court judge, Gordon Young, denied that petition in 1964. Maxwell unsuccessfully appealed that ruling to the Federal Court of Appeals for the Eighth Circuit and then, also unsuccessfully, sought

---

* Literally *habeas corpus* means "you have the body." Seeking a habeas writ is the principal means by which a state prisoner can challenge his confinement in federal court.

review in the U.S. Supreme Court in 1965.* In 1966, with LDF acting as his new counsel, he filed a second habeas corpus petition based on new evidence of racism. A second district court judge, Jesse Henley, rejected the new petition. The Eighth Circuit affirmed without holding a hearing. Maxwell appealed to the U.S. Supreme Court, which ordered the Eighth Circuit to hold a hearing. Following the hearing, the Eighth Circuit again rejected all of Maxwell's arguments in the summer of 1968. Maxwell appealed yet again to the U.S. Supreme Court, which heard oral argument in March 1969, deferred his case to the following term, heard additional argument the next May, and then in June 1970, again remanded Maxwell's case to the Eighth Circuit to determine whether jury selection procedures had been proper. Finally, in January 1971, shortly before leaving office, Winthrop Rockefeller, the reformist governor of Arkansas, commuted the sentences of Maxwell and the fourteen other men on the state's death row. Maxwell's case took ten years from start to finish. Aside from the happy ending, Maxwell's story is typical of death penalty cases, which take an average of eleven years from trial to execution.

Along this tortured and tortuous path the courts rejected all the various evidence of racism that Maxwell offered. His first attorney offered the testimony of an Arkansas prison superintendent saying that blacks were executed disproportionately. The Arkansas state courts rejected this evidence out of hand. When LDF presented Heffron's study, the federal district court judge deemed it inconclusive. Heffron's work consisted largely of interviews with court clerks. LDF later improved its earlier efforts with the assistance of Marvin Wolfgang, a sociologist from the University of Pennsylvania. Wolfgang led LDF to hire students from the Law Students Civil Rights Research Council and sent them to the south to collect data during the summer of 1965. The

---

* In the federal system, the trial courts are known as district courts. The intermediate appellate courts are known as the courts of appeals, or circuit courts, corresponding to numbered geographical districts—for example, the Eighth Circuit Court of Appeals covers Arkansas, Iowa, Minnesota, Missouri, Nebraska, and the Dakotas. The Supreme Court is the court of last resort.

students examined the records of rape cases in twelve southern states between 1945 and 1965 and found that 110 out of 119 defendants who received death sentences were black. In Arkansas they found that a black man convicted of raping a white woman had an approximately 50 percent chance of receiving a death sentence, while a man convicted of raping a woman of his own race was sentenced to die only 14 percent of the time. The disparity could have been due to other forces, so the students examined the effect of twenty-nine other aggravating and mitigating factors, such as the defendant's age and the amount of force used. From this evidence Wolfgang concluded that the odds were less than one in a thousand that the race disparity was random. Even this more sophisticated analysis failed. Judge Jesse Henley, the Eisenhower Republican who presided over the second habeas trial, questioned the sample size of the study and the choice of variables. More generally he questioned the use of statistics, which he called "elusive things at best," and added, channeling Mark Twain, "it is a truism that almost anything can be proved by them."

After the Supreme Court ordered the Eighth Circuit to rule on Maxwell's appeal, Harry Blackmun, then an appellate court judge, ominously dismissed Maxwell's statistical evidence. Professor Wolfgang's study is "interesting and provocative," Blackmun wrote, but "we are not yet ready to condemn and upset the result reached in every case of a Negro rape defendant in the State of Arkansas on the basis of broad theories of social and statistical injustice." Blackmun said he felt LDF's pain. "We can understand and appreciate the disappointment and seeming frustration which Maxwell's counsel must feel in again failing to prevail on a still more sophisticated statistical approach. They will ask themselves just how far they are required to go in order to prevail." But Blackmun offered little hope: "We are not certain that, for Maxwell, statistics will ever be his redemption." History would prove him sooth.

Twenty years later, in *McCleskey v. Kemp*, the Supreme Court would reject the most comprehensive and sophisticated analysis ever conducted of racism in capital sentencing. David Baldus, of the University of Iowa, his faculty colleague George Woodworth, and Charles

Pulaski of Arizona State University examined more than 2,400 murder cases in Georgia during the 1970s, coding for the effect of 230 potentially aggravating or mitigating variables. Baldus, Woodworth, and Pulaski found that a defendant who killed a white person was 4.3 times more likely to receive the death penalty than a defendant whose victim was black, and that this race consciousness was evident both in decisions by prosecutors to seek the death penalty and by juries in deciding whether to impose it. Still, the Eleventh Circuit Court of Appeals and the Supreme Court rejected the evidence.

They did so because rejecting a punishment on the basis of racism would undermine the entire criminal justice system. If systemic evidence of racism was deemed sufficient to strike down the death penalty, why would it not call into question life imprisonment without parole or prison sentences of shorter length? If race affected prosecutor and jury decisions in death penalty cases, as the Baldus study proved, then surely it affected decisions in noncapital cases too. No court ever dared strike down a penalty on the basis of statistical evidence because establishing such a precedent would fundamentally undermine the existing order. Instead, to prove racism, judges would require a showing of discrimination in the specific case. With respect to systemic evidence of discrimination, courts would say something vague and unsatisfying, such as what the Arkansas Supreme Court said in *Maxwell*—"the statute for rape applies to all citizens"—and leave it at that.

The reluctance of courts to admit racism would remain a thorn in LDF's side for the duration of the capital campaign. LDF would consistently have to fight the perception that it was trying to radically subvert the system. Efforts by conservatives and state and federal government attorneys to substantiate this perception—and LDF's counterefforts to fight it—would be an issue in *Furman* and the defining dynamic of the 1976 cases.

THE SECOND CONSEQUENCE OF LDF's dominance was that it brought Anthony Amsterdam to the issue. If LDF was the most important law firm in the United States, Tony Amsterdam was surely the most important individual lawyer. No other attorney in American history has had such a profound influence on civil rights issues. In addition to playing a role in every major Supreme Court death penalty case argued since 1965, Amsterdam won important victories limiting the ability of police officers to stop and frisk suspects, protecting free speech, and in defense of the civil rights of the Black Panther Bobby Seale. He argued dozens of cases before the Supreme Court, once three in a single week. Amsterdam's staying power is extraordinary. His chief rival for title of Most Influential Lawyer of the Twentieth Century, Thurgood Marshall, ultimately left LDF for a judicial career. Amsterdam, by contrast, is a lifer. His influence has extended over six decades and continues to this day. He wrote an amicus brief for the ACLU in *Miranda* in 1965,* and consulted with Seth Waxman, the former U.S. solicitor general, before Waxman's 2005 Supreme Court oral argument in *Roper v. Simmons*, the case that struck down the death penalty for juveniles.

Amsterdam was raised in West Philadelphia, a middle-class melting pot of Jews, blacks, and Italian Americans. His father, Gustave, who had been a military lawyer during World War II, worked as a corporate executive. Amsterdam's son Jon, an education reformer in Philadelphia, recalls his grandfather "as a New Dealer, a pragmatist who believed you could fix things if you could assemble the details. Like his son, he was hard working and a little bit distant." Amsterdam's mother, Valla, raised the family and volunteered for various organizations. Though they descended from a line of rabbis, the Amsterdams were not religious and named their son Anthony, which identified him more with the Italians in the neighborhood than the Jews. Young Tony liked to play sports, especially basketball, and occasionally competed in pickup games with Wilt Chamberlain.

Shortly after Tony turned twelve, he contracted bulbar polio, an

---

* An amicus brief is a submission by an amicus curiae, literally "a friend of the court," presenting information or expertise that may be helpful to the court. Courts have complete discretion whether to allow amicus briefs.

uncommon version of the virus that attacks the nerves of the brain stem. Though Amsterdam avoided paralysis, he was confined to an iron lung for several days and spent weeks in quarantine. He has blocked out many details of the experience, but it clearly shaped him. During his absence Tony's teammates elected him boxball captain. Amsterdam returned for the end of the season "mightily inspired to play better."

From that point on, it seemed he did everything better. At Haverford College he majored in comparative literature, devoured seventeenth century French poetry, and graduated summa cum laude. "I pushed myself very hard," he recalled, "but not to study in the sense of folks who are trying to accomplish something." After graduation, he attended University of Pennsylvania Law School, though without any firm sense of why he wanted to be a lawyer. He spent much of his time at law school auditing art history classes at Bryn Mawr College, where he developed a special fondness for sixteenth and seventeenth century European mannerist paintings. Son Jon says, "Tony's not just a law nerd, he's very aesthetically attuned." Tony took nature walks. He also wrote poetry, painted watercolors, and considered becoming an art historian. But he was drawn to the law and excelled at it. During his time away from his creative pursuits, he became editor in chief of the law review. After graduating first in his class in 1960, he headed to the Supreme Court to clerk for Felix Frankfurter.

By the time Amsterdam reached the Supreme Court, Frankfurter was eighty years old and in failing health. As a result he entrusted Amsterdam with even more than the substantial responsibility clerks normally have. Though Amsterdam wouldn't acknowledge it, he drafted much of Frankfurter's dissent in *Baker v. Carr*, a seminal voting rights case, which the justice cared passionately about. Congressional districting was precisely the sort of issue Frankfurter believed the Court should avoid. Brennan's 1962 opinion striking down Tennessee's gerrymandering scheme marked the end of Frankfurter's dominance on the Court. Two weeks after the announcement of the decision, Frankfurter suffered his stroke. Amsterdam blamed the case. At the time Amsterdam couldn't appreciate the irony of his work on *Baker*. The Court's rejection of Frankfurter's doctrine of judicial restraint opened the door to the arguments he would later make in the death penalty cases.

At the end of Amsterdam's clerkship, Frankfurter recommended him to the U.S. Attorney for the District of Columbia, where Amsterdam worked for a year as a prosecutor, "to learn something from the inside," as he put it. Then, at the age of twenty-six, Amsterdam returned to his alma mater as a law professor, where he began to build his unparalleled reputation.

The secret of Amsterdam's success was that he outworked everyone. Tall, rail thin, with a long, patrician nose and fine hair brushed to the side, Amsterdam sat in his office, crowded with books, chain-smoked thin cigars, swilled strong black coffee and diet soda, and burned the candle at both ends. Michael Meltsner says he worked hard at LDF, but nothing compared to Amsterdam. The people around him believed that Amsterdam read every decision by the circuit courts of appeals and slept only a few hours a night.

Impossibly, Amsterdam's reputation for competence exceeded his reputation for diligence. The tales of his prodigious memory sound apocryphal. In one infamous incident Amsterdam was arguing a case before the D.C. Circuit Court of Appeals when he referenced an old Supreme Court case, which he cited from memory by page and volume. The judge wasn't buying Amsterdam's argument and dispatched an assistant to find the case. He couldn't locate it and questioned Amsterdam's citation. "Your honor," said the young prosecutor, "your volume must be misbound." Sure enough, it was.

Everyone in this universe has a Tony Amsterdam fish story. In one, Amsterdam dictated a brief from memory from a pay phone at four o'clock in the morning. A second tale is the sort to drive high achievers mad. Two months before law school graduation, Amsterdam hadn't begun his required law-review note. The paper he dashed off, "Void for Vagueness Doctrine in the Supreme Court," reshaped First Amendment law.

Everyone in this universe also shares the same ultimate judgment of Amsterdam. Edward Lazarus, author of a memoir of his year clerking for Harry Blackmun, called Amsterdam "the finest lawyer of his generation." Franklin Zimring, a lawyer and criminologist at the University of California, says, "Amsterdam was, and deserved to be, as early as 1968, for American academics, its only genuine rock star. He was a hero to many people, and a hero of mine. He was a phenomenally gifted lawyer and litigator." Dershowitz calls Amsterdam a "terrific lawyer and a contemporary role model." Seth Waxman says, "God broke the mold when he created Tony."

AMSTERDAM GOT INVOLVED with LDF shortly after the Central Park lunch. One of LDF's early death penalty cases was an appeal by Charles Hamilton, a black man who had been sentenced to die for breaking into a home with intent to rape. Caleb Foote, a Berkeley law professor and social activist, assisted LDF on the case. He was unable to make a strategy meeting in New York and asked Amsterdam to go in his place.

Amsterdam had not previously debated the death penalty and didn't have a position on it. "I didn't start by becoming an abolitionist. I really had never given it much thought," he recalled. It was the framing of the death penalty as a race issue that attracted Amsterdam. His real interest was inequality or, as he called it, "underdogism." Amsterdam told *Time* magazine that a free society must pay attention to all views. "After the revolution, I will be representing the capitalists," he said.

At the Hamilton meeting Amsterdam impressed LDF. "They seemed to think my ideas were useful," Amsterdam recalled with characteristic understatement. Greenberg invited Amsterdam to speak at an LDF conference for cooperating attorneys at Dillard University in New Orleans. Amsterdam dazzled everyone there and soon began consulting with LDF more extensively.

Amsterdam's interest in race issues and LDF's conception of the death penalty mutually reinforced each other. Amsterdam urged LDF to expand upon Heffron's research, and it was at his initiative that LDF hired the sociologist Marvin Wolfgang to study sentencing in southern rape cases. Amsterdam worked closely with Wolfgang, and soon became the lawyer with the most in-depth knowledge of the statistical evidence of racism. When the Eighth Circuit heard Maxwell's appeal, it was only natural that Amsterdam would argue the case.

From LDF's standpoint the argument went exceedingly well. Just before it began, one of Blackmun's clerks quietly told Meltsner and Amsterdam that his boss "personally hated the death penalty and was torn up by the cases coming up." At the argument Amsterdam focused on the problem of discriminatory application. Blackmun thrust several pointed questions at Amsterdam, each of which Amsterdam parried successfully. When Blackmun asked Amsterdam why he thought the Constitution precluded executing a black man for raping a white woman, but didn't preclude executing a white man for raping a black woman, Amsterdam replied that "once the Negro situation was remedied, the white situation would take care of itself." When Blackmun criticized Wolfgang's study for being too small and for not including anyone from Maxwell's county in the sample, Amsterdam said that statistical methods required only that the sample be representative, not comprehensive. "I had to explain to him that he didn't know his mathematics," Amsterdam recalled later.

The irony of Amsterdam's statement, "he didn't know his mathematics," is that Blackmun had a math degree from Harvard. While the *Maxwell* argument may have been a success from LDF's standpoint, it also marked the beginning of a complicated relationship between Amsterdam and Blackmun. Amsterdam grated on Blackmun, whose files contain many condescending asides concerning LDF's lead counsel. "I suspect I am too far removed from academic days to understand the professorial mind," Blackmun wrote after reading one Amsterdam brief. He complained in his bench notes that Amsterdam's "voice squeaks" and once jotted this single word during an Amsterdam oral argument: "Ugh." But Blackmun also respected Amsterdam. As a judge Blackmun kept notes on the attorneys who appeared before him. Following the *Maxwell* argument, Blackmun wrote, "tall, 28, suave" and assigned Amsterdam a grade of A-. Following his retirement, Blackmun would recall Amsterdam fondly.

LDF HAD NEVER BEFORE seen an advocate with such composure and deftness on his feet. With this performance Amsterdam established himself as the de facto head of the abolition campaign, a position he would maintain through the triumph of *Furman*, the agonizing defeat in *Gregg v. Georgia*, the case that undid *Furman*, and thereafter behind the scenes, for another forty years. The legal fight he would captain can be well compared, in its length and complexity, only to the battles for the civil rights of African Americans. In many respects, though, the death penalty crusade was more complicated. Desegregation was hardly easy, but *Brown* was predicated on an unambiguous constitutional principle, and the Supreme Court had suggested a willingness to take on the issue in earlier decisions. Amsterdam and LDF had no such advantage.

The death penalty war, which continues today, would prove as heartrending and byzantine as any prolonged military campaign. It would be fought in every imaginable forum, from the lowest tribunal in remote Alabama to the hallowed halls of the Supreme Court. It would be fought at the federal level and in almost every state. It would be fought in the streets and in the ivory tower of the academy. These scholarly battles could themselves have consumed several lifetimes, as the abolitionists sought to collect and marshal data to address the various factual issues that would shape public and judicial opinion. Did the death penalty deter? Was it cost effective? Could it be fairly applied?

It was a leviathan of an undertaking, without precedent in American history. No one thought it could be done, not even many of the lawyers at LDF, who understood the difficulty of overcoming centuries of precedent. If Arthur Goldberg couldn't persuade his colleagues, how could they? "The legal acceptance and historical force of the death penalty were considered a given," said Jack Himmelstein, a young LDF attorney. "It was the power of Tony Amsterdam's mind and heart that said, 'That doesn't have to be the case.'"

CHAPTER 3

SURCEASE OF SORROW

IN THE SUMMER OF 1966 TONY AMSTERDAM FUNDA-
mentally changed the terms of the capital campaign. That July,
Governor Faubus signed six death warrants, set September 2 as
the execution date, and then left Arkansas to attend a convention.
LDF knew Faubus well from his opposition to *Brown*. But while
Faubus was a segregationist, he hadn't signed an execution warrant
in many years, and his actions caught LDF off guard. Amsterdam
and another LDF attorney, Norman Amaker, scrambled to file new
habeas corpus petitions for Maxwell and their other Arkansas client, Luther Bailey. At the eleventh hour Byron White granted a
stay, sparing Maxwell and Bailey. The other four men Faubus condemned had no representation. Amsterdam could not abide this. "I
said, 'What the hell! Are we going to let these guys die?' It was like
somebody was bleeding in the gutter when you've got a tourniquet."
LDF intervened and secured stays for them. LDF had secured many
stays, but these were different: The other four men condemned by
Faubus were white.

Until that moment, all of LDF's capital appeals involved blacks.
Generally speaking, LDF only accepted cases involving color discrimination. "Race was always the factor," Greenberg said. Amsterdam
wanted this to change. The quantum shift had a potential upside and

downside: It might attract attention to the cause, but it also jeopardized LDF's funding. Most of LDF's benefactors contributed to the organization because of its mission. Extending representation to whites was a huge gamble.

Michael Meltsner liked to gamble. Growing up in the Rockaways and, later, Manhattan, he and his father sometimes bet on horse races and prizefights. When it came to the decision to extend representation to whites, though, Meltsner didn't weigh the odds. "For me personally, there was never any question that I wasn't making neat and nice distinctions in a cost-benefit sense," he recalled. "Once you were involved with representing people on death row, you did it until you dropped. The greatest good for the greatest number was a factor, but one of many. More important was just the kind of person I was." LDF director Jack Greenberg echoed the sentiment. "People thought that capital punishment was sufficiently horrible that you didn't have to count up the numbers." Amsterdam and LDF saw the representation of whites as a moral imperative. "Once we had the power to get stays, we felt a legal and moral obligation to extend representation to other clients, many of whom had suffered the same injustices," Amsterdam said. Another LDF attorney, James Nabrit, said, "Our legal arguments created a lifeboat for people. Everybody was in the lifeboat, so LDF had an obligation to help them all." From this point on, in capital cases LDF represented whites and blacks.

Professor Eric Muller of the University of North Carolina argues that LDF should have paused longer to weigh the pros and cons. In his view representing whites placed LDF in an untenable position. LDF's central thesis remained that the death penalty should be ended because of systemic racism. Raising this argument on behalf of white people seemed odd, and in Muller's view diminished LDF's credibility. "To any observer, race had always been the top issue on LDF's agenda," Muller said. "Now race stood to be either submerged within, or entirely eclipsed by, the larger issue of a state's power to kill certain of its citizens." These larger philosophical issues were beyond LDF's expertise and diverted the organization's focus from the unqualified

evil of racism to the ambiguous moral question of whether the government may legitimately take human life.

Meltsner argues that these liabilities made LDF's decision all the
more admirable. LDF understood that representing whites diverged
from its historical role, and still it took on the fight. "Look, this was a
civil rights organization," Meltsner said in 1985. "Its contributors and
staff were there to represent black people. The clients we were representing at the broadened stage would have been drawn from the most
racist segments of society. It's to the credit of the organization that it
never let things like that stand in the way."

WHILE LDF PERCEIVED REPRESENTING whites to be a moral
imperative, increased funding played an important role in its decision.
The death penalty had never been a draw for money. In 1966 this
changed too. Under the leadership of its new president, McGeorge
Bundy, the Ford Foundation solicited proposals to support poverty
law. Leroy Clark proposed creating a spinoff, the National Office for
the Rights of the Indigent, to bring test cases on behalf of the poor.
Meltsner suggested including criminal justice issues in the application.
LDF won the grant, totaling one million dollars. Though capital punishment had not been an explicit part of the application, Greenberg
approved use of the money for the death penalty campaign. It was
highly significant that the Ford money was tied to poverty, not race.
Representing whites presented no conflict.

In relative terms the Ford grant was huge. The total annual budget of LDF in 1960 was less than five hundred thousand dollars. It
did everything on a shoestring budget. To that point Meltsner and his
colleagues effectively had been working on the death penalty cases in
their spare time. Now they envisioned hiring a managing attorney for
the capital cases to oversee all the litigation and systematically collect
the data needed to make the case against capital punishment. LDF also
wanted to begin to attract some attention to its work in the mainstream
press. Finally it had the resources to make this someone's full-time job.

Meltsner recommended that Greenberg hire twenty-six-year-old Jack Himmelstein, a Harvard Law School graduate who had spent one of his summers working at LDF. Himmelstein had most recently been on a fellowship in England, where he studied psychiatry and law at the Anna Freud Clinic. Himmelstein leaped at the opportunity to work for LDF, accepting the job even before learning what his assignment would be. When he was told that he would be working on the capital campaign, Himmelstein initially believed, to his disappointment, that he had been assigned to work on fund-raising. When he learned the truth he was greatly relieved.

The irony of hiring Himmelstein was that on the death penalty campaign, which LDF continued to conceive of principally as a race issue, the four principal attorneys would be white.* Today this would be almost inconceivable. But this was merely one of many respects in which civil rights work in the 1960s was different than it is now.

Then Meltsner, Himmelstein, and Greenberg were among a handful of attorneys who earned a living doing public-interest litigation. In their day, no career path existed for the civil rights attorney. When Meltsner tried to get a job at the ACLU while he was a law student, he was told the national office already had an attorney. Meltsner's mother-in-law, a federal judge, and one of his professors encouraged him to change direction. After miraculously landing the position at LDF, Meltsner shared the good news with a fellow Yale law student. The classmate wondered whether working for a "Negro organization wouldn't be more social work than law." Today many law students go on to do civil rights work. The ACLU has a full-time staff of more

---

* At the time LDF did not discuss this issue much, though some controversy surrounded Greenberg's appointment as director in 1961. Marshall chose Greenberg as his successor over Robert Carter, an African American and later a federal district court judge. Derrick Bell said that Greenberg "should have recognized the symbolic value of his position to the black community and turned over the leadership of LDF to a black lawyer." But Bell, an unconventional thinker who opposed *Brown*, was out of step with his colleagues on this issue. LDF's staff overwhelmingly supported Greenberg.

than forty attorneys and a national network of five thousand volunteer lawyers. LDF has a staff of dozens. The offices are better than they used to be, too.*

When Himmelstein began work at LDF in the spring of 1967, he sat at an institutional desk in the front half of Meltsner's spartanly furnished office. Himmelstein faced his chair away from the window so he wouldn't be distracted by the traffic in Columbus Circle. He had as much to do as he could handle. Himmelstein's first project was to help Amsterdam construct a "Last-Aid Kit," a comprehensive collection of forms, including draft petitions for habeas corpus, sample applications for stays of execution, and legal briefs laying out every imaginable argument against the death penalty. The goals were to increase LDF's visibility and to build a more extensive network of cooperating attorneys.

Himmelstein succeeded resoundingly. After he and Amsterdam distributed the kits in late 1967, demand for LDF's assistance swelled. In 1966 LDF had been handling the appeals of a handful of death-row inmates. By the end of 1967 LDF represented more than fifty condemned men and was involved indirectly in dozens of other cases.

As LDF took on new cases, it gradually expanded its mandate. Soon it began representing murderers as well as rapists. As with the decision to represent whites, LDF decided to represent murderers because of a perceived moral imperative, and again made no cost-benefit calculation. This too departed from the way it generally did business.

Historically LDF pursued change incrementally. *Brown*, for example, had been the culmination of a strategy that first focused the courts on discrimination in graduate school programs. Confronting racism in

---

* The pay was the one respect in which civil rights work was better then than it is now. When he started at LDF, Meltsner earned an annual salary of six thousand dollars, not much less than he would have earned at a top law firm. The salary was so generous that Meltsner offered to take less. Greenberg refused the offer and told Meltsner never to take less money for doing good.

primary and secondary schools only came later.* The rough equivalent in the death penalty context would have been to concentrate on rape. The evidence of discrimination against black rapists was overwhelming. On the other hand, discrimination against black murderers had not yet been proved. For this reason grouping rapists with murderers might be to the rapists' detriment. Meltsner said, "A general challenge to capital punishment tended to lump together men who had killed with men who had not, creating a situation in which the fate of the non-killers would be likely to hinge on the fate of the whole." Goldberg had confined his memorandum to rapists for this strategic reason. LDF, though, wasn't willing to be patient. "With people who stood to be executed, we weren't willing to commit ourselves to a forty-year strategy," Meltsner said. "*Brown* was fine, but it took a little too long for a scenario where people were getting executed."

THE DEATH PENALTY CAMPAIGN had evolved. Now LDF opposed executions not just to aid individual clients but also to publicize the plight of the condemned and to pressure judges into rendering favorable decisions. They wanted to overwhelm the courts. Meltsner said the appeals functioned "like sand poured in a machine." In 1967, Amsterdam advanced his own audacious proposal: LDF would stop all executions in the United States.

Amsterdam's plan became known as "the moratorium strategy," a concept that would serve many purposes for LDF. It would be its calling card for fund-raising efforts, help attract lawyers and laypeople to

---

* Thurgood Marshall and LDF exploited a disparity they did not fully understand. "Those racial supremacy boys somehow think that little kids of six or seven are going to get funny ideas about sex or marriage just from going to school together, but for some equally funny reason youngsters in law school aren't supposed to feel that way," Marshall recalled. "We didn't get it, but we decided that if that was what the South believed then the best thing for the moment was to go along." Thus LDF won its first victories against segregation in a graduate school of education and a separate but obviously unequal law school in Texas.

the cause, and become an important courtroom argument. In many ways the moratorium would become synonymous with the abolition movement. It would be so central to LDF's success that people invariably thought it began as a calculated strategy as opposed to a knee-jerk reaction to a perceived injustice. "In hindsight, it's easier to think about this as a campaign, but it wasn't," Amsterdam said. "The Faubus decision to get into all capital cases was a major decision and even that was made incrementally."

As a practical matter halting executions was a daunting challenge, in many respects more ambitious than Meltsner's lunchtime decision to try to persuade the Supreme Court to rule the death penalty unconstitutional: Meltsner and his colleagues only needed to prevail in one forum. Amsterdam proposed to stop every execution, everywhere. This would require him to become involved, either directly or indirectly, in every capital case in the United States. Achieving a moratorium would take a tireless, superhuman effort.

The moratorium also had a potential downside. Some individual defendants might suffer for the greater good. John Boger, who ran LDF's capital punishment project in the 1980s, says judges are wary of movements. A judge is less likely to be receptive to the arguments made by an individual defendant when he or she knows that a decision will impact other similarly situated defendants. Here LDF did make a cost-benefit calculation. It believed the benefits outweighed the risks.

Amsterdam believed that if he could put his finger in the dike and stop executions in the United States, then courts—most important, the Supreme Court—would be reluctant to authorize an execution out of fear it would open the floodgates. Judges wouldn't want so much blood on their hands. "The reason for the moratorium strategy was that we knew there was a difference between asking a court to stop an ongoing system and one where executions were not occurring," Amsterdam said in 2010 at his NYU office, surrounded by an assortment of two-liter soda bottles. "We wanted to change the momentum so that we had inertia on our side."

✦ ✦ ✦ ✦

INDEED, SLOWLY, THE MOMENTUM began to shift. LDF experienced its first major success in a class-action lawsuit in Florida. Tobias Simon, a Miami attorney and the chairperson of the Florida ACLU chapter, initiated the lawsuit following Republican Claude Kirk, Jr.'s, election as governor in 1965. Kirk, like Ronald Reagan in California, had run on a law-and-order platform and, during a visit to the Florida State Prison, told inmates, "If I'm elected, I may have to sign your death warrants." Florida's death row held more than fifty people. Simon feared that he wouldn't be able to "keep tabs" on them all if Kirk began authorizing executions.

Simon approached LDF with the idea of filing a class action raising the procedural concerns outlined in the Last-Aid Kit. Amsterdam was skeptical. Class actions are generally used in civil cases by people lacking the resources to sue on their own; one had never been filed successfully in a criminal case. Over Amsterdam's objection Simon filed the petition in April 1967 and shocked LDF by winning a temporary stay from a federal district court judge. William McRae, Jr., a Kennedy appointee, ruled that the lawsuit had enough merit that no one should be executed until he could determine whether the inmates could receive an adequate hearing on their claims in state court. If they could, the federal court had no jurisdiction. If they couldn't, it might be appropriate for a federal court to intervene.

At this point LDF got involved. Amsterdam, Greenberg, and Simon flew to Boston to discuss class actions with Harvard Law professors Benjamin Kaplan and Albert Sacks, one of the drafters of the Federal Rules of Civil Procedure. They regarded Simon's argument as a long shot, but saw no legal reason why it couldn't work. Back in New York Amsterdam drafted a brief relying on research by Simon and some volunteers who had interviewed and tested the inmates. On average they had finished eight years of school and had a mean IQ of 88. Given these limitations Amsterdam argued that their rights would be protected only if the case proceeded as a class action. "They will be heard together or they will be electrocuted individually," Amsterdam told McRae. "There is no third possibility."

McRae bought LDF's argument and certified Florida's death row as a class. This didn't mean McRae would ultimately uphold the constitutional arguments raised by the class members, but in death penalty litigation buying time for one's client is half the ballgame. McRae's decision created a moratorium on executions in Florida. In fact the Florida case would drag on long enough for the prisoners to benefit from the Supreme Court's ruling in *Furman* years later.

Around the same time, LDF supported a second class-action petition in California, where Ronald Reagan had signed off on the state's first execution in four years. The California judge, Robert Peckham, didn't certify the class, but he did require the state to notify LDF when it scheduled an execution. This would give LDF time to file habeas petitions, a procedural improvement it regarded as a substantial victory.

As LDF BEGAN TO experience success, it asserted with increasing confidence its vision of how the capital campaign should be conducted. The steps the organization took had the indirect consequence of elevating the moratorium from a strategy to a movement, even as it sometimes placed LDF in the odd position of opposing legal arguments intended to help death-row inmates.

This conflict first manifested itself with respect to further class actions. Florida and California proved the potential of such lawsuits. Lawyers around the country and the ACLU, now finally in the game, wanted to bring more. LDF discouraged them. Reflecting years later, Meltsner and Amsterdam each offered practical reasons for having opposed additional class actions. "We were scared of this thing proliferating," Meltsner said in 2010. But the principal downside of such proliferation appeared to be LDF losing its exclusive grip on the abolition movement. When Jack Greenberg implored ACLU legal director Melvin Wulf in July 1967 to refrain from filing other class actions, he offered no substantive explanation, saying only, "It may be premature to do anything in other jurisdictions before the California and Florida cases jell." Amsterdam expressed a similarly vague sentiment to another ACLU lawyer, William Friedlander. "I would approach the thought of a class suit in the way porcupines are said to make love—very gingerly."

Amsterdam explained the basis of LDF's concern in a strongly worded letter to a Louisiana lawyer who proposed to begin a class action in his state. "In the Florida and California actions, we have just about gotten our toes on the beach," Amsterdam wrote. "What we do not need—what would be a disaster in these two cases involving 110 human lives—is the backwash of some third lawsuit which, if it fortuitously lands before an unsympathetic district judge in a third state, could result in a decisive dismissal with an opinion saying we are all wet." Amsterdam argued that the costs outweighed the benefits. An adverse decision in Louisiana might hurt LDF's chances in Florida, which was in the same federal circuit. On the other hand, no one had been executed in Louisiana in three years. "The plain fact is that death cases are not occasions for venturesomeness in litigation," Amsterdam continued. "Test litigation is well and good, but not when human life is at stake. I cannot see a class action as anything but a gratuitous gamble."

Of course LDF was engaged at that moment in two such gambles in Florida and California. The entire capital campaign might reasonably have been called "test litigation."

LDF'S POSITION WAS EVEN more problematic with respect to the appeal of William Witherspoon, who challenged his Illinois conviction for murdering a police officer on the ground of jury bias. The judge in Witherspoon's case had struck all prospective jurors who expressed any reservations about capital punishment. This process, gruesomely called "death qualification," looked more or less the same in every state with the death penalty. Albert Jenner, a prominent Chicago attorney who had served as president of the Illinois Bar Association and counsel to the Warren Commission, took on the case. Jenner argued that death qualification created a jury more prone to convict than an ordinary jury. As evidence Jenner cited a then-unpublished study by the psychologists Faye Goldberg and Cody Wilson, which used college students as jurors in mock trials, and found that the students who supported capital punishment were significantly more likely to vote to convict than those who didn't. Witherspoon's case made it all the way to the Supreme Court.

Amsterdam drafted a ninety-four-page amicus brief arguing that the Supreme Court should *not* address the constitutionality of death qualification. He called the evidence "tentative" and urged the Court to refer the issue to a lower court for further review. Amsterdam added that LDF had arranged for the pollster Louis Harris to study the question more carefully. Behind the scenes Amsterdam worried that the Court would reject Jenner's argument, and that the loss would sap momentum from the moratorium. Meltsner argued in his memoir that "concern for the five hundred other men on death row forced them to take this position." He said it would be better to wait for the scientific evidence to fully develop, and for a case where LDF represented the defendant. "This was an issue of control, of getting the issues before the Court in the right order," Meltsner said.

Yet in *Brown*, LDF had no compunction about relying on psychologists Kenneth and Mamie Clark's famous doll study (the Clarks presented to young children four plastic, diaper-clad dolls, identical except for color, and found that the children attributed more positive characteristics to the white dolls). Though the research hadn't been widely accepted, Thurgood Marshall and Robert Carter offered the Clark study as evidence that segregation damaged the development of black children.* How was this calculated gamble, the sort lawyers make routinely, any different from Jenner's?

LDF differentiated *Brown*. Losing *Brown* would have been devastating, but the situation of black schoolchildren wouldn't have been made any worse. By contrast an adverse decision in *Witherspoon* would undermine the moratorium. Everyone on death row in the United

---

* The study has since been replicated many times.

States had been sentenced under jury-selection procedures similar to Witherspoon's. If the Supreme Court upheld the constitutionality of this practice, LDF would lose an essential weapon from its arsenal. The public also might believe that the Court had fixed the problems with capital punishment.

Notably absent from this calculus were William Witherspoon's interests. Sitting on death row, Witherspoon had nothing to lose from raising the jury-selection issue. Furthermore, if the argument prevailed, Witherspoon would be entitled to a new trial, not just to resentencing. LDF's amicus brief infuriated Jenner. They had treated him as if he were some backwater shyster. To Jenner LDF's position could be explained only as an act of ego. He wrote Greenberg an angry letter, accusing LDF of aggrandizing itself at the expense of defendants. Amsterdam replied with what Meltsner called an "F-U letter."

WAS JENNER'S ANGER JUSTIFIED? The American Bar Association (ABA) imposes a duty on lawyers similar to what the Hippocratic Oath requires of doctors with respect to their patients. Under the Model Code of Professional Responsibility, lawyers are expected to "zealously represent their clients within the bounds of the law." The complication is that identifying the patient—or the client—is often a matter of perspective. For example, an epidemiologist is more concerned with the health of an entire population than an individual's. While a personal physician would treat his or her patient with the most aggressive antibiotic available, an epidemiologist would employ drugs strategically. Any ethical confusion is resolved by clear labeling. No one seeks treatment for a cold at the Centers for Disease Control.

The root of Jenner's outrage was that during the abolition campaign, LDF often acted as both epidemiologist and personal physician. Greenberg acknowledged "the possible submerging of special claims of individuals." This was vividly evident with respect to the Eighth Amendment argument. Counterintuitively, arguing that the death penalty was cruel and unusual wasn't a key part of LDF's strategy. Their lawyers believed the argument should be held back to allow the pressure of the moratorium to build, and to educate the Supreme Court, through repeated lawsuits, about the problems with capital punishment. But to a man facing execution, the argument was like a new drug, and what cancer patient in a study wants the placebo? If LDF was representing *his* interests, it would argue the Eighth Amendment. How could *he* be worse off?

On the other hand LDF represented hundreds of men who otherwise would have had no attorney. Not many Albert Jenners volunteered to take on capital appeals. Surely LDF's slightly less than maximally zealous representation—tempered only by holding back arguments it thought the Supreme Court would reject—was better than any alternative these men had.

THIS TENSION BETWEEN LDF's obligation to its individual clients and its desire to steer the abolition campaign in the manner it thought best would recur time and again. It would even be present at the "coming out" of the moratorium: the National Conference on the Death Penalty, held in Manhattan on March 3, 1968. LDF invited more than one hundred abolitionist attorneys and scholars to the conference. Meltsner said a central purpose of the conference was to give the "movement for legal abolition a cohesion that it had lacked." It was also an effort to rein lawyers in.

In early 1967, in connection with their discussion of further class actions, Melvin Wulf of the ACLU broached the idea of a death penalty conference with Greenberg. Amsterdam encouraged Greenberg to agree, though not for the obvious reason. Amsterdam saw the conference as a means to keep potential competitors at bay. "Such a conference will do *something* to help contain the people that might be typing away at massive draft petitions in dark corners of the continent," Amsterdam wrote Greenberg. "And the sooner the conference, the more it is likely to coordinate energies and to discourage those that should be discouraged." The ACLU held a prominent place on Amsterdam's list of worries. "It is no small thing to keep Melvin Wulf himself in line with our containment policy. He has considerable power over ACLU branches, and has stop-or-go authority with regard to some of the people we most need fear initializing litigation." Amsterdam thought the conference could stall rivals indefinitely. "Discussions about format, invitees and the invitation-issuing and response-receiving process eat up time."

So the conference went forward. The attendees were treated to rousing speeches by Caleb Foote, Yale criminal law expert Steven Duke, and Greenberg. LDF's director recounted the history of his organization's efforts against the death penalty, reminding the audience that not long ago every southern capital trial had been a potential lynching. Greenberg then delivered a stirring discourse on the evils of executions: "The battle over capital punishment may be seen as a microcosm of the conflict between those in authority who believe in violence as a means of coping with society's problems and those who oppose the use of violence. We have seen it in war. We have heard it in political promises to get tough with crime in the streets. Reasonable force may sometimes be the only possible way to cope with violence. However, violent force, employed after the fact, legitimizes a method of coping with issues that is the antithesis of the right procedures of a just society.

"We do not know how to solve all of society's ills, and particularly all of the problems of crime. But we do know that one way not to do it is to kill needlessly. If the goal of this litigation is achieved, we will have spared a few lives that, thereafter, will be spent in prisons. We will perhaps make it possible, in some cases, for men whose innocence is established years from now to go free. Most important of all, we may make a small contribution to advancing the day when man's problems are dealt with by reason and persuasion and not by brute force."

When Greenberg finished inspiring, though, he urged restraint. He implored the lawyers not to file any new class actions. "In other states," he said, "where the number of condemned men is so much smaller, resort to class actions has been deemed inappropriate." When Amsterdam took the podium, he spent most of his time discouraging the attendees from raising Eighth Amendment arguments in their cases, encouraging them to focus instead on procedural claims. By the end of the conference, everyone had a clear sense of where the moratorium movement was heading, and an even clearer sense of who was in control.

WHATEVER ITS PHILOSOPHICAL MERITS, the moratorium steadily gathered momentum. Public opinion began to shift. Gallup first asked the question, "Are you in favor of the death penalty for a person convicted of murder?" in 1936. In that poll 59 percent answered affirmatively and 38 percent negatively. Over following polls, support for the death penalty consistently hovered around 50 percent.* In the mid-1960s the numbers began to change. In January 1965 Gallup found 45 percent support for capital punishment, the lowest level ever recorded. In May 1966 the statistic slipped further to 42 percent. This remains the lowest level of support for capital punishment ever recorded in America. The following year support for the death penalty increased to 54 percent. Gallup explained the surge as a reaction to Richard Speck, who raped and murdered eight student nurses in Chicago during the summer of 1966. Indeed, in subsequent polls, the level of support dropped again.

The decline couldn't be dismissed easily. Conventional wisdom said that fear of crime drove support for capital punishment. If this were true, passion for the death penalty should have been surging. These were the turbulent sixties. Urban riots, campus unrest, and political violence dominated the headlines. In 1968 Americans overwhelmingly identified crime as the top domestic problem. Eighty-one percent of respondents to a survey agreed with the proposition that law enforcement in the United States had "broken down." Martin Luther King and Robert Kennedy were assassinated in the span of

---

* The notable exception is a November 1953 poll, which showed 68 percent support for capital punishment. That poll, taken five months after the executions of Ethel and Julius Rosenberg, is widely viewed as a referendum on their case.

three months. Yet, in the first poll after their deaths, support for the death penalty dropped.

At the state level capital punishment appeared to be crumbling. In 1965 West Virginia and Iowa eliminated the death penalty, joining Hawaii, Alaska, and Oregon, which had already ended capital punishment. New York and Vermont limited the application of the death penalty to extraordinary crimes, such as murder by a prisoner under a life sentence. During the late 1960s twenty states considered proposals to end capital punishment. Abolition in New Mexico was considered certain.

The rate of executions slowed. During the 1950s states put to death an average of seventy-two people per year. In 1965 they executed seven. In 1966 they executed one. In 1967 two executions were conducted, including that of Luis Monge in Colorado. Monge would be the last man executed in the United States until 1977.*

International opinion coalesced against the death penalty. By 1968, more than 70 nations had rejected the death penalty, including most of Western Europe. America's closest allies, Great Britain, Australia, and Canada each ended executions during the late 1960s. To some, the end appeared inevitable. In June 1967, *Time* reported that it was only a matter of time before the United States succumbed to the worldwide trend. *Time* wrote, "By inches, the death penalty is dying in the U.S."

DURING THE SPRING OF 1968 the Court delivered two decisions that further buoyed LDF. In April, the Court struck down part of the Federal Kidnapping Act, which held that the death penalty could be imposed only following a jury trial. Thus, if a defendant waived his right to a jury trial, he faced a maximum sentence of life imprisonment. Potter Stewart's opinion said this created an unconstitutional incentive for a defendant to waive his Sixth Amendment right to trial

---

* Though the moratorium clearly had an effect, the rate of executions had started to slow before it began. The Warren Court's strengthening of protections for criminal defendants played a role.

by jury. The decision, *U.S. v. Jackson*, gave LDF another tool to attack state laws, many of which had similar provisions. LDF also took heart that Stewart only struck down the penalty provision of the Kidnapping Act. Prisoners would be resentenced, not retried. LDF thought this demonstrated Stewart's concern with public perception, which LDF shared. It would be damaging if people believed that LDF's work freed dangerous criminals.

LDF began to hope that Stewart might be cultivated as an ally. Though Stewart had been appointed by Eisenhower, and had dissented from several landmark Warren Court decisions, including *Miranda*, he had generally proved himself to be a strong defender of civil rights and in 1968 wrote a decision outlawing refusals to sell property for racially discriminatory reasons. He appeared to be guided less by philosophy and politics than the facts of a particular case or issue.

In June, Stewart wrote the opinion overturning William Witherspoon's death sentence because a jury "culled of all who harbor doubts about the wisdom of capital punishment" could "speak only for a distinct and dwindling minority." It now seemed clear that Stewart had substantial reservations about the constitutionality of capital punishment. He favorably cited Earl Warren's language in *Trop* regarding evolving standards of decency. Furthermore, in a footnote on the split of popular opinion regarding the death penalty, Stewart included this excerpt from *Reflections on Hanging*, an abolitionist tract by the Hungarian novelist-essayist Arthur Koestler: "The division is not between rich and poor, highbrow and lowbrow, Christians and atheists; it is between those who have charity and those who have not. The test of one's humanity is whether one is able to accept this fact—not as lip service, but with the shuddering recognition of a kinship: here but for the grace of God, drop I."

Many people thought *Witherspoon* meant the end of capital punishment in America. Prosecutors thought it would be impossible to secure a capital sentence without a death-qualified jury. Stanley Kirk, district attorney of Wichita Falls, Texas, said, "I'm so mad, I'm speechless. We don't know what to do." William Bolton, attorney general of Georgia, said he thought *Witherspoon* would "definitely end capital punishment in Georgia." The *Dallas Morning News* reported that *Witherspoon* "may eliminate the death penalty for capital crimes."

Even to those who thought that juries might still deliver death sentences, *Witherspoon* seemed a bad omen. Joe Patterson, attorney general of Minnesota, said, "It looks like the Supreme Court has set about to repeal the various death penalty statutes in the states." William Saxbe, attorney general of Ohio, said, "This is another nail in the coffin which is finally going to do away with capital punishment." Shortly after the Court announced *Witherspoon*, Lyndon Johnson's attorney general, Ramsey Clark, asked Congress to abolish capital punishment. This marked the first (and last) time in American history that a president had taken this position. Shortly thereafter the California Supreme Court announced that it would hear a challenge to the death penalty under the state's constitution.

By THE SUMMER the momentum seemed overwhelming. June 1968 marked one year since the last execution in America. Amsterdam believed the backlog was putting enormous pressure on the Supreme Court. The longer he and LDF stopped executions, the more difficult it would be for the Court to start them up again. "Once we stopped the executions, the courts would then have to face the awful reality that a decision in favor of capital punishment would start the bloodbath again," Amsterdam said. Meltsner felt the moratorium had exposed the dispensability of capital punishment. He said, "For each year the United States went without executions, the more hollow would ring claims that the American people couldn't do without them; the longer death-row inmates waited, the greater their numbers, the more difficult it would be for courts to permit the first execution." From his vantage point Dershowitz praised the moratorium strategy as a way of emphasizing to the Supreme Court "that by approving the death penalty they would be killing hundreds of people." Amsterdam said, "We forced the courts to deal with the constitutional questions."

Indeed, in October, the Court granted certiorari in *Boykin v. Alabama*, an appeal by a twenty-seven-year-old black man who had been sentenced to die after pleading guilty to armed robbery. This would be the first time in its history that the Supreme Court considered the proportionality of death as a punishment. LDF didn't represent Boykin, but the Court granted LDF leave to file an amicus brief. This pleased LDF, as did the choice of case. Meltsner called it "potentially far-reaching." Dershowitz and Goldberg thought Boykin "presented the strongest possible setting for a cruel and unusual punishment holding." Most important, at long last Tony Amsterdam would be able to argue to the Supreme Court, and indirectly to the American people, that the death penalty was cruel and unusual punishment.

All that remained was to write the argument.

TWO ASPECTS OF BOYKIN'S arguments were obvious. Boykin's guilty plea made no sense since it exposed him to the death penalty. Three justices of the Alabama Supreme Court had questioned whether Boykin understood what he was doing when he pled guilty. LDF would make this point first.

Second, LDF would emphasize that Boykin had been sentenced without standards. The jury simply had been handed two forms—one for life and one for death—and told by the judge, "You can use either one form or the other when you arrive at your verdict." This was more or less how it worked in every death penalty state. The argument that standardless sentencing violated the Constitution flowed from a 1966 case, *Giaccio v. Pennsylvania*. Jay Giaccio was charged with criminally firing a weapon at another person. The jury acquitted him because the weapon was a starter pistol that only fired blanks, but it fined him $230 under a one-hundred-year-old law that allowed juries to decide, without guidance, who should pay the costs of a prosecution. The Court found the absence of standards fatal. Hugo Black wrote for the majority, "A law fails to meet the requirements of the Due Process

Clause if it is so vague and standardless that it leaves the public uncertain as to the conduct it prohibits."

Giaccio was not a death penalty case, but LDF thought the argument was even stronger for capital cases because capital juries decided guilt and sentence simultaneously. These "single-phase trials" created a catch-22 for defendants. To get in background evidence that might encourage a jury to be lenient toward him, such as good character or past abuse, a defendant needed to testify. But testifying meant waiving his Fifth Amendment rights and opening himself up to cross-examination on guilt. To make matters worse, it was virtually impossible to overturn a sentence on appeal.

In mid-December the Eighth Circuit dealt these arguments a setback when it rejected William Maxwell's second habeas petition. Harry Blackmun began his majority opinion with a personal note, which his childhood friend Warren Burger had encouraged him to write. "The author of this opinion is not personally convinced of the rightness of capital punishment and questions it as an effective deterrent." But Blackmun concluded the death penalty was "a policy matter" for legislatures, not judges, to decide. With respect to split trials, Blackmun said they were rare and wouldn't be required "until the Supreme Court tells us otherwise." Regarding standards, Blackmun argued that *Giaccio* didn't apply. Giaccio couldn't have been certain what behavior Pennsylvania's law prohibited. No one could have been unsure what the Arkansas rape statute made illegal.

Blackmun's interpretation of *Giaccio* was unhelpful, but it wasn't the final word, and LDF thought the Supreme Court might go the other way. In a concurrence to *Giaccio*, Stewart wrote that the decision cast doubt "upon the settled practice to leave to the unguided discretion of a jury the nature and degree of punishment to be imposed upon a person convicted of a criminal offense." Stewart had shown sensitivity to the public's perception of the Court: Standardless sentencing was a problem ordinary people could understand. LDF likewise always had public relations on its mind. When *Time* interviewed Amsterdam about the constitutionality of capital punishment, he focused on the absence of standards.*

The final argument in Boykin's brief would be that capital punishment violated contemporary standards of decency. Making this argument was more complicated, and presented a thorny public-relations issue. LDF wanted to argue that they, a tiny group of Ivy League–educated lawyers, knew what was moral better than approximately half of the American people. Articulating this without sounding elitist posed a daunting challenge. To meet it, LDF turned once again to the singular talents of Tony Amsterdam.

AMSTERDAM HAD UNUSUAL WORK HABITS to say the least. When it came to writing briefs, he was an enigma. He would disappear with stacks of cases and resurface, often weeks later, with a finished product. In December 1968 Amsterdam went into seclusion to draft LDF's *Boykin* brief. During this period he read debates on capital punishment from nineteenth-century Great Britain. England imposed the death penalty for a wide variety of crimes but rarely carried out executions. Most offenders were pardoned for various reasons, some legitimate, some manufactured. This peculiar history triggered an epiphany. Americans tolerated the death penalty because they believed that our criminal justice system, like its British predecessor, created the threat of executions but rarely carried them out. Amsterdam wrote that the key was the "distinction between what public conscience will allow the law to *say* and what it will allow the law to *do*—between what public decency will permit a penal statute to threaten and what it will allow the law to carry out."

Amsterdam's brief laid out a four-step argument. Point one: Statistics demonstrated that states imposed the death penalty only on "unhappy minorities, whose numbers are so few, whose plight so invis-

---

* Although, with striking candor Amsterdam added that if the Court were to require standards, "I admit that I will probably be among the lawyers who will then challenge the standards as inadequate."

ible, and whose persons so unpopular, that society can readily bear to see them suffer torments which would not for a moment be acceptable as penalties of general application to the populace." Point two: Because of this sporadic and discriminatory application, one couldn't conclude that the public tolerated executions. Three: It was also reasonable to infer that the public wouldn't tolerate frequent executions. Four, and therefore finally: "Contemporary standards of decency would condemn the use of death as a penalty if such a penalty were uniformly, regularly and even-handedly applied."

Boykin vividly illustrated the randomness of the death penalty. More than two hundred thousand robberies had taken place in 1967, but Boykin was among a handful of robbers on death row. It was as if Boykin were the unlucky loser of an execution lottery. Surely the American people wouldn't tolerate this system if they were aware of it. Amsterdam wrote: "Herein is found the difference between the judgment which the legislator makes, responding *politically* to public conscience, and the judgment which a court must make under its obligation to respond *rationally* to public conscience. To put the matter another way, nothing in the political process protects the isolated individual from being cruelly treated by the state. But it is the precise business of the courts to disallow the application to them of penalties so harsh that the public conscience would be appalled by their less arbitrary application."

When Meltsner read the first draft of the brief, he thought it changed the game. *Boykin* gave the Court a basis to overturn the death penalty without disrespecting the American people. Moreover Amsterdam had gone to extremes to make it clear that LDF wasn't asking the Supreme Court to set aside the death penalty in all cases. Court briefs generally contain a section of "issues presented." Amsterdam's draft contained a section titled "issues not presented." First among the issues not presented was that "the death penalty is cruel and unusual punishment for murder." Second, "whether the death penalty might be shown to be cruel and unusual punishment on other grounds than urged here." Amsterdam explained that LDF had sought hearings on the physical and psychological effects of capital punishment in other courts, and that this developing evidence wasn't before the Court. Through these uncharted waters Amsterdam proceeded gingerly. "If, as we submit, none of these issues is presented in this case," he wrote, "we know that the Court would not want inadvertently to prejudice their subsequent presentation."

Meltsner believed that Amsterdam's unconventional tactic successfully narrowed the issue. Even on the eve of its first audience with the Supreme Court, LDF had its eyes on the larger picture. It refrained from arguing against the death penalty for murder for the same reason it had emphasized procedural arguments in prior cases. The Supreme Court might not yet be ready to rule the death penalty unconstitutional. Losing *Boykin* would be a disaster. Winning on narrower grounds would extend the moratorium and allow pressure to continue to build. "Sometimes arguing a position you don't have the stuff to support undermines your case. This is the essence of framing," Meltsner said. He believed that Amsterdam had framed the issue masterfully, and that LDF had a fighting chance for success.

Then, though it hardly seemed possible, the news got better still. On December 16 the Supreme Court announced that it would hear William Maxwell's appeal too. The justices didn't certify the race question, but they did ask for argument on the constitutionally of standardless sentencing and single-phase trials.* The moratorium strategy had worked better than anyone had ever dreamed. It moved the death penalty to the top of the Supreme Court's agenda and secured these fighters from the streets of New York a championship bout years before they would otherwise have earned one. And, though Tony Amsterdam and his colleagues would never know it, they almost landed a knockout in the first round.

---

* When the Court grants certiorari—or "certifies" a case—it can pick and choose among the legal issues presented.

CHAPTER 4

A NEAR KNOCKOUT

O N THE MORNING OF MARCH 6, 1969, THE FIRST HINT of spring in the air, William Brennan woke shortly before six, dressed casually, and walked the streets of Georgetown. Brennan had repeated this routine every morning for thirteen years since his physician diagnosed a heart problem. The doctor said brisk walking would help Brennan lose weight and reduce stress. That morning, though, Brennan felt as much anxiety as he had since becoming a justice. Later, at the courthouse, they would be conferencing the death penalty cases, and Brennan had no idea which way they would go.

Capital punishment was an issue of conscience for Brennan, though it hadn't always been so. Brennan was born in Newark to Irish Catholic immigrants. His father was a brewery worker turned union organizer, and later a local public official. Bill Brennan, Sr., a larger-than-life figure, often expressed concern about the use of government power against individuals. Brennan inherited his father's gregarious personality. He also inherited his sympathy for underdogs, but it took some time for this to express itself in his professional life.

After graduating from Harvard Law School in 1931, Brennan went to work at a law firm in New Jersey. There he made his name representing management in labor disputes. He earned his stripes representing United Color & Pigment, a Newark factory, against claims that it had violated collective-bargaining practices. Soon he became his firm's expert on the National Labor Relations Act.

When Brennan took the bench in 1949, he displayed no special sensitivity to civil liberties. As an appellate court judge Brennan wrote an opinion holding that a criminal defendant had no right to be present in the courtroom when the jury read its verdict. With respect to the death penalty, he had given the issue little thought. Starting out as a lawyer during the Depression, Brennan had taken on the cases of a few indigent defendants to make some extra money. In one Brennan represented a woman who found her husband in bed with another man, went into the kitchen, got a knife, and killed him. Brennan worried that a jury might view the moment she went into the kitchen as sufficient evidence of premeditation, and give her the death penalty on that basis. This threat got Brennan thinking about the issue. But when he became a judge he wasn't ready to act upon his reservations. In the ongoing debate between Frankfurter and Black, Brennan was squarely in the Frankfurter camp. As a justice of the New Jersey Supreme Court he advocated for judicial restraint.

When Dwight Eisenhower appointed Brennan to the U.S. Supreme Court in 1956, the president believed he was appointing a conservative Democrat. Brennan had come to Ike's attention in 1954 when Francis Cardinal Spellman, the powerful archbishop of New York, impressed upon Eisenhower the need to preserve a Catholic presence on the Court. Two years later Brennan delivered a speech on judicial efficiency at a conference organized by the Department of Justice and impressed Attorney General Herbert Brownwell. When Sherman Minton retired in 1956 Brownwell advocated promoting Brennan to the Court, and the president agreed.

Initially Brennan pleased Eisenhower. During his first term Brennan joined a concurrence by Frankfurter in an appeal by a black man facing a possible death sentence for burglary. The majority excluded two confessions, which were obtained following five days of questioning the defendant, who had no education and no attorney. Frankfurter and Brennan said the Court could interfere with state proceedings only when the police offended "fundamental fairness." Brennan agreed, too, with Frankfurter's view that the Court shouldn't intervene regarding the death penalty. In 1960 Brennan voted against hearing the appeals of Dick Hickock and Perry Smith, two Kansas parolees convicted of the quadruple murder depicted in Truman Capote's *In Cold Blood*.

Soon, though, Brennan became Brennan, the driving force behind the Warren Court's transformative expansion of civil liberties. Many scholars regard Brennan as the most influential justice of the twentieth century, and its greatest liberal champion. By 1969, when the Court heard *Boykin* and *Maxwell*, Brennan was firmly and vocally against the death penalty.

THE EVOLUTION OF BRENNAN'S worldview is often mistakenly attributed to his Catholicism. In part this is because Brennan emphasized "human dignity" as the fundamental value protected by the Constitution. This language mirrored that of John Ryan, a prominent theologian whose 1906 book, *A Living Wage*, had influenced Brennan's father. But by the time Brennan became a justice of the Supreme Court, religion played little role in his life. He neither quoted Catholic thinkers nor attended Mass regularly. He encouraged his children to have non-Catholic friends, and all three married outside the church. Brennan's mother didn't accept the principle of papal infallibility. As a judge Brennan took pains to separate his private religious beliefs from his jurisprudence. He voted with the majority in *Engel v. Vitale*, a fiercely unpopular 1962 decision striking down a nondenominational prayer that the New York State Board of Regents ordered to be read each school day. Cardinal Spellman condemned the Court's interpretation of the First Amendment prohibition again laws respecting the establishment of religion. Alabama Democrat George Andrews spoke for millions of Americans when he said, "They put the Negroes in the schools, and now they've driven God out."

Brennan's perception of his role led to repeated criticism from the church, which in turn led Brennan to feel further alienated. In 1963 the Court ruled mandatory Bible readings in public schools unconstitutional. Brennan wrote a seventy-page concurrence, laying out the history of the Court's treatment of religion. It was his effort to explain to Catholics that the law required him to break with the Church's wishes regarding school prayer. Brennan's tome didn't accomplish its purpose. John Russell, the bishop of Richmond, scolded Brennan at the Red Mass at Saint Matthew's Cathedral in Washington, D.C.* Brennan's wife, Marjorie, fumed at the rebuke.

Later, at a Sunday Mass at Epiphany Church, Brennan alone declined to stand for the decency pledge, because his judicial duties required him to examine obscene material. He appeared shaken by the experience, and when his clerk, Robert O'Neill, asked him about it the next day, Brennan said, "You have no idea what it's like to be the only person who refuses to stand. Everybody turns and looks at me. It's a terrible experience." By the early 1970s the rift between Brennan and the church was complete. In *Roe v. Wade*, Brennan voted with the majority even though he "wouldn't under any circumstances condone an abortion in my private life." He saw no conflict, and recalled, "It never crossed my mind—never, not the slightest—that my faith had a damn thing to do with how I decided the abortion case."

In truth, if a religion influenced Brennan's transformation, it was more likely Judaism, which became part of his life through his closest friend in Washington, David Bazelon. Brennan and Bazelon met at William Douglas's fifty-eighth birthday party, shortly after Brennan joined the Court, and the two became fast friends. They bonded over baseball, and attended many games together, sometimes with Douglas and Lyndon Johnson. Bazelon lived near Brennan and often joined Brennan on his morning walks.

---

* Red Mass is celebrated annually for judges, attorneys, law professors, students, and government officials. The Mass requests guidance from the Holy Spirit for all who seek justice. At Saint Matthew's, Bishop Russell said, "Separation of church and state, which we all cherish in our country, never meant the divorce of government from religion or the separation of law from morality."

Bazelon was well connected and became Brennan's entrée to the Washington liberal establishment. They lunched together often at the fabled cafeteria in Milton Kronheim's liquor warehouse on V Street. The guests sat on plastic chairs, and Kronheim's chef, Annie Ross, prepared simple lunches of soup, fried chicken, and cornbread. But the guests included the capital's most prominent politicians and judges.

Through Bazelon and Kronheim, Brennan came to know Edmund Muskie, Abraham Ribicoff, and J. Skelly Wright, who had offered crucial support for *Brown* during his time as a federal district court judge in Louisiana. Bazelon also solidified Brennan's relationship with Arthur Goldberg, with whom Bazelon, a fellow native of Illinois and descendant of Russian Jewish immigrants, had a close connection. This would become Brennan's circle of friends and his professional network. Bazelon and Wright became his conduit for clerks. Brennan even invested with Bazelon, Wright, Goldberg, and his colleague Abe Fortas in several real estate deals.

From the beginning Bazelon had his fingerprints all over the death penalty debate, influencing Brennan's views in explicit and subtle ways. It was Bazelon who put Dershowitz to work on his first capital case. At Kronheim's, Bazelon introduced Dershowitz to Brennan. It was as much this connection as his familiarity with Brennan's son that emboldened Dershowitz to reach out to Brennan in 1963, and that, in turn, led Brennan to take the extraordinary step of having a weighty conversation about a pending issue with another justice's clerk.

Bazelon spoke often on the subject of crime and criminals, and sent his speeches to Brennan, who read them with care, underlining key passages. Bazelon openly sympathized with the social and economic plight of criminals. Soon Brennan began quoting Bazelon in his own speeches. By the mid-60s, Bazelon's influence and Brennan's growing confidence in his own role had changed the justice's worldview. In May 1963 he delivered to the D.C. Circuit annual meeting a speech about the criminal justice system that could have come out of Bazelon's mouth: "The issue," Brennan said, "really comes down to whether we should further whittle away the protections of the very people who most need them—the people who are too ignorant, too poor, too ill-educated to defend themselves." The following year in New York City Brennan told the Jewish Theological Seminary, "Law is again coming alive as a living process responsive to changing human needs. The shift is to justice and away from fine-spun technicalities and abstract rules." On the death penalty specifically Brennan had a coming out of sorts in 1965, when he wrote to Norman Redlich of the New York Committee to Abolish Capital Punishment, saying that the group's efforts to end the death penalty were "gratefully encouraging." By the end of the decade he was ready for the Court to confront the issue head on. He began working on his brethren behind the scenes, and kept a close eye on the abolition campaign.

In the spring of 1968 things appeared to have been going quite well, but during the summer things took a turn for the worse. In June, Earl Warren resigned. Though only seventy-seven, Warren wanted to make sure a Democrat could pick his replacement, and he doubted the 1968 presidential election would go the right way. LBJ picked his friend Abe Fortas—then an associate justice—to replace Warren. Fortas faced substantial opposition. It emerged that he had helped draft LBJ's 1966 State of the Union address—several months after taking the bench— and had received a substantial honorarium for conducting a summer seminar at American University in violation of Court rules. Republicans and southern Democrats filibustered his nomination, using it as opportunity to lambast the Warren Court. When it became clear that he didn't have enough support to be confirmed, Fortas withdrew his name. By this time the new term had begun. Johnson asked Warren to stay on as chief justice. After Richard Nixon narrowly defeated Hubert Humphrey, he agreed that Warren should stay on for the remainder of the term. Warren's lame-duck status left the Court in limbo. Brennan felt a sense of helplessness. "There just wasn't a thing you could do," Brennan recalled. "Not a thing."

With respect to the death penalty, shortly after taking office Nixon's new attorney general, John Mitchell, said he was "not opposed to capital punishment." At the end of January 1969 the California Supreme Court upheld the constitutionality of capital punishment under its state constitution. This greatly disappointed Brennan. The California court was the most liberal in the nation, and the deciding vote in a four-to-three decision had been cast by Stanley Mosk, a liberal former attorney general and an outspoken opponent of capital punishment. The abolitionists had held out great hope for Mosk, whose judicial heroes were Brennan, with whom he served on a committee at NYU, and Goldberg, with whom he socialized regularly. Nevertheless Mosk took a position similar to Blackmun's and said the question whether to employ the death penalty should be left to the legislature. "Naturally, I am tempted to join in judicially terminating this anachronistic penalty," Mosk wrote, citing his work against the death penalty as attorney general. "However, as a judge I am bound to the law as I find it to be and not as I might fervently wish it to be."

By that March morning in 1969, even Brennan couldn't guess which way the Court would go. Two days earlier Tony Amsterdam had argued powerfully to the Court that Arkansas' standardless sentencing procedure was effectively random. Amsterdam said, "I think this Court would not sustain a sentencing procedure which provided that every man convicted of rape should roll the dice and if it came up seven or eleven he would die; any other number, he would live. What Arkansas has done is worse because I assume that the dice would not decide on the grounds of race." It was powerful rhetoric, but most of the justices didn't buy it. Fortas asked Amsterdam how it would be possible to construct standards. White pointed out that judges routinely sentenced defendants without standards. Stewart and Warren seemed to be focused on death qualification, though it hadn't been raised in the briefs. The questions dispirited Brennan. If Stewart and Warren weren't on board, then the cause was lost.

When he finished his walk, Brennan showered, ate breakfast, read the *New York Times* and *Washington Post*, and drove to the courthouse. In his chambers Brennan greeted the other clerks and his secretary,

Mary Fowler. At ten o'clock a buzzer sounded, signaling the start of conference. Brennan grabbed a bite of chocolate (his guilty pleasure), and stepped down the hall to the conference room, where he shook the hand of each of his colleagues with a bit less verve than usual.

He wasn't expecting much.

THE CONFERENCE ROOM WAS one of the treasures of the Supreme Court. Everything about it inspired seriousness and awe. Three twin-tiered chandeliers hung from forty-foot-high ceilings. A trio of windows, shrouded by dark rose tapestries, ran the height of the room, allowing in light, which illuminated white-oak bookshelves containing bound volumes of the Court's opinions. Above the mantel of a black marble fireplace hung a portrait of John Marshall, the longest-serving chief justice and the architect of judicial review, the doctrine that obligates a court to invalidate a law if it violates the Constitution and that transformed the Court from a ceremonial body to an equal partner in American government.

Most of the furniture dated back to the opening of the courthouse in 1935. A long mahogany table dominated the room. It sat on a mammoth rug, surrounded by nine high-back leather chairs, each bearing the name of a current justice. That morning, like every morning, the stewards had set each place at the table with a wooden pencil tray, a green felt blotter, and ample yellow legal pads. By tradition the chief justice sat at the head of the table. Warren faced the senior associate justice, Black, then in his thirty-second term on the Court. The other justices filled in the table, three on the side nearest the window, four on the side closest the bookcase. The stewards had wheeled in several trays. One contained a silver urn of coffee; the others held the briefs for the day's cases.

Some of the most important conversations in the nation's history had occurred in this room. *Brown*, *Miranda*, and *Korematsu*—upholding the internment of Japanese Americans in World War II—had been decided here, as had, for better or worse, every major case of the preceding thirty-five years. On Fridays the justices gathered to discuss the cases that had been argued during the week and to vote. By custom the chief justice spoke first, followed by others in descending seniority. When it came to vote, they reversed the order, and the most junior justice announced his position first. The chief justice then assigned someone to write the majority opinion. If the chief was not in the majority, the privilege fell to the senior judge in the majority. Assignments could make or break a case. The right justice could build a coalition where none appeared possible. The wrong one could drive a seemingly assured majority apart. Each justice took this responsibility seriously.

Shortly after ten o'clock Earl Warren called the conference to order. Brennan had a famously close relationship with Warren, but even he didn't know which way Warren would go. Warren sometimes claimed to be against the death penalty, and had voted with the majorities in *Witherspoon* and *Jackson*, but he also had deep reservations about the Court taking on the issue, as he indicated to Goldberg in *Rudolph*. Furthermore this didn't seem like the sort of issue for a holdover chief justice to take on.

To Brennan's astonishment, Warren came out firing against the death penalty. "The jury cannot be given the absolute right to give life or death without standards to guide their choice," he said. "Death seems to be reserved usually for the poor and underprivileged. No person of any affluence is ever executed. The jury should have ground rules. Now they have absolute discretion." Brennan felt the way the fans at Forbes Field must have felt that magical day in 1935 when Babe Ruth emerged from his stupor and thrilled them with four hits, including the three final home runs of his career. Warren appeared liberated, not restricted, by his status as a lame duck, and reconnected to his core principles. The Chief's sole reservation was that Boykin and Maxwell shouldn't be released from prison. "We should follow the *Witherspoon* formula and not send everyone back for a new trial," he said. "The only issue attacked here is the death penalty. I would not reverse the conviction, but simply convert it to a life sentence." In his

mind Brennan kept score as if it were a baseball game. Just like that, it
was one-to-nothing for Brennan's team.

Across the table Hugo Black shook his head. Warren's thinking had
evolved since 1963, but Black's hadn't. Black remained committed to
originalism and the constitutionality of the death penalty. "I disagree
with the Chief," Black said. "The Court is usurping the power of the
legislature. The only issue here is whether the death penalty is valid.
We can't formulate standards. They are too vague. The policy question
is not for us. The Constitution gave the states the power and we can't
overrule them." The game was tied at one all.

William Douglas put the abolitionists back ahead. Douglas said
he agreed "with the Chief and with Matthew Tobriner's dissent on
the California Supreme Court." Justice Tobriner, a 1962 appointee of
Democratic governor Pat Brown, had written, "If a civilized society
cannot say why one man should be executed and another not, it does
not rationally, logically take life. Instead, it grossly denies due process
of law, inflicting death on the basis of a trial that is capricious, discriminatory and guess-infected."

Dressed in a three-piece suit tailored in London, with the gold watch
chain of his namesake grandfather who had also served on the Court
draped from his vest, John Harlan spoke next. Brennan had a warm
relationship with Harlan, too. They had shared cigarettes and golf and
summered at each other's homes. Brennan didn't know what to expect
from his friend, though. Harlan had made it clear time and again that
he didn't like the direction of the Warren Court. He took particular
exception to Brennan's efforts in *Baker v. Carr*, the voting-rights case
that ended Frankfurter's era. In 1963 Harlan told the ABA: "Some
well-meaning people apparently believe that the judicial rather than
the political process is more likely to breed better solutions of thorny
problems. This is a compliment to the judiciary but untrue to democratic principle." On the other hand Harlan prided himself on taking
each case on its own merits. Brennan also had a vague sense that Harlan found the death penalty distasteful.

When he spoke Harlan expressed tepid support for reversing Maxwell's conviction. He just wasn't sure on what basis. Harlan thought single-phase trials were constitutional but said, "I can't go along on the standards point." Requiring standards would undermine the jury system. "Some acts provide the death penalty unless the jury recommends mercy," Harlan said. "This introduces the compassion of the jury, and seems to me to put the case against standards in its most striking form. Do juries need standards to exercise their mercy power? What should the standards be? I can't see why the standards wouldn't reach the Executive's commutation power. Why not standards here, too? And then where do we stop as to standards? Won't we be in the business of second-guessing? That is a legislative problem." Finally Harlan indicated that the excessiveness of death as punishment for robbery didn't concern him. Brennan went next and said that he, like Douglas, agreed with the Chief in both cases. Now it was four-to-one for Maxwell, and three-to-two for Boykin. The next vote would be crucial. On deck was Potter Stewart.

Brennan also had a strong relationship with Stewart. They had met at a judicial conference many years earlier and struck up a friendship. When Eisenhower nominated Stewart to the Court, Stewart called Brennan for advice. On the bench, though, Stewart molded himself on Harlan, not Brennan. He considered himself a judge's judge, meaning that, like Harlan, he decided each case on its individual merits. Stewart professed no overarching philosophical principles and disliked ideological labels. Brennan, in his view, was too "reflexively liberal."

On the death penalty, though, Stewart had given the most encouraging signals. LDF and the public only knew part of it. What they didn't—and couldn't—know, was that Stewart had been almost single-handedly responsible for *Witherspoon*. Initially the Court voted to deny certiorari for Witherspoon. After Stewart threatened to dissent, Warren took another look at the petition and changed his vote. Later the Chief praised Stewart for "delving more deeply into the record." Stewart's effusive opinion, with its reference to Koestler's *Reflections on Hanging*, caused a rift on the Court. Publicly Hugo Black said, "If this Court is to hold capital punishment unconstitu-

tional, I think it should do so forthrightly, not by making it impossible
for States to get juries that will enforce the death penalty." Privately
Black told his wife that he thought Stewart's opinion was terrible.
Byron White echoed the sentiment. "If the Court can offer no better
constitutional grounds that those provided in the opinion," he said,
"it should refrain its dislike for the death penalty and leave the decision to the other branches of government."

Stewart's comments at conference disappointed Brennan. Stewart
said that he would reverse Maxwell's death sentence, but only because
of problems with jury selection. LDF hadn't raised these problems, but
Stewart felt the Court could address them anyway and had asked LDF
about jury selection at oral argument.* Now Stewart said, "The *Witherspoon* issue is here, and I would dispose of the case on that basis."
This might be a good result for Maxwell, but if Stewart's view prevailed it meant the Court wouldn't address the more significant issues.
Stewart told his colleagues that LDF's argument regarding standards
didn't persuade him. He felt the standards and single-phase trial issues
were inextricably linked. "It seems to me," Stewart said, "that if you
have standards you must have a bifurcated trial because in a unitary
trial the jury can't know anything about the defendant. If a jury is
prejudiced, no instructions will curb it." Stewart also didn't appear
concerned with the excessiveness of the death penalty for robbery.

---

* Stewart's question at oral argument once again confronted LDF with the dilemma
between representing the interests of the client and the movement. LDF had excluded
the jury selection argument from its brief to focus the Court on the race issues. When
Stewart asked about the jury-selection procedures at Maxwell's trial, Arkansas' attorney general admitted that the process was illegal under *Witherspoon*. When Warren
later asked Amsterdam whether he had any objection to the Court reviewing the
trial transcript, it became clear that the Court had substantial interest in resolving
Maxwell under *Witherspoon*.

Amsterdam responded to the dilemma by trying to have it both ways. He told
the Court that he welcomed consideration of the *Witherspoon* issue, but implored the
justices not to ignore Maxwell's other arguments. If the Court failed to act on the
constitutionality of Arkansas' sentencing proceedings, Amsterdam said, "It would
be inhumanity second only to killing this man."

Byron White agreed with Stewart. He didn't see the death penalty for robbery as unconstitutional. Regarding *Maxwell*, White said
simply, "I would reverse on *Witherspoon* and go no further." At this
point it was clear that Boykin's proportionality argument was going
nowhere. For Maxwell it was six-to-one to reverse his sentence, but of
those six, three wanted to decide the case under *Witherspoon* and avoid
the more important issues.

The junior justices didn't help Brennan's cause. Fortas said he agreed
with Harlan: The Constitution didn't require jury standards. Privately
Fortas and Marshall believed that if the Court required standards, the
standards would favor prosecutors. On the other hand Fortas thought
the Constitution required split trials. He said, "A unitary trial violates due process in a rudimentary sense, because the jury is kept from
relevant facts it should know on the life or death punishment issue."
Finally Marshall said, "I would go on *Witherspoon*. I go with John
Harlan on the unitary trial question. That places too great a burden on
the defendant's Fifth Amendment rights. I reverse." What this meant
wasn't exactly clear.

In the final tally Boykin had only three votes. Maxwell had eight
votes in his favor, but no consensus as to reasoning. White and Stewart would reverse based solely on *Witherspoon*. Harlan, Marshall, and
Fortas would reverse on the bifurcation issue. If the Court reached
bifurcation, Stewart felt it must then also address standards, though he
preferred to address neither issue. Only Douglas, Warren, and Brennan wanted to reverse on both standards and bifurcation.

All in all the conference couldn't have been more confusing. Douglas returned to his office and wrote that the discussion was not "very
conclusive or illuminating." To make matters worse the next day Harlan wrote Warren and said, "I am not at rest on my yesterday's vote to
reverse this case on the basis of the split-trial issue." Harlan asked that
the case be held over for further discussion.

Brennan understood that Warren's choice to write the majority
opinion would determine the fate of the cases. Reconciling the frac-
tured views of the individual justices would require a master politician

with supreme mediation skills and a deft personal touch—someone, though Brennan would never say this, like Brennan himself. Instead Warren selected Bill Douglas.

It was difficult to imagine a worse person for the job.

NO ONE COULD DENY that William O. Douglas was a genius. From Yakima, Washington, a small railroad town of six thousand people, Douglas earned a scholarship to Whitman College, a liberal arts academy in Walla Walla. At Whitman he excelled as a student and debater, and after a brief stint teaching, he earned a place at Columbia Law School, from which he graduated near the top of his class.

His legal career was meteoric. Douglas was held back—if one can use this term with respect to a man who became a Supreme Court justice—only by his own Hamletesque capacity for indecision. Following his graduation from law school in 1925, Douglas went to work at Cravath, DeGersdorff, Swaine & Wood, one of the top firms in the country. After four months Douglas decided he didn't like Cravath and returned to Yakima. He then decided he didn't like that either and moved back east. He tried Cravath again, still didn't like it, and finally became a professor at Yale Law School. His restlessness continued. After teaching for several years Douglas set his sights on government work. He fashioned himself into an expert on securities law with an eye to earning a position in the Roosevelt administration. In 1934 he led an investigation for the Securities and Exchange Commission. A year later, he became its chief. In Washington, D.C., Douglas forged substantial political alliances with Franklin Roosevelt's confidants Tommy Corcoran, Harold Ickes, and Joseph Kennedy, among others, and secured an invitation to the president's infamous poker games. In 1939 FDR appointed Douglas to replace Louis Brandeis. This would have satisfied most attorneys, but Douglas had his sights set still higher. In those days the Court sometimes served as a holding pen for politicians with larger ambitions. Douglas, then forty, believed he would someday become president.

He did not, and again his hamartia—his "macaroni spine" as he called it—was to blame. FDR nearly offered Douglas the vice presidential nomination in 1944. In 1948 Harry Truman did offer Douglas the slot on the ticket—three times—but Douglas hemmed and hawed. He weighed his own presidential run and worried about his financial future should Truman lose. Fear of not having enough money drove many of Douglas's odd career moves. Douglas's father, a minister, died when Bill was six years old, and left his mother little money. Douglas supported his education by working menial jobs, including stints as a janitor, a waiter, and picking fruit in a cherry orchard. He even claimed that when he started law school, to get to New York City from Yakima he tended sheep on a train. Ultimately Douglas told Truman, to the president's great dismay, that he wouldn't accept the nomination. The story more or less repeated itself in 1960. Douglas could have been Lyndon Johnson's running mate had he signed on early, and his joining the team might have helped LBJ prevail in the primary. But as always, Douglas wanted to be offered the crown without risk, and of course in politics this is generally impossible.

So Douglas was relegated to a career on the Supreme Court, where he spent thirty-six years, the longest tenure of any justice in American history—and the most prolific. During his time on the bench Douglas wrote 1,186 opinions. In his spare time he authored thirty-two books on subjects ranging from the environment to foreign relations to the nature of justice. Hugo Black told his clerks, "I'm just an ordinary person, but Bill is a genius. He can get more done in an hour than I can get done in a week."

As a jurist Douglas was a visionary. His view of privacy, first advanced in a 1952 lawsuit against a streetcar company that broadcast loud radio programs—and which Douglas alone supported under a constitutional "right to be let alone"—was the germ of *Roe v. Wade.* He defended freedom of speech and religion fiercely, taking absolutist stances against the restrictions of obscenity and blue laws, which required businesses to be closed on Sundays. His highly evolved view of equal protection held that the Constitution protected not

just discrimination on the basis of race, but also class. An avid hiker
and committed environmentalist, Douglas took the unconventional
position in 1972 that inanimate objects, such as forests and streams,
should have standing to sue in court. With characteristic—though
not entirely unfounded—hubris, Douglas saw himself as the heir of
Louis Brandeis. He ranks among the handful of most important civil
libertarians in the history of the Court, rivaled during his era only
by Brennan.

On a personal level, however, Douglas was a nightmare. For start-
ers he habitually exaggerated and lied. His memoirs are littered with
inaccuracies, too numerous to discount as the product of advancing
age. Douglas's brilliant biographer Bruce Allen Murphy said that in
the course of his interviews he "could not find a single person who
could confirm a single account dealing with them in one of Douglas's
books." Describing the unique challenge of his project, Murphy wrote,
"Douglas's life was the stuff of novels. Unfortunately for me, he had
written those novels in the form of his memoirs."

Douglas was hell on his family. He divorced three times (no other
Supreme Court justice had ever been divorced), had countless affairs,
and was largely estranged from his two children. He met his third
wife, Joan Martin, at Allegheny College when he was sixty-three and
she was a senior. After they married two years later, Douglas almost
immediately became dissatisfied with Martin and began looking to
replace her. He married for the fourth time, at the age of sixty-eight,
to a twenty-two-year-old cocktail waitress, Cathy Heffernan, whom
he had known for two days.* At the time Douglas met Heffernan, he
was carrying on an affair with Elena Leonardo, a young artist working
in a Yakima travel agency. Within one week of marrying Heffernan,
Douglas regretted the decision and renewed his courtship of Leonardo. Douglas sometimes hit his wives. He abused his students, who
recalled him as a "mean son of a bitch," as well as his law clerks and
secretaries, who lived in fear of the buzzers on their desks, which they

---

* Heffernan later became a lawyer.

recalled sounding like a dentist's drill, used to summon them to the justice's chamber, where he would berate them mercilessly. One former clerk, Scot Powe, recalled waking up in the middle of the night, "bolt upright, because I heard that buzzer in my dream." Douglas called clerks "the lowest form of human life."

Douglas got along little better with his colleagues on the Court. Early on, he and Frankfurter developed a mutual hatred. Frankfurter's friendship with former justice Robert Jackson revolved substantially around ridiculing Douglas. Douglas in turn referred to Frankfurter as "the Little Giant" or "Der Führer." Time only made his edges rougher. His caustic wit spared no one. He openly clashed with Warren Burger, often ridiculing him to his face; condemned Potter Stewart as a patrician; and called Thurgood Marshall "spaghetti spine."

Douglas's style couldn't have contrasted more sharply with Brennan's. Brennan maintained warm relations with almost everyone on the Court, even those with whom he disagreed. Harlan would remain among his closest friends, despite his conservativism. So too Black, even after they drifted apart ideologically. Time and again Brennan proved himself a master Court politician. Against the odds he held together majorities in *Baker v. Carr, New York Times v. Sullivan* (the seminal case on defamation of public figures), and *Cooper v. Aaron* (striking down Orval Faubus's use of the National Guard in Little Rock). Through negotiation, subtle manipulation, and compromise, Brennan became the most influential figure in the Warren Court, in some ways more influential than the chief justice himself.

Douglas had no such inclination. The totality of his career suggested that Douglas cared more about being right than being effective. During his thirty-six years on the Court, Douglas wrote 486 dissents. This meant he dissented at twice the normal rate. Even more remarkably, in more than half the cases in which he dissented, Douglas wrote only for himself. This figure is off the charts. Right or not, Douglas was persuading no one. Someone favorably inclined to Douglas's point of view might excuse this as the necessary consequence of taking an unpopular but correct position. But even after the appointment of

Goldberg gave Warren a workable liberal majority, Douglas remained at odds with his liberal brethren. He chastened them for not going far enough in their decisions. Brennan said of Douglas, "His great mistake was his insistence—and he repeated it time and time again—'I have no soul to worry about but my own.'"

Douglas's intransigence on the Court is somewhat puzzling. During his time in academia and government service, Douglas demonstrated substantial skills in forging political alliances. His biographer Murphy speculates that his failure to become president plagued Douglas and tainted his tenure on the Court. Perhaps the only way he could make sense of devoting his lifetime to the Court was to see himself as a unique visionary, ahead of his time. Perhaps it was because his massive ego, cultivated by a doting mother, and relentless ambition, fueled by an absent father, simply didn't allow him to play well with equals. Whatever the true cause of his discontent, after his aspirations of high office disintegrated, Douglas defined himself as a loner.

In 1969 Douglas's temper and sense of anomie from the Court were more acute than they had ever been. During the previous spring he had begun to suffer from insomnia, often waking up in the middle of the night with his heart racing. In early June he collapsed during oral argument. At Walter Reed Hospital doctors installed a pacemaker. Douglas began to sense the end was near. For a man who prized himself on his physical fitness, and who perpetually sought the fountain of youth through his travels and romantic conquests, this truth was intolerable. William Douglas began to look back on his life, and he didn't like what he saw. That term, at a lunch with the law clerks, Walter Dellinger, later U.S. solicitor general, asked Douglas whether he would become a justice if he had it to do all over again. "Absolutely not!" Douglas cried. "The Court as an instrument is too peripheral, too much in the backwater. You're just too far out of the action here," he said. The clerks pressed him. What about the revolutionary decisions of the Warren Court? "Irrelevant," Douglas replied. "All of the ability to affect action is elsewhere." As he denounced the significance of his career, Douglas's eyes betrayed to the clerks a deep and profound sadness.

To bring an end to the death penalty in America in 1969, the Court needed a conciliator at the peak of his skills. What it had was a maverick at the height of his dissatisfaction and isolation.

To forge a winning coalition in *Maxwell*, Douglas's safest strategy would have been to focus solely on the unconstitutionality of single-phase trials. At conference Marshall, Fortas, Warren, and Brennan had indicated support for this argument. With Douglas's own vote he would have a bare majority. If Harlan stuck to his original position, the vote would be six to three. Perhaps if Harlan came around, Stewart might too. This was the safe, sensible course of action.

Instead Douglas swung for the fences. In late March, Douglas sent Brennan the draft of his opinion. It struck down Maxwell's conviction because of both the single-phase trial and the absence of standards. Brennan urged Douglas to focus on single-phase trials. Douglas replied that split-phase trials without standards wouldn't accomplish much. "What good would it do to focus the jury on punishment without guidelines to focus their deliberations?" he asked. Brennan thought it would accomplish quite a bit. Split-phase trials without standards were better than single-phase trials without standards. Moreover the decision needed to be understood in context. A victory of any kind would preserve the momentum of the moratorium. Douglas wasn't listening.

Brennan tried to limit the damage. In an April 1 letter Brennan implored Douglas to "sharpen his discussion" of single-phase trials. Douglas needed to make clearer the defendant's dilemma between taking the stand and being cross-examined about his guilt or not testifying regarding his punishment. More important, Brennan implored Douglas to say that the standards question need only be reached if the Court deemed single-phase trials constitutional. "I think the standards discussion would be clearer if it was made plain that this is a separate and independent inquiry necessary to decision," wrote Brennan. Dividing the issues would make it possible for Marshall, Harlan, and Fortas to reverse Maxwell's sentence without agreeing to the standards argument. Douglas met Brennan partway: He divided his opinion into separate sections, though the arguments still referenced each other.

On April 4 Douglas circulated his draft to the conference. His argument regarding standards appealed to common sense: "The law normally gives a jury guidelines" with respect to such questions as "which party is at fault in an automobile accident," he wrote. Granting a jury or judge undefined discretion was "lodging in its hands a naked and arbitrary power." It was a fine argument, but it seemed as if Douglas hadn't attended the conference. The only thing he wrote that responded to his colleagues' concerns was to make clear that if Maxwell's sentence were reversed, he wouldn't be entitled to a new trial.

In the cover memo to his draft, Douglas defended including both arguments. "The case has bothered me considerably," he wrote. "As I recall, there never were more than four votes to hold that standards were constitutionally necessary. There was, however, a majority holding that a bifurcated trial was constitutionally required. As I got deeper into the two problems they became inseparable to me."

Douglas's personal appeal didn't help. No one budged. Fortas wrote Douglas on April 7, copying the conference, saying that the standards argument didn't persuade him. "I am certainly with you with respect to the infirmity of a unitary trial," Fortas wrote. "But I continue to think that requiring standards is inadvisable and will be productive of results that I consider undesirable." Fortas declared: "The basic fact is that it is impossible, as far as I am concerned, to state standards which would justify capital punishment." He offered a further strategic reason behind his position. "I think that if standards are legislated, the result will be to substantially increase the number of cases of imposition of the death penalty."

Here Brennan would have compromised. Instead Douglas replied testily. "I have set forth my views," he wrote, again copying the conference. "Perhaps those who insist that there be standards before costs can be assessed"—referring to *Giaccio*—"can explain why standards are necessary for the assessment of costs but not for assessment of the death penalty. But that is a fact which surpasses my limited capacities."

Douglas's petulance would have been inappropriate under any circumstances, but particularly with respect to Fortas, who was Douglas's best ally on the Court. Fortas had been Douglas's student and colleague at Yale, his chief of staff during Douglas's early committee work for the SEC, a key member of the campaign that led Roosevelt to appoint Douglas to the bench, and later a supporter of Douglas's vice presidential and presidential ambitions. It made no sense to attack Fortas, but Douglas was Douglas.

Soon Douglas's majority began to disintegrate. On April 9 Harlan announced that he didn't think the lack of standards made the Arkansas statute "constitutionally infirm." He remained open on the single-phase-trial issue but said he needed more time and had "not yet come to rest on the precise scope of what due process would require in this regard." On April 21 Marshall announced that he agreed with Fortas regarding standards. "In this area," Marshall said, "we do not yet have the skills to produce words which would fit the punishment to the crime." Stewart circulated an opinion, which White joined, saying that the case should be resolved on *Witherspoon* grounds.

Finally Douglas abandoned the standards argument. On April 22 he circulated a new draft opinion overturning Maxwell's sentence solely because of the single-phase trial. Fortas joined, and now Douglas had a majority. Black circulated a caustic dissent, echoing his sentiment from *Witherspoon*: "If this Court is determined to abolish the death penalty, I think it should do so forthrightly, and not by nibbles." But neither Black's dissent nor Douglas's opinion would ever be published. Douglas's delay had cost him the case.

Two weeks after Douglas circulated his revised opinion, *Life* magazine published a story reporting that Fortas had accepted twenty thousand dollars from a foundation run by Louis Wolfson, a Las Vegas financier. Two years earlier Wolfson had been convicted of perjury and obstruction of justice, and he served one year in a federal prison. Experts speculated that the payment to Fortas had been a bribe to secure Fortas's help with the SEC. For Wolfson the incident would be only a bump in the road, but for Fortas it would be the end of his career. On May 13, after intense political pressure, Fortas resigned.

Now Douglas had only four certain votes for Maxwell. To form a majority he needed either Harlan's or Stewart's support. The day after Fortas's resignation, Brennan circulated a concurring opinion, adding the standards issue as an independent basis for reversing Maxwell's sentence. "Due process requires pre-existing standards for penalty determinations," Brennan wrote. "Without such standards, the convicted offender would be in the Kafkaesque situation of having his life at stake and not knowing which arguments will hurt him and which might save him." More than the substance of Brennan's opinion, what mattered is that Brennan had circulated a concurrence, thereby suggesting that the *Maxwell* majority remained intact. Brennan did this strategically, to make it seem life as normal in the aftermath of the Fortas scandal. For a while it worked. Nine days later Warren joined the concurrence. Douglas soon followed suit.

Ultimately, however, Brennan's ploy failed. Though Harlan had tentatively supported the single-phase trial issue, he said he wouldn't "provide the fifth vote in such a crucial case." Harlan said he thought the case should be postponed until Fortas's replacement took the bench. Shortly thereafter Stewart said he agreed. With that the hopes of forming a majority died. At that point even Douglas pushed to table the case, and on May 26 the Court put *Maxwell* over to the following term. One week later the Court decided *Boykin* for the defendant on the narrowest possible ground, that his plea had been involuntary.

BY THE TIME *Maxwell* came up for reargument, the Supreme Court had a new captain at the helm. On May 21, 1969, Richard Nixon appointed Warren Burger as chief justice with the aim of restoring law and order in the Court and the nation.

Burger, like Douglas, had pulled himself up by his bootstraps. He was raised on a family farm on the outskirts of St. Paul, Minnesota. Burger's high school classmates elected him president of the student council, and Burger earned admission to Princeton. He couldn't afford it, though, and instead attended night school at the University of Minnesota and, later, night classes at St. Paul College of Law. Burger supported himself through college and graduate school by selling life insurance. Following law school he went to work at a Minnesota law firm. In his spare time he got involved with politics as a supporter of Harold Stassen, first managing Stassen's successful 1938 gubernatorial campaign and then his failed 1948 presidential bid. At the 1952 Republican convention, Burger supported Eisenhower and caught Ike's eye. The president brought Burger to Washington, where he spent three years as an assistant attorney general before Eisenhower appointed him to the D.C. Circuit Court of Appeals in 1956.

On the Court of Appeals, Burger feuded with David Bazelon. Their mutual antipathy traced back to Bazelon's landmark opinion in *Durham v. United States*, which expanded the insanity defense. Burger thought the decision opened the door to lawlessness. Burger referred to Bazelon as "Baz" and dismissed him to colleagues as misguided, pathetic, and a menace to society. In return Bazelon despised Burger. "It was a blood feud," Brennan later said. "There isn't any doubt about that." He had his own negative experience with Burger when they taught a two-week seminar for appellate judges at NYU. They quarreled over criminal procedure, as Burger openly criticized the Warren Court. Brennan felt that Burger, knowing of Brennan's friendship with Bazelon, went too far and had allowed his animosity for Bazelon to infect the discussion.

Brennan couldn't have been more discouraged by Burger's selection as chief justice. He understood that the tide had turned. With respect to the death penalty, there could be little doubt which way Burger would vote. Fortas's replacement would be no better. After his nominations of Clement Haynsworth and G. Harrold Carswell failed, Nixon put forward Burger's childhood friend Harry Blackmun. William Rehnquist, then an assistant attorney general whose responsibilities included vetting judicial nominees, assessed Blackmun as a true conservative. At his confirmation hearing on April 29, 1970, Blackmun told the Senate Judiciary Committee that he personally disliked the death penalty but would vote to uphold it as a judge. Blackmun would have to recuse himself from *Maxwell* since he had written the Eighth Circuit's opinion, but his nomination didn't bode well for the bigger picture.

Going into the *Maxwell* reargument on May 4, 1970, Brennan held out little hope for a favorable outcome. The questions from his colleagues only made him more pessimistic. After Amsterdam finished his opening statement, Burger asked, "Isn't your burden here to show not that the procedures you seek are wise or sound, but that they are compelled by the Constitution?" Stewart asked, "Did Arkansas merely extend mercy when it changed from mandatory to discretionary capital punishment?" White questioned why standards should be required for capital cases but not for other cases. "Isn't sentencing without standards just as bad in non-capital cases?" he asked. "Are you attacking all jury sentencing?"

Amsterdam did his best. "Where more is at stake, due process is more exacting," he replied to White. "I do not think the jury can be given the absolute right to decide life or death. Why do we expect that twelve men off the street, who have never sentenced before and never will again, can sort this out even-handedly?"

Burger asked, "But isn't the process the same when jurors determine negligence in an accident case?"

"In such a case, the judge instructs the jury about the legal standard of care," Amsterdam replied. "I would be surprised if research into such cases did not discover that there was a strong correlation between the presence of faulty brakes and jury verdicts of negligence. But we did a study in Arkansas rape cases and found that the death sentence was associated only with race."

"Don't all these statistics about racial discrimination suggest that legislative bodies have advantages over courts in this area?"

"That's why we think the Constitution requires standards."

"Once you get standards, won't you be asking us to review them?"

It was that kind of day.

✦ ✦ ✦ ✦

THE ENSUING CONFERENCE ON May 6 dashed Brennan's fad-
ing hopes. Burger began by saying that he "saw no way of shaping
standards." He said, "I wish there were some, but the search is too
elusive. The jury is the agency for mitigating the harshness of judges."
Burger then referred to the American Law Institute's Model Penal
Code, which had developed some guidelines. He said, "The Model
Penal Code has useful appeal, but on analysis it does not hold up. It is
impossible to articulate all that is relevant. The jury is the conscience
of the community, and that is it." Burger summarily dismissed bifurcation. "I am not sure it is a useful device, and I am not sure whether
it helps a defendant. It is not a blessing to the accused. It is also not a
component of due process." For Maxwell it was all bad news. Burger
didn't even see a *Witherspoon* problem.

Black recapitulated what he had said a year earlier: "If one wants a
jury trial, he must want the variety of views that it gives. Anyway, this
is only a fight to abolish capital punishment, and it is not unconstitutional. It is a matter for the legislature and not the courts."

Burger interjected, "I would vote in Congress to abolish capital
punishment."

Everyone else more or less maintained their positions from the previous year. Douglas said, "I reverse on standards and bifurcation."
Harlan said standards weren't required. "Is it unconstitutional to dele-
gate an unstandardized judgment to a jury to be reached as they see fit,
laying aside only their personal biases?" he asked, and then answered
his own question, "I don't think so." On bifurcation, Harlan's views
had crystallized. "I have gone both ways. At the end of last term, I
thought that bifurcation was not necessary. Now I think that it is," he
said. "It violates basic due process to disallow a defendant from getting
into the hopper all of the elements bearing on punishment. This is one
of the clearest cases of denial of fundamental fairness that I have seen."

Brennan said he would reverse on both standards and bifurcation.
Regarding standards, he wrote a note to himself, "How about a para-

graph from the jury's point of view. Twelve men are taken off the street
and asked to play God. What are they to draw on? The life or death
decision is wholly outside their normal experience."

Stewart said he thought the Constitution required neither bifurcation nor standards. "But," he said, "unlike John, I think that if you
have bifurcation you must have standards." Stewart again said that he
wanted to decide the case under *Witherspoon*. White said he thought
that Maxwell's failure to put in any evidence regarding his penalty
fatally undermined his bifurcation argument. Harlan didn't think this
should prejudice his case. "There was no tender of evidence, but the
state of the law precluded it," Harlan said. "He should have a bifurcated trial if he wants it." Finally Marshall said that he had changed his
opinion on standards and would now vote to reverse on both counts.
Blackmun had recused himself and didn't speak.

When they tallied the votes, the justices had split four to four on
bifurcation, and five to three against requiring standards. Stewart,
though, had said that if split-phase trials were required, then he would
vote for standards. This confused matters, and the justices decided to
put the central issues over to the following term in a new case, so that
Blackmun could participate.

On June 1 the Court set aside Maxwell's sentence under *Witherspoon*, and remanded the case yet again to the district court. In a brief
collective and anonymous opinion, the justices made clear that they
were expressing "no view whatever with respect to the two questions
originally specified in our grant of certiorari," and announced that
they were granting certiorari in *McGautha v. California* and *Crampton
v. Ohio*, "in which these two questions will be considered at an early
date in the 1970 Term." Crampton had raised the Eighth Amendment
argument in his brief, but the Court chose to ignore it.

THE CHOICES OF *MCGAUTHA* and *Crampton* disappointed Brennan. These were highly aggravated murder cases. Dennis McGautha
shot a store owner in the course of a robbery. James Crampton, a drug

addict, shot his wife while she sat on the toilet. By selecting murder cases instead of a rape or a robbery, the Court had made it more difficult for LDF to present its arguments about process in the most sympathetic light. Furthermore California was one of the few states with bifurcated trials. Meltsner said, "The facts of the two cases did not augur well for the result sought by the anti-capital punishment lawyers." To make matters worse LDF didn't represent either defendant and had not been much involved in either case. It would be restricted to filing amicus briefs. All of the effort on *Maxwell* had come to nothing. The decision, Brennan said, "went down on the books as a minor footnote to *Witherspoon*."

To Meltsner, *Maxwell* and *Boykin* illustrated the fragility of the momentum for abolition. Years later, when he learned how close he and LDF had come to winning, he saw the cases as a turning point. *Maxwell* had been an opportunity for the Court to take "a measured step toward abolition," he said, a way to toe the water and see how the public would react to its involvement with the issue. Now, framed around the legitimacy of the death penalty for murder, which a majority of Americans favored, it was all or nothing. If the *Crampton* and *McGautha* appeals were lost, as Brennan and LDF thought was likely, then executions would resume. With only the Eighth Amendment argument left in LDF's holster, it was clear from the Court's repeated ducking of the issue that it wasn't going to get them anywhere. In the course of a single year, all the gains achieved through the moratorium appeared to be slipping away.

CHAPTER 5

TO LICENSE A LAUNDRY, TO LICENSE A LIFE

W HEN THE SUPREME COURT HEARD *McGAUTHA V. California* on November 9, 1970, death penalty supporters had their own superstar to advocate their cause. Ronald George, the deputy attorney general of California, was only thirty, but he had sterling credentials and experience beyond his years. The son of a successful speculator and a Sorbonne-educated stay-at-home mother, George graduated near the top of his class at Beverly Hills High School, and then attended the Woodrow Wilson School at Princeton University.

George had intended to enter the diplomatic service but changed direction after a summer in West Africa. He traveled to Nigeria with a friend whose father was stationed in Lagos, and spent several months hitchhiking with tourists, missionaries, and Foreign Service officers. The experience disillusioned George, who found that diplomats interacted very little with the local population. When he came home he enrolled at Stanford Law School "not for the noblest of motives," he recalled, but "to postpone the decision of what to do with my life."

George's life changed direction in a class with Stanford professor Gerald Gunther, an oracle of constitutional law, a disciple of the legendary judge Learned Hand, and the author of the most influential casebook of the twentieth century. Gunther inspired countless young lawyers including Ruth Bader Ginsburg and David Souter. Following the class, George found himself increasingly attracted to public-interest law. Though he could have made much more money working in private practice, George said he wanted to do something with "social relevance." When Stanley Mosk, then the California attorney general, offered him a position following graduation, George leaped at the opportunity.

In the attorney general's office, George quickly gained notice as a rising star. In 1968 the U.S. Supreme Court granted certiorari in *Chimel v. California*, a case George had been handling involving the proper scope of a search incident to arrest. George had to fight to keep the case from being assigned to an older attorney, but he succeeded, and at the age of twenty-eight argued his first case before the Supreme Court. The opportunity so racked George's nerves that he forgot to pack cufflinks, and so, when he faced the justices for the first time, the sleeves of his shirt were held together by paperclips. Though the Court ruled against California in *Chimel*, George's performance impressed his superiors. The following year they assigned him a case where the Court narrowed *Chimel*. With two oral arguments under his belt, including one victory, George had a reputation in his office as a consti-tutional law expert. When the Court granted cert in *McGautha*, it was natural to assign the matter to him.

Years later George would become an outspoken critic of his state's death penalty system and of capital punishment generally. In 1991 he would be named a justice of the California Supreme Court and, five years later, its chief. During his tenure George found particular fault with what's often called the "death row phenomenon"—the excruci-ating years prisoners spend awaiting execution.* He once had the *New York Times* quote of the day for his pithy explanation of the dynamics of capital punishment in his home state: "The leading cause of death on death row in California is old age."

In 1970, however, Ronald George was a different man. "My think-

---

* Albert Camus condemned capital punishment on this basis, but not everyone cred-ited the argument. In a note to himself regarding the phenomenon Blackmun asked, "Does this imply that a man convicted and sentenced should be executed forthwith?"

ing on the death penalty evolved—perhaps I didn't have the insight I later did," George said following his retirement in 2010. At the time of *McGautha*, he had no firm position on the morality of capital punishment. This may have worked to his advantage, and certainly differentiated him from the other attorneys involved in the capital cases. George simply saw himself as the representative of a democratically achieved outcome. "My attitude has always been that any government entity is entitled to a vigorous defense," he said.

While the Court had given LDF permission to file an amicus brief, it denied Amsterdam's request to argue the case. So George's opponent on *McGautha* was Herman Selvin, sixty-six, a graduate of Berkeley Law School who headed the litigation department at Loeb & Loeb and took McGautha's case pro bono. George thought quite highly of Selvin. "He was a very fine advocate, and had a reputation as one of the finest attorneys in California," he recalled. But Selvin wasn't Tony Amsterdam, and that day George got the best of him.

Every first-year law student learns some version of this ancient primer: "If you don't have the law on your side, argue the facts; if you don't have the facts on your side, argue the law; if you have neither the facts nor the law, argue the Constitution." Selvin didn't have the facts, so he argued the law. In an effort to minimize the stakes, Selvin began by saying that his argument did not "implicate the constitutionality of the death penalty per se," but rather California's "standardless procedure." He drew an analogy to a long line of Court decisions requiring states to define criminal conduct clearly, and said the Court would definitely find unconstitutional a statute saying "that murder was simply any killing that in the absolute discretion of the jury was determined to be deserving of some kind of punishment." Selvin couldn't have known that he was making the same argument that Douglas made in his angry memo to Fortas, which ultimately undid *Maxwell*.

The Court didn't buy it. Warren Burger laid down a land mine for Selvin, and asked whether it would be unconstitutional if the death penalty were mandatory for murder.

"I am inclined to say that on balance it would not be," Selvin answered, referencing the practices prevailing in colonial times.

Selvin had fallen into a trap, which Burger delighted in springing. "Well, if the death penalty were mandatory and were not unconstitutional, then you are here because California is more lenient than it might have to be."

Selvin laughed, understanding what had happened. "Well, it is capriciously more lenient," he said, trying to make the best of a bad position. "The trouble is that the penalty for murder has not been fixed by law," he explained. "Now that's quite a different thing from saying the penalty is death but someone has the power to dispense clemency. In that case an argument could be made that the requirement of standards does not apply because there is no constitutional right to mercy. But there is a constitutional right to know what it is that you can and can't do, and what happens to you if you do it."

This was almost certainly the best argument that could be made. From a defendant's standpoint, what was the difference whether juries punished arbitrarily or granted mercy arbitrarily? Either the law should permit both types of randomness or neither. Neither Burger nor Blackmun accepted the argument, though. In his notes Blackmun assigned Selvin a grade of B-.

When George took the podium, he argued with the confidence of a man who had the facts *and* the law on his side. "I think it is very important to approach this case as a living reality, and not in a factual vacuum," he said. "This is not a metaphysical exercise. We are dealing with the rights of one individual and specific facts." The facts were bad, George reminded the Court. "This was an unnecessary, cold-blooded execution. The owner offered no threat. He was unarmed. He was five foot, three inches tall, 135 pounds, fifty-two years of age. He could have been robbed without a weapon."

More important, George said, were the procedural protections McGautha had been afforded. He ran through the litany of measures California employed to prevent arbitrariness. "First of all," he said, the jurors had been instructed that "they would not take into account the race of the defendant, no bias, nothing. Secondly, there are special rules as far as the admissibility of evidence is concerned." For example, "prosecution evidence is excluded where it's merely inflammatory. Thirdly, there is a very wide scope of evidence allowed in mitigation. Fourthly, no hearsay evidence is permitted on the issue of penalty."

George explained that even the prosecution's closing argument was restricted. For example, "The prosecution is precluded from mentioning such things as the fact that the defendant might be out on parole in seven years if he gets a life sentence. He is not allowed to argue that the death penalty is considered by some to be a deterrent. He is not allowed to argue that the trial court might reduce the punishment nor that the state supreme court or the governor might do that. This is thought to dilute the jury's sense of responsibility," he explained, adding that California had a special rule that "any substantial error whatsoever requires reversal." George took a deep breath and said, "The death penalty is a very selective thing in California."

Whatever arbitrariness resulted, George explained, was the product of the jury system. Juries have complete discretion and operate in secrecy. Sometimes they reached arbitrary or confusing decisions, but "the jury is free to do this under any system," George said. "Under a system of fixed standards, they can still do it. They can be told don't consider his race, don't consider the expression on his face, and they can still do that and there is no system divisible by man that can preclude that possibility." In his notes Blackmun underlined the point: "*Even with standards, a jury is free to do as it pleases.*"

If anything, George said, standards would disadvantage defendants because "it is impossible to make an exhaustive list of all mitigating circumstances." Thus, he explained, "juries would feel inclined to say, well, we find two of these things here, the man has a prior record, he shot more than one victim, I guess this isn't the proper case for the exercise of our mercy function."

This back-and-forth recurred time and again throughout the capital cases. LDF cried, "The system is arbitrary and unfair." To which supporters of capital punishment replied, "The jury system is arbitrary, which is quite a different thing from saying that it is unfair. Juries dispense mercy, which is arbitrary by its nature." Then they turned to Amsterdam or whoever argued the case and asked, "Are you against the jury system?" To this the abolitionists never developed a convincing response.

Indeed George's argument quieted the bench. Blackmun asked whether McGautha had said what standard the Constitution required. "Not a specific one," George replied, "but I would like to read you what petitioner advances as his suggestion. I quote: 'Consideration of penalty could be centered around the objectives of punishment with a view to choosing that one which, having regard to the circumstances of the case and the character and temperament of the defendant, would most nearly further rather than frustrate them.'" George lowered his voice. "Now, I inquire if this is any kind of a standard? I don't know what a jury would do in trying to follow this." George's argument put the standards issue to bed. Blackmun gave him a B+.

When James Crampton's lawyer, John Callahan, took the podium, what few questions the justices asked him focused on the bifurcated-trial issue. This argument went no better for Callahan than the standards argument went for Selvin. Callahan stated the defendant's dilemma. "If he invokes his Fifth Amendment right, the jury decides his punishment without ever hearing from the man whose life they hold in their hands. If he waives his Fifth Amendment right, he is subject to impeachment as to his credibility, and in Ohio this includes a great range of inquiry."

Burger again didn't see this as a death penalty issue. "Every defendant in every criminal case is somewhat chilled or otherwise discouraged about taking the stand, isn't that true?" he asked.

"Not all, sir, but yes most."

Stewart piled on: "Mr. Callahan, was there any request for a bifurcated trial?"

"There was no request made in this case, Your Honor."

By the time Melvin Resnick made Ohio's case, the justices seemed to have moved on. For the last ten minutes of Resnick's argument they

didn't ask him a single question. Blackmun gave Resnick a C, the lowest grade of the session. Meltsner called it a "quiet day in court—too
quiet." He and Himmelstein presumed the Court would rule against
them, and they began planning for the aftermath. Greenberg advocated convening a second national conference. Several of the lawyers
thought this would be more trouble than it was worth, but this time
Greenberg didn't envision a show. He wanted to brainstorm and generate publicity. LDF had raised almost no money for its death penalty
work other than the Ford Foundation grant. Greenberg thought he
could get the Rockefeller Foundation to pay for the new conference,
and that the attention it would generate might attract other support.

LDF needed the money. It anticipated a long, tough road ahead.

FOUR DAYS AFTER ORAL ARGUMENT Burger opened the *McGau-*
tha conference by exposing what he saw as the true motives behind
the appeals. "This is an oblique attack on capital punishment," Burger
said. "Abolition of capital punishment is what this case is really all
about." The new chief had experienced no epiphanies during the week.
"The argument did not give us a set of standards," Burger said. "Bifurcated trials are a dubious thing. Some states have abandoned them, one
has adopted them. That is enough for me to refuse to put bifurcation
into a constitutional requirement. I affirm."

Black's position hadn't changed since the previous year: "A bifurcated trial is not required under the Constitution, and I doubt its wisdom from the defendant's viewpoint. I affirm." Fortas had made a
similar argument in *Maxwell* regarding standards. Black was the first
to make it with respect to splitting trials. Though LDF treated the
benefits of standards and bifurcated trials as axiomatic, one could
imagine that each could leave defendants worse off. With standards
the specifics made all the difference. Lenient standards would help
defendants. Strict standards would hurt them.

Bifurcated trials are more difficult to game. The potential benefit
to defendants is that when the jury decides guilt, it doesn't hear all

of the aggravating evidence—including, notably, the defendant's prior record. But jurors also don't hear mitigating evidence, which might lead them to find a defendant not guilty. The question before the Court was whether the benefits of bifurcation outweighed the costs. As a former trial lawyer Black appreciated that aggravating evidence often slips in during the guilt phase of trials, though mitigating evidence rarely does.* A defendant might thus prefer to have all of the evidence come in at once.

After Douglas said he would reverse in each case, Harlan explained that he thought the case boiled down to a single issue: "Is there a constitutional right of allocution?" he asked rhetorically. At common law—the ancient law of England based upon societal customs and case law—a defendant in a felony case had a right, called "allocution," to be asked why judgment shouldn't be passed against him. During *Maxwell*, Harlan had waffled regarding bifurcation. Now he resolved that bifurcation equated with allocution, which common law required but the U.S. Constitution didn't. "This is all that bifurcated trial means," Harlan said. "The United States' brief has convinced me that I should affirm both cases."

Brennan spoke simply. "I reverse in each case," he said.

Stewart felt less conflicted than the year before. *Witherspoon* hadn't been violated, and since there appeared to be little support for requiring standards, he didn't need to press his argument that requiring standards also required bifurcating trials. "I affirm in each case," Stewart said. "In Ohio, if there is a doubt as to guilt no jury will impose death. You can get anything in that you want to get in where guilt is clear." White followed and said he, too, would affirm.

Marshall said, "I'll go with Bill Douglas to reverse in both cases."

Blackmun didn't find the cases troubling. In a memo to himself, five

---

* A simple example: Suppose a prisoner who had been abused as a child escaped and committed a murder. It would be nearly impossible for a prosecutor to prove the murder without mentioning that the defendant had escaped from prison, which is a common aggravating factor. On the other hand the defendant's abusive experience would have no relevance during the guilt phase.

days before oral argument, Blackmun wrote, "A reading of the bench memorandum and of the brief here somewhat surprises me, for the case seems to me to have in its present posture less substance than I had anticipated. Noticeably absent is the Eighth Amendment." Of course this was because the Court hadn't certified the Eighth Amendment issue. Blackmun told his colleagues, "*McGautha* is less difficult than I thought. Many protective devices are used in California's procedure. I affirm. *Crampton* is harder. It comes down to whether allocution is of constitutional dimensions. I think not. I will affirm."

This conference had none of the confusion that had attended *Maxwell*. A clear six-to-three majority supported affirming both convictions, and Burger assigned the opinion to John Harlan.

ON FEBRUARY 25, 1971, Harlan circulated his draft. His opinion characteristically emphasized the Court's limited role. "Our function is not to impose on the States what might seem to us a better system for dealing with capital cases," he wrote. "Rather, it is to decide whether the Constitution proscribes the present procedures in such cases." Harlan explained why standardless sentencing didn't violate the Fourteenth Amendment, "despite the undeniable surface appeal of the proposition." The issue needed to be understood in historical context. At common law no distinction existed among the various sorts of homicide, all of which were eligible for the death penalty. Juries thus often responded by acquitting defendants in cases where they regarded death as an inappropriate punishment (lawyers refer to this as "nullification"). States responded to nullification by grading homicides and making the death penalty available only for "first-degree" murders. Still juries nullified. Thereafter, when a jury thought a prosecutor had overreached, it simply found a defendant guilty of a lesser-degree homicide. Finally states capitulated and made the jury's mercy power explicit. In short, jury-sentencing discretion had evolved as a response to jury discretion in convicting.

This history revealed Crampton's and McGautha's arguments as a cagey lawyer's move. Their attorneys understood that the Supreme Court would never restrict a jury's power to dispense mercy. To shift the issue to restricting punishment, rather than restricting mercy, they emphasized the infrequency with which juries imposed the death penalty. Harlan exposed the ruse. Even if juries were merciful 99 percent of the time, this didn't change the nature of their action. The only solutions were to eliminate jury discretion—which no one favored—or to control it. Harlan said such a limitation was impossible. No one could distinguish in plain language the people who deserved to live from those who deserved to die.

Mercy was an act of grace and by its nature couldn't be codified. Imagine someone trying to explain the factors that led them to give money to this beggar, but not another, or why they sent their child to her room on this occasion but not another. Harlan wrote, "To identify before the fact those characteristics of criminal homicides and their perpetrators which call for the death penalty, and to express these characteristics in language which can be fairly understood and applied by the sentencing authority, appear to be tasks which are beyond present human ability." He added, "For a court to attempt to catalog the appropriate factors in this elusive area could inhibit the scope of consideration, for no list of circumstances would ever be really complete. The infinite variety of cases would make general standards either meaningless boilerplate or a statement of the obvious that no jury would need."

With respect to split-phase trials, Harlan argued that neither defendant had suffered from the absence of a right of allocution. "An accused can put before the jury a great deal of background evidence with at best a tenuous connection to the issue of guilt. The record in Crampton's case does not reveal that any evidence offered on the part of the defendant was excluded on the ground that it was relevant solely to the issue of punishment." Even if evidence had been excluded, Crampton was no worse off than any defendant. Trials are always cruel to some extent, Harlan said, echoing Burger. A defendant always faces the dilemma of whether to testify or exercise his Fifth Amendment rights. In the end Harlan said that Crampton's argument came down to the complaint "that the death verdict will be returned by a jury which never heard the sound of his voice." Harlan dismissed this as "largely symbolic."

Harlan ended by restating his first point. "Before we conclude," he wrote, "it is appropriate for us to make a broader observation. It may well be that bifurcated trials and criteria for jury sentencing discretion are superior means of dealing with capital cases if the death penalty is to be retained at all. But the Constitution, which marks the limits of our authority in these cases, does not guarantee trial procedures that are the best of all worlds, or that accord with the most enlightened ideas of the infant science of criminology, or even that measure up to the individual predilections of members of this Court. The Constitution requires no more than that trials be fairly conducted and that guaranteed rights of defendants be scrupulously respected. Certainly the facts of these gruesome murders bespeak no miscarriage of justice."

Harlan's opinion caused more consternation among the clerks than the justices. Daniel Edelman, a Harvard graduate who had followed Blackmun from the Eighth Circuit, wrote Blackmun that Harlan's "proposed opinion is certainly a fine piece of work and has already been carefully edited." But, he said, "The prospect of the hundreds of executions that may follow this decision is horrifying to me personally. I think it will also be horrifying to the country." Blackmun didn't change his vote, and neither did any of his colleagues.

BLACK CIRCULATED A SIMPLE to-the-point concurrence. The framers supported the death penalty, therefore it was constitutional. "The Eighth Amendment forbids 'cruel and unusual punishment,'" Black wrote. "In my view, these words cannot be read to outlaw capital punishment because that penalty was in common use and authorized by law here at the time the Amendment was adopted. It is inconceivable to me that the framers intended to end capital punishment by the Amendment. Although some people have urged that this Court should amend the Constitution by interpretation to keep it abreast of modern ideas, I have never believed that lifetime judges have any such legislative power." LDF could take heart that Black's dissent hadn't attracted any other signers, but that was more likely because cert hadn't been granted on the Eighth Amendment issue than because of distaste for Black's position.

DOUGLAS AND BRENNAN ISSUED disgruntled dissents. Douglas reminded Black of what he wrote thirty years earlier in *Chambers v. Florida*, Black's first major opinion in what was, coincidentally, Thurgood Marshall's first Supreme Court victory. The case concerned four black men who confessed to the murder of a white man after a week of questioning, sometimes with ten police officers in the room, and without an opportunity to speak with a lawyer. Overturning the conviction, Black wrote, "Tyrannical governments had immemorially utilized dictatorial criminal procedure and punishment to make scapegoats of the weak, or of helpless political, religious, or racial minorities and those who differed, who would not conform and who resisted tyranny." Douglas quoted the language verbatim.

Brennan argued that Harlan had framed the issue incorrectly. Harlan's admonition that the Court must respect legislative actions had no relevance since no legislature had acted. "We are not called upon to determine the adequacy or inadequacy of any particular legislative procedure designed to give rationality to the capital sentencing process," Brennan wrote. "For the plain fact is that the legislatures of California and Ohio have sought no solution at all. We are not presented with a State's attempt to provide standards, attacked as impermissible or inadequate. We are not presented with a legislative attempt to draw wisdom from experience. We are not presented with the slightest attempt to bring the power of reason to bear on capital sentencing. We are faced with nothing more than stark legislative abdication."

Like Douglas, Brennan beckoned to the Court's past, to *Yick Wo v. Hopkins*, an 1886 decision where the Court held that a law which was neutral on its face nevertheless violated the equal protection clause because it had been applied in a discriminatory manner. San Francisco had given its board of supervisors the power—with no governing standards—to issue or to deny laundry permits. Uniformly the board declined to grant permits to Chinese applicants. Yick Wo, who had operated a laundry for many years, sued and won. Brennan drew the connection. "Not once in the history of this Court, until today, have we sustained against a due process challenge such an unguided, unbridled, unreviewable exercise of naked power," he wrote. "Almost a century ago, we found an almost identical California procedure constitutionally inadequate to license a laundry. Today we hold it adequate to license a life."

With equal passion Brennan challenged Harlan's claim that humans lacked the capacity to construct standards. "I think it is fair to say that the Court has provided no explanation for its conclusion that capital sentencing is inherently incapable of rational treatment," he wrote. One could imagine simple, clear standards. For example, a legislature could say that only murderers of police officers would be eligible for the death penalty. Any jury could understand this clear, objective guideline. "I see no reason whatsoever to believe that the nature of capital sentencing is such that it cannot be surrounded with the protections ordinarily available to check arbitrary and lawless action."

The majority simply refused to look beyond the status quo, Brennan said, quoting "The Problem of Capital Punishment," Felix Frankfurter's 1956 essay. "As to impossibility, all I can say is that nothing is more true of the legal profession than that the most eminent among them, for 100 years, have testified with complete confidence that something is impossible which, once it is introduced, is found to be very easy of administration." Brennan said he had no problem with discretion, "but discretion, to be worthy of the name, is not unchanneled judgment; it is judgment guided by reason and kept within bounds. Otherwise it is the law of tyrants. It is always unknown. It is different in different men. It is casual, and depends upon constitution, temper, passion."

Finally Brennan rejected the notion that the cases called upon the Court to determine the proper boundaries of state authority. "What they do call upon us to determine is whether the Due Process Clause requires the States"—again Brennan used Black's own words—"to make certain that men would be governed by *law*, not the arbitrary fiat of the man or men in power."

Douglas praised Brennan's draft. "Your dissent is magnificent," he wrote, and signed on. Several days later Marshall joined, too. Even Harlan respected the dissent. Much of it was written by Brennan's clerk, Mike Becker, a graduate of Harvard College and University of Pennsylvania Law School, where he was editor in chief of the law review, and another alumnus of David Bazelon's chambers. Becker wrote the dissent with Stewart, Black, and Harlan in mind, and it was his idea to pepper the opinion with quotes from their opinions. Harlan jokingly told his clerks to add to his opinion a sentence, "Everything to the contrary is hereby overruled."

ON MAY 3, 1971, THE COURT published *McGautha*. Even though they had been expecting the worst, the decision hit LDF hard. More than three years had passed since Colorado gassed Luis Monge to death. LDF now faced the prospect of executions resuming. Several governors, including Ronald Reagan, said they would hold off until the Supreme Court resolved the Eighth Amendment argument, which still had never been addressed. Nevertheless the moratorium was on tenuous ground.

When LDF's leaders and more than one hundred attorneys gathered on May 15 at Columbia Law School, the mood was gloomy. Greenberg opened the conference with ritualized words of encouragement. Himmelstein presented a giant brief, which he had been working on since February in the event they lost *McGautha*. But Amsterdam told the attendees they should expect no help from the Court. LDF would litigate all of its 120 pending capital cases, and they would aggressively assert the Eighth Amendment issue—they had no reason to hold back now—but Amsterdam saw no chance of a major victory. The new justices had revealed their cards.

The best the attorneys could hope for, Amsterdam said, was to win new trials for their clients. Many prisoners had been condemned by juries selected in violation of *Witherspoon*. LDF could also raise arguments along the lines of *Boykin*. The previous December the Fourth Circuit ruled the death penalty unconstitutional for a rapist who hadn't endangered the life of his victim. Perhaps the Supreme Court might be persuaded to rule the death penalty unconstitutional for particular crimes and criminals. Amsterdam saw little hope, though, of successfully arguing that the death penalty violated the Eighth Amendment.

Dramatically Amsterdam urged a shift to grass-roots tactics. He and his colleagues outlined LDF's new three-point plan. First, LDF would support a proposal in Congress to impose a two-year moratorium on executions. Second, they would try to encourage governors to take the clemency process more seriously. Third, Hugo Bedau, a philosopher at Tufts University and the president of the American League to Abolish Capital Punishment, would organize a network for public education and lobbying.

LDF's few successes over the past year had been at the state level. Shortly before the previous Christmas, Himmelstein and Amsterdam had met with Arkansas governor Winthrop Rockefeller urging him to commute William Maxwell's sentence. At the end of the session Rockefeller said that he had made up his mind before the meeting started, but he enjoyed Amsterdam's presentation too much to cut him off. Rockefeller commuted not just Maxwell's sentence, but the entirety of Arkansas' death row. LDF believed this victory could be repeated elsewhere.

Indeed, three weeks after Rockefeller's blanket commutation, Pennsylvania's outgoing attorney general, Fred Speaker, followed suit and removed the electric chair from the death chamber. "I believe killing criminals is a disgusting indecency and demeaning to the society that tolerates it," Speaker said. When Milton Shapp, the new governor, took over, he said Speaker had lacked the authority to remove the chair. This was bluster. The chair could have been replaced at any time, and Shapp promised not to execute anyone during his term.

At approximately the same time, the National Commission on Reform of Federal Criminal Laws, chaired by former California governor Edmund "Pat" Brown, issued its proposed revision of the federal code and recommended eliminating the death penalty. Shortly thereafter the Alabama Court of Appeals effectively ended executions in the state by interpreting an ancient statute to mean that executions could only be carried out in a particular prison that had been destroyed four years earlier. LDF felt the grass-roots strategy had potential.

Goldberg and Dershowitz had reached the same conclusion six months earlier. The focus of the abolition movement needed to shift to the state level and to influencing legislatures rather than courts. Even before the Court announced *Maxwell*, they had seen the writing on the wall. In the June 1970 issue of the *Harvard Law Review*, Goldberg and Dershowitz criticized the Court for avoiding *Boykin* and *Maxwell* and for its reluctance to address the constitutionality of capital punishment. Their primary message, though, was an exhortation to states not to become complacent. State courts and legislatures, they said, should resist the temptation to "assume that the only proper forum of judicial interpretation is the judiciary."

Brennan soon began sounding the same theme in his own speeches to bar associations. The Supreme Court was the ultimate arbiter of the U.S. Constitution, but nothing precluded a state court from interpreting its own state constitution to be more protective of civil liberties. And of course nothing prevented a legislature from being more protective still. Any state—or Congress—could eliminate the death penalty at any time. Goldberg and Dershowitz's article spurred Senator Philip Hart of Michigan and Representative Emanuel Celler of New York to propose that all state and federal executions be suspended for two years. Hart and Celler said the bill would give states an opportunity to take a deep breath before resuming executions.

By the summer of 1971, all the abolitionists had reached the same conclusion: What hope they had rested with the people. Goldberg and Dershowitz ended their article by noting that "the basic Eighth Amendment question now hangs in an uncomfortable limbo." Neither they nor anyone else had any delusions about how the Court would answer it.

INSIDE THE COURT the liberal justices saw things more or less the same way. Brennan was dismayed. Years later he said, "In candor, I must admit that when *McGautha* was decided it was not just a lost skirmish, but rather the end of any hope that the Court would hold capital punishment to be unconstitutional."

Brennan saw *McGautha* as part and parcel of the new direction of things. One after the other, the gains of the Warren Court appeared to be slipping away. In *Harris v. New York*, Burger's majority opinion held that police could use confessions obtained in violation of *Miranda* to impeach the credibility of defendants who testified at trial. Brennan's dissent called the opinion "monstrous." In *Labine v. Vincent*, Black upheld a Louisiana law prohibiting illegitimate children from sharing in their parents' estate. In *Rogers v. Bellei*, Blackmun supported a law depriving children born outside the United States of their American citizenship if they failed to live in the country for five continuous years between the ages of fourteen and twenty-eight. During the entire 1960s Brennan had filed sixty-seven dissents. In the 1970–71 and 1971–72 terms alone, he dissented seventy-two times. His anger filtered into his opinions, which the *New York Times* called "increasingly vinegary."

It didn't help Brennan's mood any to see Hugo Black's health failing. Black was cranky and suffering from chronic headaches. Losing Black wouldn't make a difference with respect to the constitutionality of the death penalty, but it was difficult to imagine that Richard Nixon would nominate a replacement who would be as protective of civil liberties as Black had been.

Soon Brennan would be alone. At a conference shortly before the summer, the justices discussed what to do with the pending capital cases, asking one another whether executions could resume. Stewart said they couldn't because many appeals raised the Eighth Amendment issue, which the Court hadn't decided. But Brennan was the only justice who said he thought the death penalty was cruel and unusual punishment. Since the result of an Eighth Amendment case was obvious, Brennan suggested the Court not drag the process out. The Court should simply issue a denial of cert in the remaining capital cases, to which he would append a short dissent. Douglas and Marshall agreed with Brennan. Each said he wouldn't endorse the Eighth Amendment argument. Douglas made clear that his *Boykin* vote had turned on the fact that the case involved a robbery. Had it been a murder, Douglas said he would have voted the other way. This story could very well have ended there—were it not for Hugo Black.

At the age of eighty-five, Black wouldn't be satisfied with quiet vindication. He had long predicted that the Court would strike down the death penalty someday, not because of the merits of the legal arguments but in capitulation to the fear of executing the men waiting on death row. He wanted the Court to validate explicitly his long-standing position that the death penalty was constitutional because the Founding Fathers so intended. Single-handedly Black turned the conference around. He argued that Burger should seize the moment while he had the upper hand, and "once and for all make it clear to the nation that the death penalty and all its aspects pass constitutional muster." How could he have foreseen what would happen next?

Douglas certainly didn't. The conference ended with an agreement that Brennan and White would "find four clean cases" for review. Douglas circulated an angry memo to his colleagues threatening to dissent from the grant of cert. The idea of dissenting from a *grant* of certiorari had virtually no precedent in Supreme Court history, and Douglas shared Black's bottom line, but Douglas perceived intellectual dishonesty, which he couldn't countenance. He was outraged that the Court hadn't followed Brennan's proposed course of action: "For the life of me, I do not see how anyone would entertain the thought that as a matter of constitutional law the death penalty was prohibited in a straight clean-cut first-degree murder case."

Douglas obsessed about the issue for most of June. Over the course of the month, he circulated nine drafts of his dissent. Early versions made the constitutionality of the death penalty seem axiomatic. "These cases do not present a substantial federal question," he wrote in draft number five. "Naturally the question of life and death is of supreme importance, however, the issue is one for the executive and legislature, not the judiciary. It is incredible that we should waste everyone's time for one more year in order to say so." Douglas concluded, "I personally think it is monstrous for society to take one life because a defendant took one. But I do not see any mandate under the Constitution for judges to be the arbiters of the wisdom or folly, the ethics or barbarity of capital punishment. If it is progress we want, then our task is to release these cases and let them no longer fester here."

In his sixth draft Douglas emphasized the unfairness to defendants of creating a false sense of hope. "There is much that could be done if the cases were denied," Douglas wrote. "Beyond the Eighth Amendment issue, which most do not even raise, they have absolutely no chance of securing any review by this Court. Their claims would be better served by denying certiorari now and allowing them to present any new claims to the lower courts."

In yet another draft Douglas characterized raising the hopes of the men on death row as cruel and unusual. In his final draft, the ninth, Douglas denounced the motives of his colleagues. He wrote, "The purpose of granting certiorari in these cases is not to explore the problem in all of its constitutional, sociological, and penological aspects, but to announce in draconian fashion that capital punishment passes muster."

As usual Douglas persuaded no one.

BRENNAN AND WHITE PICKED four cases from the two hundred pending red-covered cert petitions. Part of their charge was identify a range of cases wide enough to give the Court room to maneuver. They thus selected two rape cases and two murder cases. In a memo to the Conference, Brennan and White noted that their choices left open the possibility of upholding the constitutionality of the death penalty for murder but finding it cruel and unusual for rape.

Among the pending rape appeals, Brannan and White chose *Jackson v. Georgia* and *Branch v. Texas*. LDF represented Lucius Jackson. Brennan and White thought it was only fair for LDF to participate, and its presence would ensure that the Eighth Amendment argument was presented cogently. Elmer Branch's case stood out to Brennan and White because, though Branch's victim was elderly and black, in their words, she "suffered no special injury." The implication was that if the Court couldn't find the death penalty excessive for Branch then it couldn't find it excessive for any rapist. Jackson's case was more aggravated. He had escaped from prison when he broke into a home and raped the owner. Both Branch and Jackson were black.

The first of the two murder cases selected by Brennan and White was gruesome. Ernest Aikens had committed two rape-murders in Ventura County, California. Aikens was represented by Jerome Falk—a prominent California attorney and a former Douglas clerk—with an assist from LDF. It's less than clear what the justices meant by a "clean" capital case, but *Aikens* probably didn't fit the bill. One of Aikens's victims was five months pregnant; the other was an elderly neighbor of his in her sixties. The state also had introduced evidence at trial that Aikens shot a gay man who had picked him up on the road. *Time* said the case "chillingly demonstrates another kind of horror"—in contrast to the horrors of execution highlighted by abolitionists—and described Aikens as "brutal and remorseless." Ominously the magazine added, "Psychiatrists have unanimously pronounced him fearfully sane and unlikely ever to be rehabilitated."

Finally Brennan and White chose *Furman v. Georgia*, another LDF case. The facts weren't quite as bad as *Aikens*, but they were bad. On August 11, 1967, the Mickes, a white couple, awoke to a load noise in their Savannah home. Thinking it might be their eleven-year-old son sleepwalking, William Micke went downstairs to put him back to bed. Soon his wife heard a loud sound and her husband's scream. She gathered her five children, locked them in the bedroom and cried for help. A neighbor heard her, came to her aid, and together they called the police. When the officer arrived he found Mr. Micke's body on the floor, with a bullet through his chest. As the police searched the vicinity William Furman—a black man—emerged from a wooded area near the Mickes' house and began to run. The police caught Furman, searched him, and found on his person a .22-caliber pistol, the same weapon used to kill Micke.

Furman claimed that the killing had been an accident. He said that he fled when Micke came downstairs, and on his way out of the house tripped over a loose electrical cord on the back porch, inadvertently discharged his gun, and hit Micke through the back door. The all-white jury convicted Furman in less than two hours. It's impossible to know whether they bought Furman's story. They might have believed him and convicted him nevertheless. Furman would still have been eligible for the death penalty under the felony-murder rule, which makes someone committing a felony responsible for all the consequences of his actions, even if unintended. LDF said this demonstrated yet another deficiency of standardless sentencing: An appellate court couldn't determine whether the jury believed Micke's death had been intentional or accidental.

But that was an argument for another day. The justices all agreed with Brennan and White's choices. Douglas even withdrew his dissent—his bluster often faded when it conflicted with his summer vacation. On June 28 the Court granted certiorari in *Furman, Aikens, Jackson,* and *Branch,* and set argument for October 12, 1971, the first argument day of the new term. The order made it clear that the justices would finally confront the elephant in the room. The Court certified a single question: "Does the imposition and carrying out of the death penalty in this case constitute cruel and unusual punishment in violation of the Eighth and Fourteenth Amendments?"

THOUGH HE DIDN'T GO through with his dissent, shortly before leaving for his retreat in Goose Prairie, Washington, Douglas assigned his clerks their "summer research project." He did this each June to make sure they enjoyed no respite. This year's project focused on capital punishment. "The question of the death penalty has been a hobby of mine for some years," Douglas wrote. "I have always thought it was extremely unwise as public policy to enforce it. That of course is a far cry from saying that it is cruel and unusual punishment under the meaning of the Eighth Amendment." So, Douglas said, "We need a solid piece of work this summer on the sociological, penological, psychiatric and legislative aspects of this whole problem." To Douglas, "solid" meant original thinking. He made clear that he was "not interested in a collection of cases to show what judges have decided on the matter because judges by and large are pretty ignorant people." Without a doubt Douglas believed this would at most amount to a dissent from the decision Black wanted and a majority of the Court was sure to reach.

Brennan didn't know about Douglas's work. He could have used some good news. In addition to Burger undoing everything he had worked for since joining the Court, Brennan's wife, who had only recently recovered from treatment for throat cancer, had experienced a relapse. This latest round of radiation left her unable to eat normally, and she was in constant pain that prevented her from sleeping. Though Brennan was happy and gregarious by nature, when he left for his own summer vacation on the first of July, he was deeply dispirited. Before departing for Nantucket, Brennan directed Mike Becker to draft a memo explaining why the death penalty was cruel and unusual. Becker had done a spectacular job on the *McGautha* dissent, and it was natural for Brennan to turn to him, but Brennan had no hope that Becker's research would change the outcome of the 1971 cases. Rather, he expected that when he returned in the fall it would serve as the basis for a solo dissent.

In every imaginable way Brennan was alone.

PART TWO

DEATH

1971–1972

CHAPTER 6

YOUNG
LAWYERS

T HE SUMMER OF 1971 WAS THE BEST AND WORST TIME
to be a Supreme Court law clerk. Generally speaking, clerking
for a justice is a young lawyer's dream. In 1971 clerks earned $15,000
a year and they worked around the clock, but, to a person, former
clerks reflect on the experience as the best of their life. The job offers
a front-row seat to history and the opportunity to shape landmark
constitutional decisions.

Not surprisingly the competition for these positions is fierce. Of
the fifty thousand students who enter law school each August, only
approximately thirty make it to the Supreme Court.* For women the
odds are even more daunting. Though today approximately half of all
law students are women, only 30 percent of judges are women, and
merely 20 percent of law partners. During the 1950s, '60s, and '70s,
the legal profession was downright brutal for women. When Ruth
Bader Ginsburg graduated from Columbia Law School in 1959—tied
for first in her class—she had trouble landing a job. She was saved only
by the intervention of her professor, the great Gerald Gunther, who
promised a New York federal district court judge that he would replace
Ginsburg with a male clerk if she didn't work out. The situation was

* At the time, each associate justice got three clerks. The chief justice was allowed five.

no better on the Supreme Court. During the 1971 term, one of the twenty-six clerks was a woman. Though William Brennan supported a woman's right to choose and authored arguably the Court's most important decision on equal protection of women, he didn't hire his first female law clerk until 1974. At one point Brennan told friends he would resign if a woman were made a justice.

Also unsurprisingly the survivors of this cruel winnowing are the most remarkable lot. The clerks for the 1971 term would go on to become titans of the legal, business, and academic worlds. Stewart's clerk, Benjamin Heineman, became general counsel of General Electric. White's clerk, David Kendall, represented Bill Clinton during the Whitewater investigation and his impeachment hearings and is one of the most prominent litigators in the U.S. Paul Gerwitz, a Marshall clerk, became a Yale Law School professor. His colleague, Barbara Underwood, the sole woman clerk that term, is solicitor general of New York. Blackmun's clerk, George Frampton, is one of the nation's leading environmentalists.

Disproportionately, clerks are liberal. William Rehnquist identified and decried this trend in the 1950s, following his own clerkship for Justice Robert Jackson. In an essay in *U.S. News & World Report*, Rehnquist described the passion and bias of his "intellectually high-spirited" former colleagues. "Some of them are imbued with deeply held notions about right and wrong," Rehnquist wrote, "and some in their youthful exuberance permit their notions to engender a cynical disrespect for the capabilities of anyone, including the Justices, who may disagree with them." Rehnquist believed the clerks' left-wing politics negatively influenced the Court. "Some of the tenets of the 'liberal' point of view, which commanded the sympathy of a majority of the clerks I knew were: extreme solicitude for the claims of Communists and other criminal defendants, expansion of federal power at the expense of State power, and great sympathy toward any government regulation of business—in short, the political philosophy now espoused by the Court under Chief Justice Earl Warren." The cohort of clerks for the 1971 term was no exception to Rehnquist's rule.

From a liberal's perspective, though, the summer had gone badly. In July, Hugo Black checked into Bethesda Naval Hospital suffering from inflamed blood vessels. Several weeks later, John Harlan took the room next to Black, complaining of excruciating back pain. Soon Harlan learned that he had spinal cancer. On September 17 Black resigned from the Court. Harlan followed six days later. Two days after that Black died of complications from a stroke. Harlan survived just three months longer.

Their replacements were more conservative. Richard Nixon wanted a southerner to fill Black's seat. He first considered West Virginia senator Robert Byrd, a former Klansman who filibustered the 1964 Civil Rights Act. John Mitchell convinced Nixon that neither Congress nor the public would support someone who had never passed the bar, as Byrd had not. Nixon then considered Virginia representative Richard Poff, who had signed the Southern Manifesto in protest of *Brown*. Poff withdrew his name for personal reasons. Next, Nixon turned to Herschel Friday, a municipal-bond lawyer from Arkansas whose firm represented Little Rock in its effort to block desegregation. An ABA screening committee deemed him unqualified. Nixon then considered Mildred Lillie, a California Court of Appeals judge. The ABA screening committee deemed her unqualified, too. Advocating against these prospective nominees, Burger reminded Nixon and Mitchell that—at least in his view—"the Court as an institution has been sorely damaged in this last decade." Burger also said he would resign if Nixon appointed a woman.

Finally, Nixon turned to Lewis Powell, a former ABA president who had the organization's strong support. Nevertheless Powell possessed his own problematic record on race. He had been chairman of the Richmond school board during a period when the pace of desegregation had been, as Powell later characterized it, "more measured than civil rights leaders would have liked." This put it mildly. Civil rights leaders viewed the school board's action as open defiance of *Brown*. Whether this was accurate or not, Powell clearly was no friend of the civil rights movement. In 1966 he published an article titled

"Civil Disobedience: Prelude to Revolution"—also in *U.S. News & World Report*—criticizing Martin Luther King and civil disobedience. "Those who preach, practice and condone lawlessness are the enemies of social reform and of freedom itself," he wrote. Powell was as white as they came. He sat on the board of Philip Morris, lived in a colonial mansion, and belonged to the restricted Country Club of Virginia. Sadly, from the perspective of the liberal clerks, Powell was the more moderate of the two nominees.

Nixon's choice to replace Harlan, William Rehnquist, also emerged late in the process. As deputy attorney general Rehnquist participated in vetting Nixon's candidates for Black's seat. He was surprised when John Mitchell's deputy, Richard Kleindienst, told him to skip a meeting regarding the second seat because "we're going to be talking about you." Rehnquist had stellar academic credentials—he was valedictorian of his class of Stanford Law School—but he, too, had displayed racial insensitivity. During his clerkship for Justice Jackson, Rehnquist wrote a memorandum, titled "A Random Thought on the Segregation Cases," in which he defended the separate-but-equal doctrine. Rehnquist wrote, "I realize that it is an unpopular and unhumanitarian position, for which I have been excoriated by 'liberal' colleagues, but I think *Plessy v. Ferguson* was right and should be reaffirmed. To the argument that a majority may not deprive a minority of its constitutional right, the answer must be made that while this is sound in theory, in the long run it is the majority who will determine what the constitutional rights of the minority are."

This memorandum became a subject of controversy at Rehnquist's confirmation hearing. In his testimony Rehnquist characterized the memo as a statement of Jackson's "tentative views for his own use." Jackson's longtime secretary, Elsie Douglas, called Rehnquist's testimony a "smear of a great man," and said that her former boss didn't ask for his clerks' views. Whatever the truth, Kleindienst thought Rehnquist wouldn't have been confirmed but for Nixon's decision to send Powell and Rehnquist's names to Congress together. Democrats understood that if they rejected the package, Nixon's next nominees might be less "moderate." The liberal clerks despaired. Clearly the Court was about to shift to the right. Alan Dershowitz told the *New York Times* that civil rights organizations expected "lean years ahead."

With respect to capital punishment, the outlook was bleak. Many of the clerks cared passionately about the death penalty, and the stakes of its constitutionality were higher than ever. More than seven hundred people now sat on death row, waiting for the Court to decide whether executions were cruel and unusual punishment. *Furman v. Georgia* would be the case of the year, but from the clerks' perspective it was an all-but-lost cause. In the lunchroom the consensus was that LDF couldn't prevail. The numbers didn't work out. Powell, Rehnquist, Burger, and Blackmun would each support the death penalty. That meant LDF would need to carry each of the five remaining justices.

A clean sweep seemed impossible. Only Brennan's vote was secure. Some clerks thought Douglas and Marshall might be persuaded. Others thought Stewart would come around, too, but his own clerks wouldn't dare guess. One of them, William Jeffress, later a top Washington litigator who represented Vice President Dick Cheney's aide I. Lewis "Scooter" Libby, among others, said Stewart had proved unpredictable time and again. In any event Stewart's vote would only make it four to four. LDF also needed Byron White's support, which was utterly implausible. White had dissented in *Witherspoon*, advocated deciding *Maxwell* on *Witherspoon* grounds, rejected the Eighth Amendment argument in *Boykin*, and voted with Harlan in *McGautha*. Why would he change direction now?

Shortly after summer vacation Mike Becker presented the memorandum he had been asked to prepare to his boss, Brennan. Becker argued that death was a unique punishment because it treated a criminal not as a person, but "a thing to be toyed with and discarded." Despite the powerful language, Brennan remained resigned to filing a solitary dissent. He said that he intended to put the death penalty out of his mind until the oral arguments in January. It was too depressing to think about sooner.

✦ ✦ ✦ ✦

THE SUMMER OF '71 WAS also the best and worst time to be a young civil rights lawyer. Like his counterparts on the Supreme Court, Jack Himmelstein was undercompensated. He earned an annual salary of $6,000. Considering that he worked more than eighty hours per week, this came out to about $1.50 per hour, slightly less than the minimum wage of $1.60. The salary was enough to afford the rent on a small apartment in then-shabby Greenwich Village and not much else. Himmelstein wasn't complaining, though. He understood how lucky he was.

A decade had passed since Michael Meltsner's Yale classmate asked him whether working for a Negro organization wouldn't be more social work than law, but civil rights work remained an uncommon career path. Himmelstein had almost as much trouble finding a public interest job as Meltsner had. When Himmelstein joined LDF's staff, he was the eighth lawyer in the office. Himmelstein appreciated his good luck and loved every second of his job. He, too, had a ringside seat for the legal battle of the century.

But as the summer ended, the fight wasn't going well. Like the law clerks, almost everyone at LDF thought *Furman* was a lost cause. Meltsner was despairing. He had once held out hope for Blackmun, based on his conversation with Blackmun's clerk before *Maxwell*. "In my innocence I thought that translated into a vote when serendipity took him to the Supremes," Meltsner said. *McGautha* put that to rest. Blackmun was a lost cause, as were Burger, Rehnquist, and Powell. The choice of *Furman* greatly troubled Meltsner. Since Furman's murder appeared to have been an accident, it seemed the Court wanted to say that it would tolerate capital punishment even in a minimally aggravated case. Himmelstein handicapped the case the same way. Greenberg did too.

Only Tony Amsterdam was hopeful. "I expected to win," he said in 2010. It seems implausible that Amsterdam could have believed this, given the pessimism of his colleagues and the general direction of things. It also contradicts what he said at the Columbia Law School conference following *McGautha*. Perhaps the summer rejuvenated Amsterdam. Amsterdam had moved to Stanford Law School two years earlier, and Northern California summers can work magic. More likely Amsterdam had convinced himself that he would win because in order to continue working at his breakneck pace he needed to believe he would win.

Amsterdam pinned his hopes on White and Stewart. Regarding Stewart, Amsterdam saw *Witherspoon* as a bellwether. In reversing Witherspoon's sentence but not his conviction, Stewart had constructed an unprecedented remedy. Amsterdam believed this reflected Stewart's underlying dissatisfaction with capital punishment. Amsterdam also believed Stewart feared constitutionalizing criminal procedure. "He was worried about the creeping socialism of due process," Amsterdam said. "As a Frankfurter clerk, I could understand that."

In Amsterdam's view the key to winning the case was advancing an argument that appealed both to Stewart's antipathy for capital punishment and to his view of the Court's proper role. Amsterdam said, "We thought Stewart was leery of general due process, but we believed Stewart resisted the legal analysis in *McGautha*, not the result. If we could give him a confinable legal basis for striking down the death penalty, he would." Amsterdam thus made the strategic decision not to try to overturn *McGautha*. "We thought Stewart in particular would not budge," Amsterdam said.

Trying to win *Furman* without upsetting *McGautha* put LDF in an odd position. LDF's critiques of single-phase trials, standardless sentencing, and discrimination were all arguments about process, and most naturally raised under the due-process clause of the Fourteenth Amendment. In *McGautha* the Court upheld the death penalty under the Fourteenth Amendment. What could LDF say to persuade Stewart the death penalty violated the Eighth Amendment but not the Fourteenth?

Amsterdam's answer was another epiphany. He would argue that while the Fourteenth Amendment required fair procedures, the Eighth

Amendment required fair results. It was a jesuitical distinction, but a brilliant one. It gave Stewart a basis to uphold *McGautha and* strike down the death penalty. It also preserved the relevance of LDF's procedural concerns.

This notion that the Eighth Amendment required fair outcomes had almost no law to support it, but Amsterdam thought it was a natural anyway. "We thought the idea advanced in *Furman*—don't look at what's on the books, look at what happens—pointed to the Eighth Amendment. We also articulated to ourselves, though not publicly, that our ultimate weapon against the death penalty was Occam's razor." Amsterdam explained, "We took up, one by one, a series of aspects of criminal procedure that were common to capital prosecutions and to non-capital prosecutions and we argued that each procedure produced intolerable results in the capital-prosecution arena." This invited the judges to ask, "What exactly is the real problem? Can it be that there is something wrong with each of these separate procedural aspects of capital prosecutions or is the real problem capital punishment itself—an unreasoning, vengeful monster that inevitably resists all efforts to restrain it by normal, fair, rational, evenhanded process?"

OVER THE SUMMER Amsterdam wrote the brief in *Furman* and the other two cases in which LDF represented the defendant, *Aikens v. California* and *Jackson v. Georgia*. By this time Amsterdam unilaterally ran the drafting process. Sometimes LDF lawyers gave memoranda to Amsterdam, but these amounted to suggestions. "Tony would say, 'You did a great job,' and then totally rewrite a brief," Jack Himmelstein recalled. Amsterdam no longer required sign-off from LDF before submitting a legal document. In the language of the U.S. Attorney's office, where Amsterdam had worked for a year, Amsterdam was LDF's death penalty section chief. Jack Greenberg said, "Amsterdam was so manifestly inventive and smart that everyone deferred to him." In July, Amsterdam outlined the research to be done in preparation for writing the brief, which was due in court on August 26. Amsterdam liked to think before writing and tended not to revise much. "My first draft is slow," he said, "but it's pretty close to the end product." So a lot of groundwork needed to be done.

The first project was to demonstrate that the death penalty was against public policy and enlightened public opinion. This assignment went to Hugo Bedau, the Tufts philosophy professor who had taken a leadership role at the recent conference. Bedau reviewed the sociological literature on deterrence, drafted a ten-page memo on the international abandonment of capital punishment, and explained the role of scientists and learned men in the abolition movement.

At Amsterdam's request Douglas Lyons, the head of Citizens Against Legalized Murder (CALM), prepared a summary of suffering on death row and detailed gruesome execution scenes. Lyons was merely twenty-six years old, but Amsterdam regarded him as the perfect man for the job. CALM was everywhere during the late '60s. The organization held vigils outside prisons, delivered testimony on Capitol Hill, and kept tabs on the men on death row. Its letterhead featured Burt Lancaster, Truman Capote, and Steve Allen. From its level of activity one would have thought the organization had a staff of dozens. In truth Lyons ran CALM by himself, from his dormitory at the University of California, aided only by the credibility of his father, Leonard, a nationally syndicated columnist and movie reviewer. Time and again, Lyons had demonstrated his tenacity and competence, and that summer did so again.

Finally LDF attorneys took charge of researching the history and interpretation of the Eighth Amendment. One task was to show punishments that had been tolerated in 1791. Another was to review the language and holding of every Eighth Amendment Supreme Court decision. Amsterdam wanted to demonstrate the legal relevance of the victim's suffering. A penalty acceptable for one type of crime or criminal might not be acceptable for a different type of crime or criminal. Amsterdam suspected the Court had taken *Branch* and *Jackson* to signal its openness to ruling the death penalty unconstitutional for rape.

On August 18, a week and a day before the due date, Amsterdam began writing the brief. In a Stanford seminar room, he spread out the research memos and, together with his former student Jeffrey Mintz, got down to business. Eight days is an impossibly short time to write any three briefs, let alone three on the constitutionality of capital punishment, but this was Tony Amsterdam. Sustaining himself on coffee and thin cigars, he worked day and night at a pace no ordinary human could maintain. His secretary couldn't keep up. After she went home, exhausted, Mintz and Amsterdam finished typing the briefs. Amsterdam didn't type well, and so these legal briefs, which rank among the most famous in American history, were prepared by hunting and pecking. His son Jon recalled his father burning the midnight oil with twin Remington typewriters side by side on his desk—"one for the text and one for the footnotes." At ten thirty on August 25, the night before the deadline, Mintz took the briefs to the San Francisco airport and deposited them on the last plane to Washington, D.C. In the morning another of Amsterdam's former students picked up the briefs and delivered them to the Court.

The principal brief in *Aikens* used LDF's historical background work to prove that the Eighth Amendment must evolve. "To deny this dynamic character would produce inconceivable results," Amsterdam wrote. A thirty-page appendix summarized punishments that had been employed during the eighteenth century. Amsterdam wrote, "If the Constitution does not forbid capital punishment today upon the theory that it was widely allowed by law and practice in 1791, then the Eighth Amendment also does not forbid today—and will never forbid—the stocks and the pillory, public flogging, lashing and whipping on the bare body, branding of cheeks and forehead with a hot iron, and the stilting, cropping, nailing and cutting off of ears. Further discussion of a static theory of the Eighth Amendment seems unnecessary."

The standard should be "evolving standards of decency that mark the progress of a maturing society," as Warren suggested in *Trop*. The trick remained to explain how standards of decency condemned capital punishment when a majority of the American public supported it. For this Amsterdam relied on the argument from his *Boykin* brief. Americans supported the threat of capital punishment but not its imposition. LDF emphasized this point to the American public in making the case for abolition. "If a penalty is generally, fairly and uniformly enforced, then it will be thrown off the statute books as soon as the public can no longer accept it," Amsterdam told *Time* in January. "But when the penalty is enforced for a discriminatorily selected few, then all the pressures which normally exist to strike an indecent penalty off the books no longer exist," he added. "The short of the matter is that when a penalty is so barbaric that it can gain public acceptance only by being rarely, arbitrarily and discriminatorily enforced, it plainly affronts the general standards of decency of the society."

To drive home the standards point in the brief, Amsterdam offered every imaginable argument. He said that the international community had abandoned capital punishment. He claimed that society's most enlightened men and women condemned it, citing everyone from Albert Camus to the Archbishop of Canterbury. He pointed to the diminishing use of the death penalty in the United States—a trend that, of course, he had fostered through the moratorium. Finally he identified the secrecy of executions as the ultimate evidence of Americans' inner revulsion at the death penalty. "We hide our executions because we are disgusted to look at them, because the view of them would make men sick," he wrote. "Could the Court today sustain a *public* execution as consistent with the Eighth Amendment?"

The brief explored the penal practices of Liechtenstein and Monaco, but racism, the issue that had enticed Amsterdam into the death penalty business, played only a minimal role until the end of the one-hundred-page brief. There Amsterdam presented four pages of statistics showing discrimination in capital rape and murder cases. "Those who are selected to die," he wrote, "are the poor and powerless, personally ugly and socially unacceptable. In disproportionate percentages, they are also black."

Racism now served principally as an illustration of the central paradox of the American death penalty. The death penalty was considered constitutional because the public didn't oppose it, but the public didn't oppose it because it was used so infrequently. In turn, this made racism difficult to prove since statistics require large data sets to generate significant results. Amsterdam wrote, "A state can discriminate racially and not get caught at it if it kills men only sporadically."

Finally Amsterdam argued that the Eighth Amendment acted as a safeguard to prevent obvious injustices where other constitutional guarantees failed. He wrote, "If a state invokes a particular penalty sufficiently rarely that no regular pattern of its use develops, the state *may* be acting discriminatorily; it *likely will be* acting in a fashion that the penalty falls most harshly on the poor and disadvantaged; but it *surely will be* acting in a way that escapes the safeguards of the Constitution." That is, unless the Eighth Amendment stepped in to fill the void.

The legal merits of this last argument can be debated. Certainly no case had suggested the catchall function of the Eighth Amendment. As a strategic gambit, though, its usefulness is difficult to challenge. The argument preserved LDF's procedural objections, gave the justices a vehicle to express their concern with racism, and another plausible basis to rule the death penalty unconstitutional without overturning *McGautha*. In his definitive history of the death penalty in America, UCLA Professor Stuart Banner called Amsterdam's argument "brilliant."

With the brief done, LDF's thoughts turned to oral argument on October 12. Amsterdam made preparations to travel to New York, where he would meet for two days with Himmelstein and Greenberg, who would be delivering the argument in *Jackson*. Amsterdam didn't generally rely much on dry runs or "moots," as attorneys call practice sessions. By this point he knew the law and the arguments backward and forward. Still, Amsterdam would be arguing *Furman* against Ronald George, the same attorney who had argued *McGautha*, where he had proved himself formidable to say the least.

Furthermore, several important questions remained to be resolved. In *Jackson*, Greenberg would be arguing that the death penalty for rape was used only in certain areas of the country against blacks and, hence, was unusual. Since the evidence of racism in rape cases was more developed than in murder cases, this created a possible tension between Amsterdam and Greenberg's arguments. It was important that they not step on each other's toes. Also, while Amsterdam knew that standards of decency shouldn't be measured by the intentions of the framers, he hadn't settled entirely on what to say regarding how they should be measured. There was much to think about, but then, following Harlan and Black's resignations, the Court postponed the oral arguments to January 17 of the new year. After weeks of frenetic activity, suddenly Amsterdam had nothing to do but wait.

MEANWHILE, GEORGIA DEPUTY ATTORNEY GENERAL Dorothy Beasley couldn't believe her own luck. In 1967 she followed her husband to Georgia from the D.C. area, where she attended law school. One attorney after another told her that Atlanta law firms wouldn't hire women and that she shouldn't bother applying. Beasley landed a job, though, and later found the nerve to ask Arthur Bolton, the state attorney general, for a position in his office. Bolton hired her, and in December 1971, at the age of thirty-three, Beasley made her first argument to the Supreme Court in *Doe v. Bolton*, a companion case to *Roe v. Wade*. Now she would be arguing *Furman*. Over the course of two months Beasley argued two of the most important cases of the twentieth century.

Later in life Beasley became the chief judge of the Georgia Court of Appeals and an opponent of capital punishment. In 1971, though, she supported the death penalty and believed she had the Constitution on her side. "I didn't see how the Supreme Court could strike the death penalty down as cruel and unusual," she said later. "My feeling was that it would be looked at as a necessary evil."

Ronald George loved his job, too. Like the Supreme Court clerks and the lawyers at LDF, George felt the quality of his experience more than compensated for the deficiencies in his salary. In the appellate bureau, George had the luxury of time to think about cases. He could research arguments thoroughly and polish his written product. Best of all, the job got him into the Supreme Court years before he ever would have at a big law firm. At thirty-two, he had argued five cases before the Court. His parents saw him twice, and he won each case but the first.

George handicapped the capital cases somewhat differently than Beasley did, though. Despite having won *McGautha*, George felt less confident this time around. He had a healthy respect for Tony Amsterdam. In George's opinion the LDF brief was "a monumental treatise on the death penalty." Furthermore, he thought the simple fact that the Court had granted certiorari didn't bode well. "My general view was that if the Supreme Court granted certiorari on behalf of a defendant, you had an uphill fight," he said in 2010. "I had the sense that the Court wanted to change procedures."

Among the pending cases, George thought he had the most favorable facts. Aikens had been tried without a jury. Jerome Berenson, the well-respected judge who presided over the trial, took the unusual step of stating the aggravating and mitigating factors he weighed in deciding the sentence. George thought that the Court might have selected *Aikens* to illustrate a constitutionally permissible death penalty scheme. He was eager to argue the case, but after the Court postponed the matter for Rehnquist and Powell, George too had nothing to do but wait.

Then, in December, the California Supreme Court unexpectedly took an interest in the appeal of a death-row inmate named Robert Anderson. The Court asked Amsterdam and George to file their *Aikens* briefs and called for oral argument on short notice. *Anderson* was a notorious case. On a rainy morning in 1965 Anderson walked into a pawnshop and asked to see a rifle. The sixty-one-year-old store manager, Louis Richards, handed Anderson a Remington mountain rifle and began preparing a bill. While he was writing, Anderson grabbed a box of ammunition and loaded the weapon. Richards told Anderson to take the gun. Anderson responded by fatally shooting Richards and chasing a second store employee. The police surrounded the store, whereupon ensued the longest shootout in San Diego history. At trial Anderson offered little in defense other than a vague allegation that the storeowners had been racist. The jury deliberated for nine hours and sentenced Anderson to die in the gas chamber.

The horrifying facts of Anderson's case were typical of what George saw in death penalty cases. On the other hand, the California Supreme Court's sudden interest in the case, which had been languishing in the California system for six years, was extraordinary. On January 7, just ten days before the *Furman* argument, the California Supreme Court heard argument in *Anderson*. Amsterdam and Jerome Falk raised the usual arguments on Anderson's behalf: The jury had been improperly selected, standardless sentencing violated the state and federal Constitutions, and the death penalty had a disproportionate impact on the poor and minorities. The California justices, though, appeared most interested in the cruel and unusual punishment argument, even though it hadn't been a central part of LDF's brief.

George sensed something was up. The only logical explanation for the California court's action was that it was considering ruling the death penalty unconstitutional. If the highly respected California court quickly struck down capital punishment, then the U.S. Supreme Court couldn't help but take notice. As George flew to Washington, D.C., he felt that the wind had turned against him.

GEORGE WAS MORE RIGHT than he realized. As he traveled east for oral argument, Thurgood Marshall was putting the finishing touches on a draft opinion striking down the death penalty under the Eighth Amendment. Not even Brennan foresaw that Marshall would turn 180 degrees from his earlier expressions of support for the constitutionality of capital punishment.

Having grown up on the streets of Baltimore, Marshall had a dim view of the street criminal. He told one law clerk, "I hate the death penalty. But I also hate the bastards who escape because we don't use the death penalty." When Michael Meltsner, who was hired by Marshall, told Marshall that he thought criminal sentences should be reviewable on appeal, Marshall replied, "I'm in favor so long as I can raise them as well as lower them." Meltsner has said, "Marshall was not sentimental about criminals in the way that white liberals sometimes are."

That summer, though, Marshall converted. It was a natural time for Marshall to reflect on his life and judicial career. In June, Marshall had an appendectomy. It was his second hospital stay in as many years. Marshall spent the summer recovering at his home in northern Virginia, where his was the first black family in the affluent community of Lake Barcroft, a purgatory for Marshall. By nature and nurture, Marshall was an urban creature. While at LDF, Marshall lived in Morningside Gardens, an apartment complex on the edge of Harlem. When he moved to Washington to become solicitor general, Marshall and his wife, Cissy, rented a small townhome near L'Enfant Plaza. Marshall liked 64 G Street, but in D.C. he began drinking more frequently and wandering the streets. In 1968 Cissy decided to move the family to the suburbs. They borrowed $52,000 and bought a five-bedroom ranch. One neighbor told the *Washington Star* they weren't happy about the Marshalls moving into Lake Barcroft since it "might be encouragement for more of the same." Needless to say Marshall didn't exactly feel at home.

This was appropriate in many ways, as Marshall didn't exactly feel at home in the Supreme Court either. As chief attorney for LDF, Marshall had barnstormed the country, speaking to large and adoring audiences. After John Kennedy appointed him to the Second Circuit, Marshall almost immediately disliked it. He found the life of a judge tedious and isolating. He stared for hours out the window of his chambers, watching the giant construction ball across the street, daydreaming. Things briefly got better when he became solicitor general in 1965, fulfilling President Johnson's desire that when young people came into the Supreme Court and asked who was that "Negro" up there arguing, somebody would say, "He's the solicitor general of the United States." He rarely dealt with civil rights issues, but at least he was back on the front lines, doing what he did best, winning twenty-nine of the thirty-two cases he argued before the Court. When LBJ offered to nominate him to be a justice in 1967, Marshall wanted to be the man to integrate the Supreme Court, but he worried about the prospect of once more becoming isolated.

As he feared, Marshall again felt cut off. A hedonist, Marshall had always lived hard. He had prodigious appetites for food, wine, and tobacco. On the road for LDF, Marshall played cards until the wee hours and haunted nightclubs. Being a judge cramped his style. During his tenure as solicitor general Marshall solidified his relationship with LBJ over bourbon and Dr Pepper. But this life ended forever when Marshall became a justice.

With increased distance from his friends, Marshall's health began to deteriorate. Without social contact to distract him, Marshall smoked constantly and drank more. He often had three martinis at lunch. He grew fat. By the early 1970s Marshall weighed more than 230 pounds. Concerned citizens wrote to him about his poor health. He replied to one that he was down to three cigarettes a day. "So I guess there is no need to worry," he said. Marshall ventured outside the Court infrequently. He gave away his tickets to Nixon's second inaugural. He began to watch television excessively. He was trapped in the suburbs and trapped inside his own body. As he recovered from surgery, Marshall had lots of time to think. He no doubt recalled the three cases that had shaped his view of the death penalty.

The first occurred in 1933, during Marshall's third year in law school. Charles Hamilton Houston, Howard Law School's dean, asked Marshall to help him represent George Crawford, a black man accused of murdering two white women in Virginia. Marshall accepted eagerly, but what he saw appalled him. The prospective jurors were all white. At trial the prosecution produced neither the murder weapon nor a single witness. Nevertheless the jury found Crawford guilty, and the circuit court rejected his appeal. Houston regarded the representation as successful because Crawford had escaped the death penalty. Marshall later explained that from his mentor he learned, "If you get a life term for a Negro charged with killing a white person in Virginia, you've won."

During his first year in private practice in Baltimore, Marshall represented James Gross who, together with two accomplices, was charged with killing a barbecue-stand owner in Prince Georges County. The trial appalled Marshall again. The jurors didn't care that his client had only been the getaway driver. They sentenced all three men to die. The trio's ringleader, Donald Parker, later had his sentence commuted to life imprisonment, but Gross was hanged in 1935. The only way Marshall could explain this disparity was that Parker had white attorneys. Marshall felt ashamed at his failure and enraged at the arbitrariness of the system.

Later, in Marshall's first criminal case at the NAACP, he represented W. D. Lyons, a black sharecropper accused of killing a married couple on New Year's Eve, 1939. Two white men confessed to the murder, but their admission created a problem for Oklahoma governor Leon Chase Phillips. The confessors were inmates who had been given unsupervised weekend passes to visit bars and whorehouses. Convicting them would make the governor look bad. Phillips sent his brutish aide, Vernon Cheatwood, to clean up the mess. Cheatwood ordered the confessors released, arranged for their exit to Texas, and announced a search for the true perpetrator. Several days later the police arrested Lyons. Lyons said he had been hunting rabbits near the victims' home and had nothing to do with the murders. Thereupon Cheatwood began a series of vicious thrashings using a hardwood nightstick wrapped in leather, which he called a "niggerbeater." After pounding Lyons for several days, and depriving him of food and sleep, Cheatwood confronted Lyons with the victims' charred remains. Superstitious about bones, Lyons tried to crawl away. Cheatwood held his face in the remains and told him that only admitting the crime would stop the torture. At this point Lyons confessed. An all-white, all-male jury convicted him in five hours. The jury sentenced Lyons to life in prison, but Marshall had no idea why they didn't impose the death penalty. The experience confirmed to Marshall the arbitrariness of the death penalty, which he came to regard as the worst vestige of legal racism in America.

Yet Marshall was skeptical about using the law to implement social change, and after he became a judge in 1961, he initially didn't oppose capital punishment. On the Second Circuit Court of Appeals, Marshall upheld a death sentence. In his first year on the bench, he heard the appeal of Nathan Jackson, who was convicted of murdering a police officer in a shootout following robbery. Jackson was wounded himself, and his sentence stemmed largely from a confession he gave five minutes after receiving Demerol prior to surgery. Jackson argued that the injection made the confession involuntary. The Second Circuit upheld his sentence on the theory that Demerol takes fifteen minutes to work. Marshall concurred in the opinion. His clerk for that term, Ralph Winter, said Marshall "was not against the death penalty when I worked for him."

Though he had transformed civil rights in America, Marshall believed courts shouldn't run too far ahead of public opinion. Following *Brown*, against the advice of his colleagues, Marshall urged patience implementing integration. He wasn't an ideologue. Marshall considered himself an advocate for human rights, not African American rights. He deplored Malcolm X's separatism and Martin Luther King's excessive eagerness. He was, in his own words, "the ultimate gradualist." Marshall believed that people would reject overreaching decisions. He also believed that courts lacked the ability to micromanage complex social issues, and that judges lacked basic insight into the people they were trying to help.

Marshall didn't explain his transformation to his clerks or his family, but Brennan clearly had a profound influence on his thinking. They were the closest of friends on the Court, traveled in the same circles, often lunching together at Kronheim's. It's thus possible to trace an elegant line to Marshall's conversion through Brennan, Bazelon, and Goldberg. For years, no doubt empowered by Bazelon, Brennan had argued to Marshall that he shouldn't feel restrained as a justice as he had as an appellate court judge. The Supreme Court had a different and unique responsibility, Brennan argued, because it was a defendant's final place of appeal.

That summer, as Marshall reflected on his mortality, something clicked. Quietly he asked his clerks to draft an argument, following

Trop, that standards of decency had evolved to where the death penalty should be rejected under the Eighth Amendment. Marshall conceived of the secret draft as a "present" for his best friend, and he resolved to gift it to Brennan in his darkest hour: the morning of the oral argument in *Furman*.

CHAPTER 7

BOILING
IN OIL

S HORTLY AFTER TEN O'CLOCK ON THE MORNING OF January 17, 1972, the marshal of the Supreme Court, dressed in formal morning clothes, bellowed for order. "Oyez! Oyez! Oyez!" he cried. "All persons having business before the Honorable, the Supreme Court of the United States are admonished to draw near and give their attention, for the Court is now sitting. God save the United States and this Honorable Court!"

Eight lawyers had gathered at the front of the courtroom. *Aikens v. California* would be argued first. Tony Amsterdam took his place at the counsel table stage right, in the traditional place of a petitioner. To his left sat Jack Himmelstein, nervously rummaging through a file. At the opposite table sat Ronald George, rubbing his hands together. It was a cold, blustery day, and in his haste to make court on time, George had forgotten a coat.

Behind the counsel tables Dorothy Beasley and the attorneys involved in the remaining cases took seats on red couches. To their right, interspersed among the courtroom's Siena marble columns, the law clerks sat on folding chairs, eager witnesses to history. In the back of the room a frieze depicted the struggle between good and evil. Everyone's eyes, though, were on the giant mahogany bench, guarded by twin American flags and shrouded by enormous red curtains.

Behind these giant curtains Lewis Powell had his own first-tee jitters. Only ten days ago Powell and Rehnquist had taken coffee in a waiting room with their wives, Josephine and Nan, and were then sworn in as justices. Rehnquist embraced the appointment. Powell, though, had misgivings. Jo hated leaving Richmond, and Lewis wondered whether he had the right stuff. He had never been a judge before, and his legal expertise was in railroad mergers. Powell had never given much thought to either the Constitution or the death penalty.

Powell recognized that capital punishment would be the issue of the year. On his first day on the job, Marshall visited Powell's chambers, slapped him on the back, and asked him whether he had prepared his death penalty opinion. Powell didn't take it as a joke. Marshall had obviously made up his mind. "My wife Cissy is after me and thinks we should string them all up," Marshall said. "But you'll see what I've written."

Shortly thereafter Burger lobbied him more forcefully. The Chief gave Powell a copy of Douglas's unpublished dissent from the grant of certiorari. Powell filed this document from the previous term, noting that it might be "of some historical interest." Burger's views notwithstanding, Powell felt certain that a majority of his new colleagues wanted to rule the death penalty unconstitutional. This made him uneasy. Powell's instincts said the issue should be left to states to decide.

Standing to Powell's right, William Brennan felt nervous too, though for different reasons. Brennan had detected the same shift in momentum as did George. He found it impossible to keep his vow not to think about the issue. Shortly after recess Douglas's clerks told Brennan's clerks that Douglas would vote against the death penalty and had been a secure vote all along. Around the same time White told Brennan that he was "not sure how he would come down." Brennan began to hope of forming a three-way dissent. Every vote mattered. Even if the Court upheld the death penalty, sharp division might encourage legislative action.

Earlier that morning the news got better still when Marshall presented his gift. The brief took Brennan completely by surprise. Normally Brennan had outstanding reconnaissance, but he hadn't heard even a rumor of Marshall changing position. When Brennan showed Marshall's draft to his clerks, they said they neither had any knowledge of it nor insight into what had changed Marshall's mind. Even better yet, Marshall told Brennan that he had given a copy of his draft to Stewart. This gave Brennan hope that Stewart might be persuadable. At the very least Marshall believed Stewart could be turned. Infected by optimism, Brennan began to wonder whether he might also turn Blackmun, with whom he had begun to develop a close relationship. As Burger gave the cue for the justices to step forward, Brennan dreamed for the first time of forming a majority against capital punishment.

AT NINE MINUTES PAST TEN, the justices emerged in sets of three, through hidden gaps in the curtains, creating the illusion that nine old men in black robes had appeared out of nowhere. When they had taken their seats, Warren Burger called the case. "Mr. Amsterdam," he said, "you may proceed whenever you're ready."

Without notes to act as a crutch, Amsterdam took a deep breath and swung for the fences. "Thank you, Mr. Chief Justice. This case and the three cases that follow present the question of whether the penalty of death is a cruel and unusual punishment within the Eighth and Fourteenth Amendments." Amsterdam spoke in the clear, confident voice of a man who had appeared before the Supreme Court many times. "The briefs canvass a broad range of considerations, but I think the real nub of this controversy is the scope of judicial review. Respondents primarily support the death penalty on the ground that it has been put there by the legislatures of forty-one states and the federal government, and that those legislatures are the primary keepers of the national conscience in penal matters.

"I agree with all of that," Amsterdam said. But it was one thing for the Court to respect a legislative action, and another to capitulate to it. "Although deference and circumspection to legislative judgment is vital," he continued, "abnegation of judicial judgment is impermissible, because the very existence of the Eighth Amendment belies the idea that legislatures are totally free in their choice of penalogic methods. If one thing is plain, it is that the clause is a restriction on legislation. The question is what are those limitations on legislative judgment? How stringent are they?"

The answer to this question had always been "not very stringent," because, with the exception of *Trop*, the Court had always determined standards by the Founding Fathers' intentions. If the Court adhered to this view, then the battle would be over before it began. Amsterdam had to get the justices to embrace Earl Warren's view that standards of decency changed over time.

"History, although relevant, cannot be controlling, because of the evolutionary nature of the guarantee," Amsterdam said. "California, Georgia and Texas have all made the point that at the time the Eighth Amendment was written capital punishment was widely in use. All of this misconceives our submission, which is not that when the Eighth Amendment was ratified in 1791 it was intended then and there to do away with capital punishment, any more than it was intended then and there to do away with whippings or brandings or cutting off of ears, any more than the equal protection clause, when originally put into the Constitution, was intended to give equal rights to indigents or to women." He added, "The arguments made by the states to sustain capital punishment would, I think, equally sustain branding of confidence men on the forehead with the letter 'C' or cutting the hands off of pickpockets."

But if the intentions of the Founding Fathers didn't control, what did? The vagueness of the phrase "cruel and unusual" had been recognized for two hundred years. During the debate over the Bill of Rights, William Smith of South Carolina objected to the Eighth Amendment as too indefinite. Yet, during that time, no one had set forward a viable standard. The two obvious options, public opinion and judicial opinions, wouldn't help LDF. Many academics had noted the absurdity of predicating constitutional protections on polls. The constitutional scholar John Hart Ely of Harvard Law School said, "It makes no sense to employ the value judgments of the majority for protecting minorities from the value judgments of the majority." Inviting the judges to use their own moral judgment wouldn't help much either on a bench with four Nixon appointees.

Amsterdam found a third way. "Branding and cutting the hands off of pickpockets, I think, would plainly be condemned by the Eighth Amendment. But, it behooves us to ask why," he said. "Is it simply because we would be shocked? I don't think so. I think it is because there are objective bases for making a determination under the Eighth Amendment." The word "objective" was transformative: This standard had never been suggested before.

Amsterdam defended it. "The problem of construing the Eighth Amendment is where does the Court get standards? Formulations such as the notion that a punishment may shock the conscience invite subjective judgment. All of the parties agree that it is not the purpose of the Constitution to allow judges to write their own penological reflections into it. Specifically, we think that the question under the Eighth Amendment is whether the punishment applied to a particular individual would, by all available objective indications, be unacceptable to general contemporary conscience and standards of decency, if it were generally and uniformly applied to any reasonable proportions of persons subject to penalty for that crime."

In these last two sentences Tony Amsterdam displayed the full measure of his brilliance, possibly won the case, and certainly changed the history of the death penalty in America. Requiring the Court to consider tangible evidence of social norms transformed the Eighth Amendment inquiry into a quasi-scientific enterprise, ostensibly rendering judges' personal views irrelevant.

Much of *Furman* wouldn't survive, but this concept of measuring cruelty by "objective indications" would endure, even though forty years of subsequent case law would make it clear that one subjective judgment had replaced another. Who was to say what social norms should count? The answer to this question inevitably depended on a judge's views about capital punishment. Justices who favored the death penalty generally emphasized the importance of state legislation and public opinion. Justices against the death penalty focused on international opinion. In 1988 Antonin Scalia said that the constitutionality of capital punishment boiled down to the feelings and intuition of the justices—just as it had before *Furman*.

Some scholars would argue that Amsterdam's answer *hurt* the abolition movement in the long run. The truth was that by most objective indications the public *supported* the death penalty. Amsterdam attempted to finesse this by saying that objective indications should count only if the penalty was uniformly applied to reasonable proportions of persons. Since this wasn't true in the United States, American polls shouldn't count. Nevertheless, for Amsterdam to prevail, the Court needed to credit only the indicators he favored—international opinion and the views of elites. If the Court ever expanded the universe of relevant social norms to include polls, then the constitutionality of the death penalty would appear to be beyond debate. In Amsterdam's defense he had every reason to believe that the Burger Court regarded the constitutionality of the death penalty as undebatable. What could he lose by making this argument?

Amsterdam's standard, that the Court consider only evidence of a penalty applied to reasonable proportions of persons, had essentially been fabricated. Nevertheless Douglas seized upon it. "Is there anything in the record which shows the kind of people on which the death penalty is imposed?" he asked. "I mean their annual income, their race, their religion, their social status. Or are we just in the dark on that?"

"There is nothing in the record," Amsterdam answered. "But there are some published materials, which I think are judicially noticeable."*

"Are there any standards in any of these places for the exercise of discretion by the judge or jury?"

"No, Mr. Justice Douglas. It is entirely optional."

---

* A court can take "judicial notice" of a fact that is so well known or published in such an authoritative source that its truth isn't in doubt.

Feeling some momentum, Amsterdam seized the opportunity to expand upon Douglas's interest in the procedural issues. "I think our standard assigns a proper function to the Eighth Amendment in the constitution of a democracy," he said. "The problem in a democracy is that legislation can be arbitrarily, selectively, and spottily applied to a few outcast pariahs, whose political position is so weak, and whose personal situation is so unpopular, and who are so ugly, that public revulsion which would follow the uniform application of the penalties doesn't follow."

"You don't raise the question of the due-process clause of the Fourteenth Amendment?" Douglas asked.

"There is not, within the scope of the grant of certiorari, any due-process question, and the question was not raised below."

"At no stage in the proceeding?"

"No," Amsterdam said. Douglas's persistence was good news. He was either considering reversing *McGautha* or revisiting the procedural issues that had been raised there.

Stewart changed subjects to ask the obvious question. "One of the things that bother me in these cases—I think it's more than a matter of semantics—is the fact that in the due-process clause the deprivation of life is expressly permitted. And there are at least three other places in the Constitution where the death penalty is mentioned."

"I agree that it's more than a semantic problem."

"And we're not talking about what the practice was at the time the Constitution was adopted," Stewart continued. "I'm talking about the words of the Constitution."

Amsterdam had prepared for this question. "Your Honor, I don't think that one can say that language in the Constitution, which by inference permits the death penalty, meant to project a continuing permission of it," he replied. "I'm not urging that when anybody put this language in the Constitution they meant to throw over capital punishment. I think that what they meant to do was to put in several guarantees of rights, which would grow and evolve as society grew and evolved."

"Thank you," Stewart said.

Amsterdam was feeling better and better about things. Even Stewart appeared to have an open mind. Emboldened, Amsterdam focused the Court on the rarity of executions. This was the best evidence of societal norms, he said. "There is a striking contrast between the broad extent to which the penalty of death is authorized by law, and the relative infrequency with which the sentence is actually imposed and carried out. Even before the national campaign began, during the sixties executions in the United States dropped to an average of almost twenty a year, down from an ordinary norm of 175 or 150 during previous decades. Now what you are talking about is a population of 200 million people, forty-three jurisdictions which actually use the death penalty for some crime, only one hundred people convicted of capital punishment, and only twenty actually executed."

A red light on the judges' podium flashed, indicating that Amsterdam's time had nearly expired. "I will, with the Court's pleasure, reserve the continuation of this theme for the argument in the *Furman* case," Amsterdam said, and he surrendered the podium to Ronald George.

GEORGE UNDERSTOOD THAT HIS back was against the wall. Amsterdam had obviously scored some points. He had insidiously integrated procedural concerns into a debate about the Eighth Amendment. Douglas obviously bought into Amsterdam's arguments about racism and inequality. George expected this, but Stewart, too, appeared engaged and even sympathetic to Amsterdam's position. This was an unwelcome surprise.

George needed to shift the Court's focus. Doing this would be challenging under the best of circumstances, but in this case George was operating at a substantial disadvantage. Because LDF also represented William Furman and Lucius Jackson, their lawyers would have other turns before the Court. This would be George's only shot: He needed to make every second count.

George began by reminding the justices of first principles. "The basic issue before the Court is not whether the death penalty is socially, morally or politically desirable but, instead, whether there is some specific provision in the Constitution that bars California from determining that the death penalty should be available as a possible form of punishment for the offense of murder." George continued, "The petitioner comes here bearing a heavy burden of establishing that the California legislature lacks any permissible basis upon which to conclude that the protection of society requires the availability of the death penalty for the most serious of crimes—the willful and malicious taking of human life. Professor Amsterdam takes the position— or at least he did ten days ago when he and I were before the California Supreme Court—that even if it could conclusively be established that the death penalty does deter, that it would still be cruel and unusual punishment."

Potter Stewart interrupted. "Well, certainly you would agree that deterrence is not the sole criterion of whether a punishment is cruel or unusual."

Here was another bad sign. George had the controlling case on his side. If the Court simply issued a short opinion saying it was following *McGautha*, this would be a resounding victory. Benign disinterest by the justices would be ideal. Instead George had what lawyers call a "hot bench." That it was Stewart leading the charge—instead of, say, Brennan or Marshall—made matters worse. Stewart was obviously taking seriously the distinction between the Fourteenth Amendment, which had been at issue in *McGautha*, and the Eighth.

George tried to answer Stewart's question, but he couldn't get a word in. Stewart had begun what would have been called, if this were a trial, a withering cross-examination.

"In other words," Stewart continued, "I suppose that disemboweling, burning at the stake, drawing and quartering, might all serve as deterrents, even if you imposed them for petty larceny. But that wouldn't answer the question, would it?

"The execution would have to be done in a humane manner," George said. "I think one of the key aspects of that term is the definition of cruelty in terms of *unnecessary* cruelty and *unnecessary* pain."

"Is it your submission that if it can be shown that a punishment serves as a deterrent and if in a rational person's judgment no more pain or torture is inflicted than is necessary, then it's automatically constitutionally valid?"

"Yes."

"And this would, therefore, be true of horsewhipping?"

"No. Unnecessary cruelty, I think."

"No, no," Stewart said. "If rational people would conclude that the best deterrent for petty larceny was fifty lashes, then it would not be cruel and unusual so long as fifty-one lashes were not imposed?"

"If rational people could so conclude," George replied skeptically. "We start with the proposition that the death penalty was clearly constitutional during the period in which the Eighth Amendment was adopted. So one must ask rhetorically, can the Constitution be unconstitutional in its recognition of capital offenses?"

Marshall joined in. "Do you think that the word 'unusual' means what it meant then or what it means now?" It seemed to be coming from all angles now.

"Cruelty implies something barbarous, more than the extinguishment of life," George answered. "The cruelty against which the Constitution protects a convicted man is cruelty inherent in the method of punishment, not the necessary suffering involved in any method employed to extinguish life humanely."

"With all due respect, Mr. George, I was talking about the word 'unusual,' not the word 'cruel,'" Marshall said.

"In 'unusual,' I think we mean something that is not customary for that type of offense."

"As of then, or as of now?"

"As of 1791."

"Whatever was not unusual in 1791 is not unusual today?"

"I'm saying whatever was not unusual and cruel. There might have been certain things that were usual in 1791 but that were cruel."

"You just will not stick with 'unusual.' You have to tie 'cruel' with it all the time."

"I think that the two concepts are intermeshed." George had no choice but to respond to Marshall this way, otherwise California would appear to be in favor of flogging.

"Why is the word 'unusual' there?"

"*Weems* is a very good example," George replied, referring to the 1910 case in which the Court set aside a fifteen-year sentence for falsifying documents. "Perhaps you might call it cruel, but the Court seemed to stress that it was highly unusual."

"Of course, you didn't have gas chambers in 1791," Marshall said.

"That's right."

"Well, how am I going to measure the gas chamber? You said I have to consider what was not unusual in 1791. I can't do that with the gas chamber."

"We're not talking, I think, about methods of execution. We're talking about a certain kind of proportionality," George said. "Applied to the offense of murder, it's clear that there is no cruel and unusual punishment, certainly not under our humane method. There's no intentional cruelty. In fact, the death that comes to such a prisoner is, perhaps, less cruel than the death by natural causes that comes to us all eventually."

"Except nobody knows," Douglas said. George had a fair point, though: Everybody dies, and everybody suffers to some extent. Some modes of execution might be merciful by comparison.

"Nobody knows," George repeated. "But, with the state of our medical knowledge today, I think that we can assume."

"Is the gas chamber faster than a bullet, which is the way they used to do it?" Douglas asked. The subject of death was very much on his mind.

"I don't think speed is the only criterion. The test is unnecessary cruelty. And just because some rather primitive corporal punishments were in use at the time the Eighth Amendment was enacted does not mean that they and capital punishment must stand or fall together," George said. "There was never any sanctifying of tortures in the Constitution, as there is of capital punishment, in the Fifth Amendment's use of 'capital offenses' and 'taking life.'"

Stewart said, "Of course, the Fifth Amendment also talks about 'jeopardy of limb' in the double-jeopardy provision. I suppose you wouldn't use that to argue that today government could cut off the arm of a thief, would you?

"No. But I don't think that's what the framers intended to sanctify."

"What do you think the word 'limb' meant then?"

"I don't think they would necessarily mean the taking off of a limb. I think they would mean, perhaps, certain corporal punishment that did survive and might survive today."

"Such as what?"

"I'm not convinced that any form of whipping would necessarily be unconstitutional. You know, twenty lashes for murdering somebody might not be cruel and unusual today."

Finally Stewart relented. The questioning had gone on for ten minutes, though to George it seemed longer. Understanding that the argument wasn't going his way, like the best quarterbacks, he changed tactics in the middle of the game. Instead of continuing to quarrel over the language of the Constitution, George conceded Amsterdam's argument that standards of decency must evolve, but said they hadn't evolved to the point of rejecting capital punishment.

"Even if we assume that the meaning of 'cruel and unusual' can change from decade to decade," George said, "I would submit that our standards have not evolved to the point where the imposition of the death penalty to murder is inconsistent with our standards." George called out LDF's position as a litigation tactic. "Professor Amsterdam's fixation with the phrase, 'evolving standards,' is quite understandable. It provides the only escape from the historical reality of capital punishment being recognized as a legitimate form of punishment for three hundred years in this nation."

George argued that the notion of "objective" standards was a sham. "It's not clear which point petitioner wants us to focus on in determining these standards. It is clear that he conveniently ignores that forty-one states have capital punishment," he said. "So what does Professor Amsterdam choose to focus his attention on? He cites at great length what Mozambique and Liechtenstein are doing. What relevance does this have to determining what our provision means?"

George continued, "This is not a time for due process by head count. What is particularly ridiculous is for petitioner to focus upon the small number of executions as a supposed indication of the declining popular acceptance of the death penalty. At most, the number of executions is an indicator, perhaps, of the evolving standards of our judiciary. It's not an indication of popular feeling. A much more accurate barometer of the evolving standards of our times are the juries who consistently, steadily, and even increasingly in California, are returning death penalty verdicts."

Stewart rejoined the debate. "It is suggested that one reason juries these days are imposing the death penalty with a little more liberality is that they think the penalty will not be carried out."

"Neither my own experience nor anything I have read supports that," George replied. "If there is this great trend away from capital punishment, why is that not reflected in our democratically elected legislature?" he asked. "I think that basically Professor Amsterdam seeks to consider himself some sort of self-appointed guardian of the evolving standards of decency. They have the truth, and all these other indications should be disregarded."

"I also object when it comes to the issue of burden of proof," George added. "We have set forth evidence of deterrence. Our burden isn't to establish deterrence, but we have shown that there is a reasonable basis upon which the legislature can conclude that the death penalty does deter." George continued, "Now I would submit, of course, that the death penalty would be a greater deterrent if executions were being carried out."

Finally George returned to the real facts of the case. "I don't have to dwell at length upon Mr. Aikens' crimes. They are terribly brutal. No remorse. No mental problems. He was intelligent, had an education, but he committed three brutal murders. So I would close with the statement of Justice Holmes, 'If a thing has been practiced for two hundred years with common consent, it will need a strong case to affect it.' Petitioner has not made a strong case. He has made no case at all."

George concluded, "With the plea that we consider things on a constitutional level—without the emotional rhetoric of political, personal or moral feeling as to the desirability of the death penalty—we would submit that the judgment should be affirmed in this case."

It was another brilliant performance. In the heat of the moment, in front of the justices of the Supreme Court, George had sensed the shift in the tide, changed tacks, and turned the case around. Burger thanked George and called Amsterdam back to the lectern. The ball was squarely in Amsterdam's court.

AT THE PODIUM Amsterdam made his own on-the-spot judgment. Stewart's questions had exposed the problem with the government's position. If the Court deferred to legislatures, then the Eighth Amendment meant nothing. George had clouded this with his argument. The question was how to reclaim the strategic advantage. One potential route was to show how George had misstated the law even as he claimed to concede it. Instead Amsterdam invited the justices to travel down George's path and see the inconsistencies it led to.

"I perhaps should make clear our position on the question asked by Mr. Justice Stewart as to whether if there were shown to be any legitimate legislative basis for a punishment, that would itself end the Eight Amendment claim. The answer, in my judgment, is unmistakably no." Amsterdam explained, "We don't urge that a legislature could not find a basis for boiling in oil. That, I think, really presents the question very squarely. Mr. George takes the position that if boiling in oil came before this Court, even though the legislature might find it was a deterrent, that somehow the Court couldn't say it was a cruel and unusual punishment.

"I want simply to point out to the Court who is arguing subjective standards here and who is arguing objective standards," Amsterdam said. George had accused Amsterdam of constructing a legal test specifically to find capital punishment unconstitutional. In fact George had created his own legal doctrine to avoid taking the unpalatable position that torture might be constitutional. Amsterdam asked, "How could this Court say that boiling in oil is unnecessary if a legislature finds that in order to deter some particularly serious crime that the horrible prospect of being boiled in oil is all that will do it? I think that it is the respondents and not the petitioners who are urging the Court to react at that visceral level. Our proposition is, I think, the much more objective one. It looks not to what society says but to what it does. We don't reject the fact that forty-one states have it on their statues. But one must ask, 'What do they do with it?'"

Amsterdam responded to George's ridicule of his references to other nations. "Now let's look at this thing if we may for a moment in the world picture. We're not talking about Mozambique and Liechtenstein." He emphasized each syllable of these names, mimicking the dismissive tone George had used in his own argument. "We are talking about a progressive trend which has brought virtually every nation in the Western Hemisphere to abolish the death penalty. We are talking about a progressive trend which has caused all English-speaking nations, except some of the American states and four states in Australia, to abolish the death penalty."

Burger asked, "By what process did they do it in these places?"

"It is different in different places," Amsterdam replied.

"But it isn't a process which is generally one done by courts in these countries, is it?"

"No, no. Unquestionably not."

Burger seemed to attach weight to this distinction, although popular rejection would more meaningfully reflect changed standards than rejection by the courts. He continued, "If the Court undertakes to accept your general proposition, could it make exceptions for certain crimes or would it be obliged to follow an all-or-nothing approach?"

Amsterdam presumed Burger meant to ask whether the Court could find the death penalty unconstitutional for some crimes but not others. "I believe that it could, rationally," Amsterdam replied, "although I do not think it should or can on the indicators available to the Court."

"But could the Court, for example, make an exception as to homicides committed by life-term prisoners? Could it make that kind of narrow exception?"

"That is a different question," Amsterdam said. "I don't think the Court could take a general statute, like California's, and say, 'Well, they can apply it in some cases and not in others.' But a different question would be presented if a narrower statute were presented."

Courts are not generally in the business of rewriting laws, but this didn't seem to bother Burger: "You're aware, of course, that many proponents of capital punishment, among them the former Director of the U.S. Prison Bureau, are very strongly against capital punishment, but prefer to retain it for homicides of a fellow prisoner or of a prison guard?"

Amsterdam understood where Burger was going: He wanted to expose LDF as being against even the limited use of the death penalty. Many people believed that the death penalty for prisoners—especially those who had been sentenced to life without possibility of parole—presented a special case. Without the threat of execution, how could they be deterred?

Marshall came to Amsterdam's aid. "Isn't it true that in New York there is such a statute?" This is how justices speak to one another during oral argument. By his question Marshall meant to tell the Chief that nuance was possible; California and Georgia simply hadn't chosen to exercise it.

After Amsterdam agreed with Marshall, Burger put him back on the spot. "Do you think we could accept your general argument and still find such a statute that did not offend the Constitution?"

"I think a line might be drawn, but I see no occasion to draw it in these cases because no such statute is presented. The problem with those limited statutes is that we've had insufficient experience with them," Amsterdam told Burger. "But one darn well knows what the testimony of public opinion is with regard to general statutes punishing murder with death. Juries don't apply the death penalty in perhaps more than one out of twelve or thirteen cases in which they could, and maybe half or a third of those people are actually executed."

Rehnquist joined in for the first time. "You said one out of twelve or thirteen death verdicts is returned. Were those cases in which the prosecution had asked for death or was it just that death could have been returned under the statute if the prosecution had asked for it?"

"It is impossible to know," Amsterdam admitted.

"In how many jurisdictions does the judge impose sentence?" asked Blackmun.

"To my knowledge there are two jurisdictions, Maryland and Illinois, where the imposition of the death penalty requires the concurrence of the judge and the jury," Amsterdam replied. "In all other jurisdictions it is the jury that makes the decision."

"Now this is not true in my home state," said Blackmun, opening another chapter in his strange history with Amsterdam.

"Oh, I am then quite misinformed," Amsterdam answered, tactfully declining to mention that Minnesota had abolished the death penalty in 1911. "I had understood that it was. This matter is rather thoroughly canvassed in the briefs in *Maxwell v. Bishop*."

Amsterdam had less than ten minutes remaining. During these final moments the justices returned to the issues most on their respective minds. Douglas asked again, "Is there anything in the record that indicates what kind of people Georgia executes?"

"There is no evidence that was presented, but the figures are perfectly plain: Georgia executes black people." Amsterdam added two important points: First, the record didn't contain such evidence because LDF hadn't been permitted to present it. "We have been asking for an evidentiary hearing on all of these facts in all of these courts for a long time. Nobody has ever given us one." Second, because states primarily executed poor black people, the issue didn't generate public outrage. "When it is this group of people who suffers, realistically the pressure on legislatures is not the same."

Burger returned to the issue most on his mind. "You were speaking of pressures on legislatures. What are the figures now, the total number in death row?'

"The latest available figure to me is 697."

"Well, seven hundred people on death row would put quite enormous pressure on public opinion, would it not?"

"I don't think so," Amsterdam replied. "I think public opinion has been lulled in a very significant way by the failure of executions in recent years. I think the public has in large measure stopped thinking about the problem."

"Well," Burger said, "I was at least suggesting the possibility that if you didn't prevail here, that pressure would be reactivated, would it not?"

"I'm quite confident it wouldn't until you started killing people. The public is quite graphic in the way it thinks about things. Put one execution out there, people get very excited. But tell them that tomorrow a life may be taken, when one hasn't been taken since June 2, 1967, and they don't think about it," Amsterdam said. "And even if you had public sentiment activated, you are not capable of generating public disapprobation of a penalty which is applied to ugly minority-group members."

Time had expired. "Very well, Mr. Amsterdam," Burger said.

Amsterdam stepped away but Stewart called him back. "Before you sit down, Mr. Amsterdam, I want to make sure I understand your ultimate argument. It is that even assuming retribution is a permissible ingredient of punishment, even assuming rational people could conclude that the death penalty is the maximum deterrent, even assuming we're dealing with somebody who is not capable of being rehabilitated, an incorrigible person, even assuming rational people can conclude this punishment is the most efficient and the most inexpensive and that it assures the most complete isolation of the convicted man from ever getting back into society—even assuming all of those things, you say it is still violative of the Eighth Amendment?"

"That is correct, Your Honor."

"That's what I understood you to be arguing."

Amsterdam said nothing further. He had made his point.

BEFORE THE CHIEF JUSTICE called her forward, Dorothy Beasley felt nervous. The waiting was the hardest part. Years later she said, "I never felt more alone in my life. No one can help you." Following Amsterdam didn't help. "I was overwhelmed by his argument and his manner. He was a very powerful figure." Once the red light came on, though, Beasley felt a sense of calm. The Court felt like a holy place to her, and this was a transcendent issue.

She began with a textual argument. "To rule the death penalty a cruel and unusual punishment," she said, "would take a constitutional amendment because the Fourteenth Amendment, as well as the Fifth, would be rewritten so that we would have the proposition, 'No state may deprive any person of life, nor may any state deprive any person of liberty or property without due process of law.'"

Marshall interrupted and picked up on Stewart's earlier line of questioning. "Could the state boil them in oil?"

"I think no, Your Honor," Beasley said. "We had at the beginning of our country the understanding that it may not impose torture and that of course would be torture, as would horsewhipping."

"What is the standard that you use?"

Beasley answered this question differently than George. "I think it is the same standard that has been used by this Court in so many due-process clause cases: Is it a matter of fundamental fairness?" She said, "I think that so long as the State utilizes fundamental fairness, those penalties may be used."

Beasley then addressed the evolving nature of cruelty. "Mr. Justice Marshall, you asked about whether the meaning of 'unusual' has changed. I would submit that it has not," she said. "I think the death penalty itself is outside of consideration because it is specifically reserved to the states in the Fourteenth Amendment. However, if we are going to measure whether in contemporary society the death penalty is regarded as cruel and unusual, I think petitioners are using the wrong guidelines." Referring to Amsterdam, she said, "He talks about the world community, but we don't know why these countries did away with the death penalty."

"Where then does the standard of decency come from?" Douglas asked.

"I don't think it's that far removed from fundamental fairness, which to me is the basic standard."

"What would you say of a statute that allowed the death sentence to be imposed except on those people who make more than sixty thousand dollars a year?"

"That would be discriminatory. That's not looking at the crime."

"You think 'cruel and unusual' carries with it a connotation of nondiscrimination?"

This was a trap: Douglas's question adopted Amsterdam's notion that the Eighth Amendment required procedural fairness.

"Oh yes indeed," Beasley replied. "It should be applied in a nondiscriminatory matter." Beasley hadn't anticipated the Court focusing on this issue. "I took nondiscrimination as a given," she recalled in 2011. "These people did what they did. We thought the issue was whether the death penalty was constitutional."

"Are there any statistics as to what kind of people Georgia executes?" Douglas asked again.

"I don't think you could say that there's any one class that has been discriminated against. Moreover, even if there were shown to be discrimination," she said, "that would not invalidate the death penalty per se, but would be a violation of the equal protection clause." She added, "I think their proof falls far short of the kind of case this Court has considered."

"Has your supreme court ever considered the question?"

"It hasn't had the opportunity to do so," Beasley replied. "In *Furman*, the argument wasn't even made in the lower court." Furthermore she explained that LDF's statistics concerned the period between 1930

and 1968, and failed to take account of the vast changes in their criminal justice system. "We are safeguarding criminals with greater due
process," she explained. "How many of them have not been executed
because of jury discrimination or illegal confessions?"

Beasley ascended to her conclusion. "We think this is a question for
the legislature to determine," she said. "There is, in many cases before
this Court, a presumption of regularity and constitutionality that has
been overlooked." She pointed to Amsterdam. "He has the burden to
show that the legislative enactment is unconstitutional, and I think he
has not done so, not with respect to the death penalty in the abstract,
which is what he contends should be declared unconstitutional."

AMSTERDAM HAD SAVED THREE precious minutes for rebuttal.
He chose to remind the Court of the true relevance of racism. "I essentially don't disagree with Mrs. Beasley that juries are, in many ways the
conscience of the community," Amsterdam said. "Our whole case rests
on what juries and prosecutors have done, and what they have done is
to refuse to impose the death penalty. The question then arises, why
don't we leave them that way?

"The reason why juries can't be permitted to go on doing what
they've done and slowly, inexorably do away with the death penalty
themselves, is that in individual and particular cases there are going to
be regressions, depending largely on the color of the defendant's skin
and the ugliness of his person." Amsterdam raised his voice. "Our point,
I repeat again, is not discrimination. We haven't proved it. On these
records, we couldn't prove it. What I am saying is that the rare, arbitrary infliction of punishment escapes all other constitutional controls,
and escapes the public pressures to keep legislatures acting decently."

Burger thanked Amsterdam and announced that the case was submitted. Blackmun scrawled his grades for the morning—an A- for
Amsterdam, a B for George. Sexism filtered into even the grading. Beasley didn't receive a score, only a synopsis of her appearance—"white
dress, youngish" and the notation, "nice girl."

✦ ✦ ✦ ✦

AFTER LUNCH THE COURT heard argument in the rape cases. It
was good theater but not nearly as compelling as the morning show.
Mel Bruder, a Dallas attorney, represented Elmer Branch, and again
emphasized the racial disparity in the imposition of the death penalty.
Charles Alan Wright, a University of Texas law professor, argued that
the Court should be pleased that juries applied the death penalty so
selectively. In response to a question from Stewart, Wright said the
evidence of racism troubled him, but the Court couldn't go back on
McGautha. "Having decided so recently and decisively that jury sentencing is proper, I would think you'd need quite a powerful showing
to change the Court's mind."

In *Jackson*, Jack Greenberg focused on the rarity of the death penalty for rape. In America only southern states employed it, and almost
entirely against black men who raped white women. In the world only
three other nations had it on the books. Greenberg declined, though,
to invite the Court to strike down the death penalty for rape and not
murder. Here was yet another example of the conflict in LDF's roles.
Lucius Jackson would have been entirely satisfied with an opinion
striking down the death for rape. Instead Greenberg said the death
penalty was unconstitutional for all crimes.

Beasley had the last word. She argued that Greenberg's evidence of
discrimination was beside the point. He had made the same mistake
as Douglas. Only discrimination in the case at hand should concern
the Court. Jackson had made no such claim. Thus the only evidence
before the Court was his crime. With respect to the merits of using
the death penalty to punish rape, Beasley again reminded the justices
that they were not sitting as legislators considering policy. Rape, she
said, was a heinous crime with permanent effects on the victim. It was
rational for a state to punish it severely.

Shortly after three o'clock Burger adjourned the Court. Exhausted,
George and Amsterdam exited the Court building to face the press.
As they walked down the front steps, George reflected on the experi-

ence. He was impressed by Amsterdam's intellect, persuasiveness, and thoroughness. "I considered it a privilege to argue against him," he said years later. "It was a totally positive experience dealing with him."* On the marble steps of the courthouse Amsterdam and George gave brief interviews to local radio and television stations. Then George went to his hotel room and fulfilled a promise to telephone his mother and say how the argument had gone. By the time he called, Mrs. George had already seen the coverage of the argument. "At least Tony Amsterdam had the sense to wear a coat," she said. George nodded. He thought this was only the beginning of Amsterdam's good sense.

---

* As it turned out, this would be George's last argument before the Court. He would be appointed a judge several months later.

CHAPTER 8

NINE
LAW FIRMS

B YRON WHITE SAID ALMOST NOTHING DURING THE oral arguments. Nevertheless, one observer said White's face turned ashen after hearing the evidence of discrimination. In his chambers, White proclaimed Amsterdam's oral argument to be the best he had ever heard. White often told his clerks, "You can't run the criminal justice system from the courthouse," but the unequal application of the death penalty troubled White and he no longer knew how he would vote.

Meanwhile, the lives of the seven hundred men on death row, whose fates depended on the Court's decision, were keeping Potter Stewart up at night. As a general practice, after a red-labeled petition had been denied, and the execution carried out, the justices received a death notice via interoffice mail. Stewart thought of receiving seven hundred such notifications at once. Could he bear it? Could the nation bear it? Stewart's gut told him the death penalty was wrong. It treated people as objects. Its random application only made matters worse.

Stewart believed it was only a matter of time before society rejected capital punishment. In 1968 he thought his *Witherspoon* decision would set in motion a chain of events that would end the death penalty. This hadn't happened, of course, but in Stewart's view the political process simply needed more time. He wished the Court had never granted cert in these cases. Now that they had the central ethical issue before them, though, how could the justices uphold the constitutionality of capital punishment as practiced?

On the other hand, Stewart wondered, how could the Court overturn the death penalty without looking foolish? Amsterdam had valiantly crafted an Eight Amendment standard that made racism relevant. But who was he kidding? LDF's position was still based on procedural concerns. If the Court credited any of these, it would appear to repudiate *McGautha*. Stewart's heart told him that the Eighth and Fourteenth Amendment issues were different. His brain told him that the two arguments couldn't be distinguished. Stewart didn't know what to do.

AT CONFERENCE ON THE MORNING of Friday, January 21, Warren Burger predictably began by endorsing the constitutionality of capital punishment. "All of us have reservations about the death penalty," Burger said, but "the Constitution contemplated the death penalty and affirmatively recognized its existence." Burger summarily rejected LDF's argument: "It is not compromised by the infrequency of the use of capital punishment. The infrequency of capital punishment is not synonymous with 'unusual' and the argument does not impress me," he said, indicating that he would affirm in the homicide cases. "Rape is a closer question. Where there is rape without bodily harm, it is difficult. There are cruel rapes and mild rapes. I affirm in all cases."

Douglas took the opposite position. "We are locked in where reversal is almost mandatory," he said. Douglas liked nothing more than tweaking Burger, whom he regarded at best as a buffoon and at worst a malicious dissembler. One month earlier, at the conference on *Roe v. Wade*, Burger professed uncertainty over the constitutionality of abortion. Douglas believed that Burger had lied so that he could assign the opinion to Blackmun, the justice least likely to command a majority.

Douglas called it "an action that no Chief Justice in my time would ever have taken." Point by point Douglas contradicted Burger's argument. "*McGautha* was a wild card," Douglas explained. "There was complete jury discretion without any standards whatever. Statistics show that the death penalty is used primarily against minority groups. The lack of standards makes the system discriminatory. If it is discriminatory in practice, it is 'unusual' under the Eighth Amendment. I reverse."

Brennan also stayed true to form. "The Eighth Amendment reflects a gradually changing concept," he said. "Before the Civil War, the movement for the abolition of the death penalty was great. Since the beginning of this century, the feeling has increased. The death penalty is the ultimate word. There are no standards of decision making. Imposition of the penalty is susceptible to infrequent, selective use. The aggregate of those receiving the penalty shows the selectivity of the sentence." Brennan's use of the word "aggregate" drew directly from Amsterdam's formulation of the Eighth Amendment. He concluded, "If a state enacted a law making the death penalty mandatory, the case might be different, but legislatures would never do that."

Bombshells followed. Stewart sided with Brennan and Douglas. He said, "As of now, I cannot uphold the constitutionality of the death sentence. Someday the Court will hold that the death sentence is unconstitutional. If we hold it constitutional in 1972, it would only delay its abolition." Stewart expressed regret that the Court would need to decide the issue instead of the people, and said he saw no distinction between murder and rape. Suddenly, it was three to one against the death penalty.

White shockingly made it four to one. "The way the death penalty now operates in this country is impermissible," he said. "The nut of the case is that only a small proportion is put to death," adding, "I can't believe that it is meted out fairly." One by one White restated LDF's arguments. Regarding public opinion, he said, "Steadily, the jury has rejected the death penalty." Regarding crime prevention, he asked rhetorically, "Can you deter Joe by killing John?" With respect to retribution, he said, "We should not give sanction to the idea of a man getting his deserts. We should not legalize the death penalty at this time in our history."

Marshall revealed his cards. Briefly he summarized his gift to Brennan. "The death penalty is available to anyone who is low man on the totem pole," Marshall said. "The Eighth Amendment was intended to be considered in light of contemporary history. I reverse." For the first time in American history, a majority of the Supreme Court had expressed the view that the death penalty violated the Eighth Amendment. No confetti fell, though.

The conference continued. True to his own form, Harry Blackmun equivocated. "Minnesota abolished capital punishment in 1911. It got along as well as other states. I believe in evolving standards," Blackmun said. "On the other hand, in *Maxwell* I said while I was personally against the death penalty, it was a legislative decision. We have repeatedly said that the death penalty is permissible. If you knock it out, it is knocked out for assassinators of presidents, for treasonable acts, and so forth. I am disturbed that not a word was said in argument about the victims and their families. I am inclined to affirm shakily. I am not at rest. I might join a reversal opinion, but not now."

Powell suggested that he too opposed the death penalty personally, but that precedent proved the Court lacked the power to overturn it. "The Eighth Amendment has been discussed in only ten cases, and in only one did we indicate that this Court had power over state decisions. Eight of our earlier cases contain dicta that the death penalty is constitutional.* The Constitution itself contemplates the death sentence." He added, "The fact that our legislative guardians have abdicated their responsibilities hoping that this Court would take the problem off their backs can't justify our doing the job for them. Standards haven't reached the point where we can say that they ban the death penalty. I

---

* Dicta are things a court says that are unessential to the decision in a case, and hence not legally binding.

reject seeing this Court freeze the Eighth Amendment into banning the death penalty."

Finally Rehnquist indicated his support for capital punishment. He saw the issue as cut and dried. "To hold that the death penalty is bad, we would have to go beyond forty-one legislatures. I can't do that," he said. "We crossed the bridge in *McGautha*. If it is good law, I will follow it. As a legislator, I would keep it. I am not torn by the problem and I affirm."

It appeared to be five to four in favor of reversing the death penalty until Burger abruptly announced that he was changing his vote. Douglas must have wondered whether this was another ruse by the Chief to retain the right to assign the opinion, which otherwise would fall to the senior judge in the majority, Brennan. The conference couldn't have changed Burger's mind. Douglas's suspicion must have grown when Burger laid out his plan for going forward. The Chief proposed that each justice write his own opinion. This procedure had no precedent, but Burger defended it on the basis that no coherent rationale had emerged during the discussion. Douglas didn't buy it, but Burger insisted, and the conference capitulated.

Burger insisted too on absolute secrecy. He went "berserk" on this point, in Brennan's view. Burger had heard that during *Brown*, Warren took drafts of the opinion to the printer himself and personally delivered them to the justices. According to legend, the process was so secretive that no secretary or law clerk knew in advance which way the case would come out. Burger thought the death penalty cases should be treated the same way. Brennan and several others opposed this. The conference compromised that the justices wouldn't report to their clerks the discussion or votes from the conference. When the buzzer sounded, signaling the end of the session, the justices retreated to their individual chambers. No one knew what to do next.

IT IS IMPOSSIBLE TO KNOW whether Burger changed his vote as a ploy. The Chief ran a closed shop. His clerks didn't talk much with the other clerks, and Burger swore them to a lifetime confidentiality oath. During the research for this book, Burger's were the only clerks who refused interviews, each citing his vow of fealty. In donating his papers to William & Mary College, Burger specified that they not be made available to researchers until 2026.

If Burger's reversal was a ploy, it was a good one. Having the justices write their own opinions exacerbated a preexisting way of doing business on the Court that makes forming majorities difficult. This was why Douglas so forcefully opposed Burger's plan. Journalists and scholars often speak of "the Supreme Court" as a monolithic entity, like a presidential administration, but, unless one is referring to the physical building, this doesn't describe reality. The justices of the Supreme Court are almost entirely autonomous. With the notable exception of Felix Frankfurter, the justices did little lobbying. Referring to Bob Woodward and Scott Armstrong's controversial and groundbreaking account of the Burger Court, published in 1979, one former clerk said, "You would think from reading *The Brethren* that people are constantly running down the hall talking to one another. Actually, justices don't think that much about what the other justices are doing. They spend little time with them and they rarely see each other."

Even a unanimous decision doesn't necessarily reflect consensus among the justices. A unanimous opinion may create the appearance of solidarity and have a single operative effect. For example, *Brown* ended legal segregation. But justices come to a decision for their own individual reasons, as nine social-situated actors, each enormously complex in his own right. And what is unanimity? Justices often have different understandings of a decision's meaning. The aftermath of *Brown* offers conclusive evidence of this.

In essence the justices operate nine independent law firms, which interact with one another only sporadically and clumsily, most often when a justice assigned to write the majority opinion tries to build a consensus. Burger's directive meant that even this rudimentary dialogue wouldn't occur. The justices in the majority didn't speak with the justices in the minority. They didn't even discuss the case with the others on their own side. For months, on the most important case of the term, arguably one of the most important cases in American history, the justices of the Supreme Court worked in complete isolation.

WHILE THE JUSTICES SAID little to one another, most spoke openly with their clerks. Several immediately violated Burger's directive and discussed what had happened at conference.

In Brennan's office speculation turned to evaluating the strength of the slim majority. Brennan asked his clerks to do some reconnaissance. They learned that Marshall's clerks had been working on his opinion since the summer. Marshall's vote appeared reliable, although his clerks didn't know what had changed their boss's mind. Brennan's clerks also learned that Douglas had been committed since the beginning of the term. Brennan expressed confidence in Stewart's support—"Potter will not pull the switch on 600 people," he told his clerks—but Stewart's *McGautha* vote couldn't be dismissed. Even if everything fell apart, the worst-case scenario appeared to be a three-way dissent.

The best-case scenario was more difficult to gauge. Conceivably they could get to seven votes. If Brennan could establish a firm majority against the death penalty and a consensus rationale, he thought things could snowball in a positive direction. Blackmun wouldn't want to cast the deciding vote to reverse, but might join five or six others. Brennan held out a small hope that the same was true for Powell. These possibilities depended, though, on a preexisting majority, which in turn depended on White.

Brennan had a good relationship with White. White had a reputation for being stern and aloof, but Brennan cut through that veneer with his Irish charm. The two men had sat next to each other on the bench since White joined the Court in 1962. They frequently traded wisecracks, often to the chagrin of Blackmun, who complained about White's volume. White rarely spoke with the other justices, but he occasionally dropped by Brennan's chambers to chat about cases. Cordial relations, though, wouldn't necessarily translate into a vote. White didn't share Brennan's view of the proper role of the Court.

He thought Brennan was not respectful enough of legislatures, and bestowed upon Brennan the title "deputy prime minister." Brennan in turn regarded White as too invested in being right, and not enough in building coalitions. Generally speaking he was a wild card, and Brennan didn't regard his vote as dependable. Sure enough, the week after conference, White announced that he was withdrawing his vote without offering a reason. Now the tally was four to three against the death penalty.* With no majority on either side, the fate of the death penalty hung in limbo.

IN POTTER STEWART'S CHAMBERS the justice sat down with his law clerks, Ben Heineman and William Jeffress, told them about the conference, and discussed his state of mind. "I'd like to strike down the death penalty statutes," Stewart said, "but I don't know why." Stewart was inclined to write a brief opinion—a "short snapper," he called it— saying that the death penalty treated people as a means to an end and hence was "flat out cruel and unusual." At the same time Stewart said he understood that the case was a classic dialogue with other government institutions, and that expressing this sentiment alone wouldn't do. With these vague and contradictory directives, Stewart asked Heineman to take a shot at drafting an opinion.

EVEN MEASURED AGAINST THE extraordinary standards of Supreme Court clerks, Ben Heineman stood out. He had graduated magna cum laude and Phi Beta Kappa from Harvard College, where he was editorial chairman of the *Crimson*. After that he attended Oxford on a Rhodes Scholarship and then Yale Law School, where he became editor in chief of the *Yale Law Journal*. Later, as general counsel for General Electric, he supervised a staff of eleven hundred attorneys.

Heineman couldn't have been more excited by the death penalty

* Recall that Burger withdrew his vote, making it five to three in favor of Furman.

assignment. He viewed *Furman* as the case of the term. The briefing had been amazing, the advocacy at oral argument extraordinary. At Yale, Heineman had been mesmerized by a seminar on constitutional theory taught by Robert Bork and Alexander Bickel, two of the most influential legal scholars of the twentieth century. Here was an opportunity for Heineman to put that theory into practice.

Intellectually the assignment was daunting. If the Court was going to rule the death penalty unconstitutional, it needed to construct a theory for doing so. Heineman anticipated months of work ahead of him. He couldn't have asked for a better supervisor, though. Heineman and Jeffress admired Stewart and appreciated his collaborative working style. After an opinion had been drafted, Stewart would sit side by side with the clerk who had prepared it and review his proposed changes. While they worked, Stewart often smoked a cigarette, though he was always trying to quit.

Sometimes for lunch Stewart took his clerks to the Alibi Club, headquartered in an unmarked row house on I Street, just a few blocks from the White House. With only thirteen members, the Alibi ranked among the most exclusive organizations in the capital. Unanimous consent was required to admit someone new, and then only upon the death of an existing member. The club kept membership secret, often not revealing the affiliation until a member died. Former Supreme Court justice Stanley F. Reed had belonged, as well as CIA director Allen Dulles, and his brother, Secretary of State John Foster Dulles. On the right day Heineman and Jeffress could see former secretary of state Dean Acheson or Senator Prescott Bush, both nearing the end of their lives. Gen. George C. Marshall—World War II Army Chief of Staff and later secretary of state—had once been a member, too. It was living history, and Stewart's clerks were grateful for the opportunity to witness it, just as Dershowitz had been thrilled to lunch at Kronheim's cafeteria.

But liking Stewart and understanding him were different matters. He appeared to have changed his mind since supporting *McGautha* the previous term. Heineman and Jeffress could only speculate why.

One explanation was that Stewart hadn't really changed his mind. According to both Heineman and Jeffress, Stewart saw an essential difference between *McGautha* and the 1971 cases. He opposed the death penalty as a matter of principle, not because of flawed process. Thus he could reconcile supporting the death penalty under the Fourteenth Amendment while opposing it under the Eighth. But this couldn't be the entire story. In *Witherspoon*, Stewart had attempted to engineer the end of capital punishment through a procedural decision. Something had changed.

That something was John Harlan, whom Stewart admired above all other justices. He often told Heineman and Jeffress how much he respected Harlan. Robert Deitz, later counsel to the director of the CIA, clerked for Stewart in 1976, and asked him whether he had any mentors. Stewart cited only Harlan. Since *McGautha*, Harlan had resigned and died, and his absence clearly affected Stewart's conduct in the death penalty cases. Stewart himself would never admit to this connection, but the evidence is substantial.

Stewart's connection with Harlan grew from common blue-blooded origins. His father, James Garfield Stewart (named after the assassinated president, an Ohio Republican), was a prominent Cincinnati lawyer and politician who served two terms as the city's mayor and later became a justice of the Ohio Supreme Court. On the occasion of Potter's birth, the Stewarts received a congratulatory letter from President William Howard Taft. They lived in a mansion with a forty-six-foot-long living room, and educated Potter at the exclusive University School; Hotchkiss, a boarding school in Connecticut; and finally Yale, where he was a member of Skull and Bones. Following his graduation from college, Stewart spent a year at Cambridge on a Henry Fellowship, an exchange program among Harvard, Yale, Oxford, and Cambridge, before going on to Yale Law School.

Harlan's father was a prominent Chicago attorney active in Republican politics. His grandfather was a justice of the U.S. Supreme Court, best known for dissenting from *Plessy v. Ferguson*, the decision reversed by *Brown*. The younger Harlan attended boarding school in Canada, and then Princeton University, where he was a member of the Ivy Club, editor of the college newspaper, and president of his junior and senior classes. Harlan won a Rhodes Scholarship and, following graduation, spent three years at Balliol College, Oxford, studying jurisprudence. He then attended New York Law School.

Both men excelled at law school, and each joined a top law firm— Stewart to Debevoise & Plimpton, Harlan to Root, Clark & Bird (later Dewey Ballatine). Each volunteered for World War II and served with distinction. Stewart, a naval navigator, received three battle stars. Harlan, an air force colonel, received the Legion of Merit. After the war each entered public service. Stewart served two terms on the Cincinnati city council, the second as vice mayor, and seemed destined to succeed his father until President Eisenhower appointed him to the Sixth Circuit Court of Appeals in 1954. In New York, Harlan served stints as an assistant U.S. attorney, special assistant attorney general for New York State, and chief counsel to a state commission investigating the influence of organized crime before Eisenhower nominated him to the Second Circuit Court of Appeals in 1954. Though they were separated by sixteen years in age, they joined the Supreme Court, each on Eisenhower's nomination, only three years apart.

After they were transplanted to Washington, D.C., Harlan and Stewart created similar lives for themselves and their families. Harlan, with his wife and daughter, lived in a Victorian home in Georgetown. Stewart, with his wife and three children, lived in the tree-lined streets of northwestern D.C., near the tony Chevy Chase Country Club, of which he was a member. The Harlans kept a New York City apartment, a summer home in Weston, Connecticut, and a fishing camp in Quebec. The Stewarts maintained a vacation home in New Hampshire. Both men enjoyed golf and baseball, and shared a sense of humor. Once a year the justices would gather in Room 22-B, in the basement of the courthouse, to view the dirty movies that had been submitted as exhibits in the obscenity cases. Stewart would sit next to Harlan, who was nearly blind, and narrate the action. Periodically Harlan would exclaim, "By George, extraordinary!" They also shared a judicial demeanor. Stewart had been viewed as a front-runner to succeed Earl Warren, but after Warren retired Stewart asked Nixon not to consider him for chief: He didn't want the publicity that came with the job. Harlan was equally self-effacing.

Despite these substantial connections, the core of Stewart and Harlan's bond was a shared view of the proper role of a judge. Stewart prided himself on deciding each case on its own merits. One former law clerk said of Stewart, "His most consistent philosophy was his skepticism about the virtues of apparently consistent philosophies." Jeffress said, "Stewart was a guy who made distinctions. He was first and foremost a good lawyer and wanted to be remembered that way." He added, "Stewart was really a human being. As contrasted with Scalia and Thomas, people who have this overriding judicial philosophy, Stewart was never like that. There were an awful lot of gray areas." Asked about his judicial philosophy by reporters, Stewart said, "Oh, I really don't know what it is. I'd like to be thought of as a lawyer."

This was precisely the trait Stewart valued most in his friend. At a reunion of Harlan clerks at the Century Association, shortly after the tenth anniversary of Harlan's death, Stewart emphasized that while commentators described Harlan's judicial character as "scholarly" and "conservative," in his own opinion, this "missed the full measure of Harlan," who "was much more than a scholar." He was, Stewart said, "in the best sense of the word, a lawyer." Throughout his career Stewart repeated this theme of taking each case on its merits, and he urged judges to respect state legislatures. In another speech Stewart said, "The Court is not a council of platonic guardians given the function of deciding our most difficult and emotional questions according to the justices' own notions of what is good or wise and politic." It's easy enough to imagine these words flowing from Harlan's agile pen.

The most commonly cited evidence of Stewart's lack of an overarching philosophy is that he dissented from *Griswold v. Connecticut*, establishing a privacy right regarding contraception decisions, but voted with the majority in *Roe v. Wade*. In an article following Stewart's death, Heineman explained these votes as linked by Stewart's high regard for precedent and his view of himself as a balance wheel on the Court. Not everyone bought it, though.

With respect to the death penalty Michael Meltsner perceived Stewart to be "something of an enigma." From an outsider's perspective this was an understatement. Most justices had an apparently consistent ideology on capital punishment. For example, in the six crucial cases of the late '60s and early '70s—*Jackson, Witherspoon, Boykin, Maxwell, Crampton*, and *McGautha*—Marshall, Brennan, and Douglas voted for the defendant each time. In their short time on the Court, Burger and Blackmun had established themselves as consistent supporters of capital punishment.

Stewart's record was a mishmash. He voted for the defendants in *Jackson* and *Witherspoon*. In the Court's private deliberations on *Boykin*, he had been for the state but joined the reversal following Abe Fortas's resignation. In *Maxwell* he had been against standards unless bifurcation was required, in which case he thought standards were imperative. In the Court's final decision in *Maxwell*, remanding the case to Arkansas, Stewart voted for the defendant. In *Crampton* and *McGautha* he sided with the state. The only justice whose record on capital punishment resembled Stewart's was Harlan. Like Stewart, Harlan voted for the defendant in *Jackson*. Like Stewart, he had been for the state in *Boykin* during conference, and then joined the reversal after Fortas stepped down. He, too, had a complicated view in *Maxwell* but ultimately joined Stewart in voting to remand. And, of course, Harlan had been for the state in *McGautha* and *Crampton*. The only case in which they had differed was *Witherspoon*.

Mutual influence among justices is difficult to measure scientifically. Professors Harold Spaeth and Michael Altfeld of Michigan State University quantified the question by focusing on justices' success in attracting joiners to their dissenting and concurring opinions. These special opinions, Spaeth and Altfeld argue, are the purest test of a justice's influence. Authors and signers of majority opinions often have complicated motivations. Authors may want to secure other assignments in the future. Potential joiners can exert substantial control over the author and force him or her to bend to their will or risk breaking a coalition. With special opinions, however, justices are free agents. No one can be forced to write one, no one can be prevented from writing one, and quid pro quos are difficult to imagine.

Examining special opinions during the Warren and Burger courts, Spaeth and Altfeld found that justices joined one another about 10 percent of the time. Harlan and Stewart supported each other at almost triple that rate. During Stewart's time on the Warren Court, Harlan was the only justice on whom Stewart had a significant influence. Harlan, in turn, influenced only Stewart. Each was significantly influenced only by the other, and by Thurgood Marshall. In *Miranda*, Stewart (and White) joined Harlan's vociferous dissent. In *Escobedo v. Illinois*, a landmark decision on the right to counsel, Stewart dissented on virtually the same basis as Harlan. Yet again, in *Katzenbach v. Morgan*, a decision that ended literacy tests for disenfranchised minorities, it was Harlan and Stewart alone in dissent.

This mixture of statistical and anecdotal evidence is hardly conclusive, and other pairs had more substantial bonds. On the Burger court Brennan joined Marshall almost 48 percent of the time, and Marshall joined Brennan more than 57 percent of the time. During their first term together on the Court, in seventy-two non-unanimous cases, Blackmun and Burger voted the same way sixty-nine times.* At the opposite end of the spectrum, Earl Warren didn't join any of Felix Frankfurter's 188 special opinions.

Stewart dismissed the idea that Harlan's death affected his behavior, but under Spaeth and Altfeld's metrics, while Stewart had been an influence only on Harlan during the Warren Court, on the Burger Court he would be the most influential justice, having a significant effect on Douglas, Marshall, Brennan, and, remarkably, Rehnquist. Philip Kurland, a professor at University of Chicago Law School and former Frankfurter clerk, called 1971 "the year of the Stewart-White

---

* For this, and their shared heritage, Burger and Blackmun were nicknamed the "Minnesota Twins."

Court." Harlan's departure from the Court seems to have led to Stewart's florescence. His clerks believed that Harlan's absence had saddened the justice—and liberated him. As Heineman went to work on the assignment of his young lifetime, he set out to write an opinion that would unshackle Stewart's core moral principles.

AS HEINEMAN HIT THE BOOKS, Brennan and his clerks, Gerald Goldman, Paul Hoeber, and Taylor Ashworth, began drafting their own opinion. The starting point was Mike Becker's memorandum, which emphasized human dignity. The Eighth Amendment, wrote Becker, "serves to protect society as a whole from the inevitably brutalizing, dehumanizing impact that results from society's deliberately treating any human being in ways that deny that person's essential dignity and humanity." Becker had never discussed this concept with Brennan, but he believed his strength as a clerk was an ability to anticipate what a judge would say about an issue and capture the tone he would want to use. Indeed, the theme of human dignity would figure prominently in Brennan's final opinion.

Brennan needed to explain how the Constitution protected human dignity while making no mention of it. To this end he embraced Warren's formulation of evolving standards of decency. This flowed naturally from Brennan's own evolution. By 1972 Brennan had conclusively rejected originalism. He expressed this in many ways. "Current justices read the Constitution in the only way we can: as twentieth-century Americans," he told one group. The intention of the framers mattered, he told another, but "the ultimate question must be: What do the words of the text mean in our time?" At a Georgetown University symposium, Brennan said, "The genius of the Constitution rests not in any static meaning that it might have had in a world that is dead and gone, but in the adaptability of its great principles to cope with current problems and current needs."

To evidence the change in standards of decency, the opinion needed to show that capital punishment had been the subject of persistent controversy, and was used less and less frequently in part because of the substantial pain associated with its infliction. The draft Marshall showed Brennan discussed this history at length, and the clerks thought Brennan might simply endorse Marshall's recitation of this background.

It wasn't enough, though, to say that standards of decency had evolved. How were current standards to be measured? This question vexed Brennan's clerks. Marshall said the measuring stick should be fully informed public opinion. He supposed that citizens would oppose the death penalty if they knew the true facts about its application. This theory, which came to be known as the "Marshall Hypothesis," had the benefit of empowering the Court to reject a punishment favored by the overwhelming majority of Americans. Amsterdam had suggested this standard during oral argument. Dershowitz and Goldberg put it forward explicitly in their now widely read article in the *Harvard Law Review.* "Were capital punishment, like criminal punishment of narcotic addiction, better understood, prevailing moral standards might well condemn it." Brennan and his clerks were reluctant to endorse this reasoning, though. They thought the theory was condescending to ordinary people.

They were also reluctant to accept Amsterdam's argument that the core of the problem with the death penalty was that its infrequent application masked discrimination. Brennan and his clerks felt that this argument opened the door to mandatory sentences. Moreover, Brennan wanted to steer clear of racism, an instinct he had displayed often on the Warren Court. For example, in *New York Times v. Sullivan,* a libel action brought by the white city commissioner of Montgomery, Alabama, against the *Times* and the Committee to Defend Martin Luther King, Brennan's opinion followed the lead of the attorney for the *Times,* Herbert Wechsler, and made no mention of race. In *Miranda,* Brennan persuaded Warren to delete a proposed reference to the defendant's race. Brennan's note to the Chief said, "I wonder if it is appropriate in this context to turn police brutality into a racial problem. If anything characterizes the group this opinion concerns it is poverty rather than race."

While he didn't want to mention race, Brennan proposed to mirror the legal standard the Court used in discrimination cases. Under the equal-protection clause, states were required to show a compelling justification for any law that treated blacks and whites differently. In their *Harvard Law Review* article, Goldberg and Dershowitz suggested that this approach could be extended to Eighth Amendment cases. "Even when the death penalty is imposed for the taking or endangering of life," they wrote, "its constitutionality must depend upon the state's ability to demonstrate a compelling justification for using it instead of a less severe penalty." Brennan proposed developing this reasoning into a fully realized constitutional test.

The remaining issue was how much space to devote to the threshold question of the Court's role. Brennan's clerks were inclined to address it fully. Federalism questions were likely to be on Powell's mind. A persuasive opinion on this point might convince him.

THOUGH BRENNAN'S CLERKS DIDN'T know it, they had a potential accomplice inside Powell's chambers. Powell had assigned *Furman* to Larry Hammond, a graduate of the University of Texas Law School, where he was editor in chief of the law review. Hammond had originally been hired by Hugo Black. When Powell succeeded Black, he asked Hammond to stay on.

At their first meeting Powell told Hammond that he wanted the clerks to assume that he knew nothing regarding constitutional law. Powell said he knew tax law well and would handle those cases himself, but in all other cases would rely heavily on his clerks. Over time Hammond developed enormous respect for Powell. Powell also adopted a transparent, inclusive working style that contrasted sharply with his predecessor's. Black had ordered that all of his papers be burned. At the beginning of his tenure Powell decided that his own papers would be public. Consistent with this spirit of openness, Powell treated his clerks as partners. *Furman* would be Hammond's primary responsibility for the next six months. He worked closely with Powell on the case and described the process, in retrospect, as a "collaborative undertaking."

Powell's vote wasn't open for discussion, though. In their first meeting regarding the case, Powell said "he would vote against the death penalty if he were a legislator, but death is mentioned several times in the Constitution and that trumped, even though the Constitution is a living document." In notes that he took during the oral argument, Powell wrote that Amsterdam's position regarding standards of decency had been "overkill." Powell also questioned what the public really felt. "The anti-death penalty movement—waged with the fervor of a crusade—has in fact accomplished little in terms of averting public support," he wrote in a note to himself. "It has been singularly successful in the law reviews, the scholarly journals, and some of the press. But if the standard is the public—and not just an elite segment—the crusade has not had notable success." The only policy concern that resonated with Powell was the inferior representation received by defendants facing death sentences. This created intolerable arbitrariness. But, as one might expect from a former president of the ABA, Powell thought better lawyering could fix the problem. He believed that more competent attorneys would make the process rational.

At the first meeting, Powell also asked Hammond his position on the cases. "Honestly, I had not formed a view," Hammond said in 2010. He had neither thought about the death penalty much in law school nor had he worked on a capital case during his appellate clerkship. His instinct was to follow his boss's lead. In his initial bench memorandum to Powell, Hammond wrote, "On balance, while I am taken by the notion of a continuum of development in the public's rejection of the death penalty, and while it bothers me that we must permit the exercise of the penalty today—at the expense of several hundred souls—because either society's conscience has not developed or the lawyers have failed to prove its development, the case for abolition does not meet sufficiently high standards of proof to permit a definitive conclusion as to the public's position." In the margins Powell wrote, "Very good summary."

Powell had listened carefully to White and Stewart's comments at conference. He felt that the key to persuading them—and thus to winning the case—was to demonstrate that the issue was outside the Court's proper jurisdiction. Powell instructed Hammond to compile a history showing that the Founding Fathers had accepted capital punishment, and that the Court had always presumed its constitutionality. He asked Hammond to pay special attention to comments at the Constitutional Convention, in the *Federalist Papers,* and in the debates surrounding the Reconstruction civil rights amendments. Powell said he also wanted to understand the evidence for and against deterrence. LDF had submitted several longitudinal studies of murder rates in states that enacted the death penalty, showing little effect. Powell's instincts told him that these studies proved nothing.

It took Hammond weeks to get a handle on the issues. Poring through the briefs and historical documents, Hammond worked day and night. He desperately wanted to please his boss. But as January receded into a bitter February, Hammond began to develop a gnawing sense that Powell might have it wrong. Hammond didn't share his boss's confidence that better lawyering would reduce arbitrariness. The more he worked on the cases, the less Hammond believed that the death penalty could ever be applied rationally.

ON FEBRUARY 18, 1972, the California Supreme Court said precisely this. Just one month after oral argument in *Anderson,* the California high court struck down the death penalty under its state constitution, which prohibited "cruel *or* unusual punishments." The decision said many things to warm Tony Amsterdam's heart. It said that cruelty must be measured by evolving standards of decency or nailing ears and boring holes in tongues would still be permitted. It said, as Marshall had, that opinion polls must be dismissed because the public was too removed from the issue. The death penalty was falling out of favor both with American juries and in the international community. As administered, it imposed a torturous and lingering death. "It degrades and dehumanizes all who participate in its processes," the court concluded. "It is unnecessary to any legitimate goal of the state and is incompatible with the dignity of man."

The decision attracted widespread attention. California had the largest death-row population of any state—107 people, including the serial killer Charles Manson and Robert Kennedy's assassin, Sirhan Sirhan. The six-to-one decision carried extra weight because it had been written by the chief justice, Donald Wright, a conservative Reagan appointee. It also created the appearance of an emerging trend.

Anderson benefited LDF in an additional, practical way. The decision meant the Supreme Court wouldn't decide *Aikens*, as the case was now moot. *Aikens* was the most aggravated of the four cases, and LDF had worried about it the most. Meltsner said LDF "heaved a collective sigh of relief because some of the justices, especially Burger, and the public at large, would have made a great deal of hay out of Aikens' crimes."

Behind the scenes Burger resisted removing *Aikens* from the docket, though he had no real argument. Burger worried that *Anderson* would cause some damage. Many lawyers regarded the California Supreme Court as the nation's most innovative judicial body. Amsterdam said, "The California Supreme Court is to the courts what UCLA is to basketball." Blackmun thought *Anderson* would be a turning point, and later said so in his *Furman* dissent. Brennan even wondered to his clerks whether *Anderson* might bring Burger around. Perhaps Burger would see this as an opportunity to be the chief who presided over the end of the death penalty. This could be his defining legacy, as ending segregation had defined Earl Warren's tenure. At the very least Brennan thought the California decision would solidify the resolve of the more reluctant members of the tenuous majority, including Potter Stewart.

IN STEWART'S CHAMBERS Heineman presented the justice with his draft opinion. Heineman had devoted the majority of his discussion to questioning retribution as a legitimate aim of punishment. This seemed consistent with Stewart's statement that the death penalty should be rejected because it treated people as a means to an end. Stewart, however, didn't buy it. He said, "Nice try, Ben, but I think retribution is a legitimate purpose of punishment, and I can't strike the penalty down forever." Stewart told Heineman that he wouldn't commit himself to the position that the Constitution barred the death penalty in all cases. In some circumstances, it was appropriate—or at least constitutional—for the state to put people to death.

Heineman accepted Stewart's judgment. This was Stewart's decision to make, after all. But if Stewart wasn't willing to express his core moral concern, Heineman wondered what ultimately would serve as the basis for his boss's opinion. Stewart didn't appear to have much room to maneuver. Heineman hoped his draft wouldn't die and, privately, offered a copy to Brennan's clerk, Paul Hoeber.

BRENNAN AND HIS CLERKS had the draft of their opinion ready by mid-March. It began by arguing that the intent of the framers with respect to the cruel-and-unusual-punishment clause couldn't be determined conclusively. Brennan suggested that its true meaning was noble, and its basic underlying concept "is nothing less than the dignity of man." He wrote, "The State, even as it punishes, must treat its members with respect for their intrinsic worth as human beings. A punishment is cruel and unusual if it does not comport with human dignity."

Brennan outlined a four-part test to determine whether a punishment was consistent with human dignity and the Eighth Amendment. The first principle was that "a punishment must not be so severe as to be degrading to the dignity of human beings." Physical pain was but one factor among many in this judgment; mental anguish counted too. Second, "the State must not arbitrarily inflict a severe punishment." This principle made racism relevant, but Brennan grounded it differently than LDF had. "This principle," he wrote, "derives from the notion that the State does not respect human dignity when, without reason, it inflicts upon some people a severe punishment that it does not inflict upon others." The third principle was "that a severe punishment must not be unacceptable to contemporary society." Rejection by society indicated that a severe punishment didn't comport with human dignity. Finally, Brennan said, "a severe punishment must not be excessive." In this context "excessive" meant unnecessary. Just as the second principle had made relevant evidence of racism, which wouldn't ordinarily seem germane to an assessment of cruelty, this last prong of the test incorporated the entire public policy debate about capital punishment. All the evidence on deterrence, or the lack thereof, suddenly became part of the constitutional calculus—at least for Brennan.

Brennan's test owed a heavy debt to Gerald Gottlieb's 1961 law review article. Though he referenced Gottlieb only once, and then for a short article Gottlieb had written in 1969 on the cruelty of waiting on death row, the influence couldn't be denied. The fourth principle of Brennan's test came very close to a requirement of necessity that Gottlieb had outlined in 1961. The problem of irreversibility and the dignity of man had also figured prominently in Gottlieb's article. Brennan closed his opinion by restating this central theme. "Death is truly an awesome punishment," Brennan wrote. "The calculated killing of a human being by the State involves, by its very nature, a denial of the executed person's humanity. The contrast with the plight of a person punished by imprisonment is evident. An individual in prison does not lose the right to have rights. A prisoner remains a member of the human family. Moreover, he retains the right of access to the courts. His punishment is not irrevocable." By contrast, Brennan said, "When a man is hung, there is an end of our relations with him. His execution is a way of saying, 'You are not fit for this world, take your chance elsewhere.'"

On March 14, before circulating the opinion to the entire Court, Brennan privately sent copies of his draft to Stewart and White. Stewart quickly complimented the draft as excellent. Stewart told Brennan that he thought the opinion "did the job" and said that he would likely join it, though he said he might add language to the effect that "the

death penalty was impermissible because it treated people as objects."
White said nothing.

AT THE END OF MARCH the justices began sharing opinions.
Douglas and Marshall circulated their opinions first, followed by
Brennan on March 29. Marshall's opinion closely resembled the draft
he shared with Brennan in January. Douglas's opinion focused almost
exclusively on the discriminatory imposition of the death penalty. In
language mirroring Amsterdam's, Douglas said we knew "the penalty
to be selectively applied, feeding prejudices against the accused if he
is poor and despised, and lacking political clout, or if he is a member
of a suspect or unpopular minority, and saving those who by social
position may be in a more protected position." In effect, Douglas said,
American law had created a caste system. "In ancient Hindu law, a
Brahman was exempt from capital punishment," he wrote. "Punishment increased in severity as social status diminished. We have, I fear,
taken in practice the same position, partially as a result of making the
death penalty discretionary and partially as a result of the ability of the
rich to purchase the services of the most respected and most resource-
ful legal talent in the Nation."

Douglas emphasized the disadvantages of the individual defendants.
Furman had only finished sixth grade, was mildly retarded, and had
been diagnosed having psychotic episodes. Branch was mildly retarded,
too, and had completed only five years of school. Furman, Branch, and
Jackson were each black. Douglas bought into the essence of Amsterdam's argument: The Eighth Amendment dealt with the consequences
of punishment, not just procedural protections. In what would become
the most famous passage from his opinion, Douglas concluded:

A law that stated that anyone making more than $50,000 would be
exempt from the death penalty would plainly fall, as would a law
that in terms said that blacks, those who never went beyond the fifth
grade in school, those who made less than $3,000 a year, or those

who were unpopular or unstable should be the only people executed. A law which in the overall view reaches that result in practice has no more sanctity than a law which in terms provides the same.

Despite the vivid example, Brennan's clerks didn't think Douglas's opinion was very good. It was rambling and disorganized. Douglas began with a discussion of whether the Fourteenth Amendment had incorporated the Eighth Amendment, a question no one perceived as central to the case. He drew lessons from Norman England. His argument regarding racism relied on congressional testimony and textbooks, rather than state-specific data. Most damningly, Douglas made almost no effort to deal with *McGautha*. He baldly said, "The seeds of the present cases are in *McGautha*. Juries have practically untrammeled discretion to let an accused live or insist that he die."

Douglas's own clerks shared Brennan's clerks' assessment. They didn't think the opinion represented their boss's best work. The draft hadn't gone through Douglas's normal vetting process. Usually he reviewed every word of an opinion countless times, often torturing his clerks by ordering one revision after another. This opinion had been written quickly and, in the view of his clerks, haphazardly. But no one was going to say that to Douglas. From Brennan's standpoint Douglas's vote mattered much more than his rationale, since Stewart and White were going to decide the case.

At the end of the month Heineman gave one of Brennan's clerks a memorandum containing Stewart's reactions to Brennan, Marshall, and Douglas's opinions. This document was more tepid than the unqualified praise Stewart had earlier offered Brennan. Stewart questioned whether Brennan's separation of "cruel" and "unusual" made sense. He also felt that the four prongs of Brennan's test should be measured cumulatively. In other words, a punishment could fail the test even if it didn't offend each factor individually. Most pointedly, Stewart, through his clerk, said that Brennan's test obviously had been designed to generate a particular result.

To this charge Brennan would almost certainly have pled guilty.

He wouldn't have been the first Supreme Court justice to commit this crime. Overall Stewart's response encouraged Brennan. Stewart had not backed off his inclination to join the opinion, and Brennan was more than happy to modify the test in the manner Stewart had proposed. The question remained, as ever, which way White would come down. Brennan told his clerks to sit tight for a while and see which way the wind blew.

ON APRIL 24 BURGER circulated his opinion. He began with a familiar apology: If he were a legislator he would either join Brennan and Marshall or would restrict the death penalty to the most awful crimes. As a judge, however, "our constitutional inquiry must be divorced from personal feelings." Burger offered his own history of the Eighth Amendment, which differed from Brennan's. Burger said that nothing in the constitutional debates and subsequent case law suggested any interrelationship between the terms "cruel" and "unusual." His interpretation rendered the evidence of racially disparate application irrelevant. "I do not suggest that the presence of the word 'unusual' in the Eighth Amendment is merely vestigial," Burger wrote. "But where, as here, we consider a punishment well known to history," he argued that it defied law "to rely on the term 'unusual' as affecting the outcome of these cases."

Burger felt that Marshall, Douglas, and Brennan had drawn the wrong lesson from America's experience with capital punishment. The diminishing frequency with which juries imposed death sentences proved the system had been refined. Public policy arguments about deterrence were irrelevant. States were responding to a complex question, and their judgment was entitled to deference. "If it were proper to put the States to the test of demonstrating the deterrent value of capital punishment, we could just as well ask them to prove the need for any other punishment," Burger said. "Yet I know of no convincing evidence that life imprisonment is a more effective deterrent than twenty years' imprisonment, or even that a ten-dollar parking ticket is a more effective deterrent than a five-dollar parking ticket."

Brennan and Douglas's opinions were really due-process arguments. Ironically, they seemed to be saying that the jury system "had yielded more mercy than the Eighth Amendment can stand." Taking this position to its logical extension, states could respond by making the death penalty mandatory. This struck Burger as counterproductive. "If this is the only alternative that the legislatures can safely pursue," he said regarding the ruling, "I would have preferred that the Court opt for total abolition."

Finally Burger offered a simple answer to Amsterdam's argument that standards of decency must evolve or the Court would have to sanction the barbaric practices of the eighteenth century. "Punishments such as branding and the cutting off of ears, which were commonplace at the time of the adoption of the Constitution, passed from the penal scene without judicial intervention because they became basically offensive to the people and the legislatures responded to this sentiment," Burger wrote. "Beyond any doubt, if we were today called upon to review such punishments, we would find them excessively cruel because we could say with complete assurance that contemporary society universally rejects such bizarre penalties."

After the opinion had been circulated one of Burger's clerks broke his vow of silence and quipped, "There will be no boiling in oil so long as this Court sits."

HARRY BLACKMUN SOON JOINED ranks with Burger and issued his own personal disavowal of the death penalty. Because of Burger's privacy and the secrecy he demanded from his clerks, it would never be possible to determine the authenticity of his repudiation of capital punishment. Blackmun's sincerity is easier to validate. His operating style contrasted sharply with Burger's.

Blackmun was an extraordinarily hard worker and a creature of habit. He arrived at Court by seven o'clock each morning in a bright blue Volkswagen Beetle, to which he was so attached, and so strongly identified with, that one would join his funeral procession in 1999. Once at the Court, Blackmun ate breakfast in the cafeteria with his clerks (the same thing each morning—one scrambled egg and two pieces of raisin toast), a tradition many recall as their fondest memory. Then he worked until seven o'clock in the evening and took home a briefcase full of papers. He kept meticulous notes of judicial conferences, oral arguments (including lawyer grades), and his private reflections. He wrote himself a memo before oral argument on almost every case he heard. Researchers thus have a rare window into Harry Blackmun's soul.

Blackmun's clerk's aside to Amsterdam and Meltsner following the *Maxwell* argument didn't reflect a mere passing fancy on Blackmun's part. In 1966, seven years after he joined the Court of Appeals and one year before the *Maxwell* argument, Blackmun and his colleagues heard the appeal of Duane Pope in a highly publicized case about which almost everyone in the Midwest had an opinion. Pope, a college football star at McPherson College in Kansas, crossed state lines to rob a bank in Nebraska. During the robbery Pope shot three employees, including the seventy-seven-year-old president of the bank. Pope then traveled to Las Vegas, where he gambled, and to Tijuana, where he watched a bullfight. Then he turned himself in. Pope's lawyers claimed insanity at trial, and the appeal revolved around how the trial judge had handled the psychiatric evidence, which the jury had rejected in sentencing Pope to die.

The assignment went to Blackmun, who could find no basis for overturning the conviction. But Blackmun questioned the death penalty and added a paragraph at the end of his draft opinion arguing that Pope was an appropriate candidate for executive clemency. The other judges hearing the case called Blackmun's remark "gratuitous," which Blackmun took umbrage, despite the fact that neither of the other judges meant it as an insult. They had also praised the opinion as brilliant, and Blackmun had invited their responses with a cover memo indicating his own doubts about the paragraph. Still, Blackmun wrote Burger, his childhood friend (with whom he maintained a regular correspondence), that he "got into a real hoedown about capital punishment," and, months later, that he continued to kick himself for withdrawing the comment.

When the Burger Court took up the issue, Blackmun's views remained more or the less the same: Capital punishment was bad public policy, but it was not the Court's role to correct it. In April 1971, with *McGautha* looming, Blackmun sat at his desk and retyped a passage from Felix Frankfurter's opinion in *Haley v. Ohio*, a 1948 appeal by a fifteen-year-old boy who had been sentenced to die, based in large part on a confession he gave after an all-night interrogation. Frankfurter's opinion set aside the boy's confession as involuntary but didn't challenge the constitutionality of the death penalty. "I disbelieve in capital punishment," Frankfurter wrote, "but as a judge I could not impose the views of the very few States who through bitter experience have abolished capital punishment upon all the other States." At the bottom of the passage Blackmun typed his initials, endorsing the statement as his own.

Five months later, after examining the new capital cases for the first time, Blackmun reiterated this view. "Were I a legislator, I would vote against the death penalty," he wrote in a memorandum to himself. "It does not mean, however, that if a State in its wisdom chooses to impose the death penalty for high crimes, such as treason, and certain types of murder, such as killing by malice aforethought, I could say that such is violative of the Eighth Amendment. I would disagree with the policy, but I cannot throw it out, at this point at least, on constitutional grounds." Revealingly, Blackmun added, "One could say that the Court is being cowardly about this."

At the end of his career Blackmun would proclaim himself a principled opponent of capital punishment and its constitutionality. When he retired from the bench in 1994, he was widely regarded as the most liberal justice on the Court. By the middle of the 1970s, Blackmun sided with Brennan more often than he did with Burger. Between

1975 and 1980, Blackmun agreed with Brennan in 55 percent of cases. Between 1986 and 1990 Blackmun voted with Brennan and Marshall more than 95 percent of the time. Many Americans knew Blackmun solely as the author and protector of *Roe v. Wade*, the Court's most controversial and substantial expansion of civil liberties. In 1972, though, Blackmun was not yet Blackmun. During his first term on the Supreme Court, Blackmun voted with Burger in almost every case. Abolitionists later would wonder what might have been if the evolution of Blackmun's views had begun sooner.

What took so long? Part of the answer is that with Harry Blackmun nothing happened quickly. Blackmun could be principled and articulate, but he was also thin skinned and craved external affirmation. Some of this traced back to his childhood. As a boy Blackmun battled depression and hypochondria. Even as an adult he could be uncomfortable with strangers, and often expressed doubt whether he deserved his seat on the Court. Garrison Keillor called him "the shy person's justice."

At the outset of his career on the Supreme Court, when Blackmun faced the conflict between personal belief and perceived duty that every justice confronts, he defaulted to his most familiar and comfortable models: his law school professor Felix Frankfurter, and his childhood friend Warren Burger. On the eve of Blackmun's swearing-in, Burger sent a welcoming letter, which well summarized Burger's view of the role of the Court: "All good ideas do not spring from the Constitution, and all dubious ones are not prohibited by it. It is not a code." Over and over Burger counseled Blackmun not to wear his heart on his sleeve.

In 1972 the conservatives were still winning the battle for Blackmun's soul. *Roe* preoccupied him that year. On May 18 he circulated the first draft of his opinion. It proposed to strike down the Texas abortion statute on the narrowest possible ground: that the law, which banned abortion unless "for the purpose of saving the life of the mother," was so vague as to be unconstitutional. Brennan and Douglas would pressure him relentlessly to go further, and the following term

Blackmun would succumb. Indeed, the seeds of Blackmun's transformation had already been planted, as Brennan sensed when he handicapped the death penalty cases in the fall, but they would not be sown before *Furman* was decided. Blackmun's *Furman* opinion would be heartfelt, manifest the same internal turmoil he displayed in *Maxwell*, and take a long time to produce, but it would be in favor of the constitutionality of capital punishment all the same. "Cases such as these provide for me an excruciating agony of the spirit," Blackmun wrote finally. "I yield to no one in the depth of my distaste, antipathy, and indeed, abhorrence for the death penalty, with all its aspects of physical distress and fear of moral judgment exercised by finite minds." As a legislator he would vote against the death penalty, but "the authority should not be taken over by the judiciary in the modern guise of an Eighth Amendment issue." Blackmun presumed that he would be in the minority and added, finally, "Although personally I may rejoice at the Court's result, I find it difficult to accept or to justify as a matter of history, of law, or of constitutional pronouncement."

ON MAY 12 LEWIS POWELL circulated his opinion. In the end it ran fifty pages, which was long even for a majority opinion, and this was designed as a dissent. He devoted much of the draft to a discussion of judicial function. Powell, like Burger, didn't believe that the Court should decide an issue so tied to individual ethical beliefs. Powell called the decision an act of "judicial fiat," reflecting "a basic lack of faith and confidence in the democratic process." Like Burger, Powell tried to demonstrate that the death penalty was imposed more commonly than LDF claimed, and he proudly listed the justices who had supported capital punishment in prior cases.

While Powell became highly invested in his opinion after circulating it, the clerk who drafted it, Larry Hammond, moved in the opposite direction. He thought the opinion he had helped write was in error. "I do not know a person who can defend the results in the death penalty cases," Hammond said in 2010. At the time he was deeply troubled.

Powell didn't know this. He had asked Hammond's opinion at the outset of the case but not since, and now Hammond didn't know how to broach the subject. They had precedent for amicable disagreement. Hammond worked with Powell on *Keyes v. School District No. 1*, where Powell opposed forced busing, which he and his coclerk, William Kelly, supported. This disagreement hadn't affected the clerks' working relationship with their boss. To Hammond the death penalty cases felt somehow different. It was one thing for a justice to ask an opinion and for the clerk to respond; it was quite another to simply blurt out that one's views had changed and accuse the justice of deciding a case incorrectly. So Hammond said nothing.

After Powell circulated his opinion, Stewart and White praised the draft. As the favorable comments filtered in, Powell reported them to Hammond, as one would to a confederate. Hammond again held his tongue. He felt increasingly disingenuous.

After Marshall circulated a second draft of his opinion, largely in response to Powell's own, Hammond reviewed Marshall's revision and presented it to Powell with a cover memo. "If this is the extent of the argument to be mounted against your opinion, you must be right," Hammond wrote. He thought no changes were required, although, he said, "We might think about sharpening the discussion of the time-aged problems surrounding the underprivileged in this country."

Hammond expressed similar disdain with respect to a draft that Blackmun shared with Powell. "Although it makes no attempt to analyze the tough questions, it is clearly the best piece of writing that Justice Blackmun has produced in the last two years," wrote Hammond. "I find myself in close accord and sympathy for his view. He expresses as well as can be expressed the tension between the sure knowledge that capital punishment does not offend the Constitution and the non-judicial instinct that tells us that overruling the death penalty might be one of the great humanitarian acts of this century."

Of course Hammond didn't have a vote in the death penalty cases. Among those who did, it was four to four. None of the back-and-forth had changed the core reality. Everything still came down to Byron White.

SINCE JANUARY, WHITE HADN'T said a word regarding the death penalty. His clerks claimed not to know what he was thinking. They said only that the pressure of the capital cases had broken his resolve to end his forty-year smoking habit, and White was a man whose resolve didn't easily break.

Brennan viewed white's silence as ominous. He worried about whether the majority would hold. Brennan thought about what could be done to solidify Stewart's support. Brennan was prepared to compromise on treating "cruel" and "unusual" as separate components, and told his clerks to say so. But on May 29 Stewart's clerks said that such a change was unnecessary. Heineman and Jeffress reiterated that Stewart was firm, but probably wouldn't join Brennan's opinion no matter how it was modified. They said once again that Stewart was going to write a "short snapper," agreeing with what Brennan said in his draft, but that it was "enough for Stewart that the death penalty treated people as things."

Brennan thus gave up attempting to satisfy Stewart, and thought instead about how to respond to Burger and Powell's drafts. First Brennan decided to scrap his discussion of judicial review. This had been aimed at trying to persuade Powell. Clearly there was no longer any point in that. Instead Brennan began his opinion with a discussion of the cruel-and-unusual-punishments clause. Burger and Powell each had charged that the clause had limited application. Brennan thought this was important to refute, and bolstered the discussion of *Weems*, the 1910 case George referenced during oral argument. Brennan said *Weems* established that the Eighth Amendment wasn't limited to "punishments practiced by the Stuarts." A constitutional provision, wrote Brennan, "is enacted, it is true, from an experience of evils, but its general language should not be necessarily confined to the form that evil had theretofore taken. Time works changes, brings into existence new conditions and purposes. A principle to be vital must be capable of wider application than the mischief which gave it birth."

Then, satisfied that he and his clerks had done the best that could be done on this point, Brennan resumed waiting. In early June one of White's clerks told Brennan's clerks that White was continuing to keep to himself on the issue. The clerk said he was sure that nothing Brennan could write would make any difference to White. White would decide what he would decide. Ominously, though, White's clerk reported that the smart money in his chambers said that White would ultimately vote to uphold the death penalty. Heineman and Jeffress felt the same way.

On June 7, a Wednesday, the justices convened to toast White's birthday. Stewart told Brennan that he was going to meet with White about the death cases and promised to report back. Again Brennan waited anxiously but heard nothing from Stewart, concluding that Stewart either hadn't spoken with White or that White had sworn him to secrecy.

Later that day Blackmun shared a revised draft of his opinion with Powell, including a cover note he intended to circulate. The note said that Blackmun considered the opinion a dissent based on the conference vote. If the case came out the other way, Blackmun might have to rethink his language about rejoicing in the result.

Powell shared Blackmun's note with his clerk. Hammond didn't understand why Blackmun chose to characterize his opinion as a dissent. "I don't know why he has taken this approach," Hammond wrote. "Conceivably he has done so for the same reasons that you initially did, because, without solid assurance, it appeared that the majority might lean the other way. Or it might be that he knows the outcome from conference with Justice White." Hammond thought Blackmun should withhold the draft.

Nevertheless, on Thursday Blackmun circulated the note, and it created the confusion Hammond predicted. Brennan, Heineman, and Jeffress briefly wondered whether Blackmun knew something they didn't regarding White. They concluded he didn't and that Blackmun had simply been placed in an odd position by Burger's directive and by White's silence. But no one knew anything for sure. Brennan began pacing again. With a conference scheduled for the next day, Brennan felt more worried than at any point that term. It was the eleventh hour, and White had still not said a word.

WHITE ONLY ADDED TO the mystery with his behavior at the conference on June 9. The primary subject of the meeting was whether to postpone the abortion cases until the following term. Blackmun had been pushing for reargument since the beginning of the year. *Roe* and its companion case, *Doe v. Bolton*, had been argued on December 13, three weeks before Powell and Rehnquist joined the Court. Blackmun argued that the case needed to be heard by the full bench. Only Burger agreed, and so the abortion cases moved forward, slowly.

To the liberal faction of the Court it appeared that Blackmun was dragging his feet to force reargument. It had taken him nearly five months to produce his first drafts, and those narrowly focused opinions were nightmares to the liberals, though not entirely surprising. Brennan had offered his clerks three-to-one odds that Blackmun wouldn't stick to his professed prochoice position.

Brennan, Stewart, and Marshall attempted to move the cases forward by praising Blackmun for his palatable effort in *Doe*, and ignoring his proposal to dismiss *Roe* as too speculative to warrant relief. Blackmun wasn't having it, though. On the last day of May he again moved for reargument in both *Roe* and *Doe*, "although it would prove costly to me personally, in light of energy and hours expended."

At the conference Blackmun now drew a connection between the abortion and capital cases. He noted Powell and Rehnquist's absence from the oral arguments, and the need for a maximally legitimate decision. His emphasis, though, was that the American people wouldn't tolerate the Court declaring unconstitutional both the death penalty and antiabortion laws. The justices would be seen as defending the lives of criminals while condemning the unborn. This juxtaposition occurred naturally to Blackmun, as he simultaneously worked on his *Furman* and *Roe* opinions, but the others hadn't considered it. Powell added his support to Rehnquist's and Burger's, and *Roe* was put over.

Blackmun's reference to the capital cases triggered a controversy. Douglas said his notes showed five votes to uphold the death penalty: Burger, Blackmun, Powell, Rehnquist, and White. Blackmun, whose meticulous note taking was well known, said his records showed that White had voted the other way. This was why he had circulated his opinion as a dissent. Powell and Rehnquist confirmed Blackmun's recollection. They had framed their opinions as dissents for the same reason. For several minutes the justices debated which way White had voted.

White never said a word.

LATER THAT AFTERNOON Stewart told Heineman that he was going to White's chambers. This was a resounding gesture by Stewart. During his early days on the Court, Black and Frankfurter had lobbied him relentlessly. Locked in their to-the-death battle, each man desperately wanted to cultivate Stewart as an ally. Stewart resented it, particularly Frankfurter's patronizing style, and vowed that he would never behave similarly.

But Stewart believed an exception had to be made. White was no newcomer, which distinguished the situation in his mind. More important, the cases had reached a crisis point: They needed to be decided, and Stewart wanted to win. In the months since oral argument, Stewart had become entrenched in his position. So Stewart walked to White's chambers and the two men spent the remainder of the afternoon behind closed doors.

Their conversation is lost to history. Neither man ever repeated what was said to their clerks or the other justices. They gave no interviews about it. Nevertheless they reached a clear agreement. Stewart would abandon his moral position against the death penalty and draft an opinion striking down the Georgia death penalty because of its sporadic use. White, in turn, would cast the deciding fifth vote against capital punishment, and write that the death penalty was not applied frequently enough to accomplish any social aim. The emphasis of both opinions would be on the death penalty's application.

It was a peculiar bargain. Neither man got what he wanted. It may be true that White wanted nothing, so this statement may have no meaning as applied to him, but Stewart sacrificed a great deal. He would never get to write his "short snapper." In fact his published opinion in *Furman* would take no moral position on the death penalty. Furthermore, his new position created the risk that states would respond by applying the death penalty more frequently. From Stewart's standpoint it was an uncomfortable pact. Not a deal with the devil, but to a man who claimed to oppose capital punishment, one with devilish consequences. Why Stewart made this pact is a historical puzzle. To begin to solve it, one must first attempt to understand Stewart's bargaining partner: the brilliant, incomparable, and utterly enigmatic Byron White.

CHAPTER 9

WHIZZER

F ROM HUMBLE BEGINNINGS, BYRON WHITE LIVED ONE of the extraordinary lives of the twentieth century. No one could have predicted his success. White was born in Wellington, Colorado, a tiny hamlet an hour's drive north of Denver, consisting primarily of sugar-beet farms. His father, Al, managed a lumber company. His mother, Maude, was a stay-at-home mom. Neither parent graduated from high school. Each nevertheless valued education first, and had high expectations for their two sons. Ultimately each accomplished more than any parent dared dream.

The Whites' elder son, Sam, made straight As and was valedictorian of his Wellington High School class. Sam earned a scholarship to the University of Colorado, where he excelled at football and won a Rhodes Scholarship. He later attended medical school and became a founding researcher in the field of blast biology, the study of how atomic explosions affect people over time. Colleagues regarded him as a visionary, and his research had broad implications for bomb-shelter design and treatment of radiation victims. But, as Sam said in college to anyone who would listen, "If you think I'm good, just wait until you see my little brother."

Byron admired his brother above all others and emulated him magnificently. Like Sam, Byron finished at the top of his high school class and received a full scholarship to University of Colorado, where he too excelled at football. While Sam was merely excellent at sports, Byron was stellar. He possessed an extraordinary physique. One of his friends said White "looked like a Greek god—only made of pale oak, not marble."

Whizzer, as Byron was known to his great dismay, was a consensus all-American in his senior year. Like Sam, he won a Rhodes Scholarship, but Byron went his brother one better. After the Pittsburgh Pirates football club made White their first-round draft pick, White convinced Oxford to postpone his fellowship for a semester so he could play professional football. Impossibly, during his rookie season, White led the National Football League in rushing.

Following Oxford, White attended Yale (the only law school to which he applied), with semesters off to star for the Detroit Lions. In 1943 he joined the navy and served with distinction as an intelligence officer in the Pacific theater. On the last day of his tour, a kamikaze struck his ship, a fast carrier called the *Bunker Hill*. The boat in flames, White lifted a beam to free pinned men, carried out others who were suffocating, and helped extinguish the fire.

When he returned home, White, with some assistance from his former Yale professor William Douglas, landed a clerkship in the chambers of the chief justice of the Supreme Court, Fred Vinson. Vinson had been Harry Truman's secretary of the Treasury until Harlan Fiske Stone's sudden death in 1946. Vinson and White seemed like a natural team. Vinson was an affable man and a sports enthusiast who had played semiprofessional baseball. But White was turned off by his clerkship experience. He took particular exception to Felix Frankurter's overbearing manner and to Hugo Black's result-oriented jurisprudence. When his clerkship year ended, White fled Washington and took a job practicing law in Denver.

His biography could very well have ended there. He expressed no greater aspiration than raising a family and getting his name out of the newspapers. William Douglas sometimes said similar things, threatening to retreat to Yakima or into private practice, but Douglas's protestations rang hollow given the manner in which he led his life.

With White it was all real. For fifteen years he lived entirely out of the limelight. He didn't aspire to political office or a judgeship, and only grudgingly acknowledged his athletic career. He wasn't even a litigator, the flashy sort of lawyer who shows up in court to woo juries. He was a transactional attorney, working behind the scenes on behalf of his clients. This almost certainly would have remained his destiny were it not for JFK.

White met Kennedy at Oxford, and the two struck up a casual friendship. During World War II their paths crossed again. Kennedy was also stationed in the South Pacific as commander of *PT-109*, a small motor-torpedo boat, which was infamously split in two by a Japanese destroyer and sunk near Guadalcanal. Kennedy heroically rescued the surviving members of his crew, though his earlier actions may also have contributed to the accident. As fate had it, White was charged with reviewing the incident. His account cleared Kennedy.

When Kennedy publicly ruminated about running for president in 1960, White began to think about what he could do for Kennedy. Kennedy, in turn, began to think about what White could do for him. Colorado was very much in doubt. Few people knew Kennedy, and most state party officials favored Adlai Stevenson or Missouri senator Stuart Symington. When JFK visited Colorado for the first time, in 1956, he had a four-hour layover at the airport. No one recognized him. In 1960 Kennedy asked White to run the state primary campaign for him. True to form, White delivered, and after Kennedy won the Democratic nomination, White headed Citizens for Kennedy and Johnson during the general election.

Both John and Robert Kennedy held White in high regard, and White's work on the campaign only increased their esteem for him. Both brothers wanted White to work for the administration. Bobby pushed hard for White to join him at the Department of Justice. White accepted, and served as RFK's chief deputy until JFK promoted him to the Supreme Court in 1962. In their time together, Robert Kennedy trusted White and relied on him heavily. During the Freedom Summer, White acted as the administration's point person. White's friendship with each of the Kennedy brothers endured. Soon after Lee Harvey Oswald assassinated JFK, White had a comforting arm around Bobby's shoulder. When Bobby was assassinated, his death affected White deeply, causing him to reconsider the path of his life.

White and the Kennedy brothers' mutual trust was undergirded by a shared skepticism of ideology. The Kennedys deplored dogmatic thinking and had no patience for grand theory. Harris Wofford, one of JFK's advisers, said, "I think John Kennedy's central principle in politics was his desire to see the maximum intelligence brought to bear on public problems. He had no ideology and, if anything was put off by too far-reaching ideas."

So it was with White. He deplored labels. At a meal with friends during the campaign, one of White's friends said the country needed a liberal after the Eisenhower years. White dismissed the idea. He said, "I've never understood what people mean when they say that—'liberal.' Labels mean nothing. They don't make policy and they don't decide practical problems." When a reporter asked him before his judicial confirmation hearing whether he was a liberal, White, who detested reporters, replied, "The proof will be in the judging." After the hearing another journalist asked White to define the role of the Supreme Court. "To decide cases," he said. Indeed, Bobby Kennedy said that White's substantive legal views played no role in his selection as justice. JFK simply considered White "his kind of person." This fierce resistance to ideology persisted throughout White's career. On the evening of his retirement in 1993, a reporter asked White whether he was a conservative or a centrist. White replied, "Being a conservative or a centrist is all in the minds of the speaker. It just depends on what you think—and if you think I'm one, you're right, but other people might think I'm something else and they're right."

THE IDEOLOGY OF REMAINING nonideological traced its roots all the way back to Charles Darwin. While Darwin is commonly associated with the "theory of evolution," the word "evolution" scarcely appears in Darwin's great book, and many mid-nineteenth century scientists were already "evolutionists" in the sense that they believed change in nature occurred gradually (albeit directed by God). Darwin's true sedition was to reorder the universe, as part of his larger project to undermine slavery. Since Plato, scientists had asked what species *should* look like. Darwin said they instead should ask what species actually *do* look like. His work promoted empirical study to a place of prominence it had never before enjoyed.

Others recognized that if scientific method could and should be applied to biology, it could and should be applied to other disciplines. Over time the tendrils of Darwin's insidious ideas caressed the minds of the leaders of every academic field. Notably, William James began to test behavioral questions in the laboratory. He also denied the possibility of objective knowledge, or "truth," as it had been conventionally understood. "True" beliefs were those that proved useful to the believer, James said, and truth was verifiable only insomuch as it corresponded with actual things. These ideas became, essentially, American pragmatism.

In the legal universe Darwin's influence manifested itself as legal realism. Its principal founder, Oliver Wendell Holmes, began his career as an attorney in Boston and a professor at Harvard Law School, where he joined the Metaphysical Club, a discussion group that nurtured critical, empirical thinking, founded by the Harvard mathematician Chauncey Wright. Its members included Francis Ellingwood Abbott, a philosopher who attempted to bring theology in line with scientific method; John Fiske, another philosopher whom Darwin himself called the most lucid he had ever encountered; and James. Like Darwin, Holmes deplored slavery. Holmes fought in the Civil War, and his most closely held belief, which stemmed from that experience, was that dogma was dangerous. "Certitude leads to violence," Holmes said famously. "I detest a man that knows that he knows."

In the late 1800s, no institution dominated the legal universe as much as Harvard Law School, and no individual represented claimed to know so much as Harvard's dean, Christopher Columbus Langdell.

An amateur botanist, Langdell believed that lawyering was a science and that the law could be reduced to a set of rules and principles. Harvard students learned the law by studying bound volumes of appellate court decisions, which were organized around concepts. This sort of study made sense because lawyers and judges were engaged in a scientific enterprise. Formalists, as Langdell and his followers were known, spoke of a judge "finding" or "discovering" the correct result in a particular case. In their view a judge made no law when he or she (though almost certainly he) decided a case. Public policy considerations were irrelevant, as were a judge's idiosyncratic prejudices. A formalist would say, with Calvinistic severity, that a decision reached in conflict with first principles was, simply, "wrong."

Holmes rejected all this. Darwin said that man, not God, orders the universe. Holmes said that man, not God, made law. Legal rules, he argued, are never so comprehensively written or clear cut that they dictate the result in a particular case. A decision is always a matter of interpretation, and judges, like all human beings, are affected in viewing facts by their place in society, their background, and even their mood.

Holmes laid his philosophy out most clearly in *The Common Law*, published in 1881. There he said that judges decide cases by reacting to the facts, and then work out legal reasoning to justify the outcome they want to reach. The real basis of a decision is often an "inarticulate major premise" that has nothing to do with the law. Jerome Frank, an early realist, famously said that a judge's decision might be determined by what he had for breakfast. A judicial decision is effectively a rationalization of the judge's intuitive hunch about what is right. Frank dismissed the myth of certainty as a childish effort to create a father-controlled universe.

As a Supreme Court justice, Holmes remained true to his beliefs. In 1905 Holmes memorably dissented from the Court's decision in *Lochner*, setting aside a law restricting the hours bakers could work on the basis of "liberty of contract," though it was nowhere mentioned in the Constitution. Holmes argued that the majority had enacted its own economic philosophy, not neutrally interpreted the Fourteenth Amendment as they pompously claimed. "General propositions do not decide concrete cases," he wrote. In other words, ideologies don't dictate results, results dictate ideologies. The essence of realism is that to understand the law, one needs to work from the bottom up, not the top down.

HOLMES WAS A HARVARD MAN, but Yale was where legal realism came of age, and its florescence coincided with Byron White's time there. White graduated from Yale (magna cum laude) in 1946. During the 1930s and '40s, at least a dozen prominent legal realists made their scholarly home at Yale, including two men White would later join on the Supreme Court, Douglas and Fortas. Even Yale didn't carry realism through to its logical extension, however. Until the late nineteenth century, law had been regarded as a craft, which could be mastered by apprenticing to a practitioner. The fact that Langdell's formalist universe could only be comprehended via formal academic training had profound implications for the profession. The prohibitive cost of law schools closed the door on poor would-be attorneys. For the law schools own bottom lines, however, formalism was great news. The case method was cheap. Since legal principles could be deduced from books rather than experience, law schools could employ professors rather than practitioners, and they could teach many students at once. In the 1870s Harvard Law School had a professor-student ratio of one to seventy-five.

To be consistent in its rejection of Harvard's legal philosophy, Yale would have rejected the case method. Instead Yale professors embraced the case method even as they repudiated formalism. In fact their dominant scholarly activity was revising casebooks. William Douglas wrote five, directing his efforts to studying how businesses operated in the real world. He organized his casebooks around functions rather than abstract concepts. Law, Douglas said, consists of what legal actors do in the real world. Douglas also advocated that judges end all pretense of objectivity. He thought judges should explicitly say that they were imposing their preferences through their decisions.

At Yale realist scholars branched off in many different directions. Some emphasized the importance of collecting data to show how the law functioned. A subset of this group, which included Douglas, went one step further and argued that the law should be employed to achieve desirable social outcomes. (Though one might ask, desirable to whom?) Other realists devoted their energies to exposing the ambiguities of language and the grandiosity of formalist claims that legal principles could be mathematically deduced. Some tried to find a middle ground. Realism was pervasively influential. Every lawyer accepted some of its tenets.* But it means different things to different people.

WHITE NEVER EXPOUNDED ON what realism meant to him. He said little generally, and was so fiercely anti-ideological that he would have resisted identifying himself as a realist even though it was an ideology that rejected ideology. White did, however, identify three professors who had the greatest influence on him: Arthur Corbin, Wesley Sturges, and Myres McDougal. Legal realists defy simplistic labels, but Corbin, Sturges, and McDougal were among the more conservative realists in the sense that they believed law impacted judicial behavior, a principle rejected by radical realists, and that law shouldn't be an agent of social change. They also shared a pedagogical style that emphasized meticulous attention to facts, resistance to generalities, and disdain for authoritative propositions.

---

* Realism influenced even Felix Frankfurter, the ultimate proponent of judicial restraint. In his classroom at Harvard, Frankfurter integrated history, politics, and sociology into his lectures, arguing that law could only be understood in context. This is a decidedly realist impulse. Frankfurter also supported using the law to achieve progressive ends. Where he parted ways with most realists was his position that legal change should be engineered by legislatures, not judges. Many realists regarded this position as internally contradictory. On the other hand Frankfurter had a legion of devotees, many of whom identified themselves as realists, and some of whom resided at Yale.

In attempting to quantify the influence of Corbin, Sturges, and McDougal on White, it's significant that White remained friends for years with all three. When Sturges retired, White sent a glowing encomium. "His classes were intense and consuming experiences, and his driving analysis was a kind of classroom surgery. Learn 'the law' we did, or what the cases said it was. He inoculated with a hardy skepticism and this he hoped would be lasting protection against a flabby mind operating on flabby principle." By contrast, when Fred Vinson died, White neither attended the memorial service nor participated in an oral history project devoted to the former chief justice's life.

McDougal survived White, and at the end of White's judicial career praised him for "asking the hardest questions I've ever had." He also testified to White's identification with realism. "He was a very realistic fellow," McDougal said in 1993. "He wanted to examine the facts of a particular case and the policies that are relevant to a particular case, and that is just the essence of American legal realism."

The beginning of understanding Byron White thus is to understand that he didn't want to be understood. David Frederick, a former White clerk said, "Being non-ideological and non-doctrinaire was clearly very important to White, just as was being his own person and not worrying about his place in history." Another clerk said White's judicial philosophy is best found in "the elusive originality embedded in the particular." White took realism's skepticism regarding classifications to a different level. His attempt to defy all labels, schools, and intellectual boxes was a conscious effort to remain unpredictable. David Kendall, a former LDF attorney who played a key role in litigating *Gregg*, was one of White's clerks for the 1971–72 term. Kendall said, "White grew up thinking law was not this thing in the sky that you derive by the Langdell method." He would arrive at decisions by "inductive reasoning." This meant, "With each case, White would spread a deck of cards with every conceivable factual variation. He tried to resolve those variations, narrowing them, and work inductively to what the rule in the case should be. He would ask a number of questions about a situation and vary it a little bit, then a little bit more. White believed law could be discerned by looking carefully at consequences."

At times White went to extremes to avoid being pigeonholed. His opinions were often obfuscatory. During the 1971 term a clerk presented White with a draft. "You write very well. Justice Jackson had that problem too," White told the clerk, and then rewrote the opinion to make it more opaque. White was known to remove legal reasoning from opinions drafted by his clerks. This occurred most famously in *Pennsylvania v. Union Gas Co.*, a decision upholding a lawsuit against the state of Pennsylvania. Three justices felt the case violated the Eleventh Amendment's guarantee of sovereign immunity. Four justices, including Brennan, felt that Congress had the right to override that immunity. In casting the deciding vote, White wrote, "I agree with the conclusion reached by Justice Brennan, although I do not agree with much of his reasoning. Accordingly, I would affirm." The concurrence is law school legend.

From his very first case on the bench, *Robinson v. California*, White made clear that he intended to walk his own path. Lawrence Robinson was a heroin addict convicted under a California law making it criminal for a person to "be addicted to the use of narcotics." By six to two the Court held that the statute criminalized illness and was hence cruel and unusual. Stewart wrote the majority opinion, and analogized California's law to the criminalization of mental illness or leprosy. The state, Stewart said, couldn't punish the status of addiction.

White loosed a withering, sarcastic dissent. Writing solely for himself, he accused the majority of misstating the issue. Robinson, White said, hadn't been convicted for his status as an addict. The record showed he had last used drugs eight days before his arrest. Given this evidence of self-control, the state could reasonably conclude that he wasn't beyond help. White ridiculed the Court's interpretation of the Eighth Amendment. "I deem this application of cruel and unusual punishment so novel that I suspect the court is hard put to find a way to ascribe to the Framers of the Constitution the result reached today."

This was a jab at Black and his crusade to extend the Bill of Rights to its fullest possible limit.

The opinion set the tone for his judicial career. During White's first decade on the Court, he dissented from almost all of the Warren Court's landmark decisions expanding the constitutional rights of criminal defendants. With Harlan and Stewart, he demurred from *Miranda*. White wrote a stinging opinion suggesting that because of the new required warnings, a killer would be returned to the streets and kill again. He dissented in *Malloy v. Hogan*, which held that the privilege against self-incrimination applied to the states. He dissented from *Massiah v. United States*, which excluded confessions elicited by police after formal charges had been filed. He dissented yet again in *Escobedo v. United States*, holding that criminal suspects have a right to an attorney during a police interrogation. He publicly criticized *Mapp v. Ohio*, a historic decision extending the exclusionary rule to federal courts. To Earl Warren's biographer Bernard Schwartz, White said, "I wasn't exactly in his inner circle."

On privacy rights White's record would be enigmatic. He voted with the majority in *Griswold*, the watershed 1965 decision striking down a Connecticut law prohibiting the use of contraceptives. But he dissented from *Roe v. Wade* and every subsequent case recognizing a woman's right to terminate a pregnancy. He was intensely critical of the reasoning in *Roe*. White told Ira Rothgerber, his closest friend, that he viewed *Roe* as "the only illegitimate decision the Court rendered during his tenure." White said, "In every other case, there was something in the Constitution you could point to for support. There, nothing."

Similar contradictions abounded. White strongly opposed discrimination on the basis of sex, but in 1986 wrote the majority opinion in *Bowers v. Hardwick*, upholding Georgia's ban on sodomy. He called the claim that the Constitution gave homosexuals the right to engage in sodomy "at best facetious." Under the First Amendment he said pornography wasn't speech, but later voted to protect nude dancing, which he said had an "expressive component." He supported ending segregation in public schools under *Brown*, but dissented from a decision holding that federal law also prohibited discrimination in private schools.

At the end of White's career, Powell said he thought that White's rightward drift would have "disappointed President Kennedy." But calling White a conservative would be too simplistic. With respect to race, White supported affirmative action and consistently voted to uphold *Brown* and enforce its mandate. On the other hand, in *McCleskey v. Kemp*, White joined the majority in rejecting a challenge to Georgia's death penalty on the basis of statistical evidence of racism.

He defied conventional explanation.

MANY LEGAL SCHOLARS CONDEMNED White for lacking a guiding vision. In an op-ed in the *New York Times*, Yale professor Robert Cover suggested that White had been better as a running back. After White retired in 1993, Cover's colleague Bruce Ackerman said White "had the arduous sincerity of a fellow out of his depth." Jeffrey Rosen, the influential legal critic of the *New Republic*, dismissed White as "uninterested in articulating a constitutional vision." Rosen ridiculed White, with whom he had interviewed for a clerkship, for asking him superficial questions about his physical fitness and marital status. White's defenders had little to point to other than his commitment to judicial minimalism. Responding to Rosen, Harvard's Mary Ann Glendon pointed out that legal journalism offer no awards "for ordinary heroism." She wrote, "What made White hard to classify, of course, were the very qualities that made him an able and conscientious judge—his independence and his faithfulness to a modest conception of the judicial role."

Rosen argued that White's jurisprudence, such as it was, could only be understood by his need to prove himself the smartest guy in the room. "White's jurisprudence was essentially reactive and obsessed with scoring points," Rosen wrote. "Rather than defending his own positions, he focused his energies on attacking the arguments of his opponents." Rosen's argument cannot be dismissed easily. From the beginning of his academic career, White worked tirelessly to prove his intellectual credentials. At his fraternity house in college, he took the outrageous step of trying to have study hours enforced. At Yale his work ethic was notorious: He studied fourteen hours a day. Decades later, classmates vividly recalled White's slope-shouldered figure, green eyeshade in place, reading in the library for hours on end. One classmate called White's relentless concentration "eerie."

Perhaps White's work ethic was inbred, a product of his competitive instincts. Perhaps it stemmed from his desire to live up to his brother's enormous reputation. Perhaps it was born of insecurity about his sports career. Part of White believed that because he had been a star athlete, no one took him seriously as a lawyer. He went to lengths to distance himself from his football-playing past. White's biographer and former law clerk, Dennis Hutchinson, tells the story of then–deputy attorney general White out for lunch at Hammel's, a restaurant near the Department of Justice Building. As the waitress poured the coffee, she looked at White and asked, "Say, aren't you Whizzer White?"

White replied softly, "I was."

White's behavior on the Court could often be explained only as an effort to prove his intellectual superiority. He could also be petulant and petty. It's almost impossible to reconcile White's protection of nude dancing other than as a personal intellectual joust with Rehnquist and Scalia, with whom White voted consistently for many years but fell away from at the end of his career. Like a detective, White sought to find obscure facts in cases, subtle procedural points that might make a difference, and spring them upon his colleagues. Spaeth and Altfeld's research on judicial influence concluded that White influenced no one and was influenced by no one.

His conduct with his clerks had the same overtones of competiveness. He boasted to his clerks, "I never agonized over a case in my life"—although Rex Lee, later president of Brigham Young University, said White routinely wavered. He would sometimes challenge his clerks to see who could write an opinion the fastest. Late into life he played basketball with the clerks, who feared his brutish elbows.

Robert Deitz recalled White as exceedingly unpleasant. He might talk about sports but never about court business. His mission in life appeared to be to vanquish others.

The influence of legal realism and a desire to impress are not mutually exclusive. Rather, they are mutually reinforcing. Legal realism's demand for nuance and factual specificity would appeal to a young man who wanted to demonstrate his superior intelligence. To someone invested in being an intellectual maverick, realism would give a philosophical basis to justify his natural proclivity.

WHEN STEWART WENT TO MEET with White on the afternoon of June 9, he could hardly have been surprised that White had staked out an idiosyncratic position on the death penalty. Stewart knew White well. They had been one year apart at Yale, and had served together on the bench for a decade. Stewart would have foreseen that White would reject the views of the other members of the majority.

The concept of human dignity, central to Brennan's opinion, would not have appealed to a realist. It was abstract and sounded too much like religious dogma. Oliver Wendell Holmes had rejected an objective notion of human dignity, writing to his friend Harold Laski, "You respect the rights of man. I don't, except those things a given crowd will fight for—which vary from religion to the price of a glass of beer. I also would fight for some things—but instead of saying that they ought to be I merely say that they are part of the kind of world that I like—or should like."

So, too, White would have rejected Marshall's categorical rejection of retribution as an end of punishment, just as he would have rejected a blanket endorsement of the principle. Either position was, again, too dogmatic. It was up to states to determine the aims of punishment. White shared Douglas's concern with arbitrariness, but inductive reasoning proved that the death penalty couldn't be rejected solely because it was used disproportionately against southern blacks and the poor. If the Court set aside capital punishment on this basis, how could it not also set aside other punishments, which were surely also discriminatorily imposed? This would lead to anarchy. It was easy to guess what White would reject. Guessing what he would support was more complicated.

White told Stewart that he objected to the death penalty because states used it too infrequently to achieve any legitimate social goal. On what those ends might be, he saw no limit. A state could embrace the death penalty for retribution or deterrence or simply because it didn't want to spend money to house dangerous criminals. It wasn't the Court's place to judge these ends. But the Court could assess whether a punishment related rationally to the legislature's stated objective. On this score the death penalty failed. Because states executed so few criminals, capital punishment couldn't act as a deterrent. It couldn't achieve retributive justice since it treated an unlucky few much more harshly than others. And it couldn't incapacitate on any meaningful scale.

It was the sort of argument only White could make: brilliant, grounded in the facts of the case, nonideological—and perhaps finally more invested in scoring points than making good law. It embraced no philosophical position on the death penalty. White simply argued that the death penalty had to help achieve whatever goal the state embraced, and no goal was advanced by the practice of executing a few randomly selected criminals.

Stewart immediately saw the obvious response. States could evade White's criticism by executing more people. A mandatory death penalty would be a complete response to White's critique. White, however, wouldn't budge. He wouldn't consider taking a blanket position against capital punishment. If the tenuous majority in *Furman* proposed an outright ban on the death penalty, White would go with Powell and vote to uphold the Georgia statute.

It was thus White's road or none at all. Clearly Brennan and Marshall weren't going to be persuaded to compromise, and Douglas had become entrenched in his own position in the way that only he could. On the other side none of the Nixon appointees was going to budge either. If a compromise was to be struck, it would have to be between Stewart and White.

Stewart had hoped to express his basic moral sentiment about capital punishment, and Stewart found the threat of mandatory death penalty statutes even more morally repugnant than the Georgia death penalty scheme. But he needed to decide where to put his chips. For a variety of reasons Stewart thought that even an imperfect opinion, written along the lines White proposed, would end the death penalty in America. Even if a few states wrote new statutes, Stewart doubted they would make the death penalty mandatory. All the evidence suggested that public opinion was turning against the death penalty. It had been five years since the last execution in the United States. It hardly seemed possible that states would polish their electric chairs and start executing criminals again.

Stewart had been wrong before, of course. He had thought *Witherspoon* would nudge the states toward abolition. That hadn't worked out, but *Witherspoon* had slowed things down. Stewart believed that America needed one final push. Furthermore, time was running out. The term was almost over, and the brief history of constitutional litigation of the death penalty showed how quickly things could change on the Supreme Court. The fragile majority that existed to strike down the death penalty might never form again.

So Potter Stewart signed on. Stewart told White that he would articulate a narrower basis for the decision, and suggested that neither of them address mandatory sentences in their opinions. This appealed to White, and the two men agreed to write their opinions along these lines.

CHAPTER 10

LIGHTNING BOLTS

W HEN STEWART RETURNED TO HIS CHAMBER THE
clerks immediately knew that the tectonics of the case
had shifted. "When he came back, Stewart had basically taken the
due-process position," Heineman recalled. Soon the entire courthouse
knew something big was brewing. Stewart's and White's chambers had
shifted into high gear. Early Friday evening Heineman asked Brennan's clerks for their research on mandatory death penalty statutes. On
Saturday one of White's clerks visited Brennan's chambers to borrow
other research. Brennan's clerks concluded that White was writing,
though White's clerk denied this. Over the weekend all three of Stewart's clerks were in the office. One reported to Brennan's clerks that
Stewart was writing, but said he had been sworn to secrecy and could
say no more.

Indeed, Stewart was writing. He had pitched camp in his study,
staring out at the trees in his backyard, but he found little peace. The
opinion wouldn't flow easily. Stewart's deal with White constrained
him from saying what he wanted to say. Furthermore, the case had
evolved so peculiarly that Stewart felt an obligation to many people.
Stewart's drafts from the weekend reflect substantial inner turmoil.

Because so little time remained before the end of the term, Stewart's
opinion needed to be short. He couldn't recapitulate the complicated

historical issues involved. Stewart felt the need to explain this, and his first draft began, "The opinions of other Justices have set out in admirable and thorough detail the origin and judicial history of the Eighth Amendment and the origin and history of capital punishment. I simply express gratitude and admiration for the tasks the authors of these opinions performed." This would become the third paragraph of his final opinion, absent the "gratitude" sentence, which he deleted. The final opinion would begin with what originally began the second paragraph: "The penalty of death differs from all other forms of criminal punishment, not in degree but in kind. It is unique in its absolute renunciation of all that is embodied in our concept of humanity."

Stewart's heart may have been with Brennan and Marshall, but he devoted more space to praising Powell. This flowed from his commitment not to express a moral view. On the law Powell had the most coherent position, and Stewart praised him twice. Stewart explained that the issue before the Court was a narrow one, and not "whether in the words of my Brother Powell, capital punishment is unconstitutional for all crimes and under all circumstances." He wrote, "If that were the question before us, I would be hard put to disagree with Mr. Justice Powell's thoroughly documented position, premised as it is upon the root principles of stare decisis,* federalism, judicial restraint and—most importantly—separation of powers."

Stewart's internal conflict manifested itself most dramatically with respect to mandatory statutes. The issue wasn't before the Court, so Stewart could have ignored it, but his conscience compelled him to admit that his position might authorize a mandatory death penalty. His angst was palpable. "I should suppose that a legislature could rationally determine that certain criminal conduct was so atrocious that society's interest in deterrence wholly outweighs any consideration of reform or rehabilitation, and that despite inconclusive empirical evidence, only the penalty of death will provide maximum deterrence."

---

* The doctrine of following rules established in prior decisions; this is essentially the doctrine of precedent. In Latin, "to stand by things decided."

In the final draft Stewart added the word "automatic" before "penalty" to make clear he meant mandatory statutes.

While Powell earned praise, Stewart distanced himself from Marshall. "I cannot agree with Mr. Justice Marshall that retribution is an impermissible ingredient of punishment," Stewart wrote. "The instinct for retribution is part of the nature of man, and channeling that instinct in the administration of criminal justice serves an important purpose in promoting the stability of a society governed by law." Later Stewart thought better of the personal reference to Marshall, and deleted it.

Stewart readily discredited the other majority opinions, but he found it more difficult to explain his own position. Why was the death penalty unconstitutional? As Stewart sought for language to illustrate the arbitrariness of the statutes before the Court, he settled on the words "capricious," "wanton," and "freakish," and the metaphor that would come to represent *Furman*. "Death sentences are cruel and unusual in the same way that being struck by lightning is cruel and unusual," Stewart wrote. "For, of all the thousands of people convicted of rapes and murders, in the last ten years just as reprehensible as these, the petitioners are among a capriciously selected handful upon whom the sentence of death has been imposed." Stewart concluded, "My concurring Brothers have demonstrated that if any basis can be discerned for the selection of those few sentenced to die, it is the constitutionally impermissible basis of race. But racial discrimination has not been proved and I put it to one side. I simply conclude that the Eighth Amendment cannot tolerate the deliberate extinguishment of life under legal systems that permit death sentences to be so wantonly and freakishly imposed."

This language remained largely intact except for minor changes to the time period, which changed from "the last ten years" to "1967 and 1968," and the reference to thousands, which Stewart deleted. In the end Stewart softened "deliberate extinguishment of life" to "the penalty of death." Little else changed. This opinion, which set the course of the death penalty in the United States for forty years, was written, more or less, in two days.

✦   ✦   ✦   ✦

DURING THE REMAINDER OF the weekend, Stewart fought off his clerks' efforts to salvage what they could from the situation. Heineman and Jeffress each felt that Stewart could say less regarding mandatory statutes. "The language commits you more firmly than you need to be committed to the validity of mandatory death penalty statutes," Heineman told Stewart. He also questioned whether the retribution discussion might be "replaced by a more tentative statement." "After all," he said, "except perhaps for Marshall, no one says that retribution is not a permissible goal of punishment." Heineman also suggested revising or removing the sentence beginning "for I should suppose." Why did Stewart need to suggest that the death penalty might be an effective deterrent?

Finally Heineman questioned Stewart's central metaphor. "Is the bolt of lightning image the correct one?" Heineman asked. "The lightning bolt is random, but is it arbitrary in the sense we mean when talking about executions?" It wasn't as if the death penalty were applied randomly among citizens. Executions were random among murderers. Perhaps a better analogy would have been to the unlucky few struck by lightning while holding up a golf club in a thunderstorm.

White was pushing Stewart in a different direction, however. Over the weekend the two justices spoke and exchanged drafts. White's first draft so tenuously opposed the death penalty that it seemed to endorse mandatory sentences. As a compromise Stewart proposed to include further language complimentary of Powell's opinion if White would change his language regarding mandatory sentences.* White agreed.

Despite their modest victories, Stewart's clerks weren't happy. They felt that their boss's opinion was even weaker than White's, which was really saying something. White's clerks were discouraged by their own

---

* In his final opinion, Stewart's favorable references to Powell softened somewhat. The key sentence—that Stewart would be "hard put to disagree" with Powell's "thoroughly documented position"—didn't appear, and the characterization of deterrence was weakened substantially, as Heineman had suggested.

boss's opinion, which contained no footnotes and seemed not nearly as carefully written as White's usual work. Furthermore, even with the negotiated changes, White's opinion only tepidly rejected capital punishment. He made the limits of his opinion clear from the start. "In joining the Court's judgments, I do not at all intimate that the death penalty is unconstitutional per se or that there is no system of capital punishment that would comport with the Eighth Amendment. That question, ably argued by several of my Brethren, is not presented by these cases and need not be decided." White's clerks tried to get him to drop the words "at all," but he refused.

White made clear that his sole concern was the infrequent use of the death penalty, and not because sporadic application suggested racism or classism. The sole problem with a rarely used death penalty was that it couldn't accomplish any aim of criminal justice. "I begin with what I consider a near truism," he wrote. "The death penalty could so seldom be imposed that it would cease to be a credible deterrent or measurably to contribute to any other end of punishment in the criminal justice system." Though White's opinion no longer explicitly invited mandatory statutes, it did invite states to impose the death penalty more frequently, which hardly seemed better.

WHILE WHITE AND STEWART drafted, negotiated, and revised through the weekend, Brennan remained in the dark. Stewart hadn't spoken with him since saying that he planned to speak with White. Brennan took this as a bad sign. On Monday, thought, Larry Hammond told Brennan's clerks that Powell thought White and Stewart were going to vote against the death penalty. Only a few days earlier, Hammond had said Powell believed White and Stewart would join his opinion. Brennan didn't know what to believe.

In his chambers Brennan's clerks continued to revise part three of their boss's opinion. After abandoning the effort to persuade Powell, the opinion had been restructured. The new first part was intended to show that the death penalty cases were "run of the mill," as the clerks put it.

The Court had every right to decide the issue. Any other view would render the cruel and unusual punishments clause "little more than good advice." The second part presented the four-part test for determining the cruelty of a punishment. The third part applied the test to the death penalty. A punishment didn't have to be completely degrading or completely offensive to be unconstitutional. It was sufficient that it be substantially degrading and offensive. Brennan's clerks regarded this as the weakest point of the opinion. They also recognized that the opinion would never be perfect. By Tuesday, the thirteenth, they had resolved to let it go.

That afternoon, Ben Heineman called and said to expect a "real surprise." At approximately four o'clock, Heineman delivered drafts of both Stewart and White's opinions. "It isn't everything," Heineman said, "but it's better than nothing." Brennan sat down in the clerks' office and read the opinions aloud, starting with White's. They immediately recognized that White's opinion opened the door to mandatory statutes. This didn't bother Brennan or his clerks. Given where White had started, they couldn't have hoped for any more, and neither Brennan nor his clerks believed states would pass mandatory statutes. Even if they did, there was every reason to believe the Court would strike them down. Within the realm of the possible, White's opinion was the best imaginable.

Stewart's opinion was more sobering. Brennan saw what Stewart had sacrificed to make a deal with White; the opinion was a far cry from the promised short snapper. Stewart, like White, didn't suggest that the death penalty was unconstitutional. Like White, too, he said the problem was the infrequent application of the death penalty. Stewart, though, went further than White in opening the door to mandatory sentences. If mandatory sentences "were the question before us," Stewart wrote, "It would not be easy for me to conclude, in light of those principles, that no legislature could ever constitutionally specify death as the penalty for certain designated criminal conduct."* Quietly Brennan said to his clerks, "Potter had to pay a price to get Byron."

---

* The fate of this language is a mystery. Brennan's clerks mention it in their case history, but the language doesn't appear in the final version of Stewart's opinion.

✦ ✦ ✦ ✦

AFTER WHITE AND STEWART circulated their opinions, everyone on the Court understood what had happened. On his copy of
Stewart's draft, next to the complaint that the death penalty was
unconstitutional because it was imposed in a wanton and freakish
manner, Blackmun jotted, "Oh, now, PS." It was now clear which side
would prevail, and the justices in the minority circled their wagons.
On Wednesday, Blackmun indicated that he would sign on to Burger,
Powell and Rehnquist's opinions, in a document known on the Court
as a "join memo." The same day Powell sent join memos to Blackmun,
Burger, and Rehnquist. On Thursday, the fifteenth, Rehnquist recip-
rocated Powell's gesture and also joined Burger. The next day Burger
joined Blackmun, Powell, and Rehnquist.

Rehnquist had displayed no doubts about the death penalty since
joining the Court, and he didn't now. His opinion was simple and to
the point. "The Court's judgments today strike down a penalty that
our Nation's legislators have thought necessary since our country was
founded. My Brothers Douglas, Brennan, and Marshall would at one
fell swoop invalidate laws enacted by Congress and forty state legislatures." Rehnquist acknowledged that Stewart and White had relied on
different reasoning, but this didn't cure the central problem. "Whatever its precise rationale, today's holding brings into sharp relief the
fundamental question of the role of judicial review in a democratic
society. How can government by the elected representatives of the
people co-exist with the power of the federal judiciary, whose members are constitutionally insulated from responsiveness to the popular
will, to declare invalid laws duly enacted by the popular branches of
government?"

Unlike Blackmun and Burger, Rehnquist offered no apologies for
his opinion. He didn't proclaim that he would oppose the death penalty if he were a legislator, as Blackmun did, and he didn't join Blackmun's dissent. Marshall had cited the risk of executing an innocent
person in his litany of arguments against the death penalty—"we have

no way of judging how many innocent persons have been executed but we can be certain that there were some." Rehnquist turned this argument on its head. The more worrisome error was mistakenly ruling a statute unconstitutional. "Human error there is bound to be, judges being men and women, and men and women being what they are," Rehnquist wrote. "But an error in mistakenly sustaining the constitutionality of a particular enactment, while wrongfully depriving the individual of a right, nonetheless does so by simply letting stand a duly enacted law. The error resulting from a mistaken upholding of an individual's constitutional claim is more serious. For the result in such a case," he said, "is to impose upon the Nation the judicial fiat of a majority of a court of judges whose connection with the popular will is remote at best."

The only open question among the other Nixon appointees was whether to endorse Blackmun's repudiation of the death penalty as public policy. Powell had praised Blackmun's opinion as "superb—sensitive, well written, and unanswerable," and had sent a join memo. But on Saturday, June 17, Powell informed Blackmun that he wouldn't join his opinion after all. "As you know, I have the greatest admiration for what you have said so eloquently," Powell wrote, but he wouldn't sign on to the opinion because of "its manifest personal character." Shortly thereafter Burger and Rehnquist formally told Blackmun that they wouldn't join either. In the end Blackmun would be alone among the Nixon appointees in expressing moral reservations about the death penalty. But this hardly seemed to matter. The death penalty was on its way out.

THE JUSTICES HAVE LONG had a saying, "An agreement is one thing, an announced decision is another." With Bill Douglas on the bench, this adage took on new significance.

The lack of a meeting of the minds among the justices in the majority created an uncommon procedural problem. Usually a line of reasoning persuades at least a plurality of the Court. This becomes the central—

lawyers would say "controlling"—rationale. In *Furman*, however, no such rationale prevailed. In fact, no opinion had persuaded even a single other member of the majority. Thus no opinion could be said to be controlling. The Court needed to explain its holding, so the majority decided to lay out the procedural outcome of the cases in a short, collective statement called a *per curiam*.* Midweek, Brennan circulated a simple draft to the other justices in the majority.

On Thursday, the fifteenth, Douglas telephoned Brennan and approved the proposed language. To Brennan it sounded like business as usual. By this time Douglas had retreated to his summer home in Goose Prairie. His absence angered some of the other justices. *Furman* was an important case to say the least. But Douglas's mind was made up, both about the case and his summer vacation, and he claimed to be frustrated with White's delay. Since leaving, Douglas had said very little about the case, and nothing about the agreement between White and Stewart. Brennan expected no trouble since the cases were going the way Douglas wanted.

On Friday, however, Douglas called Brennan in a state of agitation. That Douglas called on consecutive days was noteworthy in itself since the nearest phone was thirty miles from his Goose Prairie hideaway. Douglas had read the opinions overnight and worked himself into a frenzy. Douglas still harbored resentment over losing *McGautha*. Having had the opportunity to absorb White and Stewart's opinions, he couldn't stop obsessing about the inconsistency between their positions in *Furman* and what they had said in *McGautha*. How could Stewart and White say that the Fourteenth Amendment didn't require standards, but then attack the Georgia death penalty scheme for being standardless?

The inconsistency, of course, stemmed from the great compromise. If Stewart had issued his snapper, Douglas would have had no cause to quarrel. Douglas could have disagreed with Stewart's reasoning and he could have continued to fault him for his vote in *McGautha*,

---

* Latin for "by the court."

but there would have been no inconsistency between his positions in *Furman* and *McGautha*. The Eighth Amendment unlike the Fourteenth invited moral judgments. But Stewart hadn't taken an ethical position. Following his agreement with White, Stewart had taken a procedural concern—arbitrariness—and presented it as an Eighth Amendment problem. This contradicted *McGautha*, which held that the Constitution didn't require standards, the best check against arbitrariness.

To make matters worse, neither Stewart nor White had explained the inconsistency. Stewart referenced *McGautha* only once, in the twelfth footnote to his opinion, and not very satisfyingly: "We expressly declined in that case to consider claims under the constitutional guarantee against cruel and unusual punishment." This hardly explained how a procedural argument, rejected in a due-process case, had become, just one year later, a winner in an Eighth Amendment case. White made no effort to explain the contradiction. When White read the draft of his opinion to his clerks, one of them said that he thought it overruled *McGautha* without saying so. The justice scowled as the other clerks waved to their colleague to drop the point. White's final opinion made no mention of *McGautha*.

On the phone Douglas told Brennan that he couldn't abide this and would attack White and Stewart for their flip-flop. Brennan urged Douglas to drop the issue. However clumsily, the Court had reached the result Douglas favored. Furthermore White and Stewart's reasoning came closer to Douglas's than either his or Marshall's did. Racism, the focus of Douglas's opinion, was another type of arbitrariness. What could be accomplished by exposing Stewart and White? Doing so would be solely an act of spite with potentially disastrous consequences.

Douglas said that he didn't care. He told Brennan that he didn't believe White would vote against the death penalty in the end. It seemed impossible that Douglas could believe this since White had already circulated his opinion. Nevertheless, Douglas said that he thought White would ultimately vote with the Nixon appointees.

Douglas wasn't the only one who thought this. Powell still hoped that White would turn around at the eleventh hour.

After he hung up Brennan dispatched his clerks to Douglas's chambers. Sure enough, Douglas's clerk, Richard Jacobson, reported that a missive would be coming, attacking Stewart and White for their inconsistency.* Brennan's clerks asked Jacobson to share whatever Douglas wrote before Douglas published anything. Jacobson agreed.

Later in the day Jacobson delivered a copy of Douglas's draft. Years later Brennan's clerks recalled it as violent. They pleaded with Jacobson to try to tone it down. In a bizarre sequence of events, possible only in Douglas's dysfunctional chambers, Jacobson revised the opinion and pouched it to Goose Prairie. Douglas then reviewed it and communicated his satisfaction with the revision not to his clerk but to Brennan, the only person Douglas deemed worthy of telephoning from Washington State.

The modified language would become the eleventh footnote to Douglas's opinion. "I should think that if the Eighth Amendment prohibits the imposition of the death penalty on petitioners because they are among a capriciously selected random handful upon whom the sentence of death has been imposed"—as Stewart argued in his opinion—or because "there is no meaningful basis for distinguishing the few cases in which the death penalty is imposed from the many cases in which it is not"—as White had argued—"statements with which I am in complete agreement, then the Fourteenth Amendment would render unconstitutional capital sentencing procedures that are purposely constructed to allow the maximum possible variation."

This modified statement posed less of a threat. It wasn't personal. As rewritten by Jacobson, the footnote's main point seemed to be that *McGautha* had been wrongly decided, not that White and Stewart

---

* Douglas hadn't communicated this directly to Jacobson, with whom Douglas refused to speak. Years later Jacobson couldn't recall why, though this isn't as odd as it might seem. Each term Douglas ostracized a member of his staff. The prior year it had been Dennis Brown, though neither Brown nor anyone else ever knew why. During the 1971 term Jacobson was the odd man out.

were hypocrites. "The tension between our decision today and *McGautha* highlights, in my view, the correctness of Mr. Justice Brennan's dissent in that case, which I joined," Jacobson wrote on Douglas's behalf. Still, Supreme Court justices had thin skins. Brennan held his breath and waited for White's and Stewart's reactions.

From Brennan's standpoint, the worst didn't come to pass. After reviewing the revised draft of Douglas's opinion, Stewart said the new language didn't bother him. Stewart reiterated that he saw the Eighth and Fourteenth Amendment issues as distinct, Douglas's footnote notwithstanding. He wouldn't change his opinion. As for White, an oblique charge of intellectual inconsistency wasn't cause for him to waver.

After several days, when it became clear that White's vote was indeed secure, Brennan finally exhaled a sigh of relief. The reality hit home when Brennan had a short word about the capital cases with Burger. The Chief spoke of the decision as a fait accompli. With apparent sincerity Burger told Brennan that he wished the Court had struck down the death penalty completely. While he disagreed with the decision from a constitutional standpoint, Burger said he also felt some measure of relief at the prospect of finally resolving the issue. Death penalty cases took up a disproportionate amount of the Court's time. In Burger's view, however, the Stewart-White compromise meant that the death penalty question soon would return. "I had hoped it was all behind us," Burger told Brennan, "and even though I thought the decision would be wrong, I was really relieved. But now we will get it all back." States would enact mandatory death sentences for certain crimes, Burger said, and he expected that the Court would uphold these new statutes.

Brennan didn't agree with either aspect of the Chief's predictions: Warren Burger didn't exactly have his finger on the pulse of America. What Brennan took from the conversation was that the white flag had been waved. *Furman* was over. Brennan related the conversation to his clerks and, with a shake of his head, said he couldn't believe that just one year ago his had been the only vote to rule the death penalty unconstitutional.

✦ ✦ ✦ ✦

On Monday, June 19, the justices agreed to hand the cases down the following week. Each of the dissenters said they wanted time to revise to respond to Stewart and White's opinions. In turn Stewart and White said they might have to respond to the responses. Brennan's sense of closure dissolved. Every day the Court waited to announce its opinion gave White additional opportunities to change his mind. The sooner the Court got the decision out, the better.

Throughout the week rumors circulated that Burger and Powell were going to deliver strong attacks against Stewart. At a conference on Thursday, June 22, Stewart said that if such an attack were to come, he would need ample time to respond, no matter how long this delayed the cases. Brennan now had another issue to worry about. Then, at a group lunch on Friday, Burger proudly told his colleagues that the opening sentence of his revised opinion would be, "The Court holds today that the death penalty is not unconstitutional in all cases."

"You can't correctly say that," Powell said.

"Well, this will flush it out," the Chief replied.

Stewart and White said they would wait until they saw the actual sentence before deciding how to respond. Stewart said, though, that if Burger published the sentence he proposed at lunch, then he would definitely revise his own opinion in response. Once again the prospect of substantial delay loomed. From Brennan's point of view, Stewart and White's posture at lunch offered the only silver lining: Neither showed any sign of wavering; to the contrary, Burger's proposal got their dander up.

After lunch Powell retreated to his chambers, despondent and discouraged. He entered Hammond's office and sat down in an overstuffed leather chair, reserved for these visits.

"I have lost the Court," Powell said quietly.

Hammond could see the anguish on Powell's face. Powell claimed not to have held a strong view at the start of the case, but over the course of the year he had become convinced of his position. Lawyers often become invested in the correctness of their arguments; in Powell's case the disappointment ran deeper because it was his first case on the bench. Once he had taken a position and advocated among his brethren for the result he favored, Powell wanted to win. By nature lawyers are competitive, and Powell was no exception.

Hammond felt bad for his boss but pleased at the same time. He was by now completely convinced that Georgia's death penalty statute should be rejected.* Hammond tried not to show his delight. But, by his own assessment, Hammond had a poor poker face, and it apparently betrayed his sense of relief.

Powell took note, and said, sadly, "You're not with me, are you?"

Hammond shook his head. For the remainder of the day Hammond obsessed about the encounter. Before leaving for the evening, he tendered his resignation to Powell. Generally they spoke every day, even on Saturdays and Sundays, but the following weekend Powell was silent. Hammond figured this meant the obvious, and that his resignation would be accepted.

WHILE POWELL REFLECTED ABOUT the case and what to do about Hammond, on Saturday, Burger sent around his revised opinion, now clearly marked as a dissent. The advertised opening sentence didn't appear. Rather, Burger strengthened the parts of his opinions telling states how they might respond to the Court's decision. One possibility was to enact mandatory statues. Another, he said, was to

---

* Fighting the death penalty would become the defining cause of Larry Hammond's life. Following his clerkship Hammond became an assistant special prosecutor for the Watergate investigation and then held a top position in Jimmy Carter's Justice Department. After entering private practice in Arizona, Hammond helped found the Arizona Justice Project, which offers representation to poor defendants in capital cases. In 2010 Hammond won the Morris Dees Justice Award from the University of Alabama for his work.

guide jury discretion: "Legislative bodies may seek to bring their laws into compliance with the Court's ruling by providing standards for juries and judges to follow or by more narrowly defining the crimes for which the penalty is imposed."

This point could be debated in light of *McGautha*, but Burger framed *McGautha* as being primarily about the impossibility of constructing standards, rather than their undesirability. Burger recalled that Harlan had said the factors involved in sentencing were too complex to be reduced to a formula. It was still worth a shot, Burger said: "If such standards can be devised or the crimes more meticulously defined, the result cannot be detrimental." Once again Brennan and his clerks worried that Stewart and White would be tempted to reply. Surely they hadn't intended to invite states to develop new standards.

On Monday, however, White said that he wouldn't respond to Burger. His opinion would remain exactly as written. Later Stewart said that he also wouldn't respond to the Chief. Both Stewart and White said they didn't want to give Burger an opportunity to delay the cases further. At a conference that afternoon the justices agreed that the decisions would come down on Thursday, the twenty-ninth, provided that the print shop could meet the deadline. This was a substantial challenge given that Powell still hadn't circulated his final draft and that the opinions now collectively ran over six hundred pages. Brennan skeptically reported the proposed schedule to his clerks: "I'll believe it when I see it."

Later that afternoon Powell circulated his new draft, but it contained no major revisions. Powell had apparently done some soul-searching over the weekend. The only change he made to his opinion was to add an opening section that summarized the rationales laid out by the individual members of the majority and his conclusion that these rationales, neither individually nor collectively, offered a sound basis for rejecting Georgia's death penalty statute. Powell said states should be allowed to decide the issue. "The majority's ruling encroaches upon an area squarely within the historic prerogative of the legislative branch. It is the very sort of judgment for which the judiciary is ill-equipped. I can recall no case in which this Court has subordinated national and local democratic processes to such an extent." Powell's revision was hardly a bombshell. Around the same time Powell handed Hammond a letter rejecting his resignation. Instead he asked Hammond to stay on for an additional year. Hammond agreed.

On Tuesday morning Stewart circulated his final draft, which softened some references to Powell's opinion and made clearer that he and White weren't addressing mandatory sentences. At approximately the same time Burger announced that everything needed to be at the print shop by noon. Brennan's clerks raced down with a few minor corrections. Around four o'clock they reviewed the revised draft and made two further changes. They asked to see one final draft, but the printer said this wouldn't be possible. Brennan and Stewart each added a final sentence to his opinion. That was that.

With a case of such magnitude, everyone has the instinct that they should be doing something, but beginning late in the afternoon on June 28, nothing more remained to be done. Brennan felt incredulous, anxious, and more excited than he had in years. "It was all over at last," his clerks wrote in their history of the term. "We kept pinching ourselves to make sure it had really happened. It was a great day for the country." Marshall, more excited, too, than he had been in ages, recalled the sense of accomplishment following *Brown*. Stewart, wondering whether he had made the right decision, spent the end of the day pacing anxiously in his chambers. That night he found it difficult to sleep.

A RED-LETTER DAY

O N THE MORNING OF JUNE 29, 1972, ASIDE FROM the justices and their clerks, no one in the United States expected the Supreme Court to rule the death penalty unconstitutional. *Time* magazine said "educated guessers" expected the Court to uphold capital punishment for murder, though it thought the death penalty for rape might fall. The *New York Times* reported little optimism among death-row lawyers. Any hope that the Court would find the death penalty to be cruel and unusual, the *Times* said, was "based more on wishful thinking than any real expectation." In March, Anthony Lewis wrote, "The Supreme Court as it stands is unlikely to uphold the arguments of the abolitionists." The *New Republic* would later refer to *Furman* as one of the biggest surprises in Supreme Court history.

This isn't to say that the pundits saw no prospect of ending the American death penalty. To the contrary, many thought capital punishment was on the way out. Shortly before *Furman*, *U.S. News & World Report* reported increased support for abolition. In June the sociologist James McCafferty published a collection of essays noting that politicians and corrections officers increasingly favored abolition. In the *National Review*, Donald Zoll, a well-known conservative professor, lamented "mounting zeal for abolition" and the likely success of the movement. Following *McGautha*, though, Court watchers uniformly believed that if change was going to occur, it would have to come from the bottom, form the emerging groundswell of public opinion against the death penalty.

No expert could have known that it was precisely this surge of public opposition to capital punishment that had emboldened Potter Stewart to make his fateful deal with Byron White. Years later Stewart would express no small measure of anger at how wrong the putative experts had been.

But this was yet to be. On this fateful Thursday, the liberal justices, LDF's lawyers, and abolitionists across America experienced the most joyous day of their lives.

THEIR DELIGHT WAS WARREN BURGER'S misery. It was drizzling outside when Burger called the Court to order at ten o'clock. The morning weather suited his mood. Grudgingly Burger read the one-paragraph per curiam decision: "Certiorari was granted limited to the following question: Does the imposition and carrying out of the death penalty in these cases constitute cruel and unusual punishment in violation of the Eighth Amendment? The Court holds that the imposition and carrying out of the death penalty in these cases constitute cruel and unusual punishment in violation of the Eighth Amendment. The judgment in each case is therefore reversed insofar as it leaves undisturbed the death sentence imposed, and the cases are remanded for further proceedings."

From his seat, William Brennan thought Burger made reading this briefest of opinions seem like a chore. He even detected Burger placing a slight emphasis on the words "these cases," to show that the decision didn't create a legal barrier to resurrecting the death penalty. It was the puniest act of protest. Burger's recitation couldn't possibly make any difference. Most of the key attorneys weren't even in the courtroom that day. *Furman* would be known to posterity solely by the written product. Lawyers and law students would dissect the published opinions, not the chief justice's verbal inflections. But that was Warren Burger. Brennan smiled.

When Burger finished reading the per curiam, attorneys raced to a room reserved for members of the Supreme Court bar to get a copy of the complete opinion. Reporters jostled outside, anxious for details. They wanted to know, and to tell the American people, precisely what the Court had decided.

WHAT THEY FOUND, FIRST, was that each justice had taken a lot of space to say what he wanted to say. *Furman v. Georgia* was, at the time it was decided, the longest decision in Supreme Court history. At 66,233 words, *Furman* was longer than many novels, including *The Great Gatsby*, *The Red Badge of Courage*, and *Fahrenheit 451*.

What the lawyers and reporters found next was that no two justices in the majority agreed with each other. William Douglas thought the problem was racism. Brennan and Thurgood Marshall thought the problem was the death penalty itself, though for different reasons. Brennan emphasized the violation of human dignity. Marshall emphasized the illegitimacy of retribution and his assessment of public opinion. Stewart and White appeared to think the problem was that the death penalty wasn't used often enough to serve any societal purpose.

Oddly, several of the justices in the majority had distanced themselves from their colleagues. Stewart cited Louis Brandeis's avoidance doctrine, first articulated in *Ashwander v. Tennessee Valley Authority*, a 1936 case about the development of the Wilson Dam, to argue that the Court shouldn't have addressed the constitutionality of the death penalty per se since the case could be decided on other grounds. Taking up the mantle of the great liberal Brandeis was an odd play by Stewart. In *Ashwander*, Brandeis had advocated judicial restraint to stop a conservative Supreme Court from striking down progressive reforms. Stewart invoked the doctrine to limit a progressive Court's effort to override conservative state legislation. His position evoked

Felix Frankfurter, for whom he had little love. White, no friend of Frankfurter either, said he agreed.

The majority only saw eye to eye regarding result. Years later, Michael Meltsner would say, "*Furman* was decided on a basis and in a manner no one could have predicted." Even the justices in the minority seemed to have substantial disagreements with one another. Each had written separately, and while Warren Burger, Lewis Powell, and William Rehnquist had joined one another's dissents, none had seen fit to join Harry Blackmun's opinion, which expressed moral reservations about the death penalty. They left their colleague dangling in the wind.

It was the oddest of decisions indeed.

SOON WORD OF *FURMAN* began to spread. Reports of the Court's decision appeared on the news ticker. Today the Supreme Court posts its decisions online; people around the world have access in a matter of moments; commentators weigh in almost immediately. In 1972 information didn't travel nearly so quickly. All that was reported initially was the fact of the decision.

At LDF headquarters in Columbus Circle, callers jammed the switchboard trying to gather details of the opinion. LDF's lawyers knew no more than anyone else. They and their secretaries gathered around transistor radios, trying to learn the details of the decision. How far had the Court had gone? Would the decision apply only to the defendants whose appeal the Court had heard, or to others? Soon LDF learned that the decision had broad application. Citing *Furman*, the justices had vacated the sentences in each of the 120 capital cases pending before the Supreme Court. This meant that almost everyone on death row in the United States would be entitled to be resentenced. When this became clear, the attorneys, secretaries, and custodians rejoiced. They hugged one another and cried tears of joy.

Douglas Lyons, the organizer of CALM, shouted into the phone, "This place looks like we just landed a man on the moon!" The analogy was apt. The campaigns to land a man on the moon and to end capital punishment had much in common: Each was audacious, each began and ended at approximately the same time, and each shared the ultimate commonality, an appeal to the aspirational spirit of humanity. This can be appreciated regardless of one's political views. Both John Kennedy and Michael Meltsner undertook something very hard and succeeded against the odds.

IN RAIFORD, FLORIDA, NEAR Jacksonville, at the Florida State Prison Farm that housed the state's death row, Leslie Horton, awaiting execution for rape, was enjoying a family visit when a guard entered the room and asked, "Can you stand some more good news today?" To Horton's astonishment the guard announced, "The Supreme Court has just abolished the death penalty."

The other death-row inmates at the prison farm soon returned from watching a morning showing of *Dirty Harry*. On the 11:15 news broadcast, they heard that Furman had won his appeal. The inmates began to hoot and holler and rattle the doors of their cells. Some shouted, "Right on, Mr. Justices!" Some cursed Richard Nixon. Many wept with joy.

IN THE GEORGIA DIAGNOSTIC and Classification Prison, sixty miles southeast of Atlanta, Lucius Jackson, was awaiting his own execution. He had raped a woman while holding the pointed ends of scissors at her throat. Late in the morning Jackson learned that he had prevailed on his appeal. Shortly thereafter he told a reporter, "I've been thinking about nothing but death for a long time. Now I can think about living."

ALAN DERSHOWITZ, ON LEAVE for the year at the Center for Advanced Study at Stanford, was on vacation in Yellowstone National Park when word reached him of the decision. He found a pay phone and called Arthur Goldberg. "We did it," Goldberg said. "It was all worth it." The following morning Dershowitz managed to secure a copy of the *New York Times*, with its six-column headline proclaiming the end of the death penalty. Forty years later Dershowitz counts it among his most treasured possessions, and shows it each term to his first-year class on criminal law at Harvard Law School.

THE TWO MEN WHO HAD the most to do with ending capital punishment were at opposite ends of the continent. In Cape Ann, Massachusetts, Michael Meltsner was on vacation with his family. The Meltsners had rented a granite house near Folly Cove, a rocky inlet where rum smugglers used to bring their goods ashore during Prohibition. Meltsner was seated at the kitchen table, writing. His nine-year-old daughter, Jessica, was seated across the table from him reading a book. His wife, Heli, in her ninth month of pregnancy with their second daughter, was out seeing her obstetrician. In the background the radio played. Shortly before noon Meltsner heard a report on *Furman*. He was shocked, amazed, and exhilarated. Jessica Meltsner had seen her father argue a Supreme Court case, and he explained to her what had happened.

"Wow!" she said.

Meltsner did what came naturally. He walked across the table, picked up his daughter, and gave her a giant hug and kiss.

THREE THOUSAND MILES AWAY in California, Tony Amsterdam was on Pacific Coast time. That week he got up at five o'clock in the morning each day and made a point of checking the radio first thing. As of nine o'clock, there was no report of a decision. Amsterdam had an appointment and left the house by car. He was driving on a highway south of San Francisco when, just past ten, he heard the news.

Amsterdam pulled his car over and took a deep breath. The word "relief" trivializes what he experienced. "When you represent people under sentence of death, you're always walking around with a dozen, fifty lives on your shoulders," Amsterdam said years later. "I remember the feeling of weight being lifted, knowing that these guys—you worry about each and every one separately—would live. I thought to myself, thank God. We could have lost that one. That job is done. Those guys are going to live." As Amsterdam sat there, captivated by the beauty of the California coastline, he "felt free for the first time in years."

From experience Amsterdam knew that the newspapers would be calling soon, and he wondered what to say. What words could adequately summarize his personal experience of working around the clock for nearly a decade, and then seeing his dream realized? What words could capture what, in his view, the Court had done for the United States? In that moment Amsterdam recalled what he told his former client Earl Caldwell, the investigative reporter for the *New York Times* who the FBI had tried to force to disclose his sources within the Black Panthers. The case touched the heart of Caldwell's profession, the privilege between a journalist and his sources. Anticipating a ruling in his favor, Caldwell asked his lawyer what to say. Amsterdam counseled him, "Just say, 'I am relieved.'"

NOT EVERYONE WAS HAPPY. That afternoon fate brought together three of the most prominent defenders of capital punishment, Dorothy Beasley, Charles Alan Wright, and Lewis Powell. They had gathered at the Greenbrier Hotel in West Virginia for the annual conference of the Fourth Judicial Circuit. The Fourth Circuit, legendarily collegial, included Powell's home state of Virginia, and Powell maintained a close connection with its lawyers and judges throughout his career. Following his retirement the court's home base, in Richmond, would be named in his honor.

In the afternoon Beasley and Wright saw Powell at a reception. Beasley thought Powell looked profoundly tired and troubled. Tired was understandable. Powell had made the four-hour drive from Washington, D.C., to White Sulphur Springs following the announcement of

Furman. Beasley, though, sensed a deeper weariness. It seemed to her as if Powell had taken the death penalty cases personally. She and Wright walked over to the justice, who greeted them warmly.

"What does it mean?" Beasley asked Powell.

"I don't know," he said.

THAT EVENING LDF CELEBRATED at its headquarters on Columbus Circle. A rock band, named the Eighth Amendment in the spirit of the evening, played in the law library into the morning. Jack Himmelstein got drunk for the first and only time in his life, and joined his colleagues in shouting the names of the men LDF had saved, one by one. Like hockey fans chanting the names of revered goaltenders, they emphasized each syllable of the names of the formerly condemned:

WILL-IAM WITH-ER-SPOON.
BIL-LY MAX-WELL.
ER-NEST AI-KENS.
LU-CIUS JACK-SON.
EL-MER BRANCH.
WILL-IE FUR-MAN.

And so on into the night.

IN THE MORNING thoughts turned to the future. On the Supreme Court the justices believed that, for better or worse, the death penalty in America was over. White had incorporated this view into his opinion. The death penalty, he wrote, "has for all practical purposes run its course." White was the *New York Times* man in the news at the end of the month, as he had "suddenly become the unpredictable swing member of the Supreme Court. Sometimes Justice White sides with the liberals, holdovers from the Warren Court. Sometimes he sides with the conservatives, appointees of Richard Nixon. Whichever way he goes, the result is a five to four vote."

Stewart told his clerks that "the death penalty in America was finished." Notwithstanding his comments to Brennan, Burger shared Stewart's view. His dissent had outlined the road map to reinstating the death penalty. He wrote that states had "the opportunity and indeed unavoidable responsibility" to reconsider their statutes. But Burger also told his clerks, "There will never be another execution in the country."

Douglas wrote to Thomas Leonardos, a Brazilian legal scholar who had extended congratulations on the decision, "Thanks very much. I hope total abolition is what we accomplished."

After digesting the opinions the press certainly thought so. Most journalists understood "randomness," which had been discussed at some length, to have been a code word for discrimination. Everyone understood where the Court stood on this issue. Few reporters thought that states would revive the death penalty or that the Supreme Court would uphold such legislation. An editorial in the *Miami Herald* said, "The decision is a turning point in American justice and perhaps in the national attitude towards violence, crime, and punishment." The prevailing sentiment emboldened Jack Greenberg to tell the *New York Times*, "There will no longer be any more capital punishment in the United States."

DERSHOWITZ AGREED WITH GREENBERG'S view, more or less. Yet after reading and reflecting on the opinions, Dershowitz felt a sense of foreboding, as did Goldberg following his own first careful reading. As a matter of law *Furman* permitted the imposition of the death penalty if nonarbitrary sentencing schemes could be constructed. Simply giving every murderer the death penalty would accomplish this end. But Goldberg wasn't overly worried. He felt it was "extremely doubtful that the death penalty would be legislatively renewed on the mandatory and even-handed basis which might meet the objections of

Justices Douglas, Stewart and White." Like Stewart, he believed that the United States had been nudged in the direction it wanted to go anyway. Having reached the moral end point, Americans would surely not return to their atavistic past.

Tony Amsterdam, too, saw the problems with *Furman*. He had no idea what had gone on behind the scenes in the Supreme Court, but the decision looked political, pitting the five Warren Court holdovers against the four Nixon appointees. It might not have been so bad if the majority had reached a consensus, but the majority opinions lacked a single common thread. Even the core moral basis for the holding was unclear. The Court was more fragmented than it had ever been in its history. *Furman* had none of the authority of *Brown*.

Amsterdam saw the loopholes. They were obvious. Surely some states would attempt to respond to *Furman* by enacting revised statutes. But even if some states did respond to *Furman* by attempting to construct guidelines or, unthinkable as this was, by simply making the death penalty mandatory, it would take years for these new laws to wend their way through the system. By the time states implemented new statutes and the Court heard an appeal, more than a decade would have passed without an execution in America. Surely the justices wouldn't allow a return to barbarism. Perhaps support for the death penalty would increase a bit following *Furman*, but it wouldn't be enough to reverse the arrow of progress. Amsterdam slept soundly.

In the morning he wrote a letter to his friend and colleague Michael Meltsner. "The battle resumes again tomorrow," Amsterdam wrote, "but we can afford a moment's respite today. That moment gives me the chance to say a word of deep gratitude. Your part in the capital punishment struggle was at the heart of everything that has been won. You started it, and largely kept it going with your ideas, incredible labors, and tireless commitment."

But Amsterdam was wrong: The new phase of the battle wouldn't resume tomorrow.

It had already begun.

PART THREE

RESURRECTION

1972–1976

CHAPTER 12

SOBERING UP

*F*URMAN OUTRAGED SUPPORTERS OF THE DEATH PENALTY. They began discrediting the decision almost immediately after the Supreme Court announced it. Republican leaders emphasized the limits of the holding. At a press conference on June 30, Richard Nixon told reporters that he hadn't read all nine opinions, but he had read Warren Burger's dissent and concluded from it that the death penalty remained viable. "The holding of the Court must not be taken to rule out capital punishment," Nixon said. He added that he continued to believe in the deterrence value of the death penalty and hoped that *Furman* wouldn't preclude executing kidnappers and hijackers. Ronald Reagan said he believed the Court's ruling did not prohibit a death sentence in the case of "cold blooded, premeditated, planned murder."

Others marginalized the justices who decided the case. In Alabama, Jere Beasley, acting as governor while George Wallace convalesced from Arthur Bremer's assassination attempt, said, "A majority of this nation's high court has lost contact with the real world." Representative Sam Nunn of Georgia, a Democrat in the middle of his first Senate campaign, said *Furman* proved that justices should run for office every six years. Lester Maddox, the segregationist former governor of Georgia, then the lieutenant governor because the state constitution barred him from running for a second term, called *Furman* a "license for anarchy, rape and murder."

Law-enforcement officers predicted *Furman* would increase crime. Memphis police chief Bill Price said that potential criminals who had "hesitated to pull the trigger before just might go ahead and do it now." Ken Brown of the California Correctional Officers Association advocated amending the Constitution. "We're in kind of a state of shock," Brown said. The *New York Daily News* urged legislators to readopt the death penalty, with its "old time" severity, and see "what the Supreme Court does about that." On the House floor New Hampshire representative Louis Wyman said, "Society is entitled to the protection of the deterrent of capital punishment. What about those prison guards who face the lifers who have nothing to lose now? What about the man who assassinated Senator Kennedy—or President Kennedy? What about the atom spies who committed treason? These cases demand the death penalty." On the same day Nixon gave his press conference, legislators in five states announced plans to enact new death penalty statutes. Several congressmen suggested that they would introduce a constitutional amendment to supersede *Furman*.

Supreme Court decisions often produce moments such as these. Politicians proclaim the decision bankrupt. They announce plans for new legislation and constitutional amendments. Predictions of doom are made. Inevitably this anger subsides. In 1968 *Witherspoon*, the jury-selection case, sparked similar outrage. That talk proved to be all bluster. Following *Furman*, though, supporters of the death penalty backed up their words with action. The decision sparked a veritable tidal wave of reaction.

WITHIN SEVERAL WEEKS a committee of the National Association of Attorneys General (NAAG) began discussing a new model death penalty statute. Alabama's attorney general, Bill Baxley, figured prominently in these efforts. Baxley's fervent support of the death penalty illustrates the fierce headwind the Court's decision faced in being embraced by the public.

Baxley, a Democrat, graduated from the University of Alabama Law School in 1964 and shortly thereafter became district attorney of Houston, his home county. In 1971, at the age of twenty-eight, Baxley won election as state attorney general. At the time he was the youngest attorney general in U.S. history. While in office Baxley proved himself a staunch defender of civil rights. He appointed the first black assistant attorney general in Alabama history. Most famously he reopened the investigation into the 1963 bombing of the Sixteenth Street Baptist Church in Birmingham, in which four young black girls died. Baxley convicted Robert Chambliss, also known as Dynamite Bob, who allegedly also firebombed the homes of several black families. For his efforts Baxley earned a rebuke from the Ku Klux Klan, which made him an "honorary nigger" and threatened him by letter. Baxley replied, "My response to your letter of February 19, 1976, is—kiss my ass."

Baxley's subsequent political career bolstered his liberal bona fides. In 1978 he lost the gubernatorial primary to Fob James, a former Republican who supported states' rights, criticized the teaching of evolution in schools, and fought against a federal court order requiring the removal of a Ten Commandments plaque from a courthouse. Baxley ran as a moderate. Later, in private practice, Baxley devoted substantial time to representing poor clients, and would be recognized as one of the five hundred fellows of the International Academy of Trial Lawyers. In short, Baxley was the sort of politician who should have embraced *Furman*.

Instead Baxley deplored the decision. He believed the death penalty acted as a deterrent. Furthermore he was outraged by the Court's intrusion into state business. The political reality, though, was that Baxley couldn't have believed anything else and survived. In a 2010 interview Baxley candidly said that even if he privately opposed capital punishment, he would have supported it publicly. Opposing the death penalty wasn't politically tenable in Alabama politics. In Baxley's experience George Wallace offered the most vivid illustration of this reality.

Privately Wallace opposed capital punishment. In 1964 Wallace, newly elected, told Baxley, then a law clerk, that he thought the Supreme Court should rule the death penalty unconstitutional. Publicly, though, Wallace supported it. When Wallace launched a third-party presidential bid in 1968, "getting tough on crime" was a major plank in his American Independent Party platform. Wallace didn't win, but he profoundly influenced the campaign. The Republican Party essentially co-opted Wallace's position on public safety. Later, as governor, Wallace signed one of the many new death penalty statutes passed in response to *Furman*. Such was the politics of crime in the South.*

Baxley says that he tried to memorize every line of *Furman* and

---

* Circumstances reunited Wallace and Baxley for an extraordinary episode. Baxley served one term as lieutenant governor, from 1983 through 1987, coinciding with Wallace's final gubernatorial term. In 1983 prison officials presented Wallace the execution warrant of John Louis Evans for signature. Evans was a recidivist offender who had been paroled in 1976 and, by his own admission, embarked on a two-month crime spree during which he committed nine kidnappings and thirty armed robberies. During one of these robberies, of a pawnshop in Mobile, Evans and a fellow inmate killed the store owner in the presence of his two young daughters. For this Evans received a death sentence.

Wallace couldn't bring himself to sign the warrant. In Baxley's view the 1972 assassination attempt against Wallace greatly changed him. Indeed, following his recovery, Wallace declared himself born again, recanted his segregationist views, and apologized to civil rights leaders. Wallace said that while he had once sought power and glory, he now sought love and forgiveness. During that final term he appointed a record number of black men and women to government positions.

Wallace's reservations about the constitutionality of capital punishment had evolved into full-blown opposition. On the eve of Evans's execution, Wallace called Baxley in tears. Wallace said that he had been up all night "praying the Bible," and couldn't bring himself to sign the warrant. Baxley said, "This is not an innocent man whose blood would be on your hands." Wallace repeated that he didn't think he could sign. Baxley told Wallace that if he commuted the sentence he would convene a press conference the next morning and brand the commutation a farce. Wallace may have been softened by age and found God through his brush with death, but he was still a politician. Wallace signed the order. Evans was Alabama's first execution after *Gregg*.

that the NAAG committee took the decision seriously. He interpreted *Furman* as a mandate to curb jury discretion as much as possible. The challenge in Alabama, and the South generally, "was to prevent legislatures from passing a rogue statute." Many Southern leaders were treating *Furman* with extreme cynicism. Larry Derryberry, attorney general of Oklahoma, told *Time*, "The trick is how to write a law the U.S. Supreme Court will approve."

Baxley doubted the NAAG would reach consensus on a model statute. By the end of 1972, Baxley's committee had drafted nineteen proposals. These ranged from a constitutional amendment to a law making the death penalty mandatory for special crimes such as murder by contract or killing a police officer. It seemed impossible they would agree on a single model statute. Baxley had no doubts, though, about the general direction of things. Alabama would pass a revised death penalty statute, and clearly other states would too. In December the attorneys general voted thirty-two to one to one in favor of a resolution calling on Congress and states to enact new statutes which could withstand constitutional muster. A majority of the attorneys believed that a mandatory statute was most likely to accomplish this. Larry Derryberry said, "We determined that the alternative for reinstating the death penalty most likely to be favorably considered by the Supreme Court is one that would impose a mandatory death sentence for certain offenses." National newspapers reported on the NAAG vote and suggested a new momentum behind the death penalty.

In truth, this was only the beginning.

IN GEORGIA, DOROTHY BEASLEY quickly began working with the state house judiciary committee to draft a revised statute. Beasley had many discussions regarding *Furman* with the NAAG committee, on which she served with Charles Alan Wright, the professor who had argued *Branch v. Texas*. No one believed the death penalty was finished. The question was how to meet the Court's concerns.

Beasley took the signals from the dissents. Georgia would split trials into a guilt phase and sentencing phase. It would provide for automatic review of death sentences by the Georgia Supreme Court. Finally, it would adopt a list of aggravating factors. A jury would need to find at least one of these present before it could impose a death sentence.

Many of Beasley's discussions with Georgia legislators concerned what to include on this list. Some aggravating factors seemed obvious, such as killing a police officer or murdering for monetary gain. Several politicians worried, though, that they would cause offense by their omissions. Ultimately support built for a catchall aggravating factor including murders that were "heinous, atrocious and cruel." Privately Beasley worried that the list had become too inclusive and subjective.

IN FLORIDA, *FURMAN* REVERSED the sentences of ninety-six death row inmates. Almost immediately, politicians began pushing for a special legislative session to reinstate capital punishment. Two legislative options had been advanced. The state attorney general, Bob Shevin, favored a mandatory statute. Others favored guiding the discretion of the jury, with a provision for bifurcated trials, not unlike the statute under consideration in Georgia.

Governor Reubin Askew responded by creating a special task force. The staff of the Committee to Study Capital Punishment included four law school professors—Charles Ehrhardt of Florida State, Harold Levinson of the University of Florida, William Smiley of Stetson, Thomas Wills of the University of Miami—and Phillip Hubbart, a public defender. Askew charged the committee to assess the likelihood of the Supreme Court upholding these new laws.

The committee unanimously rejected both possibilities. It said that the Court would reject either approach "out of respect" for *Furman*. As evidence they cited the example of John Harlan, who dissented from many seminal Warren Court decisions, including *Miranda*, but later voted to uphold them as precedent. The committee felt that in a new appeal, some or all of the four *Furman* dissenters would follow Harlan's lead and either vote to abolish capital punishment outright or restrict its use to the most heinous crimes.

Furthermore the committee felt that each of the new proposed statutes was bad public policy. Neither law did anything to curtail plea bargaining, the jury's ability to convict a defendant of a lesser included offense, or executive clemency. Each of these introduced substantial discretion and randomness into sentencing. If capital punishment were to be reinstated, the committee said, it needed to be part of a comprehensive rethinking of criminal justice.

Almost no one heeded the committee's concerns. Beginning on November 28, in a whirlwind four-day special legislative session, the Florida House of Representatives unanimously passed a death penalty bill. The Senate passed a different bill by a vote of thirty-six to one. The House version provided that death sentences should be determined by a three-judge panel, including the guilt-phase trial judge. Certain factual findings by the panel triggered a mandatory death sentence. The Senate version placed discretion in the hands of the jury. A conference committee forged a compromise. The final statute retained jury participation, but rendered this recommendation advisory to the judge, who could reject the proposed sentence based on his interpretation of the aggravating and mitigating evidence.

When Governor Askew signed the law on December 8, 1972, Florida became the first state to reenact a death penalty statute after *Furman*. It had been less than six months since LDF's historic victory. In the *Journal of Criminal Law & Criminology* former committee members Ehrhardt and Levinson condemned the new law as "seriously defective" and "an expedient response to election-time politics." The professors wrote, "Constitutional problems were brushed aside by Florida lawmakers and other leaders of opinion." The outrage fell on deaf ears. Legislators around the country didn't view Florida's new law as problematic. To the contrary, it became a model for other state statutes.

❖ ❖ ❖

IN CALIFORNIA, SUPPORTERS OF the death penalty took a different route to resurrection. The state constitution allowed for amendment by ballot initiative. In late spring, before the Court announced *Furman*, Ronald Reagan and his attorney general, Evelle Younger, put forward Proposition 17. The measure proposed to restore all death penalty laws that had been in effect before February 17, the day the California Supreme Court decided *People v. Anderson*. In other words, it would reverse *Anderson*. Proposition 17 also deemed the death penalty not to violate the cruel-or-unusual-punishment clause or any other provision of the California constitution. This unusual proposal would effectively exempt capital punishment from state judicial review.

Predictably Amsterdam threw himself into the California campaign. After Reagan announced Proposition 17, he scheduled a strategy session for July 7 with the leaders of California's abolition movement. After the Court announced *Furman*, most of these organizers questioned the point of the meeting. Amsterdam persisted. He said *Furman* didn't preclude new state legislation, and so the session went on as planned.

The mood at the July 7 meeting was grim. One after another, California abolitionists told Amsterdam that Proposition 17 would pass. The California court's decision in *Anderson* had spared Sirhan Sirhan and Charles Manson, among others. This presented a daunting public relations problem, to say the least. In a curious way *Furman* had made the situation worse. *Furman* galvanized public opinion in favor of capital punishment while undermining the resolve of abolitionists. Most potential donors believed that *Furman* had ended the death penalty, and so were reluctant to contribute to the campaign against Proposition 17. They believed that their money could be used better elsewhere. Following the meeting, Amsterdam told Meltsner, "The group had me seriously wondering whether winning *Furman* was a good thing after all."

Nevertheless the California campaign went on, and Amsterdam played a visible role. In the press he took exception to deciding constitutional rights by referendum. "Proposition 17 represents a use of the amending process hitherto virtually unknown in this country," he told the *Times*. "Its sponsorship by self-styled conservatives is ironic since it breaks with venerable American traditions insofar as it cuts down a fundamental Bill of Rights guarantee in a hasty reaction to a judicial decision interpreting that guarantee." Rights, he said, shouldn't be hastily changed. "The real source of our security lies in the unwritten principle that they will not be triflingly amended—except after the most mature experience and reflection."

Despite Amsterdam's efforts the vote wasn't close. The pessimists had been right. On November 7 Proposition 17 passed with 67.5 percent of the vote. Justice Stanley Mosk condemned the decision. "The people of California responded quickly and emphatically to callously declare that whatever the trends in the nation and the world, our state does not deem the retributive extinction of a human life to be either cruel or unusual." Mosk, though, was wrong to single out the citizens of his state. In voicing their strong support for the death penalty, Californians were hardly alone.

PUBLIC-OPINION POLLS SHOWED a dramatic increase in enthusiasm for capital punishment. Since the mid-1950s, support for the death penalty had never exceeded 54 percent in any individual poll. In the last Gallup poll taken before *Furman*, in March 1972, 50 percent of respondents said they favored the death penalty, while 41 percent said they opposed it. The level of support, and the spread between support and opposition, was consistent with the most recent poll in December, 1971, which showed 49 percent for and 40 percent against, and a 1969 poll, which came in at 51 percent for and 40 percent against. These results suggested stable attitudes regarding the death penalty. In the first Gallup poll taken after *Furman*, in December 1972, support for the death penalty increased to 57 percent the highest level of support in twenty years. The spread between pro and con, which had been just nine points in March, had nearly tripled.

Polls by Louis Harris reflected the same hardening of support for capital punishment. In the last Harris poll taken before *Furman*, in 1970, 47 percent of respondents supported the death penalty, with 42 percent opposed. Harris's results, like Gallup's, were stable. His immediate prior poll, in 1969, came in at 48 percent pro and 38 percent con. In the first Harris poll following *Furman*, 59 percent of Americans said they favored capital punishment versus 31 percent opposed. In two years the spread had more than quintupled. Harris characterized this as a "sharp increase in sentiment." LDF's leaders might have convinced themselves that Gallup's results were aberrational, but they couldn't dismiss Harris's. When LDF studied conviction-proneness, in an effort to keep the Supreme Court from deciding the issue in *Witherspoon*, it was Harris to whom they had turned.

By the end of 1972 everyone recognized the trend. In December *Newsweek* reported "The Rebirth of Death." A few weeks later, an editorial in the *New York Times* noted "the tide of reaction sweeping across America." The *Times* editorial board deplored the resurgence of the death penalty, writing, "It is a break with more than forty years of an essentially liberal momentum that has carried this nation forward to a more just and humane society." The board pointed an accusing finger at the president: "A coalition of fear and reaction in state legislatures and in Congress is blithely being incited by the Nixon Administration to outflank the court with reactionary new laws. The politicians who embrace the new reaction say that they are only sweeping out the criminals and the chiselers. In reality, they are turning their backs on the American credo of optimism, compassion, and faith in liberty under law."

Richard Nixon certainly wasn't about to listen to the *Times* editorial board. Shortly after New Year's Day, Nixon's attorney general, Richard Kleindienst, announced that the president would ask Congress to pass a law making the death penalty mandatory for kidnapping, assassination, bombing a public building, hijacking an airplane, and killing a prison guard. He said this "would be a constitutional capital punishment statute." Kleindienst, a close friend of William Rehnquist's from their days in Arizona politics, admitted that he didn't think the death penalty did much. "Generally speaking, I don't believe the death penalty accomplishes an overriding social purpose." But Kleindienst felt it could deter highly premeditated crimes such as those covered by the new law.

Nixon used his March radio address to attack the justices in the *Furman* majority, and called on Congress to pass his proposal. "The time has come for soft-headed judges and probation officers to show as much concern for the rights of innocent victims as they do for the rights of convicted criminals," Nixon said. The *Times* columnist Tom Wicker called Nixon's behavior a "splendid way to reap political benefit from the fear of crime."

In 1973 Nixon deemed the nation's affairs too complex to address in a single State of the Union message. On March 14, in the sixth installment of this address, Nixon told Congress that he favored "automatic imposition of the death penalty when it is warranted," and that the Supreme Court had objected to capital punishment only "as it is applied arbitrarily and capriciously." Nixon said his new statute would have specific and even-handed rules. One week later the president formally transmitted his bill to Congress. It provided for bifurcated trials and specified aggravating and mitigating circumstances. If a jury found an aggravating factor but no offsetting mitigating factor, the defendant would be sentenced to death automatically. If it found a mitigating factor, the defendant would be spared. The bill quickly received a favorable review from the Senate Judiciary Committee, which deemed the death penalty a "valid and necessary social remedy against dangerous types of criminal offenders."

At the state level, momentum for capital punishment surged. In early February, Washington reinstated the death penalty. Later that month the Georgia legislature passed its revised law. Governor Jimmy Carter said he would sign it despite "some questions of its constitutionality." On March 2 Kansas passed a mandatory death penalty statute.

Soon thereafter Governor Dale Bumpers signed Arkansas' new law, followed shortly by Deleware's Sherman Tribbitt. In April the British House of Commons rejected a proposal to restore death penalty, but on April 6 Nevada restored capital punishment. Two weeks later Connecticut did too. Texas came next, on May 29, followed by Louisiana on June 12, despite Governor Edwin Edwards's "serious reservations" about whether the Supreme Court would uphold the new statute. Arizona, Idaho, Indiana, Nebraska, Oklahoma, Utah, and Wyoming all followed suit soon.

By the end of 1973 three quarters of the former death penalty states had either reinstated the death penalty or had a bill under consideration to do so. Though Michigan hadn't executed anyone in 127 years, its legislature was debating a return to capital punishment. Even Massachusetts, the only state to vote for George McGovern in the 1972 presidential election, passed a death penalty statute. Although the Republican governor, Francis Sargent, vetoed the bill, its success in the legislature vividly illustrated how far the pendulum had swung.

Indeed newspapers reported overwhelmingly positive reactions to politicians who mentioned reviving the death penalty. The liberal Republican governor of New York, Nelson Rockefeller, received "thunderous" applause when he called for a return to capital punishment. So, too, did Nevada governor Mike O'Callaghan, who received an ovation during his state of the state speech precisely once: when he implored the legislature to bring back the death penalty.

State courts appeared to be treating *Furman* with disdain. *Furman* had been more confusing than any other decision in Supreme Court history, but at least it seemed clear that the decision invalidated all the state death penalty laws then in existence. In January 1973, the Supreme Court of North Carolina said otherwise. North Carolina's original death penalty statute made the death penalty mandatory for murder. In 1949 the state had passed a provision giving juries discretion. In *State v. Waddell* the North Carolina Supreme Court held that the 1949 amendment could be separated from the remainder of the law. *Furman*, it said, invalidated the 1949 amendment, not the original statute. In other words *Furman* had converted North Carolina's discretionary death penalty law into a mandatory one. Abolitionists couldn't have imagined a more ironic or implausible interpretation of *Furman*.

THE FALL OF 1973 should have been a season of celebration for LDF. In September, Random House published *Cruel and Unusual*, Michael Meltsner's history of LDF's litigation campaign.

The book's origins are a romp through the New York literary establishment of the 1970s, a story filled with coincidences that illustrate the interconnectedness of the liberal intelligentsia of that era. During the mid-1960s Meltsner had lunch with Victor Navasky, the legendary publisher of the *Nation*, and, at the time, an editor on the *New York Times Magazine*. Meltsner knew Navasky from Yale Law School and had worked on Navasky's satirical magazine, *Monocle*, a legend in its own right. At lunch Meltsner told his friend that a history of RFK's Justice Department would make a great book. Navasky agreed and suggested they write it together. Meltsner, still working around the clock at LDF, didn't see how he could find the time. So Navasky wrote the book on his own. After reading *Kennedy Justice*, which became a finalist for the National Book Award, Meltsner thought, "Maybe I can try my hand at something like this, and come halfway close to what he did." He began jotting down recollections. "I have rotten handwriting, and often I can't read my own notes," Meltsner said, "but I scribbled and threw things in a drawer." Year after year the drawer filled.

In 1970 Meltsner left LDF to join the Columbia Law School faculty. Becoming an Ivy League law professor sounds uncharacteristically conventional for an iconoclast, but once again Meltsner was blazing his own trail. Columbia had invited him to begin a legal-services clinic in Morningside Heights. Together with Gary Bellow of Harvard, Meltsner became the leader of a movement to make clinical experience a standard part of American law school education.

Legal realism notwithstanding, law students in 1970 studied law the way Christopher Langdell wanted it to be taught. They read casebooks that excerpted appellate court decisions and synthesized them into coherent wholes. In 1972 *Newsweek* wrote, "Until recently, most law schools assiduously cultivated their isolation from the outside world." Forty years later most schools offer a "clinical experience," which gets law students into the real world for a semester, and offer a standard path to tenure and promotion for so-called clinical professors. When Meltsner began teaching, however, he had no idea what standards Columbia would use to measure his performance. Law professors generally write books and articles, so it was only natural that Meltsner's thoughts turned to his desk drawer.

The stack of scrawled notes became a first draft, which Meltsner sent to Atheneum Books. Atheneum's editor, Richard Kluger, liked Meltsner's idea, but his boss rejected the proposal. Kluger referred Meltsner to Random House, where editor Joe Fox was extraordinarily well qualified to shepherd a book about constitutional law.* Fox had been the editor of *Gideon's Trumpet*, Anthony Lewis's best-selling account of *Gideon v. Wainwright*, the Supreme Court decision guaranteeing criminal defendants the right to an attorney. Fox signed the book and encouraged Meltsner to polish his manuscript right away.

So Meltsner began revising *Cruel and Unusual* before he knew how the story would turn out. When he heard about *Furman*, it was *Cruel and Unusual* that he was working on at the kitchen table of the granite house in Cape Ann. The news that came over the transistor radio that June morning meant his story would have a happy ending. The chorus of glowing praise following the book's publication in September was a triumph for Meltsner. The *Columbia Law Review* praised it as

---

* Kluger also mentioned that he wanted to write his own book, about *Brown*. Meltsner told him to go for it, though he privately doubted Kluger could do it. At Kluger's invitation Meltsner reviewed a draft of Kluger's manuscript. Meltsner said it was "as great an honor as I've ever received." *Simple Justice* also became a finalist for the National Book Award, and Kluger later won the Pulitzer Prize for *Ashes to Ashes*, his history of the cigarette industry.

"lucid and absorbing," *Time* as a "rousing intellectual adventure story," and in *Business Week*, Dan Moskowitz said Meltsner's "explanations of court procedures and legal maneuvers set a new standard for all who write about the law for a mass audience."

Tony Amsterdam said that even the rave reviews understated the book's value. On October 1 Amsterdam wrote Meltsner with his personal assessment. "It is a beautiful book, Michael, and the world is richer for it. But I am not sure that any but the initiated will ever know how *really* good it is since some of its incredible achievement can only be understood by those in a position to appreciate its astounding accuracy, unstinting honesty, and its perceptions into the dynamics of which the celebrants were largely unaware. It is a playwright's genius to make his audience comprehend what the players do not."

Yet the happy ending of *Cruel and Unusual* was being rewritten. Meltsner found himself spending more time explaining the turn in public opinion than taking credit for LDF's astonishing success in *Furman*. In December, Meltsner testified before a New York Assembly committee considering a new death penalty statute. He acknowledged that "several states have reenacted capital punishment" but argued that the new statutes didn't adequately curtail arbitrariness. "Capital punishment," Meltsner said, "has reached the humpty dumpty stage and cannot be put together again." But the tsunami didn't subside. Several months later Meltsner argued in a *Times* op-ed that LDF was the victim of its own success. Support for capital punishment, he wrote, "is inversely related to the number of legal killings. The more executions are held, the less the public likes the death penalty." In his view the national movement to restore the death penalty was "as much a response to the rarity of executions as a desire for more."

Meltsner's colleagues offered similar arguments to discount the backlash. Amsterdam contended that the moratorium had "taken the edge off abolitionist sentiments." He said, "Abolitionists get excited about executions in the same way that law and order people get excited about murders. In a period where a nice, juicy execution has not been performed for years, people are sleeping on their duffs." Hugo Bedau told *Time* magazine, "It is unclear that the public wants executions. What they want seems to be an occasional execution."

The truth was, though, the backlash blindsided LDF. Jack Greenberg admitted that he and his colleagues had not prepared for the aftermath of *Furman*. Arthur Goldberg was far more believable than Amsterdam or Bedau when he conceded that recent developments proved his proclamation of capital punishment's demise "overly sanguine." For no one was buying LDF's spin.

In the winter of 1974 Gallup registered 63 percent in favor of the death penalty. Now no one could dismiss the polling shift as a blip. This was the highest level of support since Gallup's November 1953 poll, taken shortly after the executions of the Rosenbergs. The next Gallup poll showed 66 percent support. In a Harris poll support crossed the two-thirds threshold. Harris's result was his highest since he began polling the question.

On March 13, 1974, the U.S. Senate approved President Nixon's death penalty bill by a vote of fifty-four to thirty-three, following eight hours of deliberations. The *Times* characterized the debate as "emotional," but said it appeared that "most members had made up their minds long ago." That same month Congress approved the death penalty for airplane hijackers. Another seven states—Illinois, Mississippi, New Hampshire, North Carolina, Ohio, Pennsylvania, and South Carolina—passed new death penalty laws.

In the fall the U.S. Supreme Court reentered the melee and announced that it would hear the appeal of Jesse Fowler, who had shot a man in a drunken rage, and been sentenced to die under North Carolina's now-mandatory death penalty law. The Justices set argument for April 21 of the following year. The choice of case seemed somewhat odd, since it concerned the North Carolina Supreme Court's interpretation of *Furman*, and not *Furman* itself, but in context it was bad news. By this time twenty-nine states had passed new capital punishment laws, and a dozen others had them in the pipeline. The Marshall Hypothesis had been conclusively disproved. Not even Marshall himself could deny that the American public had emphatically expressed its preference for capital punishment. Potter Stewart and Byron White had challenged states to either curtail randomness or use the death penalty more frequently. The states had responded with new statutes that either guided jury discretion or were mandatory. From LDF's perspective an entire decade of progress was in jeopardy.

CHAPTER 13

BEHIND THE BACKLASH

O NE MIGHT NATURALLY ASSUME THAT THE FERVOR OF public support following *Furman* was related to increased crime or increased fear of crime, but that theory is almost certainly incorrect.

It is true that between 1972, when the Court decided *Furman*, and 1974, when the Court announced it would hear *Fowler*, violent crime increased.* Fear of crime also rose during the same period. This statistic should most directly affect public attitudes regarding law enforcement, as it is the perception of crime, not the reality of crime, which should lead the public to become more punitive. Indeed, in a January 1973 poll, 51 percent of people said they thought there was more crime where they lived than there had been the year before (compared with 27 percent who said there was as much crime, and 10 percent who said there was less), and 74 percent of respondents said courts didn't deal harshly enough with criminals. (As a point of comparison, 48 percent answered yes to this question in 1965.) Fifty-seven percent of respondents said that they supported the death penalty. Given the increase following *Furman* in both crime and fear of crime, and sup-

---

* In 1972, 18,670 murders occurred in the United States, a rate of 9 per 100,000 citizens. In 1974, 20,710 Americans were victims of murder, 9.8 per 100,000. Over the same two years, rape increased by approximately 20 percent from a rate of 22.5 to 26.2 per 100,000.

port for the death penalty, it might seem natural to presume a causal relationship.

But if one looks beyond 1973 and 1974, the theory collapses. In the mid-1960s, the United States experienced an unprecedented surge in crime, which dwarfed the increases of the mid-'70s. Between 1963 and 1970, violent crime more than doubled.* Robberies tripled. Nevertheless support for the death penalty languished. In Gallup's May 1966 poll, more people opposed the death penalty than supported it. In the last poll of the decade, the death penalty had a bare majority of support, 51 percent. Most criminologists "lag" data. That is, they presume it takes time for the public to learn about and respond to a change in social conditions, and adjust their studies accordingly. Even if one presumes a two-year lag, which is far longer than any researcher believes is required to model reality accurately, the decline in support for capital punishment during the late '60s cannot be explained.

A long-term view of the post-*Furman* data conclusively refutes the crime-punitiveness connection. After the Court's decision in 1972, support for capital punishment increased substantially. It spiked to 57 percent following *Furman*, rose to 66 percent in 1976, 75 percent in 1985, and peaked at 80 percent in 1994. Yet between 1976 and 1985, crime dropped in the U.S. The 1994 poll result is particularly remarkable. After a brief resurgence between 1985 and 1990, crime had been dropping steadily in the United States for four years when Gallup recorded this all-time high level of support for capital punishment.

What stands out most in the public opinion data is the spike in support for the death penalty following *Furman*. For more than a decade support for capital punishment had been languishing. Even with rising crime rates, it had fallen below 50 percent in two polls. Then, following *Furman*, it surged by seven points, and in the next poll, by nine more. Almost uniformly, academics point to the *Furman* decision itself as the inciting force for the public backlash. University

---

* The murder rate increased from 4.6 to 7.9 per 100,000 citizens; rape from 9.4 to 18.7 per 100,000.

of Central Florida Professor Robert Bohm, a leading death penalty researcher, says, "Although other factors may have had an effect, public discontent with the *Furman* decision was decisive." Harvard Law School's Carol Steiker agrees, writing, "The Supreme Court's decision in *Furman* itself played a bigger role in bolstering support for capital punishment than did rising homicide rates." So the question becomes: Why was the public so angry with the Supreme Court about *Furman*?

THE MOST SIGNIFICANT CONTEXT is race. In 1972 the Supreme Court was already under heavy fire because of its decision the preceding term in a desegregation case called *Swann v. Charlotte-Mecklenburg Board of Education*.

High school history textbooks point to the 1954 landmark case of *Brown v. Board of Education of Topeka, Kansas*, as the beginning of desegregation, and the high-water mark of anti–Supreme Court sentiment. Indeed, "Impeach Earl Warren" billboards famously lined the highways of the deep South throughout the '60s. But the truth is that *Brown* had almost no impact on individual lives. So little happened in its aftermath that LDF was compelled to return to the Court one year later and demand that states move more quickly in implementing the decision's mandate of an end to "separate but equal" schools. In *Brown II* the Supreme Court famously ordered the Topeka school board to move with—Felix Frankfurter's phrase—"all deliberate speed." This was intended, and widely interpreted, as a retreat from *Brown*.

After *Brown II* once again little changed, and the ideal of a fully integrated public school system remained abstract. John J. Parker, a Fourth Circuit judge who had been nominated to the Supreme Court by Herbert Hoover in 1930 and missed confirmation by one vote, argued that the *Brown* decisions prohibited segregation, but didn't require integration. In 1963 the Supreme Court rejected Judge Parker's view and required integration in *McNeese v. Board of Education*. Still, little changed. Many states responded to *McNeese* by implementing so-called "freedom of choice" plans. Under these schemes, students were assigned to schools by race and then given the option to change schools. Almost no one exercised this right. In a 1968 decision, *Green v. County School Board of New Kent County*, the Court struck down freedom of choice systems. In New Kent County, a rural district near Richmond, no white student had opted for the black school, and few African American students chose to attend the white school. The Court said districts had an affirmative obligation to integrate schools. "The burden on a school board today is to come forward with a plan that promises realistically to work *now*," Brennan wrote for the majority. All deliberate speed, finally, was in the past.

Yet data revealed that people's lives still didn't change. For all of the progress in the law's treatment of race, American schools and neighborhoods remained rigidly segregated. A decade after *Brown*, barely more than 1 percent of Southern black schoolchildren attended schools with whites. In their seminal book, *American Apartheid*, Douglas Massey and Nancy Denton developed an index of segregation, essentially the percentage of blacks who would need to be relocated to achieve an evenly integrated community. Even in putatively progressive cities, the numbers were daunting. In 1970 New York the segregation index was 81 percent. In Atlanta it was 82.1 percent. In Chicago it was an astonishing 91.9 percent. To most white Americans integration was an idea, not a reality.

Swann changed all this. The Charlotte-Mecklenburg school district was unusually large, covering more than 550 square miles. Although it had ended legal desegregation with a neighborhood-based school assignment plan that was approved by the court, the overwhelming majority of students continued to attend segregated schools. Of the 21,000 black students in the Charlotte school system, merely 2 percent attended schools with whites. More than two-thirds of black students attended schools that were more than 99 percent black. In 1965 Julius Chambers, a Charlotte lawyer associated with LDF, brought suit on behalf of James Swann, the six-year-old son of a theology professor. Judge Braxton Craven dismissed Swann's claim because, in his view, the Constitution didn't require that school districts actively increase racial mixing. After *Green*, Chambers refiled the suit and received a more favorable audience from Judge James McMillan. McMillan opposed busing on principle, but said the law superseded his personal views. He approved a plan, authored by Dr. John Finger of Rhode Island College's Education School, which relied on a combination of strategies to integrate Charlotte schools. This included dividing the city into pie-shaped wedges, creating "satellite zones," and, most controversially, busing. Following the decision the Charlotte community shunned Judge McMillan. Julius Chambers's home and office were bombed.

In 1971 the Supreme Court approved the so-called "Finger plan," despite its reliance on "awkward, inconvenient and even bizarre" measures. Behind the scenes Warren Burger assigned the decision to himself and tried to limit the holding with a tepid endorsement of McMillan's decision. Brennan, Douglas, Harlan, Marshall, Stewart, and Black all reacted strongly. Rather than lose the Court, Burger capitulated, and the decision, as published, ruled that preservation of neighborhood schools couldn't justify continued racial imbalance. In other words the Supreme Court endorsed busing.

Now whites felt it. Federal courts across the United States began issuing desegregation plans relying heavily on busing. Integration increased geometrically. During the 1968–69 school year, 14.4 percent of black children in Alabama attended schools with whites. By 1972–73 the figure was 83.5 percent. White reaction was hostile. *Common Ground*, J. Anthony Lukas's Pulitzer Prize–Winning account of busing in Boston, begins with a federal district court decision issued in the aftermath of *Swann*. Judge Arthur Garrity required any district more than 50 percent white to be racially balanced. Famously Garrity ordered that the entire junior class of South Boston High School, mostly working class white children, be bused to Roxbury High School, located in a black ghetto. Violent protests erupted; armed riot police patrolled the city of Boston. State troopers remained stationed at South Boston High School for three years, as they did in Charleston and other cities hostile to integration. White parents taunted black children with racial epithets. George Wallace won the 1972 Demo-cratic primaries in Florida and Michigan on an antibusing platform.

So virulent and complete was this hostility that by the end of the decade, whites had succeeded in utterly alienating American blacks. At the beginning of the 1970s the majority of African Americans said they wanted to live in racially mixed neighborhoods and have their children attend integrated schools. By the end of the decade two out of three black Americans said they felt closer to African blacks than they did to American whites. Stokley Carmichael and the Black Panthers rejected assimilation as an ideal, and in the early 1970s their popularity soared. Whites felt no better about blacks, and held the Court to blame. An integrated race-blind America appeared to be an impossible ideal.

HOSTILITY TO THE SUPREME COURT reached an even higher pitch after it decided *Roe v. Wade.* The justices first heard argument on the case one month before *Furman*, in 1971, but Harry Blackmun agonized over his opinion for months, persuaded his colleagues to put the case over until the following term, and a decision didn't issue for nearly two years. The announcement of *Roe* on January 22, 1973, coin-cided with a further acceleration of pro–death penalty sentiment. This was almost certainly no coincidence. A mid-1973 Harris poll showed a nine-point increase in support for capital punishment, though nothing material had changed since the previous poll, taken at the start of the year. The six-month period following the announcement of *Roe* was the most fecund in American history for capital punishment support-ers in terms of state statutes passed. The link was antipathy for the Supreme Court.

Roe was enormously polarizing. Feminists and liberals cheered, but the substance of the decision outraged millions of Americans, as did the fact that the Court had intruded yet again on an issue of conscience. Following *Roe* the Court received more than two thousand letters a day, which piled up in the courthouse hallways. Protesters began to follow William Brennan and Blackmun at public appearances.

Ironically, Blackmun had been predisposed against *Roe*. In his preargument memo to himself on *Roe*, Blackmun wrote that he was "inclined to uphold the statute at this point." But as Blackmun dithered, his mind gradually changed. He asked his daughters for their opinion and in return got an earful and a headache, which sent him to bed. After the Court postponed the case, Blackmun spent the summer of 1972 researching abortion at the Mayo Clinic, where he had been general counsel. Because of this experience Blackmun felt he was uniquely qualified to deal with the case's medical issues, and it was at this revered medical center that Blackmun's conversion occurred. Initially Blackmun saw the case as turning on a doctor's right to perform abortions, not a woman's right to privacy, or a fetus's status as a person. At the Mayo library Blackmun learned that doctors in ancient Greece and Egypt had performed abortions, and that the Hippocratic Oath didn't forbid them. He changed his mind when he learned that a legal abortion in the first trimester posed less risk to a woman than did carrying the pregnancy to term. After he settled on the outcome of the case, his clerks John Rich and George Frampton persuaded Blackmun to frame the decision around privacy rights rather than the rights of doctors.

In the end Blackmun would be intensely proud of his decision in *Roe*, but he would also endure a prolonged public shaming. He received bags of hate mail and repeated death threats. One among many: "I am preparing myself for sacrifice. You and I will enter eternity together before the year is over. I dress well, belong to no political party, and have a pleasant middle-age prosperous appearance. I am ready to die." In 1985 someone fired a handgun through Blackmun's living room window. The shot showered Blackmun's wife with glass and lodged itself in the chair where she had just been sitting.

Blackmun battled depression at various points in his life, and the backlash to *Roe* hurt his feelings greatly. To his longtime friend Vern Trocinski, a priest on the faculty of College of Saint Teresa, in Winona, Minnesota, Blackmun wrote, "I understand the critical letters, but I do not understand the vilification and personal abuse which has come to me from some quarters." To Alquinn Toews, director of chaplain services at Rochester Methodist Hospital: "I have never before been so personally abused and castigated." A churchgoing Methodist, Blackmun didn't understand how the public could fail to differenti-ate between personal conviction and judicial obligation. Blackmun's conscience told him to vote against *Roe*, but he supported women's right to choose out of duty. So, too, his conscience told him to vote for *Furman*, but again he supported capital punishment out of constitu-tional obligation. Surely, Blackmun thought, people understood that legislating morality wasn't the Supreme Court's role. When Reverend Trocinski wrote Blackmun that *Roe* had strained their friendship, Blackmun implored Trocinski to see the distinction. "The Court's task is to pass only upon the narrow issue of constitutionality," Blackmun wrote. "We did not adjudicate that abortion is right or wrong or moral or immoral. I share your abhorrence for abortion and am personally against it." Neither Trocinski nor anyone else bought it. To the day Blackmun retired, hate mail poured in. To add insult to injury, schol-ars denounced the decision as intellectually bankrupt.

The other justices didn't understand the public's rage any better. Lewis Powell was shocked. His biographer, John Jeffries, said Powell made the same calculation in *Roe* that Stewart had made in *Furman*. "By constitutionalizing abortion, Powell meant to anticipate popular sentiment, not to supplant it," Jeffries wrote. "By leaping over the leg-islative muddle, the Court would achieve quickly, cleanly, and without wrenching divisions, the solution toward which the country as a whole was clearly aimed." Powell attempted to console Blackmun, and told him he found the scholarly reviews of his opinion offensive. In truth neither understood how much damage the Court had suffered.

RICHARD NIXON DID. While Blackmun and his colleagues felt blindsided by the antipathy to *Swann* and *Furman* and *Roe*, Nixon felt vindicated. He had predicted it all. It is all too easy, given Watergate, to dismiss Nixon, but the fact remains he achieved in 1972 a complete and stunning victory, more lopsided than every presidential election save Franklin Roosevelt's 1936 triumph over Alf Landon, and James Monroe's 1820 victory over John Quincy Adams. Perhaps more than any other politician in American history, Richard Nixon had his finger on the pulse of the nation, and he understood precisely what the American people thought of the Supreme Court.

This understanding evolved initially from a book called *The Real Majority: An Extraordinary Examination of the American Electorate*, by Richard Scammon, an election analyst who had been director of the Census Bureau under John Kennedy, and Ben Wattenberg, a former speechwriter for LBJ. Wattenberg would later become a prominent conservative, but at the time of the book's publication in 1970, both he and Scammon were moderate Democrats, and each author intended the book as a warning to the Democratic Party, which in their view was losing touch with the American electorate. Scammon and Wattenberg said Democrats "owned" the economic issue, meaning Social Security and employment policy, but were squandering credibility with voters on social issues—crime, drugs, and morality. The "real majority" was economically liberal but socially conservative.

Scammon and Wattenberg illustrated their argument with a picture of the voter at the center of the electorate: "a 47-year-old Catholic housewife in Dayton, Ohio, whose husband is a machinist." Such blue-collar families had historically voted Democratic, but because of their increasing concern over social issues, were increasingly defecting to the Republican Party. Scammon and Wattenberg wrote, "To know that the lady in Dayton is afraid to walk the streets alone at night, to know that she has a mixed view about blacks and civil rights because before moving to the suburbs she lived in a neighborhood that became all black, to know that she does not have the money to move if her neighborhood deteriorates, to know that she is deeply disturbed that her son is going to a community junior college where LSD is found on campus—to know all this is the beginning of contemporary political wisdom."

In 1972, two years after Scammon and Wattenberg published *The*

Real Majority, the sociologist Stanley Cohen, of the London School of Economics, popularized the phrase "moral panic" in *Folk Devils and Moral Panic*. The book is widely regarded by British scholars as the most influential criminology text of the late twentieth century. Moral panic results when a condition or group of people emerges as a threat to societal values. The response is characterized by widespread concern, hostility toward the offending parties ("folk devils," in Cohen's terms), consensus that the group poses a threat, and a lack of proportion to the actual threat posed. Sociologists view witch hunts, McCarthyism, and mistreatment of Muslims following the September 11 attacks as instances of moral panic. Cohen cited fear of crime as a paradigmatic example of a force that could generate moral panic. Indeed, the response to rising crime in the early '70s reflects every feature of Cohen's phenomenon. Cohen adds that moral panics can be started or exacerbated by journalists and politicians who may have a vested interest in advertising the perceived threat. Using a term coined by the sociologist Howard Becker, Cohen refers to such actors as "moral entrepreneurs."

Richard Nixon was a moral entrepreneur. On Pat Buchanan's recommendation, Nixon read *The Real Majority* in August 1970, while vacationing at the western White House in San Clemente, California. The book influenced Nixon enormously, and for the remainder of his term and throughout the ensuing presidential campaign, he spoke often of the Dayton housewife. Nixon believed that the key to understanding this hypothetical woman was her deep mistrust of liberals, bureaucrats, and big government. She, like the silent majority, believed that government programs didn't help people like herself. To his chief of staff, H. R. Haldeman, Nixon said, "We've had enough social programs: forced integration, education, housing. People don't want more on welfare. They don't want to help the working poor, and our mood has to be harder on this, not softer."

On the basis of this reasoning Nixon instructed his attorney general, John Mitchell, to adopt a tougher, meaner-spirited stance toward black militants and student protesters. He began dismantling federal

programs. He vetoed the Clean Water Act and cancelled federal housing programs. He introduced revenue sharing, which offered direct,
unconditional grants to state and local governments. It was an unprecedented surrender of control over policy areas that had traditionally
been the province of the federal government. For this program political scientists coined the sui generis term, "devolution."

In 1972 small government was Nixon's central campaign theme,
and following his historic reelection victory, he declared at his second inaugural, "Government must learn to take less from people so
that people can do more for themselves." The president didn't openly
attack the Supreme Court, but his subtext was clear: It was illegitimate
for the Court, or any other federal government institution, to impose
its values on the people. The justices were agents of unwanted social
change, and through their decisions on busing and capital punishment
had sought to aid and protect a population that whites regarded as
dangerous and undesirable.

THE COURT DIDN'T LEAD public opinion, as Powell had hoped
with respect to abortion, and as Stewart had hoped with respect to
the death penalty. To the contrary, the Court's decisions entrenched
people in the views they already held. *Roe*, for example, galvanized
both support for and opposition to abortion. Washington University's Charles Franklin and Liane Kosaski showed that following Blackmun's decision, people who initially supported discretionary abortion
became more supportive, and individuals who opposed it became
more strongly opposed.

Professors Timothy Johnson and Andrew Martin found a similar
effect with respect to *Furman*. People became more committed to
whatever opinions they held prior to the ruling. In absolute terms public support for the death penalty increased in the wake of *Furman*. At
the same time esteem for the Supreme Court dropped. The most useful data comes from the General Social Survey (GSS), a wide-ranging
interview on American attitudes administered by the National Opin-

ion Research Center (NORC) at the University of Chicago. In 1973 the GSS began asking Americans about their confidence in a variety of institutions and figures. That year 32 percent of respondents reported great confidence in the Court. This compared to 30 percent for the presidency and 24 percent for Congress.*

Generally speaking, over the thirty-seven years the GSS has tracked these attitudes, confidence in the judiciary has run 10 to 25 percentage points ahead of the legislature and the executive. In 1973 the spread between the Court and the presidency was merely 2 percentage points.† Overall the GSS tells a story of declining confidence in government from which the Court has largely been immune, except in 1973. It's highly likely that support for the Court might have been even lower that year had it not been for the Court's decision to strike down Nixon's claim of executive privilege regarding the Watergate investigation.

YET, IF FRUSTRATION WITH the Supreme Court was really born out of underlying resistance to the Court's position on race and social issues, why was the public's antipathy expressed in the campaign to revive capital punishment, rather than against the busing and abortion decisions, which most directly challenged the real majority's social values?

The answer is perhaps a simple one: *Furman* was perceived as more vulnerable than the race and abortion cases. The race decisions— *Brown, Brown II, Green,* and *Swann*—had each been unanimous. *Roe* was seven to two, and the majority articulated a shared, if not entirely persuasive, theory of constitutional law. None of this was true in *Furman*, which was patently the product of a sharply divided Court, driven by politics.

---

* Unfortunately there are no such figures available for the years preceding *Furman, Roe,* and *Swann.*

† The presidency would only again come as close as 7 points—in 1977, a year of generally high confidence in the federal government, coinciding with Jimmy Carter's election.

Professor Robert Burt of Yale highlights the sharp contrast between the Court's message regarding capital punishment and desegregation. In the race cases, Burt said, the justices "put aside differences to shape the message they thought the country needed." Even Frankfurter and Black got along on that shining day in 1954. *Furman* generated no consensus. Each individual justice was isolated, and the decision didn't even link coherently with the other recent capital cases. Burt wrote, "Since there is no majority of the Court on the ultimate issue presented in these cases, the future of capital punishment in this country has been left in an uncertain limbo." Stanford Law School professor Robert Weisberg calls *Furman* "not so much a case as a badly orchestrated opera, with nine characters taking turns to offer their own arias."

Moreover, as a purely practical matter, it was possible for the states to respond to *Furman*. With respect to the race and abortion cases, their hands were tied. *Roe* energized the right-to-life movement. Many states enacted laws limiting or regulating abortion, but no state interfered with a woman's constitutional right to choose during the first trimester of a pregnancy. The race decisions were similarly immune. Dwight Eisenhower sent the army into Arkansas rather than let Orval Faubus defy the Supreme Court. Kicking and screaming, the South had been dragged forward through history. *Furman* was more vulnerable, and those aggrieved by the Court's race decisions sublimated their anger into the effort to revive capital punishment.

For, whatever the justices may have intended, everyone understood *Furman* as having been about race. Years later Clarence Thomas, no foe of the death penalty, said he understood *Furman* as having revolved around concerns over racial discrimination. John Paul Stevens viewed the history the same way. Thurgood Marshall saw both *Furman* and *Roe* as cases about race. (His views on the latter were shaped by his experiences living in Baltimore and Harlem, where he heard stories of penniless black women dying at the hands of unqualified abortionists.)

Unfortunately for opponents of the death penalty, the Court's views on race were a step ahead of the public. Franklin Zimring says this is often the case because justices are isolated from the public and because cases take so long to make their way through the system. "There's an odd lag time with the Supreme Court." According to Zimring, "*Furman* was hanging by a thread and meanwhile the country was going from the sixties to the seventies. *Furman* and *Roe* were really culturally 1968 decisions." But while *Roe* would endure, *Furman*, because of Stewart's compromise, lacked the intellectual coherence to withstand the onslaught of public hostility. And thanks to Warren Burger's dissent, the states had a playbook telling them how to respond.

THOSE WHO HAD WORKED so hard for the abolition of capital punishment had good reason to ask themselves: Given the backlash, was the litigation campaign worth it? After its stunning victory in *Furman*, LDF had far less success before the Supreme Court. It prevailed in *Woodson v. North Carolina*, a companion case to *Gregg*, in which the Court ruled mandatory death penalty statutes unconstitutional. The following year LDF's rising star, David Kendall, argued and won *Coker v. Georgia*, ruling the death penalty unconstitutional for rape. Five years passed before abolitionists won another major case, and that victory—on capital punishment for felony-murderers—was short lived, undermined another five years later when the Court upheld the death sentences of Ricky and Raymond Tison over the protestations of their lawyer, Alan Dershowitz. It wasn't until 1987 that abolitionists achieved another clear and lasting victory. During this era, Tony Amsterdam moved to the background, fretting about his usefulness as the public face of the cause. "By the mid-nineteen eighties," Amsterdam wrote, the justices "came to view the Fund's lawyers as abolitionist zealots, embarked on a crusade against the death penalty for its own sake."

During the two decades following *Gregg*, support for the death penalty reached all-time highs. In 1994, 80 percent of Americans said they supported the death penalty. During the 1980s executions reached a pace that hadn't been achieved since the 1950s. In 1983 sixty prisoners were executed in the United States. James Q. Wilson, a prominent political scientist at Harvard, was one of many academic commentators who saw the *Furman* victory as Pyrrhic:

> In a curious way, *Furman* has had the opposite effect of what many who favor abolishing the death penalty had hoped. For decades, the death penalty was slowly withering away as judges and juries exercised ever more discretion in reaching their verdicts in capital cases. This withering away pleased abolitionists, though of course they wished it would proceed even faster. And as executions became less common, they seemed to become more arbitrary. The result, it was supposed, would be a Court-imposed end to all executions under any circumstances. Instead we have a rush of new laws that may well rescue, by making more predictable, the use of capital punishment.

Some say LDF's money and energy could have been better directed toward legislative reform. Yet once the ACLU got involved against the death penalty, its efforts didn't yield much. Aryeh Neier, executive director of the ACLU from 1970 through 1978, points to lack of money as the problem. "If resources comparable to those LDF invested in litigation had been made available for a state legislative campaign, a good many states might have been persuaded to repeal their death sentence laws," Neier says.

Others go further in criticizing LDF's strategy. The political scientists Lee Epstein and Joseph Kobylka suggest that LDF may have done more harm than good by failing to respond to the changed reality following *Furman*. Eric Muller says LDF should first have created a political consensus against the death penalty before making the constitutional case. In his controversial 1991 book *The Hollow Hope*, University of Chicago political scientist Gerard Rosenberg goes a step further, arguing that courts are incapable of effecting social change. For example, Rosenberg finds no evidence that *Brown* ended segregation in schools, or that *Roe* materially increased access to legal abortions, or that *Miranda* reduced illegal confessions. If gains are to be made, he argues, they must be achieved in the political arena or in the court of public opinion.

Yet the fact remains that LDF's leaders saw themselves not as the leaders of a social movement but as lawyers. In his 2006 memoir, *The Making of a Civil Rights Lawyer*, Michael Meltsner says LDF didn't represent every death row inmate in the United States, "but even if we had, we would not, of course, have let them die without a judicial appeal." Asked in 2010 whether LDF should have refrained from raising the Eighth Amendment argument, Amsterdam said, "I never asked that question, because if I thought I could win on behalf of one of my clients, I didn't give a fucking shit about anything else. After *McGautha*, we had no choice but to raise the Eighth Amendment argument." He added, "We didn't have the kind of relationships with other groups which would cause us to ask that question. We were not linked to a community and structure where we might have thought about the issue." As late as the early '70s the ACLU still wasn't doing very much, and many of the anti–death penalty organizations and capital representation projects, which would later create the network Amsterdam lacked, had yet to be formed.

LDF understood that in representing killers, they had taken on unsavory characters, light-years apart from the "well-dressed church-going blacks they had represented in Alabama." But they never saw the public's recoil from *Furman* coming. In a 1985 interview Jack Greenberg said, "LDF did not worry about the backlash." Another LDF attorney said, "We were surprised at the explosion." The journalist Paul Reidinger said, "No one expected the legislative response to the decision." Amsterdam said in 2010, "The thing that surprised me in retrospect was the political reaction."

LDF's surprise is believable. Litigation of this magnitude is a war with many fronts. Public opinion mattered to LDF, though in a different way than it would to the leaders of a social movement for whom shifting public opinion is the entire game. To a lawyer, public opinion is merely one fact among many to be managed in the context of a lawsuit. Lawyers care about public opinion only to the extent that it matters to judges. Going into *Furman*, the Court had given LDF little indication that public attitudes would affect its decision. Opinion polls hadn't factored in *McGautha*, hadn't been discussed during the oral arguments in *Maxwell* and *Boykin*, and had been referenced only tangentially in Stewart's *Witherspoon* decision. Indeed, public opinion played no role in the published decisions in *Furman*, other than Marshall's argument about what it would be if the public were better informed. It played an important role only in Stewart's private ruminations.

In any event LDF had no capacity to alter public opinion, but its failure to anticipate the backlash left it inadequately prepared to meet the frenzied pace of work that followed. *Furman*, with its diverse opinions and dissents, opened battle in many new theatres, and amplified the importance of the conflict in several old ones. Douglas's opinion stressed the racial disparity of capital sentencing, a disputable question of fact. White's opinion said that the death penalty as employed didn't deter, again a factual question. Stewart suggested that the death penalty would withstand muster if arbitrariness could be curtailed. Again this presented a factual question. Were it not for the backlash, these skirmishes might have been contested over the course of decades, as LDF enlisted academics to gather information and attempt to answer these questions definitively. But the avalanche of public opinion meant that the Court couldn't or wouldn't defer revisiting the issue. Thus, from 1973 through 1976, LDF found itself fighting many battles at once, several of which were, from its standpoint, premature. As always LDF was outmanned, and as these new battlegrounds opened like holes in a dike, the organization's lack of time and resources became more of an issue than ever before.

CHAPTER 14

PROVING DETERRENCE AND RATIONALITY

B YRON WHITE'S *FURMAN* OPINION FOCUSED ON DETER- rence. His central premise was that states used the death penalty so infrequently that it served neither the utilitarian nor the retributive goals of punishment. Marshall and Brennan doubted that even a regularly used death penalty could reduce murder.

The majority's skepticism about the potential utility of capital punishment were based largely on the research of University of Pennsylvania sociologist Thorsten Sellin, one of the fathers of modern criminology and a founder of the Bureau of Justice Statistics. During his influential career, which stretched more than six decades, Sellin vigorously opposed the death penalty. In 1951 he testified to Britain's Royal Commission on Capital Punishment that the death penalty served neither deterrence nor retribution. Over the next two decades Sellin authored more than twenty articles on capital punishment, a widely read book, and debated the issue hundreds of times. In *Furman*, Marshall referred to Sellin as "one of the leading authorities on capital punishment," and laid out his work in detail.

Sellin, Marshall said, urged that if the death penalty deterred, four hypotheses should be true: One, murders should be less frequent in states with the death penalty than those without it, other factors being equal. Two, murders should increase when the death penalty is abolished and decline after it's restored. Three, the deterrent effect should be greatest in communities where an execution occurred. Four, law-enforcement officers should be safer in death penalty states. Sellin's research, which consisted primarily of comparing contiguous states with similar populations and economic conditions, differing only in that one retained capital punishment while the other didn't, indicated that none of these propositions was true. In fact, some evidence suggested that executions *encouraged* crime.

Though Marshall acknowledged several flaws in Sellin's research, relating principally to problems with the available data, he felt that the weight of the evidence favored the abolitionists. Marshall deemed Sellin's work "not convincing beyond all doubt, but persuasive." More important, he said uncertainty should be resolved in the abolitionists' favor. Marshall wrote, "We would shirk our judicial responsibilities if we failed to accept the presently existing statistics and demanded more proof."

The majority didn't agree on much in *Furman*, but on this point found common ground. Brennan didn't require data to justify his position, but nevertheless credited Sellin's work and dismissed the deterrence hypothesis. Douglas cited Sellin and, following Marshall's lead, relied heavily on empirical evidence in reaching his conclusion that the burden of executions fell disproportionately on poor blacks. In the crucial opinion, Stewart called the deterrence evidence "inconclusive," but said "many statistical studies have indicated that there is little, if any, measurable deterrent effect."

IN HIS OPINION Marshall effectively wrote the opposite of a "Brandeis brief." The term originated in the 1908 case *Muller v. Oregon*, where Louis Brandeis, then a Boston lawyer, used research to convince the Court to uphold an Oregon statute limiting women's work hours. Brandeis's famous submission collected hundreds of empirical studies to show that long workdays negatively affected women's health.

The decision marked the first time the Supreme Court relied upon social science data.

Over succeeding decades the practice became more common. In *Brown* the Warren Court cited LDF's psychological, sociological, and economic data. Biological evidence played an important role in *Roe*. But in each instance where the Court credited social science data, it was either as a basis for balancing competing interests, as in *Roe*, or, more commonly, to find a legislative action rational. *Furman* marked the first time the Court employed social science data to declare a statute *unconstitutional*.

The Nixon appointees didn't take kindly to Marshall's innovation. Upholding and rejecting legislative action on the basis of tenuous empirical evidence were quite different matters. Finding a statute reasonable didn't restrict lawmakers. If the 1908 Oregon state legislature enacted a questionable law to protect women, nothing prevented the 1909 Oregon state legislature from repealing or modifying it. Striking down a statute as unreasonable foreclosed the debate for all time—or at least until the Supreme Court reversed itself, which it doesn't often do. The Court's conservative members took exception. Regarding the *Furman* majority, Powell said, "What they are saying, in effect, is that the evolutionary process has come suddenly to an end; that the ultimate wisdom as to the appropriateness of capital punishment under all circumstances, and for all future generations, has somehow been revealed."

Warren Burger felt social science had little to offer the death penalty debate. "Comparative deterrence," he wrote, "is not a matter that lends itself to precise measurement." Criminologists couldn't prove deterrence one way or the other. Moreover, in Burger's view, most of the "research" was veiled advocacy. Scholars tended to find evidence that supported their political views. Furthermore, Burger rejected Marshall's premise that doubt should be resolved against the state. "To shift the burden to the States is to provide an illusory solution to an enormously complex problem."

This question of where the burden of proof should be placed—either on the states to prove a statute reasonable or on the challenging party to prove it unreasonable—is crucial. If the government is required, as it is, to prove that a criminal defendant is guilty beyond a reasonable doubt, then defendants have a fighting chance. If, instead, it were on the accused to prove his or her innocence, defending oneself would become vastly more problematic. Just as innocence can be as difficult to prove as guilt, reasonableness can be as daunting to demonstrate as unreasonableness. This was the intuition behind Burger's memorable example regarding parking tickets.

Unsurprisingly the Nixon appointees didn't put much stock in Sellin's research. Burger characterized the social science data as an "empirical stalemate." Blackmun said, "The statistics prove little, if anything." Powell said the studies "tend to support the view that the death penalty has not been proved a superior deterrent" but didn't approach the showing required to find the penalty unconstitutional. Unanimously the dissenters said the uncertainty should be resolved in favor of the states.

LDF UNDERSTOOD THAT FOR the new round of cases it would need better evidence than it offered in *Furman*. Hugo Bedau, on sabbatical leave from the Tufts Philosophy Department, took the lead. A prolific scholar, and an outspoken opponent of capital punishment, Bedau became in the years following *Furman* as central to the abolition movement in the academic community as Tony Amsterdam was in the legal universe. More or less every academic who had an interest in ending capital punishment interacted with Bedau.

In October 1972 Bedau attended an LDF conference, where Amsterdam and Jack Himmelstein announced LDF's three-prong strategy going forward. They would continue litigation, lobby to block new death penalty bills, and make greater efforts to develop empirical evidence. In Bedau's words, Amsterdam and Himmelstein "made clear the interests of lawyers in new social science research on all aspects of the death penalty." Bedau needed no further encouragement.

Bedau was a force of nature. During the next four years he had a hand in more than twenty studies of capital punishment–related issues. Several offered support for Marshall's hypothesis regarding public opinion. The most prominent of these, published in the *Stanford Law Review* by Yale's Neil Vidmar and Phoebe Ellsworth, argued that the evidence suggested Marshall's conjecture had been correct. The more specifically researchers questioned death penalty supporters, the weaker their support. Other studies looked at the psychological torture involved in death-row confinement, expanded earlier explorations of racism, and reexamined jury decision making. Bedau and LDF cast their net widely. After hearing a radio news report about the dismissal of a murder charge, Amsterdam asked Bedau to solicit research on journalistic coverage of criminal cases. At one point Bedau sought funds to get the renowned psychologist Lawrence Kohlberg involved in death penalty research.*

The principal concern, though, always remained deterrence. It was appropriate that this would be Bedau's central focus since deterrence was what first got Bedau interested in capital punishment. In the early '60s Bedau's wife represented a liberal advocacy group at a death penalty conference sponsored by the New Jersey legislature. A representative argued there that if New Jersey abolished capital punishment, while New York and Pennsylvania didn't, then "murderers would swarm across the Delaware and Hudson Rivers." When Bedau's wife

---

* Bedau and LDF so obsessively attended to the discussion in the academic community that they even exerted influence over the reviews of Michael Meltsner's book. University of Pittsburgh law professor Welsh White sent LDF a draft of his review of *Cruel and Unusual* for comment. LDF deliberated internally whether to discourage White from mentioning guided-discretion statutes, lest the reference cast the new laws in a favorable light. The final review, published in the *Columbia Law Review*, made no mention of guided-discretion laws, and emphasized mandatory statutes as the principal response to *Furman*.

told him the story that evening, he expected to hear that one of Princeton's sociologists had rebutted this improbable claim regarding deterrence, but she said no social scientist replied. In fact she had searched the library and found nothing useful to laypersons. In that moment Bedau, then a newly minted Harvard Ph.D., resolved to become a public resource. His 1964 volume, *The Death Penalty in America*, collected data on capital punishment for the first time. It would go through four editions and become one of the best-selling books ever on the subject.

In early 1973 Bedau and Berkeley's Elliot Currie secured a $32,000 grant from the Russell Sage Foundation to collect death penalty research and organize a series of conferences. They spent a day at the University of Pennsylvania Center for Studies on Criminology and Law, another at the Center for the Study of Law and Society at Berkeley, and a third at Stanford Law School reviewing psychological research. Informed by these discussions, Bedau sought further funding from Russell Sage to establish a Project in Social Science Research on Capital Punishment at the University of Pennsylvania, headed by Marvin Wolfgang, who had spearheaded LDF's research on racism in southern rape cases. The renowned Wolfgang may have been a draw for foundation support, but in the new round of litigation he and the other criminologists Bedau and Currie interviewed were poor allies. The academic universe was changing, and the scholarly debate for the new court battles would be governed by different rules. By aligning themselves with the historical leaders of criminology, LDF effectively carried a sword to a gunfight.

AT THE TIME the academic field of criminology was poorly equipped to answer the question whether the death penalty deterred. In an article in *Public Interest*, Daniel Patrick Moynihan offered a generally bleak assessment of the state of social science in the '70s. "Perhaps the first thing a jurist will wish to know about the social sciences is: How good are they? How well do they predict? The answer must be that the social sciences are labile in the extreme. What is thought to be settled in one decade is as often as not unsettled in the very next; and even that 'decent interval' is not always observed." Moynihan concluded, "It is a melancholy fact that recurrently even the most rigorous efforts in social science come up with devastatingly imprecise stuff."

Criminology and its allied discipline, criminal justice, were especially vulnerable to criticism. These were social sciences in their infancy. Criminal justice departments were populated by a hodgepodge of scholarly types: some former practitioners—police and correction officers who taught about best training practices—a handful of lawyers, a smattering of philosophers, and a few sociologists, such as Sellin.

Some defended the multidisciplinary nature of criminal justice as an advantage. It encouraged the field to consider issues from different perspectives. Criminal justice departments wouldn't interpret the question "does the death penalty deter" in a strictly positivist manner. Their philosophers would ask, "Should deterrence be a goal of punishment?" The lawyers would ask, "Does the Constitution allow it to be a goal of punishment?" The practitioners would ask, "How can it most effectively be implemented?" To these questions they would offer many cogent answers. But they were poorly equipped to answer the basic empirical question, "Does it work?"

In his seminal 1975 book, *Thinking About Crime*, James Q. Wilson examined the research on the efficacy of criminal rehabilitation programs. Wilson concluded that the entire body of research showed nothing one way or the other. Ridiculing criminologists' inability to say anything conclusive about deterrence (or anything else), Moynihan said, "The profession, in a word, has a way to go." Prior to *Furman* no one had studied the deterrence question with the precision that would be demanded in the harder sciences.

In a curious way this lack of rigor had been useful to LDF. A study based on more arcane methodology might have been inaccessible to a Supreme Court justice. Sellin had studied deterrence by comparing homicide rates in neighboring states. Any nonspecialist could understand this. "Prior to 1974, the literature on the subject of deterrence was easily researchable by a lawyer and understandable by a lawyer," Amsterdam said. For years he had been carrying on a casual conversation about deterrence with Wolfgang and his mentor, Sellin. The dialogue was at a level Amsterdam could comprehend and participate in fully.

This would soon end.

THE SEEDS OF THE REVOLUTION were planted in a 1968 article by Gary Becker, an economist who had recently moved from Columbia University to the University of Chicago. Becker was a graduate of Princeton and the University of Chicago, where he studied with Milton Friedman. In 1967 Becker received the John Bates Clark Medal, awarded biannually to the outstanding American economist under forty. In 1992 he received the Nobel Prize in Economics.

Becker's interest in criminology began when, rushed for time one day, he weighed the costs and benefits of illegally parking in a convenient spot. Becker roughly calculated the risk of getting caught and possibly fined, and opted—rationally in his view—to park illegally. In that moment it struck Becker that his thinking likely mirrored an ordinary criminal's. His intuition that criminals made cost-benefit calculations became the basis for his seminal article, "Crime and Punishment: An Economic Approach."

Viewed from the twenty-first century, Becker's insight seems unremarkable. The idea of applying economic theory to explain the actions of ordinary people became less threatening through Steven Levitt and Stephen Dubner's 2005 best seller, *Freakonomics*. (Indeed, Levitt cites Becker as a major influence.) In the context of the '60s, however, Becker's work was highly subversive. His vision of the would-be criminal as a calm, rational actor ran against the common wisdom that criminal behavior resulted from mental illness and social oppression. Becker happily toppled this totem. "A useful theory of criminal behavior," he wrote, "can dispense with special theories of anomie, psychological inadequacies, or inheritance of special traits." In Becker's analysis crime is simply an action with pros and cons, like any other.

Becker's work transformed the intellectual landscape and opened criminology to a new cohort of academicians. Economists, with their superior capacities in mathematics and statistics, joined the conversation. Many in the criminal justice community lamented the homogenizing influence of the quantitative mind. But, like it or not, the economists came, they saw, and they counted, inspired by the titanic figure of Gary Becker.

AMONG THOSE STIRRED BY Becker was Isaac Ehrlich, a young economist Bedau met in a pub under the el-train in Chicago in the course of his Russell Sage–funded research, who ominously told Bedau that he would soon publish research proving deterrence. Ehrlich possessed formidable credentials. He did his undergraduate work at Hebrew University in Jerusalem, earned distinction for his Ph.D. dissertation at Columbia, and while teaching at the University of Chicago doubled as an associate at the National Bureau of Economic Research. Ehrlich had studied with Becker at Columbia and followed his mentor to Chicago. In the early '70s Ehrlich decided to use econometrics to test capital punishment's deterrent effect. This empirical demonstration that criminals respond to penal sanctions would help prove their rationality and confirm Becker's hypothesis.

Deterrence, though, is a tricky phenomenon to model for several reasons. First, many factors influence murder rates. What economists call the "murder function"—the relationship between murder rates and certain variables—is imperfectly understood, and in the early '70s had been described only rudimentarily. Second, if the death penalty has a deterrent effect, it's surely quite small (otherwise, it wouldn't be so difficult to prove). Third, when crime drops, it's difficult to determine whether it's the result of deterrence or simply locking up dangerous people who would otherwise have committed additional crimes. And this only scratches the surface of the list of challenges.

Nevertheless Ehrlich got results. He defined a murder function based on the probability of apprehension, the probability of conviction given arrest, the probability of execution given conviction, the unemployment rate, the labor participation rate, real per capita income, and the proportion of the population between ages fourteen and twenty-four. Examining homicide rates between 1933 and 1967, Ehrlich found a positive correlation between executions and homicide rates. In other words, the more executions, the more murders—the opposite of what he had set out to prove.

Thorsten Sellin might have stopped here, but Ehrlich's mathematical expertise allowed him to go further. He was able to control for the effect of the other variables bearing on homicide rates by using the statistical technique of multiple regression. While simple regression isn't mathematically complex, multiple regression is complicated, particularly without computers. This is part of what dissuaded criminologists from tackling deterrence.

Using multiple regression, Ehrlich found a statistically significant deterrent effect associated with executions. Specifically he found an average elasticity of the murder rate to the conditional probability of execution between -0.06 and -0.065. This wouldn't mean much to an ordinary person, so he put it in plain terms. Between 1935 and 1969, Ehrlich said, each additional execution prevented between seven and eight murders.

IN THE SPRING OF 1973, Ehrlich circulated a working paper at the National Bureau of Economic Research bearing the ominous title, *The Deterrent Effect of Capital Punishment: A Question of Life and Death.* Word of Ehrlich's findings spread quickly.

In the office of the U.S. Solicitor General one of the attorneys saw a television interview with Ehrlich and brought the study to Robert Bork's attention. Impressed, Bork inserted Ehrlich's results into his lengthy amicus brief in *Fowler.* Ehrlich's work wouldn't be published until the spring of 1975, when it appeared in the *American Economic Review,* but Bork saw no reason to wait for the validation of peer review. Common sense told him that the death penalty deterred. In his *Fowler* brief Bork wrote that Ehrlich offered "important empirical support for the a priori logical belief that use of the death penalty decreases the number of murders." He asserted that Sellin's earlier studies suffered from "investigatory flaws," which Ehrlich's methodology corrected. Bork said Ehrlich's work showed "that there is sense to the process."

Brian Forst, a young researcher at the Institute for Law and Social Research, reacted differently. Forst also had recognized the significance of Becker's work and in the early '70s began his own study of deterrence. Though they worked independently, Forst analyzed almost precisely the same data sets as Ehrlich. Forst, however, reached the opposite conclusion. He found no evidence that capital punishment deterred.

When he learned of Ehrlich's work, Forst was disappointed. In the competitive world of academic research, being first is extremely important. "I thought I had a novel idea to apply econometric analysis to this question," Forst recalled in 2010. After reading Ehrlich's results, Forst questioned his own analysis. "It stymied me," Forst said. "I asked myself, 'How can it be that we are relying on the same data and yet reaching different conclusions?' I felt I must have done something wrong." Forst doubted himself all the more when he learned that Ehrlich's work would be published in the *American Economic Review*, a leading journal. The more Forst reviewed his calculations, however, the more convinced he became that Ehrlich had made the error. Ehrlich's findings depended on very specific analytic choices. If one suspended any of these conditions, the deterrent effect disappeared. Even a small change in the time period studied appeared to defeat his results. "The data is so subtle," Forst explained, "that you get different results if you use different assumptions."

Forst called the *AER*'s highly respected editor, Martin Feldstein, with whom he had studied in Chicago, and urged that the journal reject Ehrlich's paper. "I don't know how this got through your screens," Forst told Feldstein, "but the article is a crock." Forst knew Bork had cited Ehrlich's work. He told Feldstein that bad research might lead to executions, but Feldstein wasn't interested. The article had been peer-reviewed, he said. If the results were suspect, that would emerge in future papers. "Feldstein was a true believer," Forst said.

The cause in which Feldstein believed, however, wasn't capital punishment. Rather it was the idea that all actors are rational and responsive to incentives. This explained his willingness to publish inconclusive results. Forst believed the same principle motivated Ehrlich to overreach. "I don't think it was malicious," Forst said. "I think it was such a strong a priori belief in the theory of deterrence."

BRIAN FORST WASN'T THE only one questioning Ehrlich's results. Criminal justice scholars were generally skeptical of deterrence. They trusted neither Ehrlich's methodology nor his results. More broadly, they didn't believe that economic models applied to criminals. Ehrlich's work, in his own words, rested "on the presumption that offenders respond to incentives." Many criminologists and abolitionists rejected this premise. Tony Amsterdam told the California Commonwealth Club: "You and I ask ourselves: are we not afraid to die? Of course! Would the threat of death, then, not intimidate us to forbear from a criminal act? Certainly! Therefore, capital punishment must be a deterrent. The trouble with this intuition is that the people who are doing the reasoning and the people who are doing the murdering are not the same people. You and I do not commit murder for a lot of reasons other than the death penalty. Those who are sufficiently dissocialized to murder are not responding to the world in the way that we are, and we simply cannot intuit their thinking processes from ours."* Amsterdam wrote Forst that he suspected capital murderers might be risk seekers, not risk avoiders. To such people "a gamble involving enormous negative stakes may be more attractive than an otherwise identical gamble with smaller negative stakes." Thus,

---

* Later research supported Amsterdam's view. For example, Mark Fleisher of Illinois State University found that young boys prone to criminal behavior think exclusively about the present. Hence, deterrence cannot work. In a similar vein, James Q. Wilson wrote, "Changing incentives will not alter the behavior of poorly habituated people." This disagreement over first principles underlies the tension between economists and criminologists, which persists to this day.

Amsterdam said, "the institution of the death penalty may cause the minority who are predisposed to murder to be even more inclined to commit the crime than before."

LDF was in a legal and political battle, though, not an academic debate. Given time, it might be possible to respond to Ehrlich's study with a regression-based analysis disproving deterrence or psychological research proving that Becker's model didn't apply to criminals. But developing such data would take years and lots of money. Bedau estimated his Project in Social Science Research would cost nearly seven hundred thousand dollars over four years. It was hardly guaranteed the Russell Sage Foundation would fund the effort, and even in Bedau's best-ease scenario, the project wouldn't begin until 1974. Jesse Fowler's case might be argued and decided before Bedau's project got going. Furthermore, states were passing new death penalty statutes every month: Time was of the essence.

The only practical option was to discredit Ehrlich's work. Since the concepts weren't accessible to ordinary folks, the abolitionists resorted to vouching. They recruited scholars to explain why Ehrlich's methodology was inferior to Sellin's. Here the abolitionists had several things working in their favor. Sellin was a beloved figure, Ehrlich a virtual unknown. Sellin's methodology was familiar and accessible, as evidenced by Marshall's neat description of it; Ehrlich's was novel and impenetrable.

Following the circulation of Ehrlich's results, Bedau organized a special meeting at Yale on April 5, 1973. Franklin Zimring, who had recently coauthored a book on deterrence, hosted the gathering. The attendees included Hans Zeisel, University of Iowa statistician James Cole, and Northeastern University professors William Bowers and Glenn Pierce. Bedau charged them with writing critiques of Ehrlich's work. The professors immediately understood the project's importance. "If you're Tony Amsterdam," Zimring later explained, "as a litigator, you want to make sure you cover all the bases, that you have every horse saddled."

The researchers left with an agreement to publish critiques of

Ehrlich's work, though everyone recognized this as an imperfect solution. Negative appraisals of Ehrlich's study might help, but they were a distant second best to affirmative evidence showing that capital punishment didn't deter. Since they lacked the time to develop this evidence through research, they were resigned to play defense by creating uncertainty. How the Court would resolve the confusion was anyone's guess.

THE ABOLITIONISTS GOT A BREAK when in early 1975 the *Yale Law Journal* announced that it would devote the year's final issue to deterrence. Other law reviews had rejected Bedau's team's pieces, perhaps because of their technical nature, but the *Yale Law Journal*'s editor, John Spiegel, had received a National Science Foundation Graduate Fellowship in economics and was undaunted by the mathematics involved in the new research. Though Spiegel had no ideological predisposition, he recalled that his fellow editors thought "we should rush this into print, as the cases obviously would be decided in 1976."

In their article "Comparison of the Work of Thorsten Sellin and Isaac Ehrlich on the Deterrent Effect of Capital Punishment," Cole and his collaborator, David Baldus, rejected Ehrlich's approach. They said Sellin's matching technique was limited but nevertheless superior to Ehrlich's regression analysis. Generally speaking Baldus and Cole doubted that economists had the ability to accurately model the predictors of murder, and offered a quaint, Luddite's view of statistics. "Many questions are best studied by simpler methods," they wrote. Ehrlich's bias was clearly evident from his regression equation, which wasn't prepared to deal with abolition as a policy option. If the risk of execution were zero, it would predict an infinite murder rate. Ehrlich also computed execution risk as a function of the number of actual executions, as opposed to simply examining whether a state had the death penalty on the books, as Sellin had, even though legal status was the factor "directly controlled by courts and legislatures."

Baldus and Cole also faulted Ehrlich for relying on national crime figures. They offered the example of a simplified nation, consisting of only three states—two with the death penalty, and one without. If the risk of execution went down in one of the two death penalty states (while remaining constant in the others) and the murder rate went up in the state without the death penalty (while remaining constant in the others), a national analysis would suggest a deterrence effect since the overall murder rate would have increased while the overall execution risk would have decreased. Yet this wouldn't accurately describe reality. The increased murder rate couldn't be attributed to the decrease in executions since they occurred in different states. Though simple, the example accurately modeled the gross disparity between punishment in the South and the remainder of the United States—a difference that made Sellin's regional approach essential.

Overall, Baldus and Cole argued that courts should rely on social science data with great caution. They noted "a certain danger in relying on academic work, designed to promote inquiry and further research, as a basis for deciding disputes in a court of law—especially where the stakes involved are high and the implications for society are great." Daniel Moynihan made a similar argument in his article in *Public Interest*, noting that social science and law have different missions. "In the end," Moynihan wrote, "Social science *must* be a quantitative discipline dealing with statistical probabilities. Law, by contrast, enters the realm of the merely probable at some risk." Moreover, Moynihan wrote, "Social science is rarely dispassionate and social scientists are frequently caught up in the politics which their work necessarily involves."

Most of LDF's leaders and its academic supporters had mixed feelings about launching a broadside attack on social science evidence. The argument was a double-edged sword. LDF had relied on empirical evidence before and surely would again. Indeed, in 1987, LDF came within one vote of persuading the Supreme Court to reverse Warren McCleskey's conviction solely because of statistical evidence of racism. In the case, which would have revolutionized American criminal law, David Baldus was the key witness, offering testimony about his groundbreaking, comprehensive study of race and capital sentencing in Georgia in the early 1980s. His study relied heavily on regression.

✦   ✦   ✦   ✦

WILLIAM BOWERS AND GLEN PIERCE took a different tack in their *Yale Law Journal* article. Their critique focused on the choices Ehrlich made in implementing his regression analysis and the reliability of his data. Ehrlich used FBI crime statistics that were widely regarded as problematic.* Bowers and Pierce said Ehrlich should have used data from the Census Bureau. They also faulted Ehrlich's arrest-and-conviction data, which police commonly resisted transmitting to the FBI. In the 1960s more than three-quarters of agencies didn't report arrests, even fewer reported convictions, and those that did were disproportionately from large jurisdictions. Years later Pierce summarized the problem succinctly: "The data was crap."

Most important, the crime data from the 1960s drove Ehrlich's results. Between 1962 and 1969 the national murder rate increased by almost 60 percent. This overlapped almost precisely with the period during which LDF stopped executions. Ehrlich implied a causal link, which Bowers and Pierce doubted. It was highly probable that something other than the moratorium had driven the increase in crime. As Forst pointed out, Ehrlich had failed to consider the effect of long prison sentences—the most common alternative to capital punishment—as a deterrent. Sure enough, actual time in prison had declined during the '60s. Nor had Ehrlich considered that whatever force had led to shorter prison sentences and fewer executions might itself be the cause of the crime increase. Perhaps potential criminals had perceived that governments were soft on crime. Increased availability of guns might also have contributed to the rise in homicide, but was omitted from Ehrlich's model. Furthermore, many other

---

* Specifically, Ehrlich relied upon Uniform Crime Reporting System (UCR), which has been managed by the FBI since 1930. By the '70s the UCR was the standard metric of crime rates. Many agencies, though, had been slow to join the network. A presidential commission on law enforcement warned that UCR data prior to 1958 were unreliable, and especially so prior to 1940. To compensate, the FBI readjusted the figures but didn't fully explain its calculations.

kinds of crime increased during the '60s. Relatively speaking homicide had increased the least.

If the death penalty deterred, as Ehrlich claimed, it should be discernible over any time period. The opposite was true. If data from the '60s were excluded from the analysis, "all empirical support for the deterrent effect of capital punishment disappeared." Ehrlich could have downplayed the impact of the '60s on his results. Instead Bowers and Pierce contented that Ehrlich manipulated his data to accentuate the impact of the '60s crime figures. He accomplished this by using the logarithm of execution rates rather than the natural number of executions.* If Ehrlich's analysis had been performed properly—that is, by analyzing only 1940 through 1963, without logarithmically transforming executions—it would have showed no deterrent effect.

EHRLICH FOUGHT BACK. He defended his data choices. FBI data were superior to census data because the UCR included only willful felonious homicides. Regarding the relevant time period, Ehrlich simply had selected the longest time period for which the necessary data were available. It was Bowers's and Pierce's subjective judgment—a wish, really—that the late '60s were idiosyncratic. In the '60s executions stopped and murder increased. "The sharp movements in the rates of change are, of course, not my invention," Ehrlich said. He went on to attack Bowers and Pierce as hypocritical, and eviscerated Baldus and Cole for failing to understand the methods they had criticized.† Regarding Sellin, Ehrlich said his reliance on legal status as opposed to actual risk of execution damned his results.

What differentiated Ehrlich from his critics, he said, was that he

---

* A logarithm is the exponent to which a base must be raised to produce a given number. At the lower range of a variable, logarithmic transformation accentuates variations. For example, in logarithmic form, the difference between 1 and 2 executions per 1,000 convictions is greater than the difference between 350 and 650 executions per 1,000 convictions.

† Readers can find more detailed explanations of these issues in the endnotes.

wasn't involved in the capital punishment debate. If Ehrlich had an agenda, it was merely to show that "in the aggregate, potential offenders respond to both negative and positive incentives." Ehrlich was convinced that economics could inform and elevate the debate, and he expressed concern that his critics would "baffle the lawyer pondering the merits of using an economic approach to law or of using statistical techniques to study legal questions."

With respect to the death penalty as policy, Ehrlich had little to say. "I have not claimed that my research settles the issue of the deterrent effect of capital punishment. Nor have I advocated the use of capital punishment." Much else needed to be considered. "As I stressed in my paper, the issue of deterrence is but one of a myriad of issues relating to the efficiency and desirability of capital punishment as a social instrument for combating crime." But, "research on the issue undoubtedly will benefit in the long run from legitimate attempts to use more efficient data and statistical techniques than those heretofore employed in studies of capital punishment." Indeed, many of his most vocal critics acknowledged Ehrlich as an innovative contributor to the debate.

SO WHO WAS RIGHT? The following issue of the *Yale Law Journal* published an assessment of the deterrence exchange, written by the Yale economist Jon Peck, by all accounts an honest broker. Peck agreed with Ehrlich's logarithmic transformations. He also sympathized with Ehrlich's inclusion of the 1960s data. On the larger question, Peck said Baldus and Cole were clearly wrong to prefer Sellin's methodology. Ehrlich's regression analysis could be faulted, but the alleged deficiencies didn't call into question the general reliability of regression. Matching, on the other hand, imposed "relatively little structure on the problem" and was therefore "less likely than the econometric approach to find effects which are weak." This last point was crucial since everyone agreed that if the death penalty deterred, the effect was minimal. Overall Peck felt that Ehrlich hadn't proved deterrence conclusively, but he accepted Ehrlich's results.

In 1976 the National Academy of Sciences convened a panel on deterrence chaired by Carnegie Mellon professor Al Blumstein, one of the most influential figures in the field of criminal justice, and including what Franklin Zimring called "a who's who of American econometricians." The panel's final report, issued in 1978, faulted both Sellin for failing to control for the demographic, cultural, and socio-economic factors that influence homicide and Ehrlich for depending too much on the 1962–69 crime increase. Since other crimes increased as much as homicides, one could easily conclude that an independent third cause had led to both the trends in executions and homicide. Overall the panel concluded that "the available studies provide no useful evidence on the deterrent effect of capital punishment."

In the criminal justice community, Ehrlich's work was largely discredited. In 1974, Yale's Charles Black pronounced that deterrence would never be proved or disproved conclusively. Writing by himself, Forst strongly criticized Ehrlich: "Ehrlich's findings are the product of his strong a priori belief in the theory of deterrence. A sufficiently strong a priori belief in anything can induce even the most well-intentioned of scientists to gravitate towards findings that support the belief." This reflected the prevailing sentiment about Ehrlich's work within the criminal justice community.

The work on deterrence partially undid Ehrlich's career: He didn't get tenure at the University of Chicago. Franklin Zimring, who was there during the '70s, attributed this to Ehrlich's deterrence work. "There was no scandal," Zimring said. "Just not enough theory to get him tenure. There was not enough there there. What you get credit for in this process is what Becker had done, the theory, even though all of the good economics of crime is empirical work." Some abolitionists took heart from Ehrlich's misfortune. After he heard the news, the sociologist Hans Zeisel put his arms around two of his colleagues and said, "He didn't get tenure."

In the economics universe, however, Ehrlich had ample support, and his career thrived. Ehrlich would become a distinguished professor at the State University of New York at Buffalo and the chairperson of its Economics Department. Over the next three decades he would write more than eighty peer-reviewed articles and be listed among the one hundred most cited economists. He would also be appointed as a researcher at the National Bureau of Economic Research.

In 1976 James Yunker, a professor at Western Illinois University, published an article finding deterrence in the *Journal of Behavioral Economics*. The following year Dale Cloninger of the University of Houston also replicated Ehrlich's results. Since then more than two dozen studies have been published in prominent journals finding evidence that the death penalty prevents murder. Some of these have detected an even stronger effect than Ehrlich found. A team of researchers at Emory University concluded in 2003 that each additional execution saves eighteen lives. Almost all these investigators would pay homage to Ehrlich's "seminal research."

On the other hand, many of these studies have been discredited, and many others have offered affirmative evidence that the death penalty doesn't deter. Forty years later the academic community remains sharply divided. Much of the current controversy focuses on the use of a newly popular econometric technique—instrumental variables analysis—which critics say is too sensitive to changes in model specifications to offer consistent, reliable results. It sounds eerily familiar—both in substance and in the level of rancor—to the debate over Ehrlich's research. Different people and different intellectual communities had and have different perceptions of who held the better hand in the debate over deterrence in the '70s. Generally speaking, economists have been sympathetic to Ehrlich, while criminologists have been skeptical. Even today, only the boldest of scholars would claim that the debate has been settled.*

RATHER THAN "WHO WAS RIGHT?" it is more saliently asked, "Who prevailed?" While the former cannot conclusively be answered even today, the latter lends itself to some more definitive observations.

---

* An endnote offers an overview of the current academic debate.

Ehrlich's work gave a colorable basis for making the argument that the death penalty deterred. Ernest van den Haag, a lecturer at the New School of Social Research and NYU, carried this banner for death penalty supporters. Van den Haag was one of the nation's most outspoken and audacious conservatives, with influence beyond his credentials. In March 1972, shortly before the Court announced *Furman*, a subcommittee of the House Judiciary Committee held hearings on a proposed two-year moratorium on executions. Van den Haag was among a handful of academics invited to testify.

During his career van den Haag argued to abolish child labor laws, on the premise that the evils they were designed to prevent had passed, and argued for continued school segregation, in part on the basis of blacks' supposed genetic inferiority. For years he contributed to the *National Review*. But support for capital punishment was his true passion, and van den Haag advertised Ehrlich's work in countless speeches, op-eds, and in his enduringly popular 1975 book, *Punishing Criminals: Concerning a Very Old and Painful Question*.

Van den Haag offered a wholesale defense of capital punishment on utilitarian and retributive grounds. The death penalty worked, and it gave defendants what they deserved. He dismissed the argument that the death penalty discriminated against the poor and black. "If true," he told Congress, "the suggestion would be nonetheless wholly irrelevant. It concerns the unfair way in which the penalty is distributed, not the fairness or unfairness of the penalty." But the cornerstone of van den Haag's argument was that some criminals, notably prisoners sentenced to life without parole, could only be deterred by the death penalty. "Common sense," he wrote, "lately bolstered by statistics, tells us that the death penalty will deter murder, if anything can. People fear nothing more than death. Therefore, nothing will deter a criminal more than the fear of death. Death is final. But where there is life there is hope."

The counterstudies received far less coverage than Ehrlich's work. Baldus, Cole, Bowers, and Pierce's papers may have influenced the academic community, but few ordinary people read the *Yale Law*

Journal (nor do they absorb reports by NAS panels). Furthermore, in politics, repeating an unfavorable message—even if to reject it—can be damaging in and of itself. Slowly the deterrence idea got through. An April 7, 1976, *Washington Post* editorial noted a change in the attitude of left-leaning scholars and politicians. The *Post* noted that even Morris Udall, the liberal Arizona congressman, had begun calling for measures to remove criminals from society, in part because of Ehrlich's work. So too had the Committee for the Study of Incarceration, formed in the aftermath of the Attica uprising, and also perceived as left of center. When Governor Reagan praised President Nixon for pushing to restore the death penalty, he premised his argument on deterrence. "The President certainly is reflecting the concerns of a great many Californians who agree that the death penalty is a deterrent to crime," Reagan said. New York governor Nelson Rockefeller matter-of-factly referenced deterrence in urging his state to restore capital punishment. Public support for the deterrence idea crept upward. Harris polls in mid-1973 and early 1977 found that almost 60 percent of respondents thought the death penalty deterred.*

In *Gregg*, Potter Stewart's opinion would say that the evaluation of social science data should be left to the states. Though he would deem the deterrence research inconclusive, Stewart nevertheless would offer his hunch as to the truth. Channeling van den Haag, Stewart delivered the death blow:

---

* This belief—or misconception—had a profound impact on attitudes. In the 1973 survey Harris asked whether respondents would support capital punishment if it could be proved that a long sentence was as effective a deterrent as the death penalty. Support for capital punishment slipped from 59 percent to 35 percent. It took many years for abolitionists to rebut the belief in deterrence. It wasn't until 2000 that a majority of Americans believed the death penalty didn't deter. Even still, when during a 2000 presidential debate, Jim Lehrer asked the candidates whether they "believe that the death penalty actually deters crime," George Bush said, "I think the reason to support the death penalty is because it saves people's lives." Al Gore didn't disagree.

We may assume safely that there are murderers, such as those who act in passion, for whom the threat of death has little or no deterrent effect. But for many others, the death penalty undoubtedly is a significant deterrent. There are carefully contemplated murders, such as murder for hire, where the possible penalty of death may well enter into the cold calculus that precedes the decision to act. And there are some categories of murder, such as murder by a life prisoner, where other sanctions may not be adequate.

WHILE THE FIGHT OVER deterrence raged, LDF fought an equally vital battle against the insidious notion that the death penalty could be applied rationally. In *McGautha* John Harlan answered the question whether a nonarbitrary sentencing system could be established with a resounding no, calling the task of articulating the characteristics of who should live and who should die beyond human ability. From this Harlan concluded that the decision whether and how to sentence people to die should be left to individual states and juries. In *Furman* Potter Stewart and Byron White drew the opposite conclusion. Because states lacked rational, predictable sentencing guidelines, the death penalty served no public purpose, was unfair, and hence must be scrapped.

Over the course of the next four years, thirty-five states responded to Stewart and White's opinions by passing new statutes designed to curtail arbitrariness. As the states thought through what might satisfy the Supreme Court, they considered three principal reforms. Some states implemented two. Others, notably including Georgia, did all three. First, a state could split capital trials into separate guilt and sentencing phases. Single-phase trials confronted defendants with a cruel dilemma, which had been a central issue in *Crampton*. If a defendant testified to offer mitigating evidence, he faced cross-examination regarding his alleged crime. Split-phase trials resolved this, and conventional wisdom said they also created greater rationality. Following

Furman, eight states implemented bifurcated trials, including Florida and Georgia.

Second, states could create a special sort of appellate review to correct egregiously unjust death sentences. LDF doubted that state courts would take this function seriously. Also, defining an unjust death sentence seemed as difficult as establishing standards for who should die in the first place. Nevertheless, as part of its reform package, Georgia included an automatic appeal to its Supreme Court.

Third, states could establish criteria for deciding which murderers received the death penalty. Every state engaged in this exercise to some extent. Some simply made the death penalty mandatory for murder, as Burger suggested in his *Furman* dissent. This solution, though, did nothing to curtail the charging discretion possessed by prosecutors and police. Mandatory laws also increased the possibility of nullification. For these reasons many attorneys general thought the Court would reject mandatory laws. Only seven states, including North Carolina, went in this direction.

Twenty states attempted to rationalize sentencing by specifying facts and circumstances that made some murders and murderers worse than others. Among these states, eleven, including Louisiana, made this process part of the guilt determination by building special circumstances into the definition of death-eligible murders. The federal government and nine other states, including Georgia, resolved the process during the penalty phase by creating aggravating factors, of which a jury needed to find at least one to sentence a murderer to die. The question was whether states could write these factors in clear, comprehensible language and meet Harlan's challenge.

To this end attorneys general found guidance in the Model Penal Code (MPC), a project of an organization of lawyers, judges, and professors known as the American Law Institute (ALI). The main work of the ALI is drafting "restatements," which explain the prevailing legal rules in different jurisdictions. Often the restatements themselves become a sort of law, and are commonly relied upon by lawyers in arguing cases and by judges in deciding them. Between 1923 and 1944 the ALI published restatements of agency, contracts, property, torts, and trusts. When it attempted to draft a restatement of criminal law, however, it concluded that the field was a hodgepodge with no consistent rationale. The ALI said the United States needed a model criminal code.

Two prior efforts to construct such a code had failed. In the early nineteenth century Edward Livingston, a prominent lawyer and politician who served both as mayor of New York City and a Louisiana senator, promulgated a code based on the utilitarian principles of the eighteenth-century Italian philosopher Cesare Beccaria. In other words, punishment should be employed only to the extent it produced more good than harm. Under this standard Livingston proposed to eliminate capital punishment and to make hard labor an avenue to better prison accommodation rather than a sanction. By the standards of his time, Livingston's code was uncommonly humane, and it found few supporters. Another nineteenth-century lawyer, David Dudley Field, fared somewhat better. New York adopted Field's Code in 1850, and eighteen other states followed suit. Unlike Livingston, though, Field had no aspirations of reform. He simply wanted to make existing law more readable for practicing attorneys.

The MPC, by contrast, was both transformative and highly influential. In the two decades following the MPC's publication in 1962, thirty-four states reformed their criminal codes based upon its recommendations. Philosophically the MPC blended utilitarian and retributive considerations with an emphasis on rehabilitation. Its most substantial innovation was to emphasize the mental state, or *mens rea*, of the defendant. Before the MPC, states had sometimes required a guilty mind, sometimes not. The MPC said a defendant couldn't be found guilty unless he or she had acted purposely, knowingly, recklessly, or negligently. The clarity and simple rationality of the approach had great appeal. People who acted with more blameworthy intent deserved more punishment and most needed to be deterred. Also because the MPC graded punishment on the basis of its four defined mental states, it was easier to apply than most state codes and gave judges more flexibility in determining.

With respect to the death penalty, the MPC laid out an ostensibly rational system. It required bifurcated trials. It specified mitigating factors, such as the defendant's lack of prior criminal history. It exempted defendants who were under eighteen years old at the time of their offense and people whose mental or physical condition demanded leniency. Finally it required that one of eight aggravating circumstances be found as a precondition to a death sentence. These included aspects of the murderer's status (for example, he was an escaped prisoner), characteristics of the murder (for example, it created a risk of death to many persons), and the murderer's motivation (for example, killing for monetary gain).* With minor modifications the MPC became the model for Georgia's death penalty statute and the laws in the nineteen other states that took the guided-discretion route. After the Court approved Georgia's death penalty statute and rejected mandatory laws on the same day, the MPC became the basis, essentially, for every American death penalty statute.

That the states found guidance in the MPC is ironic since the death penalty fundamentally rejected the MPC's rehabilitative philosophy and its principal architect, Herbert Wechsler, who directed the ALI from 1963 to 1984, opposed the death penalty as a matter of principle. Though Wechsler played no direct role in the capital cases, he influenced them profoundly, and his career offers an important contrasting perspective on how the capital campaign might have been conducted.

---

* Throughout the death penalty debate, different people drew different lessons from the MPC's standards. During the *Maxwell* orals Amsterdam cited the MPC to Fortas as an example of how standards might be constructed. In *McGautha* Harlan cited the MPC's vagueness to prove that standards couldn't be constructed and, hence, shouldn't be required. In his *Gregg* opinion Stewart would say that the MPC proved that standards could be drafted.

✦ ✦ ✦ ✦

BORN IN NEW YORK in 1909, Wechsler entered City College at sixteen, excelled at language studies, and applied for a professorship. But his father, a lawyer, wanted his son to follow in his footsteps. By chance, Samuel Wechsler knew the head of City College's French Department and convinced him not to give his son a job. Herbert instead enrolled at Columbia Law School, where he became editor in chief of the law review and later, following a clerkship for Justice Harlan Stone, a faculty member. During the 1940s Wechsler joined the Justice Department, where he served as assistant attorney general in charge of the War Division. In this role he advised American judges at Nuremberg and helped develop the framework for trying Nazi war criminals.

Wechsler was Jewish and, like Alan Dershowitz and Arthur Goldberg, opposed capital punishment. His concerns, however, were primarily practical. Wechsler believed the death penalty didn't help control crime. In fact he believed the death penalty might "brutalize" ordinary citizens by encouraging violent behavior. Wechsler further believed that the death penalty encouraged jury nullification. Wechsler's path diverged from Dershowitz and Goldberg's in other, more significant ways. While Dershowitz and Goldberg remained passionate, highly visible opponents of the death penalty throughout their lives, Wechsler publicly supported capital punishment.

To understand why, one needs to understand Wechsler's worldview, in which the public's moral beliefs had to be respected lest people lose confidence in the law. From behind his horn-rimmed glasses Wechsler often reminded colleagues that when a crime occurs, it is "the general community whose values have been disturbed." If the community didn't believe that justice had been done, then it would reject the outcome and make things right. Wechsler wrote, "The desire for revenge, the belief that retributive punishment is just, and the feeling that examples must be made of those guilty of shocking crimes are to a very considerable degree entrenched in the general population." Wechsler was a retributivist for utilitarian reasons: He believed offenders must be given what they deserved to satisfy the public.

Wechsler's tenure in Nuremberg cemented his world view. Assisting prosecutors, Wechsler concluded that the demand for revenge against Nazis was so great—rising, as he put it, "like a plaintive chant" from desolated, postbellum Europe—that failure to prosecute them would lead to "indiscriminate violence" and "a blood bath beyond power of control." The reason to try the Nazis, he wrote in 1947, was to provide a mechanism to keep "the application of violence" out of private actors' hands.

The fear of public backlash and vigilantism recurred as a theme throughout Wechsler's work. In their seminal casebook on criminal law, Wechsler and his colleague Jerome Michael wrote that lenient treatment of offenders could lead to lynching, and the idea informed Wechsler's MPC work. In a commentary to one of the early drafts, Wechsler wrote, "A penal law will neither be accepted nor respected if it does not seek to repress that which is universally regarded by the community as misbehavior." In a 1959 article in the *Harvard Law Review*, Wechsler argued that even though the Supreme Court possessed the awesome authority of judicial review, it mustn't act like a "naked power organ" lest the public reject its judgment. To preserve its credibility, Wechsler argued that the Court needed to rely upon "neutral principles"—that is, standards that were generally and equally applicable to all cases. Controversially, Wechsler suggested that *Brown* represented a departure from neutral principles, specifically by the Court's selective acceptance of social science data.

His unconventional, conservative view of *Brown* didn't mean that Wechsler opposed change. To the contrary, he is widely regarded as one of the great liberal reformers of the criminal law. Wechsler, though, believed the path to progress was educating or reorienting public opinion. The law could only follow, not lead, the public will. John Jay College of Criminal Justice professor Stanley Ingber vividly imagines the Court's "legitimacy account," into which deposits are made when the Court decides cases "consistent with popularly embraced values," and from which withdrawals are made when the Court attempts "to educate and direct society rather than conform to and follow it." This well describes Wechsler's view.

So, in his public discourse, Wechsler favored retaining the death penalty solely and precisely because the people overwhelmingly supported it. The ALI's advisory committee on the death penalty originally supported excluding capital punishment from the MPC. At Wechsler's urging the full council rejected the recommendation. Wechsler said political support for capital punishment would evaporate only after a majority of voters favored abolition. Ultimately the MPC finessed the question by outlining what a capital-sentencing statute should look like if the state chose to retain capital punishment. On this latter question, it took no position, as Wechsler believed that retaining the death penalty would help the MPC gain acceptance with the public.*

Wechsler maintained this same perspective throughout his career. When Wechsler served on Governor Nelson Rockefeller's Commission to Revise New York's Penal Law in 1961, New York was the only state with a mandatory death penalty for first-degree murder. A majority of the committee wanted to end capital punishment. Wechsler urged caution. He viewed the committee's other work reforming culpability, justification, and excuse as more important, and thought ending capital punishment would compromise its credibility. Once again he argued that the public's desire for revenge needed to be respected. Premature abolition could be counterproductive, as Delaware's experience proved: The state abolished capital punishment in 1958, then reinstated it two years later following a gruesome, highly publicized triple murder. Wechsler thought the pattern easily could repeat itself in New York.

Wechsler effectively confronted the same dilemma that Potter Stew-

* Wechsler made a similar compromise regarding incest, which he believed, based on a review of scientific evidence, shouldn't be a crime. He nevertheless included it in the MPC because he thought its inclusion necessary for the code to gain popular acceptance.

art faced in his negotiations with Byron White. Each had to decide how to reconcile his moral feelings about the death penalty with the world as it was. Stewart placed his chips on the idea that the Supreme Court could push public opinion. Wechsler, on the other hand, consistently accommodated the public will.

History validated Wechsler's judgment. The MPC was as a huge success. The *New York Times* commended it, the legal community embraced it, and ultimately it influenced every criminal code in the country. What makes this irony particularly cruel and unusual, though, is that Wechsler's compromise, including a modified death penalty in the MPC, helped undo Stewart's compromise. Even though the MPC designated the capital punishment provision as optional, the MPC's inclusion of a more structured death penalty gave it an imprimatur of credibility. Wechsler thus helped create the appearance that the death penalty could be applied rationally.

LDF HAD ONLY MODEST success refuting the claim that aggravating factors made capital sentencing less arbitrary. In June 1974 the *Harvard Law Review* published a note largely critical of the new laws. "In Georgia, all decisions not to impose the death penalty are justifiable. Conversely, all decisions to impose a capital sentence are also justifiable, so long as one aggravating factor is found. These statutes appear similar to those statutes which were condemned in *Furman*." The note's author, David Silberman, submitted a draft for comment to LDF, which prevailed upon him to clarify that capital punishment might be unconstitutional regardless of how states structured jury discretion.

Later that year Charles Black published *Capital Punishment: The Inevitability of Caprice and Mistake*, in which he argued that the new death penalty statutes had done nothing to curtail arbitrariness. "What Georgia has done is to lay down a smoke-screen of plenteous words, which, on hasty reading, mask the fact that exactly the same old unbridled jury discretion is there, if only the jury, guided by court and prosecutor, can grope its way through the verbal haze." Michael Meltsner published an op-ed saying, "Discretion has not been eliminated, it has merely become less visible." John Hart Ely, later wrote regarding the new statutes, "In less serious circumstances, this would be amusing." In truth, however, none of these critiques had been substantiated by research. LDF tried to recruit Lee Hamilton of the Russell Sage Foundation, among others, to test the effectiveness of the new standards, but there simply wasn't time.

Academics later had more to say on this issue. Ultimately it's an empirical question whether bifurcated trials and aggravating factors curtail arbitrariness. It's not an easy question to answer, but it's a factual question all the same: Were death sentences more predictable and consistent after *Furman* than they were before?

The sister-brother team of Carol and Jordan Steiker, of Harvard and the University of Texas, respectively, analyzed the issue in a 1995 *Harvard Law Review* article, in which they argued that *Furman* and *Gregg* accomplished nothing. Each Steiker is a former Thurgood Marshall clerk, well published, and an active opponent of capital punishment. Collectively the Steikers, who often write together, are the most influential legal scholars in the death penalty community. Though the Steikers' analysis isn't quantitative, it's persuasive. They begin by asking how death penalty statutes could have generated more predictable sentences, and offer two possible answers. First, states might have reduced the number of murderers eligible for the death penalty, a function the Steikers call "narrowing," and ostensibly the purpose served by enumerating aggravating factors. Second, states could treat similar cases similarly, which the Steikers term "channeling." In practice, the Steikers say, neither goal has been achieved.

Regarding narrowing, the devil again is in the details. To narrow successfully, states need to select a few clear, restrictive aggravating factors. Murdering a police officer is an example of a specific, objective aggravating circumstance that eliminates many defendants, as most murderers don't kill police officers. Indeed, murdering a police officer is an aggravating circumstance in every death penalty state. So, too, though, is murdering someone in an especially "heinous, atrocious or cruel" manner. This is less useful. What murder *isn't* heinous, atrocious or cruel?* The Steikers find abundant evidence of similarly vague, broad aggravating circumstances. Furthermore, they say, states often list so many factors that, even if they are individually useful, collectively they include so many types of murders and murderers as to ultimately eliminate no one. With respect to channeling, the problem is that after a murderer is found to satisfy an aggravating circumstance, it's left to the jury to decide whether the aggravating evidence outweighs the mitigating evidence, for which task they receive no guidance. For example, juries have complete discretion to decide which police killers live and which die. Thus receiving the death penalty remains as much a matter of chance as before *Furman*.†

David McCord of Drake Law School attempted to quantify the question by creating a culpability index derived from factors juries widely regard as meriting harsher punishment, such as torturing a victim, and factors juries generally perceive as mitigating, such as a defendant's mental impairment. McCord found that both before *Furman* and after, defendants with the highest culpability scores were routinely sentenced to die and defendants with the lowest scores were routinely spared. At the intermediate levels of culpability, however, he found greater consistency after *Furman*. Though McCord opposes the death penalty, he says *Furman* must at least be acknowledged as a partial success, particularly in the sense Stewart and White laid out in their

---

* In some instances, the Supreme Court has struck down "heinous, atrocious, and cruel" and similar aggravating factors as unconstitutionally vague. In other cases, though, the Court has upheld such factors either because they had been explained in case law or because a judge made the sentencing determination (and presumably requires less guidance than a juror).

† The counterargument is that the nature of the arbitrariness has changed. Prior to *Furman* the risk was that a jury might sentence to die a defendant who didn't deserve death. After *Gregg* the risk is that a jury will fail to sentence someone who deserves to die. Academics sometimes refer to this as the difference between overinclusion and underinclusion. It's arguably analogous to the distinction between convicting an innocent person and setting free a guilty man, errors the American criminal justice system treats as different in kind.

opinions. McCord writes, "The populations of death rows since 1972 very likely comprise a more carefully selected and worse collection of malefactors than before 1972."

In 2009, the ALI repealed the MPC's death penalty provision, in part because of research by the Steikers. The repeal, however, was almost certainly as much as a political statement as it was a validation of scholarly research.

RATHER THAN WHO WAS right, it again may be more saliently asked, Who prevailed? To this question, the answer is, resoundingly, the proponents of capital punishment. Georgia's Supreme Court said that its state's new statute controlled discretion "by clear and objective standards so as to produce non-discriminatory application." Other state courts reached similar conclusions.

The Steikers point to the veneer of predictability as the lasting legacy of *Furman* and *Gregg*. They write, "The Court's doctrine, a facade, is successful at making participants in the criminal justice system and the public at large more comfortable with the death penalty than they otherwise would be or should be." Founding legal realists would have ridiculed the idea that a legal system could rationally determine who should live or die. One can readily imagine that Oliver Wendell Holmes would have branded the guided-discretion statutes a folly of formalism (and the entire enterprise a charade). Holmes's essential insight is that the law cannot operate formulaically. Abstract principles don't decide concrete cases. Even in the post-*Gregg* world, juries, police and prosecutors retain enormous discretion, which no words can constrain.

Yet, the myth of rationality had (and has) substantial power. While public support for the death penalty surged after *Furman*, it skyrocketed following *Gregg*. Almost certainly this was because the public believed the courts had "fixed" the system. The Steikers term this process "legitimation," crediting the idea to the sociologist Max Weber and the Italian political theorist Antonio Gramsci. The appearance of a rational system made, and makes, actors within the criminal justice system—prosecutors, judges and executioners—more comfortable with their respective roles. It also makes people more tolerant of the exercise of power by the state. Stanford's Robert Weisberg says, "A penalty trial that looks legally sophisticated offers some comforting illusions about the moral order of our public law, and might thereby earn for the death penalty at least some grudging political respect it does not deserve."

Standards may help legitimate the death penalty not only at the macro social level, but also at the micro level of jury deliberations. In a beautiful essay, "Deregulating Death," Professor Weisberg, formerly a Stewart clerk and an LDF adviser, argues that the Supreme Court reduced the anxiety judges and juries feel about sentencing people to die by making it appear as if "the sanctions they inflict follow inevitably from the demands of neutral, disinterested legal principles, rather than from their own choice and power." Weisberg sees an essential difference between assessing guilt, a factual question, and punishment, a subjective moral judgment. To Weisberg, Stewart's language about the need for greater reliability in death sentences makes no sense. After all, what is a "reliable" death sentence? This is what Harlan meant to get at in *McGautha*. Sentencing a man to die is an existential moment, through which one cannot be guided. This truth is antithetical to the lawyer's basic instinct to codify and rationalize. Harlan was saying lawyers should be honest about the limitations of the law, instead of offering false comfort through the illusion of formalism.

It seems only natural to ask, then, whether standards made capital defendants better off.* In answering this, Weisberg contrasts the dia-

---

* LDF's lawyers never asked this question for at least three reasons: First, standards were viewed as having substantial potential to combat racism. Because LDF saw the death penalty as foremost a problem of race, standards had greater superficial appeal than they might otherwise have had. Second, LDF employed the standards argument as a means to an end, not as an end in itself. LDF's ultimate goal was to end the death penalty, not improve its administration. Finally, LDF didn't have the benefit of history. They didn't know how standards would be written. A death penalty reserved solely for terrorists or hijackers would have been an unambiguous improvement. The vague, broadly inclusive standards that states actually wrote were less useful.

logue between judge and jury in two capital cases. The first is from a 1939 Ohio trial, conducted under the sort of single-phase, standardless scheme rejected by *Furman*. The judge instructed the jury that if it found the defendant guilty it would have "one further duty to perform, and that is, you will determine whether or not you will extend or withhold mercy." After deliberating for a while, the jury returned with a question and this exchange occurred:

THE FOREMAN: What are grounds for granting mercy?

THE COURT: That rests solely and wholly in your sound discretion. You should determine whether or not in your discretion mercy should be granted from a consideration of the evidence, the character of the crime and the attending circumstances.

THE FOREMAN: What are extenuating circumstances? Are they something which we can determine in our own judgment alone?

THE COURT: No. If there are any, you must determine them from the evidence.

THE FORMAN: Well, then, may we consider sociological matters and environment in determining this question of granting mercy?

THE COURT: No. They have nothing whatever to do with this case.

Juxtapose that exchange against this prosecutor's argument to the jury in a 1981 California capital case:

You have a scale in front of you. One is for aggravation and one is for mitigation. If the scale tips towards mitigation, then you are bound by law to impose the sentence of life without possibility of parole. But if on the other hand that scale tips at all towards the factors in aggravation outweighing the circumstances in mitigation, then you are bound by law to impose the sentence of death in this case.

Which sort of rhetoric better serves the defendant? As Weisberg notes, the first instruction is an anti-instruction. It places the full weight of the decision on the jury. The second argument, typical of the sort made after *Gregg*, presents a legal formula. It makes the decision to sentence a defendant to death almost mathematical in nature, and easier.

WHILE HE DIDN'T COMMENT specifically on the American system of capital punishment, in gross and subtle ways, this facade of rationality to the American practice of capital punishment evoked the themes that occupied the pervasively influential French philosopher Michel Foucault toward the end of his life. Foucault, who had a long-standing interest in punishment and opposed the death penalty with passion, was fascinated by the concepts of "rationality" and "science." Foucault argued that scientific method wasn't inherently better than any other mode of thought. Its propositions were no more objectively true than any others. Arguments grounded in the scientific method were merely privileged. They had power, but power is different from truth.

Giving punishment the imprimatur of scientific validity was supremely problematic to Foucault, who in a 1980 interview said:

> What is most dangerous in violence is its rationality. Of course violence itself is terrible. But the deepest root of violence and its permanence come out of the form of the rationality we use. The idea had been that if we live in the world of reason, we can get rid of violence. This is quite wrong. Between violence and rationality there is no incompatibility.

This is what Harlan meant when he cited in *McGautha* the "irreconcilable conflict" between the rule of law and the death penalty. It's what Norman Mailer, author of the great death penalty novel *The Executioner's Song*, meant when he said, "Capital punishment is to the rest of all law as surrealism is to realism. It destroys the logic of the profession."

No one can say conclusively whether the justices actually believed the MPC to be an improvement over standardless sentencing statutes. Years later Harry Blackmun, Lewis Powell, and John Paul Stevens all expressed varying degrees of regret about the 1976 death penalty decisions, but at the time what they said expressed great confidence in the improvements that states had made following *Furman*. Potter Stewart's *Gregg* opinion would include a spirited defense of the merits and rationality of the new sentencing schemes. He would reference, and dismiss, his friend and mentor Harlan's metaphysical skepticism about whether meaningful standards could be constructed, citing the MPC. "While some have suggested that standards to guide a capital jury's sentencing deliberations are impossible to formulate," Stewart wrote, "the fact is that such standards have been developed." Though Stewart conceded that the MPC's standards were imperfect, he said that in the new death penalty regime, sentences wouldn't be as random as lightning strikes:

> No longer can a Georgia jury do as Furman's jury did: reach a finding of the defendant's guilt and then, without guidance or direction, decide whether he should live or die. While some jury discretion still exists, the discretion to be exercised is controlled by clear and objective standards so as to produce non-discriminatory application.

This confidence would pervade the criminal justice system for decades and vex abolitionists. In merely four years' time the dominant discourse had shifted from a widespread belief that death sentences couldn't be fairly imposed to a quiet assurance in the rationality of guided discretion, even though the transformation lacked empirical support, was condemned by the legal community, and was premised on the life's work of a man who opposed capital punishment.

CHAPTER 15

THE LION
IN WINTER

W HEN THE DRAMA RESUMED, WILLIAM DOUGLAS
wrote, before exiting the stage, a final, peculiar chapter to the
history of his tenure as a justice, a postscript that would rank among
the strangest episodes in Supreme Court history and stamp Douglas's
theretofore uneven legacy on capital punishment as indelibly and sur-
passingly bizarre. The episode began shortly after the Court announced
that it would hear *Fowler v. North Carolina*, in December 1974.

Ebenezer Scrooge had nothing on Bill Douglas. At holiday time
Douglas often reminded his clerks of how little he had had as a child
and pushed them to work harder. That year, however, shortly before
Christmas, Douglas invited his staff to take some time off and glee-
fully announced that, on New Year's Eve, he and his wife would be
flying to the Bahamas for vacation. Better still, Douglas boasted that
he would be doing no work in the Caribbean. He would be carrying
only one item of reading material with him: James Michener's most
recent novel, *The Drifters*, about the travels of six young men through
the Iberian Peninsula, Morocco, and Mozambique.

In Nassau, though, a convention of lawyers had checked into the
same hotel as the Douglases. The justice felt he wouldn't get a moment's
peace if he wandered the grounds, and announced to his wife that he
would remain in the room for the duration of their stay. Cathy went

downstairs to buy magazines. When she returned she found her husband writhing in pain, half unconscious, and unable to move the left side of his body. A local doctor concluded that Douglas had suffered a massive stroke.

From his own vacation retreat in Vail, Colorado, President Gerald Ford dispatched a military jet to transport the judge he had tried to impeach to Walter Reed Army Hospital in Washington, D.C. There Douglas harassed the doctors and nurses and presently resumed dictating opinions from his bed and terrorizing his clerks. By all accounts he appeared to be recovering quite well. In mid-January, however, Douglas took a substantial turn for the worse. His kidneys began to fail, causing fluid to pool in his lungs. Fearing that a blood clot might kill him, the doctors confined Douglas to an aluminum stretcher, which tipped him upside down. Douglas became paranoid. He interpreted his medical treatment as torture, foisted upon him by his enemies on the far right. He also became badly confused. When William Brennan visited him, Douglas told his colleague that he had been visited by a black man.

"Who?" asked Brennan.

"A black man who sits on the Court."

"Thurgood Marshall?"

"No," Douglas said. "A black man who spells his name with a 'u.'"

He meant Harry Blackmun, of course.

When Douglas finally returned home in early spring, speculation abounded about his possible retirement. Neither of his first two public appearances did anything to quell the rumors. At his first oral argument on March 24, Douglas's eyes appeared glassy. When he gave an interview later that day, he seemed confused and spoke with slurred speech. Douglas retreated to his chambers and, then, to his home. For the next month he made only a handful of appearances at the courthouse. The other justices had held off scheduling *Fowler* for oral argument, pending Douglas's convalescence, but by March they couldn't wait any longer. They didn't expect Douglas to attend the hearing, but he had other ideas.

On April 21, 1975, Douglas dramatically appeared at the courthouse for the oral arguments in *Fowler*. Shortly before one o'clock, while the other justices walked to their seats, the marshals of the court lifted Douglas out of his wheelchair into his new, specially equipped seat at the bench. His appearance heightened the already electric sense in the room, and horrified the gallery at the same time. Douglas's face was ashen and gaunt. He looked to be near death.

FOWLER WASN'T THE WHOLE ballgame, but it was nevertheless the case of the year. The issue before the Court was a narrow one: whether North Carolina's Supreme Court had correctly interpreted *Furman* when it converted the state's death penalty statute into a mandatory one. The view expressed by the North Carolina court in *Waddell* wasn't idiosyncratic. Delaware's attorney general interpreted *Furman*'s mandate the same way.

The stakes were thus high. If the Court ruled in North Carolina's favor, the death penalty would be restored in some states without any legislative action. Furthermore, it would suggest the constitutionality of mandatory statutes. Though Burger had alluded to this possibility in his *Furman* dissent, he didn't speak for the Court or other states. The Massachusetts Supreme Court had just taken up the issue of mandatory sentences.*

Of course the case made all the difference in the world to Jesse Fowler, a black man who got into a fight over a dice game with John Griffin, another black man. Griffin broke Fowler's nose and pounded him while he lay on the ground. Later Fowler returned and shot Griffin in the presence of Griffin's two children. Fowler unsuccessfully claimed self-defense, and thanks to the North Carolina Supreme Court's ruling in *Waddell*, found himself facing the gas chamber. Now he spent his days in Cellblock F of the Central Prison in Raleigh in a

---

* *Furman* invalidated Massachusetts' discretionary death penalty for murder, but left intact its mandatory death penalty for rape.

six-by-eight-foot cell, which he shared with another inmate. He rose each morning at 6:30, ate breakfast from 7:45 to 8:00, lunch from 11:30 until noon, enjoyed one hour of recreation in the prison yard, had fifteen minutes for dinner, then lights out at 10:00. Twice a week he was allowed to shower. Once a week he was allowed to watch television for three hours. On Sunday mornings he was visited by his father and stepmother, who prayed with Fowler before driving to church. The rest of the time Fowler sat in his cell and pondered his fate.

So Fowler had a huge stake. But his case didn't present a challenge to the constitutionality of capital punishment. From a strategic standpoint the main importance of his appeal was to take the Court's temperature. The backlash had accelerated over the prior year. By the morning of Fowler's argument, thirty-one states had reintroduced capital punishment. Death rows were filling up faster than anyone could have imagined. Since *Furman*, prosecutors and juries had sentenced 253 people to die. The political tide had turned so completely that during the upcoming presidential campaign, both the incumbent, Gerald Ford, and the Democratic Party nominee, Jimmy Carter, would support the death penalty. After winning the Nobel Peace Prize in 2002, Carter, a devout Christian, would call for an end to capital punishment. In 2005 he would tell Larry King that he "did not believe Jesus Christ would approve a death penalty." But for a candidate for national office in the mid-1970s to oppose capital punishment was toxic.

Fowler would be the first opportunity to see how public reaction had affected the Court and whether the justices had the stomach to resume executions. The case would also be the first chance for the attorneys to feel one another out, for the dramatis personae had changed since *Furman*. North Carolina was represented by Jean Benoy, a burly assistant attorney general, who proudly believed in his state's right to use capital punishment. "I think executing is a fit and proper punishment myself," Benoy told *Ebony*. "I think that a society has a right to defend itself, to defend its citizens, and if that means putting some people to death who cause a threat to society, I think it can do that."

Ominously the solicitor general, Robert Bork, had filed an amicus brief. It was here that Bork presented Ehrlich's research on deterrence. Bork's participation signaled to the Court that the federal government had an interest in the death penalty. This didn't bode well for LDF. The United States hadn't participated in either *McGautha* or *Furman*. Having this particular solicitor general involved was doubly problematic from LDF's standpoint: Bork was a force to be reckoned with.

The American public knew Robert Bork for his role in the Watergate so-called Saturday Night Massacre. When Richard Nixon ordered Attorney General Elliot Richardson to fire Special Prosecutor Archibald Cox, Richardson resigned rather than carry out the order. After Richardson's deputy, William Ruckelshaus, rejected the order as fundamentally wrong and also resigned, Bork, the solicitor general, became acting attorney general and carried out Nixon's order.

The legal community knew Bork as a prodigious scholar and professor at Yale Law School where he taught from 1962 through 1981, with the exception of his time in government service. Bork's seminars at Yale were highly popular, and, during his time on the faculty, he taught many of the most influential lawyers and politicians of his generation, including John Bolton, Anita Hill, and Hillary Rodham Clinton. Bork produced an influential treatise on antitrust law and dozens of law-review articles, advancing his judicial philosophy that the Constitution should be interpreted based on the framers' original understanding of the document. Despite the obvious connection, Bork rejected the legacy of Hugo Black, whom he blamed (with Douglas) for the Warren Court's excesses. Instead Bork saw himself as a disciple of Alexander Bickel, a renowned advocate of judicial restraint.

With respect to the death penalty, Bork, like Benoy, was a true believer, and had personally lobbied to file the amicus brief. His submission ran seventy-eight pages and, in addition to aggressively making the case that the death penalty deterred, offered a vigorous defense of states' right to decide the issue for themselves. Even had Bork not been known by his reputation, the clarity and force of his language made clear that he would be a formidable opponent for Tony Amsterdam.

While this wouldn't be the championship match, it would be a crucial final tune-up. The attorneys entered the ring like prizefighters and, when Burger called the Court to order at one minute past one o'clock in the afternoon, the lawyers began feeling each other out.

AMSTERDAM THREW THE FIRST JAB. "May it please the Court," he said, "we believe that the arbitrary selectivity permitted and encouraged by North Carolina procedures for the trial of capital cases involves the same sort of latitude for imposition of the death penalty, the most extreme penalty known to the law, that this Court condemned in *Furman*. It is true that the procedures under which the selected decisions are made are different, but the decision to avert or to impose the death penalty is no less arbitrary."

With this argument Amsterdam tipped his hand on a vexing and critical strategic issue. In presenting Fowler's appeal, LDF could have focused on the absurdity of the North Carolina Supreme Court's interpretation of *Furman*. How could an anti–death penalty decision mean that more people should receive the death penalty? Another possible tactic would have been to direct the Court's attention to the inhumaneness of a mandatory death penalty, which deprived defendants of the possibility of mercy. Amsterdam, though, had his eyes on a larger prize.

Hugo Bedau said that Amsterdam viewed *Fowler* as an opportunity to "consolidate and widen *Furman*." Amsterdam argued that even mandatory death penalty schemes remained arbitrary and, hence, violated the Court's 1972 decision. To uphold Fowler's appeal on this basis, the Court would have to reaffirm and expand on its commitment to *Furman*. Neither of these steps would be required if the Court confined its decision to the absurdity of the North Carolina Court's interpretation of *Furman* or the inhumanity of mandatory sentences.

LDF surely had the ammunition to make the arbitrariness argument. Even a mandatory death penalty scheme was rife with discretion: in a prosecutor's decision to indict, in what crime he charged the defendant with, in whether or not he offered a plea bargain. Juries retained discretion. They could always convict a defendant of a lesser offense, and no standards governed this decision. Governors had complete leeway to grant or withhold clemency. Amsterdam pointed out all this.

But this line of reasoning was fraught with peril. Every criminal case involved prosecutorial discretion. Every criminal case involved jury discretion. Amsterdam's argument challenged the legitimacy of the criminal justice system. Moreover, he seemed to be arguing against leniency, particularly when he pointed out the problems with clemency. Amsterdam said, "What is interesting is the extraordinary use of clemency in North Carolina, where virtually two-thirds of persons sentenced to death, over long periods of time in this century, have been commuted. So the effect of gubernatorial discretion is to avert the infliction of the death penalty in a very, very large percentage of the cases." Amsterdam's longtime antagonist Harry Blackmun immediately noted the oddness of this position. "Do I understand your argument on executive clemency, then, is directed toward its use, not its existence?"

"No," Amsterdam replied. "What we are saying is that, if you take a look at the North Carolina procedure as a whole, then you have to appreciate that very little or no difference exists between the North Carolina practice under *Waddell* and the practices which this Court struck down in *Furman*."

Having gone down this road, Amsterdam had no other move to make, but the reply left him in a tenuous position. In *Furman* Amsterdam and LDF had objected to imposing the death penalty on undeserving defendants who were being treated arbitrarily more harshly than other defendants. Now Amsterdam was objecting to sparing people who deserved to die: It sounded as if Amsterdam opposed mercy. His position might be logical, but the argument resonated in a different emotional register. Moreover, it again sounded like an indictment of the entire system. The law depended on mercy, from the simple act of a police officer excusing a speeder to the governor setting aside the sentence of a man in prison for forty years.

Blackmun explored the contradiction: "I want to be sure about my logic here, or yours. Isn't the argument you're now making about executive clemency equally applicable to any other crime, so that if it prevails you demolish the entire criminal justice system?"

In reply Amsterdam toed the waters on a theme that would play a central role in these next rounds of the fight: He argued that death is different. "I think that there is a constitutional difference between capital and non-capital cases," Amsterdam told Blackmun. "The death penalty is unique. Not only in the law under *Furman*, but in fact." Brennan had made this point in his *Furman* opinion. Stewart had mentioned it too, but it hadn't commanded a majority.

By the end of Amsterdam's presentation, the risks of his line of argument had become obvious. If a majority of the justices remained committed to *Furman*, then Amsterdam had gained the upper hand. If the decision had less than solid support, Amsterdam stood on far shakier ground. In *Furman* the arbitrary procedures at issue had been specific to the death penalty. The questions whether trials should be split into guilt and penalty phases, and whether juries should be given guidance in sentencing, applied principally to capital cases. Juries rarely decide punishment in other cases. In *Fowler*, however, Amsterdam had criticized as arbitrary procedures that were common to all criminal cases. Blackmun was right: Amsterdam had attacked the American criminal justice system.

Amsterdam made the decision to go down this road with imperfect information. All lawyers operate under uncertainty, and in this situation Amsterdam had even less information than usual. He could only guess how much support *Furman* had. Amsterdam didn't know, of course, about Stewart's deal with White or how much White had wavered before voting with the majority. He could only speculate about how the Court would respond to the public backlash. Ample precedent existed for justices voting to uphold precedents with which they had initially disagreed. Harlan had voted against *Miranda*, but later repeatedly voted to uphold the decision under stare decisis. Amsterdam had a reasonable basis for his gamble.

In retrospect, though, even Amsterdam would recognize that he placed his chips on the wrong color. "We made the serious mistake of taking the rationales of the majority justices in *Furman* seriously and believing that they took them seriously," Amsterdam recalled bitterly. "We did not think for one moment that *Furman* was the end of capital punishment. That's what Jack Greenberg told the press, but it was a sagacious public-discourse advocate's attempt to launch a self-fulfilling prophecy, not an expression of our actual expectations. Nevertheless," he said, "we did entertain a faith that was almost as naive. We didn't understand the depth of the hypocrisy of which the justices were capable. If the rationales articulated by the swing justices in *Furman* were respected and applied with intellectual honesty to a realistic perception of the North Carolina procedure after *Waddell*—and to Jesse Fowler's case in particular—the argument in *Fowler* would have been a winner."

JEAN BENOY, NORTH CAROLINA's advocate, faced his own tactical dilemma following Amsterdam's argument. Should he respond by defending North Carolina's system against the arbitrariness charge? Or should he concede arbitrariness and instead concentrate on further exposing Amsterdam's argument as a critique of the entire criminal justice system? The choice turned on Benoy's own perception of the firmness of the Court's commitment to *Furman*. If *Furman* had solid support, then it made most sense to defend North Carolina's process. If *Furman* was shaky, though, Benoy might be wise to pick up on Blackmun's question. Of course North Carolina's deputy attorney general knew nothing more about the private ruminations of the justices than did LDF. Benoy put his chips on the same color as Amsterdam, and conceded *Furman* as precedent.

Benoy began by arguing that Amsterdam had overstated the degree of discretion afforded to prosecutors and judges. He pointed to a state law that required the removal of a prosecutor (called a solicitor in North Carolina) if he didn't perform his sworn duty. With respect to clemency, Benoy said no evidence had been offered to show a pattern of discrimination. "If in some future point of time a governor started commuting the sentences of all whites, all the rich, then this Court could intervene in a proper case." But it was quite different, he said, "to just wipe it out with no presentation of facts, on the assumption that it is discriminatory."

This argument didn't resonate with the bench. Stewart questioned how such a case could ever be proved given that grand-jury proceedings were secret and gubernatorial clemency unreviewable. Marshall doubted that the law required further evidence of discrimination.

"General Benoy, do you know of any time in the history of North Carolina that a Negro's death sentence had been commuted?" Marshall asked.

"No, sir."

"What's the percentage of Negroes in North Carolina?"

"I believe it's about 20 or 30 percent."

"And what's the percentage on death row?"

"It's about 50/50, as I understand it."

"It gives you no problem?"

"No, sir. It doesn't give me a bit of a problem, Your Honor. There are things far more important in the State of North Carolina—"

"Than race," said Marshall.

"—than the race of a man who kills and rapes," said Benoy. "There's not one aspect of racial overtones in the system of justice in the State of North Carolina."

This Thurgood Marshall could not bear. Having spent the majority of his life combating southern racism, he couldn't allow Benoy's claim to pass unchallenged. The subsequent exchange is unforgettable.

"How many Negroes do you have on your judicial system?" Marshall asked.

"Let's see," the deputy attorney general replied. "I believe there—I don't know if the last Negress, there was a Negro woman who was a judge."

"A neg-what?"

"A Negress," Benoy repeated. "A Negro woman who was a judge in Guilford County."

"You're still using 'Negress' down there?"

"Well, Your Honor, I'm a Caucasian, and I see nothing wrong with using the word 'Negro.' That's the name of a race of people."

"All right. In what are those . . . trial courts . . . like magistrates or something?"

"No sir. We have district court judges who are blacks."

"Name them!" cried Marshall.

"I don't know, Your Honor," Benoy said. "I don't know them, and I'm not on intimate terms with them."

"You have Negro solicitors?"

"Yes, sir."

"I'd like you to name just one of those."

"You mean the elected solicitor?"

"Yes, sir."

"I don't believe there is an elected solicitor himself."

"I don't either," said Marshall.

Undaunted, Benoy defended the fairness of North Carolina's system. "The underlying policy of North Carolina is that we dignify the life of a black man with the same high degree that we value the life of a white man. And when we say that a mandatory penalty for rape shall be death that means if you rape a black woman in North Carolina, you're going to get the gas chamber for it," he said. "North Carolina dignifies the sexuality of a black woman to the same high degree it does a white woman. And we make no apologies for that to anyone."

Marshall wasn't impressed.

Benoy's argument encountered less resistance when he commented on the problematic extension of Amsterdam's argument, which went to "the very crux of the criminal justice system in the United States." Benoy said that if the Court questioned the constitutionality of jury or prosecutorial discretion, "you have then done away with the criminal justice system in the United States as we know it."

✦ ✦ ✦ ✦

WHEN HE TOOK THE LECTERN, Robert Bork made clear that he had no dog in the fight between North Carolina and Jesse Fowler. "Mr. Chief Justice," Bork said, "A good deal of the argument has been taken up with matters peculiar to North Carolina law in the facts of this case, and of course the United States has no interest whatever in that." Bork had injected himself into the case for one reason only: to make sure the Supreme Court didn't expand *Furman* and strike down the death penalty under the Eighth Amendment. Bork said, "The United States is here merely to ask that whatever the outcome of this particular case, the Court make it clear that capital punishment is constitutional, and that the more prudential judgments about its general use lie with the elected representatives of the people."

Bork, unlike Benoy, went right to the central tension in Amsterdam's position. He reminded the Court that the framers had included the death penalty in the Constitution and, by its requirement of indictment by grand jury and trial by petit jury, had embraced the people's judgment at every stage. "So, the constitutional criminal justice system breathes discretion at every pore," Bork said. "And, in fact, I can't understand that a constitutional system that presupposes discretion somehow makes unconstitutional a constitutional system that presupposes the allowability of the death penalty. My mind boggles at the proposition that one part of the constitutional system renders another part of the same system unconstitutional."

Discretion, said Bork, is really another word for mercy, and mercy is universally regarded as a virtue of criminal justice. "We have been looking at discretion here from the wrong end," Bork argued. "The discretion which is in the system is not the defect of the system, it is indeed the genius of the system." He added, "As the system now stands, it is utterly impossible for one person or several persons, acting out of prejudice or out of stupidity, to inflict the death penalty. But at every stage it is possible for a small group to stop the death penalty from being inflicted, and at several stages it's possible for one person to stop the death penalty from being inflicted." Bork cited a recent article in the *Stanford Law Review*, by University of Chicago law professor Harry Kalven, which Bork claimed to show that juries made rational decisions. This argument was a stretch. Kalven's article was based on research he had conducted with Hans Zeisel, LDF's longstanding ally. In fact Kalven and Zeisel's research said very little about the basis of jury decisions, and Zeisel surely would have disavowed any pro–death penalty implications of the research. None of the justices called Bork on this, though.

In fact the only resistance Bork encountered arose when he argued that LDF and the abolitionists were trying, as they had in *McGautha* and *Furman*, to have the Court substitute its judgment for that of legislators. "This case is merely the latest in a series of cases in which the opponents of the death penalty have attempted to get this Court to make a political judgment that the political branches of the state and federal governments have been unwilling to give them," Bork said.

In reply Stewart noted that it was North Carolina's Supreme Court, not its legislature, which had sentenced Fowler to die. Bork replied that LDF should have raised this distinction so that Benoy could reply to the point. "I hate to bring it up myself," Bork said.

In his rebuttal Amsterdam invoked Charles Black to counter Bork's characterization of discretion as a virtue. "Of course, whether you regard something as a genius or a defect depends on whether you're standing at the long end of the stick or the short end of the stick," Amsterdam said. "Charles Black made this point very strikingly in his recent book. He said that a yes answer to the question whether the defendant shall live or die, given by a jury, sounds good. Somebody escapes death. The trouble is that if you turn the coin around, some-body suffers death, because the jury did not find him guilty of a lesser offense rather than the capital charge." Amsterdam concluded, "The defects in the system are not accidental, they are endemic."

It wasn't Amsterdam's best argument, but perhaps the best that could be made, and likely good enough if the justices were predisposed to upholding *Furman*. If they weren't, losing *Fowler* would only be the beginning of LDF's problems.

THROUGHOUT THE ARGUMENT, through the thrust and parry of the duel between two of America's most brilliant and influential lawyers, William Douglas sat silently. His mouth hung open and he listed to one side in his chair. During the ninety-minute debate he asked not a single question. He communicated precisely once, when he attempted to write a note to one of his clerks, but Douglas couldn't separate the page, and he began beating the pad against the bench until a marshal came to his aid. At the end of the argument, after his colleagues exited, the court officers wheeled Douglas down from the podium.

The next day Douglas checked in at the Rusk Institute in New York for a lengthy rehabilitation. He missed the conference on *Fowler*, which deadlocked four to four in his absence. From his bed at the Rusk Institute, he drafted his *Fowler* opinion on a yellow legal pad, as was his wont. Douglas worked differently from the other justices. He didn't rely on bench memos, and he drafted his own opinions. This system worked fine when he was in good health. Now, though, Douglas's law clerk, Alan Austin, could barely make out anything Douglas had written. The first page indicated that Douglas would be dissenting; the rest of the opinion consisted of sentence fragments, which Austin and Douglas's secretaries spent the next several weeks deciphering and massaging into a short opinion.

The other justices didn't know how to handle the situation. Douglas would certainly retire or die, but no one had any idea how long he might hold on. On June 24 the Court put *Fowler* over to the following term. The *Times* reported the adjournment on the front page, and even though the Court had offered no official explanation for the postponement, the article correctly concluded that Douglas's illness had caused the delay. Douglas didn't pick up on this, though. In late spring he asked Austin to see the other opinions circulating in *Fowler*. Austin said there were none, and that the Court had put the matter over to look for a different case on the constitutionality of the death penalty. A healthy Douglas surely would have seen through this, but in his condition he accepted the explanation, and remained adamant that he would participate in hearing and deciding the next round of death penalty cases. In early summer Douglas asked Brennan to "pass on to conference that I am unsettled as to what disposition to recommend in the capital cases."

In August, Douglas traveled to Goose Prairie, hoping the mountain air would revive him, but when his car reached the ranch house, Douglas could barely get himself out the door. His son offered to help, but Douglas refused him: "I'll be goddamned if they carry me into the Double K." Douglas made it into the resort, but it would be the last time he ever walked. Nevertheless he continued to work. His new clerk, Robert Deitz, shipped bags of certiorari petitions to Goose Prairie, even as Burger told Deitz at tea that he and the other Douglas clerks might not have a job when the term started. Burger had visited Douglas at the Rusk Institute in July, and though he told the press Douglas had made great progress, he privately thought the opposite and desperately wanted his colleague to quit.

Nevertheless Douglas hung on. In early September lawyers in a California criminal case sought an injunction to prevent state investigators from accessing grand-jury records. A Supreme Court justice had no business hearing a state matter, but Douglas announced that he would do so at the Yakima County Courthouse. After the oral arguments the lawyers awaited a decision. Douglas sat silent for ten minutes and then invited the attorneys to visit him at his home in Goose Prairie. "It is a very beautiful place," he said, "with pristine air and abundant wildlife, the climate is salubrious." After the hearing Douglas's friends and family pressed him to retire. They recruited Douglas's good friend Charles Reich, a former Black law clerk and a Yale law professor, to try to persuade the justice to step down. Douglas told Reich that his life would be over if he resigned: He would fight on.

In October the other justices took away Douglas's vote. They agreed among themselves that no case would be decided by a five-to-four vote with Douglas in the majority. The act had no precedent. Other justices had been persuaded to retire, but none had been stripped of his power. Brennan recalled the decision as "horribly difficult." Byron White believed the action to be without basis. No formal rules govern the retirement of justices, who are seated for life. Potentially a justice could be removed as incompetent, but in White's view this was Congress's decision to make. He took particular exception to the Court's secrecy. White wrote to his colleagues, "I do hope the majority is prepared to make formal disclosure of the action it has taken." The majority was not, and the decision remained secret until the publication of Woodward and Armstrong's *The Brethren* in 1979.

Impossibly Douglas soldiered on. He wanted to last long enough to hear the new death penalty cases. He took the bench on the first Monday in October, the start of the 1975 term, and dozed on and off throughout the arguments. He had a cot installed in his chambers so he could nap following morning sessions. At the end of the month Burger doled out the term's first set of assignments—none to Douglas. The same week doctors at Walter Reed Hospital told Douglas that his condition would never improve. He wouldn't walk again, they said, and he would live the remainder of his life in constant pain.

Defiant as ever, on the following Wednesday, Douglas took the bench. He made it halfway through the arguments, then asked to be taken to his office. In the afternoon he again lasted only part of the session. On Thursday he traveled to the Rusk Institute for a second opinion. The doctors there agreed that he wouldn't walk again, though they felt rest might abate the pain. Douglas raced back to Washington for Friday conference, but again the pain overwhelmed him, and he needed to return to his office. Finally, on Wednesday, November 12, 1975, William O. Douglas resigned from the Supreme Court. His messenger delivered his letter to President Ford. At lunchtime, while the justices were celebrating Blackmun's birthday in their private dining room, Burger announced to his brethren that Douglas had stepped down. One by one the justices walked over to Douglas's wheelchair, shook their colleague's hand, and bade him farewell.

Even then Douglas wasn't done. Caught up in the spirit of the moment, the justices wrote Douglas a fond letter in the aftermath of his retirement. "We shall expect you to share our table as usual," they wrote. "For you remain Senior Justice Emeritus." Douglas took them literally. At the end of the month, after his successor, John Paul Stevens, had been sworn in on December 19, Douglas returned to the courthouse, settled into his new office and, as he had done for four decades, buzzed for his clerks. When Douglas found out that Burger had assigned Deitz to White and Stewart, leaving him only a part-time clerk, he wrote the Chief an angry letter. Douglas received no reply but persisted in acting like a justice. He circulated an opinion in *Buckley v. Valeo*, the case dealing with the constitutionality of the 1974 campaign-finance reform law. Burger wrote Douglas that as a retired justice he wasn't allowed to participate in deciding pending cases unless invited to do so by the full conference. Undeterred, Douglas ordered his part-time clerk to release his opinion to the press. The clerk refused and alerted Byron White to Douglas's plan. White told Burger, who instructed the staff of the Court to ignore Douglas's pleas for help.

Douglas still wouldn't be deterred. In January 1976, the justices held a special Saturday conference and calendared five death penalty cases for oral argument. These cases, unlike *Fowler*, were the real deal. They represented the full spectrum of state responses to *Furman*. Every issue would be on the table, including the constitutionality of mandatory statutes, whether guided-discretion laws had curtailed arbitrariness, and the ultimate issue: whether the Eighth Amendment tolerated the death penalty under evolved standards of decency. These cases would decide the future of the death penalty in America for the foreseeable future.

In March, Douglas wrote a memo to his colleagues that he would be writing an opinion in the new death penalty cases. Then he called Brennan and said that he wanted to sit for the oral arguments. Brennan told him that this would be impossible, as there were only nine chairs.

"Bring in a tenth," said Douglas.

"No," said Brennan. "John has taken your place."

"Not you too," Douglas said, and hung up.

The justices decided they had to put an end to this behavior. Burger drafted a letter saying that Douglas no longer had any business with the Supreme Court. Since he had resigned, Douglas could no longer sit for oral arguments, vote, participate in conference, or publish opinions. Burger had the letter carried to each justice for his signature and then hand-delivered to Douglas.

Finally Douglas accepted that he was no longer a justice of the Supreme Court. Perhaps this was because the message finally got through. More likely, it was because when Douglas sat down to draft his promised opinion in the new capital cases, he only managed to scratch out two pages of thoughts, which dealt mostly with his anger over being excluded from the Court's deliberations.

Approximately four years later, on January 19, 1980, Douglas died following complications from pneumonia. He was buried five days thereafter at Arlington National Cemetery on the basis of a record of military service that was—depending on one's level of sympathy for the fallen lion—either completely fabricated or merely dramatically overstated.

CHAPTER 16

THE SAUSAGE FACTORY

THE SUPREME COURT IS AN ENIGMATIC INSTITUTION, but no aspect of its work is so mysterious as the decision to grant or not to grant certiorari. Later in the process, when a case is decided on the merits, a written record is created. This record is undeniably imperfect. Published opinions often don't reflect a judge's actual reasoning. Potter Stewart's opinion in *Furman* is a vivid example. If it were accurate, instead of saying, "death sentences are cruel and unusual in the same way that being struck by lightning is cruel and unusual," Stewart's decision either would have begun with the principle, "The death penalty is immoral," or in full disclosure, would have included a note saying, "I am taking this position to secure Byron White's vote." But flawed though they are, published opinions at least offer something for lawyers and scholars to study, and even the most cynical legal realist would concede that published opinions have some connection to a judge's true beliefs. Arbitrariness may not have been Stewart's primary concern in 1972, but it did concern him.

With cert decisions, on the other hand, the Court almost never creates a written record. Arthur Goldberg's dissent in *Rudolph v. Alabama* offers a rare example of a Supreme Court justice making public the reasons for his vote, and even this document only reflected some of Goldberg's views. It would be two decades before Goldberg published the complete memorandum that Alan Dershowitz prepared during the summer of 1963, and even that article excluded the research Dershowitz had conducted on racism in capital sentencing. Generally speaking, petitioners to the Supreme Court are given only a thumbs-up or thumbs-down decision on their request to be heard.

These would-be litigants are legion, and the competition to be heard by the Supreme Court is furious. During Warren Burger's tenure as chief justice, the Court heard approximately 150 cases per year, one of the highest rates in Supreme Court history. By contrast the 2009 Roberts Court heard only 73 cases. Even at the relatively breakneck pace maintained by Burger and his colleagues, the Court still granted little more than 1 percent of the cert petitions it received.

The fact that no standards govern the cert process is a source of great frustration to lawyers. When it comes to deciding cases, judges are guided by a body of case law that can be accessed and researched. For cert this isn't true. Other than a few congressionally defined areas in which it is obliged to decide appeals, the Court has complete freedom to choose the cases it will hear, and, since it hasn't constrained itself by publishing standards, it isn't bound by precedent. An attorney cannot argue to the Court that a case should be heard because cert was granted previously in a similar case. What little guidance lawyers have is based upon Rule Ten of the Rules of the Supreme Court of the United States, which unhelpfully begins by noting that "a writ of certiorari is not a matter of right, but of judicial discretion." It goes on to enumerate circumstances that might inform a decision to grant cert. Most notable among these is whether a dispute exists among the circuit courts of appeals. But the fact that such a dispute exists is hardly a guarantee the Court will hear a case, and many cases are heard that don't involve a dispute among circuit courts. Justice Frank Murphy once said, "Writs of certiorari are matters of grace."

Not surprisingly the black box of the cert process has been the subject of substantial attention in the academic community. Scholars have advanced an abundance of theories to explain justices' behavior regarding cert. Sidney Ulmer, a prolific political scientist at the University of

Kentucky, found evidence to support what he called the "error correction strategy." A justice unhappy with a lower-court decision votes to grant cert, while a justice who is happy with the decision votes to deny. Glendon Schubert, another widely published political scientist, argues that justices base their votes on a prediction of whether, if cert were granted, the Court would reach their favored outcome. University of North Carolina's Saul Brenner argues that justices act in the manner Schubert describes only if they are inclined to affirm a lower-court decision. If they want to reverse, they may as well roll the dice and grant cert. The worst that can happen is the bad decision is affirmed. Yet another study shows that the filing of an amicus brief dramatically increases the chance of the Court hearing an appeal. Though these studies emphasize the significance of different actors, they all share the same methodological bent: Each relies on numerical data to retroactively construct a theory of judicial behavior.

H. W. Perry, a political scientist at the University of Texas, suspected that political scientists might be missing something by relying exclusively on quantitative evidence. So Perry talked to people. Over a three-year period in the late 1980s, Perry interviewed sixty-four former law clerks, five Supreme Court justices, and sixteen other court officers. He published his findings in an accessible and highly engaging book, *Deciding to Decide*.

Perry found that none of the prevailing political science models well explained the cert process. Problematically, in Perry's view, none of the studies paid adequate attention to the crucial role played by law clerks in deciding whether to hear a case. Furthermore, Perry said prior studies ignored the influence of the solicitor general, to whom the Court gave great deference. If the solicitor general wanted a case heard, the Court almost inevitably complied. Most important, Perry found that justices act dramatically differently depending on their attitude about a case. If a justice cares deeply about the outcome of a case, then he or she acts strategically, along the lines contemplated by Ulmer, Schubert, and Brenner. In the majority of cases, however, the justices have no investment in the outcome. In these instances they tend to operate in a mode Perry terms "jurisprudential," and vote on the basis of more practical, institutional factors such as whether a conflict exists among the circuit courts. Regardless of whether a justice is operating in the jurisprudential mode or the outcome mode, he or she will almost always consider whether a particular case presents an issue clearly and whether a better case is in the pipeline. In short, Perry found that justices sometimes act as politicians, as the political scientists expect, but sometimes also act merely as lawyers, a conclusion that makes political scientists uncomfortable.

Perry's book is instructive in countless respects, but three lessons are vital here. First, his study demonstrates the importance of qualitative research; that is, for actually speaking with the actors. Not everyone agrees. *Deciding to Decide* is widely regarded as the seminal book in its field, invaluable for capturing the language that justices and clerks use to talk about the cert process and actual cases, but it's not without its detractors. Perry relates two memorable critiques of his work by his senior colleagues. One said, "Well, if you want to spend your time doing this, that's fine, but it's not social science." Another, more vividly, "This is mindless gossip mongering, and ipse dixit inside dopesterism." Twenty years after the publication of *Deciding to Decide*, qualitative researchers continue to struggle to be treated as first-class academics. Many more quantitative studies of judicial decision making have been published, but very little qualitative work.

Perry is a political scientist, but the disapprobation for qualitative research is even more acute among legal scholars. Although nearly every lawyer accepts the adage "We are all realists now," law-review articles are dominated by analyses of published opinions. Almost no one speaks to the parties involved. With respect to the history of the death penalty, very little has been written. What does exist, true to form, are explorations of what the justices wrote in *Furman* and *Gregg*. This single-minded focus on published decisions is bound to create an incomplete picture.

Second, *Deciding to Decide* nurtures skepticism for simple models. Political scientists favor broad theoretical frameworks, such as Ulmer's "error-correction strategy" or Schubert's "outcome model." Perry's messy model of the cert process has two primary branches with thirteen decision points. The same tension is evident with respect to scholarly work on capital punishment. The few existing studies of the death penalty cases by political scientists attempt to fit the history within an overarching framework, which bear names like the "attitudinal model" and the "legalist model." Perry would say these scholars are missing all of the nuance, and surely he would be right. What two-word title could explain Stewart's behavior in *McGautha*, *Furman*, and *Gregg*?

Finally, and most saliently, Perry found that the law clerks and justices uniformly treated capital cases specially. One clerk colorfully told him, "There was always special treatment whenever the petitions dealt with a capital case. They had a big pink sticker on them." Even Perry's detailed and nuanced decision tree, which so admirably attempted to model real life, couldn't explain what happened next inside the Court. As in so many other regards, the death penalty cases defied both simple and complex explanation.

BEFORE THE JUSTICES FOUGHT their behind-the-scenes battle regarding which of the new death penalty cases they would hear, Warren Burger charged the Court's motion counsel, Georgetown Law School graduate James Ginty, with reviewing the pending capital cases. The motion counsel reports directly to the chief justice, and generally handles appeals that come in outside the ordinary cert process. Though it departed from standard practice for the motions counsel take on this sort of task, everyone viewed this situation as unusual, and none of the other justices made an issue over Burger's decision.

On January 8, 1976, Ginty circulated a memorandum summarizing his findings. Forty-eight capital cases now awaited action by the Court, thirty-nine of which had been placed on hold pending *Fowler*. The queue on death row had grown substantially. As of November, 376 persons in twenty-eight states were under sentence of death.

Given the variety of state laws, it was widely perceived that the Court would grant cert in several capital cases. Ginty, though, felt it would be best to take up only one. In his view it should be from a state that had passed a mandatory statute, preferably North Carolina or perhaps Louisiana. Ginty wrote, "Ideally, the capital punishment issues should be given plenary consideration in a single-issue case involving a mandatory death penalty statute which presents facts raising little doubt as to the otherwise constitutional appropriateness of the sentence." This would allow the Court to most directly address the statutory response that had been invited by the dissenters in *Furman*, and by Stewart and White. Most important, it would force the Court to consider once and for all whether the death penalty violated the Eighth Amendment.

If the justices were inclined to reach beyond the mandatories, Ginty felt a Georgia case would be a logical choice. Ten appeals were pending from Georgia's law. In his summation, Ginty said the Georgia law gave juries considerable discretion "in the consideration of mitigating factors which are not defined by the statute." Thus, he said, the statute appeared open to a "*Furman* discretion equals arbitrariness argument." Since the Georgia Supreme Court had held that the new statute satisfied *Furman*, and since the statute resembled those enacted by many other states, Ginty concluded "the Court sooner or later will have to take a discretionary statute to answer the questions raised by *Furman*."

Among the Georgia cases, Ginty identified *House* as a particularly good candidate for Supreme Court review. Jack House had raped and choked to death two seven-year-old boys. House didn't challenge the constitutionality of his conviction, so the Court could focus solely on the penalty-phase issues. A second Georgia case, *Gregg*, involved a robbery and an execution-style killing of a car driver. Ginty thought the facts of the case were "straightforward," but perhaps not appropriate for the Court because *Gregg* presented probable cause and *Miranda* claims that "might distract from the death penalty issue." Ginty also proposed, as possible alternatives, *McCorquodale*, an extremely brutal case, and *Mitchell*, in which the defendant shot a fourteen-year-old boy without provocation. *Mitchell* had the advantage of being a single-issue case—the constitutionality of the death penalty was the sole basis for appeal—but the case had racial overtones, which Ginty thought might complicate matters. Mitchell, a black man, had suggested that his white attorney hadn't represented him well.

Finally Ginty thought the Court might also need to hear a Florida case. The Florida statute improved on the Georgia statute by identifying the kinds of mitigating evidence that could be considered, although it contained a broad exception that allowed the admission of any evidence "relevant to sentence." Furthermore, a Florida jury's recommendation was merely advisory to the judge, who could impose whatever sentence he saw fit. Ginty thought this might also be problematic. Still, several states had emulated the Florida approach, so the justices might conclude they needed to address it. Among the Florida cases Ginty targeted the appeal of Carl Songer, who had been convicted of shooting a police officer.

IN LEWIS POWELL'S CHAMBERS the justice assigned review of the death penalty cert petitions to law clerk Christina Whitman, a brilliant graduate of the University of Michigan, where she had been editor in chief of the law review, amassed the highest grade-point average in the school's history, and in her spare time earned a second graduate degree, in Chinese literature. Powell asked Whitman to examine all the pending cases and offer recommendations regarding which should be heard.

After studying the petitions Whitman agreed with Ginty's conclusion that the Court should hear a North Carolina case. She preferred the appeal of James Woodson, who had been sentenced to die for participating in the robbery of a convenience store. During the crime Woodson's coconspirator, Luby Waxton, shot and killed the store owner. Woodson had been drinking on the evening of the break-in and had been urged by Waxton, under threat of death, to join in.

Whitman had her own agenda in recommending this case. Like Larry Hammond, she opposed capital punishment. In *Woodson* she perceived an opportunity. One fact of the case would trouble even the most ardent supporter of capital punishment: Waxton avoided the death penalty by pleading guilty to a lesser offense and testifying against Woodson. Whitman thought this highlighted the arbitrariness inherent in even a mandatory-sentencing scheme.

Among the Georgia cases Whitman preferred *Gregg* to *House*. She thought the brutality of House's crime would cloud the death penalty issue. Gregg's offense was far less aggravated. Though the case involved legal issues relating to probable cause and *Miranda* warnings, Whitman didn't think these issues had substantial merit. Whitman thought *Roberts v. Louisiana* manifested a similarly moderate degree of aggravation and would thus also be a good candidate.

Among the Florida cases Whitman preferred the appeal of Charles Proffitt, who had stabbed a man in the course of burglarizing his home. Ginty had considered a case called *Gardner*, but Whitman found the facts horrifying and didn't endorse it. She regarded Ginty's recommendation of *Songer* as reasonable, but felt *Proffitt* would better focus the Court on the strengths and weaknesses of the Florida statute.

Finally Whitman recommended also granting Jerry Jurek's appeal from the Texas death penalty statute. Jurek had been sentenced to die for raping and choking to death a ten-year-old girl. The Texas law was an odd hybrid. Following a finding of guilt in a murder case, the Texas law required the jury to answer three questions about the murder. If the jury answered all of these affirmatively, then a death sentence would be imposed. Because of this structure the law superficially appeared to function as a guided-discretion statute. But each of the three questions, including "whether there was a probability that the defendant would commit criminal acts of violence," were so broad that the law was effectively mandatory. In fact Whitman thought *Jurek* might be taken in lieu of the North Carolina and Louisiana cases.

On Friday afternoon, January 16, the day before the special Saturday conference, Powell reviewed Whitman's memorandum and jotted down his own thoughts on the cases. Powell agreed with each of Whitman's conclusions, with one notable exception. Whitman favored *Woodson* because it highlighted the arbitrariness of mandatory laws. "What could be more random than sparing the life of the actual murderer while executing his accomplice?" she asked. Powell reached the opposite conclusion. "Not good case to take because the actual murderer pled guilty in plea bargaining to lesser offense," he wrote to himself. "Also, petitioner is black. Victim is white. I would not grant any North Carolina case."

THE JUSTICES BEGAN THEIR special Saturday session at 9:30 in the morning on January 17, 1976. There had been talk of starting later, a concession to the weekend, but Burger had plans to speak that evening at a Virginia Bar Association meeting in Williamsburg, and so the justices gathered early.

Consensus reigned for much of the session. The justices all felt that they needed to address the full range of state responses and thus would need to hear several cases, most likely at least five, including at least one each from Georgia, North Carolina, Louisiana, Florida, and Texas. The justices further agreed that the grants of cert should be limited to a single issue. Whichever appeals they heard should consider only whether the statute in question constituted cruel and unusual punishment. The bulk of the conversation revolved around which cases to choose. Again the justices found themselves largely in agreement. Everyone had focused on *Woodson* as the North Carolina case, *Roberts* as the Louisiana case, and *Jurek* from Texas. With the exception of *Jurek*, this all followed from Jim Ginty's recommendations.

Discussing the Florida cases, Stewart raised a concern with *Songer*. He thought the "other" issue raised in Ginty's memorandum could bollix things. The sentencing judge had relied on materials outside the record. Ordinarily this might not be a major issue, but in a capital case Stewart felt it took on a "quite different coloration." Stewart recommended *Proffitt* instead. Powell readily agreed, as this had been the case he and Whitman preferred, and the other justices eventually followed suit.

The judges parted ways regarding Georgia. Burger surprised his colleagues by arguing to take the state's most brutal case, the appeal of Timothy McCorquodale, who had been convicted of one of the most depraved and horrific crimes imaginable. McCorquodale mutilated, tortured, raped, murdered, and then desecrated the corpse of a seventeen-year-old named Donna, whom McCorquodale's friend Leroy had met on the Atlanta strip. McCorquodale and Leroy accused Donna of being a "nigger lover," and they decided that she needed to be taught a lesson.

Ginty had considered this case but ranked it lower in his memorandum. He felt that the death penalty issue couldn't be presented clearly as LDF had raised several other issues on McCorquodale's behalf, including a Fourth Amendment argument, a claim of prosecutorial misconduct, and a substantial *Witherspoon* issue. More important, Ginty regarded the facts of the case as too extreme. In her own memorandum to Powell, Whitman said she found the crime to be so horrible that she couldn't finish reading the statement of facts. She counseled Powell against taking *McCorquodale*, arguing that the gruesomeness of the case would divert attention from what she called "the real questions."

Burger wanted to take the appeal for precisely the reasons Whitman wanted to reject it. The viciousness of McCorquodale's crime would help to illustrate the sort of criminals who received death sentences. The horrible facts would be an effective rejoinder to the liberals' effort to humanize the so-called victims of capital punishment. Burger believed he had the votes to support taking the case. Brennan and Marshall would clearly oppose granting cert, but Burger could obviously count on Rehnquist's vote and almost certainly Blackmun's too. Stewart seemed likely to oppose granting cert, based on his original position in *Furman*, but Burger only needed one more vote. Although he couldn't be sure, he had high hopes that Stevens and White would support taking the case.

Powell, however, was a sure thing. Indeed, by every theory of judicial decision making, Burger should have been able to count on Powell's vote. Sidney Ulmer would have predicted a yes vote, as a way of correcting the error of *Furman*. Glendon Schubert's strategic model would have suggested an affirmative vote based on the likelihood of prevailing after the grant of cert. Powell wasn't a sure thing, though, and that he wasn't illustrates the limitations of quantitative models of behavior, and the limitations of pigeonholing intelligent, ambitious men. Powell's position surprised Warren Burger. To the chief justice it appeared to be a change of heart. The plain fact, though, is that Burger didn't understand his man.

LEWIS POWELL WAS THE firstborn child of Louis Franklin Powell, who managed box companies, and Mary Lewis, a doting stay-at-home mother. They lived in Forest Hill, a suburb of Richmond, Virginia, on the James River's southern bank. Powell's personality manifested itself early. Consistent with the man he would become, young Lewis was thin with poor eyesight, well-mannered, quiet, fastidious, and very, very smart. He was also fiercely ambitious. Powell's drive is noted less often than Byron White's because of the differences in their deportment. White's competitiveness evidenced itself everywhere: in his brute physicality, in his terse opinions, and in his gruff dealings with law clerks, who didn't know what to make of him. By contrast Powell's clerks revered their genteel justice. He would leave notes reminding them to take care on trips. He tolerated dissent, as evidenced by his interactions with Hammond and Whitman. His colleagues on the Court grew to love him, too, in a way they never did Whizzer. In her 2003 memoir, Justice Sandra Day O'Connor wrote, "For those who seek a model of human kindness, decency, exemplary behavior, and integrity, there will never be a better man." It would be a mistake, though, to confuse his southern chivalry with a lack of drive. The fire in Powell's belly burned hot.

Powell's ambition manifested itself early. Lewis believed that his father preferred his sister, Eleanor. At the age of fifteen Lewis announced to her, "I am going to prove to Daddy that some day I will amount to something." (Even after he became a justice, Lewis felt hurt by his demanding, unaffectionate father's too-frequently-expressed disbelief that his son had made the Supreme Court.) At Washington and Lee University, he became managing editor of the student newspaper, head of his fraternity, and in his senior year, president of the student body. He set his sights on law school because he enjoyed studying the past and, he said, "It seemed clear to me that soldiers and lawyers made most of the history." Military service intensified Powell's drive. He served with distinction in army intelligence, playing an important role in the Enigma project, deciphering and interpreting German messages. Powell rose to the rank of colonel and commanded as many as forty men.

When Powell returned home following the war, he found that being a subordinate partner in his Richmond practice no longer satisfied him. Powell wanted to be in charge. In 1953 he and his partners terminated their senior colleague, Wilt Marks, the firm's second-highest earner. Powell's show of strength during the coup boosted him to the most powerful position in his firm. Thereafter Powell implemented a plan to broaden his local influence and to develop a national reputation. He became president of the Richmond School Board and devoted more time to the ABA. In 1963 he won election as the organization's president, and served a popular term. In 1965 LBJ appointed Powell to the President's Crime Commission. Powell's stock rose further. Four years later Richard Nixon considered appointing Powell to the Supreme Court, following Clement Haynsworth's failed nomination, but Powell asked John Mitchell to withdraw his name from consideration. Powell and his wife didn't want to leave their home in Richmond, and Powell worried that he wouldn't be able to afford the pay cut he'd have to take as a justice. In 1971, however, he finally accepted Nixon's invitation to succeed Hugo Black.

A specter of racism clouded Powell's nomination. Powell had attended all-white schools and churches, and at the time of his nomination, Powell's law firm employed no black attorneys. Furthermore, the Richmond School Board had resisted *Brown* during Powell's tenure as president. At the time Powell said, "I am not in favor of, and will never favor compulsory integration." Powell told the Judiciary Committee that questioning the status quo never occurred to him. Racial segregation was fact. The Senate accepted Powell's defense and confirmed him with only one negative voter, Oklahoma senator Fred Harris, who called Powell "an elitist who has never shown any deep feelings for little people."

Generally speaking, though, Powell offered Nixon a safe choice. Powell approached the law practically: Washington and Lee wasn't Yale; his law professors adhered strictly to formalism and taught law as a science. Charles McDowell, Powell's favorite professor, asked one hundred yes-and-no questions on a final. Yale never would have tolerated this sort of exam. During his law school years Powell characteristically took careful notes, which he kept in meticulously organized files. The preserved record of Powell's education shows close attention to the results of cases, but little to the reasoning employed.

Powell spent a postgraduate year at Harvard, where he encountered Felix Frankfurter, but the experience hardly affected him. In Frankfurter's seminar on administrative law, Powell recorded Frankfurter's message that "we get nowhere by analytical dialectics," but, characteristically, didn't internalize it. Powell's biographer, John Jeffries, says Powell "was unreceptive to the influence of abstractions" and that "his legal training was, at least at the conscious level, overwhelmingly nonideological."

It was thus entirely natural that Justice Powell approached capital punishment without Burger or Rehnquist's passion. When Marshall asked Powell whether he had written his death penalty opinion, he not only hadn't written one, he hadn't formed one either. Powell had never worked on a death penalty case. The only serious thought he had given to the issue had been as part of Johnson's crime commission. The commission didn't oppose capital punishment, despite pressure from its staff. Powell's reasoning on the issue mirrored Herbert Wechsler's. He thought coming out against the death penalty would "adversely affect the credibility and weight" of the commission's proposals on education and police training, which Powell regarded as far more important. In Powell's view capital punishment wasn't a problem of "large dimensions."

On the Court a strong disapprobation for judicial activism led Powell to support the constitutionality of capital punishment. Powell had been trained to interpret the Constitution as if it were a statute, controlled by close reading of the text and, as necessary, references to its drafters' intentions. Since the framers clearly hadn't opposed capital punishment, this ended the matter for Powell.

Powell's judgment excluded any ethical dimension and any intuition about capital punishment's usefulness as a deterrent. This differentiated him from the conservatives. While Burger and Rehnquist agreed that states should decide the issue, they also believed capital punishment to be an important check against crime. Powell simply believed that the Supreme Court shouldn't decide the issue. "All he really cared out of this was that capital punishment not be declared unconstitutional," Whitman said. "He cared very little about the specifics. He thought all the cases trying to constrain judges more were too technical. He had a lot of confidence in how people did their jobs, because of how he did his job."

Powell thus rejected *McCorquodale* in part because he lacked Burger and Rehnquist's connection to the issue. They wanted to make an emotional appeal. Powell found this inappropriate. In fairness, the left acted no better. Brennan and Marshall approached capital punishment emotionally, too, and Powell took offense at Brennan's caustic dissents. But this didn't justify Burger's action. Powell thought the issue of capital punishment demanded dispassionate thinking. He told Whitman that he regarded any other behavior as "sleazy." Though Powell wanted to reach the same result as Burger, he wouldn't resort to the same means to get there.

A second force behind Powell's resistance to *McCorquodale* had more to do with interpersonal dynamics than with the case's facts. Though Burger didn't know it, Powell intensely disliked the Chief. He found Burger's opinions incoherent, and he had serious doubts about

Burger's intellectual capacity for the job. Furthermore, as did all his colleagues, Powell found Burger overbearing and bombastic. A theme of *The Brethren* is the universal dislike of the Chief. More than anything else, Burger's colleagues resented his attachment to the ceremony of his job. Burger loved the pomp of being chief justice. He took great pride in changing the shape of the bench from a straight line to a gentle U, so the justices could see one another. He renovated the courthouse's interior courtyards, redecorated the cafeteria, and delighted in making public appearances. His colleagues felt this distracted Burger from the actual work of a justice. They also found Burger manipulative and dishonest. Sometimes Burger miscounted or misreported votes. Sometimes he switched positions so that he could remain in the majority and control the assignment, as in *Roe*. Forty years later law clerks from the era still express scorn for Burger.

Burger put Powell off quickly. Shortly after Powell joined the Court, Burger chastised him for failing to read the record in a case, saying that if Powell had, he would have agreed with Burger's position. Powell, meticulous and diligent, didn't take this criticism lightly. Following conference, Powell returned to his chambers and immediately reread the record. Powell concluded that the Chief either hadn't read the record himself or, worse still, had lied. Burger's public rebuke of him struck Powell as beyond the pale. In another case Powell wrote an opinion ruling that a state couldn't prohibit resident aliens from joining the lawyers' bar. Burger dissented, and repeatedly told Powell that the decision would harm the image of attorneys. Powell couldn't believe Burger would take such a problematic, illogical position. He also resented the Chief's unannounced visits to his chambers, when Burger would sit and chat for hours while work piled up. The two men couldn't have been more dissimilar. Powell was a gentleman. Burger was a boor. Powell prided himself on maintaining an open mind. Burger was an ideologue. Nothing evidenced this better than his support for hearing *McCorquodale*.

In this moment in early 1976, Powell perceived an opportunity. At the time neither the liberal nor the conservative faction of the Court possessed a workable majority. The liberal pillars, Brennan and Marshall, had two votes. The Nixon appointees had three. How White voted in any particular case was essentially random, but even if he joined Burger, the conservatives still had only four votes. This could ensure that a case would be heard, but not an outcome. To assure victory Burger needed Powell, Stewart, or the newest member of the Court, Stevens. If Powell could bring the three of them together, their alliance would effectively control the Court.

Powell had no tangible objective. He didn't aspire to become chief justice. His worldview was such that he didn't even seek an outcome in any particular case. But Powell fiercely wanted to be intellectually relevant. Jeffries wrote, "His lifelong desire for control—of himself, of his family, of his friends, and of his firm—had not ceased with his ascension to the bench."

The courthouse politics favored Powell. He felt confident that he could count on Stewart, his closest friend among the justices. They shared a history of military service, socialized regularly, and maintained an open dialogue about cases. Powell said, "I felt particularly free to talk to Potter, and when I was having difficulty making up my mind on a case, whether we voted the same way or not, I felt free to talk to him." Most important, they shared a common view of the Court and its role. Both men idealized John Harlan and his commitment to judicial restraint. Both men shared a dim assessment of Burger's leadership. In Powell's view *Furman* was a departure for Stewart, and he could be expected to reverse course in 1976. Based on what Powell knew, he had a sense that John Paul Stevens would share his and Stewart's view of the Court's proper role.

Powell's hopes bore fruit. *The Brethren* ends shortly after the announcement of the Court's decision in *Gregg*, concluding with the sentence, "The center was in control." Powell was at the center of this center, and would reside there for the remaining eleven years of his career. From 1976 until his retirement in 1987, he would be in the majority more than any other justice on death penalty cases, and his influence would extend to every area of the Court's work. He would effectively determine all of the abortion cases following *Roe*: In eighteen subsequent decisions Powell was always in the majority. He single-handedly crafted the constitutional law of affirmative action in *Bakke*, striking a middle ground between quotas and some regard for race in admissions. He cast the deciding vote in *Bowers v. Hardwick*, the 1986 decision upholding Georgia's sodomy laws, and played an instrumental role in shaping the Court's position on gender discrimination.

Powell's reach and influence on constitutional law were profound. The American University legal historian Herman Schwartz argues that the Supreme Court of the 1970s and '80s should be referred to as the "Powell Court." Brennan sent a copy of this comment to Powell with a note adding, "and so completely the truth." In 1985 Burt Neuborne, the ACLU's legal director, referred to Powell as "the most powerful man in America."

POWELL'S RISE TO PROMINENCE began at the special January conference. Following the meeting he returned to chambers, proudly told Whitman that *McCorquodale* had been rejected, and then announced the five cases in which cert had been granted. Among the Georgia cases the Court would hear *Gregg*. Florida still wasn't decided, but it almost certainly would be *Proffitt*. The Court would hear two appeals from mandatory laws, *Woodson v. North Carolina* and *Roberts v. Louisiana*. Finally the Court would hear *Jurek v. Texas*.

Whitman momentarily felt relieved and proud. Powell had substantially transformed the debate by steering the Court to more moderate cases that didn't involve emotional issues, such as torture or racial discrimination, and her memorandum had played a role. But when Powell told Whitman that she would retain the death penalty assignment for the remainder of the term, she felt a sinking in the pit of her stomach. Reviewing cert petitions was quite different from working on actual cases. Whitman knew how Powell was going to vote. Unlike Hammond, Whitman had long opposed capital punishment. She had already made her views known to Powell and now did so again. She asked him to give the assignment to one of her co-clerks.

Powell insisted. He trusted Whitman to do her best for him, even where they disagreed. The justice and the clerk had established a way of working well together on controversial issues as early as her interview. Whitman noted on her résumé that her husband was a union lawyer. "I'm not a great friend of unions," Powell said. "Will this be a problem?"

"No," said Whitman. "I understand that we'll disagree from time to time."

In cases where they disagreed, Whitman wrote two opinions—one representing what she believed and another presenting the best argument for his side. Whitman found Powell to be quite tolerant, as long as she was candid about her views. Thus Whitman, unlike Hammond, never considered resigning.

For his part Powell never thought of giving the assignment to anyone else. She was brilliant, open minded, and even though she didn't like it, already had experience on the capital cases. Powell had an additional reason why he wanted Whitman on the cases for the long term: She had a great relationship with Stewart's clerk, Harvard Law School graduate Ron Stern, with whom she had clerked for Harold Leventhal on the D.C. Court of Appeals. Stewart had gravely disappointed Powell with his vote in *Furman*, but the universe had changed, and Powell believed that Stewart could be converted. Close collaboration between the chambers could only help.

CHAPTER 17

TAKING
STOCK

O N JANUARY 22, 1976, THE SUPREME COURT ANNOUNCED that it would hear *Gregg, Roberts, Proffitt, Woodson,* and *Jurek.* Naturally everyone around the courthouse began handicapping LDF's prospects for success. By all accounts its outlook appeared bleak. By this time thirty-four states and Congress had passed new capital punishment laws.

The liberal clerks felt despondent. In their view the Court had become more conservative over the previous term, especially regarding criminal procedure. In *Michigan v. Mosley* the Court upheld a conviction where the police questioned the defendant about a robbery, stopped after he asserted his right to remain silent, then questioned him two hours later about an unrelated homicide. In *Faretta v. California* the Court ruled that a defendant has a constitutional right to refuse counsel. In *U.S. v. Park* the Court rejected the appeal of a company president who had been convicted of selling contaminated food even though he didn't know about the contamination. In a scathing review of the term, University of Michigan professor Francis Allen wrote, "The Court's opinions have been unphilosophic, capricious, inadequately articulated, and lacking in sensitivity." Christina Whitman said, "Brennan and Marshall were losing everything. It felt to us like the Court was veering to the right. The right wing was on a roll."

Most of the clerks believed that the justices had taken the new cases to make it clear once and for all that capital punishment didn't violate the Constitution. Whitman, too, thought LDF surely would lose. Regarding the specifics of what the justices would rule, Whitman said, "I thought they would come up with something Solomonic." In Thurgood Marshall's chambers Columbia Law School graduate Greg Diskant saw things the same way. "In my view the outcome was foregone," he recalled. Diskant was having the typical law clerk experience, working from eight o'clock in the morning through midnight, eating most of his meals at the Roy Rogers near the courthouse. Rather than think about capital punishment, Diskant preferred to focus on the term's other blockbuster case, *Buckley v. Valeo. Gregg*, he said, "was just judicial politics."

William Brennan's clerks could find no greater cause for optimism. *Michigan v. Mosley* had dispirited their boss, who decried the "distortion of *Miranda*'s constitutional principles." Desperate, he followed Dershowitz and Goldberg's lead and began to call on states to pick up the civil liberties mantle. "No state is precluded from adhering to higher standards under state law," Brennan wrote in his *Mosley* dissent, and he began to repeat the theme in speeches. Brennan had suddenly been stripped of the influence he wielded on the Warren Court, and he didn't like it one bit. A newspaper story from 1976 called Brennan "an angry, frustrated, and saddened man."

The press saw things as generally bleak for the abolitionists. *Time* cited the new death penalty statutes "as evidence of substantial popular sentiment for execution in certain specified crimes—a point that could influence the court." The magazine concluded, "Close observers of the court expect that it will vote this summer to restore executions."

The only matter in doubt was what the precise vote would be. In forecasting this the biggest question mark was John Paul Stevens. Gerald Ford had nominated Stevens precisely because he could not be pigeonholed. As the only unelected president in American history, Ford believed that he lacked the political capital to nominate a staunch conservative. After Douglas retired, Ford told his attorney general, Edward Levi, "Find me another Lewis Powell," by which he meant someone who would be perceived as nonpartisan and confirmed quickly.

By all accounts Levi succeeded. Stevens had no family political connections. His father had been a Chicago lawyer and hotelier. His mother taught high school English. Stevens attended the University of Chicago, served in the navy as a code breaker, and, following his return from the war, graduated first in his class from Northwestern Law School. After that, he clerked for Justice Wiley Rutledge, served briefly as counsel to the House Judiciary Committee, and developed a national reputation as an antitrust lawyer. Stevens caught Senator Charles Percy's eye for his work investigating a scandal on the Illinois Supreme Court, and in 1970 Percy helped secure his nomination to the Court of Appeals.

On the bench Stevens showed no signs of being an ideologue. He had a reputation for being thorough and making sophisticated arguments, and was widely regarded as a judge's judge. An ABA committee, which included the liberal Harvard Law School professor Laurence Tribe, reviewed Stevens's nomination and concluded that his appellate court opinions reflected "very high degrees of scholarship, discipline, open-mindedness, and a studied effort to do justice to all parties within the framework of the law."

LDF refrained from opposing Stevens's nomination because it perceived him to be open minded. During the 1970s LDF routinely advocated against judicial nominees whose ideology they regarded as problematic. Regarding Stevens, LDF said nothing. "We were talked out of opposing Stevens," Amsterdam recalled. "People told us he was a reasonable person who had a real streak of decency, a sense of injustice, and was fairly imaginative."

Not all his colleagues agreed with Amsterdam's judgment, but by 1976 the central dynamic at LDF had changed. On the day the Court granted cert in *Gregg*, Tony Amsterdam had been the unquestioned leader of the capital campaign for a decade. For his extraordinary intelligence Amsterdam would have commanded great deference under any circumstances. By this time, though, Amsterdam had become far more than an accomplished litigator running an important case. His status before *Furman* had been merely legendary. Now it approached divine. Amsterdam's improbable, historic victory in *Furman* was to lawyers the equivalent of Don Larsen's perfect game in the 1956 World Series, the sort of accomplishment that stretches even a child's imagination.

Amsterdam had invested and produced more than anyone else involved in the abolition movement. He also had outworked and outlasted his colleagues from the 1960s. The founders of the capital campaign had all moved on: Michael Meltsner to Columbia Law School, Leroy Clark to Catholic University, Frank Heffron to private practice in Massachusetts. Jack Himmelstein had also departed, joining Meltsner at Columbia. Only Amsterdam remained.

For the 1976 campaign a new generation of LDF lawyers assisted Amsterdam. Among these Peggy Davis and David Kendall played the most important roles. Davis, a Harvard Law School graduate, came to LDF fresh off a clerkship for federal judge Robert Carter, a civil rights pioneer who assisted Marshall at LDF and delivered part of the oral argument in *Brown*. Kendall was raised a Quaker on an Indiana farm, attended Wabash College, Oxford on a Rhodes Scholarship, and Yale Law School. Following graduation he clerked for Byron White, who assigned him to *Furman*. It was in part because of this background that Drew Days, LDF's first assistant counsel, hired Kendall. Kendall, in turn, felt connected to LDF's lawyers who had defended him following his several arrests in Mississippi during the Freedom Summer.

Kendall and Davis were every bit as brilliant as their predecessors, and they would go on to become titans of the legal world themselves, but they were young and their careers had just begun. Meltsner, by contrast, had been Amsterdam's peer. In his own way Meltsner, and arguably Himmelstein, had done and sacrificed as much for the movement as Amsterdam had. Amsterdam, in turn, respected Meltsner and Himmelstein and, on occasion, deferred to their judgment.

This time around, Amsterdam was completely in charge. This isn't to say that he operated autocratically or less than collegially. To the contrary, this cohort of LDF attorneys revered Amsterdam as much as their predecessors did. Amsterdam maintained humility about his accomplishments, and he solicited Kendall and Davis's advice. He never yelled or made demands. On the fundamental strategic questions, however, his decisions had been made, and the course he set would neither be second-guessed nor changed. Amsterdam's authority was beyond question.

And he was working harder than ever. Amsterdam's marriage had fallen apart in the course of the first capital campaign. The endless hours had taken their toll. "Work consumed his life," said Amsterdam's son Jon. Mere mortals succumbed to the stress. Nine years in the pressure cooker wore Meltsner down and drove him to teaching. "The weight of capital punishment work was palpable," Meltsner said. During his time at LDF, Meltsner logged long hours, regularly took briefs home, and lived the cases. Still, he described himself as a "part-timer" compared with Amsterdam, who, seemingly impossibly, had accelerated his pace. Amsterdam had captured his white whale, and he wasn't about to let it get away without the fight of its life. Kendall, who recalled Amsterdam as the finest lawyer he had ever met, believed there were two Amsterdams: the chain-smoking Tony he knew (often accompanied by his dogs, Brandeis and Holmes), and a clone who worked through the night while the original caught up on sleep.

When Kendall met Amsterdam for the first time at Amsterdam's Stanford University office in August 1973, a giant elephant sat in the room. Kendall's clerkship experience doubtlessly gave him insight into White's thinking about the death penalty and what arguments might appeal to him on this go-round. But though Amsterdam astonished Kendall with his intensity and his comprehensive overview of the capital cases, he never asked Kendall about White. Part of this was an expression of respect for the integrity of the clerkship experience and part was to avoid placing Kendall in an uncomfortable position. Mostly, though, Amsterdam refrained because there wouldn't have been any point: He had set LDF's direction and wasn't about to alter its heading.

Amsterdam was aware of the despair regarding the new cases, but regarded it as "a strange pessimism." He recalled, "We were sure if the Supreme Court had any balls we would win. We were confident justice was on our side. Even after our exposure to the reality that shit happens, we had some hope." Amsterdam had some objective basis for this hope. Nationally more than six hundred people waited on death row, though much of the machinery of executions had been dismantled. A prison barber cut hair in Arkansas' electric chair. Pennsylvania employed its death chamber as office space. In New Hampshire it stored vegetables. Idaho's held medical equipment. Furthermore, the Massachusetts Supreme Court had rejected a mandatory death penalty under its state constitution, in a case LDF supported. Amsterdam hoped the ruling would create a favorable climate, in the same way that *Anderson* set the tone for *Furman*. Mostly, though, his optimism could be explained only as the product of his indomitable spirit.

IN 1976 AMSTERDAM DISPLAYED the same instinct to consolidate authority that he showed during the run-up to *Furman*. For example, when the ACLU inquired about coordinating media efforts, shortly prior to *Gregg*, Amsterdam encouraged LDF to put them off, saying we had "the best possible state of affairs." The task of dealing with the ACLU went to Davis. She wrote to the organization's director, Aryeh Neier, "Maybe (I doubt it, but maybe) the public can be convinced the death penalty is a bad thing, but they cannot be convinced in the next four months." Davis then discussed with Neier the idea of a public campaign if the Court ruled the wrong way.

Davis is now a professor at NYU, where she teaches constitutional law and runs a laboratory devoted to studying professional pedagogy. Looking back, Davis saw both benefits and drawbacks to having the charismatic Amsterdam in charge: "I have never worked for anyone from whom I have learned more or who raised my professional standards as he did," she said in 2011. "I also came to learn that I work better without him." Amsterdam's dominance meant that fundamental strategic questions wouldn't be asked. "I remember thinking that the ball was in Tony's court, and not feeling very much a participant in that," Davis said.

For here was a moment when, in a different environment, the LDF team might have taken a collective deep breath and reconsidered its position. Many thorny strategic issues, including the backlash, needed to be navigated, and Amsterdam's wasn't the only course through them. Ordinarily the public's reaction to a Supreme Court decision has little legal significance. In *Gregg*, however, it would be of paramount importance because in *Furman*, Brennan had established evolved standards of decency as the standard of review. What could better reflect current standards of decency than the legislative response to the decision? Marshall said the public would oppose the death penalty if only it knew the facts. *Furman* publicized the facts, and public support *increased*.

In reply LDF's lawyers could go one of three ways: They could ignore the backlash. They could acknowledge the backlash but somehow argue that it didn't accurately reflect public opinion. Or they could concede that evolved standards of decency supported the occasional use of capital punishment and limit their efforts to contesting the arbitrariness of individual state laws and opposing mandatory statutes. Kendall, like most of his associates, thought LDF's "chances were better with the mandatories than with these statutes, which were shiny and new, and took discretion seriously, even if it were a lie." This strategy carried high risks. Capitulating on the Eighth Amendment would mean partly giving up the ship. But it also held substantial potential rewards. Framing the argument in this manner might bolster LDF's credibility with the Court and allow it to challenge the worst of the new laws more forcefully.

Jerry Jurek's appeal seemed to cry out for special treatment. Texas's statute was so unusual and so problematic that Jurek's best strategy almost certainly would have been to ignore the cruel-and-unusual punishment argument and simply expose the Texas law as a mandatory one. Jurek didn't need the Court to rule the death penalty unconstitutional in all cases. In many respects his case presented LDF a dilemma similar to what it confronted in *Witherspoon*. Jurek's interests may have been so different from the other defendants that he needed his own lawyer. Yet LDF never considered conceding the constitutionality of capital punishment or referring any of its clients to other lawyers. "Each of us was a committed abolitionist and believed that the death penalty was a brutalizing force," Davis said in 2011. "I think all of us working on the cases were too sold on our own arguments."

In its submissions to the Court, LDF's thrust remained, as it had been in *Furman* and again in *Fowler*, that capital punishment in any form violated the Eighth Amendment. In the opening to its brief, it wrote that its years of handling capital cases proved that the death penalty was discriminatorily applied. "Further study and reflection led us to the conclusion that the evil of discrimination was not merely adventitious, but was rooted in the very nature of capital punishment."

The argument that the death penalty couldn't be applied in a nondiscriminatory manner remained, as it had always been, a doubleedged sword. Perhaps the Court might deem the death penalty theoretically constitutional but say that, in practice, no state could meet *Furman*'s mandate and eliminate arbitrariness. In reaching this conclusion, perhaps they might credit LDF's experience. More likely the Court would conclude, as Harlan had, that since the problem could never be cured completely the matter should be left to states to work out for themselves. Reasonable minds could differ whether LDF should have pursued the tactics it did, but from Jerry Jurek's standpoint, the answer was clear. These complicated questions would distract the Court from the simple injustice of his case: he had been sentenced to die under a law that gave no consideration to his individual circumstances.

◆   ◆   ◆   ◆

ALTHOUGH LDF'S LAWYERS HAD their eyes on a larger prize, it
didn't entirely ignore the specific problems with the new laws. After its
opening salvo against capital punishment, LDF condemned Georgia's
procedural protections as a veneer: "The new statute merely perpet-
uates the arbitrariness condemned in *Furman*. In its parts and as a
whole, the process is inveterately capricious." It first faulted the specific
choices of aggravating factors. Georgia hadn't articulated clear, objective standards and, in the Steikers' language, didn't narrow the application of the death penalty. Troy Gregg had been sentenced under
three aggravating factors:

> One—The offense was committed while the offender was engaged
> in the commission of two other capital felonies.

> Two—The offender committed the offense for the purpose of
> receiving money and the automobile described in the indictment.

> Three—The offense was outrageously and wantonly vile, horrible
> and inhuman, in that it involved the depravity of the mind of the
> defendant.

Amsterdam's outrage jumped off the page. Almost all murders
involved the commission of another felony and depravity of mind,
and "'outrageous or wantonly vile' is on its face limitless," Amsterdam
wrote. Georgia also had created an aggravating factor for murders
involving an aggravated battery of the victim. What murder didn't?
Only Gregg's second factor might not be true of all murders. But the
existence of a single acceptable aggravating factor couldn't save the
law. Aggravating circumstances didn't exist in isolation. They functioned collectively as a scheme. On the whole, Amsterdam wrote,
Georgia's factors were "amorphous, intangible, elusive, and open to
differing interpretations in like cases depending upon the subjective
impressions or instincts of the sentencer." Furthermore Georgia's stat-

ute allowed the jury to rely on "any aggravating circumstances otherwise authorized by law." This meant an attorney could make "almost any form of argument he desires."

Appellate review sounded like a meaningful check against arbitrariness, but Georgia implemented no guidelines, which rendered the process meaningless. "Notably, but unsurprisingly," Amsterdam wrote, "the Georgia Supreme Court has made no progress (indeed, it has made no effort) toward developing coherent or even articulate standards of appellate review." In fact, in Gregg's case, the Georgia Supreme Court simply asserted that Gregg's death sentence passed muster under the statutory criteria, and appended to its opinion, as required by the statute, a list of "similar" cases it considered in reaching its conclusion. It concluded with boilerplate language that "after considering both the crimes and the defendant, the sentence of death was not excessive or disproportionate to the penalties imposed in similar cases which are hereto attached." Georgia's Supreme Court more or less followed the same procedure in every other capital case.

Even this formulaic process might have been of some use if a defendant could point to cases similar to his where a death sentence hadn't been imposed. This could never happen, though, because Georgia's process made it nearly impossible for a defendant to win. Thus no body of useful examples could evolve. "Death-sentenced appellants before the Georgia Supreme Court must necessarily play the deadly game against a stacked deck," Amsterdam wrote. "As time passes, each new death sentence is approved by comparison with previous ones which were in turn approved as comparable to others *Furman* held cruel and unusual." Furthermore, nothing had been done to curb the discretion invested in the system's other actors. The appellate court had no ability to review "the decisions of prosecutors, trial judges and juries not to sentence potentially capital offenders to death in cases indistinguishable from others in which death sentences have been imposed and are upheld." Executive clemency offered no check. The governor had absolute discretion to spare a life or not. This process constituted merely a "final lottery." Georgia's system had been dressed up, but was every bit as arbitrary as before *Furman*. Amsterdam deemed it "strewn with opportunities for whimsy and vindictiveness" and the sentencing pattern it produced was "the same kind of crazy quilt of arbitrary and inconsistent decision-making that was present at the time of *Furman*."

Amsterdam closed by noting that the system's problems would be greater in practice than in theory. Even here, though, he couldn't resist taking a final jab at capital punishment in general:

> The system we have just described is not an orderly one, even on paper. Obviously, it will be immeasurably more disorderly in the flesh. Its caprices and irregularities arise in part from the studied purpose of the Georgia legislature to retain an arbitrary discretion in capital sentencing. In another, perhaps preponderate part, they arise from the basic irrationality of the punishment which the system seeks to administer, and from the difficulty of providing for its administration in a society to which it is intolerable except in aberrant and unpredictable cases.

This final point, one might argue, undermined LDF's position regarding Georgia's statute, but this possibility wasn't discussed.

ROBERT BORK ONCE AGAIN filed an amicus brief, this time with the assistance of Frank Easterbrook and A. Raymond Randolph. Easterbrook would later become chief judge of the Seventh Circuit Court of Appeals and an influential scholar in the field of law and economics, which emphasizes the efficiency of legal rules over moral questions. Randolph joined the D.C. Circuit Court of Appeals on George H. W. Bush's nomination, and in 2008 wrote the majority opinion in *Al Odah v. U.S.*, holding that Guantanamo Bay detainees have no constitutional rights. (The Supreme Court later reversed his decision.) Bork would be nominated to the Supreme Court by Ronald Reagan in 1987, whereupon Senator Edward Kennedy, among many others, would brand him an extremist. So thorough was this vilification that the *Oxford English Dictionary* later recognized "to bork" as a synonym for defaming a person systematically so as to block him or her from public office. Following his defeat Bork became a best-selling author and an influential conservative thinker. The notable exception to this who's-who of the current and future conservative elite in the solicitor general's office was Robert Reich, former *Yale Law Journal* editor, later Bill Clinton's secretary of labor, an influential liberal economist, and a strong opponent of capital punishment.

In *Fowler* Bork had portrayed the federal government as having a limited interest in the case, and took a measured tone. This time Bork emptied both barrels. His brief ran 103 pages, not including three appendixes. It began with familiar arguments. The Constitution mentioned capital punishment in three places. Colonial states regularly executed convicts. Thirty-five states had passed new death penalty laws, and in 1974 alone 151 defendants had been sentenced to die. "How then can it be declared by this Court, by any court, that the death penalty contravenes evolving standards of decency or society's currently-held moral values?" Bork asked.

Though Bork couldn't have known this, his argument took Potter Stewart to task for his *Furman* gambit. Bork acknowledged that social mores obviously change over time. It was thus appropriate for the Court to use the word "evolved" in connection with standards of decency. But judges shouldn't anticipate the direction of change. If they did, Bork said, "They will frequently anticipate incorrectly, and fasten their own views upon the nation in the name of enlightenment. Such a theory is antithetical to the tenets of representative democracy." These cases required no speculation about social values, as the justices had an up-to-the-minute check on where the public stood. "The Court has previously spoken," Bork wrote, "and it has seen the response."

That response couldn't be dismissed as irrational. The death penalty served legitimate social aims. The solicitor general again cited Ehrlich's work as evidence that the death penalty prevented murder. Bork conceded that the deterrence research was inconclusive, and he acknowledged the critiques of Ehrlich's methodology, but Bork noted that while some studies failed to find deterrence, even Sellin found no evidence that the death penalty *encouraged* crime. This offered yet another reason to resolve doubt in the states' favor. "So long as rational men can debate whether the death penalty deters crime, legislatures should be allowed to resolve that question for themselves," Bork said.

Furthermore, utilitarian concerns aside, the death penalty constituted an important expression of society's moral outrage. It had "heavy symbolic significance," Bork wrote, and he noted that a criminal justice theory predicated solely on deterrence "would have been unable to support any punishment whatever for Adolf Hitler, had he been captured." Marshall had wrongly categorized retribution as a forbidden end. Bork cited his opinion in *Powell v. Texas* as evidence that Marshall himself didn't believe it should be precluded. Furthermore, could anyone deny the importance of permanently incapacitating someone who had raped and murdered a ten-year-old girl, like Jerry Jurek?

The brief was a tour de force. Bork vividly countered LDF's claim that the death penalty was excessive because it imposed substantial suffering. "There are a number of things we do not wish to think about that are disgusting and perhaps revolting that we also acknowledge as necessary," he wrote. "Enemas, the vivisections of monkeys, cleaning up outhouses, are all disgusting and abhorrent, but they may also be necessary. Imprisonment is abhorrent—people would find it so if they knew more about it—but it is hardly, in itself, cruel and unusual."

With equal deftness Bork parried LDF's contention that legislative actions didn't accurately reflect social values by exposing the alternative. "The blunt fact cannot be avoided with the contention that elected legislators and chief executives do not necessarily reflect the moral beliefs of the communities they represent," Bork wrote. "But they certainly reflect it more accurately than does the judiciary, which was made independent precisely to insulate judges from majority sentiment."

Bork then delivered his right to the jaw. In *Fowler*, when Amsterdam argued that the new systems were as bad as the old ones, and that discretion in capital cases produced arbitrariness, Blackmun tentatively explored the hole in this argument. Bork drove a truck through it. LDF had devoted sixty pages of its *Gregg* brief to arguing that discretion in capital cases produced arbitrary results. "This elaborate argument does not need an elaborate answer," Bork wrote, quoting Oliver Wendell Holmes. Surely LDF didn't object to prosecutorial discretion or jury discretion. The solicitor general sarcastically said, "Petitioners obviously do not contend for a system in which the prosecutor must charge a capital offense whenever there has been a killing. We would thus have the rule of the Tyrant which ancient Greece replaced with the rule of law millennia ago."

Amsterdam irrationally opposed mercy, Bork said again. Jury discretion kept people from getting harsher sentences than they otherwise might, not the other way around. "It is utterly impossible for one person or several persons, acting out of prejudice, malice or stupidity, to inflict the death penalty," Bork wrote. "But at every stage it is possible for one person or a small group of people to prevent its infliction. The multiplication of occasions for mercy is the system's great safeguard. It cannot simultaneously be the source of its unconstitutionality." Prosecutors rarely sought the death penalty, and juries rarely imposed it, but this didn't suggest that they opposed capital punishment. They just acted selectively, "reserving their ultimate punishment for those whose transgressions are most clearly established and seem to them most revolting."

No legal system could operate without discretion because no law could anticipate every possible circumstance. "The varieties of human endeavor are endless and unpredictable," Bork wrote and, echoing Harlan, added that specifying the criteria of what crimes and criminal deserved the death penalty "approaches the limit of human abilities." The opportunity for mercy was thus essential, Bork said, as he pushed LDF down the slippery slope. "Petitioners state that they are not suggesting that the selective discretion of the criminal process would be constitutionally objectionable in a non-capital case," he wrote. "With all respect, we submit that they are suggesting just that. There is not a single argument petitioners put forward that could not equally be made in regard, for example, to the penalty of life imprisonment for first-degree murder."

On this point Bork was surely right. The capital sentencing system was racist and discriminated against the poor. So too did the criminal justice system. Amsterdam couldn't advance this truth, though, for the Court would never admit it. If it did, the wheels of the criminal justice system would grind to a halt.

Bork had pinned Amsterdam into a corner.

AMSTERDAM, KENDALL, AND DAVIS had little time to prepare their response. Because the solicitor general didn't represent a party in the case, the Court allowed him to submit his brief on Thursday, March 25, just five days before oral argument. Over the weekend LDF's team gathered at the Madison Hotel to discuss strategy and moot Amsterdam.

Bork had revealed his hand. He would portray Amsterdam as chief counsel for the leftist fringe, a curmudgeon who spoke for a discredited and rapidly diminishing minority of American society. He would accomplish this by exposing Amsterdam personally as a threat to the American criminal justice system and out of touch with the mainstream. He would brand LDF's campaign a political crusade masquerading as a legal argument, pursued in a court of law because it couldn't be won in the court of public opinion. Once again, as it had throughout the civil rights movement and during the debate over abortion, LDF's liberal chic was trying to impose its way of life on the American people. Amsterdam was these extremists' champion.

Of course no name-calling could occur in civil discourse. Bork had confined himself to constitutional history, legislative history, and data. But his message came through clearly, and subtext mattered as much as text. In *Furman* Stewart's unexpressed belief that the death penalty was on the way out decided the case. LDF didn't know the behind-the-scenes story, of course, but knew it would be damaging to be branded a leftist fringe. A response was necessary.

Amsterdam and LDF faced familiar options. Once again they could scale back their goals, and concentrate their argument on the mandatory statutes or Texas's law, which came so close to being mandatory. Taking this stance would be far less subversive. The system wouldn't collapse without mandatory laws. Even Bork might tolerate this position. Perhaps LDF could go one step further and emphasize the particular deficiencies of Georgia's and Florida's laws and say how they might be improved. In other words they could fight for the best—or least awful—death penalty law. Once again LDF's team never considered this course of action.

As he rehearsed his answers, smoking cigars all the while, Amsterdam became increasingly convinced that he needed to respond to Bork's challenge the same way he responded to Blackmun during the *Fowler* argument: He needed to say that death differed categorically from all other punishments. Racism, discrimination, and arbitrariness were different in kind when a jury returned a sentence of death. Amsterdam had toed the waters with this argument in *Fowler*, and they hadn't been warm, but Amsterdam believed that if he yielded even an inch on this—if he allowed Bork to turn his argument into a rant and portray him as a "liberal crackpot," as he put it, then all would be lost. The LDF team agreed. In Kendall's view the "death is different" principle had three advantages: One, it had some basis in constitutional history. Two, it provided the Court with an avenue to issue a narrow ruling if the justices were inclined to uphold *Furman*. Three, it didn't require LDF to relinquish any ground.

This strategic decision remains the subject of intense controversy. Professors Lee Epstein and Joseph Kobylka identify this as LDF's critical error, faulting Amsterdam for failing to understand the attitudinal shift occurring in the Court and American society. They say LDF lost *Gregg* because it "doggedly clung" to what it believed—or wished—*Furman* to mean. Edward Lazarus agrees that Amsterdam's "total immersion" in the cause "rendered him tone deaf to the changing tune of the country and the Court." Michael Meltsner, now a university professor at Northeastern Law School, interprets the "death is different" principle differently. In his memoir Meltsner said Amsterdam was offering the Court a limiting principle, so that the justices could strike down the death penalty statues without undermining the entire criminal law.

To Eric Muller, Meltsner's reply exposes the fundamental flaw in LDF's abolition campaign. "The argument that death is different had the unfortunate and unintentional entailment that racism might be tolerable where death is not possible penalty," Muller said. "In some sense, LDF's commitment to the capital punishment campaign brought about a silent yet total abandonment of its general policy goals in the criminal justice system." Stanford Law professor Herbert Packer had exposed this tension in 1964, arguing that Goldberg's *Rudolph* dissent, by focusing on rape, legitimated the appropriateness of the death penalty for murder, and by focusing on racism in capital punishment, suggested that racism didn't infect the criminal justice system.

For his part, thirty-five years later, Amsterdam continues to view the "death is different" argument as having been necessary, though for his own unique reasons. "The historical dynamic is important," he said. "We understood we could be perceived as nits. We had to raise every argument on behalf of our clients, and as a result we were on records with eight different arguments against the death penalty. This gave Bork the power to say we were radical subverters of the system. Strategically, that's why we had to say that death is different." Jon Amsterdam says, however, that his father "will tell you they overplayed their hand."

IN THE END AMSTERDAM acknowledged that both sides had good arguments. From an analytical standpoint, he found it difficult to differentiate death from long prison sentences, especially life without parole.* From a metaphysical standpoint, however, Amsterdam was

---

* Many years later Amsterdam indirectly would make this argument to the Supreme Court. Though he keeps behind the scenes, Amsterdam remains heavily involved in the abolition movement, and has consulted on almost every major case of the past

certain death was different. At his NYU office, he quoted Hamlet's agonizing act three soliloquy, saying, "There is something real about death being that realm 'from whose bourn no traveler returns.'" Most importantly, at the time, it offered LDF a defensible position. The law had always treated death differently by allowing more peremptory challenges, automatic appeals, and extra scrutiny of prospective. Moreover, in older cases, Frankfurter and Harlan had each said death is different. "That was good enough for me," Amsterdam said. Soon the justices would be hearing oral argument. For LDF to prevail, it would need to be good enough for them, too.

---

thirty-five years. In 2009 he offered advice to the Equal Justice Initiative (EJI), a leading advocacy group for criminal defendants and the condemned, in a case called *Sullivan v. Florida*. Sullivan, a thirteen-year-old boy convicted of sexual assault, received a sentence of life without parole. EJI opposed the sentence as cruel and unusual. A core part of their argument was that life without parole resembled the death penalty. "The essential feature of a death sentence or a life-without-parole sentence," they wrote, "is that it imposes a terminal, unchangeable, once-and-for-all judgment upon the whole life of a human being and declares that human being forever unfit to be a part of civil society."

CHAPTER 18

THE MAIN EVENT

O N THE AFTERNOON OF TUESDAY, MARCH 30, THE weather once again conspired to set the right mood for arguing about the death penalty. Dark, ominous clouds shrouded the Supreme Court building in a malevolent haze. It would rain later that day, as it had the day before and would again for each of the following three. The unrelenting deluge soaked the capital and dampened spring spirits. Even the cherry blossoms seemed sullen.

Inside the courthouse the lawyers shed their raincoats and waited for the capital cases to be called. Under the Court's schedule the Texas and Louisiana cases would be argued first. The appeals from Georgia, Florida, and North Carolina's laws would be heard the following day. Since LDF represented Jerry Jurek, the defendant in the Texas case, Tony Amsterdam would have the first word. As he waited, Amsterdam felt the same peculiar pessimism he had felt for months. Reason told him that he wouldn't win, but he also knew that he had justice on his side.

In the lunchroom several of the justices had a last-minute bite. "I don't see why the rest of us have to sit through this again," one joked to another. "Potter, Byron and John Stevens could decide this one by themselves." Together they walked to the robing room, donned their formal togs, and entered the courtroom. When Warren Burger nodded, they emerged from behind the red curtain in their familiar trios. "We will hear argument next in *Jerry Lane Jurek v. Texas* and *Stanislaus Roberts v. Louisiana*," Burger announced. Amsterdam stepped forward to the lectern. It felt almost too comfortable. Amsterdam had been there more times than he would have liked. When the green light came on, the rest came by instinct.

"Thank you, Mr. Chief Justice. May it please the Court." Amsterdam began by reviewing what happened following *Furman*. "It may be useful at the outset to give the Court a brief description of the present state of capital statutes in the country." In his clear and confident voice, Amsterdam broke down the new statutes along four criteria: those requiring bifurcated trials, those requiring a special factual finding to impose the death penalty, those modifying the definition of a capital-eligible crime, and those making the death penalty mandatory for murder. All of the new statutes provided "an array of outlets" for avoiding the death penalty, Amsterdam said. These conditions rendered the death penalty more prone to arbitrariness than life imprisonment cases, where no "elaborate" provisions for aggravation and mitigation existed. In the notes that he kept throughout the two days of oral argument, Lewis Powell wrote, "In other words, Amsterdam doesn't like these 'elaborate' opportunities for mercy."

Approximately twelve minutes into the argument, Harry Blackmun put Amsterdam to his first serious test. "Don't you think this is compelled by the holding in *Furman*?" he asked. Blackmun meant that LDF's argument in *Furman* had encouraged the states' responses. In other words, LDF had reaped what it sowed.

"No," Amsterdam replied. "I think the very variety of responses indicate that the states could have responded by making all crimes, including jaywalking, punishable mandatorily by death. That would have been a response to *Furman* as well. The particular form which the response took was not dictated by *Furman*, although of course the response was a response to *Furman*."

"Are you surprised that we have these new statutes?" Blackmun really meant to ask, "Are you surprised that these states acted as quickly as

they did? Do you acknowledge their show of support for capital punishment as decisive? Do you admit that your predictions were wrong?"
Amsterdam understood Blackmun's true intent. His petulance made
Amsterdam think back again to their first meeting, when Amsterdam
argued *Maxwell* before the Eighth Circuit.

"No," Amsterdam replied again, "But I think it is remarkable that
the statutes are as narrow as they are." Amsterdam and David Kendall
had anticipated this question. Lawyers call this making lemonade out
of lemons.

"You can't have been surprised," Blackmun said, "as this kind of
thing was forecast in at least one opinion." Blackmun meant his own,
in which he had predicted, and lamented, the rise of mandatory statutes.* Amsterdam understood but refused to give an inch. "The form
that the statutes have assumed is indicative of something less than
a broad based acceptance of the death penalty as a regular part of
the penal armamentarium of American society." He wouldn't concede
then, or ever, that the new death penalty laws reflected a consensus.
Rather, Amsterdam argued that by restricting capital punishment to a
small number of crimes, Americans again had demonstrated that they
couldn't stomach executions.

Amsterdam's reply harkened to his *Boykin* brief, and his epiphany
that the rarity of executions proved the public supported having capital
punishment on the books, but not its use. In 1976, though, the argument that support for the death penalty was an illusion sounded quite
different than it did in 1968 and 1972. *Boykin* and *Furman* concerned
old statutes. These were brand new. Their narrowed scope didn't suggest that the public had reservations about capital punishment. Rather,
it suggested that the public had great enthusiasm for selective executions, and made state legislatures appear to have acted reasonably.

The overall picture conflicted with the argument Amsterdam
advanced next, that states had failed to take *Furman*'s mandate seri-

---

* In *Furman*, Blackmun wrote, "The reservations expressed by my Brothers Stewart
and White encourage legislation that is regressive and of an antique mold, for it eliminates the element of mercy in the imposition of punishment."

ously and continued to impose the death penalty arbitrarily. His overview of the preceding four years concluded, Amsterdam turned to Jurek and Roberts's "two constitutional submissions." First, he said, death sentences imposed pursuant to "systems of arbitrary selectivity" were cruel and unusual. Second, when "assessed against the history of this country's use of the punishment in this century," capital punishment violated the Eighth Amendment. "These are separate contentions," Amsterdam said, "although they are closely connected."

Stewart interrupted. "Is your second contention that a death sentence is cruel and unusual no matter what the technique and no matter how serious the offense and no matter how completely a fair trial he may have been given?"

"That is precisely the second contention, yes."

Burger picked up the line of questioning. "Your point, I take it, is that no statute would meet the problems posed by *Furman*, is that right?"

Amsterdam paused. During moots he, Kendall, and Davis anticipated this line of questioning and resolved to concede the constitutionality of the death penalty for what they called the "exotics"—assassination attempts, aircraft hijacking, and other rare, highly specialized crimes that generated the strongest public outrage. Taking the absolutist position that no statute could satisfy *Furman* would make their position appear overtly political and unreasonable. In the heat of the moment, though, Amsterdam failed to implement this strategic decision. "Mr. Chief Justice," he said, "the laws of each of these states demonstrates a quality of selected decision-making which is arbitrary both in its potency, its potentiality, and in fact in the way it operates."

Looking back, Amsterdam says that he intended to admit the validity of the exotics, presumably in this answer, and in the last part of his reply to Burger he suggested that it might be possible to write a death penalty law that met *Furman*'s requirements. Whatever his intention, though, the justices didn't interpret his response as a concession. In his notes Powell wrote that Amsterdam believed "no statute may validly impose the death penalty." Most of the justices interpreted Amster-

dam's reply to Stewart the same way. This lingering perception damaged LDF's prospects immeasurably.

BYRON WHITE PRODDED AMSTERDAM to address Jurek's case.
Amsterdam accepted the invitation and addressed the glaring flaw in
the Texas statute: the three so-called special questions, which suppos-
edly restricted the death penalty. "This record shows how this provision is going to be applied," Amsterdam said. On the question of
whether the defendant would constitute a continuing threat to society,
the evidence was the fact of the murder itself, and the "hearsay opinions of four local citizens in the community that the defendant had a
bad reputation for peace and order."* Amsterdam lowered his voice.
"The thing that is most devastating is that you can't even challenge the
jury's finding because the question to which it responds is so meaningless. You can say that on this record that the jury in this case found,
without sufficient evidence, the defendant was guilty of capital murder. I mean, that is a question that has meaning." But, he asked, "How
can you—even on the absurd basis on which this jury condemned this
defendant to die—say that the evidence is or is not sufficient to establish that there is a probability that the defendant may engage in future
criminal conduct? The question is devoid of intelligible meaning." In
his notes Powell wrote that he found this argument "fairly persuasive."

    John Paul Stevens interjected for the first time. "Do you think your
position on this aspect of the array of discretion is consistent with
the *McGautha* holding?" he asked. "Do you think that to distinguish
McGautha you must rely on matters such as executive clemency and
prosecutorial discretion, or may you do it just within the area of jury
discretion?"

    LDF had also anticipated this question. To the uninitiated Stevens's
query might have appeared harmless, offering an easy way to reconcile

---

* Two of the five judges on the Texas Criminal Court of Appeals voted to rule the
statute unconstitutional because of this double counting.

McGautha with *Furman*, but in fact it was a land mine. If Amsterdam said prosecutorial discretion made the difference, he would validate Bork's central critique of LDF, since prosecutorial discretion pervaded the criminal justice system. During the moots Kendall had found dealing with *McGautha* terribly awkward, and no one had a convincing way to jibe the cases, but they knew they couldn't take this bait.

Understanding the situation fully, Amsterdam replied to Stevens, "No way." He explained, "To the extent that *Furman* is not consistent with *McGautha*, neither is our position, but I don't think *Furman* is inconsistent with *McGautha*." Amsterdam unveiled his own jesuitical distinction between the two cases: "Now, *Furman*, some have said, is inconsistent with *McGautha*. Some have said that the jury discretion which was recognized in *Furman* as invalidating the death penalty statute was no more or less than the jury discretion that *McGautha* held consistent with the Fourteenth Amendment. If you take that view, and I do not, then our position is inconsistent with *McGautha*." But, Amsterdam said, "We think that *Furman* is not inconsistent with *McGautha* because *Furman* is an Eighth Amendment decision which looks to the consequences of jury discretion, rather than simply whether the procedure is good or not."

In essence Amsterdam argued that *McGautha* had been about process and *Furman* about outcomes. "I think what *Furman* did was to say that the Eighth Amendment and the Fourteenth Amendment are two very different animals," he explained. "As a matter of due process, the states are given a great deal of leeway to shape their procedures." But, Amsterdam said, "What *Furman* said was that when a procedure of that sort resulted in an arbitrary dispensation of death across the total range of those cases in which it was authorized, so that the infliction of the death penalty on a particular individual was senseless—this arbitrariness made the death penalty unusual in a constitutional sense."

Amsterdam could more easily have explained how to count angels on the head of a pin. Powell viewed his distinction as gobbledygook. "If I have correctly noted what Amsterdam says," he wrote to himself, "I find it to be incomprehensible." To the extent that Powell understood the distinction between procedures and outcomes, he saw it as a reframing of the same old argument about mercy: Amsterdam viewed it as unfair to spare some from the death penalty while others received it. Critically to Powell, Amsterdam hadn't identified any problem in Jurek's specific case. "Amsterdam is not interested in the fairness of procedure in a particular case," Powell added in his notes.

Stewart wasn't buying it either. In asking Amsterdam earlier whether he opposed the death penalty in all cases, he seemed to be begging Amsterdam to concede the exotics. Now Stewart gave him one more chance to narrow his argument, whereupon followed an exchange that many of LDF's critics identify as the defining moment of the 1976 cases.

"Mr. Amsterdam, doesn't your argument prove too much?" Stewart asked. "In other words, in our system of adversary criminal justice, we have prosecutorial discretion, we have jury discretion, including jury nullification—we have lesser included offenses, we have appellate review, and we have the possibility of executive clemency. And that is true throughout our adversary system of justice. If a person is sentenced to anything as the end product of that system, under your argument, his sentence, be it life imprisonment or five years imprisonment, is a cruel and unusual punishment because it is the product of this system. That is your argument, isn't it?"

"No," said Amsterdam.

"And why not?"

Amsterdam paused again. He had foreseen this line of inquiry, too. "I very definitely anticipated the question," Amsterdam said in 2010, "though perhaps not the exact words." In reply to Stewart, Amsterdam staked the case on the uniqueness of capital punishment. "Our argument is essentially that death is different," he said. "If you don't accept the view that for constitutional purposes death is different, we lose this case. Let me make that very clear." He raised his voice for the first time, emphasizing each word in his answer. "Death is factually different. Death is final. Death is irremediable. Death is unnullable. It goes beyond this world. It is a legislative decision to do something and we know not what we do."

AFTER AMSTERDAM RESTED, John Hill, Texas's attorney general, hammered home the point that LDF opposed the American criminal justice system. Hill was a graduate of University of Texas Law School, a former Texas Cowboy, and one of the top lawyers in the Lone Star State. During the 1960s, he won civil judgments of $3.5 million against Lockheed and $8.5 million against Braniff Airlines, in the process earning a reputation for writing masterful briefs and a down-to-earth style with juries. Hill forayed into politics as an organizer for Governor John Connally, who appointed him secretary of state in 1966. In 1968 Hill unsuccessfully ran for governor, but in 1972 he upset the incumbent Democratic attorney general. During his tenure Hill closed down the Chicken Ranch in Fayette County, the brothel that inspired *The Best Little Whorehouse in Texas*.*

Texas's attorney general addressed the Court in a slow, southern drawl. "As Justice Stewart observed, his argument indeed does prove too much," Hill said, referring to Amsterdam. "It would be an anomaly, to say the least, if we were to condemn today in this country as unconstitutional the very procedures that our Constitution created, the same Constitution that created the cruel and unusual punishment provision." Hill meant that the Constitution required juries. Thus, by implication, it required the power to grant mercy traditionally invested in them.

"The truth is, and it becomes more and more obvious as this litigation proceeds, that there are those who hold very strongly the view and the conviction that the death penalty should no longer be used for any

---

* Hill later ran another unsuccessful campaign for governor, but in 1984 won election as the chief justice of the Texas Supreme Court, in which capacity he served for four years before retiring from public life.

purpose in this country," Hill said. "However, this Court is not a super legislature. This Court is not the keeper, any more than Amsterdam is, of the social values, the conscience, and the moral standards of the people of this country."

Stevens defended Amsterdam. Texas's law hadn't been Amsterdam's principal focus, but he had pointed out its substantial flaws. "I wonder if that really is a fair statement of his argument," Stevens said. "Mr. Amsterdam says the first and third of the aggravating questions have already been answered by the jury and therefore there really is no standard guiding these. Do you have a response to that argument?"

The aggravating questions were not "idle academic gestures," Hill replied. He cited fifteen instances where a jury answered no to the deliberate-conduct question. With respect to future dangerousness, Hill reminded the Court that Jurek had kidnapped a ten-year-old girl from a lake where her grandmother had taken her to swim. He raped her, choked her to death, threw her in a river, and went off with his friends to have a beer. Hill argued that Jurek had demonstrated "such an incorrigibility" and such a lack of remorse that the jury could have deemed him a menace to society based solely on the facts of his case. "But in this instance we had more," Hill said, referencing the testimony regarding Jurek's bad reputation, which Amsterdam had rejected as hearsay. Hill dismissed Amsterdam's objection. "Your Honors," he said, "the only way we prove bad character in Texas in these cases is by hearsay." Following a brief exchange about whether Texas's aggravating factor for murder of a police officer required that a defendant know that the victim was a police officer, Hill rested.

In his notes Powell wrote, "Strong jury speech!" though he didn't mean it as a compliment. Odd as this may seem, Supreme Court justices generally don't want discussions of facts. They are in the business of establishing principles that sometimes last for centuries. Their focus is far beyond an individual petitioner's case. By and large justices have a dim view of state attorneys general and think they focus too much on the facts of particular cases and too little on the implications for the law.

✦ ✦ ✦ ✦

JAMES BABIN, LOUISIANA'S ATTORNEY GENERAL, stepped to
the podium, but he had barely begun when Burger interrupted him
in midsentence at precisely three o'clock, and said the Court would
reconvene at ten o'clock the next day. When argument resumed in
the morning, Babin struck a familiar chord. He once again portrayed
Amsterdam as fundamentally opposed to the jury system. "The juries
in Louisiana and in the United States, if the argument of the respon-
dent were to be believed, are not dependable. They will not attempt to
follow their duties that they have taken an oath to do," Babin said. "If
jurors are suspect then the jury system can no longer exist. And I certainly do not think that this Court in the *Furman* decision intended a
change in the system such as that."

Like Hill, Babin attempted to focus the Court on the vileness of the
defendant's act. Babin said he wouldn't be "arguing in a general sense,"
as Amsterdam had. "We have a case where a man killed a one-armed
man when he was engaged in the perpetration of an armed robbery. In
fact, he killed him when it does not appear that he even needed to kill
him. This is a killing which has been presented to our grand jury and
later to our jury. Your Honors, we ask that the Supreme Court affirm
that decision." Babin's argument fared no better with the justices than
Hill's had. In his notes, Powell wrote, "In a major case, Louisiana has
sent a third line—and third rate—counsel to debate Amsterdam."
Harry Blackmun, who by this time had shifted to numerical grades,
gave Babin a 75.

William James, the assistant attorney general for California, fared
little better. Arguing as a friend of the court, James said that California
feared Amsterdam's ambition. "We are concerned that these petitioners are not going to be content with trying to get this Court to hold
unconstitutional the statutes that are presently before the courts, but
they also want an all-encompassing decision declaring the death penalty unconstitutional per se and invalidating all statutes." James urged
the Court to lay down guidelines to aid state legislatures and Congress

in devising acceptable standards. Finally he reminded the justices that after the California Supreme Court rejected the death penalty "the response of the people was fairly quick." The referendum that overrode *Anderson* won 67 percent support, with 5.3 million voting.

Stevens asked James the specifics of California's new law and how often juries failed to find any aggravating circumstances.

"I know there are quite a number," James said.

"What you are telling us is that the second jury doesn't rubber-stamp the process and simply declare all of them subject to the death penalty?" Stevens asked.

"That is correct."

As James sat down, Powell wrote to himself, "No help." But the cavalry was coming.

A JOLT OF ELECTRICITY surged through the courtroom as Robert Bork stepped forward to the lectern, oozing intelligence and gravitas. In the tradition of American solicitors general, Bork had dressed for the day in a black morning coat with matching black waistcoat and striped trousers. On many men the outfit looked uncomfortable, but Bork wore it easily. He projected supreme confidence, and spoke with a degree of precision that at least matched Amsterdam's own. For the past several rounds the quality of the bout had dropped. The attorneys general were not suitable sparring partners for Amsterdam; Bork was a worthy foe in every respect.

"Mr. Chief Justice, and may it please the Court," he began, "the constitutional argument made by petitioner's counsel is rather diffused. I will try to sort out these various propositions that are being urged and attempt to show their inadequacy either singly or collectively." Bork made a strategic concession. "To begin with, we know as a fact that the men who framed the Eighth Amendment did not mean—did not intend as an original matter—to outlaw capital punishment." As an originalist Bork believed this should be the end of the Court's inquiry. But just as LDF believed Amsterdam needed to concede the exotics, lest he be perceived as extreme and unreasonable, Bork felt that he couldn't take an absolute originalist position, lest he be perceived as unreasonable himself. Thanks to the backlash, he didn't need to take this position: Even under evolved standards of decency he could win. So Bork conceded that "one cannot exclude the possibility that cruel or unusual punishment means something different today than it meant then," though he added that "the principle is one of controlled evolution. The amendment is not an uncontrolled delegation of power to the judiciary to judge punishments. There are criteria by which the judiciary judges punishments, and I will try to demonstrate that the principle of evolution which controls the case here, not only does not outlaw the death penalty, but in fact affirmatively supports it." That principle, according to Bork, was "that punishments may not be used which fall far outside the mainstream of our jurisprudence and which are rejected by the current moral consensus."

White seized upon Bork's concession. "So you accept judging the cruelty in the light of contemporary morality?"

"I do indeed, Mr. Justice White."

"Do courts have independent input into this question?"

In a masterful move Bork said no. "I think proportionality has to be judged on objective standards," he averred, embracing the test Amsterdam advanced in *Furman*. Of course Amsterdam had proposed this standard because public support for the death penalty had been slipping and states had ancient death penalty laws on the books. In 1976 the argument spun differently. Not surprisingly, Bork said, "Proportionality would be judged by the frequency with which legislatures choose." He added, "If one jurisdiction only suddenly imposed death for jaywalking, or flogging for jaywalking, I think, looking across the spectrum of the American commonwealths and seeing that that was wildly out of proportion with every other jurisdiction would be one way of judging proportionality."

"So if enough legislatures pass a law, you would say the courts have no basis to say that the penalty is disproportionate?"

"I doubt very much, Mr. Justice White, whether a court could. Disproportionateness depends in great part upon the moral understanding of the community. If the moral understanding of the community in a very widespread way views the punishment as proportionate, I don't know what independent source a court would have to look to."

"Do you think we should overturn *Furman* on that basis?"

"I was preparing to suggest that later in my argument."

"I thought so. But do you think it is required?"

"No, I don't think what I have said requires it," Bork said, "but I think other reasons make it desirable." He added, "Congress and thirty-five states have shown that the legislative will is frustrated if the death penalty is never imposed."

Bork's replies to White reflected the extent of his confidence. To win Bork didn't need the Court to overturn *Furman*. The justices could say that the new statutes satisfied *Furman* or, as Powell recorded in his notes, that *Furman* applied only to standardless discretion. Nevertheless Bork swung for the fences. Amsterdam, by contrast, offered the Court a basis to uphold *McGautha* and *Furman*, and rule the new statutes unconstitutional. He never considered asking the Court to overturn *McGautha*. When Stevens asked Bork why *McGautha* and *Furman* couldn't coexist, Bork rejected Amsterdam's distinction between process and outcomes. "I don't understand how a process which produces intolerable results can be due process," Bork told Stevens. "So it seems to me that there is a necessary contradiction between the two cases."

"Well," said Stewart, "they did involve two different provisions of the Constitution."

"That is quite true," Bork said. "But that gets us back into the position where the Constitution mandates discretion in a criminal justice system, and that discretion renders illegal a punishment which the Constitution recognizes as legally allowable."

"It certainly isn't an unusual situation," Stewart said. "Something that is perfectly permissible under one provision of the Constitution and violates another provision of the Constitution, there's nothing unusual about that."

"I think this is unique," Bork insisted. "The Fifth Amendment and the Fourteenth Amendment say, use due process of law when you impose the death penalty. To then say that the procedure by which you use due process of law makes it cruel and unusual punishment under the Eighth Amendment, so that all along there was no death penalty, seems to me to be a logical impossibility."

So what did *Furman* mean, then? "If it is not necessary to overrule *Furman* to decide these cases, why not?" Stevens asked. "Why is not *Furman* controlling?"

"Because I think *Furman* refers to standardless jury discretion—that is all it really applies to. I think the statutes that have been enacted in response to *Furman* now put standards into the process and therefore it is not necessary to overrule *Furman*." Bork delivered his coup de grace. Hill and Babin had alluded to this point. Bork took the argument to its full extension, and delivered it with punishing force, a roundhouse right to the collective jaw of Amsterdam, LDF, and everyone on death row in America. "It is not necessary to overrule *Furman*," he said decisively. "But I think counsel made it plain that he objects to every element of discretion in the system, not just jury discretion. He objects to them collectively, and if I understood him correctly yesterday, he would object to them singly." Bork continued, "There is apparently no way according to this argument that anybody could devise a system of justice in which anybody used any judgment which could then inflict the death penalty. The system—the only system that would meet counsel's objections would be one that was so rigid and automatic and insensitive that it would be morally reprehensible, and then apparently it would meet the moral standards of the Constitution."

Bork continued, "Counsel's real complaint is not that anybody is freakishly convicted and executed, but rather that some murderers are freakishly spared and given life imprisonment. In other words, the fault in the system which makes it unconstitutional is that it errs, if it errs at all, on the side of mercy, and the side of safety, and that is what we are told makes it unconstitutional—I have seldom heard logic more unintelligible. It is impossible to see how these procedures disadvantage anybody, because the persons who are not spared are not made worse off."

Finally Bork countered Amsterdam's efforts to limit the impact of his argument. "These arguments that are made against the death penalty could be made against any other form of punishment," Bork said. "There is not one of them that does not apply to life imprisonment." "Of course, it is different," he said, referring to death. But "life imprisonment is different from a year imprisonment. Life imprisonment is different from a fine."

"Well, if you made a mistake you can cancel it and undo it," Stewart said.

Bork denied this premise. Errors in long prison sentences couldn't be reversed, he said. "You can undo it to the extent you set him free when you discover the mistake, but the years are gone." Really the death penalty "is unique only because we surround it by so many precautions."

Burger seized the moment: "Precautions that were generated by *Furman*."

"That is entirely true, Mr. Chief Justice."

In Bork's view these precautions had generated increased rationality in the system. Again he cited Hans Zeisel and Harry Kalven's book as evidence that "there is sense to the process." Even if Zeisel and Kalven were wrong, Bork said the Court lacked the power to improve the system. "If we found a bias of any kind in the system, I don't know what we would do," he said. "It wouldn't be an argument for this case— because if it's true that capital punishment is inflicted disproportionately by sex or by race or by social economic group—and this hasn't been shown hereto—then it must also be true that all other punishments are inflicted with equal bias, because it is the same prosecutors, the same jurors, the same judges, the same governor."

Bork attempted to close by sounding the theme of federalism. "Ultimately, these cases are about democratic government, the right of various legislatures of the United States, to choose or reject—

according to their own moral sense and that of the people, the death penalty, in accordance with the Constitution." He concluded, "The case is merely the latest in a continuing series seeking to obtain from this Court a political judgment that the opponents of the death penalty have been unable to obtain from the political branches of government. The United States asks that the constitutionality of the death penalty be upheld."

BORK COLLECTED HIS PAPERS and stepped away from the lectern, but before he could return to his seat, Powell summoned him back to answer an additional question. Bork had impressed Powell so thoroughly that he made a note to himself to review the transcript of Bork's oral argument if he decided to write an opinion in the case. Neither man could have foreseen the irony of this moment. When Ronald Reagan nominated Bork to the Supreme Court in 1987, it was to replace Powell. And it would be Bork's commitment to originalism, the jurisprudential premise from which he concluded that the Eighth Amendment didn't bar the death penalty, that would be his undoing. (Of course this was all in the future. At the time they were unspoken allies, defending capital punishment, federalism, and judicial restraint.)

"Mr. Solicitor General," Powell said, calling to Bork, "you haven't had an opportunity to address in your oral argument the issue of deterrence." Powell cited the recent increase in murders—from 15,720 murders in 1968 to 19,510 in 1973, the most recent year for which statistics were available. Powell barely contained his emotion as he juxtaposed this 40 percent increase against the war in Asia. "It is perfectly obvious from these figures that we need some way to deter the slaughter of Americans," Powell said. "I use the word 'slaughter' because the word was used in connection with the disaster in Vietnam, in which fifty-five thousand Americans were killed over a six- or seven-year period. If the FBI figures are correct, there were more Americans killed in this country, murdered, than there were on the battlefields of Vietnam."

Powell appeared to be channeling every parent who had made their child cut his or her hair, and he vented their rage at the hypocrisy and narrow-mindedness of American liberals.

According to Bork, he "never heard a question from the bench he liked better." Bork interpreted Powell's comment as an invitation to make any additional points he wished, and Bork took full advantage of the license. "Mr. Justice Powell, it seems to me that it cannot rationally be questioned that the death penalty has a deterrent effect," he said. "Mankind has always thought so throughout its history. We know, as a matter of common sense—that all other aspects of human behavior, as you raise the cost and the risk, the amount of the activity goes down. I don't know why murder should be any different. I wouldn't have thought that anybody would have doubted that or listened to a couple of academicians who doubted it. We introduce the Ehrlich study to show that there is respectable academic evidence on the side of deterrence. But I would have thought that the judgment of the legislatures of this country—that they think it deters—is enough. It is a rational judgment. We think it is enough for this Court." Bork seized upon Powell's theme. "And I must say that, at a time when international and domestic terrorism is going up, at a time when brutal murders are going up, it is an awesome responsibility to take from the states what they think is a necessary deterrent, and save a few hundred guilty people, and thereby probably condemn to death thousands of innocent people. That is truly an awesome responsibility."

Finally Bork sat down, and the Court took the Texas and Louisiana cases under submission.

SHORTLY BEFORE HALF PAST eleven, Burger called for argument in *Woodson*. Amsterdam and Sidney Eagles, a deputy attorney general for North Carolina, stepped forward to the counsel tables. Since LDF represented neither Gregg nor Proffitt, and hadn't been invited to argue in the Georgia and Florida cases, these would be Amsterdam's final words before the justices decided the death penalty cases.

Amsterdam faced yet another critical strategic choice. Without a doubt Bork had scored points with the Court. Should Amsterdam attempt to counter Bork's arguments, or should he focus on the deficiencies of North Carolina's statute? The North Carolina law appeared to be the most vulnerable of the five. Kendall felt they had a strong chance of defeating it. Amsterdam, though, still had his eyes on the brass ring. He felt that several of Bork's assertions had to be challenged. Furthermore the questioning during *Jurek* had diverted him from making several points he had wanted to make regarding the unconstitutionality of capital punishment generally. In the end Amsterdam barely mentioned mandatory sentences during his *Woodson* argument.

Amsterdam began by confronting Bork's proposition that *Furman* couldn't comfortably coexist with *McGautha*. "Our first argument is based squarely upon *Furman*," he said. "It is arbitrary selectivity, by which I mean that certain persons are consigned to die and others are spared. Call it mercy if you will, as the Government puts it, but other people in like situations are spared with no meaningful basis to distinguish between them. This is an Eighth Amendment argument. It is not a Due Process argument, because the Eighth Amendment is not concerned with process, it is concerned with the result of process." He explained, "That is why *Furman* is consistent with *McGautha*. It is our position that *Furman* outlaws the present system because the results are no better than a lottery—the Government suggests in its brief that another way to run a system of selecting people to die would be a lottery, that is, if all people convicted of murder were in a lottery and you only kill some of them. It is our contention that *Furman* would outlaw that just as much as it outlawed the jury discretionary system."

Justice Stevens questioned Amsterdam's premise. "Is your argument predicated on the proposition that standardless sentencing is equivalent to a lottery? The solicitor general takes precisely the opposite position. Is it not a rational basis that a jury of twelve people differentiated? One found that this group should die and another group found that they should not. Is that not rational?"

"No, it is not," Amsterdam replied. "The fact is that each individual jury may come in with different standards, different approaches. There is no way to rationalize a system like that." This exchange placed Amsterdam in the familiar, uncomfortable position of opposing jury discretion, so he quickly changed subjects, announcing that he would spend the remainder of his time arguing the unconstitutionality of the death penalty in all cases. "Our second argument, a safe, square one, does not depend on *Furman*. It would be the same whether *Furman* had been decided or not. The second argument is that the death penalty is an atavistic butchery which has run its course." Amsterdam condemned the revised statutes: "The new death penalties that we are having urged on us are either totally discretionary or they are reversions, they are rollbacks—to the old mandatory death penalty system. The mandatory death penalty system was repudiated because it was intolerable and because juries would not convict—"

Blackmun cut Amsterdam off. "I thought I said that in my dissent in *Furman*, precisely that."

"Mr. Justice Blackmun, I think you got—"

Blackmun interrupted Amsterdam again. "Of course, one doesn't read dissents anyway," Blackmun said to laughter from the gallery. "You know, as a professor, that when counsel lose one case, they come up in the next one and distinguish it."

Amsterdam maintained his cool. "Mr. Justice Blackmun, I think there is quite a difference. I think that when we are now told that they system under which hundreds of people were put to death was arbitrary and uninformed and irrational, that is quite an important consideration."

"Well, I say again, as I said yesterday, hasn't your *Furman* result prompted this kind of thing which you are now so seriously complaining about?"

"We have a dialectic process going on," Amsterdam replied. "The states have responded to *Furman*, but *Furman* itself responded to what went before—mandatory capital punishment found unacceptable by the people of the country."

"I think I said that in my dissent. So you don't have to argue with me about it."

Amsterdam wondered whether he had so offended Blackmun in 1967, when he corrected his mathematics, that Blackmun held a grudge nine years later. But Amsterdam didn't worry long before Burger seized the mantle from his childhood friend.

"Mr. Amsterdam," the chief justice asked, "Would you argue for abolishing the jury system in criminal cases because it produces some irrational results?"

"No, not at all. And that's not what I'm saying—"

"That's the essence of what you are arguing now: that we should abolish the whole system of punishment because it works irrationally sometimes."

"The question is whether what is good enough for meting out remediable punishments, punishments that are within the realm of the knowable and curable, is also good enough for meting out the punishment of life and death. *Furman* said no."

"Your argument is that death is different. This is where you must end up, as yesterday when Mr. Justice Stewart asked you the question. And your answer has to be that death is different. And if it isn't different, you have to lose."

Amsterdam had gone too far down this path to change direction now. "That is absolutely correct." He repeated once more, "If death is not different, we lose on every argument we have got."

POWELL HAD BEEN SILENT for some time, but now he put Amsterdam to a stern, final test. Powell focused Amsterdam on the federal death penalty statute, which imposed capital punishment only for air piracy. Because of its narrower scope, and because air piracy occurred infrequently—"fortunately," Powell said—the federal law didn't create the same risk of arbitrariness as the state statutes. Powell inquired, "Do you make the same argument against the federal statute that you do against the North Carolina statute?" He might as well have asked, "Are you willing to deal?" Amsterdam understood the subtext: Powell had a reputation as a pragmatist.

In this moment the potential concession of the appropriateness of the death penalty for extreme crimes took on new significance. Powell's inquiry suggested that he, and perhaps others, wanted to split the baby—to do something "Solomonic," as Christina Whitman put it. The question offered Amsterdam an opportunity to weigh in on what this compromise should look like. Participating in this exercise might undermine Amsterdam's grand argument against capital punishment, but it could help Jurek, Gregg, and Woodson. It also might help make Amsterdam appear reasonable. This is why LDF had resolved to concede the exotics in the first place. But Amsterdam didn't have it in his heart. Once again his instincts took over.

"I would not make the same argument, but I think the federal statute is subject to attack," Amsterdam told Powell. "The narrower you make the statute, the more alike the people within the class are and the more arbitrary therefore it is to distinguish among them instead of treating them all the same." Once more it sounded as if no death penalty statute could satisfy LDF.

"Can you conceive of any crime to which you would consider the death penalty an appropriate response by society?" asked Powell.

"No."

"Well, let me put a case to you. If we had had jurisdiction over the commandant of Buchenwald, would you have thought capital punishment was an appropriate response to what that man was responsible for?" Powell had prepared this inquiry in advance and vetted it with Whitman, as he did each of the questions he asked during oral argument.

Amsterdam resented the question. He believed Powell had asked him this because he was Jewish. In his advocacy the subject of the death penalty for severe crimes came up often. At the *Anderson* oral argument the chief justice of California's Supreme Court, Donald Wright, had asked him several difficult questions on the topic. But in

Amsterdam's hundreds of appearances before skeptical judges, none had ever asked him whether Nazis should be executed. Amsterdam refused to admit the appropriateness of the death penalty for genocide. "We have an instinctive reaction that says, 'Kill him,'" he told Powell. "But would that crime be consistent with the Eighth Amendment against the history which the Court must now apply to that Amendment at this point in time? My answer would be, 'no.'"

Powell couldn't believe Amsterdam's answer. Powell's biographer John Jefferies said that after years of struggle, Amsterdam had become so emotional about the issue that he lost all sense of his audience. Powell pressed Amsterdam further. "So if some fanatic set off a hydrogen bomb and destroyed New York City, still you think the appropriate remedy for that would be to put him in prison, perhaps out on parole in seven years?"

"Mr. Justice Powell, there is no question in my mind that the state must have and it does have ample remedies against people who are going to set off hydrogen bombs."

"Would you be willing to put him in prison in solitary confinement for life with no parole?"

"The question is not before the Court. I think that under certain limited circumstances it may be permissible to incarcerate someone—it seems to me we are now getting constitutional and normative questions mixed up. I see no constitutional objection at all for life imprisonment without parole." In the ongoing struggle to avoid being seen as a subverter of the system, the "it may be permissible to incarcerate someone" may have been unfortunate language.

Burger seized upon the slip. "Aren't there many, many arguments that are exactly the same ones as have been presented to us in this case that total life imprisonment and solitary confinement is a more cruel and unusual punishment than death?"

"It is neither, Mr. Justice Burger, and not only do my clients, but everybody on death row appreciates the difference."

"Very well," said Burger. Amsterdam reserved for rebuttal his remaining two minutes: two minutes before the fate of hundreds of men on death row, and thousands more who might someday sit there, would be sealed.

SIDNEY EAGLES, DEPUTY ATTORNEY GENERAL of North Carolina, argued next. Eagles had attended Wake Forest for college and law school. Later he would become a judge on the North Carolina court of appeals. Eagles began by responding to Amsterdam's argument that the American people had repudiated mandatory death penalties. "Two members of the Court in *Furman* indicated a preference in that direction. And, the people—at least the people of North Carolina—have acted definitely to guarantee a mandatory death penalty in a limited series of cases."

Like his counterparts from Georgia and Louisiana, Eagles spent most of his time talking about the facts of the case. He said Woodson, Waxton, and Tucker went into a "Seven-Eleven quick mart type," asked for cigarettes, and Waxton shot the victim in the head "without any resistance on her part." During his argument Amsterdam had briefly suggested that Woodson, not being the triggerman, bore less responsibility than Waxton, who didn't receive a death sentence. Eagles fired back.

"The assertion by Mr. Amsterdam that Woodson is the least culpable defies my comprehension," said Eagles. "Much of his argument has, from time to time, but I attribute that to my limitation rather than to him." Eagles explained that Waxton and Tucker had pled guilty, while Woodson refused to bargain. This acceptance of responsibility explained the disparity in their sentences. Furthermore, Eagles called discretion a virtue, not a liability of the criminal justice system.

"The judgment that's complained of in this case—necessarily occurs in the constitutional mandate," Eagles said. "The prosecutor, the juror, the trial judge, our appellate courts, and the Supreme Court of North Carolina are all acting pursuant to obligations under our Constitution. All these things result, we believe, in a trial which is constitutionally perfect in the sense of fairness and due process to the individual being tried. Having resulted in this, over two hundred years of evolution of this country and its judicial system, we are shocked, frankly, that petitioners now say that because things are so fair and because your system is so judicious and because your system is so careful about who finally receives the death penalty, that then it's arbitrary. It's logically fallacious."

With that Eagles and North Carolina rested.

AMSTERDAM HAD ONLY TWO precious minutes remaining, and the justices had at him before he could get out more than two sentences. Stewart asked, "If in fact the North Carolina practice results in a larger number of death penalties, would you nevertheless conclude that the North Carolina statute is less vulnerable than the Louisiana statute?"

"Less vulnerable on a scale of one to one hundred, yes," Amsterdam replied, "But they are both well below the line of constitutionality, and the difference between them is small compared to the quantum jump that would have to be made to get up to constitutionality."

"Suppose the Gallup Poll and Harris Poll showed 90 percent of the people in the country favor capital punishment," Burger asked. "Do you think that enters into the constitutionality appraisal?"

"No, Your Honor. I don't think that the plebiscites cut one way or the other."

"I got the impression from what you said yesterday that we have to evaluate standards in light of what people think," Burger said.

"I think that's true, but not as a matter of plebiscite."

The red light flashed, indicating that Amsterdam's time had expired, even though he had barely had a chance to say anything he wanted to. Amsterdam asked the Court for two more minutes. Burger gave him one.

Amsterdam tried to frame LDF's position more reasonably. The organization wasn't a friend of criminals, he said. "To attack the death penalty is not to express sympathy for crime. It is not to express callousness with respect to victims. The death penalty may be the greatest obstacle to adequate enforcement of crime in this country today because it stops public conscience and makes you think we are doing something about serious crime instead of devising other methods of dealing with it.

"Secondly, we are taxed in this case and have been throughout our presentation with the notion that it is we who are seeking to have this Court use subjective gut feelings to be a super-legislature. That is not true. Our position is the only coherent analytic position of the Eighth Amendment," Amsterdam said. "If the Eighth Amendment was written to apply only to the federal government it couldn't be asking a comparative question." This responded powerfully to Bork's originalist argument. Since the Bill of Rights applied only to the federal government, the framers couldn't have intended the meaning of the Eighth Amendment to turn on a comparative assessment of state mores. The Bill of Rights wasn't extended to the states until after the Civil War, and even then the Court only applied its protections piecemeal.

Amsterdam had scored a final point. He knew it and tried to exit on that high note: "We submit simply that our argument has a coherent Eighth Amendment base, accounts for the needs of law enforcement, and protection of victims. Under that view, the death penalty is a violation of the Eighth Amendment."

He said, "Thank you for the extra time," and collected his papers, but Lewis Powell called him back. "Mr. Amsterdam," he asked. "May I give you at least another half a minute?" Burger didn't object, so Amsterdam returned to the podium. Powell still couldn't fathom Amsterdam's strategy.

"I would like to ask this question," Powell said, with his unfailing civility. "I am sure you feel that each of these five statutes is abhorrent and unconstitutional under the views that you have expressed. Let's assume for the moment that someone, somewhere, had to choose among the five. Which of the five, in your judgment—you have studied them all—would be the most likely to minimize the elements of discretion and arbitrariness that are so offensive to you?" Powell appeared to be suggesting again that the Court wanted to reach a compromise.

Amsterdam had anticipated this question, too. During the *Anderson* argument, the California Supreme Court asked him to distinguish among the various state responses to *Furman*. Amsterdam regarded it as a trap, which he called "the obverse of a slippery slope." In 2010 he said, "If we gave something away, we'd lose." Moreover Amsterdam felt that in its choices for certiorari, the Court had picked the most egregious new statutes. "The discretionaries were the worst of the discretionaries, and the mandatories were the worst of the mandatories."

Amsterdam didn't believe that the Court had any interest in delving into the nitty-gritty of state statutes. *Spencer v. Texas*, a 1967 challenge to Texas's habitual criminal statutes, had proved this to him. Under these laws a jury heard evidence of past convictions for sentencing purposes. The judge issued a limiting instruction—of debatable value— that the defendant's prior behavior shouldn't influence its decision on guilt. The Court upheld the controversial practice. Harlan's opinion said the Constitution didn't contemplate the Court examining the minutiae of state criminal procedure. He quoted Benjamin Cardozo's proposition that a state law "does not run afoul of the Fourteenth Amendment because another method may seem to our thinking to be fairer or wiser or to give a surer promise of protection to the prisoner at bar." Harlan added, "It has never been thought that this Court is a rule-making organ for the promulgation of state rules of criminal procedure. And none of the specific provisions of the Constitution ordains this Court with such authority." This became, more or less, the gist of *McGautha*, and it influenced Amsterdam's thinking profoundly.

Amsterdam accurately believed that Harlan's long shadow continued to influence the swing justices—most notably Stewart and White. "Should we have picked nits with the Texas statute when the issues were at a macro level?" Amsterdam asked rhetorically from his NYU office. He said he might have answered differently if he had been asked whether he could imagine a statute that could conform with *Furman*, but this hadn't been Powell's question. Powell asked about the five statutes as written. So Amsterdam declined the implicit invitation to deal. He paused and snickered. "None of them is close enough so that I can give a meaningful answer to that question." Amsterdam continued, "I am not trying to simply cop off the question, it's just that they don't come close enough. They are so close together in their total impact and they are so far from where they ought to be that to draw that marginal difference is essentially, I think, meaningless."

Powell gave him yet another chance. "You think they ought to be zero, I understand that, but you have no choice among the five statutes?"

"No, no," Amsterdam replied, adding that a particular problem with mandatory death penalty statutes was that "some cases go right through the mill and nobody recognizes that they have got the power and these people end up dead because nobody realized that all the discretion which is in the system, which is exercised by other prosecutors and other juries, was even available. I think that is a very bad thing. But is it worse than what goes on under a system in which overt discretion allows inconsistent judgments? I think they are both bad and as bad. That's the best I can do."

His additional time had expired.

"I thank the Court," he said.

"Thank you, Mr. Amsterdam," said Burger.

THE REST WAS DENOUEMENT. Thomas Davis of Georgia defended the selection of torture as an aggravating factor. LDF had attacked this aggravating circumstance, and many others, as broad and vague in its brief. Davis also defended the rationality of Georgia's appellate system. Powell regarded Davis's argument as able, and the best of the state arguments. He also thought the appellate review a "wise type of requirement" and he reminded himself to reread the Georgia statute.

In *Proffitt*, Clinton Curtis and Robert Shevin sounded familiar themes. On behalf of Proffitt, Curtis said the Florida statute didn't adequately curtail arbitrariness. Shevin, Florida's attorney general, attacked LDF as ideologues one final time. "I don't care what he calls it," Shevin said, referring to Amsterdam. "What he is really doing is attacking the whole system." Later Shevin added, "Even though Mr. Amsterdam stands before this Court and says, 'I am only trying to apply the Eighth Amendment in death cases,' there is no way he can foreclose someone who is under a life sentence from coming back to this Court and saying, 'Give me that same protection.' He is going to say that if you say the whole system is wrong, then it's wrong to him as well. For those reasons, we urge you to affirm his conviction, to state in effect that the whole system is not wrong." Shevin declined to attack *Furman*. Rather he said that "we provided a system that meets the arbitrariness that has been outlawed in *Furman*."

It had all been said before, and five minutes past three o'clock, a weary Burger brought matters to close. "Thank you, gentlemen," he said. "The case is submitted." The future of the death penalty now rested in the justices' hands.

When LDF debriefed after the argument, they found themselves on different pages. Amsterdam, as always, felt he had justice on his side. Davis also had some hope. She wrote a friend, "The key justices seemed open and responsive." Kendall felt more uneasy. "I did not leave the Court with a good feeling. I had mild hope, but more gloom," he said. Throughout the two days Kendall had kept his eyes on Stevens and thought he had responded with hostility to Amsterdam's argument that the death penalty resembled a lottery. Kendall thought this didn't bode well.

CHAPTER 19

THE CENTER
IN CONTROL

BACK IN THEIR CHAMBERS THE JUSTICES CONDEMNED Tony Amsterdam's presentation. Amsterdam had earned high praise for his oral argument in *Furman*. For his performance in the 1976 cases he received universal derision. "Now I know what it's like to hear Jesus Christ," William Brennan told his clerks. Lewis Powell told Christina Whitman that he thought Amsterdam was a "nut." Several of the justices felt Amsterdam had been rude to Harry Blackmun. Blackmun assigned Amsterdam a grade of 83, a substantial drop from the A- he received in 1972, and added the unkind notation, "very glib, voice squeaks." Brennan was furious with Amsterdam. He believed Amsterdam should have engaged Powell's overtures toward compromise and, generally speaking, acted less self-righteous and preachy. The clerks saw things much the same way. Stewart's clerk, Ron Stern, thought Amsterdam's response to his boss's questions hadn't been helpful. Christina Whitman expected things would go poorly for LDF when the justices discussed the cases later in the week.

Indeed things went quite poorly. At conference on Friday, April 2, Warren Burger spoke first. "On the basic question, my view remains that this is primarily a legislative prerogative. Since I could have sustained in *Furman*, I would sustain here." Burger didn't surprise anyone with his comments. Neither did Brennan, who said he "would never change his 1972 view," and that he would reverse in all of the cases.

Potter Stewart stirred things up. Near the start of the term, Stewart dejectedly told his clerk, William Jeffress, "I misjudged the passion among voters." Now, Stewart made this agonizing concession to his colleagues. "There was more to say for Bill Brennan's views at the time of *Furman* than there is now. Death statutes then were dead letters. But what thirty-five state legislatures have done since 1972 is focused on why there should be the death penalty for specific, serious offenses. This establishes what evolving standards of decency are in 1976." Furthermore, Stewart said, "these standards, in this context, should be determined by the legislative rather than judicial branch. As a matter of constitutional law, I can't say that capital punishment is invalid."

Stewart put some distance between his and White's 1972 positions. "Byron and I didn't say the same thing in *Furman*," said Stewart. "My view was: one, this penalty is different from any other, and unusual in that sense, and, two, imposed with no rhyme or reason by juries uninstructed as to standards, uninformed as to relevant considerations, and uncontrolled discretion was unreviewable. I thought Byron's view was that this was a particular defect." Stewart distinguished among the new statutes. "Georgia and Florida have clearly devised constitutionally tolerable systems," he said. "The crimes are specified, and only after conviction in a separate trial does the jury address the penalty. In both states, appellate review is carefully structured. Each step in the process is designed to minimize error and afford opportunity for review. I can't buy Amsterdam's view as to the wrongness of the opportunity for discretion. There must be discretion." For this reason Stewart rejected the mandatory statutes. "North Carolina doesn't really change post-*Furman*, retains jury irrationality, and is invalid. Louisiana allowing lesser included convictions is bad and therefore invalid. The Texas statute is close. I'm not at rest as to its validity."

White said he would affirm all five statutes. In his view each had satisfied *Furman*'s mandate. "These are very different from the pre-

Furman statutes," said White, who recalled *Furman* differently than Stewart did. White said that he and Stewart had been on the same page in 1972. "My emphasis in *Furman* was upon the infrequency of imposition. I did emphasize, as Potter did, the standardlessness, freakishness, and the lack of instructions.* I think that North Carolina and Louisiana have met the test I had in mind in *Furman*. I thought in *McGautha* that once you provided juries with standards the number of death sentences would increase, and that is what is happening." White added, "We did not take a rape case, and it must make a difference what the offense is. Any opinion must note that we don't address the death penalty in rape cases."

Blackmun agreed with White's caveat. "I am disturbed by the use of capital penalty for rape," he said. Blackmun said the evidence that North Carolina's new law had been used disproportionately against black defendants also disturbed him, but he couldn't find a constitutional basis to overturn capital punishment. Nor could he find a basis for the Court to pick and choose among the new statutes. Blackmun voted in favor of the Georgia, Florida, Texas, and Louisiana laws and passed regarding North Carolina.

After Thurgood Marshall said that he stood behind his 1972 opinion, and would reverse all five death sentences, Powell said that he supported the use of capital punishment for heinous crimes, but opposed mandatory laws. "What the country needs is for public executions to be reinstated," Powell told his colleagues. He reasoned that the public would disfavor mandatory laws if people were forced to observe executions. Powell felt more sanguine about Georgia and Florida's laws. "States have provided safeguards against systems that operated like

---

* This emergent tension between Stewart's and White's characterizations of White's *Furman* opinion is fascinating, especially since they bear little relation to what White actually wrote. White never used the word "standards." He did refer to a jury's ability to "refuse to impose the death penalty no matter what the circumstances of the crime." The point of this reference, however, was to suggest that states couldn't be aggrieved greatly by *Furman* since they had delegated so much of their authority to juries.

bolts of lightning, so *Furman* served a salutary role." Consistent with his notes during the oral argument, Powell said that automatic state supreme court review provided an important check against inconsistent jury verdicts. He would vote to uphold all five laws, although he harbored reservations regarding North Carolina. "Looking at the statutes individually, in light of Potter's and Byron's opinions in *Furman*, North Carolina raises doubt in my mind. It touches a wide sweep of crimes. I'm quite doubtful as to its validity under *Furman*. The Louisiana statute on its face is one of the best, but it does not have bifurcated trials. This is not essential, but it is a safeguard. I'll consider this further."

William Rehnquist said he would affirm all five statutes. Finally John Paul Stevens showed his cards for the first time. "*Furman* is the law for me," said Stevens. "That is my starting point, and therefore I think that the death penalty is permissible in some circumstances under an evolving standards concept. I have no doubt that capital punishment is a permissible penalty under the Constitution. I cannot agree that standards have yet evolved as Amsterdam urges. I think that Thurgood's and Bill Brennan's views will eventually become law, but not yet."

Stevens continued, "When the only issue is the Eighth Amendment, it may be unusual to make a procedural analysis. But this seems to be the basis of the Stewart-White rationale in *Furman*, and so I accept this type of analysis. When the Eighth Amendment is the only issue, one must make a procedural analysis of the total picture. That is *Furman*'s teaching for me." Amsterdam's distinction between *Furman* and *McGautha* had earned one convert.

Regarding the specific statutes, Stevens said, "To have created a monster like North Carolina is abhorrent. Moreover, neither North Carolina nor Louisiana has a separate sentencing hearing. That is a lawless use of the legal system. I originally felt the same way about the Texas statute, but I can't object to a separate jury determination, even if it is essentially standardless."

After everyone had spoken, the tallies appeared to be seven to two in favor of the Georgia and Florida laws, five to four in favor of Louisiana, five to three in favor of Texas (Stewart had passed), and a four-to-four tie on North Carolina (Blackmun had passed). The question remained who would write the opinions. Burger coveted the assignment for himself. He also considered giving Rehnquist part of the action. Since the cases presented different issues, Burger could have assigned them piecemeal. Instead Burger assigned all five cases to White, whose vote he considered least solid among the death penalty supporters. White's endless hemming and hawing in *Furman* showed his lack of resolve regarding capital punishment. Burger felt that the assignment would solidify White's support, and that his opinion would persuade Powell and Blackmun regarding North Carolina. With White's help, Burger believed the pro–death penalty forces could win all five cases.

Burger calculated correctly in one regard. White relished the assignment and expressed excitement regarding it. He gave part of the work to each of his three clerks, and he strategized with them about the prospects for pulling off a clean sweep. In presuming Powell's support, though, Burger badly miscalculated.

THOUGH POWELL HAD OPPOSED *Furman* strongly, in his notes during the April 2 conference, Powell wrote to himself, "I accept *Furman* as precedent." During his confirmation hearings, Powell told the Senate Judiciary Committee, "As a lawyer, I have a deep respect for precedent. I know the importance of continuity and reasonable predictability of the law." As a justice, Powell lived up to these words. For the duration of his tenure he supported *Roe v. Wade*, even though initially he opposed the decision with as much fervor as he opposed *Furman*. Furthermore, whether or not *Furman* had been correctly decided, Powell believed it had accomplished substantial good. His notes echoed what he told his colleagues. "It is fair to say that the result of *Furman* has been wholesome in prompting states to focus on the problem and enact standards."

At the same time, more than any other justice, Powell saw the dangers in the extension of Amsterdam's argument. If the Court validated the existence of racism in the criminal justice system—even if only with respect to the death penalty—it would be impossible to limit the damage. A balance had to be struck. In Powell's view the Supreme Court had to curtail arbitrariness and respect the humanity of defendants, without undermining the American criminal justice system or disrespecting the states. North Carolina clearly had gone too far in the wrong direction. Powell's remarks at the April 2 conference understated the degree to which North Carolina's law troubled him. At the beginning of the term Powell told Whitman that mandatory death penalty laws made him uncomfortable. He thought the system should always preserve the opportunity for mercy.

Whitman's analysis reinforced Powell's view. In a March 27 memo to Powell, she argued that the North Carolina statute demonstrated "the worst that can happen when a state takes to its logical conclusion the suggestions of Justices Stewart and White that a death penalty statute can be constitutional only if not arbitrary." North Carolina's law cast a broad net, and even a mandatory scheme left "plenty of room for the arbitrary infliction of the ultimate penalty. Whitman hadn't resolved for herself how the Court should handle the arbitrariness problem. She wrote, "My personal opinion is that arbitrariness cannot be eliminated, as I think this statute demonstrates. That line of analysis must either be dropped or carried to its logical conclusion, which is the total abolition of the death penalty. If it is not dropped, and the death penalty is upheld, some room must be left for mercy." Amsterdam would have been thrilled with what Whitman wrote next. Death is different, she said. "If I were a Justice, I would say that there is some arbitrariness inherent in our criminal justice system, that such arbitrariness cannot be eliminated and is ordinarily tolerated because it is necessary to any humane system of justice, but that arbitrariness is just not tolerable when the punishment is as severe and irrevocable as death."

This suggested that a Justice Whitman would have voted against each of the five statutes before the Court, but Law Clerk Whitman hedged, deferring to her boss. "I think that there is a great deal to be said for your position that the judgment is a legislative one when moral and policy matters such as these are involved," she wrote. "Indeed, I think that that would be my second choice." Whitman also agreed with Powell's instinct that *Furman* had done some good. She thought standards had given useful guidance to juries and appellate courts. "In sum, I don't think the effect of the language in Justices White and Stewart's opinion in *Furman* was a nullity or even harmful, except in North Carolina. But I also don't think that it can be carried much further without eliminating the death penalty altogether."

Whitman, who remains an opponent of the death penalty, views *Gregg* as "her failure case." Thirty-five years later she remembered this memo, and felt she could have done more. Many clerks expressed similar regret. So too did many of the lawyers. Peggy Davis, for example, agonized for years about whether she had done enough to assist her client, Jerry Jurek. These extraordinary men and women would become the leaders of their profession, but when these events occurred they were twenty-somethings working for gods of the legal universe. Even a young Alan Dershowitz hesitated before telling a Supreme Court justice that he was wrong.

Whitman is surely too hard on herself. Powell respected Whitman enormously, and her thinking influenced him in crucial ways. She didn't budge him on Georgia, which she believed had chosen "vague and not exclusive" aggravating factors. Nor did she shift his views of the Texas and Florida statutes, each of which she regarded as fundamentally flawed. "When does a murderer not act deliberately?" she asked Powell in a memorandum. "What kind of probability is required as to a defendant constituting a continuing threat to society?" In his own notes on the case, though, Powell wrote that the Texas statute "reflects a careful attempt to provide standards to guide a jury to its judgment." Nor did he buy Whitman's argument that Florida's scheme was fatally flawed because the jury had only vague directions regarding how to weigh the aggravating and mitigating evidence.

Regarding the Louisiana statute, however, Whitman's analysis influenced Powell profoundly. Louisiana's law superficially appeared more humane than North Carolina's because it restricted the universe of criminals subject to the mandatory death penalty. It accomplished this, however, by incorporating aggravating factors into the definition of death-eligible murder. Whitman felt this demonstrated the "tenuousness of the line between mandatory statutes and aggravating statutes." Powell had initially been inclined favorably toward Louisiana's law. He wrote to himself that Louisiana attempted to "define narrowly the crimes for which a death sanction may be imposed." After reading Whitman's memo, Powell grouped the Louisiana and North Carolina statutes together in his mind. Whitman's analysis also solidified Powell's opposition to the mandatory statutes.

This resistance represented a subtle but important shift for Powell. Powell's commitment to judicial restraint suggested deferring to North Carolina's judgment, just as Powell had wanted the Court to defer to Georgia's judgment in *Furman*. Whitman's view, and internal changes, had evolved Powell's view of where the balance needed to be struck. John Jeffries says that Powell "was less concerned about judicial restraint in 1976 than he had been in 1972." His time on the Court had taught Powell that interpreting the original meaning of the Constitution was not so cut and dried as he first believed. Powell had also grown more confident in his role and his own judgment. At a basic level, the mandatory statutes repulsed Powell. Time, and Whitman's views, emboldened him to express that sentiment.

Powell's disenchantment with Burger pushed him over the top. Powell strongly disapproved of Burger's handling of the capital assignments, which trivialized his machinations during the certiorari process. To play his gamble, and assign all five cases to White, Burger needed to be in the majority in all five cases. Powell counted five votes to overturn North Carolina's law—Brennan, Marshall, Stevens, Stewart, and himself. Powell believed that at conference he had made his opposition to North Carolina's law clear. This placed Burger in the minority, not the majority. The Chief thus had no basis to make the assignment to White. The privilege should have fallen to Brennan. Yet again Burger had breached protocol. On this occasion Powell thought Burger wrong both on process and substance. He wouldn't tolerate it any longer. The time had come to establish a working center of the Court. Shortly after the April 2 conference, Powell swung into action.

AN ALLIANCE BETWEEN POWELL and Stewart formed quickly and organically, as their close friendship had grown even stronger through work on *Buckley v. Valeo* earlier in the term. That decision had been almost as splintered as *Furman*. Together, with an assist from Brennan, they produced the plurality opinion, which upheld campaign contribution limits but struck down caps on campaign expenditures.

With respect to the death penalty both men agreed that it would be intolerable if *Furman* ended up having been for naught. Both men also regarded a mandatory death penalty as barbaric. They therefore drew a distinction among the state responses. Georgia and Florida had made a good-faith effort to comply with *Furman*; North Carolina had not.

For Powell, Stewart was both a natural and crucial ally. While Powell felt closer to Stewart than any of the other justices, Stewart's relationships extended across both sides of the aisle. He had great fondness for Rehnquist, and had regular conversations with all the justices, except Burger and Blackmun. In turn, the justices and their clerks liked Stewart. He followed sports and politics closely, had a good sense of humor, and didn't take himself too seriously.

When Powell and Stewart decided to reach out to one of their colleagues regarding the capital cases, they naturally turned to the newest justice, Stevens. Characteristically, Stewart had already established a good relationship with Stevens. When he and Powell invited Stevens to lunch at the Monocle in early April, Stevens quickly accepted.

The Monocle, located near the rear entrances to the Senate office buildings on Capitol Hill, is a Washington institution, and its regular patrons included both Richard Nixon and John Kennedy during their respective times in the Senate. On the rare occasions when the clerks could spare time to leave the Court for a nice lunch, they went to the

Monocle. Powell had specific requirements for where he would eat. He wanted to be acknowledged when he went places, but he made this difficult by wearing sneakers, hardly the standard uniform for a Supreme Court justice. Furthermore, while Powell wanted to be noticed, he didn't want too much of a fuss to be made. At the Monocle they got it just right. When Powell, Stewart, and Stevens went for their lunch, they were greeted warmly by the maître'd, Nick Selimos, and taken to a table where a waiter brought Powell his regular order, a well-done hamburger.

Down to business, each of the three men indicated his opposition to the North Carolina law. Each also said he supported Georgia and Florida's laws. The only points of dispute were Texas and Louisiana. Stewart and Stevens didn't like the Texas law; Powell supported it. On the other hand, Powell now opposed Louisiana's law, which Stewart and Stevens supported. All agreed that unanimity, at least among their trio, was crucial. *Furman* had offered states little guidance. This time they needed to lay out a consistent rationale. So they compromised. Each man agreed to oppose Louisiana's law and support Texas's.

In his investigation of certiorari, H. W. Perry found that though horse-trading is routine in other branches of government, it rarely occurs on the Supreme Court. Each justice with whom he spoke, and nearly every clerk, told him that justices don't trade votes. One clerk told Perry, "There was never to my knowledge a deal such as I'll trade a vote on Case A for a vote on Case B. That goes on in the Congress and the White House all the time. It's incredible how it doesn't go on in the Court. Cases are each decided on their merits." Woodward and Armstrong caused a stir—and earned a condemnation from Anthony Lewis—for their suggestion in *The Brethren* that Brennan stuck to what he had come to believe was an incorrect vote, in a case called *Moore v. Illinois*, rather than risk jeopardizing Blackmun's support in abortion and obscenity cases.

Neither Stewart nor Powell nor Stevens ever spoke about the substance of their conversation at the Monocle, but the outcome of their lunch is clear. Each man changed his vote in at least one of the cases.

The most convincing evidence that the troika—as Powell, Stewart, and Stevens soon came to be known—had accommodated one another and not acted purely out of principle, is *Jurek* itself. Stevens's opinion satisfied almost no one. It offered no clear explanation why Texas's statute hadn't been classified as mandatory. The decision left undisturbed a system that would become the most aggressive in the nation, with no state a close second. Between 1977 and 2008, Texas executed 423 men and women. Virginia, the next most active state, executed 102. By point of comparison, every other state in America combined to execute 611 people during the same period. Asked to reflect on his career following his retirement, Stevens identified *Jurek* as the single decision he regretted.

FOLLOWING LUNCH, POWELL RETURNED to his chambers and announced, "We've got this deal." That afternoon the troika and their clerks met in the conference room to discuss what would happen next. Whitman remembered this as the first and only time she saw the inside of the conference room. There, the three justices worked out a distribution of labor. Stevens would handle the facts. Powell would defend the constitutionality of capital punishment and take the lead writing *Gregg*. Stewart would explain why the North Carolina and Louisiana statutes didn't comply with *Furman*.

Whitman would handle the cases for Powell. Stewart gave the assignment to Whitman's friend Ron Stern. After their bosses left the conference room, Whitman and Stern spent several hours discussing the challenges they faced. Stern opposed the death penalty, and felt relieved to have been assigned *Woodson* rather than *Gregg*. Had he been assigned to *Gregg*, Stern would have wanted to change Stewart's mind. This didn't seem possible. While Stewart agonized in *Furman*, this time around he displayed no uncertainty. Stewart spoke with his clerks before the oral arguments, after the arguments, before drafting began, and many times during the writing process. His position remained consistent throughout, and he appeared to be completely comfortable with the new guided discretion statutes. "Let's have them be as guided and as rational as they can be," Stern recalled Stewart saying.

Stern felt that his work on *Woodson* helped improve the world. The decision ensured that defendants facing the death penalty were treated as individuals. Stewart believed the American public wanted this. He believed states had passed mandatory laws only because of their uncertainty over what new laws the Court would tolerate. Absent *Furman*, Stewart didn't think people would have regarded a mandatory death penalty as desirable, and state legislatures never would have passed such laws if they had known the Court would uphold guided discretion statutes. Stewart blamed Burger. His cues had misled the states.

Stewart charged Stern to research the history of mandatory statutes in the United States and North Carolina, a task Stern greatly enjoyed. Following his clerkship, Stern seriously considered enrolling in graduate school for history. From his research, he concluded that people strongly disfavored mandatory laws. Mandatory sentences had been prevalent at the time of the nation's founding. Juries often acquitted an accused murderer rather than allow him to face execution. To avoid this problem, states graded crimes. Reviving mandatory laws would renew the incentive for jury nullification. The logical solution would be to abandon mandatory sentences once and for all.

Stewart played a particularly active role drafting the final section of the *Woodson* argument, much of which evoked the original opinion he had envisioned writing in *Furman*. Stewart deemed fatal North Carolina's failure to allow for individualized consideration of each defendant. "A process that accords no significance to relevant facets of the character and record of the individual offender, or the circumstances of the particular offense, excludes from consideration in fixing the ultimate punishment of death the possibility of compassionate or mitigating factors stemming from the diverse frailties of humankind," Stewart wrote. "It treats all persons convicted of a designated offense not as uniquely individual human beings, but as members of a faceless, undifferentiated mass to be subjected to the blind infliction of the penalty of death."

Stewart characterized individualized sentencing as a "progressive and humanizing development" and deemed it essential in capital cases. The *Furman* Court had "acknowledge what cannot fairly be denied—that death is a punishment different from all other sanctions in kind rather than degree." This section of Stewart's draft vindicated Amsterdam. Stewart wrote, "This conclusion rests squarely on the predicate that the penalty of death is qualitatively different from a sentence of imprisonment, however long. Death, in its finality, differs more from life imprisonment than a one hundred-year prison term differs from one of only a year or two. Because of that qualitative difference, there is a corresponding difference in the need for reliability in the determination that death is the appropriate punishment in a specific case."

Some argued later that *Woodson* contradicted *Furman*. On the one hand, *Furman* required that the law treat like cases alike. On the other hand, *Woodson* appeared to require that each defendant be treated individually. Indeed, Stewart's logic in *Woodson* became the basis for a 1978 decision, *Lockett v. Ohio*, which gives a defendant facing capital charges license to present any mitigating evidence, no matter how remotely relevant. Critics of *Lockett* say the opinion invites juries to grant mercy on a whim.

Stanford's Robert Weisberg argues that the conflicting mandates reflect an underlying dissonance in the Court's approach to capital punishment. He explains, "To make a moral decision about a defendant is to treat him as a unique being. And the state cannot treat him as unique under a substantive criminal law, since a criminal law is necessarily a generalization about human behavior and moral desert." *Furman* and *Gregg* attempted to combat this. But, Weisberg says, "statutory descriptions of behavior, however finely drawn, are still generalizations. A death penalty law must contain intelligible generalizations if the law is to meet Harlan's challenge in *McGautha*. But no generalization can permit the moral sensitivity which the death penalty decision requires—at least on the side of mercy." In the simplest terms, a person cannot be both unique and equal.

Many view the conflict between these ideals as irreconcilable. Justice Antonin Scalia colorfully said in 1990, "To acknowledge that there is perhaps an inherent tension between this line of cases and the line stemming from *Furman*, is rather like saying that there was perhaps an inherent tension between the Allies and the Axis Powers in World War II. And to refer to the two lines as pursuing twin objectives is rather like referring to the twin objectives of good and evil. They cannot be reconciled." Nevertheless the principles that emerged from deals made over hamburgers at the Monocle would remain the twin pillars of death penalty law for decades to come. The troika, and the Burger Court, would leave it to their successors to make sense of them.

THE UNPLEASANT BUSINESS OF INFORMING White remained. Stewart, Powell, and Stevens first went to see Burger and asked that he reassign the cases to them. Burger refused. He already had circulated a memorandum to the conference, on April 24, because of what he called "time factors." The memo, drafted by Burger's clerk Kenneth Starr, didn't present itself as either a dissent or a majority opinion. It simply offered an argument. Burger said that if we "sat as a Council of Wise Men, I would urge at the very least we narrow the use of capital punishment. A constitutional inquiry, however, must be divorced from personal feelings." Burger still had hopes of a clean sweep.

This meant one of the troika still needed to tell White about the deal. Powell was out, as he and White didn't get along. Powell could sometimes be indecisive, and his hand-wringing drove White crazy. Powell, in turn, didn't appreciate White's open disapproval of him. On one occasion, while Powell pondered, White snapped a pencil in Powell's face and told Powell to make up his damned mind. In 1974 White's clerks took Powell to lunch in the hope of smoothing over the hard feelings between the chambers. Powell replied that "it would take more than one lunch to do that." It didn't seem right to ask Stevens. The duty thus fell to Stewart, who told White that he, Powell, and Stevens would be voting against the North Carolina statute, and that they would be writing a joint opinion in each of the five cases. White

said nothing to Stewart, but his clerks reported later that White felt
hurt and extremely angry.

On May 5 the justices held a special conference to discuss the death
penalty cases. Burger now acknowledged his position in the minority,
and he asked Brennan to reassign *Woodson*. Brennan declined. He presumed that he and Marshall would never agree with whatever argument the troika developed. After a prolonged uncomfortable silence,
Stewart stepped in and said that he, Powell, and Stevens would write in
all five cases, and that the others could join or dissent as they pleased.

Back in chambers, Stewart, Stevens, and Powell's clerks began
drafting. Work proceeded quickly. Powell's *Gregg* opinion recapitulated much of his *Furman* argument that states should have the freedom to decide capital punishment. As he and Whitman expanded that
statement into a full opinion, Powell told Whitman that he wanted
to say, "Society has a need to do this. Society has a need for revenge."

"You can't put in an opinion," said Whitman.

"It's honest," said Powell.

"It's wrong."

"You're just more Christian than I am."

Over time, this section would grow to read:

In part, capital punishment is an expression of society's moral
outrage at particularly offensive conduct. This function may be
unappealing to many, but it is essential in an ordered society that
asks its citizens to rely on legal processes rather than self-help to
vindicate their wrongs. The instinct for retribution is part of the
nature of man, and channeling that instinct in the administration
of criminal justice serves an important purpose in promoting the
stability of a society governed by law. When people begin to believe
that organized society is unwilling or unable to impose upon criminal offenders the punishment they deserve, then there are sown
the seeds of anarchy—of self-help, vigilante justice, and lynch law.
Retribution is no longer the dominant objective of the criminal
law, but neither is it a forbidden objective nor one inconsistent with

our respect for the dignity of men. Indeed, the decision that capital punishment may be the appropriate sanction in extreme cases is an expression of the community's belief that certain crimes are themselves so grievous an affront to humanity that the only adequate response may be the penalty of death.

To Whitman's chagrin, many people would later tell her that they liked this part of the opinion the best.*

ON THE EVE OF HIS greatest triumph, Powell's conscience began to weigh on him. Affirmative decisions in *Gregg*, *Proffitt*, and *Jurek* would mean that the six hundred men sitting on death row would face execution. This didn't sit right with Powell. For months, he had been avoiding this reality. During a conversation early in the term, Powell told Whitman that if the Court upheld the death penalty, individual state governors would pardon all the people on death row, and no one would be executed. But he had no basis for this confidence, which Whitman could only explain one way: Powell didn't want to accept responsibility for the consequences of his actions.

In mid-April, Powell floated a novel idea, which would keep blood off his hands. Powell proposed that the 1976 capital decisions apply only to future defendants and future death sentences. Defendants currently on death row would be resentenced, even if they had been condemned to die under a valid state law. In an April 16 memo to

---

* The troika didn't get overly bogged down in the specifics of what measures were required to combat arbitrariness. Powell wrote that *Furman*'s concerns could be met "by a carefully drafted statute that ensures that the sentencing authority is given adequate information and guidance." Generally, he said, this was best achieved "by a system that provides for a bifurcated proceeding at which the sentencing authority is apprised of the information relevant to the imposition of sentence and provided with standards to guide its use of the information." Powell made clear, though, that the Constitution didn't require these procedures. Rather, they had been offered as examples of a system capable of meeting *Furman*'s concerns. "Each distinct system must be examined on an individual basis," he wrote.

Whitman, Powell explained his reasoning: "I think one can at least surmise that some of the sentences were imposed by juries, and even by courts, with a rather strong belief that capital punishment would be totally outlawed by this Court." Powell added, "Indeed, I had no idea myself until the day before Conference how some of my Brothers would vote. In view of this ambiguity, I hesitate to say that every sentence of death in these states would have been imposed had the law been settled rather than unsettled." Powell's reasoning mirrored Stewart's explanation of the resurgence of mandatory death penalty laws, and Powell thought his friend therefore might sign on to his proposal.

Two weeks later Powell wrote to Stewart, "No one—no legislator, judge, or juror—could have been certain how this Court ultimately would come down on the capital punishment issue." Thus, he said, "It is at least possible that subtle, and even unconscious, influences and especially uncertainties may have pervaded legislative, judicial and jury decisions." Powell further worried how mass executions would affect the public's perception of the Court. "The stark fact is that the carrying out of several hundred executions, pursuant to validation thereof by this Court, would cause profound shock waves. My guess is that state governors, certainly for the most part, would exercise executive clemency on a broad scale. But one cannot be sure that this would be done uniformly, even within a particular state."

Powell told Whitman that Stewart was "sympathetic to the idea," and that he and Stewart had plans to "broaden the base of our discussion." Powell, however, had no legal authority for his scheme. A few Supreme Court decisions had been applied *retroactively*. For example, the Court had sometimes said that a defendant sentenced under a procedure later found to be unconstitutional should be entitled to the benefit of the revised law. In *Gregg*, however, the Court would be ruling a procedure constitutional, not unconstitutional. Limiting the application of such a decision to future cases had never been done. "The argument to make it prospective clearly came out of emotion, not logic or law," Whitman said. Powell admitted as much to her and to Stewart. "Although I have given this some thought since our last conversation, I have come up with no rationale supported by authority," he told Stewart. Powell's "tentative conclusion" was that "the Court should simply exercise its ultimate authority and responsibility even in the absence of precedent," but hoped that Stewart might be able to come up with "some more traditional and scholarly rationale." Stewart could not, and soon the idea faded away.

THROUGH MAY AND JUNE, Powell, Stewart, and Stevens tweaked their opinions. Immediately following the May 5 conference, Burger announced that the troika would be producing a single opinion, "holding that the Eighth Amendment in and of itself does not foreclose state or federal power to impose capital punishment." Two days later Stewart corrected Burger and told his colleagues that while "each opinion will reject the contention that the Eighth and Fourteenth Amendments foreclose the imposition and execution of a death sentence under any circumstances," the three justices would be producing five separate opinions: three affirmances—in *Gregg, Jurek,* and *Proffitt*; and two reversals—in *Woodson* and *Roberts.*

The opinions abounded with inconsistencies. On May 31 Powell inserted language into *Gregg* suggesting that LDF had renewed its argument regarding the overall constitutionality of capital punishment "with diminished conviction." In the final version this became: "Developments during the four years since *Furman* have undercut substantially the assumptions upon which their argument rested." Powell's language suggested the Court was overturning *Furman.* At the same time, in his *Woodson* draft, Stewart attributed great weight to *Furman.* He wrote, "*Furman mandates* that discretion must be suitably directed and limited." This suggested that *Furman* lived on.

The opinions appeared to disagree, too, on the difference death made. Stewart placed great emphasis on this point in his *Woodson* opinion, with his call to treat all criminal defendants as individual human beings. Powell, though, said that while "there is no question that death as a punishment is unique in its severity and irrevocability," it didn't undermine the appropriateness of applying it in some cases.

"We are concerned here only with the imposition of capital punishment for the crime of murder, and when a life has been taken deliberately by the offender, we cannot say that the punishment is invariably disproportionate to the crime. It is an extreme sanction, suitable to the most extreme crimes."

These tensions were obvious, but the die had been cast. At the end of June, join memos circulated with no surprises. White would write separately, concurring in *Gregg*, *Jurek*, and *Proffitt*, and dissenting in *Woodson* and *Roberts*. Blackmun said he would write separately, too, and simply reference his *Furman* dissent. On June 29 Rehnquist announced that he would join White's opinions. The following day Burger said he would do the same. Finally Blackmun said that he also would join White's dissent in *Roberts*.

BRENNAN AND MARSHALL SAID they would dissent from *Gregg, Jurek*, and *Proffitt,* and write separately in *Woodson* and *Roberts*. So began a long and lonely partnership. Over the next fifteen terms they would dissent together in 1,841 death penalty cases. Brennan sometimes engaged the reasoning of his colleagues, as he did in *McCleskey v. Kemp* and *Stanford v. Kentucky*, a case upholding the use of the death penalty against sixteen- and seventeen-year-olds. Sometimes he seemed to argue past them, as he did in *Gregg*. "The fatal constitutional infirmity in the punishment of death is that it treats members of the human race as nonhumans, as objects to be toyed with and discarded," Brennan wrote. "It is thus inconsistent with the fundamental premise that even the vilest criminal remains a human being possessed of common human dignity." Brennan quoted from Albert Camus' abolitionist essay, *Reflections on the Guillotine*: "Justice of this kind is obviously no less shocking than the crime itself, and the new 'official' murder, far from offering redress for the offense committed against society, adds instead a second defilement to the first." Marshall wrote his own dissent in *Gregg*, but thereafter almost invariably joined Brennan or simply issued a boilerplate statement, "The death penalty is in all circumstances cruel and unusual punishment forbidden by the Eighth and Fourteenth Amendments."

Because they generally refused to engage the specifics of the constitutionality of the death penalty, Brennan and Marshall became peripheral to the issue. Yale's Robert Burt calls their behavior "a kind of vigil against the death penalty—virtually a silent vigil, closer to the tradition of civil disobedients, who see themselves as prophets in a wilderness."

ON JULY 2, 1976, the Court announced the decisions. The chamber was filled to capacity that day. People had waited on line for hours, some overnight, to be among the first to hear the Court's decisions. A sense of dread permeated the crowd. Except to the justices and their clerks the outcomes of these historic cases were unknown and very much in doubt. Nevertheless many people in the audience appeared to have guessed what was coming. In their robing room the justices dressed in silence. Often they would chat with one another before entering the chamber, but on that Friday no one said a word. Marshall barely looked up. Even the climate conspired to set the appropriate milieu. On an otherwise mild stretch of weather in the nation's capital, heavy clouds gathered over the Court building, ominously shrouding the chamber in darkness. Shortly after ten o'clock the justices emerged solemnly. The marshal called the room to order, pointlessly: Everyone already had fallen silent. Several of the justices rocked back and forth in their leather chairs, anxiously waiting for the proceedings to begin.

After a few moments Warren Burger said, "The dispositions in the following cases: Gregg against Georgia, Proffitt against Florida, Jurek against Texas, and Woodson against North Carolina will be announced by Mr. Justice Stewart, Mr. Justice Stevens, and Mr. Justice Powell." The abolitionists immediately recognized this as bad news. They had held out hope for Stewart and Stevens, but there could be no question where Powell stood. A deal had been struck. Almost certainly this coalition would uphold capital punishment in part or in full.

The chamber grew deathly quiet as Burger called on Stewart to announce the first of the decisions, *Gregg*. Stewart's voice cracked and his hands shook as he summarized the opinion. Quietly Stewart read. "We consider at the outset the basic contention that the punishment of death for the crime of murder is under all circumstances cruel and unusual in violation of the Constitution.

"We reject that contention."

Justices don't generally read dissents from the bench. Thurgood Marshall read his. He first addressed what had happened in the United States during the preceding four years. "Since the decision in *Furman*, the legislatures of thirty-five States have indeed enacted new statutes authorizing the imposition of the death sentence for certain crimes," Marshall said. "I would be less than candid if I did not acknowledge that these developments had a significant bearing on a realistic assessment of the moral acceptability of the death penalty to the American people. But if the constitutionality of the death penalty turns, as I have urged, on the opinion of an *informed* citizenry, then the enactment of new death statutes cannot be viewed as conclusive. In *Furman*, I observed that the American people are largely unaware of the information critical to a judgment on the morality of the death penalty. A recent study has confirmed that the American people know little about the death penalty, and that the opinions of an informed public would differ significantly."

Marshall grew more passionate. Public opinion didn't matter because the death penalty was an excessive punishment. "An excessive penalty is invalid even though popular sentiment may favor it," he said. "The inquiry here is simply whether the death penalty is necessary to accomplish the legitimate legislative purposes in punishment, or whether a less severe penalty—such as life imprisonment—would do as well. The two purposes that sustain the death penalty as non-excessive in the Court's view are general deterrence and retribution." Marshall deemed the evidence of deterrence inconclusive, and doubted

Powell's concern that failing to execute murderers would lead to vigilantism. "It simply defies belief to suggest that the death penalty is necessary to prevent the American people from taking the law into their own hands," Marshall said. He ridiculed the idea that without capital punishment individuals would fail to realize that murder is wrong, and he urged humility as to the fallibility of man. It was one thing to say that a human being deserves death, Marshall said, and quite another for society to carry out that judgment.

The ultimate test couldn't be satisfying "society's instinct for retribution," as Stewart, Stevens, and Powell had suggested. Marshall spat, "To be sustained under the Eighth Amendment, the death penalty must comport with the basic concept of human dignity at the core of the Amendment." He explained, "The objective in imposing it must be consistent with our respect for the dignity of men. Under these standards, the taking of life because the wrongdoer deserves it surely must fail, for such a punishment has as its very basis the total denial of the wrongdoer's dignity and worth."

After Marshall finished, the justices exited as they had entered, gravely, and without a word to one another. Marshall was exhausted and despondent. He didn't even return to his chambers. Instead he drove the twenty-foot, cream-colored Cadillac that he had gifted himself following his appointment to the Court in 1967 directly to his home on Lake Barcroft. It was Marshall's sixty-eighth birthday, but he didn't feel like celebrating.

WHEN THE DECISIONS CAME DOWN, David Kendall was in the Supreme Court, near the clerk's office where they kept the court records. He knew the people who worked there from his time clerking for White. They in turn knew of his interest in the cases, and gave him copies of the decisions simultaneous with their release in the courtroom. It took Kendall a few seconds to figure out what had happened. When he absorbed it, his heart sank: They had lost almost everything.

Later that day Kendall spoke with Amsterdam, who had already reviewed the opinions. Kendall expected Amsterdam to be in despair. To the contrary, Amsterdam appeared to be in good spirits. He took great heart from *Woodson*, which he believed gave LDF the ammunition to fight another day. Amsterdam's persistent optimism, his almost superhuman ability to remain focused on "the work," as he always called it, without enjoying the occasional highs or succumbing to the lows, astonished Kendall.

The United States celebrated its bicentennial that weekend. Kendall spent Saturday and Sunday at his brother-in-law's New York City apartment, which had a magnificent view of the water. As he watched the tall-masted ships sail into New York Harbor, Kendall wallowed in self-pity. As if losing weren't bad enough—and it was quite bad—Kendall knew that his life would soon get much, much worse. *Gregg* meant that hundreds of death penalty cases would be remanded, creating a mountain of work for LDF, "and we were thinly manned as it was," Kendall recalled.

Davis felt miserable, too. *Jurek* particularly saddened her. "The decision told me that they didn't want to continue what they had started in *Furman*. Now it was hands off, leave it to the states, and *Jurek* was the proof of that." That weekend Davis obsessed about whether LDF could have done more to distinguish *Jurek* from the other cases, and began to contemplate a rehearing petition. She didn't sleep very well. She knew she had little hope of persuading Amsterdam to separate *Jurek* from the other cases. Even if she could, she thought it extremely unlikely that the Court would vote to reconsider the death penalty. The decision had been made.

THE JUSTICES CERTAINLY BELIEVED that the constitutionality of capital punishment had been resolved once and for all. The liberals retreated to lick their wounds. Friends scarcely recognized William Douglas now. Most days he sat in a reclining chair, wrapped in blankets and heating pads, lamenting his lost youth. On the best days he slept well enough to dream of hiking in the Cascade Mountains. On the worst he worried that he had grown too feeble to sound the buzzer that summoned the nurse for help.

The wind left William Brennan's sails, too. Shortly before leaving for Nantucket, he delivered a speech to the New Jersey Bar Association's annual convention at Playboy's Great Gorge Resort Hotel. One-third of the way through his call for state courts to step in where the Supreme Court had failed, Brennan sensed that the audience had little interest in his words, and sat down. "I said the hell with it, and just quit," Brennan remembered. Soon doctors found a malignant tumor on his left vocal cord.

Marshall spent much of the weekend staring out the window onto Lake Barcroft. Saturday afternoon he watched some television and played a game of Monopoly with his son. He called his friend Brennan but couldn't reach him. In the evening, Marshall retired early to bed, but couldn't settle. After he finally succeeded in falling asleep, he awoke a few hours later, around four o'clock in the morning, with chest pains. Marshall began pacing around his house, hoping to feel better, but the walking didn't help. After three hours he got worried and called a doctor, who told Marshall to get himself to a hospital. At Bethesda Naval, the medical staff ran a series of tests. Despite Marshall's obesity and his lifetime of smoking, he hadn't yet had a heart attack. He had his first that weekend, and two more over the next three days. He feared the end was near.

"Is this it?" Marshall asked the doctor.

"It sure is," the doctor replied.

THE FINALITY OF THE DECISIONS even affected Lewis Powell. Powell and his wife, Jo, spent the weekend in Richmond, Virginia, at George Gibson's annual Fourth of July party. Gibson had been one of Powell's law partners. His guests included University of Virginia Law School professor J. Harvie Wilkinson; Virginius Dabney, a well-known Richmond journalist; Tennant Bryan, the publisher of the *Richmond Times-Dispatch*; and Justin Moore, another of Powell's former law partners. All deferred to Powell, who gave a brief talk about the recently concluded term. Everyone sensed Powell's satisfaction in the decision and his new position as a leader on the Court.

Shortly thereafter, though, Powell displayed further pangs of remorse. On July 16 Amsterdam petitioned for rehearing of the capital cases, and asked for stays of execution pending reargument. LDF addressed the rehearing petition to Powell, in his capacity as a circuit justice. Jim Ginty thought the petitions should have been addressed to Stewart, as the author of the prevailing opinion. Powell disagreed. The opinion had been jointly authored by him, Stevens, and Stewart. Anyway, Stewart had left town. Powell told Ginty that he would handle the petition himself.

The Supreme Court rule is that a stay should be denied unless the justice to whom the request is made believes there will be four votes to support the rehearing petition. Powell knew this; he also knew that four justices would never vote to rehear *Gregg, Proffitt,* or *Jurek.* Nevertheless Powell wanted to grant the stay. He thought the standard of review included whether a judgment's implementation would result in irreparable harm, as it would in these cases. Furthermore Powell felt that the entire Court should formally consider the issues raised by the petition, given their magnitude. "This is the orderly and proper way," he wrote to himself.

Powell placed his first call to Burger, whose reaction was "instant and explosive." Burger said that Powell's action would shock the legal community, reflect adversely on the Court as an institution, and create an unjustified sense of expectation on death row. Burger thought the stay might even become the basis for another round of constitutional appeals. "It might trigger a further claim that creating false hope is in itself cruel and unusual punishment," the Chief told Powell.

Burger's reaction surprised and dismayed Powell, who said that he would survey the other justices. Brennan told Powell that he would grant the petition, but Blackmun, Rehnquist, and White each said he would vote to deny. Powell thought it best not to present the issue to Marshall in the hospital. On July 20 Burger circulated a memo, written in a far more civil tone than he had used on the telephone with Powell. Burger said he would be open to convening a special Court session, though he thought granting a stay would create false expectations. He repeated his concern that issuing the stay and then not granting the rehearing petition would be "inherently cruel."

Stewart told Powell that he "could take it either way." Stewart said he understood his friend's concern, but also thought Burger might be right in saying the stay would create false expectations. Stevens told Powell that he would support him no matter what.

Despite the tepid support for rehearing the cases, Powell granted the stay on July 22, although he tried at the same time to dampen expectations. "The decision to grant this stay is not suggestive of my position on the merits," Powell wrote. "It reflects, rather, only my belief in the special nature of these cases." At the start of the following term, on October 4, the Court voted to deny the petition for rehearing, and so nothing came of Powell's regrets, though it would hardly be the end of them.

THE SAME REHEARING PETITIONS caused substantial consternation behind the scenes at LDF. Losing parties routinely ask the Supreme Court for reargument, and they are routinely denied. These petitions, however, were anything but routine. The Court had announced a new direction for death penalty law. Guided-discretion statutes would be tolerated, mandatory statutes wouldn't. When LDF drafted its briefs and prepared for oral argument, this had been but one of many plausible directions the Court might take. Having seen the Court's rulings, LDF now felt it hadn't devoted sufficient attention to the question of whether the Georgia and Florida statutes offered meaningful guidance to juries. LDF wanted the Court to consider this issue more closely.

Peggy Davis had a different concern. Why had *Jurek* been grouped with the discretionary statutes? It had all the earmarks of a mandatory law. Davis fought with Amsterdam and Kendall to differentiate *Jurek* from the other cases. Perhaps Amsterdam had been right to continue his assault against the constitutionality of capital punishment, but professional ethics required LDF to do the best possible job for each of its individual clients. Jerry Jurek didn't need LDF to launch another broadside attack on capital punishment. He needed LDF to demonstrate that his case should have been decided under *Woodson*, not *Gregg*.

Davis wrote an impassioned plea to Amsterdam and Kendall. "Over and over again, during the last week I have thought: What kind of rehearing petition would I write if I represented only Jerry Lane Jurek? And every time I think about that I am troubled because I think that a much stronger attack on the Texas statute could be made." Davis acknowledged that the petition faced long odds. "Of course, the chances of success in any case on rehearing are extraordinarily slight," she wrote. "But I think there is some small chance in Texas, and I don't think our petition, which is a brilliant attack on the collective rulings, does justice to the Texas argument."

Davis's plea fell on deaf ears, and the rehearing petition would emphasize the commonalities of the cases, not the differences. Amsterdam argued that a stay in Texas, without a stay in Florida and Georgia, would be little help to LDF. Davis questioned how making the best argument for Jurek could hurt their chances in the Florida and Georgia cases, which she assessed at close to nil. She further wondered how a denial of rehearing could hurt them any more than the devastating initial losses had hurt them already, but Amsterdam wouldn't budge.

THE WEEKEND AFTER THE Court announced *Gregg*, Tony Amsterdam returned to work. At his Stanford office he began writing a detailed guide to further attacks on capital punishment. This modern Last-Aid Kit, which Amsterdam finished in one month, totaled more than one hundred pages and outlined for lawyers every plausible claim that they might raise against the death penalty. The scope of Amsterdam's project was astonishing, and he did it all in the immediate aftermath of the undoing of his greatest victory. David Kendall said, "It was one of the most incredible intellectual and emotional achievements I have ever seen."

Even more incredibly, in that document Amsterdam foretold the outcome of almost every major death penalty decision for the next forty years. The kit employed an elaborate coding scheme, and for each argument, Amsterdam included a section titled "Strength of claim/tactical considerations." For example, claim A-2-1-F argued that a death sentence violated the Eighth Amendment because it was "grossly disproportionate and excessive for the crime for which he was convicted." Assessing the strength of this claim, Amsterdam wrote, "Strong for non-homicide crimes; fair for accessorial liability; fair-to-weak for unintentional homicide." Each aspect of this prediction proved uncannily accurate.

The following term, David Kendall argued and won *Coker v. Georgia*, in which the Supreme Court overturned the death penalty for rapists of adult women. White wrote the plurality opinion, holding that rape didn't compare with murder. "Life is over for the victim of the murderer; for the rape victim, life may not be nearly so happy as it was, but it is not normally over and normally is not beyond repair." Powell, still in tumult, agreed with the conclusion because Coker's crime hadn't been excessively brutal, but dissented in part because he thought capital punishment might sometimes be appropriate "for the rare case of a rape so outrageous and serious in its consequences as to justify society's ultimate penalty."

In 1982, as Amsterdam predicted regarding accessorial liability, the Court struck down the death sentence of Earl Enmund, who had been the getaway driver for a robbery that ended in death. In 1987 as Amsterdam again predicted in his "fair-to-weak" assessment, the Court limited Enmund's precedent in *Tison v. Arizona*, a case argued by Alan Dershowitz. In *Tison* the Court said that the death penalty could be appropriate for participants in felonies who didn't kill if they nevertheless displayed reckless indifference to human life.

The new Last-Aid Kit suggested that the death penalty might be deemed unconstitutional for the insane, and in 1986, the Supreme

Court so ruled. It also suggested that executing the mentally disturbed might violate the Eighth Amendment. In 2002 in *Atkins v. Virginia*, the Court deemed the death penalty unconstitutional for the mentally retarded. The kit laid out a general strategy of challenging death sentences for vulnerable classes of offenders, which led, indirectly, to the Court's 2005 decision in *Roper v. Simmons*, barring the use of capital punishment against offenders under eighteen years of age at the time of their offense.

Amsterdam even foretold the Court's future treatment of race. Amsterdam handicapped a claim that a death sentence violated the Equal Protection Clause because it was "imposed pursuant to a pattern and practice of racial discrimination in capital sentencing" as "legally solid but factually difficult and burdensome to prove." So it would prove to be.

In 1987 LDF came within a whisker of winning *McCleskey v. Kemp*, the constitutional challenge predicated on David Baldus's regression-based study of racism in Georgia's capital system. Lewis Powell cast the deciding vote and wrote the majority opinion. Though Powell found Baldus's research persuasive, he remained concerned with the extension of LDF's argument. Prior to the oral argument, Powell's clerk, Leslie Gielow, wrote to him, "Opening the door to these types of challenges could threaten the entire operation of the criminal justice system." Powell wrote in the margin, "Yes!" Two weeks later Gielow wrote Powell that Marshall and Brennan's chambers believed that evidence of sentencing racism could support an initial showing of discrimination under the Fourteenth Amendment. Gielow wrote, "Those who agree with the Fourteenth Amendment theory recognize that there would be no way to limit its application." Powell scrawled in the margin: "Agree no way to limit." On the same day Gielow presented Powell a research memo exploring whether Eighth Amendment decisions could be restricted to capital cases. She wrote, "Because of the limitless application of a challenge like that posed by McCleskey—a tragic byproduct of social and economic deprivation—the proper inquiry as to whether a punishment is cruel or unusual cannot be made as to the system as a whole." Again Powell agreed.

By this late point in his career, Powell harbored serious reservations regarding capital punishment, but he refrained from expressing them in *McCleskey* because of the revolution it would have fomented. Powell's opinion upheld McCleskey's conviction because it hadn't been shown that racism affected his particular case. Furthermore, the disparities were the result of jury discretion, which Powell again defended. "The inherent lack of predictability of jury decisions does not justify their condemnation," Powell wrote, adding that "discretion in the criminal justice system offers substantial benefits to the criminal defendant."

Amsterdam called *McCleskey* "the *Dred Scott* decision of our time," but in 1976 he saw it coming. Amsterdam foretold, too, that executions would resume. More than six hundred men and women sat on death row in desperate need of help, and many more would be joining them soon. No one would wait for LDF to lick its wounds. An adverse decision didn't constitute an invitation for self-remonstrations or prolonged strategizing. Others could criticize if they were so inclined; academics could assess LDF's legacy: They had the luxury of time. He did not. A new race against the clock had begun.

SURE ENOUGH, ON JULY 19, in Orem, Utah, a man named Gary Gilmore robbed and murdered a gas station employee named Max Jensen. The next night he robbed and murdered a motel manager in Provo. In October a jury sentenced Gilmore to die. From the moment the jury rendered its verdict, Gilmore, who had an IQ of 133, vexed his attorneys by advocating for his own demise. He wrote poetry welcoming death and attempted suicide on two occasions, once after a court stayed his execution. The case captivated the attention of people around the world. Sting wrote "Bring on the Night," as an ode to Gilmore's death wish. Norman Mailer won the Pulitzer Prize for *The Executioner's Song*, his novel based on Gilmore's case.

On the morning of January 17, 1977, just six months after *Gregg*, five riflemen armed with .30 millimeter deer rifles fired through a sailcloth partition into which had been cut a series of slits. One of the rifles had been loaded with a blank. The other four contained steel-jacketed shells. Gilmore, freshly shaved, wearing a black T-shirt, white trousers and red, white, and blue sneakers, said, "Just do it." His last words made a permanent impression on Nike's cofounder, Dan Wieden. When the bullets found their mark, the Utah government had conducted the first legal American execution since 1967.

A little more than two years later, in May 1979, Florida governor Bob Graham signed a death warrant for John Spenkelink, a small-time criminal who murdered a misfit named Joseph Szymankiewicz. Spenkelink argued self-defense, claiming that Szymankiewicz raped and robbed him in a motel room and forced him to play Russian roulette. Spenkelink became a national celebrity. *Time* and the *New York Times Magazine* covered his story, and Alan Alda and Joan Baez, among many others, took up his cause.

Spenkelink's appeal raised several familiar issues. LDF argued that *Proffitt* only said that Florida's statute *might* be constitutional. In practice, LDF said, the new law continued to be applied arbitrarily and discriminatorily in violation of the Eighth Amendment. Millard Farmer, America's most successful abolitionist trial lawyer, begged LDF to focus instead on Spenkelink's abundant mitigating evidence. As a child Spenkelink idolized his father, a shell-shocked veteran of World War II. At the age of eleven, Spenkelink found his father dead in his garage, where he had committed suicide by asphyxiation. His criminal behavior began then, and psychologists concluded that it derived largely from this trauma. Yet Spenkelink's lawyers presented none of this evidence at trial. Farmer argued that the appeal should focus on these failures rather than larger legal issues. LDF ignored him. Generally speaking, Farmer believed LDF should devote its resources to preventing death sentences at trial, and that appeals should focus on case-specific issues rather than systemic claims. LDF ignored this too. Farmer lamented LDF's continuing influence. In his view Amsterdam's deific status blinded his followers to his errors in judgment. Farmer said, "Despite pleas in numerous forums, like flies to sweetcakes, the most brilliant and dedicated of the American legal profession continued to worship the golden casket that LDF displayed."

On May 25, 1979, protesters gathered outside the gates of the Florida State Prison Farm in Raiford. Inside they fired up the electric chair, known as "Old Sparky," returning to action after a fifteen-year hiatus. Shortly thereafter John Spenkelink's heart stopped, and he became the first man executed without his consent in the United States in a decade. Then the floodgates opened.

In the thirty-five years since 1977, American states have executed approximately 1,300 men and women. Though these executions had yet to happen, Tony Amsterdam prophesized them, and already felt their weight upon his chest. "You feel guilty about every one, simply because there has never been enough time in the day, you have never had enough skill," he said. "Hard as you try, you've got to admit that, life being what it is, maybe you could have tried harder."

WHAT MIGHT
HAVE BEEN

Almost everyone involved with this history at some point has asked a what if question. William Brennan obsessed about these at the end of his career. Many of these questions focused around Abe Fortas. LBJ offered the United Nations ambassadorship to Arthur Goldberg to make room for his friend Fortas. What if Goldberg had resisted the pressure? Then Fortas would first have emerged as a candidate to replace Earl Warren in 1968. He would almost certainly have been confirmed. Joining the Court later, Fortas would never have had the opportunity to engage in the unethical behavior that led to his undoing, and Richard Nixon would never have had the chance to appoint Warren Burger. With Fortas as chief justice instead of Burger, and Goldberg on the bench, Brennan said, "the whole face of the nation" might have been different.

One doesn't have to create such an elaborate counterfactual narrative to wonder whether the capital cases could have come out differently. Earl Warren's biographer Bernard Schwartz simply asked, "What if Justice Goldberg had used his memorandum as the basis for challenging the constitutionality of the death penalty as such?" If Goldberg had resisted Warren's requests to narrow the issue, Schwartz speculates that the Eighth Amendment issue would have been decided by the Warren Court, which he believes would have been sympathetic to the claim. Indeed, after his retirement, Warren said that he always had regarded the death penalty as "repulsive."

What if LDF had deferred its constitutional litigation campaign, and instead concentrated its efforts at the grass-roots level or in state appellate courts? Aryeh Neier, Alan Dershowitz, and many others urged some version of this course of action at one time or another. Alternatively, what if LDF had concentrated its resources on assisting defendants at trial, and, on appeal, emphasized individual rather than systemic claims?

What if William Douglas had successfully negotiated a compromise in *Boykin* and *Maxwell*? Then the issues would have been decided before Abe Fontas's undoing and prior to Burger's ascension as chief justice. What if Brennan and Douglas had prevailed over Black following *McGautha*, and the Court had summarily dismissed the pending Eighth Amendment cases? Neither *Furman* nor *Gregg* would have been decided. Were these decisions of benefit to criminal defendants?

What if Potter Stewart had issued his short snapper in *Furman*? Would Byron White have had the stomach to send hundreds of men to their death? What if Stewart and White never struck their deal? Would the states have responded to *Furman* in the same way? Would Stewart have felt as constrained as he did in *Gregg*? What if Burger hadn't played his gambit in 1976 and assigned the five cases to different justices, rather than all to White? Might individual assignments have led to different outcomes? At the least, might *Jurek* have come out differently?

Finally, what if the constitutionality of the death penalty could have been decided by each justice at the end of his life, with the benefit of his full collected wisdom? Almost certainly history would have been changed, for three of the men who decided the 1976 capital cases, including two members of the notorious troika, later changed their views on capital punishment.

✦ ✦ ✦ ✦

Harry Blackmun displayed increasing frustration with the death penalty toward the end of his judicial career. When the Court upheld a death sentence in a 1986 case, *Darden v. Wainwright*, in spite of evidence that the prosecutor referred to the defendant as an animal during his closing argument and let slip that he was on furlough from prison, Blackmun issued a scathing dissent. "This Court has stressed repeatedly in the decade since *Gregg v. Georgia* that the Eighth Amendment requires a heightened degree of reliability in any case where a State seeks to take the defendant's life," Blackmun wrote. "Today's opinion, however, reveals a Court willing to tolerate not only imperfection, but a level of fairness and reliability so low it should make conscientious prosecutors cringe."

The following term Blackmun again dissented with Marshall, Brennan, and Stevens in *McCleskey v. Kemp*. The same man who doubted that for Billy Maxwell "statistics will ever be his redemption" dismissed Powell's fear that granting McCleskey's appeal would open the door to other constitutional claims. "That is no reason to deny McCleskey his rights under the Equal Protection Clause," Blackmun wrote. "If a grant of relief to him were to lead to a closer examination of the effects of racial considerations throughout the criminal justice system, the system, and hence society, might benefit."

In 1994 Blackmun rejected capital punishment for all time. During the preceding summer Blackmun's clerk, Andrew Schapiro, proposed to Blackmun that he repudiate all further efforts to construct a constitutional death penalty law. Schapiro cited the irreconcilable tension between the no-arbitrariness mandate of *Furman* and the sensitivity to individual circumstances required by *Woodson*. He wrote, "Twenty years of applying the Eighth Amendment to the death penalty has demonstrated that the rationalizing enterprise has failed." Blackmun, on the verge of his eighty-fifth birthday, agreed, and told his clerks to find a suitable case to express this view. Schapiro's successor, Michelle Alexander, selected *Callins v. Collins*, a run-of-the-mill capital appeal where Blackmun, in the best tradition of Arthur Goldberg, dissented from the Court's denial of certiorari. With an assist from Alexander, Blackmun wrote:

> From this day forward, I no longer shall tinker with the machinery of death. For more than twenty years I have endeavored—indeed, I have struggled—along with a majority of this Court, to develop rules that would lend more than the mere appearance of fairness to the death penalty endeavor. Rather than continue to coddle the delusion that the desired level of fairness has been achieved, I feel morally and intellectually obligated simply to concede that the death penalty experiment has failed. It is virtually self-evident to me now that no combination of procedural rules or substantive regulations ever can save the death penalty from its inherent constitutional deficiencies.

Four days before filing the dissent, Blackmun went to see Brennan, by then retired and frail. Brennan read Blackmun's opinion, and said, "Thank you for the present." When the South African Constitutional Court declared the death penalty unconstitutional the following year, it cited Blackmun's opinion in *Callins* as evidence that it's impossible to design a death-sentencing system that avoids arbitrariness.

In 1995 Blackmun gave a series of interviews to his former clerk Harry Koh, then a professor at Yale Law School. Blackmun told Koh that while his personal feelings about the death penalty didn't change over the course of his career, he came to believe capital punishment couldn't be fairly applied. When asked by Koh how he would vote on *Furman* if the case were presented to him then, Blackmun called this "an interesting question." Time had reformulated his memories of *Furman*. His recollections of the case seemed almost an exercise in self-denial. "We didn't get into the death penalty in depth," Blackmun told Koh. "I wrote a dissent. The case was well argued, rather excruciating at the time, and brought one right face-to-face with the death penalty issue, on which I had felt rather strongly for some years, and in fact, I think I wrote no less than three times on the court of appeals about my distaste for the death penalty. This didn't help any, but as I remember, it went off largely on a procedural ground. It seemed to me that the main argument was that the statute was vague. I hope my memory is correct."

Time had worked its healing magic, too, with respect to the former justice's remembrances of LDF's principal attorney. Blackmun recalled Amsterdam as "a very serious, earnest advocate. There was never any humor in him when he argued, but one knew exactly where he stood. I always welcomed him and have missed him." Harking back to the oral argument in *Gregg*, Blackmun said he recalled the "death is different" argument and said, "I don't know why there was delay in getting to that statement, but he finally made the statement, and I think it was a good one." Blackmun told Koh, "Death is different. Whether Amsterdam felt it weakened his position or not, I do not know, but I thought it sharpened the analysis of the case."

Years later, when Amsterdam heard this, he commented, "I think he identified me with an idealistic part of himself that he felt it was his duty as a judge to severely repress."

AT OR AROUND THE same time, Lewis Powell underwent his own, more improbable transformation. In 1986, the year before the Court decided *McCleskey v. Kemp*, Powell showed signs of wavering on the death penalty in *Darden v. Wainwright*, the case that so troubled Harry Blackmun. Before the Court rejected Darden's appeal, it granted a last-minute stay of execution. Even though the Court had heard and rejected all of Darden's arguments in a prior appeal ten years earlier, the stay was favored by Blackmun, Stevens, Marshall, and Brennan, with whom Powell had developed a close friendship. These four votes were enough to hear Darden's second appeal, but not enough to spare his life. Under Court rules, while four votes are sufficient for cert, five are required to grant a stay. Powell thought this made no sense. He felt that Darden's claims had "no merit whatsoever," and it perturbed him that Darden's lawyers had waited until the last minute to file their stay application, as capital defense attorneys often do, to keep their clients alive as long as possible. Despite his disdain for his lawyers' tactics and his case, Powell voted to stay Darden's execution at one minute before midnight.

The following morning Powell circulated a memorandum to his colleagues. "The experience of last evening disturbs me—perhaps all of us." The majority of Powell's memo addressed the procedural anomaly regarding stay petitions, but to this discourse on Court procedure, Powell appended his current thinking regarding the death penalty. (The issue must have been gnawing at him, since it had nothing to do with the thrust of the memo.) "I have no doubt as to the constitutionality of capital punishment," Powell wrote, "but I have grave doubts as to whether it now serves the purposes of deterrence and retribution, the principle purposes we identified in *Gregg*. On his copy of the memo, Blackmun corrected the spelling of "principal," and wrote, "So do others of us!"

In 1988 Powell delivered a speech on capital punishment to the ABA's Criminal Justice Section. After recounting the history of the Court's treatment of the issue, he condemned the extraordinary delay associated with capital cases, which undermined the retributive and deterrence functions of capital punishment. "However this delay may be characterized, it hardly inspires confidence in our criminal justice system," he said. Though Powell reiterated his belief in the permissibility of capital punishment—"As a co-author of *Gregg*, and recently the author of *McCleskey v. Kemp*, I adhere to the view that the death penalty may be imposed lawfully under the Constitution"—his enthusiasm had diminished. He characterized capital punishment as a system "no other democracy deems necessary," and suggested in conclusion that "Congress and the state legislatures should take a serious look at whether the retention of a punishment that is being enforced only haphazardly is in the public interest."

In a 1990 interview Powell went further and said flatly, "If I were in the state legislature, I would vote against capital punishment." In the summer of 1991, in discussing his career with his biographer, University of Virginia Law School professor John Jeffries, Powell went further still. Near the end of the session Jeffries asked Powell whether he would change his vote in any case.

"Yes, *McCleskey v. Kemp*," said Powell.

"Do you mean you would now accept the argument from statistics?" asked Jeffries.

"No, I would vote the other way in any capital case."

"In *any* capital case?"

"Yes."

"Even in *Furman v. Georgia*?"

"Yes. I have come to think that capital punishment should be abolished."

Powell explained that capital punishment "serves no useful purpose." The concerns that Powell outlined in his speech to the ABA had changed his mind. The sporadic application of the death penalty troubled him, as did the endless litigation in capital cases and the resulting delays before execution. "It brings discredit on the whole legal system," Powell said. *Furman* and *Gregg* hadn't accomplished their stated goals. Powell had counseled the Court against getting into the business of regulating the death penalty, but since it had, and in so doing committed itself to the view that the penalty must be applied rationally, it would be better for now for the Court to admit its failure and strike capital punishment down once and for all.

AT THE END OF his own career, the third member of the troika changed his view, too. During his 1995 interview with Harry Koh, Harry Blackmun had suggested that John Paul Stevens had misgivings about capital punishment. Blackmun told Koh that Stevens was "deeply concerned about the constitutionality of the death penalty." This became the subject of widespread speculation in the legal community.

In 2008 Stevens made his reservations public in *Baze v. Rees*, a decision upholding Kentucky's lethal injection protocol. Although

Stevens said that his concerns didn't justify "a refusal to respect precedents that remain a part of our law," experience had taught him that the death penalty represented "the pointless and needless extinction of life with only marginal contributions to any discernible social or public purposes." Three goals had been outlined in *Gregg*: incapacitation, deterrence, and retribution. Each no longer applied. The rise in life-without-parole statutes meant that states no longer required executions to achieve incapacitation. "Despite thirty years of empirical research in the area, there remains no reliable statistical evidence that capital punishment in fact deters potential offenders," Stevens said. Finally, the shift to more humane methods of execution had an unintended double effect. "This trend," Stevens wrote, "while appropriate and required by the Eighth Amendment, actually undermines the very premise on which public approval of the retribution rationale is based."

In October 2010, shortly after his retirement, in an interview with Nina Totenberg of National Public Radio, Stevens said he regretted his vote in *Jurek*. "I think there is one vote that I would change, and that one was upholding the Texas capital punishment statute." Stevens said he and his allies believed they were upholding statutes that allowed the death penalty only for narrow categories of offenders, using procedures that, as he put it, "prevented loading the dice towards the prosecution." But as the composition of the Court became more conservative, the universe of defendants eligible for the death penalty expanded. Furthermore the Court tolerated more procedures that aided the prosecution. "We did not foresee how it would be interpreted," Stevens said. "I think that was an incorrect decision."

Stevens reiterated his regret in an interview with Sandra Day O'Connor, saying he would have changed only one vote from his tenure.

"What was that one about?" asked O'Connor.

"That was the Texas death-penalty case," Stevens said. "My first year on the court we decided five death-penalty cases, and we held unconstitutional the mandatory death sentences in two states and upheld the nonmandatory statutes in two other states. And I think upon reflection, we should have held the Texas statute—which was challenged in the fifth case—to fit under the mandatory category and be unconstitutional. In my judgment we made a mistake on that case."

Based on this statement, the final tally would have been five to four in favor of Jurek. Stevens didn't say that he regretted his vote in *Gregg*, so the end-of-career vote there is five to four for Georgia. But if Powell had never convened the troika, would Stevens have had the stomach to cast the deciding vote to send hundreds of people to their death? If not, as his comments to Totenberg and O'Connor suggest, then this history would have quite a different ending.

ACKNOWLEDGMENTS

WHEN I CONCEIVED THIS BOOK in 2007, I suspected there was a good story to tell about *Furman and Gregg*, but was uncertain whether I'd be able to get the access to tell it. To my surprise nearly everyone I wanted to speak with spoke with me. These conversations were thrilling, and I learned from each of them. My thanks go to all the law clerks and attorneys who shared their stories with me. Special thanks to Peggy Davis, Alan Dershowitz, Ronald George, David Kendall, and Michael Meltsner for opening their personal files to me, and to Dorothy Beasley for welcoming me and my family into her Adirondack retreat. Collectively these conversations were the greatest learning experience of my life, and I am changed by them. Even my own conception of the book has been altered. I have a sense that this potential for personal growth and evolution has implications for the ongoing debate over capital punishment.

My brilliant agent, Sam Stoloff, was the great champion of this book and I am deeply indebted to him. At Norton my sincere thanks go to Alane Salierno Mason, Denise Scarfi, and copyeditor extraordinaire Sue Llewellyn, whose life merits a book of its own. Thanks to Ursula Bentele, Stan Ingber, Jeffrey Kirchmeier, and Valerie West who read and commented on drafts of the manuscript. The book benefited in countless ways from the contributions of my friend and former graduate student, Zach Shemtob, whose smashing scholarly success is inevitable.

I am indebted in this as all my endeavors to my parents, Matt and Sherry, who have encouraged me in all my pursuits, no matter how quixotic. My dad also read and commented on an early draft of the manuscript.

This project took so long that I was single when it began and am now married with three kids. I was sustained in innumerable ways by my wonderful children Suria, Eamon, and Mattie and my bodaciously intelligent and beautiful wife, Valli, who patiently discussed every aspect of this book with me over its six-year gestation. I could never have done this without her. I am fortunate to be able to do much of my writing at home, and I also never could have finished without being able to give my magnificent Mattie periodic kisses and tickles. My next life project is to convince her that her father is not surgically attached to his ergonomic kneeling chair.

My deepest thanks go to Michael Meltsner and his incomparable wife, Heli. Michael was the first person I contacted for an interview. Having read his memoirs, I believed, as I still do, that it wouldn't be possible to tell this story without his cooperation. Michael responded by making a giant leap of faith. He opened his files to me and put me in touch with many of the people whose stories you have just read. Over the past six years we have had countless conversations about family, politics, history, sports, and almost every other subject imaginable. Amazingly, we have never discussed the morality of the death penalty (although I have a pretty good hunch where he stands). Michael's friendship was this book's greatest gift to me.

GLOSSARY OF KEY CASES

ANDERSON V. CALIFORNIA (1972)
A California Supreme Court decision outlawing the use of the death penalty under the state constitution. The decision was overturned by Proposition 17 later that year.

BRANCH V. TEXAS (1972)
A companion case to *Furman*.

BOYKIN V. ALABAMA (1969)
A constitutional challenge to the use of the death penalty for robbery that was ultimately upheld on the ground that the defendant's plea had been involuntary.

CRAMPTON V. OHIO (1971)
A companion case to *McGautha*.

FOWLER V. NORTH CAROLINA (1976)
A challenge to a North Carolina Supreme Court decision that interpreted *Furman* to transform its death penalty statute into a mandatory law. The case was argued in 1974, but postponed following

William Douglas's illness. Fowler's death sentence was ultimately set aside in 1976, following the Court's decision in *Woodson*.

FURMAN V. GEORGIA (1972)

A 5-to-4 decision, with five separate majority opinions, overturning Georgia's capital sentencing scheme. The Court consolidated *Jackson* and *Branch* with *Furman*.

GIACCIO V. PENNSYLVANIA (1966)

A unanimous decision setting aside a fine for criminally firing a weapon because of the law's lack of standards.

GREGG V. GEORGIA (1976)

A 7-to-2 decision upholding Georgia's revised capital sentencing system. Stewart, Powell, and Stevens's majority opinion emphasized that Georgia had responded to the arbitrariness concerns laid out in *Furman*. Brennan and Marshall dissented.

JACKSON V. GEORGIA (1972)

A companion case to *Furman*.

JUREK V. TEXAS (1976)

A companion case to *Gregg* in which the Court upheld Texas's revised death penalty statute.

LOCHNER V. NEW YORK (1905)

A 5-to-4 decision holding that the Fourteenth Amendment Due Process Clause implied a "liberty of contract," and therefore rejecting a New York law restricting the hours that bakers could work.

MAXWELL V. ARKANSAS (1970)

Maxwell's appeal began as a broad appeal based on racism in Arkansas's capital-sentencing scheme. It ended with a per curiam opinion reversing his sentence on *Witherspoon* grounds.

McGautha v. California (1971)

A 6-to-3 decision rejecting a challenge to California's death penalty statute under the Fourteenth Amendment. Harlan wrote the majority opinion.

Proffitt v. Florida (1976)

A companion case to *Gregg* in which the Court upheld Florida's revised death penalty law.

Roberts v. Louisiana (1976)

A companion case to *Woodson* in which the Court rejected Louisiana's revised death penalty law as effectively mandatory.

Rudolph v. Alabama (1963)

Arthur Goldberg dissented from the denial of certiorari in this appeal involving the imposition of the death penalty for rape.

Trop v. Dulles (1958)

Earl Warren wrote the majority opinion in this 5-to-4 decision rejecting the revocation of citizenship as cruel and unusual punishment, as measured by "evolving standards of decency."

Weems v. United States (1910)

A 4-to-2 decision striking down a fifteen-year sentence for falsifying public documents in which the majority said the Eighth Amendment needed to be interpreted under evolving standards of decency.

Witherspoon v. Illinois (1968)

Stewart wrote the opinion in this 6-to-3 decision overturning Illinois's capital jury selection procedure.

Woodson v. North Carolina (1976)

A 5-to-4 decision in which the Court rejected mandatory death penalty statutes. Brennan and Marshall joined Stewart, Powell, and Stevens in the majority.

NOTES

Abbreviations for Collections of Papers

AG   Arthur Goldberg Papers, Pritzker Legal Research Center, Northwestern University Law School, Chicago, Ill.

HAB   Harry A. Blackmun Papers, Manuscript Division, Library of Congress, Washington, D.C.

HB   Hugo A. Bedau Papers, M. E. Grenander Department of Special Collections and Archives, State University of New York, Albany, N.Y.

HLB   Hugo L. Black Papers, Manuscript Division, Library of Congress, Washington, D.C.

LFP   Lewis F. Powell Papers, William C. Hall Law Library, Washington and Lee Law School, Lexington, Va.

MM1   Michael Meltsner Papers, 1961–2008, Archives and Special Collections, Northeastern University Libraries, Boston, Mass.

MM2   Michael Meltsner Papers, 1965–1974, Rare Book & Manuscript Library, Columbia University, New York, N.Y.

PD   Peggy Davis Files, New York University, New York, N.Y.

PS   Potter Stewart Papers, Yale University Library Manuscript and Archives, New Haven, Conn.

TM   Thurgood Marshall Papers, Library of Congress, Washington, D.C.

WB   William Brennan Papers, Library of Congress, Washington, D.C.

WOD   William O. Douglas Papers, Library of Congress, Washington, D.C.

Prologue

ix   curing the "cancer of capital punishment": *New York Times*, "Overruling a Cancer," July 3, 1972, p. 16.

Chapter 1: *AN AUDACIOUS IDEA*

6   "None of my relatives were lawyers": An excellent overview of Justice Goldberg's early life is in David Stebenne, *Arthur J. Goldberg: New Deal Liberal*. Goldberg's formative years are discussed in pp. 4–11. The quote appears on p. 5.

8   Goldberg also worried about the problem of executing innocents: Arthur J. Goldberg, "The Death Penalty and the Supreme Court." *Arizona Law Review* 15 (1973): 355, 362.

8   sentenced under outdated principles: Goldberg wrote, "Our evolving concepts of constitutional law have required the Supreme Court frequently to hold that what was considered permissible yesterday is prohibited today. When such convictions result in the penalty of death, the dead cannot be restored to life." Ibid.

10   "The same issues that were here in 1947 are still here": Hutchinson, *The Man Who Once Was Whizzer White*, p. 339.

10   "Judges have an exaggerated view of their role": ibid., p 8.

10   "The trouble with these liberals": ibid., p. 346.

11   Goldberg's voting record: Russell W. Galloway, Jr., "Third Period of the Warren Court: Liberal Dominance (1962–1969)," *Santa Clara Law Review* 20 (1980): 773.

11   The intellectual foundation for repudiating *Lochner*: Holmes, Frankfurter, and Brandeis owed a substantial debt to James Bradley Thayer, as described in Noah Feldman, *Scorpions*, p. 105.

12   "When the people want to do something": *Time*, "Nation: Felix Frankfurter," September 7, 1962, p. 29.

14   It's inadequately framed as a battle of liberal versus conservative: Even pro-*Lochner* versus anti-*Lochner* is unsatisfactory. On the case that started everything the two men agreed on results, though for different reasons. Frankfurter developed his judicial restraint doctrine precisely to reject *Lochner*. Black would have overruled *Lochner* because the word "persons" in the Fourteenth Amendment wouldn't have been understood to include corporations.

15   "The Court must abstain from interference with State action": *Louisiana ex rel. Francis v. Resweber*, 329 U.S. 459, 464 (1947).

15   compilation of prior Supreme Court decisions on Eighth Amendment: Lain, "Deciding Death," pp. 10–12.

15   constitutionality of the firing squad: *Wilkerson v. Utah*, 99 U.S. 130 (1875); the electric chair: *In re Kemmler*, 136 U.S. 436 (1889).

16   "Therein lies the beauty of our Bill of Rights": Dershowitz recounts the conversation in *The Best Defense*, p. 306.

16   superior turkey slicer: *Forbes*, "First Job: Alan Dershowitz," May 23, 2006.

17   During his clerkship year: Dershowitz's commitment to capital punishment and his early work on the issue with Judge Bazelon are discussed in Dershowitz, *The Best Defense*, pp. 305–13.

19   the votes of four justices: The so-called rule of four is a matter of custom, not law. It is designed to prevent a majority of the Court from having complete control over the docket, and has been observed since Congress gave the Court the power to decide which appeals it would hear in the Judiciary Act of 1891.

20   it was easy enough to imagine Warren opposing capital punishment: Warren's record was mixed. As governor, he commuted the sentence of a young black man who had been sentenced to death for rape. Warren asked the trial judge whether the same sentence would have been imposed had the defendant been a white man. The judge said, "Certainly not," and Warren set aside his sentence. But he also supported legislation to curtail last-minute appeals by death-row inmates. On the discussion with the trial judge regarding race, see Earl Warren, *The Memoirs of Earl Warren* (New York: Doubleday, 1977), p. 212.

21   This is how desegregation proceeded: "Is Racial Segregation Consistent with Equal Protection of the Laws? *Plessy v. Ferguson* Reexamined," *Columbia Law Review* 49 (May 1949): 629–39; "Segregation in Public Schools: A Violation of 'Equal Protection of the Laws,'" *Yale Law Journal* 56 (June 1947): 1059–67.

21   "It may tenably be urged": Gerald Gottlieb, "Testing the Death Penalty," *Southern California Law Review* 34 (Spring 1961): 268–81. Gottlieb's article is reprinted in Hugo Bedau, *The Death Penalty in America* (New York: Anchor Books, 1964), pp. 194–213.

21   Gottlieb was the only one: The only arguable exception was Alexander Bickel, who included a passage about the death penalty in his 1962 book, *The Least Dangerous Branch* (New Haven: Yale University Press, 1962).

22   Dershowitz presented evidence: Dershowitz reprinted the published version of the memorandum in his book, *Shouting Fire: Civil Liberties in a Turbulent Age* (Boston: Little, Brown, 2002), pp. 279–189.

22   "would eliminate the well-recognized disparity": Goldberg, "Memorandum to the Conference," 493, 505.

22   "I circulate this memorandum": ibid.

24   "We read it, of course, because it is great literature": Goldberg to Dedication Dinner of the Jewish Publication Society of America, February 10, 1963, PS, Box 585.

25   Warren and Black's reaction to Goldberg's memorandum: Epstein and Kobylka, *Supreme Court and Legal Change*, p. 332.

25   Warren's judgment regarding the wisdom of the Court taking on the issue of capital punishment: See, for example, Dershowitz, *The Best Defense*, p. 308: "Warren, the astute politician who was always concerned with public acceptance of the Court's opinions, was convinced that any suggestion that the death penalty was unconstitutional would undermine the credibility of the Court's decision in desegregation and other controversial areas."

26   "a very poor time to bring the matter up": Banner, *The Death Penalty*, p. 250.

26   "Goldberg, the scholar": Simon, *The Antagonists: Hugo Black, Felix Frankfurter and Civil Liberties in Modern America*, p. 256.

27   "He did not think so, nor did I": Douglas, *The Douglas Letters*, p. 189.

27   "It would be best to let the matter sleep for a while": Epstein and Kobylka, *Supreme Court and Legal Change*, p. 332; Douglas, *The Douglas Letters*, p. 189.

27   Brennan's advice to Goldberg: Stern and Wermiel, *Justice Brennan*, p. 414.

27   Goldberg and Warren's compromise: Haines, *Against Capital Punishment*, p. 27.

28   "Alan, you are going to be very disappointed": Gordon, "Nothing Less Than the Dignity of Man," p. 33. Goldberg's response to Warren is also discussed in Meltsner, *Making of a Civil Rights Lawyer*, pp. 207–8, and in Alan Dershowitz interview (June 14, 2010).

28   the appeal of Frank Lee Rudolph: *Rudolph v. Alabama*: 375 U.S. 889 (1963).

30   he mailed copies of his memorandum: Epstein and Kobylka, *Supreme Court and Legal Change*, p. 43.

Chapter 2: THE MOST IMPORTANT LAW FIRM IN AMERICA

33   discussed the implication of Goldberg's dissent: The LDF lawyers were not yet aware of Dershowitz's memorandum.

33   "potentially far-reaching idea": *New York Times*, "3 Justices Question Legality of the Death Penalty for Rapists," Oct. 22, 1963, p. 41.

33   "an appeal to the brooding spirit of the law": *Washington Post*, "Death Penalty for Rape," Oct. 23, 1963, p. A20.

33   Polling data: Gallup has an exceedingly useful summary of its polling on the capital punishment issue available online at: http://wwww.gallup.com/poll/1606/death-penalty.aspx. Another accessible source is http://www.pollingreport.com/crime.htm. Another useful historical reference is David W. Moore, *Americans Firmly Support Death Penalty*, *Gallup Poll Monthly* 357 (June 1995): 23–25. An early, influential example of the scholarly literature on the subject is Neil Vidmar and Phoebe Ellsworth, "Public Opinion and the Death Penalty," *Stanford Law Review* 26 (June 1974): 1245.

34   "can serve only to encourage would-be rapists": Dershowitz, *The Best Defense*, p. 309.

34   "If one may venture a guess": Herbert L. Packer, "Making the Punishment Fit the Crime," Harvard Law Review 77 (1964): 1071, 1081–82.

34   "To hold that capital punishment is a method of punishment wholly prohibited": "The Cruel and Unusual Punishment Clause and the Substantive Criminal Law," *Harvard Law Review* 79 (1966): 635, 639.

34   "If we aren't able to turn these cases away": Meltsner, *Cruel and Unusual*, p. 31.

35   "capital punishment was not on the Fund's agenda": ibid., p. 15.

35   Greenberg would in turn disagree: Muller, "The Distorting Influence of Death," p. 164.

35   ACLU had no position on the death penalty: Epstein and Kobylka, *Supreme Court and Legal Change*, p. 45; Dorsen, *Frontiers of Civil Liberties*, p. 269.

36   "support the Negro revolution totally": Samuel Walker, *In Defense of American Liberties*, p. 266.

36   Fraenkel said the organization had to limit: ibid., pp. 266–67.

36   "for logically, this argument would call for the abolition": Dorsen, *Frontiers of Civil Liberties*, p. 271.

36   "inconsistent with the underlying values of a democratic system": ibid., p. 278.

36   The ACLU was heavily involved in defending conscientious objectors: Epstein and Kobylka, *Supreme Court and Legal Change*, p. 48.

37   Greenberg's first initiative: Meltsner, *Cruel and Unusual*, pp. 34–35.

38   Rockefeller . . . commuted the sentences: *Time*, "The Law: Clemency in Arkansas," Jan. 11, 1971.

38   Arkansas state courts rejected this evidence: *Maxwell v. Bishop*, 370 S. W. 2d 118 (1963).

38   Wolfgang led LDF to hire students: Haines, *Against Capital Punishment*, p. 28; Epstein and Kobylka, *Supreme Court and Legal Change*, pp. 49–51; Meltsner, *Cruel and Unusual*, p. 78; Foerster, *Race, Rape, and Injustice*, pp. 2–3.

38   The students examined the records: Marvin Wolfgang and Marc Reidel, "Race, Judicial Discretion, and the Death Penalty," *Annals of the American Academy of Political and Social Science* 407 (1973): 119–33; Epstein and Kobylka, *Supreme Court and Legal Change*, p. 50.

39   "elusive things at best": *Maxwell v. Bishop*, 257 F. Supp. 710, 720 (E. Dist. Ark. 1966).

39   "interesting and provocative": *Maxwell v. Bishop*, 398 F.2d 138, 147 (8th Cir. 1968).

42   "mightily inspired to play better": Nadya Labi, "A Man Against the Machine," *NYU Law School Magazine*, Autumn 2007, p. 14. Ms. Labi's article is the most extensively that Professor Amsterdam has spoken on the record about his life history. Other valuable sources are Meltsner, *The Making of a Civil Rights Lawyer*, pp. 201–2; Meltsner, *Cruel and Unusual*, pp. 78–86; Haines, *Against Capital Punishment*, pp. 31–32. My account is supplemented by interviews with Professor Meltsner, Jon Amsterdam, and, to a limited extent, Professor Amsterdam.

42   Amsterdam drafted *Baker v. Carr*: This is reported in, among other places, James Simon, *The Antagonists*, p. 251.

43   "to learn something from the inside": Epstein and Kobylka, *Supreme Court and Legal Change*, p. 49, referencing Frederick Mann, "Anthony Amsterdam: Renaissance Man or Twentieth Century Computer?" *Juris Doctor*, no. 3 (1973): 30–33.

43   "your volume must be misbound": Meltsner, *Cruel and Unusual*, p. 80.

44   "the finest lawyer of his generation": Lazarus, *Closed Chambers*, p. 90.

44   "God broke the mold": Labi, "A Man Against the Machine," p. 12.

44   "After the revolution, I will be representing the capitalists": *Time*, "The Law: Advocate for Underdogs," May 25, 1970.

45   "personally hated the death penalty and was torn up": Michael Meltsner interview (December 4, 2010).

45   "once the negro situation was remedied": *Maxwell v. Bishop*, 398 F.2d. 138, 148.

46   "Ugh": David Von Drehle, "Death Penalty Divide Frustrated Blackmun: Papers on Lockett Case Show How He Came to See Split Between Fairness, Consistency," *Washington Post*, March 15, 2004, p. A04.

46   "tall, 28, suave": Labi, "A Man Against the Machine."

46   Supreme Court had suggested a willingness: For example, the court had ordered
     Missouri to integrate a graduate school: See *Missouri ex rel Gaines v. Canada*, 305
     U.S. 337 (1938). Professor Meltsner discusses the foundation that the Supreme
     Court laid for *Brown* in *Cruel and Unusual*, p. 66. As Meltsner puts it, the Court
     had "chipped away at the legal foundation." Other relevant cases include *Sweatt v.
     Painter*, 339 U.S. 629 (1950), and *McLaurian v. Oklahoma*, 339 U.S. 637 (1950).

47   "It was the power of Tony Amsterdam's mind": Labi, "A Man Against the
     Machine," p. 13.

Chapter 3: SURCEASE OF SORROW

48   "Race was always the factor": Eric Muller, "The Legal Defense Fund's Capital
     Punishment Campaign: The Distorting Influence of Death," p. 162.

49   "People thought that capital punishment was sufficiently horrible that you didn't
     have to count up the numbers": ibid.

49   "Once we had the power to get stays": Anthony Amsterdam interview (January
     20, 2010). Jack Greenberg also emphasized the moral obligation that LDF per-
     ceived to extend its expertise to non-black defendants. He wrote, "Once having
     raised these claims, it was not adequate to assert them on behalf of some defen-
     dants in the hope that they would receive the benefit of a new rule announced at
     a later date. And one cannot ignore the prejudices, not merely racial, that bring a
     jury to select this man and not another for death—indeed, to select any man for
     death for any crime." Greenberg and Himmelstein, *Varieties of Attack on the Death
     Penalty*, p. 116.

49   "To any observer, race had always been the top issue on LDF's agenda": Muller,
     "The Legal Defense Fund's Capital Punishment Campaign," p. 182.

50   "Look, this was a civil rights organization": ibid., p. 181.

50   The death penalty had never been a draw for money: Jack Greenberg interview
     (November 2, 2009).

50   Greenberg approved use of the money: Greenberg, *Crusaders in the Court*, pp.
     440–44; Haines, *Against Capital Punishment*, p. 31; Epstein and Kobylka,
     Supreme Court and Legal Change, p. 54.

50   The total annual budget of LDF in 1960: Meltsner, *Making of a Civil Rights Law-
     yer*, p. 89.

51   "more social work than law": ibid., p. 29.

53   "*Brown* was fine": Muller, "The Legal Defense Fund's Capital Punishment Cam-
     paign," p. 186.

53   "like sand poured in a machine": Meltsner. *Cruel and Unusual*, p. 71.

54   A judge is less likely to be receptive to the arguments made by an individual defen-
     dant: Muller, "The Legal Defense Fund's Capital Punishment Campaign," p. 169.
     Muller references an address by Dean John C. Boger, former director of the LDF
     Capital Punishment Project, at a Yale Law School seminar (Feb. 21, 1985).

55   "If I'm elected, I may have to sign your death warrants": Mello, *Deathwork: Defending the Condemned*, p. 25; Meltsner, *Cruel and Unusual*, p. 127.

55   "They will be heard together or they will be electrocuted individually": Meltsner, *Cruel and Unusual*, p. 133.

56   McRae bought LDF's argument: *Adderly v Wainwright*, 46 F.R.D. 97 (1968).

56   "It may be premature to do anything": Epstein and Kobylka, *Supreme Court and Legal Change*, p. 55.

57   "I would approach the thought of a class suit": Schwed, *Abolition and Capital Punishment*, p. 111.

58   "concern for the five hundred other men": Meltsner, *Cruel and Unusual*, p. 122.

59   "F-U letter": Meltsner interview (December 4, 2010).

59   "the possible submerging of special claims of individuals": Greenberg, *Judicial Process and Social Change*, p. 444.

60   give the "movement for legal abolition a cohesion": Meltsner, *Cruel and Unusual*, p. 114.

60   "Such a conference": Tony Amsterdam to Jack Greenberg, July 28, 1967. See also Schwed, *Abolition and Capital Punishment*, p. 112 (LDF wanted to "restrain uniformed or careless attorneys from going into court to save a client with ill-conceived frontal attacks on the constitutionality of the death penalty.")

61   "The battle over capital punishment": Greenberg and Himmelstein, *Varieties of Attacks on the Death Penalty*, p. 120.

61   "In other states": ibid., p. 118.

63   twenty states considered proposals: A useful summary of state action from the era is in Lain, *Furman Fundamentals*, pp. 19–23.

63   "By inches, the death penalty is dying": *Time*, "Killing the Death Penalty," July 7, 1967.

64   "The division is not between": *Witherspoon v. Illinois*, 391 U.S. 510, 520 (1968).

65   "definitely end capital punishment in Georgia": Lazarus, *Closed Chambers*, p. 98.

65   "may eliminate the death penalty for capital crimes": HLB, *Witherspoon v. Illinois* case file. See also Gordon, *Nothing Less Than the Dignity of Man*, p. 46.

65   "This is another nail in the coffin": Meltsner, *Cruel and Unusual*, p. 124.

65   "Once we stopped the executions": Haines, *Against Capital Punishment*, p. 30; Wolfe, *Pileup on Death Row*, pp. 244–25.

65   "For each year the United States went without executions": Meltsner, *Cruel and Unusual*, p. 71.

65   "We forced the courts to deal": *Newsweek*, "Renaissance Lawyer," July 17, 1972.

66   The Court found the absence of standards fatal: *Giaccio v. Pennsylvania*, 382 U.S. 399 (1966).

67   "The author of this opinion": *Maxwell v. Bishop* 398 F.2d 138, 153 (8th Cir. 1968).

67   When *Time* interviewed Amsterdam: *Time*, "The Law: Advocate for Underdogs," May 25, 1970, p. 72.

68   the "distinction between what public conscience will allow the law to *say*": Brief of Amicus Curiae NAACP Legal Defense and Education Fund, *Boykin v. Alabama*, p. 38. Quoted in Meltsner, *Cruel and Unusual*, p. 182.

69   Contemporary standards of decency would condemn the use of death: ibid., pp. 39–40.

69   "Herein is found the difference": ibid., p. 39.

Chapter 4: A NEAR KNOCKOUT

71   Brennan had repeated this routine every morning: In their splendid biography of Justice Brennan, Seth Stern and Stephen Wermiel report that in 1957 Brennan "settled into a comfortable routine" of waking before six, wearing "old clothes," and walking every morning in response to his doctor's advice. Stern and Wermiel, *Justice Brennan*, p. 132. Stern and Wermiel report this practice continuing until the mid-1960s (ibid., p. 276), as does Brennan's former clerk Robert O'Neill. Andrew J. Stephens, "Chamber of Secrets: Professors Reflect on Clerking Experiences," *Virginia Law Weekly* 58, no. 15 (February 10, 2006): 1–2. C. Taylor Ashworth, who clerked for Brennan during the 1971–72 term said, "Justice Brennan was still very much in the habit of taking morning walks before coming to the Court all during the 1971 term. He would meet with his law clerks at 9:00 every weekday morning and frequently had comments based on what he thought about during his walk." Email on file with author. The weather in Washington, D.C., was nice on March 6, 1969, so it seems likely Brennan took a walk.

72   Brennan represented a woman who found her husband: Stern and Wermiel, *Justice Brennan*, pp. 410–11.

72   Brennan was squarely in the Frankfurter camp: ibid., p.102. Stern and Wermiel's biography offers a wonderfully vivid portrait of Justice Brennan as a young man.

72   appeal by a black man facing a possible death sentence for burglary: *Fikes v. Alabama*, 352 U.S. 191 (1957).

73   voted against hearing the appeals of Dick Hickock and Perry Smith: Stern and Wermiel, *Justice Brennan*, p. 412.

73   the driving force behind the Warren Court's transformative expansion of civil liberties: Dennis J. Hutchinson, "Hail to the Chief: Earl Warren and the Supreme Court," *Michigan Law Review* 81 (1983): 922, 923. Stephen Gillers, "The Warren Court—It Still Lives," *The Nation*, September 17, 1983, p. 207.

73   This language mirrored that of John Ryan: Stern and Wermiel, *Justice Brennan*, p. 166.

73   He neither quoted Catholic thinkers: ibid., p. 166.

73   He encouraged his children to have non-Catholic friends, and all three married outside the church: ibid., pp. 166–67.

73   "They put the Negroes in the schools, and now they've driven God out": Stern and Wermiel, ibid., p. 171.

74   The Court ruled mandatory Bible readings: *Abington Township School District v. Schempp*, 374 U.S. 203 (1963).

74   John Russell . . . scolded Brennan at the Red Mass: Kenneth Dole, "Bishop Raps Neutral Stand on Religion," *Washington Post*, January 27, 1964. See also Stern and

Wermiel, *Justice Brennan*, pp. 174–75. Stern and Wermiel discuss the difficulties Brennan faced in balancing his Catholicism with his role on the Court at pp. 164–77.

74 "You have no idea what it's like": Stern and Wermiel, *Justice Brennan*, p. 172 (discussing the Epiphany Church episode generally).

74 "It never crossed my mind": ibid., p. 372.

74 Brennan and Bazelon met: ibid., p. 97.

74 Bazelon . . . often joined Brennan on his morning walks: ibid., p. 179.

75 Through Bazelon and Kronheim, Brennan came to know Edmund Muskie: ibid., pp. 178–80.

75 Brennan even invested with Bazelon, Wright, Goldberg, and Abe Fortas: ibid., p. 319.

75 Bazelon . . . sent his speeches to Brennan: ibid., pp. 241–48 (discussing Bazelon's influence on Brennan generally).

75 "The issue . . . really comes down to whether we should further whittle away the protections": *Washington Post*, "Brennan Urges Greater Rights for Defendants," May 10, 1963.

76 "Law is again coming alive": Stern and Wermiel, *Justice Brennan*, p. 233.

76 "gratefully encouraging": ibid., p. 412.

76 "There just wasn't a thing you could do": ibid., p. 309 (discussing Brennan's sense of despair).

76 "not opposed to capital punishment": Fred P. Graham, "Mitchell Vows Vigorous Law Enforcement in U.S.," *New York Times*, January 22, 1969.

77 California Supreme Court upheld the constitutionality of capital punishment: *In re Anderson*, 447 P.2d 117 (Cal. 1968).

77 Stanley Mosk's judicial heroes: California State Archives State Government Oral History Program, available at http://www.sos.ca/gov/archives/oral-history/pdf/mosk.pdf, p. 90.

77 "Naturally, I am tempted": *In re Anderson*, 447 P.2d at 132 (Mosk, concurring).

77 When he finished his walk: Stern and Wermiel discuss Brennan's morning routine of eating breakfast while reading newspapers at p. 132. Brennan's taste for chocolate is discussed in ibid., p. 51.

80 "If a civilized society cannot say": ibid., p. 154 (Tobriner, concurring). The "dissent" to which Douglas referred was formally a concurrence. Justice Tobriner agreed that *Witherspoon* had been violated but said the Court should have gone further.

80 Brennan had a warm relationship with Harlan: See Woodward and Armstrong, *The Brethren*, p. 46, and Stern and Wermiel, *Justice Brennan*, pp. 148–49 (referencing shared cigarettes and interest in golf).

80 Harlan . . . didn't like the direction of the Warren Court: Stern and Wermiel, *Justice Brennan*, p. 185. Regarding *Baker*, Harlan wrote, "The independence of the Court, and its aloofness from political vicissitudes, have always been the mainspring of its stability and vitality."

80 "Some well-meaning people apparently believe": *New York Times*, "Harlan Cautions on Role of Court," August 14, 1963.

81   They had met at a judicial conference: Stern and Wermiel, *Justice Brennan*, p. 155
      (also referencing Stewart calling Brennan for advice).

81   too "reflexively liberal": ibid., p. 357.

81   "If this Court is to hold capital punishment unconstitutional": *Witherspoon v.
      Illinois*, 391 U.S. 510, 532 (Black, dissenting).

82   "It would be inhumanity": Meltsner, *Cruel and Unusual*, p. 166.

83   Fortas and Marshall believed that if the Court required standards, the standards
      would favor prosecutors: Dickson, *The Supreme Court in Conference*, p. 611.

83   not "very conclusive or illuminating": Epstein and Kobylka, *Supreme Court and
      Legal Change*, p. 63.

83   Harlan asked that the case be held over: Schwartz, *Unpublished Opinions of the
      Supreme Court*, pp. 394–444; Schwartz, *Super Chief*, pp. 734–42.

85   "macaroni spine": See Murphy, *Wild Bill*, pp. 63, 75, 194. Murphy's brilliant biog-
      raphy is the definitive account of Douglas's life and is the principal source of this
      portrait.

85   "I'm just an ordinary person, but Bill is a genius": ibid., p. 365.

85   "right to be let alone": The case in which Justice Douglas found the "right to be
      let alone" was *Public Utilities Commission v. Pollak*, 343 U.S. 451 (1952). Felix
      Frankfurter did not participate in the decision.

85   absolutist stances against the restrictions of obscenity: *Roth v. United States*, 354
      U.S. 476 (1957); against blue laws: *McGowan v. Maryland*, 360 U.S. 420 (1961).

86   "Douglas's life was the stuff of novels": Murphy, *Will Bill*, p. 515.

86   "mean son of bitch": Kalman, *Legal Realism at Yale*, p. 113.

87   "bolt upright, because I heard that buzzer in my dream": Murphy, *Wild Bill*, p.
      409.

87   "the lowest form of human life": ibid., p. 347.

88   "His great mistake was his insistence": Jeffrey T. Leeds, "A Life on the Court,"
      New York Times Magazine, October 5, 1986, p. 24.

88   Douglas defined himself as a loner: Feldman, *Scorpions*, p. 323.

88   "Absolutely not!": Murphy, *Wild Bill*, p. 351.

90   "The case has bothered me considerably": WOD, Memorandum to the Confer-
      ence, April 4, 1969, WOD.

90   "I am certainly with you": Abe Fortas to William Douglas, April 7, 1969, ibid.

91   "constitutionally infirm": Harlan to Douglas, April 9, 1969, ibid.

91   "In this area," Marshall said, "we do not yet have the skills": Marshall to Fortas,
      April 21, 1969. TM, Box 57, File 13 (*Maxwell v. Bishop*).

91   Douglas's April 22 memorandum: WOD Memorandum to the Conference, April
      22, 1969, WOD.

91   "If this Court is determined to abolish the death penalty": Schwartz, *Unpublished
      Opinions*, p. 427.

92   "Due process requires pre-existing standards": Schwartz, *Super Chief*, p. 741.

92   wouldn't "provide the fifth vote in such a crucial case": ibid., p. 748.

94   "Where more is at stake, due process is more exacting": The only available record
      of this oral argument is Meltsner, *Cruel and Unusual*, pp. 202–06.

96   the justices decided to put the central issues over to the following term: William

J. Brennan, "Constitutional Adjudication and the Death Penalty," Harvard Law Review 100 (1986): 313, 317–18.

97 "The facts of the two cases did not augur well": Meltsner, *Cruel and Unusual*, p. 228.

97 "went down on the books as a minor footnote": Brennan, "Constitutional Adjudication and the Death Penalty," p. 318.

97 "a measured step toward abolition": Meltsner, *The Making of a Civil Rights Lawyer*, p. 195.

Chapter 5: TO LICENSE A LAUNDRY, TO LICENSE A LIFE

99 "The leading cause of death": Dean E. Murphy, "San Quentin Debate: Death Row vs. Bay Views," *New York Times*, Dec. 18, 2004, p. A1.

99 "Does this imply that a man convicted and sentenced should be executed forthwith?": HAB to himself, September 14, 1971, HAB.

104 "quiet day in court": Meltsner, *Cruel and Unusual*, p. 231.

104 "This is an oblique attack on capital punishment": Banner, *The Death Penalty*, pp. 256–57. See also Dickson, *The Supreme Court in Conference*, pp. 614–616.

106 "A reading of the beach memorandum and of the brief here": HAB to himself, November 4, 1970, HAB.

106 "Our function is not to impose": See *McGautha v. California*, 402 U.S. 183, 195 (1971).

108 "largely symbolic": ibid., p. 217.

109 *Yick Wo. v. Hopkins*: 118 U.S. 356 (1886).

112 Fourth Circuit ruled the death penalty unconstitutional for a rapist: *Ralph v. Warden*, 438 F.2d 786 (4th Cir. 1970).

112 Rockefeller said that he had made up his mind: Meltsner, *Cruel and Unusual*, pp. 235–36.

112 "I believe killing criminals": ibid., p. 237.

113 The Alabama Court of Appeals effectively ended executions: *Brown v. State*, 264 So. 2d 529 (1971).

113 Goldberg and Dershowitz criticized the Court for avoiding *Boykin* and *Maxwell*: Arthur Goldberg and Alan Dershowitz, "Declaring the Death Penalty Unconstitutional," *Harvard Law Review* 83, (1970): 1773–1819.

114 "In candor, I must admit that when *McGautha* was decided": Brennan, "Constitutional Adjudication and the Death Penalty," p. 321.

114 During the entire 1960s, Brennan had filed sixty-seven dissents: Stern and Werniel, *Justice Brennan*, p. 351.

114 "increasingly vinegary": ibid., p. 351; Fred P. Graham, "Justices are Losing Their Cool," *New York Times*, April 11, 1971.

114 Stewart said they couldn't: Woodward and Armstrong, *The Brethren*, p. 206.

115 "once and for all make it clear": Banner, *The Death Penalty*, pp. 257–58.

115 "find four clean cases": Brennan, "Constitutional Adjudication and the Death Penalty," p. 322. The justices had differing recollections as to who was charged

with selecting the 1971–72 capital cases. In his 1986 lecture at Harvard Law School, referenced above, Brennan recalled the responsibility as being his and Stewart's. However, one week after the Court announced *McGautha*, William Douglas wrote a note to his law clerk saying that the conference had declined to dispose of the remaining cases by denying certiorari, and instead created a committee to pick one case from each of the three groups—rapes, robberies, and "run of the mill murders"—to be argued in October 1971. Douglas said the committee consisted of himself, Brennan, White, and Stewart. Douglas's papers offer no further evidence of his involvement in the selection of the of the 1971 term cases. Furthermore, given the timing of the post-*McGautha* conference, and Douglas's habit of leaving early for his summer vacation in the Pacific Northwest, it seems unlikely that he participated materially in the case selection process. White, on the other hand, appears to have been involved. A June 8 memorandum to the conference regarding the new cases was authored by Brennan and White. Brennan and White Memorandum to the conference, June 8, 1971, WOD, Box 1486.

115 "For the life of me, I do not see how anyone": Douglas to conference, June 3, 1971, TM, Box 64, File 5.

116 left open the possibility of upholding the constitutionality of the death penalty: Brennan and White Memorandum to the Conference, June 8, 1971, WOD, Box 1486.

117 "Psychiatrists have unanimously pronounced him fearfully sane": *Time*, "The Death Penalty: Cruel and Unusual," January 24, 1972, p. 66.

119 "not interested in a collection of cases": Urofsky, *The Douglas Letters*, pp. 194–95.

119 Brennan directed Mike Becker to draft a memo: Stern & Wermiel, *Justice Brennan*, p. 418; Becker interview (June 21, 2011).

119 he expected that when he returned in the fall it would serve as the basis for a solo dissent: Brennan, "Constitutional Adjudication and the Death Penalty," p. 322.

Chapter 6: YOUNG LAWYERS

124 Brennan told friends that he would resign if a woman were made a justice: Stern & Wermiel, *Justice Brennan*, p. 388.

124 "Some of them are imbued with deeply held notions about right and wrong": William Rehnquist, "Who Writes Decisions of the Supreme Court," *U.S. News & World Report*, December 13, 1957, p. 74.

125 "the Court as an institution has been sorely damaged in this last decade": Fred Strebeigh, *Equal: Women Reshape American Law* (New York: Norton, 2009), p. 375.

125 "more measured than civil rights leaders would have liked": Jeffries, *Justice Lewis F. Powell, Jr.*, p. 2.

126 "Those who preach, practice and condone lawlessness are the enemies": *U.S. News & World Report*, "Civil Disobedience: Prelude to Revolution," October 30, 1967, pp. 66–69.

126 "we're going to be talking about you": Woodward and Armstrong, *The Brethren*, p. 161.

126 "I realize that it is an unpopular and unhumanitarian position": William Rehnquist, "A Random Thought on the Segregation Cases," S. Hrg. 99–1067, Hearings Before the Senate Committee on the Judiciary on the Nomination of Justice William Hubbs Rehnquist to be Chief Justice of the United States (July 29–31 and August 1, 1986).

126 "smear of a great man": 132 Cong. Rec. 23548 (1986) (speech of Senator Paul Sarbanes). Available at http://www.loc.gov/rr/law/nominations/rehnquist-cj/statements .pdf.

127 "lean years ahead": "Rights Lawyers: Bracing for the Lean Years": *New York Times*, December 19, 1971, p. E8.

127 Many of the clerks cared passionately about the death penalty: Stern and Wermiel, p. 419.

132 "To deny this dynamic character would produce inconceivable results": Brief for Petitioner, *Aikens v. California*, p. 17. Available as 1971 WL 134168.

133 "If a penalty is generally, fairly and uniformly enforced": *Time*, "The Death Penalty: Cruel and Unusual," January 24, 1972. p. 66.

133 "We hide our executions because we are disgusted to look at them": Brief for Petitioner, *Aikens v. California*, p. 48.

133 "Those who are selected to die": ibid., p. 51.

134 "brilliant": Banner, *The Death Penalty*, p. 260.

137 "I hate the death penalty": Alan Dershowitz interview (June 14, 2010).

138 "He's the solicitor general of the United States": Williams, *Thurgood Marshall*, p. 314; Marshall's doubts about the Supreme Court job: ibid., p. 5.

139 A hedonist, Marshall had always lived hard: ibid., p. 193.

139 Marshall solidified his relationship with LBJ: ibid., p. 321.

139 Marshall weighed more than 230 pounds: ibid., p. 346.

139 He gave away his tickets to Nixon's second inaugural: ibid., p. 352.

139 "If you get a life term for a Negro": ibid., p. 59.

141 Marshall upheld a death sentence: ibid., p. 351.

141 The Second Circuit upheld his sentence: *Jackson v. Denno*, 309 F.2d 573 (2d Cir. 1962).

141 "was not against the death penalty": Williams, *Thurgood Marshall*, p. 351.

141 "the ultimate gradualist": ibid., p. 286.

141 Brennan had argued to Marshall: ibid., p. 351.

Chapter 7: BOILING IN OIL

144 On his first day on the job, Marshall visited Powell's chambers: Woodward and Armstrong, *The Brethren*, pp. 204–5.

144 "My wife Cissy": ibid., p. 205.

145 gave Brennan hope that Stewart might be persuadable: Epstein and Kobylka,

Supreme Court and Legal Charge, p. 76; Woodward and Armstrong, *The Brethren*, p. 216.

145 Brennan began to wonder whether he might also turn Blackmun: Stern and Wermiel say Brennan's courtship of Blackmun began in earnest in 1974, Stern and Wermiel, *Justice Brennan*, p. 383.

145 "Mr. Amsterdam," he said, "you may proceed": Because *Aikens v. California* ultimately was not decided by the Court, as discussed in chapter 8, the transcript of the oral argument is not available either from the Supreme Court or the Oyez Project. I have reconstructed the argument from a recording retained by Ronald George, which he generously shared with me.

146 William Smith of South Carolina objected to the Eighth Amendment: Michael D. Dean, "State Legislation and the 'Evolving Standards of Decency': Flaws in the Constitutional Review of Death Penalty Statutes," *University of Dayton Law Review* 35 (2010): 379.

146 "It makes no sense to employ the value judgments of the majority for protecting minorities": Ely, *Democracy and Distrust*, p. 69. Franklin Zimring and Gordon Hawkins make a similar point: "What is the significance of a curb on majority and legislative will which cannot be employed to check or restrain that will?" Zimring and Hawkins, "Capital Punishment and the Eighth Amendment," p. 941.

148 Antonin Scalia said that the constitutionality of capital punishment boiled down to the feelings and intuition of the justices: *Atkins v. Virginia*, 536 U.S. 304, 348–49. A majority of the Supreme Court claimed otherwise in *Coker v. Georgia*: "Eighth Amendment judgments should not be, or appear to be, merely the subjective views of individual Justices." *Coker v. Georgia*, 433 U.S. 584, 592 (1986). But it's hard to deny Scalia's point. Professor Corinna Barrett Lain speaks for much of the scholarly community when she says, "The Justices do not follow doctrine in any meaningful way. Doctrine follows them." Lain, "Deciding Death," 1, n 9.

148 Some scholars would argue that Amsterdam's answer *hurt* the abolition movement: William W. Berry III, "Following the Yellow Brick Road of Evolving Standards of Decency: The Ironic Consequences of Death-is-Different Jurisprudence," *Pace Law Review* 28 (2007): 15.

160 "The latest available figure to me is 697": This figure came from Doug Lyons of Citizens Against Legalized Murder, and is cited in Richard Halloran, "Death Penalties Argued in Court," *New York Times*, January 18, 1972, p. 15. In his review of Michael Meltsner's book, *Cruel and Unusual,* Hugo Adam Bedau found some uncertainty in this figure. Bedau, "Challenging the Death Penalty," *Harvard Civil Rights and Civil Liberties Law Review* 9 (1974): 626.

163 "nice girl": Greenhouse, *Becoming Justice Blackmun*, p. 106.

Chapter 8: NINE LAW FIRMS

166 the best he had ever heard: Woodward and Armstrong, *The Brethren*, p. 209.

166 "You can't run the criminal justice system from the courthouse": ibid., p. 210.

167 "All of us have reservations about the death penalty": Banner, *The Death Penalty*, p. 260.

168 "an action that no Chief Justice in my time would ever have taken": Jeffries, *Justice Lewis F. Powell*, p. 338.

168 "As of now, I cannot uphold the constitutionality of the death sentence": Del Dickson's account of the *Furman* conference is reconstructed from Douglas's conference notes. WOD, Box 1541, Case File O.T. 1971, "Argued Cases."

171 "You would think from reading *The Brethren*": Perry, *Deciding to Decide*, p. 143.

172 "Potter will not pull the switch": Woodland and Armstrong, *The Brethen*, p. 216.

173 "deputy prime minister": Stern and Wermiel, *Justice Brennan*, p. 453.

173 Brennan in turn regarded White as too invested in being right: The most vivid illustration of this is Brennan's decision to assign *Bakke*, a seminal affirmative action decision, to himself rather than White. Ibid., pp. 452–53.

173 "I'd like to strike down": William H. Jeffries, Jr., interview (October 12, 2009); Benjamin W. Heineman interview (October 23, 2009).

177 "His most consistent philosophy was his skepticism": Jefferies, *Justice Lewis F. Powell*, p. 262.

177 At a reunion of Harlan clerks: PS, Box 586.

177 "The Court is not a council of Platonic guardians": Roger K. Newman, *The Yale Biographical Dictionary of American Law* (New Haven: Yale University Press, 2009), p. 517.

177 an article following Stewart's death: Ben W. Heineman Jr., "A Balance Wheel on the Court," *Yale Law Journal* 95 (1986): 325–27.

178 "something of an enigma": Meltsner, *Cruel and Unusual*, p. 157.

178 Harold Spaeth and Michael Altfeld of Michigan State University quantified the question: Harold J. Spaeth and Michael F. Altfeld, "Influence Relationships Within the Supreme Court: A Comparison of the Warren and Burger Courts," *Western Political Quarterly* 38 (1985): 70–83. See also Michael F. Altfeld and Harold J. Spaeth, "Measuring Influence on the U.S. Supreme Court," *Jurimetrics Journal* 24 (1984): 236–47.

179 Harlan, in turn, influenced only Stewart: Spaeth and Altfeld show that Harlan also influenced Justices Charles Whittaker and Harold Burton, though they had retired by the time Stewart took the bench.

179 Blackmun and Burger voted the same way sixty-nine times: Stern and Wermiel, *Justice Brennan*, p. 353.

179 "the year of the Stewart-White Court": Hutchinson, *The Man Who Once Was Whizzer White*, p. 358.

180 "serves to protect society as a whole": Stern and Wermiel, *Justice Brennan*, p. 418.

180 "The genius of the Constitution rests not in any static meaning": ibid., p. 505. Justice Brennan delivered these remarks in 1985. The Georgetown symposium asked speakers to say how a text had affected their life.

181 "Were capital punishment, like criminal punishment of narcotic addiction": Goldberg and Dershowitz, "Declaring the Death Penalty Unconstitutional," p. 1783.

181 Brennan's opinion . . . made no mention of race: Stern and Wermiel, *Justice Brennan*, p. 221.

181 "I wonder if it is appropriate": ibid., p. 238.

182 "Even when the death penalty is imposed": Goldberg and Dershowitz, "Declaring the Death Penalty Unconstitutional," 1796.

183 "On balance, while I am taken by the notion of a continuum": Larry A. Hammond to Lewis F. Powell, undated memorandum, LFP.

184 On February 18, 1972, the California Supreme Court said precisely this: *California v. Anderson*, 6 Cal 3d 628 (Cal. 1972).

185 "heaved a collective sigh of relief": Muller, "The Legal Defense Fund's Capital Punishment Campaign," p. 178.

186 "Nice try, Ben": Jeffress interview (October 12, 2009).

186 its basic underlying concept "is nothing less than the dignity of man": *Furman v. Georgia*, 408 U.S. at 270 (Brennan, J., concurring).

189 Douglas's own clerks shared: Interview on background.

190 "our constitutional inquiry": *Furman v. Georgia*, 408 U.S. at 375 (Burger, J., dissenting).

191 "There will be no boiling in oil": 1971–72 Term History, p. 118. Brennan's clerks wrote histories of each Court term (hereafter, "Term History"). Most are available at the Library of Congress.

193 his own doubts about the paragraph: Greenhouse, *Becoming Justice Blackmun*, pp. 32–35 (discussing the Pope case generally).

193 retyped a passage: Greenhouse, *Becoming Justice Blackmun*, p. 162.

193 he was widely regarded as the most liberal justice: ibid., p. 235.

194 Blackmun agreed with Brennan in 55 percent of cases: ibid., p. 186.

194 "the shy person's justice": ibid., p. 249.

194 "All good ideas do not spring from the Constitution": ibid., pp. 51–52.

196 Stewart and White praised the draft: Jeffries, *Justice Lewis F. Powell*, p. 412.

196 "If this is the extent of the argument": Larry A. Hammond to Lewis F, Powell, May 24, 1972, LFP.

Chapter 9: WHIZZER

202 "If you think I'm good": Hutchinson, *The Man Who Once Was Whizzer White*, p. 29. Hutchinson's is the only published biography of White, and the principal source for this portrait of White's childhood and early career.

203 "looked like a Greek god": ibid., p. 136.

203 He expressed no greater aspiration: ibid., p. 227.

205 "I think John Kennedy's central principle": ibid., p. 328.

205 "I've never understood what people mean": ibid., p. 259.

205 "his kind of person": Jeffrey Rosen, "The Next Justice," *New Republic*, April 12, 1993, p. 21.

205 "Being a conservative or a centrist is all in the minds of the speaker": ABC Tran-

script 3056, March 19, 1993; Hutchinson, *The Man Who Once Was Whizzer White*, p. 444.

206 **part of his larger project to undermine slavery:** The influence of slavery on Darwin's thinking is magnificently laid out in Desmond and Moore's *Darwin's Sacred Cause*. Darwin deplored the brutality of slavery and the white man's desire "to make the black man another kind, sub-human, a beast to be chained" (p. xvii). *On the Origin of Species*, published in 1859, liberated blacks—intellectually at least—from their status as a natural underclass. The theory of natural selection showed that no species or race was inferior to another. One might be different, or better adapted to a set of environmental conditions, but not better. "It is absurd to talk of one animal being higher than another," Darwin wrote. (See Darwin, *Notebook B: Transmutation of Species*, in Paul H. Barrett, Peter J. Gautrey, Sandra Herbert, David Kohn and Sydney Smith, *Charles Darwin's Notebook, 1836–1844*, Ithaca: British Museum [Natural History] and Cornell University Press, 1987.) "I look at the term species as one arbitrary given for the sake of convenience to a set of individuals closely resembling each other." Within a species, individuals simply differed from one another, and those who possessed advantageous traits survived. While this is commonly referred to as the "theory of evolution," the true purpose of *On the Origin of Species* was to undermine the notion that a supernatural intelligence guided evolution, as Jean-Baptiste Lamarck, Herbert Spencer, and other "evolutionists" purported. The process Darwin described was natural and driven largely by luck (and hence supremely unsettling). Darwin's worldview and influence are discussed at length in Louis Menand, *The Metaphysical Club*, pp. 120–28. This is one of my favorite books, and I recommend it to anyone.

206 **the tendrils of Darwin's insidious ideas:** In history, Charles Beard looked behind the standard narrative of the American Revolution and exposed the economic motivations of the Founding Fathers. The sociologist Max Weber shifted the study of God from theology to an exploration of the social consequences of religion and its relationship to capitalism. In linguistics I. A. Richards and C. K. Ogden's *The Meaning of Meaning* exposed the ambiguity of language. In anthropology Bronislaw Malinowksi and Franz Boas shifted the focus to the functions of customs, beliefs, and institutions. In political science Charles Merriam pioneered behavioralism, a data-driven field focused on individuals rather than institutions.

A key, often-overlooked figure in Darwin's rising influence is Charles Peirce, a logician and lecturer at Johns Hopkins University, who was among the first to see the full implications of Darwin's work. Peirce recognized that Darwin's work challenged the very intellectual foundation of nineteenth-century Western culture. If, as Darwin proposed, knowledge was continually subject to observation and revision, then the concept of "knowledge" itself needed to be revised. "Certainty" needed to be ascribed a different meaning, as did the concepts of "cause" and "effect," which influenced so many fields, including the law. Facts had to be understood as guesses or predictions rather than conclusions. This was all supremely unsettling. Though Peirce underachieved in his academic career (Johns Hopkins dismissed him in 1884), he had substantial intellectual influence. Peirce studied at Harvard, and during his time there befriended Chauncey Wright, who would later found the Metaphysical Club.

206 Notably, William James began to test: James possessed one of the extraordinary minds in American history and was pervasively influential. He maintained close relationships with a who's-who of the intellectual elite, including his own godfather, Ralph Waldo Emerson, Bertrand Russell, Mark Twain, and John Dewey, who would make pragmatism a household word. During James's thirty-five-year career at Harvard, he transformed the field of psychology, which had theretofore been the domain of philosophers. James took it from the realm of speculation to experimentation. The new psychologists, as James and his colleagues were known, tested behavioral questions in the laboratory. They became committed to a functional view of human action, regarding behavior as an adaptation to environment. The new psychology was driven by evidence, attempted to apply scientific method to the study of social questions, and presumed the subjectivity of knowledge.

206 "Certitude leads to violence": Menand, *The Metaphysical Club*, p. 62.

207 Frank dismissed the myth of certainty: Kalman, *Legal Realism at Yale*, p. 8.

208 "General propositions do not decide concrete cases": *Lochner v. New York*, 198 U.S. 45, 76 (1905) (Holmes, dissenting).

208 Harvard Law School had a professor-student ratio of one to seventy-five: Kalman, *Legal Realism at Yale*, p. 12.

209 Realism was pervasively influential: Joseph Singer, "Legal Realism Now," *California Law Review* 76 (1988): 465, 467.

209 Many realists regarded this position as internally contradictory: Feldman, *Scorpions*, p. 63.

210 "His classes were intense and consuming experiences": Hutchinson, *The Man Who Once Was Whizzer White*, p. 154.

210 "asking the hardest questions": Jeffery Rosen, "The Next Justice," *The New Republic*, April 12, 1993, p. 24.

210 "He was a very realistic fellow": ibid.

210 "Being non-ideological and non-doctrinaire was clearly very important to White": Hutchinson, *The Man Who Once Was Whizzer White*, p. 457.

210 "the elusive originality": ibid., p. 7.

210 "White grew up thinking": ibid., p. 365.

211 "You write very well": ibid., p. 363.

211 *Pennsylvania v. Union Gas Co.*: 491 U.S. 1 (1989).

211 "I deem this application": *Robinson v. California*, 370 V.S. 660, 689 (1962).

212 "I wasn't exactly in his inner circle": ibid., p. 341.

212 "the only illegitimate decision the Court rendered": ibid., p. 368.

213 "disappointed President Kennedy": ibid., p. 541.

213 op-ed in the *New York Times*: Robert M. Cover, "Your Low-Baseball Quiz," *New York Times*, April 5, 1979, p. A23.

213 "had the arduous sincerity of a fellow out of his depth": Jeffrey Rosen, "The Next Justice: How Not to Replace Byron White," *New Republic*, April 12, 1993, p. 24.

213 "uninterested in articulating a constitutional vision": ibid.

213 "What made White hard to classify": Mary Ann Glendon, "Partial Justice,"

Commentary, August, 1994, p. 22. Other defenders included UCLA's Monroe Price, who said White's work demonstrated his belief that "judges should not be pre-programmed and easily predictable" (Monroe Price, "White: A Justice of Studied Unpredictability," *National Law Journal*, February 18, 1980, p. 24), and Lance Liebman, a White clerk who later became dean of Columbia Law School. Liebman wrote an essay about White in the *New York Times Magazine*, framed around twin questions. "Is he on the fence between opposing ideologies? Or is he walking a path of his own that intersects now with one group, now with another?" Liebman argued the latter, but found it difficult to define White's personal path in understandable language. (Lance Liebman, "Swing Man on the Supreme Court," *New York Times Magazine*, October 8, 1972, p. 16.)

214 "eerie": Hutchinson, *The Man Who Once Was Whizzer White*, p. 214.

214 "Say, aren't you": ibid., p. 1.

214 White influenced no one and was influenced by no one: Spaeth and Altfeld, "Influence Relationships Within the Supreme Court," Burger Courts," p. 78.

214 "I never agonized over a case in my life": Hutchinson, *The Man Who Once Was Whizzer White*, p. 349.

215 "You respect the rights of man": Menand, *The Metaphysical Club*, p. 63.

Chapter 10: LIGHTNING BOLTS

218 "When he came back": Benjamin Heineman interview (October 23, 2009).

219 "The opinions of other Justices": PS, Box 428.

221 "Is the bolt of lightning image": Benjamin Heineman to Potter Stewart, undated, PS.

222 not nearly as carefully written: Woodward and Armstrong, *The Brethren*, p. 218.

222 "In joining the Courts judgment": *Furman v. Georgia*, 408 U.S. at 310 (White, J., concurring).

222 drop the words "at all": Woodward and Armstrong, *The Brethren*, p. 218.

223 "little more than good advice": *Furman v. Georgia*, 408 U.S. at 269 (Brennan, J., concurring).

223 "real surprise": 1971 Term History, pp. 147–48.

223 "Potter had to pay a price": ibid.

224 "Oh, now, PS": David Von Drehle, "Death Penalty Divide Frustrated Blackmun: Papers on Lockett Case Show How He Came to See Split Between Fairness, Consistency," *Washington Post*, March 15, 2004, p. A04.

224 Powell sent join memos to Blackmun, Burger, and Rehnquist: PS, Box 428.

224 "The Court's judgments today": *Furman v. Georgia* 408 U.S. at 465 (Rehnquist, J., concurring).

225 "superb": Lewis F. Powell to Harry A. Blackmun, June 6, 1972, PS, Box 428.

225 "As you know, I have the greatest admiration": Lewis F. Powell to Harry A. Blackmun, June 17, 1972, PS, Box 428.

227 "We expressly declined": *Furman v. Georgia*, 408 U.S. at 310 (Stewart, J., concurring).

227 overruled *McGautha* without saying so: Woodward and Armstrong, *The Brethren*, p. 218.

228 a missive would be coming: 1971 Term History, WB, pp. 147–50.

228 "I should think that if the Eighth Amendment": *Furman v. Georgia*, 408 U.S. at 249 (Douglas, J., concurring)

229 "I had hoped it was all behind us": 1971 Term History, WB, p. 151.

230 "I have lost the Court": Hammond interview (November 9, 2009).

233 "We kept pinching ourselves": 1971 Term History, WB, p.160.

Chapter 11: A RED-LETTER DAY

234 "educated guessers" expected the Court to uphold capital punishment: *Time*, "The Death Penalty: Cruel and Unusual," January 24, 1972, pp. 54–55.

234 "based more on wishful thinking than any real expectation": "Bad News for the 648 on Death Row," *New York Times*, May 9, 1971, p. E8.

234 "The Supreme Court as it stands": Anthony Lewis, "A Legal Nightmare," *New York Times*, March 22, 1971, p. 33.

234 one of the biggest surprises in Supreme Court history: "Mixed Reviews," *New Republic*, July 15, 1971, p. 7.

234 "mounting zeal for abolition": Donald Zoll, "A Wistful Goodbye to Capital Punishment," *National Review*, December 3, 1971, p. 1351.

237 "*Furman* was decided on a basis and in a manner no one could have predicted": Michael Meltsner, *The Making of a Civil Rights Lawyer*, p. 215.

237 the justices had vacated the sentences in each of the 120 capital cases pending before the Supreme Court: *Stewart v. Massachusetts*, 408 U.S. 845, 932–41 (1972). The Court ordered the judgment in each case "vacated insofar as it leaves undisturbed the death penalty imposed, and the case is remanded for further proceedings." See also *Moore v. Illinois*, 408 U.S. 786 (1972).

237 This meant that almost everyone on death row in the United States would be entitled to be resentenced: The exceptions were defendants who had been sentenced under a mandatory death penalty statute. They were not eligible for resentencing. The California Supreme Court had vacated several such sentences in *Anderson*. How many remained on death rows is unclear. The issue is discussed in Bedau, "Challenging the Death Penalty," in note 35 and the accompanying text.

237 "This place looks like we just landed a man on the moon!": Meltsner, *Cruel and Unusual*, p. 290.

238 "Right on, Mr. Justices": Haines, *Against Capital Punishment*, p. 23; Martin Waldron, "Ruling Cheered on Florida Death Row," *New York Times*, June 30, 1972, p. 14.

238 "I've been thinking about nothing but death for a long time": *Time*, "Closing Death Row," July 10, 1972, p. 45.

239 "We did it": Dershowitz, *The Best Defense*, p. 311.

239 "When you represent people under sentence of death": Labi, "A Man Against the

Machine," p. 14. On the fate of the *Furman* commutees, see James Marquart and Jon Sorensen, "A National Study of the Furman-Commuted Inmates: Assessing the Threat to Society From Capital Offenders," *Loyola of Los Angeles Law Review* 23 (November 1989): 5–28.

241 That evening LDF celebrated: The LDF party is also discussed in Jack Greenberg, *Crusaders in the Courts*, p. 451.

241 "suddenly become the unpredictable swing member of the Supreme Court": B. Drummond Ayres., Jr., "The Swing Justice," *New York Times*, June 30, 1972, p. 16.

242 "the death penalty in America was finished": Dickson, *The Supreme Court in Conference*, p. 619.

242 "There will never be another execution in the country": Epstein and Kobylka, *The Supreme Court and Legal Change*, p. 80; Woodward and Armstrong, *The Brethren*, p. 219.

242 a code word for discrimination: The influence of race on *Furman* is discussed in Banner, *The Death Penalty*, pp. 255–66. The quote appears on p. 265.

242 Douglas wrote to Thomas Leonardos: William Douglas to Thomas Leonardos, July 21, 1972, WOD.

242 "The decision is a turning point in American justice": *Miami Herald*, June 30, 1972, p. A6.

242 "There will no longer be any more capital punishment": *New York Times*, June 30, 1972, p. 14.

242 "extremely doubtful that the death penalty would be legislatively renewed": Arthur Goldberg, "The Death Penalty and the Supreme Court," *Arizona Law Review* 15 (1973): 355, 366–67.

243 "The battle resumes again tomorrow": Anthony Amsterdam to Michael Meltsner, June 30, 1972, MM 1.

Chapter 12: SOBERING UP

247 "The holding of the Court must not be taken": Epstein and Kobylka, *The Supreme Court and Legal Change*, p. 84.

247 "cold blooded, premeditated, planned murder": Meltsner, *Cruel and Unusual*, p. 291.

247 "A majority of this nation's high court": ibid., p. 290.

247 *Furman* proved that justices should run for office: ibid., p. 291.

248 "hesitated to pull": ibid.

248 "license for anarchy, rape and murder": ibid.

248 "old time" severity: ibid.

248 "Society is entitled to the protection": *Congressional Digest*, "Controversy over Capital Punishment," January 1973, p. 11.

248 Several congressman suggested: Meltsner, *Cruel and Unusual*, p. 291.

250 Wallace . . . thought the Supreme Court should rule the death penalty unconstitutional: Baxley interview (March 3, 2010).

251 "The trick is how to write a law the U.S. Supreme Court will approve": *Time*, "The Law: Death Rattles," November 20, 1972, p. 72.

251 By the end of 1972, Baxley's committee had drafted nineteen proposals: ibid.

251 the attorneys general voted thirty-two to one: *Newsweek*, "Rebirth of Death?" December 18, 1972, pp. 23–24.

251 "We determined that the alternative": ibid.

253 a whirlwind four-day special legislative session: Epstein and Kobylka, *The Supreme Court and Legal Change*, p. 85. The Florida experience is discussed extensively by Charles Ehrhardt and other members of the Askew Commission. See Charles Ehrhardt et al., "The Future of Capital Punishment in Florida: Analysis and Recommendations," *Journal of Criminal Law and Criminology* 64 (1973): 2; Charles Ehrhardt and L. H. Levinson, "Florida's Legislative Reponse to *Furman*: An Exercise in Futility," *Journal of Criminal Law and Criminology* 64 (1973): 10.

254 "The group had me seriously wondering whether winning *Furman* was a good thing": Anthony Amsterdam to Michael Meltsner, October 9, 1972, MM 1. Also discussed in Meltsner, *Cruel and Unusual*, p. 91.

255 "Proposition 17 represents a use of the amending process": Anthony G. Amsterdam, "The Death Penalty and a Free Society," *New York Times*, November 4, 1972, p. 33.

255 Proposition 17 passed with 67.5 percent of the vote: Goldberg, "The Death Penalty and the Supreme Court," p. 367.

255 "The people of California responded quickly and emphatically": *People v. Frierson*, 25 Cal. 3d 142, 189 (1978).

256 In the last Harris poll taken before *Furman*: For a summary of polling see http://www.pollingreport.com/crime.htm. This is reproduced in my textbook, *Capital Punishment: A Balanced Examination*, 2nd ed., p. xxix. The Harris poll was taken in June 1973.

256 "sharp increase in sentiment": Louis Harris, "Majority of Americans Now Favor Capital Punishment," press release, The Harris Survey, June 11, 1973.

256 "The Rebirth of Death": *Newsweek*, "Rebirth of Death," December 18, 1972, pp. 23–24.

256 "A coalition of fear and reaction": "The Tide of Reaction," *New York Times*, January 15, 1973, p. 28.

257 "would be a constitutional capital punishment statute": "Kleindienst Sees Move to Restore Death Penalties," *New York Times*, January 5, 1973, p. 65.

257 "The time has come for soft-headed judges": "Playing to the Fear of Crime," *New York Times*, March 13, 1973, p. 39.

257 "splendid way to reap political benefit": ibid.

257 "automatic imposition of the death penalty when it is warranted": John Herbers, "Nixon Crime Plan Sent to Congress: President Asks Harsh Steps Without Pity," *New York Times*, March 15, 1973, p. 1.

257 "valid and necessary social remedy": Epstein and Kobylka, *The Supreme Court and Legal Charge*, p. 84.

257 "some questions of its constitutionality": ibid., p. 87.

258 Mike O'Callaghan, who received an ovation: ibid., p. 89.

258 *State v. Waddell*: 194 S.E. 2d 19 (1973).

259 a history of RFK's Justice Department would make a great book: Meltsner interview (December 4, 2010). Victor Navasky confirms the story of the origin of *Kennedy Justice* in his memoir, *A Matter of Opinion*, p. 83.

260 "Until recently, most law schools assiduously cultivated their isolation": *Newsweek*, "Renaissance Lawyer," July 17, 1972, p. 81.

261 "lucid and absorbing": Welsh White, "Books: *Cruel and Unusual*," *Columbia Law Review* 74 (1974): 319, 323.

261 "rousing intellectual adventure story": *Time*, "The Death Killers," September 17, 1973, p. 94.

261 "explanations of court procedures and legal maneuvers set a new standard": Dan Moskowitz, "A Tug of War for the Nation's Soul," *Business Week*, September 15, 1973, pp. 29–30.

261 "It is a beautiful book, Michael": Anthony Amsterdam to Michael Meltsner, October 1, 1973, MM1.

261 "Capital punishment," Meltsner said, "had reached the humpty dumpty stage": Testimony of Michael Meltsner in Behalf of the New York Civil Liberties Union Before the New York Assembly Standing Committee on Codes, December 4, 1973, MM2.

261 "is inversely related to the number of legal killings": Michael Meltsner, "Cruel and Unusual Punishment," *New York Times*, October 11, 1974, p. 39.

261 "taken the edge off abolitionist sentiments": Anthony Amsterdam, "The Case Against the Death Penalty," *Juris Doctor*, November 1971, p. 4.

262 "It is unclear that the public wants executions": "The Law: Reconsidering the Death Penalty," *Time*, April 12, 1976, p. 61.

262 "overly sanguine": Goldberg, "The Death Penalty and the Supreme Court," p. 367. Jack Greenberg offers a similar assessment in Muller, "The Legal Defense Fund's Capital Punishment Campaign," p. 179.

262 Harris's result was his highest since he began polling: Louis Harris, "Increasing Support for Executions," press release, The Harris Survey, February 7, 1977. The press release also offers a useful summary of prior Harris polls.

262 the U.S. Senate approved President Nixon's death penalty bill: Warren Weaver, "Death Penalty Restoration Is Voted by Senate, 54–33," *New York Times*, March 14, 1974, p. 1.

Chapter 13: BEHIND THE BACKLASH

264 that theory is almost certainly incorrect: The theory does have a handful of supporters. See, e.g., Joseph H. Rankin, "Changing Attitudes Toward Capital Punishment," *Social Forces* 58, no. 1 (1979): 194, 207. Corinna Lain also discusses the issue in her seminal article, "*Furman* Fundamentals," pp. 49–50.

264 in a January 1973 poll: "51% in Survey Say That Crime Has Increased in the Last Year," *New York Times*, January 16, 1973, p. 6.

265 After a brief resurgence between 1985 and 1990, crime had been dropping steadily: UCR crime statistics are available, among other places, at: http://www.disastercenter.com/crime/uscrime.htm.

265 academics point to the *Furman* decision itself as the inciting force: Corinna Lain offers an excellent summary in "Furman Fundamentals" at pp. 50–53.

266 "Although other factors may have had an effect": Robert M. Bohm, "American Death Penalty Opinion: Past, Present and Future," in Acker, et al., *America's Experiment With Capital Punishment*, pp. 27–54.

266 "The Supreme Court's decision in *Furman* itself played a bigger role": Carol Steiker, "Capital Punishment and American Exceptionalism," *Oregon Law Review* 81 (2002): 97, 108.

266 "widely interpreted, as a retreat from *Brown*": Meltsner, *Making of a Civil Rights Lawyer*, p. 84.

267 "The burden on a school board": *Green v. County School Board of New Kent County*, 391 U.S. 430, 438 (1968).

267 A decade after *Brown*: Rosenberg, *The Hollow Hope*, p. 50.

267 index of segregation: Massey and Denton, *American Apartheid* p. 20. See also Nathan Glazer, "A Tale of Two Cities," *The New Republic*, August 2, 1993, p. 39.

268 Integration increased geometrically: Rosenberg, *The Hollow Hope*, p. 345.

269 two out of three black Americans said they felt closer to African blacks: Schulman, *The Seventies*, p. 58.

269 The link was antipathy for the Supreme Court: On the relationship between capital punishment opinion and other contemporary social issues, see Neil Vidmar and Phoebe Ellsworth, "Public Opinion and the Death Penalty," *Stanford Law Review* 26 (1973): p. 1245.

269 Protestors began to follow William Brennan: Stern and Wermiel, *Justice Brennan*, p. 376.

270 asked his daughters for their opinion: Greenhouse, *Becoming Justice Blackmun*, p. 83 (discussing Blackmun's deliberations generally).

270 the Hippocratic Oath didn't forbid them: The oath forbids giving a woman a pessary to produce an abortion. A pessary is a medical device inserted into the vagina or rectum and held in place by the musculature of the pelvic floor. A diaphragm is a pessary.

270 "I am preparing myself for sacrifice": Tinsley E. Yarbrough, *Harry A. Blackmun: The Outsider Justice*, p. 278.

270 "I understand the critical letters": Greenhouse, *Becoming Justice Blackmun*, p. 135.

270 "I have never before been so personally abused": ibid., p. 134.

271 "By constitutionalizing abortion": Jeffries, *Justice Lewis F. Powell*, P. 352.

271 Powell attempted to console Blackmun: Hammond interview (November 9, 2009).

272 "To know that the lady in Dayton": Richard M. Scammon and Ben J. Wattenberg, *The Real Majority*, p. 491.

273 "We've had enough social programs": Schulman, *The Seventies*, p. 41.

274 Charles Franklin and Liane Kosaski showed: Charles H. Franklin and Liane C. Kosaski, "Republican Schoolmaster: The U.S. Supreme Court, Public Opinion and Abortion," *American Political Science Review* 83 (1989): 751–71.

274 Professors Timothy Johnson and Andrew Martin found: Timothy R. Johnson and Andrew D. Martin, "The Public's Conditional Response to Supreme Court Decisions," *American Political Science Review* 92 (1998): 299–309. On this subject generally, see Valeria Hoekstra, *Public Reaction to Supreme Court Decisions*.

276 Professor Robert Burt of Yale highlights: Robert Burt, "Disorder in the Court," *Michigan Law Review* 85 (1987): 1741–1819.

276 "not so much a case as a badly orchestrated opera": Robert Weisberg, "Deregulating Death," p. 315.

276 Clarence Thomas . . . understood *Furman*: *Graham v. Collins*, 506 U.S. 461, 479–84 (1993). See generally, Meltsner, *The Making of a Civil Rights Lawyer*, p. 208.

276 Thurgood Marshall saw both *Furman* and *Roe*: Williams, *Thurgood Marshall*, p. 354.

277 "There's an odd lag": Zimring interview (April 18, 2010).

277 *Coker v. Georgia*: 433 U.S. 584 (1977). Eric Muller finds irony in the decision's failure to mention race. Muller, "The Legal Defense Fund's Capital Punishment Campaign," p. 182.

277 "came to view the Fund's lawyers as abolitionist zealots": Anthony G. Amsterdam and Jerome Bruner, *Minding the Law*, p. 198.

278 "In a curious way, *Furman* has had the opposite effect": James Q. Wilson, "Is It Unusual? Is It Just? Or is it Only Cruel?" *New York Times*, October 28, 1973, p. 273.

278 "If resources comparable to those LDF invested": Neier, *Taking Liberties*, p. 198.

278 Eric Muller says LDF should first have created a political consensus: Muller, "The Legal Defense Fund's Capital Punishment Campaign," p. 177. Michael Meltsner replies in *The Making of a Civil Rights Lawyer*, pp. 194–97.

279 ". . . we would not, of course, have let them die without a judicial appeal": Meltsner, *The Making of a Civil Rights Lawyer*, p. 196.

279 "I never asked that question": Amsterdam interview (January 20, 2010).

279 As late as the early '70s, the ACLU still wasn't doing very much: Epstein and Kobylka, *The Supreme Court and Legal Change*, p. 90; Neier, *Taking Liberties*, p. 206.

279 "well-dressed churchgoing blacks": Haines, *Against Capital Punishment*, p. 30.

279 "LDF did not worry about the backlash": Epstein and Kobylka, *The Supreme Court and Legal Change*, p. 90.

279 "We were surprised at the explosion": ibid.

279 "No one expected the legislative response to the decision": ibid., p. 91; Paul Reidinger, "A Court Divided," *ABA Journal*, January, 1987, p. 50.

Chapter 14: PROVING DETERRENCE AND RATIONALITY

282 Though Marshall acknowledged several flaws in Sellin's research: Most statistics grouped all homicides together, conflating capital and noncapital killings. Furthermore, many homicides evaded detection, and police sometimes misinterpreted murders as accidental deaths or suicides. See *Furman v. Georgia*, 408 U.S., p. 349–50 (Marshall, J., concurring).

282   "We would shirk": ibid., p. 353 (Marshall, J., concurring).

282   "many statistical studies": ibid. p. 308 (Stewart, J., concurring).

283   "What they are saying, in effect, is that the evolutionary process": ibid., p. 430
       (Powell, J. concurring).

283   "To shift the burden to the States": ibid. p. 396 (Burger, J., concurring).

284   "The statistics prove little, if anything": ibid. p. 455 (Blackmun, J., concurring).

284   "tend to support the view": ibid., p. 454 (Powell, J., concurring).

284   "made clear the interests of lawyers": Hugo A. Bedau, Report to the SAGE Foun-
       dation, MM1, October 1, 1973.

285   The more specifically researchers questioned: Vidmar and Ellsworth, "Public
       Opinion and the Death Penalty," pp. 1245–70.

285   Amsterdam asked Bedau to solicit research on journalistic coverage: Anthony
       Amsterdam to Hugo Bedau et al., MM1, April 12, 1973.

285   Bedau sought funds: LDF's research projects are summarized at Epstein and
       Kobylka, *The Supreme Court and Legal Change*, pp. 92–93.

285   LDF deliberated internally whether to discourage White: Peggy Davis to David
       Kendall and Jack Himmelstein, PD, January 3, 1974.

285   "murderers would swarm across the Delaware and Hudson Rivers": Resolution on
       the Retirement of Professor Hugo Bedau. Available at ase.tufts.edu/faculty/pdfs/
       retiredfaculty/bedau.pdf

286   "Perhaps the first thing a jurist will wish to know": Daniel Patrick Moynihan,
       "Social Science and the Courts," *Public Interest* 54 (1979): 12–31.

288   "A useful theory of criminal behavior": Gary S. Becker, "Crime and Punishment: An
       Economic Approach" in *Essays in the Economics of Crime and Punishment*, ed. Gary
       S. Becker and William M. Landes (New York: Columbia University Press, 1974).

290   one of the attorneys saw a television interview: Epstein and Kobylka, *The Supreme
       Court and Legal Change*, p. 97, n. 14.

290   Ehrlich's work . . . appeared in the *American Economic Review*: Isaac Ehrlich, "The
       Deterrent Effect of Capital Punishment: A Question of Life or Death," *American
       Economics Review* 65 (1975): 397–417.

290   Bork saw no reason to wait for the validation of peer review: Epstein and Kobylka,
       The Supreme Court and Legal Change, p. 97.

292   "You and I ask ourselves": Anthony Amsterdam, "Do We Really Need to Kill
       People to Teach People that Killing People is Wrong?" *Vital Speeches* 43 (1977):
       677–682.

293   "If you're Tony Amsterdam": Zimring interview (April 28, 2010). Though Zim-
       ring hosted the meeting and recognized the significance of the research, he didn't
       personally undertake any research projects as his personal position on capital pun-
       ishment didn't turn on whether it deterred. Forst resisted too. "I didn't want to be
       an ambulance chaser," he said in 2010. "I didn't want to make my career disprov-
       ing someone."

294   "Many questions are best studied by simpler methods": David C. Baldus and
       James W. Cole, "A Comparison of the Work of Thorsten Sellin and Issac Ehrlich
       or the Deterrent Effect of Capital Punishment," *Yale Law Journal* 85 (1975): 173.

297   "all empirical support for the deterrent effect": William J. Bowers and Glenn L.

Pierce, "The Illusion of Deterrence in Isaac Ehrlich's Research on Capital Punishment," *Yale Law Journal* 85 (1975): 1996.

297 He went on to attack Bowers and Pierce as hypocritical: Specifically, Ehrlich attacked their criticism of his logarithmic transformation. Bowers and Pierce conceded that their regression results deteriorated when natural numbers were used. In Ehrlich's view they absurdly concluded from this that the death penalty didn't deter rather than that the logarithmic form was superior. Ehrlich also pointed out that eliminating the '60s data, as they urged, would have diminished his sample size and hence the reliability of the regression analysis. Isaac Ehrlich, "Deterrence, Evidence and Inference," *Yale Law Journal* 85 (1975): 209–27.

297 eviscerated Baldus and Cole: Baldus and Cole had faulted Ehrlich for not holding constant certain variables in one of his analyses. Ehrlich said these variables were exogenous and couldn't be held constant for his analysis to have meaning. In his view, the error suggested that Baldus, a law professor, and Cole didn't know what they were talking about. "This error by Baldus and Cole betrays quite a fundamental misunderstanding of the methodology which they have undertaken to evaluate," Ehrlich wrote. Ibid., p. 221.

297 Regarding Sellin, Ehrlich said his reliance: In Ehrlich's view the particular problem with relying on legal status was that in many of the retentionist states, "the execution risk was negligible throughout the entire period." It was thus unsurprising that Sellin's matching comparisons showed little variation regarding homicide risk. Therefore Sellin had no basis to justify his inference that the death penalty didn't influence homicide rates. Bowers had repeated this error in an attempt to corroborate Sellin's results. He chose nine groups of putatively similar states, noting similar patterns of crime. "However, the plain fact is that *none* of the states in eight of the nine groups had a single execution throughout the period," Ehrlich wrote. Ibid., p. 223.

298 He also sympathized with Ehrlich's inclusion of the 1960s data: Bowers and Pierce had tested Ehrlich's model over different periods, finding no evidence of deterrence. Peck deemed this fair. But he said that Bowers and Pierce had ignored the more obvious conclusion that the effect of the death penalty changed during the '60s. Indeed, Peter Passell and John Taylor had found evidence of such a change in a discussion paper circulated at the Columbia University economics department. (Though, overall, Passell and Taylor found little evidence of deterrence.) Regarding the use of national data, Peck called it routine and said nothing in Ehrlich's analysis "precluded an application of his model to more disaggregated data." If Baldus, and Cole wanted to test Ehrlich's model on state-level data, let them have at it, Peck said in effect. Regarding the alleged flaws in the data, the FBI's procedure for retrospectively readjusting data resembled the Census Bureau's practice, so this choice seemed immaterial. Jon K. Peck, "The Deterrent Effect of Capital Punishment: Erlich and His Critics," *Yale Law Journal* 85 (1976): 359–67.

298 Matching, on the other hand, imposed "relatively little structure": Matching also couldn't avoid a spillover problem. If state A had the death penalty but B didn't, potential murderers might migrate to state B. This would create the false appearance of deterrence. Ibid., p. 363–64.

299 "a who's who of American econometricians": These included MIT's Franklin Fisher, University of North Carolina professor Gary Koch, and Duke's Daniel Nagin. The panel also included James Q. Wilson, Marvin Wolfgang, Yale sociologist Albert Reiss, and psychologist Paul Meehl.

299 "the available studies provide no useful evidence on the deterrent effect": The NAS report included a review of the literature written by Forst, Victor Filatov, and Lawrence Klein, who would soon win the Nobel Prize in Economics. The trio criticized Ehrlich's work as "extraordinary insofar as it employs a vast array of manipulations." On the question of how much economics had to offer, they came down squarely on the side of the criminologists. Referring to Ehrlich's murder function, they said, "We have doubts about the insight that this approach is likely to bring to an understanding of criminal behavior." They found greater usefulness in the methodology of smoking-cancer link studies that weren't locked into a utility calculus, and that allowed for the exploration of other variables, emotional behavior, and social phenomena. "Students of econometrics ought to learn very early that significant economic conclusions can rarely be drawn from estimates of single equations."

299 "Ehrlich's findings are the product": Brian Forst, "Capital Punishment and Deterrence: Conflicting Evidence," *Journal of Criminal Law and Criminology* 74 (1983): 927, 939.

299 "There was no scandal": Zimring interview (April 28, 2010).

300 Even today, only the boldest of scholars would claim that the debate has been settled: In the academic community, all is as it was. Scholars in the field of criminal justice—which remains a hodgepodge of former policemen, corrections officers, lawyers, philosophers, and sociologists—almost uniformly believe that the death penalty doesn't deter. Over the past two decades, more than a dozen studies have been published in the leading criminal justice journals finding no deterrent effect of the death penalty. Nothing published in these journals has found any evidence of deterrence. In a 2008 survey, 88 percent of past presidents of criminological associations said they didn't believe the death penalty prevents murder. Criminal justice types continue to have little respect for the potential contribution of economists. They largely believe, as Tony Amsterdam did, that potential murderers aren't rational actors.

Among economists, however, ample support exists for the deterrence hypothesis. Many studies published in economics journals have found evidence that capital punishment prevents murder. Emory's Joanna Shepherd has been a central figure in the modern debate. In 2004 she told the House Judiciary Committee, which was considering a bill to extend the federal death penalty to terrorist acts, "In the economics literature, there is a very strong consensus. All of the modern economic studies in the past decade have found a deterrent effect." Her colleague Paul Rubin told the Senate Judiciary Committee in 2006, "All the refereed studies find a deterrent effect."

The economists regard the criminologists with reciprocal disdain, viewing them as unstructured, undisciplined, and lacking insight into criminal behavior. In 1996 Princeton's John DiLulio wrote that professional criminologists "generally lack the quantitative and formal modeling skills necessary to shed new light on old controversies or provide analytically compelling answers to methodologically complicated questions." Often the two camps act as if the other doesn't exist. Shepherd said, "Each group tends to ignore the other's research."

Many of the actors in this long-running play remain the same. Even the setting hasn't changed. The University of Chicago remains at the drama's center. In a 2006 exchange Gary Becker and his intellectual sparring partner, Richard Posner, signed on with George W. Bush and Al Gore in the deterrence debate. In the *Stanford Law Review*, the well-known University of Chicago law professor (and future Obama administration official) Cass Sunstein, and his colleague Adrian Vermeule, argued that the death penalty is morally required because of research proving deterrence.

The study of deterrence continues to vex researchers. Yale Law School's John Donohue is an intriguing and outspoken figure in the modern debate. Donohue is highly critical of the putative evidence of deterrence. It would be merely convenient, though, to group Donohue with the criminal-justice scholars. Rather, Donohue offers a cautionary note about the limited usefulness of any grouping of intellectuals, and especially the division I have drawn between criminologists and economists. Sunstein is but one example of a lawyer who credits the deterrence evidence. Donohue is an economist who doesn't. Though a law professor, Donohue holds a Ph.D. in economics from Yale. Much of his work might be classified as conservative. In 2000, Donohue and Steven Levitt published a highly controversial paper in which they argued that half of the 1990's crime drop was attributable to the Court's protection of abortion rights in *Roe*. Nevertheless, Donohue believes deterrence hasn't been proved and isn't likely to be.

Donohue uses New York's experiment with capital punishment to illustrate the problems of modeling deterrence. During the 1994 gubernatorial campaign, George Pataki ran on a pro–death penalty platform. His opponent, the three-term incumbent Mario Cuomo, had vetoed several bills aimed at reinstating capital punishment in New York. Pataki prevailed in the election, and in 1995 signed the death penalty into law. Nine years later the state's highest court declared the statute invalid under the state constitution. Between 1995 and 2004, New York juries sentenced several murderers to death, but none were executed.

Donohue asks whether deterrence studies should include New York in the control group (because no one was executed) or the experimental group (because the death penalty was on the books). Given New York's population, and that most studies weigh results by population, this threshold decision of how to classify New York is of enormous importance. The results of one study finding deterrence, by LSU's Naci Mocan and Kaj Gittings, depend entirely on whether New York is included among the sample. The model is highly sensitive, Donohue says, in the same way that Ehrlich's depended on whether one included the 1960s data. The important lesson is that Mocan and Gittings's decision to include New York was a judgment call.

Donohue next asks what potential criminals know about the death penalty. Economic models presume knowledge, but a criminal in New York would need to be highly sophisticated. Some of the district attorneys, including Robert Morgenthau of Manhattan and Robert Johnson of the Bronx, had sworn never to seek the death penalty. Complicating matters further, crime dropped more in these boroughs between 1995 and 2004 than in Brooklyn, where the DA actively sought death sentences. Would a potential offender in Manhattan or the Bronx respond to the incentives of living in a death penalty state or a non–death penalty state?

Furthermore, this is all premised on the highly debatable notion that offenders are rational. Ample research suggests that, as a group, offenders seek risk. They are more impulsive than non-offenders. Their decision making is often impaired by drug and alcohol abuse. They tend to ignore future considerations. North Carolina professor Charles Dean argues that the persistence of an orientation to the present, which most adults grow out of, explains long criminal careers. This, of course, is what Tony Amsterdam said forty years ago.

Donohue and Columbia's Jeffrey Fagan, among others, catalog a long list of thorny methodological questions. Executions happen long after murders, so how could current-year execution risk bear on current-year murder rates? Are the data reliable? Four decades later problems with the UCR haven't been resolved. States are inconsistent reporting crime to the FBI. In 1997 only 73 percent of Americans lived in jurisdictions reporting arrest records. Florida failed to report any homicides to the FBI in 1998, for only five months in 1989, and for no more than two months per year in 1997, 1998, and 1999. Yet, as Fagan points out, Florida is one of the most active death penalty states, so the omission of its data is highly material.

Finally, and most vexingly, has the murder function been properly stated? Consider Texas for a moment. The Lone Star State experienced a substantial drop in murder during the 1990s and 2000s. Some have attributed this to Texas's increased use of executions. But Texas also substantially increased incarcerations, which has also been known to reduce crime. Generally speaking, high crime rates are associated with more police, more aggressive policing, tougher gun laws, longer sentences, three-strikes laws, severe prison conditions, and harsh treatment of releasees. All these policy responses have been shown to affect murder rates. But no published murder equation comes near considering them all. When a state implements multiple crime-control measures, how can a researcher know which are generating the benefit?

More problematic, what if some measures have offsetting responses? Suppose that to combat rising crime, a state hires more police and begins executing more prisoners. The policing works but, unknown to the state, the executions incite citizens to violence, partially offsetting the benefit of the policing initiative. Not seeing the sort of results it had hoped for, the state hires even more police and executes even more prisoners. As it turns out, the policing program has increasing marginal utility, and executions have decreasing marginal utility. In other words, the new police hires stop more crime than the executions encourage. At the end of the program, the state would achieve a reduction in crime for its efforts. It might further conclude that the death penalty had caused this reduction in crime. Of course in some sense it *was* the cause of the reduction in crime. The increased use of the death penalty caused the state to hire more police officers, which in turn led to a reduction in crime. But it only brought about the crime decrease indirectly and serendipitously.

Furthermore, none of this considers the entirely plausible notion that something entirely different is driving the system. Republicans often fare better in elections following crime waves. In the example above, it's easy enough to imagine the election of a Republican as the cause of both hiring more police and increased use of the death penalty. But what if criminals are responding to the election of the Republican governor rather than the policy changes? Research suggests this is possible. Would we say then that increased policing or the election caused the crime drop? Even this doesn't resolve the causal knot. What if the governor's election was due to a set of social and economic forces that themselves affected the crime rate. How do we identify the chicken and egg then?

Disentangling causation is tricky business to say the least. In the context of the death penalty, many scholars feel these problems of what statisticians call "endogeneity" cannot be overcome. This is precisely what the NAS faulted Ehrlich for in its 1976 report. Ehrlich's results were driven by the simple facts that during the 1960s, the rate of executions and crime went up. But correlation doesn't prove causation. What if some other factor caused both the execution rate and the murder rate to decrease? Lawrence Klein and his colleagues said critically, "Ehrlich assumes that economic factors affect criminal behavior, but that criminal factors do not affect economic behavior through the economic variables that he has selected." In other words, Ehrlich didn't know his chicken from his egg.

Yet this isn't the last word on this matter. Statisticians are daunted but not paralyzed by endogeneity problems. The ideal way to deal with complex causal issues is to run a real social experiment rather than attempting to draw inferences from data. Generally speaking, running such experiments isn't ethically possible. In a 1976 article Hans Zeisel offered an entertaining example of what such an experiment might look like. A state could decree that citizens convicted of a capital crime and born on an odd-number day would be subject to the death penalty, while criminals born on even-numbered days would merely face life in prison. If persons born on uneven days committed fewer crimes, this would prove deterrence. Aside from the obvious ethical problems with randomly meting put punishment, Zeisel speculated that forward-thinking mothers might demand cesarean deliveries on even-numbered days.

A statistical method called instrumental analysis offers a possible solution. Some controversy surrounds the technique's origin. It's often attributed to Philip G. Wright, a mathematics professor, who outlined the idea in Appendix B of his breezy 1928 volume, *The Tariff on Animal and Vegetable Oils*. Others believe the credit is due to Wright's son, Sewall, an influential genetic statistician, who used instrumental analysis to analyze corn and hog cycles, which are causally tangled.

Here's the idea: Consider for a moment an illustration outside the world of crime and punishment. Imagine that an epidemiologist wants to determine the effect of drinking on mortality rates. The scientist could examine national data and would likely find that as alcohol consumption increases, so too do death rates. It would be a mistake, though, to attribute the higher mortality to increased alcohol consumption. This confuses correlation with causation. One could easily imagine that another factor—for instance, depression—is leading people both to drink and die. The challenge for the researcher is to figure out whether it's drinking or depression or something else that's driving the system.

The solution is to use an "instrument," a variable that is related to the independent variable, but not the dependent variable. In the above example the researcher might examine the impact of alcohol taxes on mortality. Alcohol taxes are useful to study because they predict alcohol consumption—taxes go up, consumption goes down—but aren't related to depression. If decreasing alcohol taxes caused death rates to increase, the rise in mortality could be casually linked to drinking.

In the 1970s, when Ehrlich conducted his pioneering research, instrumental variable analysis hadn't yet become popular. Researchers didn't immediately recognize its value. Even Philip and Sewall Wright failed to appreciate fully the usefulness of their creation for addressing causation questions. Beginning in the '90s, economists more frequently employed instruments to address endogeneity problems. In 1994 a team of researchers at Emory including Shepherd, Rubin, and Hashem Dezhbakhsh used instrumental variable analysis to address the alleged deficiencies of Ehrlich's work. The Emory team found that each execution saves, on average, eighteen lives. Over the next several years several other teams replicated their work or independently used instrumental variable analysis and found a deterrent effect to capital punishment. So the question has been answered, right?

Not so fast. Instrumental variable analysis doesn't end the causation debate; it only shifts its terms. Today the debate over deterrence research is whether the studies finding deterrence have relied upon proper instruments. "Proper" means a variable that's truly external to the system. But whether a variable is truly external is largely a matter of judgment. For example, in the earlier example, the researcher used alcohol taxes as the instrument on the theory that alcohol taxes directly affect alcohol consumption but aren't affected by the exogenous variable, depression. Who's to say, though, that depression isn't part of the system? Perhaps depression makes legislators more tolerant of taxes. Perhaps taxes cause depression. That's easy enough to imagine. If so, then the researcher doesn't have an instrument, she has a new endogeneity problem. This is the focus of the modern deterrence debate.

Consider two examples of how the Emory team responded to the critiques of Ehrlich. The NAS panel, among others, said that Ehrlich's murder function suffered from endogeneity problems. For instance, the likelihood of receiving a death sentence and the murder rate might be interrelated. One might affect the other, or they might each share a common external cause. To address this the Emory team used a proxy for the likelihood of receiving a death sentence once arrested: the Republican candidate's vote tally in the preceding election. Even if jury-sentencing rates and murder rates shared a common cause, they reasoned, this common cause wouldn't affect voting behavior. In other words, election results would be a valid instrument. John Donohue says the opposite. He points to a wealth of research suggesting that Republicans do better in elections following crime increases. Thus, he says, it's easy to imagine that voting patterns might be part of the same causal chain as crime rates and jury behavior.

A second example: The Emory team used statewide expenditures on the judicial and legal system as a proxy for the likelihood of execution given a death sentence. The idea, again, is that these expenditures aren't part of the causal chain. But Duke's Philip Cook, among others, has shown that states with lots of executions spend more on appellate appeals, which means that the likelihood of getting the death penalty is affecting the putatively exogenous variable. To illustrate this point—and to underscore how expensive the death penalty can be—New York spent $170 million on its death penalty system between 1995 and 2004, and yet executed no one.

To critics these problems are fatal. Donohue writes, "Bad instruments cannot resolve an endogeneity problem. If valid instruments cannot be found, researches must assess how acute the endogeneity issue is. If debilitating, then the researcher must conclude that valid estimation of the impact of capital punishment is not possible." Fagan agrees. "The central mistake in this enterprise is one of causal reasoning: the attempt to draw causal inferences from a flawed and limited set of observation data, and the failure to address important competing influences on murder." The debate over causation goes on. Luke must surely have said something like this in mind when he said, "Woe unto you, lawyers."

Finally it would be remiss not to note the apparent tendency of researchers to find what they want to find. Daniel Moynihan observed this effect in his *Public Interest* article, which is worth reading simply for its elegance. "Social scientists," Moynihan wrote, "are never more revealing of themselves than when challenging the objectivity of one another's work." Hans Zeisel dismissed the *Gregg* Court's conclusions as merely an effort to "bolster with reasons the unwillingness to abandon the ancient sentiment" in favor of retribution. But Zeisel and the LDF lawyers were happy enough with the Massachusetts Supreme Court's 1975 ruling in *O'Neal*, which rejected the same evidence of deterrence that *Gregg* credited. It's challenging to find any basis other than wish fulfillment to discredit the U.S. Supreme Court's decision as lacking objectivity, and yet credit the Massachusetts Supreme Court on the same score.

Whatever tiny hope exists of synthesizing this disparate body of research may rest with Joanna Shepherd of the aforementioned Emory team. In 2007 Shepherd reexamined the data that she and her colleagues had relied upon. This time, though, instead of looking at national execution risks, Shepherd looked at state-specific estimates. What she found didn't contradict her earlier findings. However, it fundamentally alters the picture those earlier findings drew. Shepherd found that deterrence exists on a national level, but that deterrence is driven by a deterrence effect in just six states. In eight states Shepherd found that executions had no impact on the murder rate. In thirteen others, they caused the murder rate to *increase*. The 2004 study's reliance on national data had masked this state-by-state variation.

How could it be that the death penalty deterred in some states but not others? The key to the answer is that the states where Shepherd observed a deterrence effect executed many more people than the states where she found either no deter-rence or anti-deterrence. Shepherd found that a threshold level of executions—at least nine during the period she studied, 1977–96—was necessary to generate a deterrent effect. One policy implication of this research is that if states want to achieve deterrence, they need to execute many people. Shepherd writes, "If a state is unwilling to establish a large execution program, it should consider abandoning capital punishment." Her work, though, says something broader about the nature of criminal behavior, and the possible damage that can be done by misapplied and misunderstood statistics.

A final example: A scientist is asked, "How quickly is that block on the table moving?" The scientist replies, "Zero miles per hour." The uninitiated observer is left with the impression of an object at rest. But this isn't the case. In fact, two men are pushing against the block in opposite directions, each with equal might. Since they are equivalently strong, the block doesn't move. The statistic—zero miles per hour—is accurate, but it doesn't give a descriptive picture of the block, which isn't at rest in the conventional sense.

If Shepherd is right, a similarly complex set of forces is at work regarding deter-rence. Statistics may help identify classes of offenders or regions where deterrence works in the aggregate. But the statements "He has been deterred" or "He was not deterred" are as misleading as the statement "The block is moving zero miles per hour." The threat of the death penalty is but one of countless social forces that impel or deter a potential offender toward or away from crime. Even the death penalty itself isn't a simple force. It may both deter a potential offender and incite him to crime. These aren't mutually exclusive possibilities. Potential criminals, like all human beings, aren't always rational or irrational. The threat of execution may deter some potential offenders, calmly calculating the costs and benefits of a contemplated crime, in the manner Gary Becker envisioned in 1968. To other potential offenders—or the same individuals in different states of agitation—the fact of executions may send a message that violence is a socially acceptable means to resolve disputes. Indeed, many studies have found support for the "brutaliza-tion" hypothesis in short-term murder-rate spikes following executions.

Shepherd's research suggests that executions do brutalize society. In fact, she says, the anti-deterrence or brutalization in non-deterrence states is substantial. In the non-deterrence states, Shepherd found that executions lead to an additional 250 murders per year. Her intuition is that executions contribute to an environ-ment of violence. The death penalty, she said, "sets an example of killing to avenge grievances, an example that some private individuals then follow."

At the same time executions deter. But with low executions rates—as in states such as California, Oregon, and Utah—the deterrence effect is small. Thus these states appear to have encouraged killing through their use of the death penalty. It is only in states such as Florida, Texas, and South Carolina, which execute many people, that "potential criminals become convinced the state is serious about the punishment" and reduce their criminal activity. When the number of executions exceeds the threshold minimum, the deterrence effect becomes powerful and out-weighs the brutalization effect. Only then does the death penalty appear to have worked. Shepherd points out that murderers executed in states that fell below the execution threshold died needlessly and induced the murder of five thousand innocent people between 1977 and 1996.

In reaching her conclusions, Shepherd incidentally came down on the same side as Baldus and Cole on the question of whether national or state level data should be used in studying deterrence. In their 1975 critique Baldus and Cole faulted Ehrlich for presuming that an execution anywhere would have an equal deterrent effect across the United States, even in states that didn't have the death penalty. Shepherd similarly argues that earlier papers' focus on national averages masked important "variation among states." It isn't that the other economics papers were wrong. They were just nondescriptive in the same way that the statement "The block is not moving" is misleading. The earlier papers blended together the large number of executions in the deterrence states with the small number of executions in the other states. It thus appeared that executions deterred crime. But this masked what was really going on—deterrence in some states, none or anti-deterrence in the others. The appearance of deterrence on a national level was driven "by a handful of high-execution, high-deterrence states," as Shepherd puts it. "In most places," she says, "capital punishment either increases murder or has no effect."

Shepherd's findings help bridge the divide between the economists who keep finding deterrence and the criminologists and sociologists who persistently don't. It could be that the results depend largely—or even entirely—on the level of aggregation of the data. To test this hypothesis Shepherd reexamined the leading studies of the past decade. Sure enough, she found that economists tended to use national data while sociologists and criminologists focused on individual states. If these researchers picked a no-deterrence state, of which there are many according to Shepherd's analysis, then, needless to say, they found no evidence of deterrence. At a personal level Shepherd said in an interview that she has no strong view about the death penalty. "For me all it ever was was that people respond to incentives—surprise, surprise. There's a big difference between finding deterrence and supporting a policy."

Richard Berk, professor of criminology and statistics at University of Pennsylvania, and one of the few figures who is highly respected in both the economics and criminology universes, suggests that the entire morass can be explained simply by whether an individual study includes Texas in its data set. If it does, the researcher will find deterrence. If it doesn't, no deterrence will be found. Since 1976 approximately eleven hundred executions have been conducted in the United States. More than one-third have been in Texas. Texas has such a large deterrent effect, and large population, that its results drive any study in which it's included.

In the end one might conclusively say this: the death penalty deters, but only some people—specifically those not deterred by the risk of life imprisonment without the possibility of parole—and only in some places and at some times and under some conditions, but we don't know where and when and what conditions, and where the effect exists it's almost certainly quite small, and almost certainly not larger or more cost effective than other penal options.

Of course this all may be answering the wrong question. Even if it were possible to determine conclusively whether the death penalty deters, this would hardly end the public-policy debate. Utilitarians would need to evaluate the cost and efficacy of the death penalty against other penal and nonpenal options. And, of course, not everyone is a utilitarian. As Franklin Zimring, author of more than thirty books and one hundred articles on criminal justice issues colorfully put it, "I don't give a shit whether the death penalty deters." This core belief isn't something that even the most sophisticated and convincing social science can alter.

301   "Common sense . . . lately bolstered by statistics": Ernest van den Haag, "For the Death Penalty," *New York Times*, p. A21.

302   "The President certainly is reflecting the concerns of a great many Californians": "McGovern Differs With Nixon's Plan for Death Penalty," *New York Times*, March 12, 1973, p. 25.

302   "I think the reason to support the death penalty is because it saves people's lives": Election 2000 Presidential Debate with Republican Candidate Governor George W. Bush and Democratic Candidate Vice President Al Gore (Oct. 17, 2000). Transcript available at http://www.debates.org.

303   "We may assume safely": *Gregg v. Georgia*, 428 U.S. 153, 185 (1976).

305   The ALI said the United States needed a model criminal code: Paul H. Robinson and Markus Dubber, "The American Model Penal Code: A Brief Overview," *New Criminal Law Review*, Volume 10, No. 3 (Summer 2007): 319–41.

306   Herbert Wechsler . . . opposed the death penalty as a matter of principle: Wechsler told this to Michael Meltsner, among others. Meltsner interview (December 4, 2010).

307   Wechsler entered City College at sixteen: On Wechsler's childhood, see Tamar Lewin, "Herbert Wechsler, Legal Giant, Is Dead at 90," *New York Times*, April 28, 2000, p. C21.

307   "the general community whose values have been disturbed": Herbert Wechsler, "Sentencing, Correction, and the Model Penal Code," *University of Pennsylvania Law Review* 109 (1973): 465, 473.

307   "The desire for revenge": Anders Walker, "American Oresteia: Herbert Wechsler, the Model Penal Code, and the Uses of Revenge," 2009 *Wisconsin Law Review* (2009): 1017, 1018 citing Jerome Michael and Herbert Wechsler, *Criminal Law and Its Administration: Cases, Statutes and Commentaries* (New York: Foundation Press, 1940), p. 16.

308   Wechsler was a retributivist for utilitarian reasons: The leading scholar on Wechsler, Professor Anders Walker of St. Louis University Law School, points to three events that helped form Wechsler's outlook. The first took place during Wechsler's childhood in New York under Prohibition. The Volstead Act, the law defining prohibited liquors under the Eighteenth Amendment, granted a ration of ten gallons of sacramental wine per family. Jewish leaders protested the infringement of their religious freedom. When the city's anti-Semitic Bureau of Prohibition refused to issue wine licenses, Wechsler's family defied the law, as Wechsler put it, "with abandon." Wechsler took from this that laws lacking popular support had no effect.

Wechsler found further support for this view during his clerkship, when the Supreme Court heard the appeal of the Scottsboro Boys. Again Wechsler saw the risk of the public taking the law into its own hands. The stakes didn't seem high when it came to families drinking sacramental wine, but the Scottsboro Boys had to be protected from multiple lynch mobs.

Wechsler became a strong advocate against Southern lynching, and later made his scholarly name by publishing an article in the *Yale Law Journal* advocating federal anti-lynching legislation. The Scottsboro Boys' case also illustrated to Wechsler the influence public opinion could have on legal matters. The International Labor Defense, which represented the Scottsboro Boys, mounted a massive propaganda campaign on behalf of their clients. Albert Einstein, H. G. Wells and Maxim Gorky each spoke out on behalf of the boys, who prevailed in their appeal before a generally conservative Court. The third event was Wechsler's experience in Nuremberg. See Anders Walker, "American Oresteia," p. 1025.

308 lenient treatment of offenders could lead to lynching: Jerome Michael and Herbert Wechsler, *Criminal Law and Its Administration*, p.16.

308 "naked power organ": Herbert Wechsler, "Toward Neutral Principles of Constitutional Law," *Harvard Law Review* 73 (1959): 1–35.

308 "legitimacy account": Stanley Ingber, "The Interface of Myth and Practice in Law," *Vanderbilt Law Review* 34 (1981): 309, 339–40.

310 "In Georgia, all decisions not to impose the death penalty are justifiable": "Note: Discretion and the Constitutionality of the New Death Penalty Statutes," *Harvard Law Review* 87 (1974): 1690–1719.

310 Silberman submitted a draft for comment: Peggy Davis to David Silberman, April 17, 1974, PD.

311 "Discretion has not been eliminated": Michael Meltsner, "Cruel and Unusual Punishment," *New York Times*, October 11, 1974, p. 39. Professor Corinna Lain summarizes the contemporary sentiment in the academic community in "Furman Fundamentals," at n. 337 and the accompanying text.

311 "In less serious circumstances, this would be amusing": John Hart Ely, *Democracy and Distrust*, p. 175.

311 LDF tried to recruit Lee Hamilton: Peggy Davis to Lee Hamilton, May 20, 1974. PD.

311 1995 *Harvard Law Review* article: Carol S. Steiker and Jordan M. Steiker, "Sober Second Thoughts: Reflections on Two Decades of Constitutional Regulation of Capital Punishment," *Harvard Law Review* 109 (1995): 355–438.

311 Murdering a police officer is an . . . aggravating circumstance: For an overview see the Death Penalty Information Center Web site, http://www.deathpenaltyinfo .org/aggravating-factors-capital-punishment-state.

313 "The populations of death rows": David McCord, "Judging the Effectiveness of the Supreme Court's Death Penalty Jurisprudence According to the Court's own Goals," *Florida State University Law Review* 24 (1996): 545, 593.

313 "by clear and objective standards": *Coley v. State*, 231 Ga. 829, 833 (1974).

313 "The Court's doctrine, a facade, is successful": Steiker and Steiker, "Sober Second Thoughts," p. 429.

313 The appearance of a rational system made, and makes, actors . . . more comfortable: Gramsci developed the idea of hegemony in an effort to explain why Marxism failed to take root in Western Europe. The gist is that people can internalize ideas and attitudes to such an extent as to make a challenge to the dominant order literally unthinkable. *Furman* and *Gregg* established a hegemony of rationality and legitimated death sentencing on multiple levels. In this way, people grew more comfortable in their roles.

314 "A penalty trial that looks legally sophisticated": Weisberg, "Deregulating Death," p. 395.

314 "the sanctions they inflict follow inevitably": Ibid., p. 393.

314 false comfort through the illusion of formalism: Weisberg says, colorfully, "We cannot mitigate our inevitable moral ambivalence about condemning people to death by dignifying our decision in the illusory language of legal science." Ibid., p. 312.

315 "You have a scale in front of you": ibid., pp. 363–64 and 378. The cases are *State v. Caldwell*, 135 Ohio St. 424, 425-27 (1939) and *People v. Hamilton*, No. 25591 (Cal. Super. Ct. Contra Costa Cty., Sept. 30, 1981) Transcript Vol. 19-B at 8.

316 mathematical in nature, and easier: Weisberg draws a direct analogy to Stanley Milgram's famous study of obedience to authority, in which a "scientist" asked volunteers to administer increasing levels of electric shock to subjects in what was presented as a learning exercise. Milgram found that the most important factor in the study participants' willingness to administer pain was the professional authority of the scientist, expressed through his language and appearance. Inadvertently LDF may have encouraged courts to play the role of the reassuring scientists, and, through standards, assuaged the angst of capital juries.

316 "What is most dangerous in violence is its rationality": Michel Foucault, "Truth is in the Future," in Sylvère Lotringer, ed. *Foucault Live (Interviews, 1961–1984)*, p. 299.

316 This is what Harlan meant: Weisberg, "Deregulating Death," p. 311.

316 "Capital punishment is to the rest of all law": Normal Mailer, "Until Dead: Thoughts on Capital Punishment," *Parade*, February 6, 1981, p. 6.

317 "No longer can a Georgia jury": *Gregg*, 428 U.S., p. 197.

Chapter 15: THE LION IN WINTER

319 "A black man who spells his name with a 'u'": Jeffries, *Justice Lewis F. Powell, Jr.*, p. 417.

320 Delaware's attorney general interpreted *Furman*'s mandate: *Time*, "The Law: Death Rattles," November 20, 1972, p. 72.

321 thirty-one states had reintroduced capital punishment: for the list see "List of the 31 States Backing Death Penalty," *New York Times*, April 21, 1975, p. 47.

321 prosecutors and juries had sentenced 253 people: Leslie Oelsner, "Supreme Court Begins Review of the Death Penalty," *New York Times*, April 22, 1975, p. 21.

321 Jimmy Carter would support the death penalty: *Newsweek*, "Carter Meets the Questions," February 2, 1976, p. 18.

321 he would tell Larry King: *CNN Live*, "Interview With Former President Jimmy

Carter," November 2, 2005, transcript available at http://archives.cnn.com/ TRANSCRIPTS/0511/02/lkl.01.html; Carter's Nobel Lecture: Oslo, December 10, 2002, available at http://nobelprize.org/nobel_prizes/peace/laureates/2002/ carter-lecture.html.

321 "I think executing is a fit and proper punishment": Carol A. Morton, "205 Prisoners Await Fate on Death Row," *Ebony*, April 1975, pp. 114–21.

322 Bork rejected the legacy of Hugo Black: Bork, *The Tempting of America*, pp. 69–100. In his book Bork quoted Arthur Schlesinger, who wrote, "The Black-Douglas wing appears to be more concerned with settling particular cases in accordance with their own social preconceptions." Ibid., p. 69.

323 "consolidate and widen *Furman*": Hugo Adam Bedau, *The Courts, The Constitution, and Capital Punishment*, cited in Epstein and Kobylka, *The Supreme Court and Legal Change*, p. 97.

331 the article correctly concluded: Warren Weaver, "Supreme Court Postpones Review of Death Penalty," *New York Times*, June 24, 1975, p. 1.

332 "pass on to the conference": Urofksy, *The Douglas Letters*, p. 195.

333 "horribly difficult": Stern and Wermiel, *Justice Brennan: Liberal Champion*, p. 384.

333 He wanted to last long enough: Greg Diskant interview (September 22, 2009).

Chapter 16: THE SAUSAGE FACTORY

337 "Writs of certiorari are matters of grace": *Wade v. Mayo*, 334 U.S. 672, 680 (1948).

338 "error correction strategy": S. Sidney Ulmer, "The Decision to Grant Certiorari as Indicator to Decision 'On the Merits,'" *Polity* 4 (1972): 429–47.

338 Glendon Schubert . . . argues: Glendon A. Schubert, "The Study of Judicial Decision Making as an Aspect of Political Behavior," *American Political Science Review* 52 (1958): 1007–25.

338 Saul Brenner argues: Saul Brenner, "The New Certiorari Game," *Journal of Politics* 41 (1979): 649–55.

339 "Well if you want to spend your time": Herbert M. Kritzer, "Interpretation and Validity Assessment in Qualitative Research: The Case of H. W. Perry's Deciding to Decide," *Law and Social Inquiry* 19 (1994): 687, 689.

340 The few existing studies of the death penalty cases by political scientists: The most important is Epstein and Kobylka, *The Supreme Court and Legal Change*.

340 "There was always special treatment": Perry, *Deciding to Decide*, p. 92.

341 "Ideally, the capital punishment issues": James B. Ginty, "Memorandum for the Chief Justice," June 10, 1975, LFP.

341 Jack House had raped: *House v. The State*, 232 Ga. 140; 205 S.E. 2d 217 (1974).

343 "whether there was a probability": *Jurek v. Texas*, 428 U.S. 262, 269 (1976).

344 "Not good case to take": Lewis F. Powell memorandum to file, "Capital Cases," January 16, 1976. LFP.

344 Burger had plans to speak: Warren E. Burger Memorandum to Conference, January 9, 1976, LFP.

344 The justices all felt that they needed: The conference is discussed in *The Brethren*, p. 431.

344 "quite different coloration": Potter Stewart Memorandum to the Conference, "Capital Cases," January 19, 1976, LFP.

345 the appeal of Timothy McCorquodale: *McCorquodale v. The State*, 233 Ga. 369 (1974). In 1980, McCorquodale escaped with Troy Gregg shortly before Gregg's scheduled execution. Gregg died during a brawl at a biker bar. According to several accounts, McCorquodale either caused or abetted in Gregg's death.

346 "For those who seek": Jeffries, Lewis F. Powell, Jr., p. ix (preface to the 2001 edition).

346 "I am going to prove to Daddy": ibid., p. 23. John Jeffries's definitive biography of Powell is the principal source of this portrait of Powell's childhood and career.

347 "It seemed clear to me": ibid., p. 30.

347 Powell had attended all-white schools and churches: ibid., p. 234.

348 "I am not in favor of": ibid., p. 140.

348 questioning the status quo never occurred to him: ibid., p. 139.

348 "an elitist": ibid., p. 240.

348 "we get nowhere by analytical dialectics": ibid., p. 41.

348 "was unreceptive to the influence of abstractions": ibid., p. 42.

348 written his death penalty opinion: Woodword and Armstrong, *The Brethren*, pp. 204–5.

349 "large dimensions": Jeffries, *Justice Lewis F. Powell*, p. 409.

349 "All he really cared out of this": Whitman interview (November 12, 2010).

349 Powell took offense: Stern and Wermiel, *Justice Brennan*, p. 443.

350 A theme of *The Brethren*: Colleagues on both the left and right ridiculed Burger. Brennan referred to Burger's statements at conference as "an unqualified disaster" and "an embarrassment" (p. 466). Stewart provided the impetus for Woodward and Armstrong's book. After Woodward relentlessly pressed Stewart for an interview, they spent two evenings together and, Woodward said, Stewart "kind of outlined the book." (J. Anthony Lukas, "Playboy Interview: Bob Woodward," *Playboy*, Feb. 1989, p. 51.)

351 "His lifelong desire for control": Jeffries, *Justice Lewis F. Powell*, p. 432.

351 "I felt particularly free to talk to Potter": ibid., p. 263.

352 the "Powell Court": Herman Schwartz, *Packing the Court*, p. 122.

352 "and so completely the truth": Jeffries, *Justice Lewis F. Powell*, p. 533.

352 "the most powerful man in America": Aric Press, "A Reagan Court," *Newsweek*, July 15, 1985, p. 69; see also Bronner, *Battle for Justice*, pp. 21–22.

Chapter 17: TAKING STOCK

354 *Michigan v. Mosley*: 423 U.S. 96 (1975).

354 *Faretta v. California*: 422 U.S. 806 (1975).

354 *U.S. v. Park*: 421 U.S. 658 (1975).

354 "The Court's opinions have been unphilosophic": Francis A. Allen, "Quiescence

and Ferment: The 1974 Term in the Supreme Court," *Journal of Criminal Law and Criminology* 66 (1976): 391, 393.

355 "No state is precluded": *Michigan v. Mosley*, 423 U.S. 96, p. 121.

355 "angry, frustrated, and saddened": UPI, "Supreme Court Shifts Away from Brennan," *Jacksonville Times-Union and Journal*, June 6, 1976.

355 "Close observers of the court": "American Notes: New Life for Death," *Time*, February 2, 1976, p. 12.

356 Find me another Lewis Powell": Jeffries, *Justice Lewis F. Powell*, p. 419.

356 "very high degrees of scholarship": *Hearings Before the Judiciary Committee on the Nomination of John Paul Stevens*, p. 19 (available at www.gpo.gov).

359 Nationally more than six hundred people: "34 States and U.S. Have Capital Punishment Laws," *New York Times*, July 3, 1976 p. 7.

359 the machinery of executions had been dismantled: Banner, *The Death Penalty*, p. 266.

359 The Massachusetts Supreme Court had rejected a mandatory death penalty: *Commonwealth v. O'Neal*, 339 N.E.2d. 676 (1975).

359 in a case LDF supported: Peggy Davis to Morris Shubow, May 29, 1974, PD.

359 "Maybe . . . the public can be convinced": Peggy Davis to Aryeh Neier, PD.

360 "I have never worked for anyone": Davis interview (January 10, 2011).

360 "chances were better": Kendall interview (December 9, 2010).

361 "I think all of us working on the cases were too sold": At the time, Davis also shared Amsterdam's instinct not to oppose Stevens. Following his nomination, she wrote to Amsterdam, "I agree that Stevens is unstoppable and Ford would get someone else in if he were stopped. I also feel that someone else would be worse. I think that there was a moderating involvement from Levi which might not be present next time."

361 In its submissions to the Court: LDF incorporated by reference its brief in *Fowler*, which emphasized the death penalty's cruelty and raised familiar arguments about its brutality and lack of usefulness.

363 "almost any form of argument": *Gregg v. Georgia*, Brief of the NAACP Legal Defense Fund, Inc., as Amicus Curiae (*Gregg* Amicus Brief), 1976 WL 178715, p. 38.

363 "Notably, but unsurprisingly": ibid., p. 44.

363 "after considering both the crimes": *Gregg v. State*, 233 Ga. 117 (1974).

363 "As time passes": *Gregg* Amicus Brief, p. 46.

364 "The system we have just described": ibid., p. 66.

365 "How then can it be declared": ibid., p. 32.

366 Bork cited his opinion in *Powell*: In *Powell* the Court upheld the conviction of a sixty-six-year-old shoeshine man who had been arrested for public intoxication and fined twenty dollars. The dissent felt that Texas had punished Powell for his illness. Marshall wrote that the most troubling aspect of the dissent's position was to establish a constitutional doctrine of criminal responsibility. "If Leroy Powell cannot be convicted of public intoxication," Marshall wrote, "it is difficult to see how a State can convict an individual for murder, if that individual, while exhibiting normal behavior in all other respects, suffers from a 'compulsion' to kill, which

is an 'exceedingly strong influence,' but 'not completely overpowering.' " Marshall was equally concerned, though, with the prospect of returning "inebriates to the streets without even the opportunity to sober up adequately which a brief jail term provides." Marshall added, "Before we condemn the present practice, perhaps we ought to be able to present some clear promise of a better world for these unfortunate people."

367 "Petitioners obviously do not contend": ibid., p. 69.

367 "It is utterly impossible": ibid., p. 81.

369 Amsterdam had toed the waters with this argument in *Fowler*: Internally LDF referred to the problem of distinguishing death from other penal sanctions as "caging the bugbear of *Tigner v. Texas*," a reference to a 1940 Frankfurter decision upholding an anti-trust prosecution, even though the law at issue excluded agricultural products. It is commonly cited for the proposition that "the Constitution does not require things which are different in fact or opinion to be treated in law as though they were the same." (Amsterdam email to author, October 9, 2012.)

369 "doggedly clung": In *The Supreme Court and Legal Change*, Epstein and Kobylka added that Amsterdam and LDF "were blinded to the necessity of strategic backtracking by the tyranny of absolutes, the belief that to win the big one is to establish for all time the precedential base for future victories" and that their recalcitrance to reexamine earlier victories "fatally constrained their ability to shift grounds when those victories came under threat." Epstein and Kobylka's discussion of LDF's strategy can be found at pp. 106–15, 127–36, and 311.

369 Edward Lazarus agrees: Lazarus, *Closed Chambers*, p. 114.

370 in his memoir Meltsner said: "Attacking discretionary decision making could undermine the criminal law, which at all levels depends on it. As difficult as would be a decision that flew in the face of popular hostility to abolition, the fallout would be small in comparison with the vituperative response to a decision that undermined the sense of safety conveyed by the entire criminal law." Meltsner, *The Making of a Civil Rights Lawyer*, p. 215.

370 "the unfortunate and unintentional entailment": Muller, "The Legal Defense Fund's Capital Punishment Campaign," p. 183. LDF might ask whether Muller means to suggest they should have done nothing. Furthermore, Jack Greenberg said in a 1985 interview that LDF made some tentative efforts to extend its critique of the criminal justice system. "After we won *Furman* there were efforts to extend the *Furman* rationale beyond capital punishment. They weren't really very extensive efforts because people were busy litigating the cases that went up in *Gregg*. But there were efforts. They got absolutely nowhere." Ibid.

370 Herbert Packer had exposed this tension: Herbert Packer, "Making the Punishment Fit the Crime," *Harvard Law Review* 77 (1964): 1071–82.

370 "overplayed their hand": Jon Amsterdam interview (January 27, 2011).

370 difficult to differentiate death from long prison sentences: I explored this question in detail in a 2004 law review article. See Evan J. Mandery, "Innocence as a Death Penalty Issue," *Criminal Law Bulletin* 40 (2004): 78–82. The obvious answer to the question "is death unique" is yes, and in some superficial ways it is. If laws are changed or new evidence is discovered or clemency granted, the person in

prison can be released, while the executed inmate cannot. But this is the extent of the dissimilarities. It isn't true that nothing can be done for the deceased. The government can attempt to restore his reputation or pay reparations to his surviving family members. Furthermore, it's not the case that the person released from prison can be made whole. This point is key.

When accident victims sue injurers, the goal of the legal system is to put these plaintiffs in the same position they would have been in but for the accident. This leads to macabre questions such as how much it is worth to lose a finger or an arm. For short-term prison sentences, this question can be answered. It is easy to imagine someone accepting ten thousand dollars to spend a night in prison or $1 million for a year. But who would take any amount of money to spend twenty or thirty years in prison? Furthermore, no state government is paying the sort of money required to make released inmates whole. Most pay nothing at all. While it's true that executed people are in a different position than people who serve finite prison sentences, whether that difference makes a real difference is another matter.

371 "There is something real": Amsterdam interview (January 20, 2010).

Chapter 18: THE MAIN EVENT

372 "I don't see why": *Time*, "The Law: Reconsidering the Death Penalty," April 12, 1976, p. 61.

375 "no statute may validly impose the death penalty": Justice Powell took detailed notes during oral arguments, which are preserved in his archives at Washington and Lee University. They are an extraordinary resource, offering his real-time reactions to the oral arguments. Justice Blackmun also kept notes, which also have been preserved in his archive, though they are in his peculiar shorthand and not as detailed as Powell's.

380 justices have a dim view of state attorneys general: Perry, *Deciding to Decide*, p. 127.

388 "never heard a question": Bork, *The Tempting of America*, p. 275.

393 Amsterdam had become so emotional: Jeffries, *Justice Lewis F. Powell*, p. 422.

397 *Spencer v. Texas*: 385 U.S. 554 (1967).

Chapter 19: THE CENTER IN CONTROL

400 "Now I know what's it's like to hear Jesus Christ": Jeffries, *Justice Lewis F. Powell*, p. 422.

400 "nut": ibid.

400 Amsterdam had been rude: Woodward and Armstrong, *The Brethern* p. 434.

402 "What the country needs": ibid.

404 Burger felt that the assignment would solidify White's support: ibid., p. 435.

404 "I accept *Furman* as precedent": Jeffries, *Justice Lewis F. Powell*, p. 424.

404 "As a lawyer, I have a deep respect": ibid., p. 291. Confirmation Hearing of Lewis F. Powell, p, 219.

405 "the worst that can happen": Christina Whitman to Lewis Powell, "Death Penalty Cases," March 27, 1976, LFP.

406 "reflects a careful attempt to provide standards": Lewis Powell memorandum to file, April 1, 1976, LFP Papers.

407 "was less concerned about judicial restraint": Jeffries, *Justice Lewis F. Powell*, pp. 424–25.

409 Powell had specific requirements: Powell's eating habits and preference for the Monocle are discussed ibid., pp. 346, 426. The Powell-Stevens-Stewart lunch is discussed at pp. 425–26. This account was supplemented by Christina Whitman (November 12, 2010).

409 "There was never to my knowledge": Perry, *Deciding to Decide*, p. 150.

410 Stevens identified *Jurek*: Sandra Day O'Connor, "Sandra Day O'Connor Interviews John Paul Stevens," *Newsweek*, December 17, 2010, p. 38.

410 "We've got this deal": Whitman interview (November 12, 2010).

411 "A process that accords": *Woodson v. North Carolina*, 428 U.S. 280, 304 (1976).

412 "To make a moral decision": Weisberg, "Deregulating Death," p. 323.

413 "To acknowledge that there is perhaps an inherent tension": *Walton v. Arizona*, 497 U.S. 639, 664 (1990) (Scalia, J., concurring). Some scholars have reconciled the cases based on the earlier-referenced distinction between overinclusion and underinclusion. The argument goes that *Furman* attempts to minimize overinclusion—that is, executions of defendants who don't deserve to die. *Woodson*, on the other hand, produces underinclusion—in other words, failing to execute defendants who deserve to die. Again, a loose parallel might be drawn to the difference between convicting the innocent and acquitting the guilty.

413 "sat as a Council of Wise Men": Warren Burger, Memorandum to the Conference, April 24, 1976, LFP Papers.

413 "it would take more than one lunch": Jeffries, *Justice Lewis F. Powell*, p. 265.

414 "In part, capital punishment is an expression": *Gregg v. Georgia*, 428 U.S. at 183, quoting *Furman v. Georgia* 408 U.S. at 308, and *Williams v. N.Y.*, 337 U.S. 241, 248 (1949).

416 "I think one can at least surmise": Jeffries, *Justice Lewis F. Powell*, p. 428.

416 "No one—no legislator, judge, or juror": Lewis Powell to Potter Stewart, May 1, 1976, LFP.

416 "sympathetic to the idea": Lewis Powell to Christina Whitman, April 16, 1976, LFP.

417 "holding that the Eighth Amendment": Potter Stewart to Warren Burger, May 7, 1976, LFP (referencing the May 5 memo).

418 "The fatal constitutional infirmity": *Gregg v. Georgia*, 428 U.S. at 230 (Brennan, J., dissenting).

419 "a kind of vigil against the death penalty": Burt, "Disorder in the Court," pp. 176–79. Brennan didn't like his new role, and over time, became frustrated even with Marshall. "What the hell happened when he came on the Court?" he asked rhetorically. "I'm not sure, but he doesn't seem to have had the same interest. He

has some areas where he does and when he really gets involved in case he just does an absolutely superb job. But when he's not interested, whatever I do, that's all right with him." (Stern and Wermiel, *Justice Brennan*, p. 431).

422 That weekend Davis obsessed: Peggy Davis to John Blue, November 10, 1976, PD.

423 "I said the hell with it": Stern and Wermiel, *Justice Brennan*, p. 436 (discussing the conference generally).

423 Marshall spent much of the weekend: MacKenzie, "Marshall: Ready For Court Term," *Washington Post*, September 5, 1976, p. 46.

423 "Is this it?" Williams, *Thurgood Marshall: American Revolutionary*, p. 360 (discussing the weekend).

424 "This is the orderly and proper way": Lewis Powell, "My Notes on My Own Views," July 20, 1976, LFP.

424 "instant and explosive": Confidential File Memo, July 26, 1976, p. 2, LFP. Also discussed in Jeffries, *Justice Lewis F. Powell*, p. 429.

425 "inherently cruel": Warren Burger to the Conference, July 20, 1976, LFP.

426 "Over and over again": Peggy Davis to Anthony Amsterdam, David Kendall and James Nesbitt, undated, PD.

427 "Life is over for the victim": *Coker v. Georgia*, 433 U.S. 584, 598 (1977).

427 "for the rare case of a rape": Jeffries, *Justice Lewis Powell*, p. 436. In *Coker*, Powell wrote, "In a proper case, a more discriminating inquiry than the plurality undertakes well might discover that both juries and legislatures have reserved the ultimate penalty for the case of an outrageous rape resulting in serious, lasting harm to the victim." *Coker*, 433 U.S. at 604 (Powell, J., concurring).

428 "Opening the door": Leslie Gielow to Lewis Powell, October 1, 1986, LFP.

428 "Agree no way to limit": Leslie Gielow to Lewis Powell, October 14, 1986, LFP.

428 "Because of the limitless application": ibid.

429 "The inherent lack of predictability": *McCleskey v. Kemp*, 48, U.S. 279, 311 (1987).

429 "the *Dred Scott* decision of our time": Adam Liptak, "A New Look At Race When Death is Sought," *New York Times*, April 29, 2008, p. A10.

431 "Despite pleas in numerous forums": http://www.goextranet.net/Seminars/Black Hole/DeathRowUSA/Spenkelink.htm. For more on Farmer see Meltsner, *The Making of a Civil Rights Lawyers*, pp. 217–20.

431 "You feel guilty about every one": Labi, "Man Against the Machine," p. 17.

Postscript: *WHAT MIGHT HAVE BEEN*

432 "the whole face of the nation": Stern and Wermiel, *Justice Brennan*, p. 317.

432 "What if Justice Goldberg had used his memorandum": Bernard Schwartz, *The Unpublished Opinions of the Warren Court*," p. 443.

433 "repulsive": Banner, *The Death Penalty*, p. 239.

434 "This Court has stressed repeatedly": *Darden v. Wainwright*, 477 U.S. 168, 188 (Blackmun, J., dissenting).

434 "That is no reason": *McCleskey v. Kemp*, 481 U.S. 279, 365 (Blackmun, J., dissenting).

434 "Twenty years of applying": this history is beautifully recounted in Greenhouse, *Becoming Justice Blackmun*, pp. 174–81.

434 Michelle Alexander selected *Callins v. Collins*: ibid., pp. 177–79.

434 *Callins v. Collins:* 510 U.S. 1141, 1145 (1994) (Brennan, J., concurring).

435 "Thank you for the present": Stern and Wermiel, *Justice Brennan*, p. 542. Linda Greenhouse reports a slightly different chronology with the thank you occurring after release of the opinion.

435 the South African Constitutional Court declared the death penalty unconstitutional: *State v. Makwanyane and Mchunu*, CCT/3/94 (1995).

435 "We didn't get into the death penalty in depth": Harry A. Blackmun Oral Interview Project, June 2, 1995, pp. 189–90 (available at lcweb.2.loc.gov).

436 "a very serious, earnest advocate": ibid.

436 "I think he identified me": Labi, "Man Against the Machine," p. 19. Amsterdam also recalled in an interview that Blackmun's wife once praised him in the Supreme Court cafeteria following one of his oral arguments.

436 Powell had developed a close friendship: Stern & Wermiel, *Justice Brennan*, p. 476.

437 "The experience of last evening": Greenhouse, *Becoming Justice Blackmun*, p. 168.

437 "So do others of us!": ibid.

437 "However this delay may be characterized": Lewis F. Powell, "Commentary," *Harvard Law Review* 102 (1989): 1035, 1040; "Congress and the state legislatures": ibid., p. 1046.

437 "If I were in the state legislature" Don J. DeBenedictis, "The Reasonable Man," *ABA Journal*, October 1990, p. 69.

438 "I have come to think that capital punishment should be abolished": Jeffries, *Justice Lewis F. Powell*, pp. 451–53.

438 *Baze v. Rees*: 533 U.S. 35 (2008).

439 "a refusal to respect precedents": ibid., p. 87 (Stevens, J., concurring).

439 "I think that there is one vote that I would change": http://www.npr.org/templates/story/story.php?storyId=130332059 (October 4, 2010). NPR has posted different versions of Totenberg's interview with Justice Stevens. In one he appears to go a bit further in his expression of remorse saying that he regrets "upholding the capital punishment statute." http://www.npr.org/templates/transcript/transcript.php?storyId=130198344 (October 4, 2010). This is almost certainly an editing error, as Stevens has never publicly expressed regret about *Gregg* elsewhere. He has, however, expressed regret about *Jurek* in many forums. See, for example, George Stephanopoulos, "Retired Justice John Paul Stevens on His 'Wrong' Vote on Texas Death Penalty Case," September 28, 2011 (http://abcnews.go.com/blogs/politics/2011/09/former-justice-john-paul-stevens-i-was-wrong-on-the-death-penalty/); Sara Olkon, "Event with Justice Stevens Recounts Remarkable Supreme Court Career," *UChicagoNews*, October 4, 2011.

439 "That was the Texas death-penalty case": O'Connor, "Sandra Day O'Connor Interviews John Paul Stevens," *Newsweek*, January 3, 2011, p. 38.

SOURCES

INTERVIEWS

Anthony G. Amsterdam
Jon Amsterdam
C. Taylor Ashworth
William J. Baxley
Dorothy Toth Beasley
Loftus E. Becker, Jr.
Hugo Bedau
Craig M. Bradley
Edward E. Carnes
Elliott Currie
Peggy Cooper Davis
Robert L. Deitz
Alan M. Dershowitz
Gregory L. Diskant
Norman Dorsen
Peter Edelman
Brian Forst
Ronald M. George
Jack Greenberg
Larry A. Hammond
Benjamin W. Heineman, Jr.
Jack Himmelstein

Richard L. Jacobson
William H. Jeffress, Jr.
David E. Kendall
Michael Meltsner
Glenn Pierce
Louis M. Seidman
Joanna Shepherd
John W. Spiegel
Ronald A. Stern
Potter Stewart, Jr.
Samuel Walker
Robert Weisberg
Christina B. Whitman
Franklin E. Zimring

SUPREME COURT TRANSCRIPTS

Transcripts of Supreme Court oral arguments are preserved in *The Complete Arguments of the Supreme Court of the United States*, maintained by University Publications of America. Another remarkable resource is the Oyez Project at Chicago-Kent College of Law, where audio recordings of many arguments can be found. The recreations of the oral arguments contained in the book are primarily based on these transcripts and recordings. I have taken some minor liberties for the sake of readability, and, of course, what I have presented are only excerpts from the various arguments. Supreme Court conferences are not taped, so historians are required to piece together what was said from the justices' notes. An invaluable resource is Del Dickson's book, *The Supreme Court in Conference*, which collects the available record and reconstructs the debates on prominent cases. The recreations of the judicial conferences in this book draw on Dickson's book and the records of the justices, especially Harry Blackmun and Lewis Powell, who kept detailed notes.

MAJOR WORKS CITED

Acker, J. R., and C. S. Lanier. "Parsing This Lexicon of Death: Aggravating Factors in Capital Sentencing Statutes. *Criminal Law Bulletin* 30, no. 2 (1994): 107–52.

Adamany, D., and Grossman, J. B. "Support for the Supreme Court as a National Policymaker." *Law & Policy* 5, no. 4 (1983): 405–37.

Amsterdam, A. G., and J. S. Bruner. *Minding the Law*. Cambridge, MA: Harvard University Press, 2000.

Assembly of Behavioral and Social Sciences Panel on Research on Deterrent and Incapacitative Effects, A. Blumstein, J. Cohen, and D. Nagin, eds. *Deterrence and Incapacitation: Estimating the Effects of Criminal Sanctions on Crime Rates*, National Academy of Sciences, 1977.

Acker, James R., Robert M. Bohm, and Charles S. Lanier, eds. *America's Experiment with Capital Punishment: Reflections on the Past, Present, and Future of the Ultimate Penal Sanction*. Durham, NC: Carolina Academic Press, 1998.

Ancel, Marc. *The Death Penalty in European Countries: Report*. Council of Europe, 1962.

Baldus, D. C., and J. W. L. Cole. "A Comparison of the Work of Thorsten Sellin and Isaac Ehrlich on the Deterrent Effect of Capital Punishment." *Yale Law Journal* 85 (1975): 170–86.

Banner, S. *The Death Penalty: An American History*. Cambridge, MA: Harvard University Press, 2002.

Barry, R. V. "*Furman* to *Gregg*: The Judicial and Legislative history." *Howard Law Journal* 22 (1979): 53–118.

Bedau, H. A. *The Courts, the Constitution, and Capital Punishment*. Lexington, MA: Lexington Books, 1977.

———. *The Future of the Death Penalty: The Need for a National Project in Social Science Research and Capital Punishment*. Unpublished Report, 1973.

Bedau, H. A., and E. Currie. *Social Science Research and the Death Penalty in America: An Interim Report*. Unpublished Report, 1973.

Berk, R. "New Claims about Executions and General deterrence: Déja Vu All Over Again?" *Journal of Empirical Legal Studies* 2, no. 2 (2005): 303–30.

Bork, R. H. *The Tempting of America*. New York: Free Press, 1997.

Bowers, W. J., and G. L. Pierce. "The Illusion of Deterrence in Isaac Ehrlich's Research on Capital Punishment." *Yale Law Journal* 85, no. 2 (1975): 187–208.

Bowers, William J., Glenn L. Pierce, and John F. McDevitt. *Legal Homicide: Death as Punishment in America, 1864–1982*. Boston: Northeastern University Press, 1984.

Brennan, W. J. "Constitutional Adjudication and the Death Penalty: A View from the Court." *Harvard Law Review* 100, no. 2 (1986): 313–31.

Brenner, S. "Granting Certiorari by the United States Supreme Court: An Overview of the Social Science Studies." *Law Library Journal* 92 (2000): 193–201.

Brenner, S., and J. F. Krol. "Strategies in Certiorari Voting on the United States Supreme Court." *Journal of Politics* 51, no. 4 (1989): 828–40.

Bronner, E. *Battle for Justice: How the Bork Nomination Shook America*. New York: Union Square Press, 2007.

Burris, S. "Death and a Rational Justice: A Conversation on the Capital Jurisprudence of Justice John Paul Stevens." *Yale Law Journal* 96, no. 3 (1987): 521–46.

Burt, R. A. "Disorder in the Court: The Death Penalty and the Constitution." *Michigan Law Review* 85, no. 8 (1987): 1741–1819.

Cameron, S. "A Review of the Econometric Evidence on the Effects of Capital Punishment." *Journal of Socio-Economics* 23, no. 1 (1994): 197–214.

Culver, J. H. "Capital Punishment Politics and Policies in the States, 1977–1997." *Crime, Law and Social Change* 32, no. 4 (1999): 287–300.

Daniels, S. "Social Science and Death Penalty Cases: Reflections on Change and the Empirical Justification of Constitutional Policy." *Law & Policy* 1, no. 3 (1979): 336–72.

Dershowitz, A. M. *Shouting Fire: Civil Liberties in a Turbulent Age*. Boston: Little, Brown, 2002.

———. *The Best Defense*. New York: Vintage, 1983.

Desmond, A. J., and J. R. Moore. *Darwin's Sacred Cause: Race, Slavery and the Quest for Human Origins*. Chicago: University of Chicago Press, 2011.

Dezhbakhsh, H., P. H. Rubin, and J. M. Shepherd, "Does Capital Punishment Have a Deterrent Effect? New Evidence from Postmoratorium Panel Data." *American Law and Economics Review* 5, no. 2 (2003): 344–76.

Dezhbakhsh, H., and J. M. Shepherd. "The Deterrent Effect of Capital Punishment: Evidence from a Judicial Experiment." *Economic Inquiry* 44, no. 3 (2006): 512–35.

Dickson, D. *The Supreme Court in Conference (1940–1985): The Private Discussions Behind Nearly 300 Supreme Court Decisions*. New York: Oxford University, 2001.

DiIulio, J. J. "Help Wanted: Economists, Crime and Public Policy." *Journal of Economic Perspectives* 10, no. 1 (1996): 3–24.

Donohue, J., and S. D. Levitt. "The Impact of Legalized Abortion on Crime." *Quarterly Journal of Economics* 116, no. 2 (2001): 379–420.

Donohue, J., and J. J. Wolfers. "The Death Penalty: No Evidence for Deterrence." *The Economists' Voice* 3, no. 5, (2006).

Donohue, J. J., and J. Wolfers. "Estimating the Impact of the Death Penalty on Murder." *American Law and Economics Review* 11, no. 2 (2009): 249–309.

———. "Uses and Abuses of Empirical Evidence in the Death Penalty Debate." *Stanford Law Review* 58, no. 1 (2006): 791–846.

Dorsen, N. *Frontiers of Civil Liberties*. New York: Pantheon Books, 1968.

Douglas, W. O. *The Douglas Letters: Selections from the Private Papers of Justice William O. Douglas*. Edited by M. I. Urofsky, with the assistance of P. E. Urofsky. Bethesda, MD: Adler & Adler, 1987.

Ehrhardt, C. W., P. A. Hubbart, L. H. Levinson, and W. M. K. Smiley. "Aftermath of *Furman*: The Florida Experience." *Journal of Criminal Law and Criminology* 64 (1973): 2.

Ehrlich, I. "Capital Punishment and Deterrence: Some Further Thoughts and Additional Evidence." *Journal of Political Economy* 85, no. 4 (1977): 741–88.

———. "The Deterrent Effect of Capital Punishment: Reply." *American Economic Review* 67, no. 3 (1977): 452–58.

———. "Deterrence: Evidence and Inference." *Yale Law Journal* 85 (1975): 209–27.

———. "The Deterrent Effect of Capital Punishment: A Question of Life and Death." *American Economic Review* 65, no. 3 (1975): pp. 397–417.

Ely, J. H. *Democracy and Distrust: A Theory of Judicial Review*. Cambridge, MA: Harvard University Press, 1980.

Epstein, L., and J. F. Kobylka. *The Supreme Court and Legal Change: Abortion and the Death Penalty*. Chapel Hill: University of North Carolina Press, 1992.

Fagan, J. "Death and Deterrence Redux: Science, Law and Casual Reasoning on Capital Punishment." *Ohio State Journal of Criminal Law* 4 (2006): 255–320.

Feldman, N. *Scorpions: The Battles and Triumphs of FDR's Great Supreme Court Justices*. New York: Twelve, 2010.

Foerster, B. J., and M. Meltsner. *Race, Rape and Injustice: Documenting and Challenging Death Penalty Cases in the Civil Rights Era*, University of Tennessee Press, Knoxville: 2012.

Forst, B. "Capital Punishment and Deterrence: Conflicting Evidence." *Journal of Criminal Law & Criminology* 74, no. 3 (1983): 927–42.

Fourcault, M. *Foucault Live: Interviews, 1966–84*. Cambridge, MA: MIT Press, 1996.

Franklin, C. H., and L. C. Kosaki. "Republican Schoolmaster: The U.S. Supreme Court, Public Opinion, and Abortion." *American Political Science Review* 83, no. 3 (1989): 751–71.

Garraty, J. A. *Quarrels That Have Shaped the Constitution*, New York: Harper & Row, 1964.

George, T. E., and L. Epstein, "On the Nature of Supreme Court Decision Making," *American Political Science Review* 86, no. 2 (1992): 323–37.

Goldberg, A. J. "Memorandum to the Conference Re: Capital Punishment October Term, 1963," *Southern Texas Law Review* 27 (1985): 493–99.

———. "The Death Penalty and the Supreme Court," *Arizona Law Review* 15 (1973): 355.

Goldberg, A. J., and A. M. Dershowitz. "Declaring the Death Penalty Unconstitutional." *Harvard Law Review* 83 (1970): 1773–1819.

Gordon, A. *Nothing Less Than the Dignity of Man: The Eighth Amendment Jurisprudence of the Warren Court*, 2003. (Unpublished, manuscript on file with author.)

Gray, I., and M. Stanley. *A Punishment in Search of a Crime*. New York: Avon, 1989.

Greenberg, J. *Crusaders in the Courts: Legal Battles of the Civil Rights Movement*. New York: Basic Books, 2004.

———. *Cases and Material on Judicial Process and Social Change: Constitutional Litigation*. St. Paul, MN: West Publishing Company, 1977.

Greenberg, J., and J. Himmelstein. "Varieties of Attack on the Death Penalty." *Crime & Delinquency* 15, no. 1 (1969): 112–20.

Greenhouse, L. *Becoming Justice Blackmun: Harry Blackmun's Supreme Court Journey*. New York: Times Books, 2006.

Haines, H. H. *Against Capital Punishment: The Anti-Death Penalty Movement in America, 1972–1994*. New York: Oxford University Press, 1996.

Hoekstra, V. J. *Public Reaction to Supreme Court Decisions*. New York: Cambridge University Press, 2003.

———. "The Supreme Court and Local Public Opinion." *American Political Science Review* 94, no. 1 (2000): 89–100.

Hutchinson, D. J. "Hail to the Chief: Earl Warren and the Supreme Court." *Michigan Law Review* 81 (1982): 922–30.

———. *The Man Who Once Was Whizzer White: A Portrait of Justice Byron R. White*. New York: Free Press, 1998.

Jeffries, J. C. *Justice Lewis F. Powell, Jr.* New York: Fordham University Press, 2001.

Kalman, L. *Legal Realism at Yale, 1927–1960*. Chapel Hill: University of North Carolina Press, 1986.

Klein, L. R., B. Forst, and V. Filatov. "The Deterrent Effect of Capital Punishment: An Assessment of the Estimates." *Deterrence and Incapacitation: Estimating the Effects of Criminal Sanctions on Crime Rates* (1978): 336–60.

Kluger, R. *Simple Justice: The History of Brown v. Board of Education*. New York: Knopf, 1975.

Lain, C. B. "Deciding Death." *Duke Law Journal* 57, no. 1 (2007): 1–83.

————. "*Furman* Fundamentals." *Washington Law Review* 82, no. 1 (2007): 1–74.

Lazarus, E. *Closed Chambers*. New York: Random House, 1998.

Lejins, P. P. "Thorsten Sellin: A Life Dedicated to Criminology." *Criminology* 25, no. 4 (1978): 975–90.

Liptak, A. "Does the Death Penalty Save Lives? A New Debate." *New York Times*, Nov. 18, 2007.

Lukas, J. A. *Common Ground*. New York: Random House, 1985.

Mandery, E. J. *Capital Punishment in America: A Balanced Examination*. 2d ed. Jones & Bartlett, 2011.

Marsel, R. S. "Mr. Justice Arthur J. Goldberg and the Death Penalty: A Memorandum to the Conference." *South Texas Law Review* 27 (1985): 467.

Massey, D. S. and N. A. Denton. *American Apartheid: Segregation and the Making of the Underclass*. Cambridge, MA: Harvard University Press, 1993.

McCafferty, J. A., ed. *Capital Punishment*. Cambridge, MA: Aldine-Atherton, 1972.

McCord, D. "Judging the Effectiveness of the Supreme Court's Death Penalty Jurisprudence According to the Court's Own Goals: Mild Success or Major Disaster." *Florida State University Law Review* 24 (1996): 545–605.

Mello, M. *Deathwork: Defending the Condemned*. Minneapolis: University of Minnesota Press, 2002.

Meltsner, M. *The Making of a Civil Rights Lawyer*. Charlottesville, VA: University of Virginia Press, 2006.

————. *Cruel and Unusual: The Supreme Court and Capital Punishment*. New York: Random House, 1973.

Menand, L. *The Metaphysical Club*. New York: Farrar, Straus & Giroux, 2002.

Michael, J and H. Wechsler. *Criminal Law and Its Administration: Cases, Statutes, and Commentaries*. New York: Foundation Press, 1940.

Moynihan, D. P. "Social Science and the Courts." *Public Interest* 54 (1979): 12–31.

Muller, E. L. "The Legal Defense Fund's Capital Punishment Campaign: The Distorting Influence of Death." *Yale Law & Policy Review* 4, no. 1 (1985): 158–87.

Murphy, B. A. *Wild Bill: The Legend and Life of William O. Douglas*. New York: Random House, 2003.

————. *Fortas: The Rise and Ruin of a Supreme Court Justice*. New York: William Morrow, 1988.

Nathanson, S. *An Eye for an Eye: The Immorality of Punishing by Death*. Totowa, NJ: Rowman & Littlefield, 2001.

Navasky, V. S. *A Matter of Opinion*. New York: Farrar, Straus & Giroux, 2005.

Neier, A. *Taking Liberties: Four Decades in the Struggle for Rights.* New York: Public Affairs, 2003.

Packer, H. L. "Making the Punishment Fit the Crime." *Harvard Law Review* 77, no. 6 (1964): 1071–82.

Passell, P. "Deterrent Effect of the Death Penalty: A Statistical Test." *Stanford Law Review* 28 (1975): 61–80.

Peck, J. K. "The Deterrent Effect of Capital Punishment: Ehrlich and His Critics." *Yale Law Journal* 85 (1975): 359–67.

Perry, H. *Deciding to Decide: Agenda Setting in the United States Supreme Court.* Cambridge, MA: Harvard University Press, 1991.

Powell, L. F., Jr. "Capital Punishment." *Harvard Law Review* 102 (1988): 1035.

Radelet, M. L., and R. L. Akers. "Deterrence and the Death Penalty: The Views of the Experts." *Journal of Criminal Law and Criminology* 87, no. 1 (1996): 1–16.

Rosenberg, G. N. *The Hollow Hope: Can Courts Bring About Social Change?* Chicago: University of Chicago Press, 2008.

Rubin, P. H. "Reply to Donohue and Wolfers on the Death Penalty and Deterrence." *The Economists' Voice* 3, no. 5 (2006).

Scammon, R. M., and Ben J. Wattenberg. *The Real Majority.* New York: Coward-McCann, 1970.

Schulman, B. J. *The Seventies: The Great Shift in American Culture, Society, and Politics.* New York: Free Press, 2001.

Schwartz, B. *Super Chief: Earl Warren and His Supreme Court: A Judicial Biography.* New York: New York University Press, 1983.

Schwartz, H. *Packing the Courts: The Conservative Campaign to Rewrite the Constitution.* New York: Scribner, 1988.

Schwartz, B. *The Unpublished Opinions of the Warren Court.* New York: Oxford University Press, 1985.

Schwed, R. E. *Abolition and Capital Punishment: The United States' Judicial, Political, and Moral Barometer.* New York: AMS Press, 1983.

Shepherd, J. M. "Deterrence Versus Brutalization: Capital Punishment's Differing Impacts among States." *Michigan Law Review* 104 (2005): 203–57.

Simon, J. F. *The Antagonists: Hugo Black, Felix Frankfurter and Civil Liberties in Modern America.* New York: Simon & Schuster, 1989.

Stebenne, D. *Arthur J. Goldberg: New Deal Liberal.* New York: Oxford University Press, 1996.

Steiker, C. S., and J. M. Steiker. "Sober Second Thoughts: Reflections on Two Decades of Constitutional Regulation of Capital Punishment. *Harvard Law Review* 109, no. 2 (1995): 355–438.

Stern, S., and S. Wermiel. *Justice Brennan: Liberal Champion*. New York: Houghton Mifflin Harcourt, 2010.

Stock James H., and Francesco Trebbi. "Who Invented Instrumental Variables Regression," *Journal of Economic Perspectives* 17 (2003): 177–94.

Toobin, J. *The Nine: Inside the Secret World of the Supreme Court*. New York: Anchor, 2008.

Turow, S. *Ultimate Punishment*. New York: Picador, 2002.

Tushnet, M. V. *Making Constitutional Law: Thurgood Marshall and the Supreme Court, 1961–1991*. New York: Oxford University Press, 1997.

United States Supreme Court. *The Complete Oral Arguments of the Supreme Court of the United States*. Frederick, MD: University Publications of America, 1952.

Vidmar, N., and P. Ellsworth. "Public Opinion and the Death Penalty." *Stanford Law Review* 26 (1973): 1245–70.

Vila, B., and C. Morris. *Capital Punishment in the United States: A Documentary History*. Westport, CT: Greenwood, 1997.

Walker, A. "American Oresteia: Herbert Wechsler, the Model Penal Code, and the Uses of Revenge." *Wisconsin Law Review* 2009 (2009) 1017–58.

Walker, S. *In Defense of American Liberties: A History of the ACLU*. Carbondale: Southern Illinois University Press, 1999.

Wechsler, H. "Sentencing, Correction, and the Model Penal Code." *University of Pennsylvania Law Review* 109, no. 4 (1961): 465–93.

Weisberg, R. "Deregulating Death." *Supreme Court Review* 1983 (1983): 305–95.

Williams, J. *Thurgood Marshall: American Revolutionary*. New York: Three Rivers Press, 2000.

Woodward, B., and S. Armstrong. *The Brethren: Inside the Supreme Court*. New York: Simon & Schuster, 2005.

Yarbrough, T. E., and A. Harry. *Blackmun: The Outsider Justice*. New York: Oxford University Press, 2008.

Zeisel, H. "The Deterrent Effect of the Death Penalty: Facts v. Faiths." *Supreme Court Review* 1976 (1976): 317–43.

Zimmerman, P. R. "Statistical Variability and the Deterrent Effect of the Death Penalty." *American Law and Economics Review* 11, no. 2 (2009): 370–98.

Zimring, F. E. *The Contradictions of American Capital Punishment*. New York: Oxford University Press, 2004.

Zimring, F. E., and G. Hawkins. *Capital Punishment and the American Agenda*. New York: Cambridge University Press, 1989.

———. "Capital Punishment and the Eighth Amendment: *Furman* and *Gregg* in Restrospect." *U.C. Davis Law Review* 18 (1984): 927–56.

INDEX

Abbott, Francis Ellingwood, 206
Abolition and Capital Punishment (Schwed),
    453*n*
abolition campaigns, 36–37, 40, 46–62, 76,
    77, 102–3, 133, 148, 150, 168, 183, 194,
    234, 243, 259, 261, 276, 284–86, 292,
    303, 306, 330, 357–62, 385, 419, 429,
    430
  ACLU's initial reluctance to become
    involved with, 35–36
  Amsterdam's behind-the-scenes consulting
    role in, 370*n*–71*n*
  Amsterdam's central role in, 46, 130, 277,
    284, 357, 358, 359–60
  Anderson decision as significant in, 185
  anti-Proposition 17 campaign of, 254–55
  bifurcated trials advocated in, 82, 103, 104
  bleak prospects for, 127, 128–29, 354, 355,
    359, 372
  class-action lawsuits in, 55–57
  conflict of individual vs. systemic claims in,
    54, 56–60, 82*n*, 164, 361, 426, 430–31,
    433
  criticisms for LDF's strategies in, 278–79,
    369–70, 429, 430–31, 433, 488*n*
  "death is different" argument of, 325,
    369–71, 378–79, 386, 391, 405, 412, 436
  deterrence theory rebuttals in, 293–94,
    299, 302*n*
  in disproving myth of "rational
    application," 303, 304, 310, 311
  Eighth Amendment argument in, 59–60,
    62, 69–70, 97, 109, 111–14, 117, 129–30,
    279, 361, 417, 426, 433, 453*n*
  "extremist" labeling of, 277, 368, 369, 370,
    398
  funding of, 50, 53, 104, 254, 278, 280,
    293
  Furman decision and reaction in, 237–38,
    239–40, 241
  grass-root tactics in, 112–13, 433
  horrors of execution highlighted by, 117,
    131, 487*n*
  increasing public support for, 234–35
  "Last-Aid Kits" in, 52, 55, 426–28
  LDF as leading voice in, 35, 37, 40, 56, 62,
    359
  LDF's decision to extend representation to
    whites in, 48–50, 452*n*
  LDF's decision to represent murderers in,
    52–53, 279
  LDF's focus on procedural claims in, 62,
    70, 97, 129, 130, 134, 149, 150, 167
  LDF's legal containment policy in, 56–57,
    58–62, 453*n*
  Maxwell's significance in, 97
  moratorium strategy in, 53–55, 56, 58, 60,
    62, 65, 70, 89, 97, 111, 112–13, 133, 137,
    296
  national conferences held in, 60–62, 104,
    111–12, 129, 131, 284–85
  1976 litigation strategy in, 358–62, 367,
    368–71, 375, 376–77, 378, 382–83, 389,
    392, 417, 425–26, 488*n*

abolition campaigns (*continued*)
post-*Furman* backlash as harmful to, 254, 263, 277–80, 360
race as initially central issue in, 37, 44–45, 48, 49–50, 51, 82*n*, 133, 314*n*
social science research used in, 38–40, 45, 58, 94, 131, 162–63, 184, 283, 284–86, 287–88, 295
see also Amsterdam, Anthony; NAACP Legal Defense Fund; *specific death penalty cases*
abortion, 74, 167, 194, 199–200, 212, 269–71, 274, 275, 276–77, 278, 352, 368, 409, 470*n*, 475*n*
death penalty vs., 199–200
Ackerman, Bruce, 213
Adams, John Quincy, 272
affirmative action, 213, 352
African Americans, 18, 48, 267, 269, 272, 279, 301, 463*n*
voting rights of, 32, 35, 36, 179
see also race issues; racism, in capital sentencing
Aikens, Ernest, 117, 136, 155, 185, 241
Aikens v. California, 117, 118, 130, 136
legal briefs filed in, 130, 132–34, 136
oral arguments in, 136, 143, 145–61, 460*n*
removal from docket of, 185
Alabama, 9, 14, 25, 28, 46, 181, 247, 249, 250, 268, 279
mandatory statute proposals in, 248, 251
Alabama, University of, Law School, 13, 249
Alabama Court of Appeals, 113
Alaska, 63
Alda, Alan, 430
Alexander, Michelle, 434–35
Alibi Club, 174
Allen, Francis, 23, 354
allocution, 105, 107
Al Odah v. U.S., 364
Altfeld, Michael, 178–79, 214, 461*n*
Amaker, Norman, 48
American Apartheid (Massey and Denton), 267
American Bar Association (ABA), 59, 80, 125, 183, 347, 356, 437, 438
American Civil Liberties Union (ACLU), 9, 15, 21, 30, 35, 36–37, 41, 51–52, 55, 56, 57, 60–61, 278, 279, 352, 359
as reluctant to join abolition movement, 35–36
American Economic Review, 290, 291

American Federation of Labor, 7
American Independent Party, 250
American Law Institute (ALI), 95, 304–5, 306, 309, 313
American University, 76
amicus briefs, 41, 58, 59, 66, 68–70, 97, 100, 290–91, 322, 338, 364, 365–68, 374
Amsterdam, Anthony, 40–46, 47, 48, 66, 67–70, 84*n*, 100, 103, 128–29, 136, 164–65, 185, 261, 277, 279, 287–88, 322, 356–60, 368, 380, 381, 382–83, 384, 385, 398–99, 405, 429, 451*n*, 476*n*, 487*n*
Anderson case and, 137, 151, 392, 397
in anti-Proposition 17 campaign, 254–55
on arbitrary and discriminatory application of death penalty, 77, 94, 133–34, 148, 150, 159, 163, 167, 168, 181, 323, 324–25, 326, 330, 362–64, 366–67, 373, 375, 376–78, 385–86, 389–90, 392, 399, 401
background and education of, 41–42, 392
behind-the-scenes consulting role of, 370*n*–71*n*
Blackmun's complicated relationship with, 45–46, 159, 374, 390, 391, 400, 436, 492*n*
Boykin amicus brief filed by, 66, 68–70, 132–33, 374
central abolition campaign role of, 46, 130, 277, 284, 357, 358, 359–60
in class-action lawsuit, 55–56, 57
"death is different" argument of, 325, 369–71, 378–79, 386, 391, 405, 412, 436, 488*n*–89*n*
death penalty statutes criticized by, 323–24, 362–64, 366–67, 373–76, 380, 390–92, 396–98, 401
deterrence effect dismissed by, 151, 156–57, 292–93, 474*n*
Eighth Amendment arguments of, 112, 129–30, 131, 132–33, 134, 145–50, 154–55, 156–61, 163, 167, 168, 184, 188, 191, 375, 389, 393, 396, 399, 426, 427–28
"evolving standards of decency" argument of, 132–33, 135, 145–48, 150, 154–55, 156–57, 162, 183, 184, 191, 393, 395, 403
Fowler oral arguments of, 323–26, 330–31, 366–67, 369
Furman briefs of, 130–34, 136
Furman decision reaction of, 239–40, 243

Furman oral arguments of, 134–35, 143, 145–50, 156–61, 163, 166, 181, 400

further class-action suits discouraged by, 56, 57

Gregg brief of, 362–64, 367

Gregg rehearing petitions and, 424

Gregg/Woodson oral arguments of, 372, 373–79, 388–94, 395–98, 400, 436

influence and legendary reputation of, 41, 43, 44, 357, 358, 430–31

"Last-Aid Kits" of, 52, 55, 426–28

LDF's containment policy and, 56–57, 58–61

Maxwell case and, 45, 46, 77, 82*n*, 94, 192, 306*n*, 374

moratorium strategy of, 53–55, 65, 112, 133

at national death penalty conferences, 61–62, 111–12, 129, 284–85

1976 abolition campaign strategy set by, 360–62, 368, 369, 375, 389, 425–26, 488*n*

"objective indicators" argument of, 147–48, 154, 156–57, 183

on post-*Furman* sway in public opinion, 261–62

in reaction to *Gregg/Woodson* decisions, 421–22

Supreme Court clerkship of, 42–43, 129

tireless work ethic of, 43, 68, 129, 132, 357, 358

as "tone deaf" to main stream attitudes, 368, 369, 393

Amsterdam, Gustave, 41

Amsterdam, Jon, 41, 42, 132, 358, 370

Amsterdam, Valla, 41

Ancel, Marc, 29

Anderson, Robert, 136–37

Anderson v. California, 136–37, 151, 184–85, 254, 359, 392, 397, 443, 466*n*

Proposition 17 in overturning of, 255, 382, 443

Andrews, George, 73

anti-Semitism, 5, 6, 482*n*

appellate review, in revised death penalty statutes, 304, 363, 378, 398, 401, 403

arbitrary sentencing, 69, 80, 102–3, 133–35, 140, 278, 429, 438

appellate review created in response to, 304, 363, 378, 398, 401, 403

clemency and, 140, 253, 324–25, 327, 363, 367, 373, 376, 378, 385–86, 389, 394–95, 412

death penalty statutes in perpetuating of, 310–12, 313, 323–24, 326, 341, 343, 344, 361, 362–64, 366–67, 373, 375, 380, 390, 391, 394, 395, 396–98, 401, 405, 430, 435

in Eighth Amendment capital punishment arguments, 133–35, 148, 149, 162, 163, 164, 167, 168, 181, 186–87, 188–89, 190, 215–16, 220, 221, 222, 224, 227, 228, 257, 377, 378, 385, 389, 396, 401, 430

Fowler and issues of, 323–25, 326–27, 328–30

Furman and issues of, 133–35, 148, 149, 150, 162–63, 164, 166, 167, 181, 184, 186–87, 188–90, 201, 215–16, 220, 221, 222, 224, 227, 228, 236, 242, 257, 276, 280, 282, 303, 323, 324, 325, 341, 361, 362, 377, 385, 389–90, 399, 401, 402, 405, 434, 444

Gregg and issues of, 360, 366–68, 369, 373, 375, 376–78, 385–86, 401, 415*n*, 444

jury discretion and absence of standards as leading to, 66–68, 77, 79, 80, 81, 82, 83, 89–91, 92, 94, 95–96, 100–103, 106–7, 108, 111, 118, 148, 168, 189, 312, 315, 385, 389–90, 391, 401, 402

poverty and, 8, 79, 133, 134, 137, 159, 188, 215, 368, 386

racism and, *see* racism, in capital sentencing

"rational application" statutes designed for curtailing of, 261, 303–17, 385, 386, 398, 399, 402–3, 411, 415*n*, 434–35, 438, 444, 484*n*

single-phase trials as leading to, 95–96, 103, 105, 107–8, 311

social science research on, 22, 94, 162–63, 168

Woodson and issues of, 343, 344, 360, 373, 375, 389, 392, 394–95

Arendt, Hannah, 8

Arizona, 231*n*, 257, 258, 302

Arizona Justice Project, 231*n*

Arkansas, 25, 32, 38, 39, 48, 67, 112, 125, 178, 258, 259, 276, 444

standardless sentencing procedure in, 70, 77, 91, 94

Arlington National Cemetery, 335

Armstrong, Scott, 171, 333, 409, 486*n*

Ashes to Ashes (Kluger), 260*n*

Ashland College, 13

Ashwander v. Tennessee Valley Authority, 236

Ashworth, Taylor, 180, 454n
Askew, Reuben, 252, 253
Atheneum Books, 260
Atkins v. Virginia, 428, 460n
Atlanta, Ga., 267
Atlantic, 9
Austin, Alan, 331–32
Australia, 63, 157

Babin, James, 381, 385
Baez, Joan, 430
Bailey, Luther, 48
Baker v. Carr, 42–43, 80, 87, 455n
Bakke case, 352, 461n
Baldus, David, 39–40, 294–95, 297, 298,
    301, 428, 473n, 481n
Baldwin, James, 18
Baltimore, Md., 137, 139, 276
Banner, Stuart, 134
Baxley, Bill, 248–51
Bazelon, David, 3, 8, 17, 19, 74–75, 93, 111,
    141
Baze v. Reez, 438–39
Beard, Charles, 463n
Beasley, Dorothy, 135, 136, 143, 240, 241
    Furman oral arguments of, 161–63, 164
    in revising of Georgia's death penalty
        statutes, 251–52
Beasley, Jere, 247
Beccaria, Cesare, 305
Becker, Gary, 288–89, 291, 293, 299, 475n,
    480n
Becker, Howard, 273
Becker, Mike, 111, 119, 127, 180
Bedau, Hugo, 112, 131, 262, 284–86, 289,
    293, 294, 323, 460n
Bell, Derrick, 32, 51n
Bellow, Gary, 259
Benoy, Jean, 321, 322, 329, 330
    Fowler oral arguments of, 326–28
Berenson, Jerome, 136
Berk, Richard, 481n
Best Little Whorehouse in Texas, 379
Bible, 14, 24, 74, 250n
Bickel, Alexander, 174, 322, 449n
bifurcated trials, 83, 95–96, 97, 103, 104–5,
    107–8, 325, 403
    post-*Furman* legislation for, 251–52, 253,
        257, 303–4, 311, 373, 415n
    sentencing standards issue as linked with,
        82, 83, 90, 96, 178
Bill of Rights, 14, 16, 146, 212, 255, 396

Birmingham, Ala., 13, 32
Black, Charles, 10–11, 16, 299, 310, 330
Black, Hugo, 4, 9, 12–15, 16, 17, 20, 22, 29,
    72, 78, 81–82, 85, 87, 91, 109, 111, 114,
    115, 119, 126, 182, 200, 212, 268, 276,
    322, 332, 347, 448n, 485n
    background and education of, 9, 12–13
    Court nomination and confirmation of, 13
    death penalty as viewed by, 15
    failing health of, 114, 125
    Giaccio decision of, 66–67
    Griswold dissent of, 15
    judicial philosophy of, 9, 10, 11, 12, 14–15,
        20, 24, 25, 80, 108–9, 203
    Maxwell case and, 80, 95, 96
    McGautha case and, 104, 108, 111, 433
    in reaction to Goldberg's death penalty
        memorandum, 25
    religious faith of, 13, 14, 24
    resignation of, 125, 135
    on single-phase trial issue, 104, 105
Blackmun, Harry, 44, 77, 99n, 114, 127, 145,
    179, 224, 284, 317, 319, 333, 404, 408,
    409, 424, 438, 460n, 489n
    Amsterdam's complicated relationship
        with, 45–46, 159, 374, 390, 391, 400,
        436, 492n
    as appellate court judge, 39, 45, 67, 94,
        108, 192–93, 374, 436
    cert dissent of, 435
    in cert petition review of statutory cases,
        345
    childhood of, 194
    confirmation hearings of, 93–94
    death penalty as viewed by, 45, 67, 94, 169,
        178, 192–93, 195, 224, 225, 237, 434–36
    in *Fowler* oral arguments, 324, 325, 326,
        366–67, 369
    in *Furman* conference, 169
    Furman dissent of, 185, 225, 374, 390–91,
        418, 435
    Furman draft opinions of, 191, 195, 196,
        198–99, 200, 224, 225, 237
    in *Furman* oral arguments, 159, 163
    in *Gregg/Woodson* conference, 402, 404
    in *Gregg/Woodson* oral arguments, 373–74,
        381, 390–91
    insecurities of, 194
    judicial philosophy of, 193, 195, 271
    law clerks of, 45, 108, 124, 128, 192, 270,
        434–35
    liberal evolution of, 193–95

Maxwell case and, 39, 45, 67, 94, 169, 192, 195, 374, 434

McGautha case and, 101, 102, 103, 104, 105–6, 108, 128

Roe v. Wade decision of, 167, 194–95, 199–200, 269–71, 274

Woodson dissent of, 418

working style of, 191–92

Black Panthers, 240, 269

Blumstein, Al, 299

Boas, Franz, 463*n*

Boger, John, 54

Bohm, Robert, 266

Bolton, Arthur, 135

Bolton, William, 64–65

Bork, Robert, 174, 364–65, 369, 370, 377, 387, 396, 485*n*

background and career of, 322

Fowler amicus brief filed by, 290–91, 322, 365

Fowler oral argument of, 329–30

Gregg amicus brief filed by, 364, 365–68

Gregg/Woodson oral arguments of, 382–88, 389

Boston, Mass., busing in, 268–69

Bowers, William, 293, 296–97, 301, 473*n*

Bowers v. Hardwick, 212, 352

Boykin v. Alabama, 66, 73, 92, 97, 112, 113, 115, 127, 132–33, 178, 280, 433, 443

Court conference on, 79–84, 178

LDF amicus brief filed in, 66, 68–70, 374

standardless sentencing issue in, 66–68, 79, 82

Branch, Elmer, 117, 164, 188, 241

Branch v. Texas, 117, 118, 131, 164, 251, 443, 444

see also Furman v. Georgia

Brandeis, Louis, 12, 13, 84, 86, 236, 282–83

Braniff Airlines, 379

Brennan, Bill, Sr., 71

Brennan, Marjorie, 74, 119

Brennan, William, 9, 24, 29, 71–78, 83–84, 86, 93, 113, 127, 137, 144, 151, 179, 193–95, 199, 211, 219, 224, 226, 227, 229, 230, 235–36, 242, 267, 268, 281, 319, 332, 333, 334–35, 349, 352, 354–55, 400, 403, 407, 408, 409, 414, 424, 432, 434, 435, 436, 460*n*, 486*n*, 490*n*–91*n*

as appellate court judge, 72

avoidance of racial issues in decisions of, 181–82

background and education of, 71–72

Baker decision of, 42, 80, 87

Bazelon's influential friendship with, 74–75, 141

in cert petition review of statutory cases, 345

Court appointment of, 72

daily routine of, 71, 454*n*, 455*n*

death penalty opposed by, 27, 71, 73, 75, 76, 115, 119

Dershowitz's meeting with, 18–19, 27, 75

"evolving standards of decency" argument of, 180–81, 360

"four clean cases" for review chosen by, 115, 116–18, 457*n*–58*n*

in *Furman* conference, 168, 170

Furman draft opinions and, 172–73, 180–82, 186–88, 189–90, 191, 197–98, 215, 216, 222–23, 233

Furman published opinion of, 236, 282, 325

Gregg dissent of, 418, 444

in *Gregg/Woodson* conference, 401

"human dignity" argument emphasized by, 73, 180, 186–87, 215, 236, 418

as influential justice on Warren Court, 73, 87, 355

judicial philosophy of, 72, 73, 180

law clerks of, 74, 75, 111, 119, 124, 144, 172, 180–81, 182, 185, 186, 189, 190, 197, 198, 218, 222–23, 228, 229, 232, 233, 355, 400, 454*n*

liberalism of, 73, 75, 81, 88, 351

and loss of influence in Burger Court, 355, 423

Marshall's secret anti-death penalty draft given to, 142, 144–45, 169

Marshall's voting partnership with, 418

as master Court politician, 87, 90

Maxwell case and, 79–80, 81, 83, 89–92, 94, 95–96, 97, 178

McGautha case and, 105, 109–11, 119, 178, 433

Mosley dissent of, 355

religion's lack of influence on, 73–75

Roe v. Wade and, 74, 194, 269

on standardless sentencing issue, 83, 89–90, 92, 95–96, 109–10

warm relations with colleagues of, 80, 81, 87, 141, 145, 172–73

in *Woodson* majority, 445

Brenner, Saul, 338

Brethren, The (Woodward and Armstrong),
171, 333, 350, 351, 409, 486*n*
Brown, Edmund "Pat," 80, 113
Brown, Ken, 248
Brown v. Board of Education, 14, 21, 28, 32,
35, 46, 48, 51*n*, 75, 78, 141, 170, 171,
175, 212, 213, 233, 243, 260*n*, 266, 267,
275, 276, 278, 283, 308, 357, 452*n*
LDF's work in, 52–53, 58
public backlash to, 25–26, 125, 266,
347–48
Brown II, 266, 275
Brownwell, Herbert, 72
Bruder, Mel, 164
Buchanan, Pat, 273
Buckley v. Valeo, 334, 355, 408
Bumpers, Dale, 258
Bundy, McGeorge, 50
Bunker Hill, 203
Bureau of Justice Statistics, 281
Burger, Warren, 67, 87, 92–93, 107, 114,
115, 119, 125, 127, 128, 144, 145, 164,
167–68, 170–71, 179, 185, 193, 194, 199,
200, 224, 225, 229, 268, 323, 332, 333,
334, 335, 337, 340, 344, 348, 349, 351,
411, 418, 419, 420, 432, 433
assigning of *Gregg/Woodson* opinions by,
404, 407–8, 413, 417, 433
background and education of, 92–93
Bazelon's feud with, 93
in cert petition review of statutory cases,
345–46
colleagues' dislike of, 349–50, 407–8,
486*n*
Court nomination of, 92
death penalty as viewed by, 95, 178
in *Furman* conference, 167, 168, 170, 173*n*
Furman decision read by, 235–36
Furman draft opinions of, 190–91, 197,
224, 230, 231–32, 237
Furman individually written opinions
ordered by, 170–71
in *Furman* oral arguments, 145, 156,
157–60, 161, 163
Furman published dissent of, 242, 247,
277, 284, 304, 320
Gregg rehearing petitions and, 424–25
in *Gregg/Woodson* conference, 400–401
in *Gregg/Woodson* oral arguments, 372–73,
375, 381, 386, 391, 393, 395, 396, 398,
399
judicial philosophy of, 194, 195

law clerks of, 170–71, 172, 191, 413
legal career of, 93
Maxwell case and, 94, 95
McGautha case and, 100–101, 103, 104,
106, 232
secrecy of, 170–71, 191, 199
as skeptical of social science, 283–84
Burger Court, 171, 193, 337, 413
mutual influence among justices in, 179
rightward swing of, 114, 127, 354–55, 439
Stewart as significant influence in, 179–80
White's emergence as swing vote in, 241–
42, 351
Burt, Robert, 276, 419
Burton, Harold, 461*n*
Bush, George H. W., 364
Bush, George W., 302*n*, 475*n*
Business Week, 261
busing, 196, 268–69, 274, 275
Byrd, Robert, 125

Caldwell, Earl, 240
California, 35, 97, 99, 100, 110, 146, 151, 153,
155, 158, 211, 240, 315, 332, 381, 480*n*
class-action suit in, 56, 57
Proposition 17 in, 254–55, 382, 443
standardless sentencing procedures in, 100,
101–2, 106, 109, 137, 445
Warren as governor of, 9, 20, 449*n*
California Commonwealth Club, 292
Callahan, John, 103
Callins v. Collins, 434–35
Calvin, John, 14
Camus, Albert, 99*n*, 133, 418
Canada, 63
capital punishment, *see* death penalty
*Capital Punishment: The Inevitability of
Caprice and Mistake* (Black), 310
Capote, Truman, 73, 131
Cardozo, Benjamin, 397
Carmichael, Stokely, 269
Carson, Rachel, 18
Carswell, G. Harrold, 93
Carter, Jimmy, 231*n*, 257, 321
Carter, Robert, 51*n*, 58, 357
case method, 207, 208, 260
Catholic Church, Catholicism, 73–74
Celler, Emanuel, 113
Census Bureau, U.S., 296
Central High School, Little Rock, Ark.,
25–26
Century Association, 177

cert petitions, 4, 19, 66, 99, 332, 336–41, 407, 436, 445
   Blackmun's dissent on denial of, 435
   in death penalty cases, 28–30, 70, 73, 81, 96, 99, 109, 115, 116–18, 136, 144, 166, 340–46, 349–51, 352–53, 458*n*
   Goldberg's dissent on denial of, 28–30, 31, 33–34, 435
   law clerks role in reviewing of, 338, 339, 340, 342–44, 345, 352–53
   motion counsel and, 340
   see also grant of certiorari
Chamberlain, Wilt, 41
Chambers, Julius, 267–68
Chambers v. Florida, 109
Chambliss, Robert, 249
Charlotte-Mecklenburg school district, 267–68
Cheatwood, Vernon, 140
Chicago, Ill., 6, 17, 267, 289
   Goldberg's childhood in, 5–6, 16
Chicago, University of, 288, 299, 356, 475*n*
Chicken Ranch, 379
child labor laws, 301
Chimel v. California, 99
CIA (Central Intelligence Agency), 7
circuit courts, 38*n*, 43
Citizens Against Legalized Murder (CALM), 131, 237
Citizens for Kennedy and Johnson, 204
civil liberties, 8, 10, 16, 17, 20, 35, 36, 72, 73, 113, 114, 194, 355
Civil Rights Act (1964), 125
civil rights movement, 7, 32, 36, 46, 125, 141, 250*n*, 272, 368
   Freedom Summer in, 36, 204, 357
   Powell's criticisms of, 125–26
civil rights workers, 51–52, 128
   salaries of, 52*n*, 128
Civil War, U.S., 5, 206, 396
Clark, Kenneth and Mamie, 58
Clark, Leroy, 33, 34–35, 50, 357
Clark, Ramsey, 65
Clark, Tom, 4, 10
class-action lawsuits, 55–57, 60
Clean Water Act, 274
clemency, 38, 68, 112, 192, 250*n*, 378, 405, 415, 416, 449*n*, 488*n*
   arbitrariness in awarding of, 140, 253, 323–25, 327, 363, 367, 373, 376, 378, 385–86, 389, 394–95, 412
Clinton, Bill, 124, 365

Cloninger, Dale, 300
Cohen, Stanley, 273
Coker v. Georgia, 277, 427, 460*n*, 491*n*
Cole, James, 293, 294–95, 297, 298, 301, 473*n*, 481*n*
Colorado, 111
Colorado, University of, 202, 203
Columbia Law Review, 21, 260–61, 285*n*
Columbia Law School, 32, 33, 84, 123, 307, 465*n*
   Meltsner on faculty at, 259–60, 357
   second national death penalty conference at, 111–12, 129
Columbia University, 288, 289, 473*n*
Commission to Revise New York's Penal Law, 309
Committee for the Study of Incarceration, 302
Committee to Defend Martin Luther King, 181
Committee to Study Capital Punishment, 252
Common Ground (Lukas), 268
common law, 105, 106
Common Law, The (Holmes), 207
Communists, Communism, 12, 35, 124
Congress, U.S., 12, 65, 95, 112, 113, 125, 126, 211, 224, 251, 275, 301, 333, 354, 381, 384, 409, 437, 449*n*
   death penalty statute proposals in, 256–57, 262
Congress of Industrial Organizations, 7
Connally, John, 379
Connecticut, 258
   contraception laws in, 15, 212
conservatives, conservatism, 12, 14, 15, 40, 87, 185, 194, 205, 213, 365, 448*n*, 475*n*
Constitution, U.S., 5, 10, 11, 14–15, 16, 29, 45, 66, 73, 78, 83, 94, 96, 100, 103, 104, 105, 106, 108, 113, 132, 134, 137, 144, 147, 151, 152, 158, 186, 194, 196, 207, 211, 212, 227, 267, 287, 379, 384, 385, 394, 397, 403, 415*n*, 437, 488*n*
   death penalty as sanctioned in, 5, 23, 149, 153, 154, 161, 167, 169, 183, 329, 349, 365
   as "evolving" document, 16, 20, 23, 108–9, 146, 180, 183, 448*n*
   language of, 149, 153–54
   "originalist" view of, 12, 14, 20, 23, 25, 80, 180, 224, 322, 349, 382, 383, 387, 396, 407

Constitution, U.S. (*continued*)
  post-*Furman* amendments proposed for,
    248, 251
  see also specific amendments
Constitutional Convention, 184
contraception, 15, 177, 212
Cook, Philip, 479*n*
Cooper v. Aaron, 87
Corbin, Arthur, 209–10
Cover, Robert, 213
Cox, Archibald, 322
Crampton, James, 96–97, 103, 106, 107–8
Crampton v. Ohio, 96–97, 103–4, 106, 107–
    8, 178, 303, 443
  see also McGautha v. California
Cravath, DeGersdoff, Swaine & Wood, 84
Craven, Braxton, 267–68
Crawford, George, 139
crime, crime rates, 62, 264*n*, 265, 272, 281–
    82, 296–97, 299, 387, 470*n*, 476*n*–77*n*,
    478*n*–79*n*
  death penalty as deterrence to, *see*
    deterrence
  "moral panic" in response to, 273
  public opinion on death penalty and,
    264–66
  see also homicide rates
criminal codes, 95, 304–6, 308, 309–10,
    313, 317
criminal justice community, 287, 299,
    474*n*
  as skeptical of deterrence, 292–93
criminology, 108, 273, 281, 283, 286–89,
    474*n*
  economic theory applied to, 288–89, 291,
    292, 293, 294, 298, 299, 300, 474*n*–76*n*,
    477*n*, 480*n*, 481*n*
  tensions between economists and, 292*n*,
    300, 474*n*–75*n*
  see also social science research
Cruel and Unusual (Meltsner), 259, 260–61,
    285*n*, 460*n*
cruel and unusual punishment, 4, 15, 24,
    59–60, 66, 108–9, 115, 116, 117, 118,
    119, 127, 135, 167, 173, 227, 234, 235,
    379, 418–19, 420, 429
  Anderson argument of, 137, 254
  Brennan's four-point test on, 186–87,
    189–90, 223
  brutality and pain of executions as, 15, 131,
    153, 181, 184–85, 186, 487*n*
  Burger's interpretation of, 190

California's abolishment of death penalty
    under, 184–85
  death penalty statutes as, 344, 361, 363,
    375
  denationalization as, 19, 20, 445
  deterrence argued as criteria for, 151–52,
    156, 157, 187, 190, 219, 222
  "evolving standards of decency" in
    measuring of, 20, 21, 22, 23, 64, 68, 69,
    131, 132–33, 135, 142, 145–48, 154–55,
    156–57, 162, 169, 180–81, 183, 184, 191,
    334, 365, 383–84, 393, 395, 401, 403,
    445, 448*n*
  false hope for death row inmates as, 116,
    424
  Furman draft opinions on, 180–82, 186–
    87, 188–90, 197, 220, 223, 224, 227
  Furman oral argument debate on, 151–54,
    161–62, 163
  life imprisonment as, 371*n*, 393
  mental anguish of death row as, 99, 131,
    186, 187, 285, 366
  Robinson v. California and, 211
  vagueness of phrase, 146–47
  see also death penalty, Eighth Amendment
    arguments on; Eighth Amendment
culpability index, 312
Cuomo, Mario, 475*n*
Currie, Elliot, 286
Curtis, Clinton, 398

Dallas Morning News, 65
Darden v. Wainwright, 434, 436–37
Darrow, Clarence, 6, 35
Darwin, Charles, 205–6, 207, 463*n*
Darwin's Sacred Cause (Desmond and Moore),
    463*n*
Davis, Peggy, 357, 358, 359–60, 361, 368,
    375, 399, 406, 422, 487*n*
  Jurek rehearing petition requested by,
    425–26
Davis, Thomas, 398
Days, Drew, 357
D.C. Circuit Court of Appeals, 3, 43, 75, 93,
    353, 364
Dean, Charles, 476*n*
death penalty, 6, 8, 11, 21, 72, 76–77,
    99–100, 135, 144
  abortion vs., 199–200
  Blackmun's views on, 45, 67, 94, 169, 178,
    192–93, 195, 224, 225, 237, 434–36
  Black's views on, 15

Brennan's views on, 27, 71, 73, 75, 76, 115, 119

Burger's views on, 95, 178

campaigns for abolishment of, *see* abolition campaigns

as constitutionally sanctioned, 5, 23, 149, 153, 154, 161, 167, 169, 183, 329, 349, 365

as cruel and unusual punishment, *see* cruel and unusual punishment

"death row phenomenon" and, 99

Dershowitz's aversion to, 16–17, 18

deterrence issue and, *see* deterrence

as disproportionate punishment, 22, 23, 28, 29, 34, 66, 69, 81, 82–83, 112, 117, 164, 187, 366, 383–84, 418, 420, 427

Douglas's "summer research project" on, 118–19

Douglas's views on, 27, 119

Eighth Amendment argument against, *see* death penalty, Eighth Amendment arguments on

Founding Fathers as accepting of, 5, 16, 108–9, 115, 152, 184, 349

Frankfurter's views on, 15, 193

Goldberg-Dershowitz memorandum on constitutionality of, 20–25, 26–28, 29, 30, 32, 34, 53, 336–37, 432

Goldberg's cert dissent on, 28–30, 31, 33–34

Goldberg's plan for abolition of, 4–5, 8, 15–16, 18

Goldberg's views on, 8, 16, 17

innocent people as victims of, 8, 23, 61, 224–25

international trend toward abolition of, 23, 63, 131, 133, 157, 162, 184, 435

juries as rarely imposing, 107, 133, 150, 159, 164, 167, 190, 222, 223, 278, 367

for juveniles, 41, 418, 428

lack of scholarly opposition to constitutionality of, 5, 20–21, 47

life imprisonment vs., 370, 371*n,* 386, 393, 412, 488*n*–89*n*

"Marshall Hypothesis" on, 181, 262–63, 420

Marshall's evolving views on, 137–38, 139–42, 145, 172

Marshall's secret draft in opposition to, 137, 142, 144–45, 169, 181

for mentally-disturbed individuals, 427–28

MPC's provisions for, 306, 310, 313

New York experiment with, 475*n*–76*n,* 479*n*

in 19th century Britain, 68

for non-homicide crimes, 18, 22, 26, 28, 29, 34, 37, 38–40, 44, 45, 66, 69, 72, 77, 81, 82–83, 94, 112, 115, 117, 133, 164, 234, 277, 320*n,* 328, 370, 402, 427, 443, 445, 449*n,* 491*n*

post-*Furman* reactionary legislation on, 248–55, 256–59, 261, 262–63, 278, 279, 302, 303–4, 311, 341, 354, 360, 365, 373–74, 384, 394, 401, 420

post-*Furman* rates in imposing of, 277–78, 321, 429, 431, 481*n*

poverty and, 8, 79, 133, 134, 137, 159, 188, 215, 301, 368, 386

Powell's views on, 144, 169, 348–49, 437–38

public opinion on, 33, 62–63, 132, 148, 155, 160, 168, 183, 184, 217, 234–35, 236, 254, 255–56, 258, 261–63, 264–66, 269, 274–75, 277–78, 279–80, 302*n,* 309, 313, 317, 355, 360, 374, 383, 420

racist application of, *see* racism, in capital sentencing

Rehnquist's support for, 170, 224

as retributive punishment, 23, 169, 186, 215, 216, 220, 221, 236, 281, 301, 305, 307–8, 309, 366, 414–15, 420, 421, 437, 439, 479*n*

for special or cases, 157–59, 375, 378, 382–83, 391–93

state-level abolition of, 63, 112–13, 159, 169, 184–85, 309, 382, 443

state-level reinstatement of, 252–53, 255, 257–59, 261, 262, 309, 321

Stevens's views on, 438–39

Stewart's views on, 29, 64, 81–83, 166–67, 173, 175, 201

supporters of, 33–34, 55, 64–65, 76–77, 98, 102–103, 247–248, 285, 475*n; see also* pro-death penalty campaigns

Trop disclaimer on, 20

viewed as states' issue, 15, 148, 169, 190, 224–25, 236, 249, 303, 321, 322, 330, 361, 366, 388, 401, 405, 414, 422

Warren's views on, 20, 79, 433, 449*n*

see also executions

death penalty cases, 17, 28–30, 41, 43, 44–45, 50, 54, 63–66, 72–73, 137, 139–41, 192–93, 229, 231*n,* 277, 333, 334, 351, 429–31, 434–35, 437, 466*n* death penalty cases (*continued*)

  abolition strategy vs. obligation to
    individual clients in, 54, 56–60, 82*n*,
    164, 361, 426, 430–31, 433

  appellate review instituted in revised
    statutes for, 304, 363, 378, 398, 401, 403

  bifurcated trials created for, 251–52, 253,
    257, 303–4, 311, 373, 403, 415*n*

  cert petitions reviewed in, 28–30, 70,
    73, 81, 96, 99, 109, 115, 116–18, 136,
    144, 166, 340–46, 349–51, 352–53,
    458*n*

  class-action lawsuits filed in, 55–57

  clemency and commuting of sentences
    in, 38, 68, 112, 140, 192, 250*n*, 253,
    324–25, 327, 363, 367, 373, 376, 378,
    385–86, 389, 394–95, 405, 412, 415,
    416, 449*n*, 488*n*

  Court's reversal of convictions in, 15

  Fourteenth Amendment arguments in,
    66–67, 70, 80, 83, 90–92, 94–96, 100–
    103, 104–11, 118, 129, 145, 146, 149,
    151, 155, 161, 162, 163, 167, 189, 191,
    218, 226–27, 228, 229, 417, 419, 428,
    434

  habeas corpus petitions filed in, 37, 38, 39,
    48, 56

  jury-selection bias in, 37, 38, 57–59, 64, 77,
    82, 112, 137

  LDF's decision to extend representation to
    whites in, 48–50

  LDF's decision to represent murderers in,
    52–53

  LDF's first attempt at representing
    defendant in, 37–39, 45, 48

  as long and arduous process, 37, 38

  Powell's proposal to apply *Gregg* decision
    only to future, 415–17

  single-phase trials issue in, 67, 70, 81, 82,
    83, 89, 90, 91, 92, 95–96, 103, 104–5,
    107–8, 129, 303–4, 315, 325

  standardless sentencing issue in, 66–68,
    70, 77, 79, 80, 81, 83, 89–91, 92, 94,
    95–96, 100–103, 104, 105, 106–7, 108,
    109–10, 118, 129, 133, 137, 148, 168,
    226, 303, 315, 325

  stays of execution granted in, 48, 55, 56,
    424–25, 429, 436–37

  see also abolition campaigns; *specific cases*

death penalty, Eighth Amendment
  arguments on, 4–5, 22–23, 34, 108–9,
  118, 119, 127, 145–64, 175, 193, 234,

  235, 329, 360, 361, 377, 396, 418–19,
  427–29, 432–33, 434, 439, 460*n*

  abolition campaign's decision to focus on,
    111–12, 113, 117, 129–30, 279, 361, 417,
    426, 433

  abolition campaign's initial avoidance of,
    59–60, 62, 69–70, 97, 109, 111, 113–14

  Amsterdam's use of, 112, 129–30, 131,
    132–33, 134, 145–50, 154–55, 156–61,
    163, 167, 168, 188, 375, 389, 393, 396,
    399, 426, 427–28

  in *Anderson* case, 137

  arbitrary and discriminatory capital
    sentencing in, 133–35, 148, 149, 162,
    163, 164, 167, 168, 181, 186–87, 188–89,
    190, 215–16, 220, 221, 222, 224, 227,
    228, 257, 375, 377, 378, 385, 389, 396,
    401, 430

  disproportionality of capital punishment
    in, 22, 23, 66, 69, 112, 117, 164, 187,
    366, 383–84, 418, 420, 427

  in *Furman* case, 129–30, 131, 132–33,
    134, 145–54, 156–62, 163, 167, 168,
    169–70, 173, 180–82, 183, 184, 186–87,
    188–90, 195, 197–98, 215–16, 219–20,
    222, 227, 228, 229, 377, 385, 389

  in *Gregg/Woodson* cases, 360–61, 362–64,
    366–67, 375, 377, 378, 382, 383–85,
    387, 389, 390, 392–94, 396, 401–2, 403,
    417, 420, 421

  human dignity emphasized in, 20, 21, 180,
    185, 186–87, 215, 236, 411–12, 418, 421

  Marshall's secret anti-death penalty draft
    based on, 137, 142

  Supreme Court's reluctance to address, 16,
    70, 96, 97, 106, 109, 111–12, 113–15,
    116, 432–33, 449*n*

  see also cruel and unusual punishment

Death Penalty in America, The (Bedau), 286

death penalty statutes, 65, 97, 162, 173, 226,
  248, 401

  biased jury-selection procedures in, 37, 38,
    57–59, 64, 77, 82, 112, 137

  "channeling" of eligible defendants in, 311,
    312

  difficulty in shaping of, 95, 107, 110, 303,
    304, 361

  felony-murder rule in, 17, 118

  Furman standards loopholes for, 201, 216,
    217, 219–20, 222, 223, 229, 231–32,
    233, 242–43, 247, 254, 257, 276, 280,
    303, 341, 373, 374, 405, 406, 411

Harlan's skepticism on feasibility of fair standards in, 107, 110, 232, 303, 304, 306*n*, 314, 316, 317, 361, 367

"narrowing" of eligible defendants in, 311–12

"special cases" argument for, 157–59, 375, 378, 382–83, 391–93

standardless sentencing procedures in, *see* standardless sentencing procedures

see also guided-discretion statutes; mandatory statutes

death penalty statutes, post-*Furman* revisions of, 248, 250, 251–53, 256–59, 260–62, 285*n*, 293, 303, 305–17, 320, 334, 341, 354, 355, 370, 373–74, 381–82, 384, 385, 386, 390, 394, 397, 416, 420, 443

aggravating factors in, 252, 253, 304, 310, 311–12, 315, 362–63, 373, 380, 382, 398, 406, 407

Amsterdam's criticisms of, 323–24, 362–64, 366–67, 373–76, 380, 390–92, 396–98, 401

appellate review added to, 304, 363, 378, 398, 401, 403

arbitrariness as inherent in, 310–12, 313, 323–24, 326, 341, 343, 344, 361, 362–64, 366–67, 373, 375, 380, 390, 391, 392, 394, 395, 396–98, 401, 405, 430, 435

bifurcated trials introduced in, 251–52, 253, 257, 303–4, 311, 373, 415*n*

cases challenging constitutionality of, *see Gregg v. Georgia*; *Woodson v. North Carolina*

Court's striking down of, 277, 312*n*, 425, 439, 445

in Florida, 252–253, 304, 342, 343, 398, 401, 402, 404, 406, 408, 409, 425, 430, 445; *see also Proffitt v. Florida*

in legitimizing capital punishment, 313–14, 374, 484*n*

in Louisiana, 258, 304, 395, 401, 402, 403, 404, 406–7, 409, 410, 445; *see also Roberts v. Louisiana*

MPC as basis for, 305–6, 310, 317

in North Carolina, 258–9, 262, 304, 320, 323, 324, 326, 328, 341, 372, 389, 392, 394, 395, 401, 402, 403, 404, 405, 406, 407, 408, 409, 410, 413; *see also Fowler v. North Carolina*; *Woodson v. North Carolina*

in Texas, 258, 343, 360–361, 369, 372, 376, 380, 401, 402, 403, 404, 406, 409, 410, 425–426, 439–440, 444; *see also Jurek v. Texas*

"rational application" of capital punishment as intent of, 261, 303–17, 385, 386, 398, 399, 402–3, 411, 415*n*, 434–35, 438, 484*n*

review of cert petitions in regard to, 340–46, 349–51, 352–53

vagueness of, 311–12, 314*n*, 315, 316, 436

Deciding to Decide (Perry), 338–40

Deitz, Robert, 175, 215, 332, 334

Delaware, 258, 309, 320

Dellinger, Walter, 88

Democracy and Distrust (Ely), 460*n*

Democrats, Democratic Party, 76, 247, 269, 272, 379

denationalization, 19–20, 445

Denton, Nancy, 267

"Deregulating Death" (Weisberg), 314

Derryberry, Larry, 251

Dershowitz, Alan, 3–5, 8, 15–19, 20–22, 44, 65, 66, 127, 174, 277, 307, 355, 406, 427, 433

background of, 16–17

Brennan's meeting with, 18–19, 27, 75

constitutionality memorandum of Goldberg and, 20–25, 26–28, 29, 30, 32, 34, 53, 336–37, 432

death penalty opposed by, 16–17, 18

Furman decision reaction of, 238–39, 242

Goldberg's cert dissent and, 28, 29, 30

Harvard Review article published by, 113, 181, 182

religious faith of, 17

social science research of, 22, 23, 26, 30, 337

desegregation, 14, 21, 32, 46, 53*n*, 126, 141, 212–13, 266–69, 271, 273, 274, 275–76, 278, 449*n*, 452*n*

busing and, 196, 268–69, 274, 275

"Finger plan" in, 268

"freedom of choice" plans in reaction to, 266–67

public backlash against, 25–26, 125, 266–69, 347–48

see also Brown v. Board of Education

deterrence, 8, 22, 131, 155, 156, 157, 158, 168–69, 187, 216, 219, 247, 281–82, 285–86, 287, 301–3, 305, 307, 349, 420–21, 437, 472*n*

deterrence (*continued*)
  abolitionist rebuttal to theory of, 293–94, 299, 302*n*
  Blackmun as unconvinced about, 67
  in constitutionality debate, 151–52, 155, 156, 157, 168–69, 187, 190–91, 222
  criminal justice scholars as skeptical of, 292–93
  in death penalty supporters' arguments, 248, 249, 257, 290–91, 301, 302, 322, 365–66, 388
  Dershowitz's study on, 22, 23
  as difficult to model for, 289, 290, 475*n*–82*n*
  econometrics applied to question of, 289–90, 291, 294, 300, 474*n*–76*n*, 477*n*, 480*n*, 481*n*
  Ehrlich's controversial study on, 289–301, 322, 365–66, 388, 473*n*, 474*n*, 475*n*, 477*n*, 478*n*, 481*n*
  execution threshold level for generating of, 480*n*–81*n*
  Furman and issue of, 151–52, 155, 156, 157, 158, 168–69, 187, 216, 219, 221, 222, 280, 281–82, 283, 284
  Gregg and issue of, 302–3, 365–66, 387–88, 437, 439
  inconclusive and contradictory evidence on, 23, 184, 282, 283, 287, 291–92, 299, 300–303, 366, 420–21, 439, 473*n*, 474*n*–76*n*, 479*n*–81*n*
  public support for theory of, 301–2
  Sellin's research on, 281–82, 284, 287–88, 291, 293, 294, 295, 297, 298, 299, 366, 471*n*, 473*n*
  Yale Law Journal articles on, 294–97, 301–2
Deterrent Effect of Capital Punishment, The: A Question of Life and Death (Ehrlich), 290
Detroit Lions, 203
Deutsch, Jan, 26
Dezhbakhsh, Hashem, 478*n*
dicta, 169*n*
DiIulio, John, 474*n*–75*n*
discrimination, class, 86
discrimination, racial, 64, 86
  see also racism
discrimination, sex, 212, 352
  in legal field, 63, 123, 124, 125, 135
Diskant, Greg, 355
district courts, 38*n*
Doe v. Bolton, 135, 199

Donohue, John, 475*n*–76*n*, 478*n*–79*n*
Dorsen, Norman, 36
Douglas, Cathy, 318–19
Douglas, Elsie, 126
Douglas, William O., 9, 18, 27, 28, 29, 74, 84–92, 115, 127, 164, 171, 172, 178, 179, 190, 194, 200, 203, 224, 225, 226, 242, 243, 268, 318–20, 322, 455*n*, 456*n*, 458*n*
  abusive and disagreeable temperament of, 86–87, 88, 318
  on arbitrary and discriminatory capital sentencing, 188–89, 215, 227, 236, 280, 282
  background and education of, 84, 85, 88, 91
  in *Boykin/Maxwell* conferences, 80, 81, 83, 95, 433
  Court vote taken away from, 332–33
  death of, 335
  death penalty as viewed by, 27, 119
  declining health of, 88, 319–20, 331–35, 422–23, 444
  discontentment of, 88, 89
  exaggerations and fabrications of, 86, 335
  Fowler opinion drafted by, 331
  in *Fowler* oral arguments, 320, 331
  in *Furman* conference, 167–68, 170
  Furman draft opinion of, 188–89, 191, 215–16, 227–29
  in *Furman* oral arguments, 148–49, 150, 153, 159, 162
  Furman published opinion of, 236, 280, 282
  grant of cert dissent of, 115–16, 118, 144
  indecisiveness of, 84, 85
  law clerks of, 86–87, 88, 117, 119, 144, 189, 228, 318, 319, 331–32, 334
  legal career of, 84, 88, 91
  legal realism of, 208–9
  marriages and affairs of, 86
  Maxwell opinion drafted by, 89–91, 92
  McGautha case and, 105, 109, 111, 172, 178, 226–27
  presidential ambitions of, 84–85, 88, 91
  reluctant resignation of, 333–35, 356
  on single-phase trial issue, 90, 95
  on standardless sentencing issue, 83, 89–90, 91, 95, 100
  strained relations with fellow justices of, 87–88, 90–91
  "summer research project" assigned by, 118–19

White and Stewart's inconsistent opinions attacked by, 226–29
at Yale Law School, 84, 208–9
Dred Scott decision, 429
Drifters, The (Michener), 318
Dubner, Stephen, 288
due process clause, 5, 83, 129, 149, 155, 161, 163, 191, 218, 385, 389, 394–95, 444
standardless sentencing and, 66–67, 80, 91, 92, 94, 95, 111, 227
Duke, Steven, 61
Durham v. United States, 93

Eagles, Sidney, 388, 394–95
Easterbrook, Frank, 364
Eastland, James, 25
Ebony, 321
econometrics, 289–90, 291, 300, 474*n*–76*n*, 477*n*, 480*n*, 481*n*
economic theory, as applied to criminology, 288–89, 291, 292, 293, 294, 298, 299, 474*n*–76*n*, 480*n*, 481*n*
Edelman, Daniel, 108
Edwards, Edwin, 258
Egypt, 270
Ehrhardt, Charles, 252, 253
Ehrlich, Isaac, 289–301, 474*n*, 477*n*, 478*n*
Forst's research as contradicting that of, 291–92
post-deterrence study career of, 299–300
problematic data used by, 296–97, 299, 473*n*, 475*n*, 477*n*, 481*n*
pro-death penalty supporters in citing of, 301, 302, 322, 365–66, 388
regression analysis of, 290, 294, 296, 298
in response to criticisms, 297–98, 473*n*
scholarly critiques of study by, 291, 294–98, 473*n*, 474*n*, 477*n*, 478*n*, 481*n*
Eichmann, Adolf, 8, 16
Eichmann in Jerusalem: A Study in the Banality of Evil (Arendt), 8
Eighteenth Amendment, 482*n*
Eighth Amendment, 4–5, 20, 21, 22–23, 108–9, 152, 153, 175, 182, 191, 197–98, 211, 219, 387, 417, 439, 460*n*
Burger's interpretation of, 190
death penalty and, *see* death penalty, Eighth Amendment arguments on
human dignity protections in, 20, 21, 180, 185, 186–87, 421
vagueness of, 146–47
see also cruel and unusual punishment

Eighth Amendment (rock band), 241
Eighth Circuit Court of Appeals, 37–38, 39, 45, 67, 94, 108, 192–93, 374
Eisenhower, Dwight, 9, 10, 25–26, 64, 72, 81, 93, 176, 205, 276
elections, U.S.:
of 1972, 272
of 2000, 302*n*
electric chair, 15, 112, 217, 359, 431
Eleventh Amendment, 211
Eleventh Circuit Court of Appeals, 40
Ellsworth, Phoebe, 285
Ely, John Hart, 146–47, 311, 460*n*
Emory University, 300
Engel v. Vitale, 73
England, Norman, 189
Enmund, Earl, 427
environmentalists, environmentalism, 18, 86, 124
Epiphany Church, 74
Epstein, Lee, 278, 369, 488*n*
Equal Justice Initiative (EJI), 371*n*
equal protection clause, 21, 85–86, 109–10, 124, 146, 162, 182, 428, 434
Escobedo v. Illinois, 26, 179, 212
Evans, John Louis, 250*n*
Evers, Medgar, 7
evolution, theory of, 35, 205–6, 249, 463*n*
Executioner's Song, The (Mailer), 316, 429
executions, 5, 9, 111, 127, 155, 160, 166, 187, 242, 250*n*, 289, 321, 355, 359, 374, 416, 439, 476*n*, 479*n*
abolition campaign's moratorium strategy for, 53–55, 56, 58, 60, 62, 65, 70, 89, 97, 111, 112–13, 133, 137, 296
"brutalization" hypothesis on, 480*n*
Ehrlich's correlation between homicide rates and, 290, 294–95, 296–97, 299, 473*n*, 475*n*, 477*n*
long death row waits before, 99, 437, 438, 476*n*
methods of, 15, 153, 439
pain and brutality of, 15, 117, 131, 181, 184–85, 487*n*
post-*Gregg* resumption of, 278–79, 429, 430, 431, 481*n*
public, 133, 402
rarity of, 63, 65, 150, 155, 159, 160, 167, 181, 216, 258, 261–62, 278, 374
state-level moratoriums on, 56, 112, 113, 114, 133, 217, 243, 261, 296, 431

executions (*continued*)
  stays of, 48, 52, 55, 56, 424–25, 426, 429,
    436–37
  in Texas, 410, 476*n*, 480*n*, 481*n*
  threshold level of, for generating
    deterrence, 480*n*–81*n*
  U.S.'s mid-century declining rates of, 63,
    65, 133, 150, 160, 181, 190, 278
executive clemency, 38, 112, 192, 250*n*, 253,
  324–25, 327, 363, 376, 378, 415, 416,
  449*n*
executive privilege, 275

Fagan, Jeffrey, 476*n*, 479*n*
Falk, Jerome, 117, 137
Faretta v. California, 354
Farmer, Millard, 430–31
Faubus, Orval, 25, 48, 54, 87, 276
FBI (Federal Bureau of Investigation), 240,
  296, 297, 473*n*, 476*n*
federalism, 182, 386, 387
Federalist Papers, 184
Federal Kidnapping Act (1948), 63–64
Federal Rules of Civil Procedure, 55
Feldstein, Martin, 291–92
felony-murder rule, 17, 118
Feminine Mystique, The (Friedan), 18
Field, David Dudley, 305
Fifth Amendment, 5, 67, 103, 107, 153, 161
  double-jeopardy provision in, 154
  due process clause in, 5, 83, 91, 92, 94, 161,
    385
Filatov, Victor, 474*n*
Finger, John, 268
Fire Next Time, The (Baldwin), 18
firing squads, 15, 430
First Amendment, 14, 43, 73, 212
Fisher, Franklin, 474*n*
Fiske, John, 206
Fleisher, Mark, 292*n*
Florida, 269, 343, 344, 352, 369, 388, 426,
  430, 476*n*, 480*n*
  class-action lawsuits in, 55–56, 57
  revised death penalty laws in, 252–253,
    304, 342, 343, 398, 401, 402, 404, 406,
    408, 409, 425, 430, 445; *see also Proffitt
    v. Florida*
Florida State Prison, 55, 238
Florida State Prison Farm, 431
Folk Devils and Moral Panic (Cohen), 273
Foote, Caleb, 44, 61
Ford, Gerald, 319, 321, 333, 355–56, 487*n*

Ford Foundation, 50, 104
formalists, formalism, 207, 208, 209, 210,
  260, 313, 314, 348, 484*n*
Forst, Brian, 291–92, 296, 299, 474*n*
Fortas, Abe, 75, 77, 83, 89, 90–92, 93, 100,
  104, 208, 306*n*
  Court nomination of, 76
  scandal and resignation of, 91–92, 178,
    432, 433
Foucault, Michel, 316
Fourteenth Amendment, 5, 145, 161, 175,
  229, 397, 417, 419, 428
  due process clause in, 66–67, 80, 83, 91,
    94, 95, 111, 129, 149, 161, 218, 227, 385,
    444
  equal protection clause in, 21, 85–86,
    109–10, 124, 146, 162, 182, 428, 434
  Furman case and issues of, 118, 129, 145,
    146, 149, 155, 161, 162, 163, 167, 189,
    191, 218, 226–27, 228
  Lochner and, 11, 207–8, 444, 448*n*
  McGautha and, 100–103, 104–11, 151,
    226, 227, 228, 377
  standardless sentencing challenged under,
    70, 80, 94–96, 104, 106, 149, 226, 227,
    445
Fourth Amendment, 345
Fourth Circuit Court of Appeals, 112
Fourth Judicial Circuit, 240
Fowler, Jesse, 262, 293, 320–21, 326, 329,
  444
Fowler, John, 320
Fowler, Mary, 77–78
Fowler v. North Carolina, 264, 318, 320–23,
  331–32, 334, 340, 443–44
  amicus brief filed in, 290–91, 322, 365
  arbitrary sentencing concerns in, 323–25,
    326–27, 328–30
  court conference on, 331, 332
  LDF's strategy in, 323–24, 325, 326, 330,
    361
  mandatory statutes issue in, 262, 320, 323,
    443
  opinions drafted in, 331
  oral arguments in, 319–20, 323–31, 366–
    67, 369
  race issues in, 327–28
  social science data cited in, 290–91
Fox, Joe, 260
Fraenkel, Osmond, 36
Frampton, George, 124, 270
Francis, Willie, 15

Francis v. Resweber, 15

Frank, Jerome, 207

Frankfurter, Felix, 8, 9–10, 11, 13–14, 15, 16,
    19, 22, 26, 29, 35, 72–73, 80, 87, 110,
    129, 171, 179, 194, 200, 203, 237, 266,
    276, 371, 456*n,* 485*n,* 488*n*
  Amsterdam as law clerk for, 42–43
  background and education of, 9
  death penalty as viewed by, 15, 193
  failing health of, 42
  Haley v. Ohio opinion of, 193
  judicial philosophy of, 9, 10, 12, 14, 15, 19,
    26, 43, 193, 209*n,* 348, 448*n*
  legal realism as influence on, 209*n*
  Lochner dissent of, 13
  resignation of, 7, 9

Franklin, Charles, 274

Freakonomics (Levitt and Dubner), 288

Frederick, David, 210

Freedom Summer, 36, 204, 357

Freund, Paul, 10, 11

Friday, Herschel, 125

Friedan, Betty, 18

Friedlander, William, 57

Friedman, Milton, 288

Furman, William, 118, 128, 150, 188, 238,
    241, 317

Furman v. Georgia, 21, 40, 46, 56, 117–18,
    127, 128–30, 137, 142, 174, 230–31,
    234, 250, 254, 269, 271, 301, 310,
    312–13, 314, 322, 324, 325, 326, 329,
    331, 339, 340, 345, 346, 351, 353, 359,
    364, 368, 369, 375, 381, 400, 403, 404,
    407, 409, 414, 420, 433, 435, 438, 444,
    458*n,* 488*n*
  abolitionists' pessimism in lead up to, 127,
    128–29
  Amsterdam's legal briefs in, 130–34, 136
  announcement of decision in, 235–37,
    247
  arbitrary and discriminatory sentencing
    concerns in, 133–35, 148, 149, 150,
    162–63, 164, 166, 167, 168, 181, 184,
    186–87, 188–90, 201, 220, 221, 224,
    227, 228, 236, 242, 257, 276, 280, 282,
    303, 323, 324, 325, 341, 361, 362, 377,
    385, 389–90, 399, 401, 402, 405, 434,
    444
  Burger's directive for individually written
    opinions in, 170–71
  confidentiality ordered in, 170, 171–72,
    199

Court conference on, 167–70, 172, 173*n,*
    184, 198, 200
  deterrence issue in, 151–52, 155, 156, 157,
    158, 168–69, 187, 216, 219, 221, 222,
    280, 281–82, 283, 284
  dissenting opinions in, 185, 224, 225, 230,
    231–33, 237, 242, 247, 277, 283–84,
    304, 320, 341, 390–91, 418, 435
  drafting of opinions in, 170–74, 180–84,
    185–91, 195–99, 200–201, 218–25,
    226–30, 231–33, 411, 433
  "evolving standards of decency" argument
    in, 131, 132–33, 142, 145–48, 150,
    154–55, 162, 169, 180–81, 183, 184, 191,
    360, 365, 401, 445
  "human dignity" argument in, 180, 186–
    87, 215, 236
  join memos in, 224, 225
  lack of "controlling" rationale in decision
    of, 225–26, 236, 237, 243, 275–76, 277,
    280, 282
  LDF's strategy in, 129–30, 134, 154, 164,
    279, 324, 361
  lengthiness of opinion in, 236
  mandatory statutes in response to, 248–49,
    250–51, 252–53, 256–57, 258–59,
    262–63, 285*n,* 303, 304, 320, 334, 341,
    373–74, 390, 394, 397, 401, 405, 406,
    411, 416, 443
  McGautha arguments as seemingly
    inconsistent with, 129, 130, 164, 167,
    175, 189, 226–29, 232, 376–78, 384–85,
    389
  negative reactions to, 240–41, 247–48,
    249, 257
  new legislation and statutory revisions in
    response to, 248–55, 256–59, 261, 262–
    63, 278, 279, 285*n,* 293, 302, 303–4,
    305–17, 320, 334, 341, 342, 354, 360,
    365, 373–74, 384, 385, 386, 390, 394,
    397, 401, 406, 411, 416, 420, 443, 444,
    445
  North Carolina and Louisiana statutes
    as not compliant with, 401, 403, 405,
    406–7, 408, 410, 417
  oral arguments in, 134–35, 136, 143,
    145–65, 166, 174, 181, 197, 400,
    460*n*
  positive reaction to, 237–40, 241, 260
  public opinion backlash to, 254, 255–56,
    258, 261–63, 264–66, 269, 274–75,
    277–78, 279–80, 321, 325, 360

Furman v. Georgia (continued)
  social science data cited in, 281–82,
      283–84
  standardless sentencing issue in, 118, 148,
      168, 189, 226, 303, 315, 325, 384, 385,
      389–90, 391, 401, 402
  statutory loopholes in, 191, 201, 216, 217,
      219–20, 222, 223, 229, 231–32, 233,
      242–43, 247, 254, 257, 263, 276, 277,
      280, 303, 341, 373, 374, 394, 405, 406,
      411
  Stewart-White compromise in, 200–201,
      215, 216–17, 218, 223, 226–27, 229, 235,
      277, 309–10, 325, 336, 433
  White as swing-vote in, 172, 189, 190, 197,
      198–99, 200, 201, 216, 227–28, 241
  Woodson as contradicting opinions in,
      412–13, 434, 490*n*

Gallup polls, 33, 62, 255–56, 262, 265, 395,
      450*n*
Gardner case, 343
Garrity, Arthur, 268
gas chamber, 137, 153, 320, 328
General Social Survey (GSS), 274–75
genocide, 393
George, Ronald, 98–100, 135–36, 137, 144,
      161, 163, 164–65, 460*n*
  background and legal career of, 98–99
  death penalty as viewed by, 99–100
  Furman oral arguments of, 143, 150–57,
      197
  McGautha oral argument of, 101–2, 134
Georgia, 64–65, 135, 146, 158, 201, 247, 317,
      343, 344, 345, 352, 388, 394, 426, 444
  discriminatory sentencing in, 40, 159, 162,
      213, 295, 428
  sodomy laws in, 212, 352
Georgia Court of Appeals, 135
Georgia Diagnostic and Classification Prison,
      238
Georgia statutes, 216, 217, 226, 231, 232,
      251–52, 257, 303–4, 306, 310, 313, 341,
      342, 362–64, 369, 372, 402, 404, 406,
      408, 409, 425, 444
  appellate review in, 304, 363, 398, 401
  see also Furman v. Georgia; *Gregg v. Georgia*
Germany, Nazi, 8, 31, 307, 308, 392, 393
gerrymandering, 42
Gerwitz, Paul, 124
Giaccio, Joe, 66
Giaccio v. Pennsylvania, 66–67, 90, 444

Gibson, George, 423
Gideon's Trumpet (Lewis), 260
Gideon v. Wainwright, 260
Gielow, Leslie, 428–29
Gilmore, Gary, 429–30
Ginsburg, Ruth Bader, 98, 123
Ginty, James, 340–42, 343, 344, 345, 424
Gittings, Kaj, 475*n*
Glendon, Mary Ann, 213
Goldberg, Arthur, 3–8, 10, 18, 47, 66, 75,
      77, 79, 88, 113, 141, 239, 262, 307, 355,
      432, 448*n*
  background and education of, 5–6, 16
  cert dissent of, 28–30, 31, 33–34, 435
  constitutionality memorandum of
      Dershowitz and, 20–25, 26–28, 29, 30,
      32, 34, 53, 336–37, 432
  Court nomination and confirmation of, 7,
      10
  death penalty as viewed by, 8, 16, 17
  end to death penalty proposed by, 4–5, 8,
      15–16, 18
  on *Furman* decision, 242–43
  Harvard Review article published by, 113,
      181, 182
  judicial philosophy of, 10–11, 16, 23
  justice chambers of, 4
  law clerks of, 8
  legal career of, 6, 7
  religious faith of, 6, 17, 24, 75
  Rudolph dissent of, 336, 370, 445
  in World War II, 6–7
Goldberg, Faye, 58
Goldman, Gerald, 180
Gore, Al, 302*n*, 475*n*
Gottlieb, Gerald, 21, 187
Graham, Bob, 430
Gramsci, Antonio, 313, 484*n*
grant of certiorari, 19, 66, 70, 96, 99, 109,
      115–18, 136, 144, 149, 167, 235, 341,
      357
  Court's mysterious process in deciding of,
      336–40, 346
  Douglas's dissent on, 115–16, 118, 144
  see also cert petitions
Great Britain, 63, 68
Great Depression, 16, 72
Greece, ancient, 270, 367
Greenberg, Jack, 32, 33, 35, 37, 44, 48, 49,
      50, 51, 52*n*, 55, 59, 60, 130, 242, 262,
      279, 452*n*, 488*n*
  Furman case and, 128, 134–35, 164, 326

further class-action suits discouraged by, 56–57, 61

national death penalty conferences and, 61, 104, 111

oral arguments of, 134–35, 164

Greenhouse, Linda, 492*n*

Green v. County School Board of New Kent County, 267, 268, 275

Gregg, Troy, 361, 362, 388, 392, 486*n*

Gregg v. Georgia, 46, 210, 250*n,* 277, 306*n,* 311, 312*n,* 313, 316, 317, 340, 341, 343, 351, 352, 354, 355, 357, 359, 392, 412, 419, 433, 434, 437, 438, 444, 488*n,* 492*n*

abolitionists' bleak prospects in lead up to, 354, 355, 359, 372

amicus brief filed in, 364, 365–68

Amsterdam's legal brief on, 362–64, 367

announcement of decisions in, 420–21

arbitrary sentencing issues in, 360, 362–64, 366–68, 369, 373, 375, 376–78, 385–86, 401, 415*n,* 444

Burger's assigning of opinions in, 404, 407–8, 413, 417, 433

Court conference on, 400–404, 405, 407, 414

"death is different" principle raised in, 369–71, 378–79, 386, 391, 405, 417, 436, 488*n*–89*n*

deterrence issue debated in, 302–3, 365–66, 387–88, 437, 439

dissenting opinions in, 418–19, 420–21, 444

drafting of opinion in, 410, 414–15, 417–18

executions as resuming in wake of, 278–79, 429, 430, 431, 481*n*

join memos in, 418

LDF's strategy in, 360–62, 367, 368–71, 375, 376–77, 378, 382–83, 392, 398, 417, 425–26, 488*n*

oral arguments in, 372–80, 382–88, 398–99, 400, 403, 435

and Powell's proposal to apply decision to future cases only, 415–17

Powell's remorse over decision in, 424, 425

rehearing petitions for, 424–26

retributive justice as issue in, 414–15, 421, 437, 439, 479*n*

troika agreement in, 408–10, 413–14, 419, 440

Woodson opinion as contradictory to, 417–18

Griffin, John, 320

Griswold v. Connecticut, 15, 177–78, 212

Gross, James, 140

Guantanamo Bay, 364

guided-discretion statutes, 108, 252, 285*n,* 304, 305–6, 310–17, 325, 334, 341, 396–98, 401, 406, 411, 417, 425, 439

aggravating factors in, 253, 304, 310, 311–12, 315, 362–63, 373, 380, 382, 398, 406

arbitrariness as inherent in, 310–12, 313, 343, 362–64, 366–67, 373, 375, 376–78, 380, 430

Court's acceptance of, 425, 444

Powell's support for, 415*n*

public's misguided belief in rationality of, 313–14, 317, 374

vagueness of, 311–12, 314*n,* 315, 316

see also death penalty statutes

Gunther, Gerald, 98–99, 123

habeas corpus petitions, 37, 38, 39, 48, 52, 56, 67

Haldeman, H. R., 273

Haley v. Ohio, 193

Hamilton, Charles, 44

Hamilton, Lee, 311

Hammond, Larry, 182–84, 195–96, 198, 222, 230–31, 233, 342, 346, 352, 353

Hand, Learned, 98

Harlan, John, 10, 26, 87, 89, 92, 111, 126, 178, 212, 252, 253, 268, 325, 361, 371, 455*n,* 461*n*

background and education of, 175–76

Court nomination of, 176

judicial philosophy of, 10, 80, 106, 108, 177, 351

legal career of, 176

Maxwell case and, 80–81, 83, 95, 96, 105, 178

McGautha opinion drafted by, 106–8, 109, 110, 127, 178, 232, 303, 306*n,* 314, 316, 412, 445

resignation of, 125, 135, 175

on single-phase trial issues, 91, 92, 95, 96, 105, 107–8

as skeptical of possibility of fair capital sentencing standards, 107, 110, 232, 303, 304, 306*n,* 314, 316, 317, 361, 367

Spencer opinion of, 397

on standardless sentencing, 81, 83, 91, 95, 106–7, 108

Harlan, John (*continued*)
  Stewart's close bond with, 175, 176–77, 178–80, 351, 397
Harrington, Michael, 17–18
Harris, Fred, 348
Harris, Louis, 58, 256
Harris polls, 58, 256, 262, 269, 302, 395
Harris v. New York, 114
Hart, Philip, 113
Harvard Law Review, 12, 34, 113, 181, 182, 308, 310, 311
Harvard Law School, 9, 12, 13, 32, 51, 71, 146, 206–7, 208, 239, 348, 357, 458*n*
  judicial restraint favored by, 10–11, 209*n*
Harvard University, 45, 464*n*
Hawaii, 63
Hawkins, Gordon, 406*n*
Haynsworth, Clement, 93, 347
Heffernan, Cathy, 86
Heffron, Frank, 33, 34–35, 37, 38, 45, 357
Heineman, Benjamin, 124, 173–75, 177–78, 180, 185–86, 189, 197, 198–99, 200, 218, 221, 223
Henley, Jesse, 38, 39
Hickock, Dick, 73
Hill, John, 379, 381
  Jurek oral argument of, 379–80, 385
Himmelstein, Jack, 47, 51, 52, 104, 111, 112, 128, 130, 134, 143, 241, 284–85, 357–58, 452*n*
Hindu law, 188
Hitler, Adolf, 366
Ho, Elizabeth, 7
Hoeber, Paul, 180, 186
Hollow Hope, The (Rosenberg), 278–79
Holmes, Oliver Wendell, 4, 11, 12, 155–56, 215, 313, 367
  legal realism of, 206, 207–8
  Lochner and, 207–8
Holmes v. Danner, 32
Holocaust, 8
homicide rates, 264*n*, 265*n*
  deterrence effect and, 281–82, 287, 290, 294–95, 296–97, 299, 387, 388, 473*n*, 476*n*
homosexuals, 212
Hoover, Herbert, 266
Horton, Leslie, 238
House, Jack, 341, 343
House case, 341, 343
House of Commons, British, 258
House of Representatives, Florida, 253

House of Representatives, U.S., 248
  Judiciary Committee of, 301, 356, 474*n*
Houston, Charles Hamilton, 139
Howard Law School, 139
Hubbart, Phillip, 252
human dignity, 20, 21, 73, 180, 185, 186–87, 215, 236, 411–12, 418, 421
Humphrey, Hubert, 76
Hutchinson, Dennis, 214, 462*n*

Idaho, 258, 359
Illinois, 159, 262
Illinois Bar Association, 6, 57
Illinois Law Review, 6
incest, 309*n*
In Cold Blood (Capote), 73
Ingber, Stanley, 308–9
Institute for Law and Social Research, 291
instrumental analysis, 477*n*–79*n*
integration, *see* desegregation
International Academy of Trial Lawyers, 249
International Labor Defense, 483*n*
interracial marriage, 28
Iowa, 63
Israel, 16

Jack, Hulan, 31, 32
Jackson, Lucius, 117, 150, 164, 188, 238, 241
Jackson, Nathan, 141
Jackson, Robert, 87, 124, 126, 211
Jackson v. Georgia, 117, 118, 131, 134–35, 164, 178, 444
  Amsterdam's brief on, 130, 132
  see also Furman v. Georgia
Jacobson, Richard, 228, 229
James, Fob, 249
James, William, 206, 381–82, 464*n*
Jeffress, William, 127, 173, 174, 175, 177, 197, 198–99, 221, 401
Jeffries, John, 271, 348, 351, 393, 407, 438
Jehovah's Witnesses, 35
Jenner, Albert, 57–58, 59, 60
Jensen, Max, 429
Jewish Publication Society of America, 24
Jewish Theological Seminary, 8, 76
Jews, Judaism, 6, 17, 24, 41, 74, 75, 307, 392, 482*n*
Johns Hopkins University, 463*n*
Johnson, Lyndon B., 18, 65, 74, 76, 85, 138, 139, 272, 347, 348, 432

Johnson, Robert, 476*n*
Johnson, Timothy, 274
join memos, 224, 225, 418
Journal of Behavioral Economics, 300
Journal of Criminal Law & Criminology,
   253
judicial activism, 9, 10–11, 14, 349
"judicial notice," 148*n*
judicial restraint, 9, 10, 12, 14, 15, 22–23, 26,
   27, 29, 43, 72, 106, 108, 209*n,* 219, 236,
   322, 351, 387, 407, 448*n*
   Trop decision as departure from, 19–20
judicial review, 78, 145, 197, 224, 308
Judiciary Act (1891), 449*n*
Jurek, Jerry, 343, 360–61, 366, 372, 375, 376,
   378, 380, 392, 406, 426, 440
Jurek v. Texas, 343, 344, 352, 354, 360–61,
   366, 372, 373, 375, 376, 378, 379–80,
   388, 389, 392, 410, 415, 417, 418, 419,
   422, 424, 444
   Davis's rehearing proposal for, 425–26
   Stevens's regret over decision in, 410,
      439–40, 492*n*
   see also Gregg v. Georgia
jury trials, 64–65, 137, 139, 140, 155, 159,
   163, 164, 192, 248, 253, 285, 379, 381,
   397
   arbitrariness of clemency in, 253, 323–24,
      367, 373, 376, 385–86, 389, 394–95,
      412
   biased selection procedures in, 37, 38,
      57–59, 64, 77, 82, 112, 137
   death penalty as rarely imposed in, 107,
      133, 150, 159, 164, 167, 190, 222, 223,
      278, 367
   guided-discretion statutes for, 108, 252,
      253, 285*n,* 304, 305–6, 310–17, 325,
      334, 341, 343, 363, 367, 373, 376–78,
      380, 397, 406
   mandatory statutes and continued use of
      discretion in, 323–24, 326, 328–30, 373,
      390–91, 394, 398, 401, 412
   nullification in, 106, 304, 307, 378, 411
   "single-phase," 67, 70, 81, 82, 83, 89, 90,
      91, 92, 103, 104–5
   standardless sentencing in, 66–68, 70, 77,
      79, 80, 81, 82, 83, 89–91, 92, 94, 95–96,
      100–103, 106–7, 108, 111, 118, 137, 148,
      168, 189, 312, 315, 384, 385, 389–90,
      391, 401, 402
Justice Brennan (Stern and Wermiel), 454*n*–
   55*n,* 460*n*

Justice Department, U.S., 72, 204–5, 214,
   231*n,* 259, 307

Kalven, Harry, 330, 386
Kansas, 257
Kaplan, Benjamin, 55
Katzenbach v. Morgan, 179
Keillor, Garrison, 194
Kelly, William, 196
Kendall, David, 124, 210–11, 277, 357,
   358–59, 360, 368, 369, 374, 375, 377,
   389, 399, 425, 426–27
   in reaction to *Gregg/Woodson* decisions,
      421–22
Kennedy, Edward, 364
Kennedy, John F., 7, 10, 138, 204–5, 213,
   238, 248, 272, 408
Kennedy, Robert F., 62–63, 185, 204–5, 248,
   259
Kennedy Justice (Lavasky), 259
Kentucky, 438
Keyes v. School District No. 1, 196
King, Larry, 321
King, Martin Luther, Jr., 32, 62–63, 126, 141
Kirk, Claude, Jr., 55
Kirk, Stanley, 64
Klein, Lawrence, 474*n,* 477*n*
Kleindienst, Richard, 126, 256–57
Kluger, Richard, 260
Kobylka, Joseph, 278, 369, 488*n*
Koch, Gary, 474*n*
Koestler, Arthur, 64, 81
Koh, Harry, 435, 438
Kohlberg, Lawrence, 285
Korematsu v. United States, 78
Kosaski, Liane, 274
Kronheim, Milton, 75, 141, 174
Ku Klux Klan, 13, 125, 249
Kurgans, Dorothy, 4, 10–11
Kurland, Philip, 179–80

Labi, Nadya, 451*n*
Labine v. Vincent, 114
labor laws, 6, 7, 11–12, 71–72, 444
labor movement, 7, 35
Lain, Corinna Barrett, 460*n*
laissez-faire capitalism, 11
Lamarck, Jean-Baptiste, 463*n*
Landon, Alf, 272
Langdell, Christopher Columbus, 206–7,
   208, 210, 260
Laski, Harold, 215

Last-Aid Kits, 52, 55, 426–28

law clerks, 3–5, 8, 9, 13, 17, 18, 25, 26, 38,
    45, 74, 75, 88, 108, 111, 117, 123–25,
    126, 127, 128, 135, 137, 141–42, 143,
    144, 145, 166, 170–71, 174–75, 177, 185,
    200, 203, 210, 214–15, 229, 230–31,
    232, 233, 234, 250, 270, 307, 311, 314,
    318, 331–32, 334, 346, 350, 354–55,
    356, 357, 358–59, 400, 401, 404, 405–7,
    408–9, 413, 419, 421, 428–29, 434–35,
    454n, 465n, 483n
  Amsterdam as, 42–43, 129
  in cert petition reviews, 338, 339, 340,
      342–44, 345, 352–53
  Douglas's abusive treatment of, 86–87, 319
  Douglas's "summer research project" for,
      119
  female minority of, 123–24
  in Furman opinion drafting process, 172,
      173–74, 180–81, 182–84, 185–86, 189,
      190, 191, 195–96, 197, 198–99, 218,
      221–23, 227, 228, 233
  in Gregg opinion drafting process, 410,
      414, 415
  liberal leanings of, 124–25, 126, 127
  long hours and small pay of, 123, 355
  in Woodson opinion drafting process,
      410–12, 414

Law Students Civil Rights Research Council,
    38–39

Lazarus, Edward, 44

LDF, see NAACP Legal Defense Fund

Least Dangerous Branch, The (Bickel), 449n

Lee, Rex, 214

legal realism, 206–11, 215, 259, 313, 336, 339

legal services clinics, 259–60

Lehrer, Jim, 302n

Leonardo, Elena, 86

Leonardos, Thomas, 242

Leopold and Loeb trial, 6

lethal injection, 438

Leventhal, Harold, 353

Levi, Edward, 356, 487n

Levinson, Harold, 252, 253

Levitt, Steven, 288, 475n

Levy, Lionel, 31

Lewis, Anthony, 234, 260, 409

Libby, I. Lewis "Scooter," 127

liberals, liberalism, 12, 14, 17, 73, 75, 81, 88,
    138, 199, 205, 241, 249, 256, 259, 269,
    345, 351, 365, 368, 422, 448n
  Blackmun's evolution into, 193–95

growing mistrust of, 273, 388
  of law clerks, 124–25, 126, 127

"liberty of contract," 11

Liebman, Lance, 465n

Liechtenstein, 155, 157

Life, 91

Lillie, Mildred, 125

Little Rock, Ark., 25–26, 87, 125

Livingston, Edward, 305

Living Wage, A (Ryan), 73

Lochner, Joseph, 11

Lochner v. New York, 11–12, 13, 207–8, 444,
    448n

Lockett v. Ohio, 412

Lockheed, 379

Loeb, William, 34

Louisiana, 57, 75, 114, 341, 343, 344, 381,
    394, 402

Louisiana statutes, 258, 304, 395, 401, 402,
    403, 404, 406–7, 409, 410, 445
  see also Roberts v. Louisiana

Lukas, J. Anthony, 268

Luther, Martin, 14

lynching, 61, 308, 414, 483n

Lyons, Douglas, 131, 237, 460n

Lyons, Leonard, 131

Lyons, W. D., 140

Maddox, Lester, 247–48

Mailer, Norman, 316, 429

Making of a Civil Rights Lawyer, The
    (Meltsner), 279, 488n

Malcolm X, 141

Malinowski, Bronislaw, 463n

Malloy v. Hogan, 212

"Man Against the Machine, A" (Labi), 451n

Manchester Union Leader, 34

mandatory statutes, 94, 100–101, 168,
    181, 191, 218, 221, 243, 306, 309,
    315–16, 323, 328, 334, 341, 343, 352,
    360, 361, 366n, 369, 389, 390–91,
    402, 407
  arbitrariness as inherent in, 323–24, 326,
      328–30, 344, 373, 390, 391, 394, 395,
      398, 401, 405, 412
  Fowler and issue of, 262, 320, 323, 443
  Furman loopholes for, 191, 216, 217, 219–
      20, 222, 223, 229, 231–32, 233, 242–43,
      257, 303, 341, 374, 394, 405, 406, 411
  history of, 411
  human dignity argument against, 411–12
  jury nullification and, 304, 307, 411

Massachusetts Supreme Court's rejection of, 359

post-*Furman* legislation on, 248–49, 250–51, 252–53, 256–57, 258–59, 262–63, 285*n*, 303, 304, 320, 334, 341, 373–74, 390, 394, 397, 401, 406, 411, 416, 443

Powell's opposition to, 402, 405, 407, 408, 445

Stewart's opposition to, 217, 219–20, 221, 408, 411–12, 445

Texas law not classified as, 361, 369, 410, 425–26

Woodson decision as rejection of, 277, 425, 439, 445

Mandery, Evan J., 488*n*–89*n*

Manson, Charles, 185, 254

Man Who Once Was Whizzer White, The (Hutchinson), 462*n*

Mapp v. Ohio, 212

Marks, Wilt, 347

Marshall, Cissy, 138, 144

Marshall, John, 78

Marshall, Thurgood, 41, 58, 87, 89, 115, 127, 137–42, 144, 151, 178, 179, 190, 194, 199, 219, 221, 224, 233, 268, 276, 319, 345, 348, 349, 351, 354–55, 403, 407, 414, 419, 434, 436, 445, 490*n*–91*n*

as appellate court judge, 138, 141

background and education of, 137, 139

Brennan's voting partnership with, 418

Court nomination and appointment of, 138–39

death penalty standards opposed by, 83, 91, 420–21

declining health of, 139, 423, 424

on deterrence issues, 281–82, 420–21

evolving views on death penalty of, 137–38, 139–42, 145, 172

in *Fowler* oral arguments, 327–28

in *Furman* conference, 169

Furman draft opinions of, 172, 188, 189, 196, 215, 216, 220, 224–25, 227

in *Furman* oral arguments, 152–53, 158, 161

Furman published opinion of, 236, 280, 281–82, 420

Gregg dissent of, 418–19, 420–21, 444

in *Gregg/Woodson* conference, 402

hard living of, 138, 139

isolation of, 138, 139

law clerks of, 124, 137, 141–42, 145, 172, 311, 355

at LDF, 31, 32, 51*n*, 53*n*, 109, 138, 139, 357

Maxwell case and, 83, 89, 96, 178

McGautha case and, 105, 111, 178

Powell v. Texas opinion of, 366, 487*n*–88*n*

public opinion "hypothesis" of, 181, 184, 236, 262–63, 280, 285, 360, 420

retributive punishment rejected by, 215, 220, 221, 236, 281, 366, 420, 421

secret anti-death penalty opinion drafted by, 137, 142, 144–45, 169, 181

social science data cited by, 281–82, 283, 293, 471*n*

as solicitor general, 138–39

Martin, Andrew, 274

Martin, Joan, 86

Marxism, 484*n*

Maryland, 159

Massachusetts, 258

Massey, Douglas, 267

Massiah v. United States, 212

Maxwell, William, 37–39, 48, 67, 70, 79, 80–81, 82, 83, 89, 90, 91, 92, 95, 96, 112, 241, 434, 444

Maxwell v. Arkansas, 37–39, 40, 45, 73, 94, 97, 113, 127, 128, 169, 178, 192, 195, 374, 433, 434, 444

Court conferences on, 79–84, 89, 90, 95–96, 106

Douglas's drafting of majority opinion in, 89–91, 92

habeas corpus petitions filed in, 37, 38, 39, 48, 67

oral arguments in, 38, 45, 46, 77, 82, 280, 306*n*

per curiam opinion in, 96, 444

reargument of, 92, 94–96

single-phase trial issue in, 81, 82, 83, 89, 90, 91, 92, 95–96, 105, 178

standardless sentencing issue in, 77, 79, 81, 82, 83, 89–91, 92, 94, 95–96, 100, 104, 178

Maxwell v. Bishop, 159

Mayo Clinic, 270

McCafferty, James, 234

McClellan, John, 7

McCleskey, Warren, 295, 429, 434

McCleskey v. Kemp, 39, 213, 295, 418, 428–29, 434, 436, 437, 438

McCord, David, 312–13

McCorquodale, Timothy, 345, 486*n*

McCorquodale v. The State, 341, 345, 349–50, 352, 486*n*

McDougal, Myres, 209–10

McDowell, Charles, 348

McGautha, Dennis, 96, 100, 101, 103, 106

McGautha v. California, 96–97, 98, 99,
    100–103, 111, 114, 127, 128, 134, 136,
    149, 151, 170, 172, 174–75, 178, 193,
    235, 279, 280, 303, 322, 340, 397, 403,
    433, 445, 458*n*
  amicus brief filed in, 100
  Court conference on, 104–6
  dissenting opinions in, 109–11, 119
  Furman arguments as seemingly
    inconsistent with, 129, 130, 164, 167,
    175, 189, 226–29, 232, 376–78, 384–85,
    389
  Harlan's opinion in, 106–8, 109, 110, 127,
    178, 232, 303, 306*n*, 314, 316, 412, 445
  oral arguments in, 100–104, 134
  single-phase trial issue in, 103, 104–5, 107–8
  standardless sentencing issue in, 100–103,
    104, 105, 106–7, 108, 109–10, 168, 226,
    227, 303, 306*n*, 316, 377, 402, 445

McGovern, George, 258

McLaurian v. Oklahoma, 452*n*

McMillan, James, 268

McNeese v. Board of Education, 266

McRae, William, Jr., 55, 56

Meaning of Meaning, The (Richards and
    Ogden), 463*n*

Meehl, Paul, 474*n*

Meir, Golda, 16

Meltsner, Heli, 239

Meltsner, Jessica, 239

Meltsner, Michael, 33, 34–35, 43, 45, 50–52,
    53, 54, 56, 58, 59, 60, 65, 66, 69, 70, 97,
    104, 128, 137–38, 178, 185, 192, 237,
    238, 243, 254, 310–11, 357–58, 452*n*,
    460*n*
  background of, 33, 49
  books written by, 259, 260–61, 279, 285*n*,
    370, 488*n*
  on Columbia Law School faculty, 259–60,
    357
  on "death is different" principle, 369–70
  Furman decision reaction of, 239, 260
  on LDF's decision to extend representation
    to whites, 49, 50

Menand, Louis, 463*n*

Meredith v. Fair, 32

Merriam, Charles, 463*n*

Metaphysical Club, The (Menand), 463*n*

Miami Herald, 242

Michael, Jerome, 308

Michener, James, 318

Michigan, 258, 269

Michigan v. Mosley, 354, 355

Micke, Mrs., 117–18

Micke, William, 117, 118

Milgram, Stanley, 484*n*

military, right to deny citizenship by, 19, 20

minimum-wage law, 11

Minnesota, 159, 169

Minton, Sherman, 26, 72

Mintz, Jeffrey, 132

Miranda v. Arizona, 41, 64, 78, 114, 179, 181,
    212, 252, 278, 325, 341, 343, 355

Mississippi, 25, 32, 36, 262

Mississippi, University of, 32

Mitchell, John, 76–77, 125, 126, 273, 347

Mitchell case, 341–42

Mocan, Naci, 475*n*

Model Code of Ethical Responsibility, 59

Model Penal Code (MPC), 95, 304–6, 308,
    309–10, 313, 317

Monge, Luis, 63, 111

Monocle, 259

Monocle (restaurant), 408–9, 413, 490*n*

Monroe, James, 272

Moore, Justin, 423–24

Moore v. Illinois, 409, 466*n*

"moral panic," 273

Morgan v. Virginia, 32

Morgenthau, Robert, 476*n*

Morocco, 19

Moses, Robert, 31

Mosk, Stanley, 77, 99, 255

Moskowitz, Dan, 261

motion counsel, 340

Motley, Constance Baker, 32

Moynihan, Daniel Patrick, 286–87, 295, 479*n*

Mozambique, 155, 157

Muller, Eric, 49, 278, 370, 488*n*

Muller v. Oregon, 282–83

"murder function," 289, 474*n*, 476*n*, 478*n*

Murphy, Bruce Allen, 86, 88

Murphy, Frank, 337

NAACP Legal Defense Fund (LDF), 30,
    31–35, 43, 44–45, 46, 48–49, 58,
    63–64, 65, 81, 104, 109, 111, 112, 127,
    128, 135, 146, 150, 158, 159, 185, 195,
    235, 253, 256, 259, 277, 284, 314, 314*n*,
    330, 331, 345, 354, 355, 364, 385, 395,
    399, 400, 422, 428, 430, 479*n*, 484*n*

in abolition campaigns, *see* abolition
campaigns
amicus briefs filed by, 58, 59, 66, 68–70,
97, 100
Boykin case and, 66, 67, 68–70
Brown campaign of, 52–53, 58, 266,
357
changing dynamic at, 256–58
Coker v. Georgia and, 277, 427
commuted sentences earned by, 38, 112
death penalty added to agenda of, 34–35
decision to represent murderers by, 52, 279
in disproving myth of "rational
application," 303, 304, 310, 311
Fowler strategy of, 323–24, 325, 326, 330,
361
funding and budget of, 34, 37, 49, 50, 53,
104, 280, 293
Furman decision reaction at, 237, 241
Furman strategy of, 129–30, 134, 154,
164, 186, 279, 324, 361
Goldberg's cert dissent and, 33–34
Gregg rehearing petitions and, 425–26
Gregg/Woodson strategy of, 360–62, 367,
368–71, 375, 376–77, 378, 382–83, 389,
392, 398, 417, 425–26, 488*n*
habeas corpus petitions filed by, 37, 38, 39,
48, 56, 67
interests of clients vs. philosophical goals
of, 54, 56–60, 82*n*, 164, 361, 426,
430–31, 433
Jackson case and, 117, 150
McGautha case and, 100, 102–3
Marshall as chief attorney at, 31, 32, 51*n*,
53*n*, 109, 138, 139, 357
Maxwell case and, 37–39, 45, 48, 67, 82,
97
offices of, 31–32, 52
and post-*Furman* public opinion backlash,
261, 262, 263, 279–80, 360
power and reputation of, 32–33, 40–41
public relations concerns of, 64, 67–68,
279, 360
rehearing petitions filed by, 424–25
social science research relied on by, 38–40,
45, 58, 94, 162–63, 184, 283, 284–86,
287–88, 295
stays of execution secured by, 48, 424–25
see also Amsterdam, Anthony
Nabrit, James, 49
Nagin, Daniel, 474*n*
Nation, 259

National Academy of Sciences (NAS), 299,
302, 474*n*, 477*n*, 478*n*
National Association for the Advancement of
Colored People (NAACP), 35, 140
Legal Defense Fund, *see* NAACP Legal
Defense Fund
National Association of Attorneys General
(NAAG), 248–49, 251
National Bureau of Economic Research, 289,
290, 300
National Commission on Reform of Federal
Criminal Laws, 113
National Conference on the Death Penalty,
60–62
National Football League, 203
National Guard, U.S., 87
Nationality Act (1940), 19
National Labor Relations Act (1935), 72
National Office for the Rights of the Indigent,
50
National Opinion Research Center (NORC),
274–75
National Public Radio (NPR), 439, 492*n*
National Review, 234–35, 301
natural selection, 463*n*
Navasky, Victor, 259
Nazis, 8, 31, 307, 308, 392, 393
Neier, Aryeh, 278, 359, 433
Neuborne, Burt, 352
Nevada, 258
New Deal, 11, 13, 14, 41
New Hampshire, 262, 359
New Jersey Bar Association, 423
New Mexico, 63
New Republic, 213, 234
Newsweek, 256, 260
New York, 11, 63, 158, 176, 258, 285, 305,
309, 444
experiment with capital punishment in,
475*n*–76*n*, 479*n*
New York, N.Y., 8, 16, 76, 267, 422
New York Assembly, 261
New York Civil Liberties Union, 36
New York Coliseum, 31
New York Committee to Abolish Capital
Punishment, 76
New York Daily News, 248
New York Law School, 176
New York Times, 33, 77, 99, 114, 127, 213,
234, 239, 240, 241, 242, 255, 256, 257,
261, 262, 310, 331
New York Times Magazine, 259, 430, 465*n*

New York Times v. Sullivan, 87, 181

New York University, 77, 93, 301

Niebuhr, Reinhold, 8

Nigeria, 98

Nike, 430

Nixon, Richard, 76, 114, 139, 147, 177, 216, 238, 271–72, 408

    Court nominations and appointments by, 92, 93–94, 125–27, 225, 242, 347, 348, 432

    death penalty bill of, 256–57, 262, 302

    on *Furman* decision, 247, 248, 257

    as "moral entrepreneur," 273–74

    1973 State of the Union speech of, 257

    Watergate scandal and, 231*n*, 271, 275, 322

North Carolina, 258–59, 262, 324, 327, 329, 342, 343, 344, 388

North Carolina statutes, 258–59, 262, 304, 320, 323, 324, 326, 328, 341, 372, 389, 392, 394, 395, 401, 402, 403, 404, 405, 406, 407, 408, 409, 410, 413

    see also Fowler v. North Carolina; Woodson v. North Carolina

Northeastern Law School, 33, 369

Northwestern Law School, 6, 356

Northwestern University, 6

nullification, 106, 304, 307, 378, 411

Nunn, Sam, 247

Nuremberg trials, 307, 308, 483*n*

NYU Law Magazine, 451*n*

O'Callaghan, Mike, 258

O'Connor, Sandra Day, 346, 439, 440

Office of Strategic Services, 6–7

Ogden, C. K., 463*n*

Ohio, 103, 105, 109, 262, 315

Oklahoma, 140, 258

O'Neal decision, 479*n*

O'Neill, Robert, 74, 454*n*

On the Origin of Species (Darwin), 463*n*

Oregon, 63, 282, 283, 480*n*

Oregon Law School, 32

originalism, 12, 14, 20, 23, 25, 80, 180, 224, 322, 349, 382, 383, 387, 396, 407

Oswald, Lee Harvey, 205

Other America, The (Harrington), 17–18

Oxford English Dictionary, 365

Oxford University, 173, 203

Packer, Herbert, 34, 370

Papcun, George, 36

Parker, Donald, 140

Parker, John J., 266

Passell, Peter, 473*n*

Pataki, George, 475*n*

Patterson, Joe, 65

Peck, Jon, 298, 473*n*

Peckham, Robert, 56

Peirce, Charles, 463*n*–64*n*

penal codes, 95, 304–6, 308, 309–10, 313, 317

Pennsylvania, 67, 112, 211, 262, 285, 359

Pennsylvania, University of, 286

    Law School, 42, 111

    Project in Social Science Research on Capital Punishment at, 286, 293

Pennsylvania v. Union Gas Co., 211

per curiam opinions, 226, 235, 236, 444

Percy, Charles, 356

Perry, H. W., 338–40, 409

Philadelphia, Pa., 41

Phillips, Leon Chase, 140

Pierce, Glenn, 293, 296–97, 301, 473*n*

Plato, 206

Pledge of Allegiance, 35

Plessy v. Ferguson, 126, 175

Poff, Richard, 125

Pope, Duane, 192–93

pornography, 212

Port Huron Statement, 18

Posner, Richard, 475*n*

poverty, 17–18, 181, 231*n*, 249

    death penalty sentences and, 8, 79, 133, 134, 137, 159, 188, 215, 301, 368, 386

poverty law, 50

Powe, Scot, 87

Powell, Josephine, 144, 423

Powell, Leroy, 487*n*–88*n*

Powell, Lewis, 128, 136, 198, 199, 200, 213, 220, 222, 225, 228, 230–31, 240–41, 271, 274, 283, 284, 317, 346–53, 356, 404–10, 419, 421, 423–25, 436–38, 489*n*, 490*n*

    background and education of, 346–47, 348

    Burger disliked by, 349–50, 407–8

    in cert petition review of statutory cases, 340, 343–44, 345–46, 349–51, 352

    Coker dissent of, 427, 491*n*

    Court nomination and appointment of, 125–27, 144, 224, 347–48, 404

    death penalty as viewed by, 144, 169, 348–49, 437–38

    fierce ambition of, 346–47, 351

in *Furman* conference, 169–70, 184

Furman draft opinion of, 182–84, 195–96, 197, 216, 219, 221, 230, 232–33, 237, 414

Gregg decision remorse of, 424, 425

Gregg opinion drafted by, 410, 414–15, 417–18, 437, 444

in *Gregg/Woodson* conference, 402–3, 404, 405, 407

in *Gregg/Woodson* oral arguments, 373, 375, 376, 377–78, 380, 381, 382, 384, 387–88, 391–93, 396–98, 400, 403

in *Gregg/Woodson* troika agreement, 408–10, 413–14, 419, 440

guided-discretion statutes supported by, 415*n*

inclusive working style of, 182–83

indecisiveness of, 413

as influential justice, 424

judicial philosophy of, 195, 348, 349, 351, 407

law clerks of, 182–84, 195–96, 198, 230–31, 233, 342–44, 345, 346, 352–53, 400, 405–7, 410–12, 414, 428–29

legal career of, 347–48

mandatory statutes opposed by, 402, 405, 407, 408, 445

McCleskey opinion of, 428–29, 437, 438

as meticulous and diligent, 350

military service of, 347, 351

as nonideological, 348

power and influence of, 351–52

precedent respected by, 404

and proposal to apply *Gregg* to future cases only, 415–17

race issues record of, 125–26, 347–48

retributive justice supported by, 414–15, 421

Roe v. Wade and, 404

Stewart's close relationship with, 351, 408

White's tense relationship with, 413

Powell, Louis Franklin, 346–47

Powell, Mary Lewis, 346

Powell v. Texas, 366, 487*n*–88*n*

President's Crime Commission, 347, 348–49

Price, Bill, 248

Price, Monroe, 465*n*

Princeton University, 93, 176, 286, 288

privacy rights, 15, 85, 177–78, 212, 270

Proffitt, Charles, 343, 388, 398

Proffitt v. Florida, 343, 344, 352, 354, 388,

398–99, 415, 417, 418, 419, 424, 430, 445

see also Gregg v. Georgia

Prohibition, 239, 482*n*

Project in Social Science Research on Capital Punishment, 286, 293

Proposition 17, 254–55, 382, 443

Protestants, Protestantism, 13, 14

PT-109, 204

public executions, 133, 402

Public Interest, 286, 295, 479*n*

Public Utilities Commission v. Pollak, 456*n*

Pulaski, Charles, 39–40

Punishing Criminals: Concerning a Very Old and Painful Question (Van den Haag), 301

race issues, 17, 28, 32, 35, 36, 58, 102, 273, 342, 428

affirmative action, 213, 352

Baxley's favorable record on, 249

Brennan's avoidance of, in Court decisions, 181–82

as central theme in abolition campaign, 37, 44–45, 48, 49–50, 51, 82*n*

desegregation cases and, 14, 21, 25–26, 32, 46, 52–53, 58, 125, 126, 141, 212–13, 266–67, 268–69, 271, 274, 275–76, 347–48, 449*n*, 452*n*

forced busing and, 196, 268–69, 274, 275

in *Fowler* case, 327–28

in jury selection procedures, 37, 38

in *Maxwell* case, 77, 94, 444

as omitted from Goldberg's cert dissent, 28, 29, 34

Powell's problematic record on, 125–26, 347–48

Rehnquist's insensitive views on, 126

White's record on, 212–13

see also civil rights movement

racism, 22, 33, 34, 36, 38, 52–53, 137, 186, 285, 301, 352, 370, 428

racism, in capital sentencing, 8, 19, 28, 36, 68–69, 77, 129, 133–35, 137, 140, 150, 159, 164, 166, 167, 181, 188–89, 190, 215–16, 220, 227, 236, 242, 276, 280, 282, 301, 314*n*, 361, 368, 369, 370, 386, 402, 430, 444, 449*n*

clemency and, 327

courts as reluctant to admit to, 40, 405, 428–29, 434

as difficult to prove, 34, 37, 40, 428

racism, in capital sentencing (*continued*)
    Georgia and, 40, 159, 162, 213, 295, 428
    McCleskey case and, 39, 213, 295, 418,
        428–29, 434, 438
    rape cases and, 18, 22, 26, 35, 37, 38–40,
        45, 53, 77, 94, 133, 134–35, 164, 449*n*
    research and statistical evidence on, 22,
        26, 29, 38–40, 45, 94, 162–63, 168, 213,
        295, 337, 428, 438
    as violation of Equal Protection Clause,
        162, 182, 428, 434
Randolph, A. Raymond, 364
Random House, 259, 260
rape, 26, 28, 97, 168, 220, 238, 341, 343
    death penalty in cases of, 18, 22, 26, 28,
        29, 34, 37, 38–40, 44, 45, 77, 112, 117,
        131, 133, 134, 164, 234, 277, 320*n*, 328,
        370, 402, 427, 445, 449*n*, 491*n*
    discriminatory sentencing in cases of, 18,
        22, 26, 35, 37, 38–40, 45, 53, 77, 94,
        133, 134–35, 164, 286
Reagan, Ronald, 54, 55, 56, 111, 185, 247,
        302, 364, 387
Real Majority, The (Scammon and
        Wattenberg), 272–73
Reconstruction, 184
Redfield, Emanuel, 36
Redlich, Norman, 76
Reflections on Hanging (Koestler), 64, 81
Reflections on the Guillotine (Camus), 418
rehabilitation programs, 287, 305, 306
rehearing petitions, 424–25
Rehnquist, Nan, 144
Rehnquist, William, 93, 128, 136, 144, 179,
        199, 200, 214, 224, 257, 345, 348, 349,
        408, 418, 424
    academic and legal background of, 126
    clerkship of, 124, 126
    Court nomination and confirmation of,
        126–27, 144
    death penalty supported by, 170, 224
    Furman case and, 159, 170, 224–25, 237
    in *Gregg/Woodson* conference, 403
    as insensitive on race issues, 126
    judicial philosophy of, 224
    on liberalism of law clerks, 124
Reich, Charles, 332
Reich, Robert, 365
Reidinger, Paul, 279
Reiss, Albert, 474*n*
Republicans, Republican Party, 76, 93, 175,
        247, 249, 250, 272, 477*n*, 478*n*–79*n*

Resnick, Melvin, 103–4
"restatements," 304–5
Rich, John, 270
Richards, I. A., 463*n*
Richards, Louis, 136
Richardson, Elliot, 322
Richmond School Board, 347–48
right to counsel, 26
right-to-life movement, 276
robbery, 97, 101, 192, 265, 341, 354, 381,
        394, 427, 429
    death penalty in cases of, 17, 22, 66, 69, 81,
        82–83, 115, 443
Robert E. Lee Klan No. 1, 13
Roberts, Owen, 11
Roberts Court, 337
Roberts v. Louisiana, 343, 344, 352, 354, 373,
        375, 381–82, 388, 417, 418, 445
    see also Woodson v. North Carolina
Robinson, Lawrence, 211
Robinson v. California, 211
Rockefeller, Nelson, 258, 302, 309
Rockefeller, Winthrop, 38, 112
Rockefeller Foundation, 104
Roe v. Wade, 74, 85, 135, 167–68, 177–78,
        194–95, 199–200, 212, 269–71, 274,
        275, 276, 277, 278, 283, 350, 352, 404,
        475*n*
    public backlash to, 269, 270–71
Rogers v. Bellei, 114
Roosevelt, Franklin D., 9, 11, 13, 14, 84, 85,
        91, 272
Roper v. Simmons, 41, 428
Rosen, Jeffrey, 213–14
Rosenberg, Ethel and Julius, 62*n*, 262
Rosenberg, Gerard, 278–79
Ross, Annie, 75
Rothgerber, Ira, 212
Roxbury High School, Boston, Mass., 268
Royal Commission on Capital Punishment,
        British, 281
Rubin, Paul, 474*n*, 478*n*
Ruckelshaus, William, 322
Rudolph, Frank Lee, 28, 34
Rudolph v. Alabama, 79, 336, 370, 445
Rules of the Supreme Court of the United
        States, 337
Rusk Institute, 331, 332, 333
Russell, John, 74
Russell Sage Foundation, 286, 289, 293,
        311
Ruth, Babe, 79

Rutledge, Wiley, 356
Ryan, John, 73

Sacco, Ferdinando Nicola, 9
Sacks, Albert, 55
San Francisco, Calif., 110
Sargent, Francis, 258
Saxbe, William, 65
Scalia, Antonin, 12, 148, 214, 413, 460*n*
    judicial philosophy of, 12, 14, 177
Scammon, Richard, 272–73
Schapiro, Andrew, 434
Schlesinger, Arthur, 485*n*
Schmitter, Aman, 11
school prayer, 7, 73, 74
Schubert, Glendon, 338, 340, 346
Schwartz, Bernard, 212, 432–33
Schwartz, Herman, 352
Scopes, John, 35
Scottsboro Boys, 15, 483*n*
Seale, Bobby, 41
Second Circuit Court of Appeals, 138, 141,
    176
Securities and Exchange Commission, 84, 91
segregation, segregationists, 14, 25, 32, 48,
    58, 126, 171, 185, 212, 250*n*, 267, 278,
    301, 348
    index of, 267
    see also desegregation
Selimos, Nick, 409
Sellin, Thorsten, 281–82, 284, 287–88, 290,
    291, 293, 294, 295, 297, 298, 299, 366,
    471*n*, 473*n*
Selvin, Herman, 100–101, 103
Senate, Florida, 253
Senate, U.S., 13, 262, 408
    Judiciary Committee of, 94, 257, 348, 404,
        474*n*
separate-but-equal, 126
separation of church and state, 74*n*
Seventh Circuit Court of Appeals, 364
sexism, 123, 124, 125, 135, 163
Shapp, Milton, 112
Shepherd, Joanna, 474*n*, 475*n*, 478*n*,
    479*n*–81*n*
Shevin, Robert, 252, 398–99
Silberman, David, 310
Silent Spring (Carson), 18
Simon, Tobias, 55
Simple Justice (Kluger), 260*n*
single-phase trials, 67, 70, 129, 303, 315,
    325

Maxwell case and issue of, 81, 82, 83, 89,
    90, 91, 92, 95–96, 105, 178
McGautha case and issue of, 103, 104–5,
    107–8
    see also bifurcated trials
Sirhan, Sirhan, 185, 254
Sixth Amendment, 63–64
Sixth Circuit Court of Appeals, 176
slavery, 206, 463*n*
Smiley, William, 252
Smith, Perry, 73
Smith, William, 146
Smith v. Allwright, 32
social science research, 58, 274–75, 284–89,
    301–2, 471*n*
    on Court cert process, 337–40, 346
    Court's rejection of evidence in, 39–40,
        302
    courts' reliance on, 281–84, 287, 295, 302,
        308
    on criminal rehabilitation programs, 287
    critics and skeptics of, 283–84, 286–87,
        295
    in Dershowitz memorandum, 22, 23, 26,
        30, 337
    on deterrence issue, 22, 23, 131, 184, 281–
        82, 283–84, 286, 287–88, 289–301,
        365–66, 388, 472*n*, 473*n*, 474*n*–82*n*
    in Ehrlich's controversial deterrence study,
        289–301, 365–66, 473*n*, 474*n*, 475*n*,
        477*n*, 478*n*, 481*n*
    endogeneity problems in, 289, 476*n*–79*n*
    Fowler case and, 290–91
    in *Furman* decision, 281–82, 283–84
    instrumental analysis in, 477*n*–79*n*
    on judicial influence among Court justices,
        178–79, 214
    LDF's reliance on, 38–40, 45, 58, 94,
        162–63, 184, 283, 284–86, 287–88, 295
    priori beliefs in, 299
    qualitative vs. quantitative evidence in,
        338, 339, 346
    on racism in capital sentencing, 22, 26, 29,
        38–40, 45, 94, 162–63, 168, 295, 337,
        428, 438
    regression analysis in, 290, 293, 294, 295,
        296, 298, 473*n*
    see also criminology
sodomy laws, 212, 352
Songer, Carl, 342
Songer case, 342, 343, 344
Souter, David, 98

South African Constitutional Court, 435

South Boston High School, 268

South Carolina, 146, 262, 480*n*

Southern California Law Review, 21

Spaeth, Harold, 178–79, 214, 461*n*

Speaker, Fred, 112

Speck, Richard, 62

Spellman, Francis Cardinal, 72, 73

Spencer, Herbert, 463*n*

Spencer v. Texas, 397

Spenkelink, John, 430, 431

Spiegel, John, 294

standardless sentencing procedures, 66–68, 70, 77, 79, 80, 106, 129, 133, 137, 317

    in *Boykin/Maxwell* cases, 66–68, 70, 77, 79, 81, 82, 83, 89–91, 92, 94, 95–96, 100, 104, 178

    in *Furman* case, 118, 148, 149, 168, 189, 226, 303, 315, 384, 385, 389–90, 391, 401, 402

    in *McGautha* case, 100–103, 104, 105, 106–7, 108, 109–10, 111, 168, 226, 227, 303, 306*n*, 316, 377, 402, 445

Stanford Law Review, 285, 330, 475*n*

Stanford Law School, 34, 98, 126, 129, 132, 286

Stanford University, 238, 358, 426

Stanford v. Kentucky, 418

stare decisis, 219, 325

Starr, Kenneth, 413

Stassen, Harold, 93

State Department, U.S., 7

State v. Waddell, 258

stay petitions, 424–25, 426, 436–37

Steiker, Carol, 266, 311–12, 313, 362

Steiker, Jordan, 311–12, 313, 362

Stephens, Andrew J., 454*n*

Stern, Ron, 353, 400, 460*n*

    in drafting of *Woodson* opinion, 410–12

Stern, Seth, 454*n*–55*n*

Stevens, John Paul, 276, 317, 334, 335, 345, 351, 355–56, 372, 399, 407, 410, 417, 419, 421, 424, 425, 434, 436, 438–40, 444

    background and education of, 356

    Baze decision and, 438–39

    Court nomination and appointment of, 355–56, 487*n*

    death penalty as viewed by, 438–39

    in *Gregg/Woodson* conference, 403

    in *Gregg/Woodson* oral arguments, 376–77, 382, 389

    in *Gregg/Woodson* troika agreement, 408–10, 413–14, 419, 440

    Jurek decision regretted by, 410, 439–40, 492*n*

    legal career of, 356

    in *Woodson* majority, 445

Stevenson, Adlai, 204

Stewart, John Garfield, 175

Stewart, Potter, 10, 27, 63–64, 67, 77, 87, 89, 91, 92, 114, 127, 130, 145, 178, 187–88, 189–90, 196, 198, 212, 224, 232, 242, 243, 263, 268, 271, 274, 351, 365, 372, 407, 416, 419, 420, 421, 424, 425, 458*n*, 486*n*

    background and education of, 175, 176

    in cert petition review of statutory cases, 344, 345

    Court nomination of, 81, 176

    death penalty as viewed by, 29, 64, 81–83, 166–67, 173, 175, 201

    in *Fowler* oral arguments, 327, 330

    in *Furman* conference, 168, 184

    Furman draft opinions of, 173–75, 180, 185–86, 197, 200–201, 218–21, 222, 223–24, 226, 227, 228, 230, 233, 345, 411, 433

    in *Furman* oral arguments, 149–50, 151–52, 154, 155, 156, 160–61, 164

    Furman published opinion of, 236, 280, 282, 303, 312–13, 314, 325, 336, 340, 341, 353, 368, 374*n*, 401, 402, 403, 405, 406

    in *Gregg* decision, 444

    Gregg opinion of, 302–3, 306*n*, 317, 340, 433

    in *Gregg/Woodson* conference, 401, 404

    in *Gregg/Woodson* oral arguments, 375, 378, 379, 380, 384, 385, 386, 391, 395

    in *Gregg/Woodson* troika agreement, 408–10, 413–14, 419, 440

    Griswold dissent of, 177–78

    Harlan's close bond with, 175, 176–77, 178–80, 351, 397

    as influential justice, 179–80

    judicial philosophy of, 29, 177–78, 236, 351

    law clerks of, 26, 124, 127, 173–75, 177, 180, 185–86, 189, 197, 218, 221, 314, 334, 353, 400, 401, 410

    mandatory statutes opposed by, 217, 219–20, 221, 408, 411–12, 445

    Maxwell case and, 81, 82–83, 94, 96, 178

McGautha case and, 103, 105, 111, 129, 164, 172, 174–75, 178, 226–27, 340

Powell's close relationship with, 351, 408

and Powell's proposal to apply *Gregg* to future cases only, 416–17

on privacy rights, 177–78

Robinson v. California decision of, 211

Roe v. Wade and, 177–78, 199

on single-phase trial issue, 82, 96, 103, 105, 178

on standardless sentencing, 82, 96, 105, 178, 303

White's *Furman* compromise with, 200–201, 215, 216–17, 218, 223, 226–27, 229, 235, 277, 309–10, 325, 336, 433

Witherspoon decision of, 64, 81–82, 129, 166, 175, 178, 217, 280

in *Woodson* majority, 445

Woodson opinion drafted by, 410–12, 414, 417–18

Sting, 429

Stone, Harlan, 307

Stone, Harlan Fiske, 203

Stromberg, Yetta, 35

Student Nonviolent Coordinating Committee (SNCC), 36

Students for a Democratic Society, 18

Sturges, Wesley, 209–10

Sullivan v. Florida, 371*n*

Sunstein, Cass, 475*n*

Supreme Court, Alabama, 66

Supreme Court, Arkansas, 37, 38

Supreme Court, California, 65, 77, 80, 99
    Anderson case in, 136, 137, 151, 184–85, 254, 382, 392, 397, 443, 466*n*
    death penalty struck down by, 184–85, 382

Supreme Court, French, 29

Supreme Court, Georgia, 252, 304, 313, 341, 363

Supreme Court, Illinois, 356

Supreme Court, Massachusetts, 320, 359, 479*n*

Supreme Court, New Jersey, 72

Supreme Court, North Carolina, 258, 262, 320, 323, 330, 394, 443

Supreme Court, Ohio, 175

Supreme Court, Texas, 379*n*

Supreme Court, U.S., 3, 5, 8, 18, 24–25, 32, 33, 34, 38, 39, 41, 43, 46, 54, 60, 63–70, 85, 111, 112, 135, 136, 137, 138, 141, 175, 177, 182, 203, 205, 234, 250, 251, 252, 258, 262, 295, 308, 314, 318, 332, 364, 370*n*, 423, 466*n*, 483*n*

abortion cases in, 74, 167–68, 194–95, 199–200, 212, 269–71, 274, 275, 276–77, 352, 404, 409, 475*n*

as ahead of public opinion on social issues, 276–77, 309, 365

amicus briefs submitted to, 41, 58, 59, 66, 68–70, 97, 100, 290–91, 322, 338, 364, 365–68, 374

assigning of opinion writing in, 79

autonomy of justices in, 171

cert petitions reviewed in, 4, 19, 66, 70, 73, 81, 96, 99, 109, 115, 116–18, 136, 144, 166, 332, 340–46, 349–51, 352–53, 407, 436, 445

conference room of, 78–79

courthouse interior of, 143–44, 350, 372–73

death penalty convictions reversed by, 15

death penalty statutes struck down by, 277, 312*n*, 445

desegregation cases in, 14, 21, 25–26, 46, 126, 171, 175, 185, 212–13, 266–67, 268–69, 271, 274, 275–76, 449*n*, 452*n*

Eisenhower nominations and appointments for, 9, 10, 64, 72, 81, 176

FDR nominations and appointments to, 9, 13

FDR's plan for packing of, 11

Ford's appointment for, 355–56, 487*n*

in granting stays of execution, 48, 424–25, 436–37

Ingber's "legitimacy account" view of, 308–9

JFK nominations and appointments for, 7, 10

join memos in, 224, 225, 418

judicial activism vs. restraint view of, 9–11, 12, 14, 15, 22–23, 26, 27, 29

labor law decisions in, 11–12

law clerks of, *see* law clerks

LBJ nominations and appointments for, 76, 138–39

motion counsel of, 340

mutual judicial influence among justices on, 178–79, 214, 461*n*

Nixon nominations and appointments for, 92, 93–94, 125–27, 225, 242, 347, 348, 432

per curiam opinions in, 226, 235, 236

Supreme Court, U.S. (*continued*)
  on privacy rights, 15, 85, 177–78, 212, 270
  public backlash against decisions of, 25–26, 73, 248, 266–67, 268–69, 270–72, 274–75, 321, 325, 360
  Reagan's nominations for, 387
  rehearing petitions filed in, 424–25
  as reluctant to address Eighth Amendment issue, 16, 70, 96, 97, 106, 109, 111–12, 113–15, 116, 432–33, 449*n*
  as reluctant to address racism in criminal justice system, 405, 428–29, 434
  rightward swing of, 114, 127, 354–55, 439
  rule of four in, 449*n*
  sexist attitudes on, 124, 125, 163
  social science data accepted in, 281–84, 287, 308
  statistical evidence of racism dismissed by, 39–40, 295, 437
  stays of execution granted in, 48, 424–25, 436–37
  treatment of religion in, 7, 73–74
  Truman nominations and appointment for, 10
  vote trading on, 409
  see also Burger Court; Warren Court; *specific cases and justices*
Supreme Court and Legal Change, The (Epstein and Kobylka), 488*n*
Swann, James, 267
Swann v. Charlotte-Mecklenburg Board of Education, 266, 267–68, 271, 275
Sweatt v. Painter, 452*n*
Symington, Stuart, 204
Szymankiewicz, Joseph, 430

Taft, William Howard, 175
Tariff on Animal and Vegetable Oils, The (Wright), 477*n*
Taylor, John, 473*n*
Tempting of America, The (Bork), 485*n*
Tennessee, 35, 42
Texas, 32, 53*n*, 140, 146, 194, 344, 388, 397, 426, 487*n*
  Criminal Court of Appeals in, 376*n*
  high rates of executions in, 410, 476*n*, 480*n*, 481*n*
Texas statutes, 258, 343, 360–61, 372, 376, 380, 401, 402, 403, 404, 406, 409, 410, 439–40, 444

  as inexplicably not classified as mandatory, 361, 369, 410, 425–26
  see also Jurek v. Texas
Thayer, James Bradley, 448*n*
Thinking About Crime (Wilson), 287
Thomas, Clarence, 177, 276
Tigner v. Texas, 488*n*
Time, 18, 44, 63, 67–68, 117, 133, 234, 251, 261, 262, 355, 430
Tison, Ricky and Raymond, 277
Tison v. Arizona, 427
Tobriner, Matthew, 80, 455*n*
Toews, Alquinn, 271
Topeka, Kans., 266
Totenberg, Nina, 439, 440, 492*n*
Tribbitt, Sherman, 258
Tribe, Laurence, 356
Trocinski, Vern, 270, 271
Trop, Albert, 19
Trop v. Dulles, 19–20, 21, 23, 64, 132, 142, 146, 445
Truman, Harry, 10, 85, 203
Tufts University, 112, 131
Twain, Mark, 39, 464*n*

Udall, Morris, 302
Ulmer, Sidney, 337–38, 339–40, 346
Underwood, Barbara, 124
Uniform Crime Reporting System (UCR), 296*n*, 297, 476*n*
unions, 7
United Color & Pigment, 71–72
United Nations, 17, 432
United Nations Report on Capital Punishment, 29
U.S. News & World Report, 124, 126, 234
U.S. v. Jackson, 63–64, 79, 178
U.S. v. Park, 354
Utah, 258, 480*n*

Van den Haag, Ernest, 301, 302
Vanzetti, Bartolomeo, 9
Varieties of Attack on the Death Penalty (Greenberg and Himmelstein), 452*n*
Vermeule, Adrian, 475*n*
Vermont, 63
Vidmar, Neil, 285
Vietnam War, 36, 387
Vinson, Fred, 203, 210
Virginia, 138, 139, 240, 410
Virginia Bar Association, 344
Virginia Law Weekly, 454*n*

Volstead Act (1919), 482n
voting rights, 32, 35, 36, 42–43, 80, 179

Waddell case, 320, 324, 326
Walker, Anders, 482n
Wallace, George, 25, 247, 250, 269
Walter Reed Hospital, 88, 333
Walton v. Arizona, 490n
War on Poverty, 18
Warren, Earl, 9, 20, 27, 28, 77, 78, 79, 81, 82n,
    92, 124, 179, 181, 185, 212, 432, 449n
  in Boykin/Maxwell conference, 79–80, 83,
    89
  Brown decision and, 25–26
  death penalty as viewed by, 20, 79, 433,
    449n
  on "evolving standards of decency," 20, 23,
    64, 132, 146, 180, 445
  Goldberg's cert dissent negotiation of,
    28–29, 432
  as governor of California, 9, 20, 449n
  as lame duck justice, 76, 79
  law clerks of, 9
  Maxwell opinion of, 83–84
  public backlash against, 25–26, 266
  in reaction to Goldberg's death penalty
    memorandum, 25–26, 27
  resignation of, 76, 177
  Trop decision of, 19–20, 23, 64, 132
Warren Court, 12, 76, 80, 87, 88, 93, 114,
    241, 243, 252, 283, 322, 355, 433, 455n
  Black-Frankfurter ideological divide on,
    9–11, 14, 15, 22, 29, 72, 200, 448n, 485n
  in expanding rights of criminal defendants,
    63n, 64, 73, 114, 179, 181, 212, 260
  members of, 9–10
  mutual influence among justices on, 179
Washington Post, 33, 77, 302
Washington Star, 138
Washington State, 11, 257
Watergate scandal, 231n, 271, 275, 322
Wattenberg, Ben, 272–73
Waxman, Seth, 41, 44
Waxton, Luby, 342–43, 394
Weber, Max, 313, 463n
Wechsler, Herbert, 181, 306, 307–10, 348,
    482n–83n
  background and education of, 307, 482n
  legal career of, 307, 308
Wechsler, Samuel, 307
Weems v. United States, 21, 153, 197, 445
Weisberg, Robert, 276, 314–16, 412, 484n

Wermiel, Stephen, 454n–55n, 460n
West Africa, 98
West Coast Hotel Co. v. Parrish, 11
West Virginia, 63
White, Al, 202
White, Byron, 10, 48, 77, 82, 91, 127, 129,
    144, 179, 187–88, 196, 202–5, 209–17,
    224, 243, 263, 333, 334, 345, 372, 397,
    413–14, 418, 424, 461n, 462n, 465n
  athletic career of, 203, 204, 214
  background and education of, 202–3, 208,
    209–10, 214
  clerkship of, 203
  Coker opinion of, 427
  confirmation hearings of, 205
  contradictory rulings of, 212–13, 226, 227,
    228–29
  criticized for lack of guiding vision, 213–14
  and expansion of criminal defendants'
    constitutional rights, 212
  "four clean cases" for review chosen by,
    115, 116–18, 458n
  in Furman conference, 168–70, 184
  Furman draft opinions of, 198, 216, 221–
    22, 223–24, 227, 228, 230, 232, 233
  in Furman oral arguments, 166
  Furman published opinion of, 236, 237,
    241, 280, 281, 303, 312–13, 341, 374n,
    401, 402, 403, 405, 406
  Furman vote as guarded secret of, 188, 197,
    198–99, 200, 222
  in Gregg/Woodson conference, 401–2
  Gregg/Woodson opinion assigned to, 404,
    407, 413, 433
  in Gregg/Woodson oral arguments, 376,
    383–84
  insecurity and competitiveness of, 214–15,
    346
  in JFK campaign and administration,
    204–5
  judicial philosophy of, 10, 172–73, 205,
    209–11, 213
  at Justice Department, 204–5, 214
  law clerks of, 124, 166, 197, 198, 210–11,
    214–15, 218, 221–22, 227, 334, 346, 357,
    358, 404, 413, 465n
  legal realism as influence on, 209–11, 215
  Maxwell case and, 83, 94, 96, 127
  McGautha case and, 105, 127
  military service of, 203, 204
  nonideological stance of, 205, 209, 210,
    211, 216, 465n

White, Byron (*continued*)
  Pennsylvania v. Union Gas Co. decision of,
    211
  petulant and gruff demeanor of, 214, 215,
    346, 413
  Powell's tense relationship with, 413
  on race issues, 212–13
  retirement of, 205
  Robinson v. California dissent of, 211
  Roe v. Wade and, 212
  Stewart's *Furman* compromise with, 200–
    201, 215, 216–17, 218, 223, 226–27, 229,
    235, 277, 309–10, 325, 336, 433
  as swing vote, 172, 189, 190, 197, 198–99,
    200, 201, 216, 227–28, 241–42, 351
  tireless work ethic of, 214
  Woodson dissents of, 418
White, Maude, 202
White, Sam, 202, 203, 214
White, Welsh, 285*n*
Whitman, Christina, 342–44, 345, 346, 349,
    352–53, 354–55, 392, 400, 410, 415–16
  Gregg/Woodson memo of, 405–7
Whittaker, Charles, 461*n*
Wicker, Tom, 257
Wieden, Dan, 430
Wills, Thomas, 252
Wilson, Cody, 58
Wilson, James Q., 277–78, 287, 292*n*, 474*n*
Wilson Dam, 236
Winter, Ralph, 141
Witherspoon, William, 57, 59, 64, 81, 241
Witherspoon v. Illinois, 57, 58, 64–65, 79,
    81–82, 83, 91, 95, 96, 97, 105, 112, 127,
    129, 166, 175, 178, 217, 248, 256, 280,
    345, 361, 444, 455*n*
Wofford, Harris, 205
Wolfgang, Marvin, 38, 39, 45, 286, 288,
    474*n*
Wolfson, Louis, 91
women, 18, 146
  as law clerks, 123–24
  legal field's sexism against, 123, 124, 125,
    135, 163
  Oregon's statute on work hours of, 282–83
  right to choose of, 124, 212, 270, 271, 276
Woodson, James, 342, 343, 392, 394
Woodson v. North Carolina, 277, 342–43,
    352, 354, 392, 418, 419, 422, 426, 439,
    444, 445

arbitrariness of death penalty statutes
  illustrated in, 343, 344, 360, 373, 375,
    389, 392, 394–95
  Burger's assigning of opinions in, 404,
    407–8, 413, 414, 417, 433
  Court conference on, 400–404, 405, 407,
    414
  drafting of opinion in, 410–12, 414,
    417–18
  Furman as contradicted by, 412–13, 434,
    490*n*
  Gregg opinion as contradictory of, 417–18
  join memos in, 418
  LDF's strategy in, 389, 392
  oral arguments in, 372–80, 381–98, 400,
    403
  troika agreement in, 408–10, 413–14, 419
Woodward, Bob, 171, 333, 409, 486*n*
Woodworth, George, 39–40
World War II, 6–7, 12, 41, 176, 203, 204,
    413, 430
  internment of Japanese Americans in, 78
Wright, Charles Alan, 164, 240, 241, 251
Wright, Chauncey, 206, 464*n*
Wright, Donald, 185, 392
Wright, Philip G., 477*n*, 478*n*
Wright, Sewall, 477*n*, 478*n*
writ of certiorari, *see* cert petitions
Wulf, Melvin, 56, 60, 61
Wyman, Louis, 248

Yakima County Courthouse, 332
Yale Law Journal, 21, 173, 298, 365, 483*n*
  deterrence articles in, 294–97, 301–2
Yale Law School, 16, 19, 33, 84, 91, 124, 173,
    174, 175, 203, 214, 215, 259, 293, 322,
    332, 348, 357, 435, 475*n*
  judicial activism favored by, 10–11
  legal realism philosophy at, 208–9
Yale University, 175
Yick Wo, 110
Yick Wo v. Hopkins, 109–10
Young, Gordon, 37
Younger, Evelle, 254
Yunker, James, 300

Zeisel, Hans, 293, 299, 330, 386, 477*n*, 479*n*
Zimring, Franklin, 44, 276–77, 293, 299,
    460*n*, 472*n*, 482*n*
Zoll, Donald, 234–35